Your Companion Site—
Even more help for studying!

bedfordstmartins.com/mckaywest

FREE Online Study Guide—Improve your performance!
Get immediate feedback on your progress with

- Quizzing
- Key terms review
- Map and visual activities
- Timeline activities
- Note-taking outlines

FREE History Research and Writing Help
Refine your research skills, evaluate sources, and organize your findings with

- *Make History* maps, documents, images, and Web sites
- History Research and Reference Sources
- More Sources and How to Format a History Paper
- Build a Bibliography
- Tips on Avoiding Plagiarism

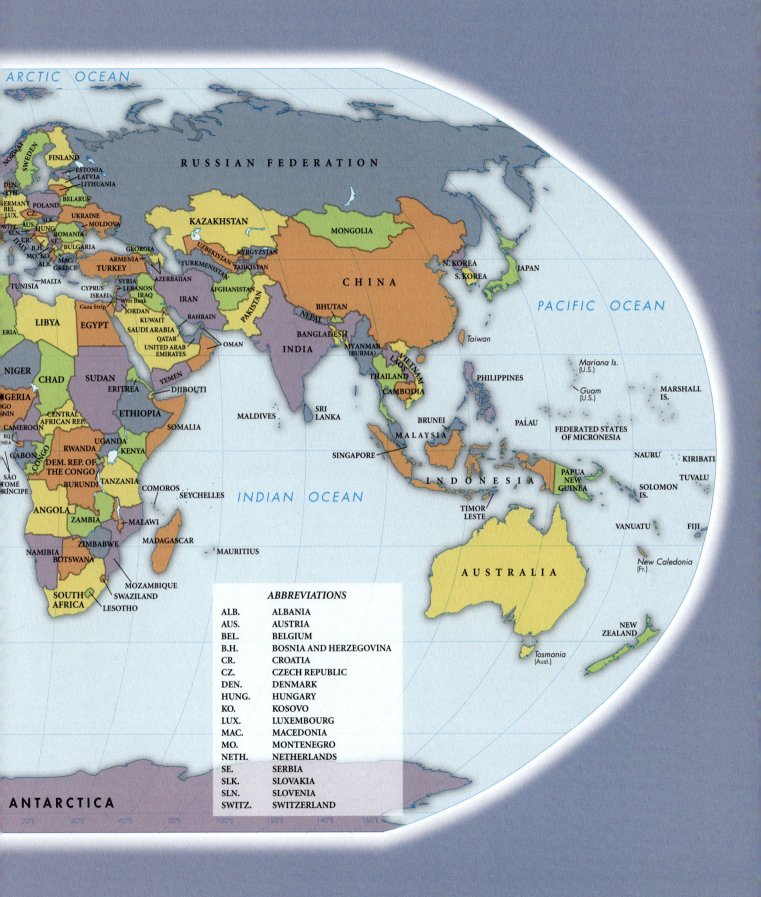

A History of Western Society

Hans Holbein the Younger, *The Merchant Georg Gisze*, 1532.

A History of Western Society

VOLUME B
From the Later Middle Ages to 1815

Tenth Edition

John P. McKay
University of Illinois at Urbana-Champaign

Bennett D. Hill
Late of Georgetown University

John Buckler
University of Illinois at Urbana-Champaign

Clare Haru Crowston
University of Illinois at Urbana-Champaign

Merry E. Wiesner-Hanks
University of Wisconsin–Milwaukee

Joe Perry
Georgia State University

BEDFORD/ST. MARTIN'S
Boston • New York

FOR BEDFORD/ST. MARTIN'S

Publisher for History: Mary Dougherty
Director of Development for History: Jane Knetzger
Executive Editor for History: Traci Mueller Crowell
Senior Developmental Editor for History: Laura Arcari
Senior Production Editor: Christina Horn
Senior Production Supervisor: Nancy Myers
Executive Marketing Manager: Jenna Bookin Barry
Associate Editor: Lynn Sternberger
Production Assistant: Alexis Biasell
Senior Art Director: Anna Palchik
Text Design: Brian Salisbury
Copyeditor: Sybil Sosin
Map Editor: Charlotte Miller
Indexer: Leoni Z. McVey
Page Layout: Boynton Hue Studio
Photo Research: Carole Frohlich and Elisa Gallagher, The Visual Connection Image Research, Inc.

Cover Design: Billy Boardman
Cover Art: Hans Holbein the Younger (1497–1543), *The Merchant Georg Gisze*, 1532. Oil on oak panel, 96.3 × 85.7 cm. Photo: Gemäldegalerie, Staatliche Museen Berlin/Bildarchiv Preussischer Kulturbesitz, Art Resource, NY.
Cartography: Mapping Specialists, Ltd.
Composition: NK Graphics
Printing and Binding: RR Donnelley and Sons

President: Joan E. Feinberg
Editorial Director: Denise B. Wydra
Director of Marketing: Karen R. Soeltz
Director of Editing, Design, and Production: Susan W. Brown
Assistant Director of Editing, Design, and Production: Elise S. Kaiser
Managing Editor: Elizabeth M. Schaaf

Library of Congress Control Number: 2010920486

Copyright © 2011, 2008, 2006, 2003 by Bedford/St. Martin's

All rights reserved. No part of this book may be reproduced, stored in a retrieval system, or transmitted in any form or by any means, electronic, mechanical, photocopying, recording, or otherwise, except as may be expressly permitted by the applicable copyright statutes or in writing by the Publisher.

Manufactured in the United States of America.

1 2 3 4 5 6   14 13 12 11 10

For information, write: Bedford/St. Martin's, 75 Arlington Street, Boston, MA 02116 (617-399-4000)

ISBN-10: 0-312-68773-7   ISBN-13: 978-0-312-68773-1 (combined edition)
ISBN-10: 0-312-64059-5   ISBN-13: 978-0-312-64059-0 (Vol. 1)
ISBN-10: 0-312-64060-9   ISBN-13: 978-0-312-64060-6 (Vol. 2)
ISBN-10: 0-312-64061-7   ISBN-13: 978-0-312-64061-3 (Vol. A)
ISBN-10: 0-312-64062-5   ISBN-13: 978-0-312-64062-0 (Vol. B)
ISBN-10: 0-312-64063-3   ISBN-13: 978-0-312-64063-7 (Vol. C)
ISBN-10: 0-312-63827-2   ISBN-13: 978-0-312-63827-6 (Since 1300)
ISBN-10: 0-312-64058-7   ISBN-13: 978-0-312-64058-3 (Since 1300 for Advanced Placement)

Brief Contents

12 The Crisis of the Later Middle Ages, **1300–1450**   338

13 European Society in the Age of the Renaissance, **1350–1550**   372

14 Reformations and Religious Wars, **1500–1600**   406

15 European Exploration and Conquest, **1450–1650**   442

16 Absolutism and Constitutionalism, **ca. 1589–1725**   478

17 Toward a New Worldview, **1540–1789**   518

18 The Expansion of Europe, **1650–1800**   552

19 The Changing Life of the People, **1700–1800**   584

20 The Revolution in Politics, **1775–1815**   618

Glossary   G-1
Index   I-1
Timeline   A History of Western Society: An Overview   I-18

Contents

Maps, Figures, and Tables   xix

Special Features   xxi

Preface   xxiii

Versions and Supplements   xxvii

12 The Crisis of the Later Middle Ages
1300–1450   338

Prelude to Disaster   340
- Climate Change and Famine   340
- Social Consequences   341

The Black Death   341
- Pathology   342
- Spread of the Disease   342
- Care of the Sick   345
- Economic, Religious, and Cultural Effects   347

The Hundred Years' War   348
- Causes   348
- English Successes   350
- Joan of Arc and France's Victory   352
- Aftermath   354

Challenges to the Church   354
- The Babylonian Captivity and Great Schism   355
- Critiques, Divisions, and Councils   355
- Lay Piety and Mysticism   357

Social Unrest in a Changing Society   358
- Peasant Revolts   358
- Urban Conflicts   361
- Sex in the City   361
- Fur-Collar Crime   366
- Ethnic Tensions and Restrictions   366
- Literacy and Vernacular Literature   367

Looking Back, Looking Ahead   369

Chapter Review   370

Living in the Past *Treating the Plague*   344

Individuals in Society *Meister Eckhart*   359

Listening to the Past *Christine de Pizan, Advice to the Wives of Artisans*   362

13 European Society in the Age of the Renaissance
1350–1550 372

Wealth and Power in Renaissance Italy 374
   Trade and Prosperity 374
   Communes and Republics of Northern Italy 375
   City-States and the Balance of Power 376

Intellectual Change 378
   Humanism 378
   Education 380
   Political Thought 381
   Christian Humanism 384
   The Printed Word 385

Art and the Artist 387
   Patronage and Power 387
   Changing Artistic Styles 389
   The Renaissance Artist 390

Social Hierarchies 393
   Race and Slavery 394
   Wealth and the Nobility 395
   Gender Roles 396

Politics and the State in Western Europe, ca. 1450–1521 397
   France 397
   England 399
   Spain 400

Looking Back, Looking Ahead 403

Chapter Review 404

Listening to the Past *Perspectives on Humanist Learning and Women* 382

Individuals in Society *Leonardo da Vinci* 391

Living in the Past *Male Clothing and Masculinity* 398

14 Reformations and Religious Wars
1500–1600 406

The Early Reformation 408
   The Christian Church in the Early Sixteenth Century 408
   Martin Luther 409
   Protestant Thought 411
   The Appeal of Protestant Ideas 412
   The Radical Reformation and the German Peasants' War 413
   Marriage and Sexuality 416

The Reformation and German Politics 419
   The Rise of the Habsburg Dynasty 420
   Religious Wars in Switzerland and Germany 421

The Spread of Protestant Ideas 422
   Scandinavia 422
   Henry VIII and the Reformation in England 422
   Upholding Protestantism in England 424
   Calvinism 425
   The Reformation in Eastern Europe 427

The Catholic Reformation 428
   Papal Reform and the Council of Trent 428
   New Religious Orders 431

Religious Violence 433
   French Religious Wars 433
   The Netherlands Under Charles V 434
   The Great European Witch-Hunt 435

Looking Back, Looking Ahead 438

Chapter Review 438

Listening to the Past *Martin Luther,* On Christian Liberty 414

Living in the Past *Uses of Art in the Reformation* 418

Individuals in Society *Teresa of Ávila* 432

Contents xv

15 European Exploration and Conquest
1450–1650   442

World Contacts Before Columbus   444
    The Trade World of the Indian Ocean   444
    The Trading States of Africa   445
    The Ottoman and Persian Empires   446
    Genoese and Venetian Middlemen   447

The European Voyages of Discovery   448
    Causes of European Expansion   448
    Technology and the Rise of Exploration   450
    The Portuguese Overseas Empire   451
    The Problem of Christopher Columbus   453
    Later Explorers   456
    Spanish Conquest in the New World   457
    Early French and English Settlement in the New World   460

The Impact of Conquest   461
    Colonial Administration   461
    Impact of European Settlement on the Lives of Indigenous Peoples   461
    Life in the Colonies   463
    The Columbian Exchange   463

Europe and the World After Columbus   464
    Sugar and Slavery   464
    Spanish Silver and Its Economic Effects   468
    The Birth of the Global Economy   470

Changing Attitudes and Beliefs   472
    New Ideas About Race   472
    Michel de Montaigne and Cultural Curiosity   473
    William Shakespeare and His Influence   473

Looking Back, Looking Ahead   475

Chapter Review   476

Listening to the Past *Columbus Describes His First Voyage*   454

Living in the Past *Foods of the Columbian Exchange*   466

Individuals in Society *Juan de Pareja*   469

16 Absolutism and Constitutionalism
ca. 1589–1725   478

Seventeenth-Century Crisis and Rebuilding   480
    Peasant Life in the Midst of Economic Crisis   480
    The Return of Serfdom in the East   482
    The Thirty Years' War   482
    Achievements in State-Building   484
    Warfare and the Growth of Army Size   485
    Popular Political Action   486

Absolutism in France and Spain   486
    The Foundations of Absolutism   486
    Louis XIV and Absolutism   487
    Life at Versailles   488
    French Financial Management Under Colbert   489
    Louis XIV's Wars   492
    The Decline of Absolutist Spain in the Seventeenth Century   492

Absolutism in Austria and Prussia   494
    The Austrian Habsburgs   495
    Prussia in the Seventeenth Century   495
    The Consolidation of Prussian Absolutism   496

The Development of Russia and the Ottoman Empire   497
    The Mongol Yoke and the Rise of Moscow   497
    The Tsar and His People   498
    The Reforms of Peter the Great   499
    The Growth of the Ottoman Empire   503

Alternatives to Absolutism in England and the Dutch Republic   506
    Absolutist Claims in England   506
    Religious Divides and the English Civil War   507
    Cromwell and Puritanical Absolutism in England   508
    The Restoration of the English Monarchy   510
    Constitutional Monarchy and Cabinet Government   510
    The Dutch Republic in the Seventeenth Century   511

Baroque Art and Music   514

Looking Back, Looking Ahead   515

Chapter Review   516

Living in the Past *The Absolutist Palace*   490

Listening to the Past *A German Account of Russian Life*   500

Individuals in Society *Glückel of Hameln*   512

17 Toward a New Worldview
1540–1789 518

The Scientific Revolution 520
- Scientific Thought in 1500 520
- Origins of the Scientific Revolution 521
- The Copernican Hypothesis 522
- Brahe, Kepler, and Galileo: Proving Copernicus Right 522
- Newton's Synthesis 525
- Bacon, Descartes, and the Scientific Method 526
- Science and Society 527
- Medicine, the Body, and Chemistry 529

The Enlightenment 530
- The Emergence of the Enlightenment 530
- The Influence of the Philosophes 531
- The Enlightenment Outside of France 534
- Urban Culture and Life in the Public Sphere 535
- Race and the Enlightenment 537
- Late Enlightenment 541

Enlightened Absolutism 541
- Frederick the Great of Prussia 543
- Catherine the Great of Russia 544
- The Austrian Habsburgs 546
- Jewish Life and the Limits of Enlightened Absolutism 549

Looking Back, Looking Ahead 550

Chapter Review 550

Living in the Past *Coffeehouse Culture* 538

Listening to the Past *Denis Diderot's "Supplement to Bougainville's Voyage"* 542

Individuals in Society *Moses Mendelssohn and the Jewish Enlightenment* 548

18 The Expansion of Europe
1650–1800 552

Working the Land 554
- The Legacy of the Open-Field System 554
- The Agricultural Revolution 555
- The Leadership of the Low Countries and England 556

The Beginning of the Population Explosion 558
- Long-standing Obstacles to Population Growth 558
- The New Pattern of the Eighteenth Century 559

The Growth of Rural Industry 560
- The Putting-Out System 561
- The Lives of Rural Textile Workers 561
- The Industrious Revolution 566

The Debate over Urban Guilds 566
- Urban Guilds 566
- Adam Smith and Economic Liberalism 568

Building the Global Economy 569
- Mercantilism and Colonial Wars 569
- Eighteenth-Century Colonial Trade 571
- The Atlantic Slave Trade 573
- Identities and Communities of the Atlantic World 575
- Trade and Empire in Asia and the Pacific 578

Looking Back, Looking Ahead 581

Chapter Review 582

Listening to the Past *Contrasting Views on the Effects of Rural Industry* 564

Living in the Past *The Remaking of London* 574

Individuals in Society *Olaudah Equiano* 579

Contents xvii

19 The Changing Life of the People
1700–1800   584

Marriage and the Family   586
- Late Marriage and Nuclear Families   586
- Work Away from Home   587
- Premarital Sex and Community Controls   588
- New Patterns of Marriage and Illegitimacy   588
- Sex on the Margins of Society   590

Children and Education   591
- Child Care and Nursing   591
- Foundlings and Infanticide   592
- Attitudes Toward Children   593
- The Spread of Elementary Schools   595

Popular Culture and Consumerism   595
- Popular Literature   595
- Leisure and Recreation   597
- New Foods and Appetites   598
- Toward a Consumer Society   601

Religious Authority and Beliefs   606
- Church Hierarchy   606
- Protestant Revival   606
- Catholic Piety   608
- Marginal Beliefs and Practices   608

Medical Practice   609
- Faith Healing and General Practice   610
- Hospitals and Surgery   610
- Midwifery   611
- The Conquest of Smallpox   611

Looking Back, Looking Ahead   614

Chapter Review   614

Individuals in Society *Rose Bertin, "Minister of Fashion"*   600

Listening to the Past *Louis-Sébastien Mercier, a Day in the Life of Paris*   604

Living in the Past *Improvements in Childbirth*   612

20 The Revolution in Politics
1775–1815   618

Background to Revolution   620
- Legal Orders and Social Reality   620
- The Crisis of Political Legitimacy   621
- The American Revolution and Its Impact   622
- Financial Crisis   624

Politics and the People, 1789–1791   625
- The Formation of the National Assembly   625
- The Storming of the Bastille   627
- Peasant Revolt and the Rights of Man   628
- Parisian Women March on Versailles   630
- A Constitutional Monarchy and Its Challenges   630
- Revolutionary Aspirations in Saint-Domingue   632

World War and Republican France, 1791–1799   633
- Foreign Reactions to the Revolution   633
- The Outbreak of War   634
- The Second Revolution   635
- Total War and the Terror   637
- Revolution in Saint-Domingue   639
- The Thermidorian Reaction and the Directory   643

The Napoleonic Era, 1799–1815   644
- Napoleon's Rule of France   644
- Napoleon's Expansion in Europe   646
- The War of Haitian Independence   646
- The Grand Empire and Its End   649

Looking Back, Looking Ahead   651

Chapter Review   652

Listening to the Past *Abbé de Sieyès, "What Is the Third Estate?"*   626

Living in the Past *A Revolution of Culture and Daily Life*   640

Individuals in Society *Toussaint L'Ouverture*   648

Glossary   G-1
Index   I-1
Timeline   A History of Western Society: An Overview   I-18

Maps, Figures, and Tables

Maps

Chapter 12
Map 12.1 The Course of the Black Death in Fourteenth-Century Europe   343
Map 12.2 The Hundred Years' War, 1337–1453   351
Map 12.3 Fourteenth-Century Revolts   360
Spot Map The Great Schism, 1378–1417   355
Spot Map The Hussite Revolution, 1415–1436   357

Chapter 13
Map 13.1 The Italian City-States, ca. 1494   377
Map 13.2 The Growth of Printing in Europe, 1448–1551   386
Map 13.3 The Unification of Spain and the Expulsion of the Jews, Fifteenth Century   401
Spot Map The Expansion of France, 1475–1500   399

Chapter 14
Map 14.1 The Global Empire of Charles V, ca. 1556   421
Map 14.2 Religious Divisions in Europe, ca. 1555   429
Spot Map The Route of the Spanish Armada, 1588   425
Spot Map The Netherlands, 1609   435

Chapter 15
Map 15.1 The Fifteenth-Century Afro-Eurasian Trading World   444
Map 15.2 Overseas Exploration and Conquest in the Fifteenth and Sixteenth Centuries   452
Map 15.3 Seaborne Trading Empires in the Sixteenth and Seventeenth Centuries   465
Spot Map Columbus's First Voyage to the New World, 1492–1493   455
Spot Map Invasion of Tenochtitlán, 1519–1521   458

Chapter 16
Map 16.1 Europe After the Thirty Years' War   484
Map 16.2 Europe After the Peace of Utrecht, 1715   493
Map 16.3 The Growth of Austria and Brandenburg-Prussia to 1748   496
Map 16.4 The Ottoman Empire at Its Height, 1566   504
Spot Map The Acquisitions of Louis XIV, 1668–1713   492
Spot Map The Expansion of Russia to 1725   498
Spot Map The English Civil War, 1642–1649   508

Chapter 17
Map 17.1 The Partition of Poland, 1772–1795   546
Spot Map The War of the Austrian Succession, 1740–1748   543
Spot Map The Pale of Settlement, 1791   549

Chapter 18
Map 18.1 Industry and Population in Eighteenth-Century Europe   562
Map 18.2 The Atlantic Economy in 1701   570
Map 18.3 European Claims in North America Before and After the Seven Years' War, 1755–1763   572
Spot Map Plantation Zones, ca. 1700   573
Spot Map India, 1805   581

Chapter 19
Map 19.1 Literacy in France, ca. 1789   596

Chapter 20
Map 20.1 The War of Haitian Independence, 1791–1804   642
Map 20.2 Napoleonic Europe in 1812   650
Spot Map The Great Fear, 1789   629
Spot Map Areas of Insurrection, 1793   635
Spot Map German Confederation of the Rhine, 1806   646

Figures and Tables

Thematic Chronology The Hundred Years' War   350
Thematic Chronology Major Contributors to the Scientific Revolution   527
Thematic Chronology Major Figures of the Enlightenment   534
Figure 18.1 The Growth of Population in England, 1000–1800   558
Figure 18.2 The Increase of Population in Europe in the Eighteenth Century   559
Figure 18.3 Exports of English Manufactured Goods, 1700–1774   571
Thematic Chronology The French Revolution   638
Thematic Chronology The Napoleonic Era   647

Special Features

Living in the Past

Treating the Plague   344
Male Clothing and Masculinity   398
Uses of Art in the Reformation   418
Foods of the Columbian Exchange   466
The Absolutist Palace   490
Coffeehouse Culture   538
The Remaking of London   574
Improvements in Childbirth   612
A Revolution of Culture and Daily Life   640

Listening to the Past

Christine de Pizan, Advice to the Wives of Artisans   362
Perspectives on Humanist Learning and Women   382
Martin Luther, *On Christian Liberty*   414
Columbus Describes His First Voyage   454
A German Account of Russian Life   500
Denis Diderot's "Supplement to Bougainville's Voyage"   542
Contrasting Views on the Effects of Rural Industry   564
Louis-Sébastien Mercier, a Day in the Life of Paris   604
Abbé de Sieyès, "What Is the Third Estate?"   626

Individuals in Society

Meister Eckhart   359
Leonardo da Vinci   391
Teresa of Ávila   432
Juan de Pareja   469
Glückel of Hameln   512
Moses Mendelssohn and the Jewish Enlightenment   548
Olaudah Equiano   579
Rose Bertin, "Minister of Fashion"   600
Toussaint L'Ouverture   648

Preface

With this, the tenth edition of *A History of Western Society*, we invite our colleagues and current and past adopters to join us in seeing the book as if for the first time. For us, this edition—undertaken at a new publishing house—has been an opportunity to revisit our original vision and to thereby realize the most thorough reconsideration of our text since we first began. *A History of Western Society* grew out of the initial three authors' desire to infuse new life into the study of Western Civilization. We knew that historians were using imaginative questions and innovative research to open up vast new areas of historical interest and knowledge. At that point, social history was dramatically changing the ways we understood the past, and we decided to create a book that would re-create the lives of ordinary people in appealing human terms, while also giving major economic, political, cultural, and intellectual developments the attention they unquestionably deserve. The three new authors who have joined the original author team—and who first used the book as students or teachers—remain committed to advancing this vision for today's classroom. With its new look, line-by-line edits aimed at increasing the book's readability and accessibility, reinvigorated scholarship, and broader definition of social history that reflects where instructors and students are now, we've rethought every element of the book to bring the original vision into the twenty-first century and make the past memorable for a new generation of students and instructors.

History as a discipline never stands still, and over the last several decades cultural history has joined social history as a source of dynamism. Because of its emphasis on the ways people made sense of their lives, *A History of Western Society* has always included a large amount of cultural history, ranging from foundational works of philosophy and literature to popular songs and stories. The focus on cultural history has been heightened in this tenth edition in a way that highlights the interplay between men's and women's lived experiences and the ways men and women reflect on these experiences to create meaning. The joint social and cultural perspective requires—fortunately, in our opinion—the inclusion of objects as well as texts as important sources for studying history, which has allowed us to incorporate the growing emphasis on material culture in the work of many historians.

These new directions have not changed the central mission of the book, which is to introduce students to the broad sweep of Western Civilization in a fresh yet balanced manner. Every edition has incorporated new research to keep the book up-to-date and respond to the changing needs of readers and instructors, and we have continued to do this in the tenth edition. As we have made these changes, large and small, we have sought to give students and teachers an integrated perspective so that they could pursue—on their own or in the classroom—the historical questions that they find particularly exciting and significant.

Textual Changes

For the tenth edition we took the time to revisit, reconsider, and revise every paragraph of the book. We paid painstaking attention to the writing, and we're proud of the results. Informed by recent scholarship, every chapter was revised with an aim toward readability and accessibility. Several main lines of revision have guided our many changes. In particular, as noted above, we have broadened the book's focus on social history to include a greater emphasis on cultural history. This increased emphasis is supported in every chapter by the use of artifacts that make history tangible and by the new Living in the Past visual feature, described below, that demonstrates the intersection between society and culture. In addition, the social and cultural context of Western Civilization has been integrated throughout the narrative, including expanded and new sections on Egyptian life, common people in Charlemagne's empire, artistic patronage during the Renaissance, identities and communities of the Atlantic world, eighteenth-century education, nineteenth-century family life, consumer society between the two world wars, life under Nazi occupation, and state and society in the East Bloc, among others.

The tenth edition continues to reflect Europe's interactions with the rest of the world and the role of gender in shaping human experience. The global context of European history is reflected in new scholarship on the steppe peoples of Central Asia, Muslim views of the Crusades, the Atlantic world, decolonization, and globalization. New scholarship on gender is woven throughout the book and is included in sections on Frankish queens, medieval prostitution, female humanists, politics and gender during the French Revolution, and gender roles during industrialization.

These major aspects of revision are accompanied by the incorporation of a wealth of new scholarship and subject areas. Additions, among others, include material on Paleolithic and Neolithic life (Chapter 1); the Neo-Babylonians (Chapter 2); the later period of the Roman Empire in the West (Chapter 7); the bubonic plague in eastern Europe (Chapter 12); the Jesuits (Chapter 14); the limits of enlightened absolutism (Chapter 17); eighteenth-century beliefs and practices (Chapter 19); expanded coverage of the peasant revolt (Chapter 20); sections on the Battle of the Somme, waging total war, and the human costs of World War I (Chapter 26); popular support for National Socialism (Chapter 27); the affluent society (Chapter 30); and up-to-date coverage of the economic downturn in Europe, the Iraq War, and the global recession (Chapter 31).

Organizational Changes

To meet the demands of the evolving course, we took a close and critical look at the book's organization, and have made several major changes in the organization of chapters to reflect the way the course is taught today. Chapter 7 now begins in 250 with the reforms of Diocletian and Constantine, and includes material on the debate over the decline of the Roman Empire in the West as well as a more comprehensive discussion of the barbarian migrations. To increase clarity, we've combined the separate chapters on absolutism in western and eastern Europe into a single chapter on absolutism and constitutionalism. Volume 2 also features a completely revised and updated post-1945 section featuring a third, new, postwar chapter, "Europe in an Age of Globalization, 1990 to the Present." In response to the growth in new and exciting scholarship for this period, the postwar chapters have been completely rewritten by new author Joe Perry with new scholarship on decolonization, consumerism as an aspect of the Cold War, new patterns of immigration and guest worker programs, the growth and decline of the welfare state in eastern and western Europe, and Europe's place in an era of increasing globalization, including the challenges to liberalism mounted by new social movements.

Features

We are proud of the diverse special features that expand upon the narrative and offer opportunities for classroom discussion and assignments, and in the new edition we have expanded our offerings to include a brand new feature created in response to current research trends that is sure to get students and instructors talking. This **NEW** visual feature, **Living in the Past**, uses social and cultural history to show how life in the past was both similar to and different from our lives today. Focusing on relatively narrow aspects of social and cultural history to write compelling stories that would encourage students to think about the way the past informs the present was both a challenge and a pleasure. The resulting thirty-one essays—one in each chapter—introduce students to the study of material culture, encourage critical analysis, and engage and inform with fascinating details about life in the past. Richly illustrated with images and artifacts, each feature includes a short essay and questions for analysis.

We use these features to explore the deeper ramifications of things students might otherwise take for granted, such as consumer goods, factories, and even currency. Students connect to the people of the past through a diverse range of topics such as "Assyrian Palace Life and Power," "Roman Table Manners," "Foods of the Columbian Exchange," "Coffeehouse Culture," "The Immigrant Experience," "A Model Socialist Steel Town," and "The Supermarket Revolution."

In our years of teaching Western Civilization, we have often noted that students come alive when they encounter stories about real people in the past. To give students a chance to see the past through ordinary people's lives, each chapter includes one of the popular **Individuals in Society** biographical essays that offer brief studies of individuals or groups, informing students about the societies in which they lived. This feature grew out of our long-standing focus on people's lives and the varieties of historical experience, and we believe that readers will empathize with these human beings as they themselves seek to define their own identities. The spotlighting of individuals, both famous and obscure, perpetuates the book's continued attention to cultural and intellectual developments, highlights human agency, and reflects changing interests within the historical profession as well as the development of "micro-history." **NEW** features include essays on Cyrus the Great; Queen Cleopatra; the Venerable Bede; Meister Eckhart; Rose Bertin, "Minister of Fashion"; Josiah Wedgwood; Germaine de Staël; and Armando Rodrigues, West Germany's "One-Millionth Guest Worker."

Each chapter also continues to include a primary source feature titled **Listening to the Past**, chosen to extend and illuminate a major historical issue through the presentation of a single original source or several voices. Each opens with an introduction and closes with questions for analysis that invite students to evaluate the evidence as historians would. Selected for their interest and importance and carefully fitted into their historical context, these sources allow students to hear the past and to observe how history has been shaped by individuals. **NEW** topics include "Cicero and the Plot to Kill Caesar," "Augustus's *Res Gestae*," "Eirik's Saga," "Perspectives on Humanist Learning and Women," "Denis Diderot's 'Supplement to Bougainville's Voyage,'" "Contrasting Views on the Effects of Rural Industry," "Abbé de Sieyès, 'What Is the Third Estate?,'" "Herder and Mazzini on the Development of Nationalism," "Lin Zexu and Yamagata Aritomo, Confronting Western Imperialism," and "The Nixon-Khrushchev 'Kitchen Debate.'" In addition to using documents as part of our special feature program, we have quoted extensively from a wide variety of primary sources in the narrative, demonstrating that such quotations are the "stuff" of history. We believe that our extensive program of using primary sources as an integral part of the narrative as well as in extended form in the "Listening to the Past" chapter feature will help readers learn to interpret and think critically.

With the goal of making this the most student-centered edition yet, we paid renewed attention to the book's pedagogy. To help guide students, each chapter opens with a **chapter preview with focus questions** keyed to the main chapter headings. These questions are repeated within the chapter and again in **NEW chapter reviews**. Many of the questions have been reframed for this edition, and new summary answers have been added to the chapter review. Each chapter review concludes with a carefully selected list of annotated **suggestions for further reading**, revised and updated to keep them current with the vast amount of new work being done in many fields.

To help students understand the material and prepare for exams, each chapter includes **NEW Looking Back, Looking Ahead** conclusions. Replacing the former chapter summaries, each conclusion provides an insightful synthesis of the chapter's main developments, while connecting to events that students will encounter in the chapters to come. In this way students are introduced to history as an ongoing process of interrelated events.

To promote clarity and comprehension, boldface **key terms** in the text are defined in the margins and listed in the chapter review. **NEW phonetic spellings** are located directly after terms that readers are likely to find hard to pronounce. The **chapter chronologies**, which review major developments discussed in each chapter, have been improved to more closely mirror the key events of the chapter, and the number of topic-specific **thematic chronologies** has been expanded, with new chronologies on "Art and Philosophy in the Hellenic Period" and "Major Figures of the Enlightenment," among others. Once again we also provide a **unified timeline** at the end of the text. Comprehensive and easy to locate, this useful timeline allows students to compare developments over the centuries.

The high-quality art and map program has been thoroughly revised and expanded. The new edition features more than **600 contemporaneous illustrations**. To make the past tangible, and as an extension of our enhanced attention to cultural history, we include over **100 artifacts**—from swords and fans to playing cards and record players. As in earlier editions, all illustrations have been carefully selected to complement the text, and all include captions that inform students while encouraging them to read the text more deeply. Completely redesigned and reconceptualized for the new edition, **87 full-size maps** illustrate major developments in the narrative. In addition, **61 NEW spot maps** are embedded in the narrative to show areas under discussion. **NEW** maps in the tenth edition highlight such topics as the Persian wars, the Hanseatic League, the Russian civil war, the Holocaust, Cold War Europe, pollution in Europe, and the Soviet war in Afghanistan, among others.

We recognize students' difficulties with geography and visual analysis, and the new edition includes the popular **Mapping the Past map activities** and **NEW Picturing the Past visual activities**. Included in each chapter, these activities give students valuable skills in reading and interpreting maps and images by asking them to analyze the maps or visuals and make connections to the larger processes discussed in the narrative. All these activities can be completed online and submitted directly to instructors at the free online study guide.

To showcase the book's rich art program and to signal our commitment to this thorough and deep revision, the book has been completely redesigned. The dynamic new contemporary design engages and assists students with its clear, easy-to-use pedagogy.

Acknowledgments

It is a pleasure to thank the many instructors who read and critiqued the manuscript through its development:

Georgia Bonny Bazemore, Eastern Washington University
John Beeler, University of Alabama
Dudley R. Belcher, Tri-County Technical College
Stephen A. Beluris, Moorpark College
Nancy B. Bjorklund, Fullerton College
Paul Bookbinder, University of Massachusetts, Boston
Edward A. Boyden, Nassau Community College
Harry T. Burgess, St. Clair County Community College
Jacqueline de Vries, Augsburg College
Daniel Finn, Valencia Community College
Jennifer Foray, Purdue University
Gary Forsythe, Texas Tech University
Lucille M. Fortunato, Bridgewater State College
Robert Genter, Nassau Community College
Stephen Gibson, Allegany College of Maryland
Andrew L. Goldman, Gonzaga University
Anthony Heideman, Front Range Community College
Jason M. Kelly, Indiana University
Keith Knutson, Viterbo University
Lynn Lubamersky, Boise State University
Susan A. Maurer, Nassau Community College
Greg Mauriocourt, Technical College of the Lowcountry
Jennifer McNabb, Western Illinois University
Elisa Miller, Rhode Island College
James M. Mini, Montgomery County Community College
Mary Lou Mosley, Paradise Valley Community College
Lisa Ossian, Des Moines Area Community College
Scott W. Palmer, Western Illinois University
Dennis Ricci, Community College of Rhode Island and Quinsigamond Community College
James Robertson, Montgomery County Community College
Daniel Robison, Troy University
Jahan Salehi, Guilford Tech Community College
Carol Longenecker Schmidt, Tri-County Technical College
Robert Shipley, Widener University
Karen Sonnelitter, Purdue University
Donathan Taylor, Hardin-Simmons University
Norman R. West, SUNY at Suffolk
Shelley Wolbrink, Drury University
Robert Zajkowski, Hudson Valley Community College

It is also a pleasure to thank the many editors who have assisted us over the years, first at Houghton Mifflin and now at Bedford/St. Martin's. At Bedford/St. Martin's, these include senior development editor Laura Arcari, with assistance from Beth Welch, for developing the new "Living in the Past" features; freelance development editor Michelle McSweeney; associate editors Lynn Sternberger and Jack Cashman; executive editor Traci Mueller Crowell; director of development Jane Knetzger; publisher for history Mary Dougherty; map editor Charlotte Miller; photo researcher Carole Frohlich; text permissions editor Sandy Schechter; and Christina Horn, senior production editor, with the assistance of Alexis Biasell and the guidance of managing editor Elizabeth Schaaf and assistant managing editor John Amburg. Other key contributors were designer Brian Salisbury, page makeup artist Cia Boynton, copyeditor Sybil Sosin, proofreaders Andrea Martin and Angela Hoover Morrison, indexer Leoni McVey, and cover designer Billy Boardman. We would also like to thank editorial director Denise Wydra and president Joan E. Feinberg.

Many of our colleagues at the University of Illinois, the University of Wisconsin–Milwaukee, and Georgia State University continue to provide information and stimulation, often without even knowing it. We thank them for it. We also thank the many students over the years with whom we have used earlier editions of this book. Their reactions and opinions helped shape the revisions to this edition, and we hope it remains worthy of the ultimate praise that they bestowed on it, that it's "not boring like most textbooks." Merry Wiesner-Hanks would, as always, also like to thank her husband Neil, without whom work on this project would not be possible. Clare Haru Crowston thanks her husband Ali and her children Lili, Reza, and Kian, who are a joyous reminder of the vitality of life that we try to showcase in this book. John McKay expresses his deep appreciation to JoAnn McKay for her keen insights and unfailing encouragement. Joe Perry thanks Andrzej S. Kaminski and the expert team assembled at Lazarski University for their insightful comments and is most grateful to Joyce de Vries for her unstinting support and encouragement.

Each of us has benefited from the criticism of our coauthors, although each of us assumes responsibility for what he or she has written. John Buckler has written the first six chapters; building on text originally written by Bennett Hill, Merry Wiesner-Hanks has assumed primary responsibility for Chapters 7 through 14; building on text originally written by Bennett Hill and John McKay, Clare Crowston has assumed primary responsibility for Chapters 15 through 20; John McKay has written and revised Chapters 21 through 25; and Joe Perry has written and revised Chapters 26 through 31, building on text originally written by John McKay.

Versions and Supplements

A History of Western Society is supported by numerous resources—study tools for students, materials for instructors, and many options for packaging the book with documents readers, trade books, atlases, and other guides—that are free or available at a substantial discount. Descriptions follow; for more information, visit the book's catalog site at **bedfordstmartins.com/mckaywest/catalog**, or contact your local Bedford/St. Martin's sales representative.

Available Versions of This Book

To accommodate different course lengths and course budgets, *A History of Western Society* is available in several different formats, including three-hole punched loose-leaf Budget Books versions and e-books, which are available at a substantial discount.

- Combined edition (Chapters 1–31): available in hardcover, loose-leaf, and e-book formats
- Volume 1, From Antiquity to the Enlightenment (Chapters 1–17): available in paperback, loose-leaf, and e-book formats
- Volume 2, From the Age of Exploration to the Present (Chapters 15–31): available in paperback, loose-leaf, and e-book formats
- Volume A, From Antiquity to 1500 (Chapters 1–13): available in paperback
- Volume B, From the Later Middle Ages to 1815 (Chapters 12–20): available in paperback
- Volume C, From the Revolutionary Era to the Present (Chapters 20–31): available in paperback
- Since 1300 (Chapters 12–31): available in paperback and e-book formats
- Since 1300 for Advanced Placement (Chapters 12–31): available in hardcover and e-book formats

Our innovative e-books give your students the content you want in a convenient format at about half the cost of a print book. **Bedford/St. Martin's e-Books** have been optimized for reading and studying online. **CourseSmart e-Books** can be downloaded or used online, whichever is more convenient for your students.

Companion Site

Our new companion site at **bedfordstmartins.com/mckaywest** gathers free and premium resources, giving students a way to extend *A History of Western Society* online. This book-specific site provides a single destination that students can use to practice, read, write, and study, and to find and access quizzes and activities, study aids, and history research and writing help.

FREE Online Study Guide. Available at the companion site, this popular resource provides students with self-review quizzes and activities for each chapter, including a multiple-choice self-test that focuses on important concepts; an identification quiz that helps students remember key people, places, and events; a flash-card activity that tests students' knowledge of key terms; and map activities to strengthen students' geography skills. Instructors can monitor students' progress through an online Quiz Gradebook or receive e-mail updates.

FREE History Research and Writing Help. Also available at the companion site, this resource includes **History Research and Reference Sources**, with links to history-related databases, indexes, and journals; **More Sources and How to Format a History Paper**, with clear advice on how to integrate primary and secondary sources into research papers and how to cite and format sources correctly; **Build a Bibliography**, a simple Web-based tool that generates bibliographies in four commonly used documentation styles; and **Tips on Avoiding Plagiarism**, an online tutorial that reviews the consequences of plagiarism and features exercises to help students practice integrating sources and recognize acceptable summaries.

Instructor Resources

Bedford/St. Martin's has developed a wide range of teaching resources for this book and for this course. They range from lecture and presentation materials and assessment tools to course management options. Most can be downloaded or ordered at **bedfordstmartins.com/mckaywest/catalog**.

HistoryClass for *A History of Western Society*. HistoryClass, a Bedford/St. Martin's Online Course Space, puts the online resources available with this textbook in one convenient and completely customizable course space. There you can access an interactive e-book and primary sources reader; maps, images, documents, and links; chapter review quizzes; interactive multimedia exercises; and research and writing help. In HistoryClass you can get all our premium content and tools and assign, rearrange, and mix them with your own resources. For more information, visit **yourhistoryclass.com**.

Bedford/St. Martin's Course Cartridges. Whether you use Blackboard, WebCT, Desire2Learn, Angel, Sakai, or Moodle, we have free content and support available to help you plug our content into your course management system. Registered instructors can download cartridges with no hassle and no strings attached. Content includes our most popular free resources and book-specific content for *A History of Western Society*. Visit **bedfordstmartins.com/cms** to see a demo, find your version, or download your cartridge.

Instructor's Resource Manual. The instructor's manual offers both experienced and first-time instructors tools for presenting textbook material in engaging ways. It includes chapter review material, teaching strategies, and a guide to chapter-specific supplements available for the text.

Guide to Changing Editions. Designed to facilitate an instructor's transition from the previous edition of *A History of Western Society* to the current edition, this guide presents an overview of major changes as well as of changes in each chapter.

Computerized Test Bank. The test bank includes a mix of fresh, carefully crafted multiple-choice, definition, short-answer, and essay questions for each chapter. The questions appear in Microsoft Word format and in easy-to-use test bank software that allows instructors to easily add, edit, re-sequence, and print questions and answers. Instructors can also export questions into a variety of formats, including WebCT and Blackboard.

PowerPoint Maps, Images, Lecture Outlines, and i>clicker Content. These presentation materials are downloadable individually from the Media and Supplements tab at bedfordstmartins.com/mckaywest/catalog and are available on *The Bedford Lecture Kit Instructor's Resource CD-ROM*. They include ready-made and fully customizable PowerPoint multimedia presentations built around lecture outlines with embedded maps, figures, and selected images from the textbook and with detailed instructor notes on key points. Also available are maps and selected images in JPEG and PowerPoint formats; content for i>clicker, a classroom response system, in Microsoft Word and PowerPoint formats; the Instructor's Resource Manual in Microsoft Word format; and outline maps in PDF format for quizzing or handing out. All files are suitable for copying onto transparency acetates.

Overhead Map Transparencies. This set of full-color acetate transparencies includes 130 maps for the Western Civilization course.

Make History: Free Documents, Maps, Images, and Web Sites. Finding the source material you need is simple with Make History. Here the best Web resources are combined with hundreds of carefully chosen maps and images and helpfully annotated. Browse the collection of thousands of resources by course or by topic, date, and type. Available at bedfordstmartins.com/makehistory.

Videos and Multimedia. A wide assortment of videos and multimedia CD-ROMs on various topics in Western Civilization is available to qualified adopters through your Bedford/St. Martin's sales representative.

Packaging Opportunities

Save your students money and package your favorite text with more! For information on free packages and discounts of up to 50 percent, visit bedfordstmartins.com/mckaywest/catalog, or contact your local Bedford/St. Martin's sales representative.

e-Book. The e-book for this title can be packaged with the print text at no additional cost.

***Sources of Western Society*, Second Edition.** This primary-source collection — available in Volume 1, Volume 2, and Since 1300 versions — provides a revised and expanded selection of sources to accompany *A History of Western Society*, Tenth Edition. Each chapter features five or six written and visual sources by well-known figures and ordinary individuals alike. Now including nineteen visual sources and 30 percent more documents, this edition offers both breadth and depth. A new Viewpoints feature highlights two or three sources that address the same topic from different perspectives. Document headnotes and reading and discussion questions promote student understanding. Available free when packaged with the text.

***Sources of Western Society* e-Book.** The reader is also available as an e-book. When packaged with the print or electronic version of the textbook, it is free.

***Rand McNally Atlas of Western Civilization*.** This collection of over fifty full-color maps highlights social, political, and cross-cultural change and interaction from classical Greece and Rome to the postindustrial Western world. Each map is thoroughly indexed for fast reference. Available for $3.00 when packaged with the text.

***The Bedford Glossary for European History*.** This handy supplement for the survey course gives students historically contextualized definitions for hundreds of terms — from *Abbasids* to *Zionism* — that they will encounter in lectures, reading, and exams. Available free when packaged with the text.

***The Bedford Series in History and Culture*.** More than one hundred titles in this highly praised series combine first-rate scholarship, historical narrative, and important primary documents for undergraduate courses. Each book is brief, inexpensive, and focused on a specific topic or period. For a complete list of titles, visit bedfordstmartins.com/bshc. Package discounts are available.

Trade Books. Titles published by sister companies Hill and Wang; Farrar, Strauss and Giroux; Henry Holt and Company; St. Martin's Press; Picador; and Palgrave Macmillan are available at a 50 percent discount when packaged with Bedford/St. Martin's textbooks. For more information, visit bedfordstmartins.com/tradeup.

***The Social Dimension of Western Civilization*.** Combining current scholarship with classic pieces, this reader's forty-eight secondary sources, compiled by Richard M. Golden, hook students with the fascinating and often surprising details of how everyday Western people worked, ate, played, celebrated, worshiped, married, procreated, fought, persecuted, and died. Package discounts are available.

The West in the Wider World: Sources and Perspectives. Edited by Richard Lim and David Kammerling Smith, the first college reader to focus on the central historical question "How did the West become the West?" offers a wealth of written and visual source materials that reveal the influence of non-European regions on the origins and development of Western Civilization. Package discounts are available.

A Pocket Guide to Writing in History. This portable and affordable reference tool by Mary Lynn Rampolla provides reading, writing, and research advice useful to students in all history courses. Concise yet comprehensive advice on approaching typical history assignments, developing critical reading skills, writing effective history papers, conducting research, using and documenting sources, and avoiding plagiarism — enhanced by practical tips and examples throughout — have made this slim reference a bestseller. Package discounts are available.

A Student's Guide to History. This complete guide provides the practical help students need to be successful in any history course. In addition to introducing students to the nature of the discipline, author Jules Benjamin teaches a wide range of skills from preparing for exams to approaching common writing assignments, and explains the research and documentation process with plentiful examples. Package discounts are available.

A History of Western Society

12

The Crisis of the Later Middle Ages

1300–1450

During the later Middle Ages the last book of the New Testament, the Book of Revelation, inspired thousands of sermons and hundreds of religious tracts. The Book of Revelation deals with visions of the end of the world, with disease, war, famine, and death — often called the "Four Horsemen of the Apocalypse" — triumphing everywhere. It is no wonder this part of the Bible was so popular, for between 1300 and 1450 Europeans experienced a frightful series of shocks. The climate turned colder, leading to poor harvests and famine. People weakened by hunger were more susceptible to disease, and in the middle of the fourteenth century a new disease, probably the bubonic plague, spread throughout Europe. Over several years the plague killed millions of people, and there was no effective treatment. War devastated the countryside, especially in France, leading to widespread discontent and peasant revolts. Workers in cities also revolted against dismal working conditions, and violent crime and ethnic tensions increased. Death and preoccupation with death make the fourteenth century one of the most wrenching periods of Western civilization. Yet, in spite of the pessimism and crises, important institutions and cultural forms, including representative assemblies and national literatures, emerged. Even institutions that experienced severe crisis, such as the Christian church, saw new types of vitality. ■

Life in the Later Middle Ages. Peasants and urban workers rose up in revolt across Europe in the fourteenth century. In this French illustration, Wat Tyler, the leader of the English Peasants' Revolt, is stabbed during a meeting with the king. Tyler died soon afterward, and the revolt was ruthlessly crushed.

CHAPTER PREVIEW

Prelude to Disaster
■ What were the demographic, economic, and social consequences of climate change?

The Black Death
■ How did the spread of the plague shape European society?

The Hundred Years' War
■ What were the causes of the Hundred Years' War, and how did the war affect European politics, economics, and cultural life?

Challenges to the Church
■ What challenges faced the Christian church in the fourteenth century, and how did church leaders, intellectuals, and ordinary people respond?

Social Unrest in a Changing Society
■ How did economic and social tensions contribute to revolts, crime, violence, and a growing sense of ethnic and national distinctions?

Prelude to Disaster

What were the demographic, economic, and social consequences of climate change?

In the first half of the fourteenth century, Europe experienced a series of climate changes that led to lower levels of food production, which had dramatic and disastrous ripple effects. Political leaders attempted to find solutions but were unable to deal with the economic and social problems that resulted.

Climate Change and Famine

The period from about 1000 to about 1300 saw a warmer than usual climate in Europe, which underlay all the changes and vitality of the High Middle Ages. About 1300 the climate changed, becoming colder and wetter. Historical geographers refer to the period from 1300 to 1450 as a "little ice age," which they can trace through both natural and human records.

Evidence from nature emerges through the study of Alpine and polar glaciers, tree rings, and pollen left in bogs. Human-produced sources include written reports of rivers freezing and crops never ripening, as well as archaeological evidence such as the abandoned villages of Greenland, where ice floes cut off contact with the rest of the world and the harshening climate meant that the few hardy crops grown earlier could no longer survive. The Viking colony on Greenland died out completely, though Inuit people who relied on hunting sea mammals continued to live in the far north, as they had before the arrival of Viking colonists.

An unusual number of storms brought torrential rains, ruining the wheat, oat, and hay crops on which people and animals almost everywhere depended. Since long-distance transportation of food was expensive and difficult, most urban areas depended for bread and meat on areas no more than a day's journey away. Poor harvests—and one in four was likely to be poor—led to scarcity and starvation. Almost all of northern Europe suffered a **Great Famine** in the years 1315 to 1322, which contemporaries interpreted as a recurrence of the biblical "seven lean years" (Genesis 42).

Even in non-famine years, the cost of grain, livestock, and dairy products rose sharply, in part because diseases hit cattle and sheep. Increasing prices meant that

Great Famine A terrible famine in 1315–1322 that hit much of Europe after a period of climate change.

Death from Famine In this fifteenth-century painting, dead bodies lie in the middle of a path, while a funeral procession at the right includes a man with an adult's coffin and a woman with the coffin of an infant under her arm. People did not simply allow the dead to lie in the street in medieval Europe, though during famines and epidemics it was sometimes difficult to maintain normal burial procedures. (Erich Lessing/Art Resource, NY)

fewer people could afford to buy food. Reduced caloric intake meant increased susceptibility to disease, especially for infants, children, and the elderly. Epidemics of typhoid fever carried away thousands. Workers on reduced diets had less energy, which in turn meant lower productivity, lower output, and higher grain prices.

Social Consequences

The changing climate and resulting agrarian crisis of the fourteenth century had grave social consequences. Poor harvests and famine led to the abandonment of homesteads. In parts of the Low Countries and in the Scottish-English borderlands, entire villages were abandoned, and many people became vagabonds, wandering in search of food and work. In Flanders and East Anglia (eastern England), some peasants were forced to mortgage, sublease, or sell their holdings to richer farmers in order to buy food. Throughout the affected areas, young men and women sought work in the towns, postponing marriage. Overall, the population declined because of the deaths caused by famine and disease, though the postponement of marriages and the resulting decline in offspring may have also played a part.

As the subsistence crisis deepened, starving people focused their anger on the rich, speculators, and the Jews, who were often targeted as creditors fleecing the poor through pawnbroking. (As seen in recent chapters, Jews often became moneylenders because Christian authorities restricted their ownership of land and opportunities to engage in other trades.) Rumors spread of a plot by Jews and their agents, the lepers, to kill Christians by poisoning the wells. Based on "evidence" collected by torture, many lepers and Jews were killed, beaten, or heavily fined.

Meanwhile, the international character of trade and commerce meant that a disaster in one country had serious implications elsewhere. For example, the infection that attacked English sheep in 1318 caused a sharp decline in wool exports in the following years. Without wool, Flemish weavers could not work, and thousands were laid off. Without woolen cloth, the businesses of Flemish, Hanseatic, and Italian merchants suffered. Unemployment encouraged people to turn to crime.

Government responses to these crises were ineffectual. The three sons of Philip the Fair who sat on the French throne between 1314 and 1328 condemned speculators who held stocks of grain back until conditions were desperate and prices high; forbade the sale of grain abroad; and published legislation prohibiting fishing with traps that took large catches. These measures remained largely a wish list and had few actual results.

In England, Edward I's incompetent son, Edward II (r. 1307–1327), also condemned speculators after his attempts to set price controls on livestock and ale proved futile. He did try to buy grain abroad, but little was available: yields in the Baltic were low; the French crown, as we have seen, forbade exports; and the grain shipped from northern Spain was grabbed by pirates. Such grain as reached southern English ports was stolen by looters and sold on the black market. The Crown's efforts at famine relief failed.

Chronology

1300–1450	Little ice age
1309–1376	Babylonian Captivity; papacy in Avignon
1310–1320	Dante writes *Divine Comedy*
1315–1322	Great Famine in northern Europe
1320s	First large-scale peasant rebellion in Flanders
1337–1453	Hundred Years' War
1347	Black Death arrives in Europe
1358	Jacquerie peasant uprising in France
1366	Statute of Kilkenny
1378–1417	Great Schism
1381	English Peasants' Revolt
1387–1400	Chaucer, *Canterbury Tales*

The Black Death

How did the spread of the plague shape European society?

Around 1300 improvements in ship design allowed year-round shipping for the first time. European merchants took advantage of these advances, and ships continually at sea carried all types of cargo. They also carried vermin of all types, especially insects and rats, which often harbored disease pathogens. Rats, fleas, and cockroaches could live for months on the cargo carried along the coasts, disembarking at ports with the grain, cloth, or other merchandise. Just as modern air travel has allowed diseases such as AIDS and the H1N1 virus to spread quickly over very long distances, medieval shipping did the same. The most frightful of these diseases, carried on Genoese ships, first emerged in western Europe in 1347, a disease that was later called the **Black Death**.

Black Death Plague that first struck Europe in 1347 and killed perhaps one-third of the population.

341

Pathology

Most historians and microbiologists identify the disease that spread in the fourteenth century as the bubonic plague caused by the bacillus *Yersinia pestis*. The disease normally afflicts rats. Fleas living on the infected rats drink their blood and then pass the bacteria that cause the plague on to the next rat they bite. Usually the disease is limited to rats and other rodents, but at certain points in history—perhaps when most rats have been killed off—the fleas have jumped from their rodent hosts to humans and other animals. One of these times appears to have occurred in the Eastern Roman Empire in the sixth century, when a plague killed millions of people. Another was in China and India in the 1890s, when millions died. Doctors and epidemiologists closely studied this outbreak, identified the bacillus as bubonic plague, and learned about the exact cycle of infection for the first time.

The fourteenth-century outbreak showed many similarities to the nineteenth-century outbreak, but also some differences. There are no reports of massive rat die-offs in fourteenth-century records. The plague was often transmitted directly from one person to another through coughing and sneezing (what epidemiologists term *pneumonic* transmission) as well as through flea bites. The fourteenth-century outbreak spread much faster than the nineteenth-century outbreak and was much more deadly, killing as much as one-third of the population when it first spread to an area. These differences have led some historians to question whether the fourteenth-century outbreak was actually not the bubonic plague, but a different disease, perhaps something like the Ebola virus. Other scholars counter that the differences could be explained by variant strains of the disease or improvements in sanitation and public health that would have limited the mortality rate of later outbreaks significantly, even in poor countries such as India. These debates fuel continued study of medical aspects of the plague, with scientists using innovative techniques such as studying the tooth pulp of bodies in medieval cemeteries to see if it contains DNA from plague-causing agents.

Though there is some disagreement about exactly what kind of disease the plague was, there is no dispute about its dreadful effects on the body. The classic symptom of the bubonic plague was a growth the size of a nut or an apple in the armpit, in the groin, or on the neck. This was the boil, or *bubo*, that gave the disease its name and caused agonizing pain. If the bubo was lanced and the pus thoroughly drained, the victim had a chance of recovery. The next stage was the appearance of black spots or blotches caused by bleeding under the skin. (This syndrome did not give the disease its common name; contemporaries did not call the plague the Black Death. Sometime in the fifteenth century the Latin phrase *atra mors*, meaning "dreadful death," was translated as "black death," and the phrase stuck.) Finally, the victim began to cough violently and spit blood. This stage, indicating the presence of millions of bacilli in the bloodstream, signaled the end, and death followed in two or three days.

Spread of the Disease

Plague symptoms were first described in 1331 in southwestern China, part of the Mongol Empire. Plague-infested rats accompanied Mongol armies and merchant caravans carrying silk, spices, and gold across Central Asia in the 1330s. The rats then stowed away on ships, carrying the disease to the ports of the Black Sea by the 1340s. Later stories told of more dramatic means of spreading the disease as well, reporting that Mongol armies besieging the city of Kaffa on the shores of the Black Sea catapulted plague-infected corpses over the walls to infect those inside. The city's residents dumped the corpses into the sea as fast as they could, but they were already infected.

In October 1347 Genoese ships brought the plague from Kaffa to Messina, from which it spread across Sicily. Venice and Genoa were hit in January 1348, and from the port of Pisa the disease spread south to Rome and east to Florence and all of Tuscany. By late spring southern Germany was attacked. Frightened French authorities chased a galley bearing the disease away from the port of Marseilles, but not before plague had infected the city, from which it spread to southern France and Spain. In June 1348 two ships entered the Bristol Channel and introduced it into England, and from there it traveled north into Scandinavia. The plague seems to have entered Poland through the Baltic seaports and spread eastward from there (Map 12.1).

Although urban authorities from London to Paris to Rome had begun to try to achieve a primitive level of sanitation by the fourteenth century, urban conditions remained ideal for the spread of disease. Narrow streets filled with refuse and human excrement were as much cesspools as thoroughfares. Dead animals and sore-covered beggars greeted the traveler. Houses whose upper stories projected over the lower ones blocked light and air, and extreme overcrowding was commonplace. When all members of an aristocratic family lived and slept in one room, it should not be surprising that six or eight persons in a middle-class or poor household slept in one bed—if they had one. Closeness, after all, provided warmth. Houses were beginning to be constructed of brick, but many wood, clay, and mud houses remained. A determined rat had little trouble entering such a house.

People were already weakened by famine, and standards of personal hygiene remained frightfully low. Fleas and body lice were universal afflictions: everyone from peasants to archbishops had them. One more bite

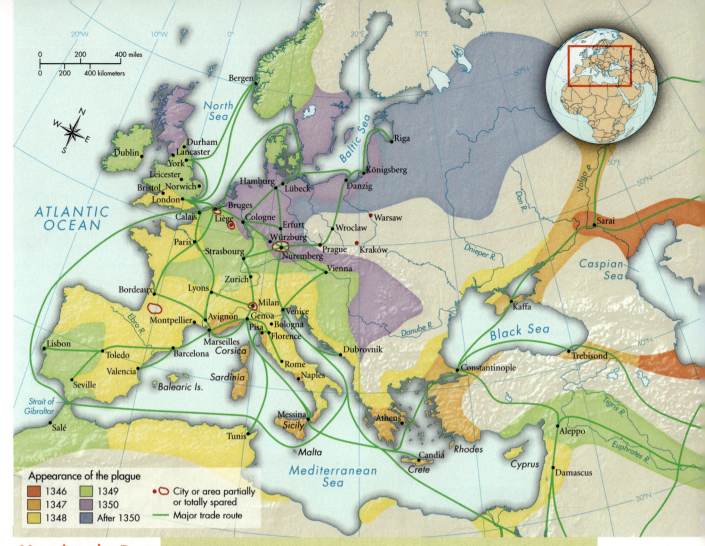

Mapping the Past

Map 12.1 **The Course of the Black Death in Fourteenth-Century Europe** The bubonic plague spread northward across Europe, beginning in the late 1340s with the first cases of disease reported in the ports of the Black Sea.

ANALYZING THE MAP When did the plague reach Paris? How much time passed before it spread to the rest of northern France and southern Germany? Which cities and regions were spared?

CONNECTIONS How did the expansion of trade that resulted from the commercial revolution contribute to the spread of the Black Death?

To complete this activity online, go to the Online Study Guide at bedfordstmartins.com/mckaywest.

---

did not cause much alarm, and the association among rats, fleas, and the plague was as yet unknown. If that nibble came from a bacillus-bearing flea, an entire household or area was doomed.

Mortality rates can be only educated guesses because population figures for the period before the arrival of the plague do not exist for most countries and cities. Of a total English population of perhaps 4.2 million, probably 1.4 million died of the Black Death. Densely populated Italian cities endured incredible losses. Florence lost between one-half and two-thirds of its population when the plague visited in 1348. Islamic parts of Europe were not spared, nor was the rest of the Muslim world. The most widely accepted estimate for western Europe and the Mediterranean is that the plague killed about one-third of the population in the first wave of infection.

Nor did central and eastern Europe escape the ravages of the disease. One chronicler records that, in the summer and autumn of 1349, between five hundred and six hundred died every day in Vienna. As the Black Death took its toll on the Holy Roman Empire, waves of emigrants fled to Poland, Bohemia, and Hungary, sometimes taking plague with them. In the Byzantine Empire the plague ravaged the population. The youngest son of Emperor John VI Kantakouzenos died just as his father took over the throne in 1347. "So incurable was the evil," wrote John later in his history of the Byzantine Empire, "that neither any regularity of life, nor any bodily strength could resist it. Strong and weak

Treating the Plague

LIVING IN THE PAST

MEDIEVAL PHYSICIANS BASED TREATMENTS FOR THE PLAGUE on their understanding of how the body worked, as do doctors in any era. Fourteenth-century people — lay, scholarly, and medical — attributed the disease to "poisons" in the air that caused the fluids in the body to become unbalanced. The imbalance in fluids led to illness, an idea that had been the core of Western ideas about the primary cause of disease since the ancient Greeks. Certain symptoms of the plague, such as boils that oozed and blood-filled coughing, were believed to be the body's natural reaction to too much fluid.

Doctors thus recommended preventive measures that would block the poisoned air from entering the body, such as holding strong-smelling herbs or other substances, like rosemary, juniper, or sulfur, in front of the nose or burning incense. Treatment concentrated on ridding the body of poisons and bringing the fluids into balance. As one fifteenth-century treatise put it, "everyone over seven should be made to vomit daily" and twice a week wrap up in sheets to "sweat copiously." The best way to regain health, however, was to let blood: "as soon as [the patient] feels an itch or pricking in his flesh [the physician] must use a goblet or cupping horn to let blood and draw down the blood from his heart, and this should be done two or three times at intervals of one or two days at the most." Letting blood was considered the most effective way to rebalance the fluids and also to flush the body of poisons.

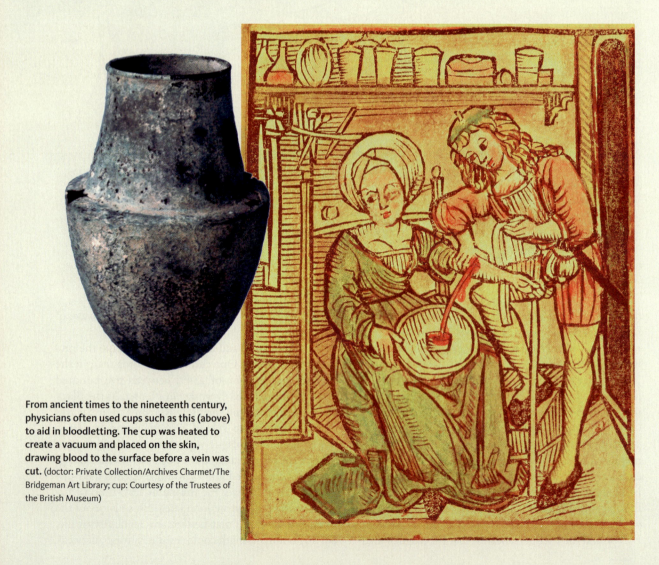

From ancient times to the nineteenth century, physicians often used cups such as this (above) to aid in bloodletting. The cup was heated to create a vacuum and placed on the skin, drawing blood to the surface before a vein was cut. (doctor: Private Collection/Archives Charmet/The Bridgeman Art Library; cup: Courtesy of the Trustees of the British Museum)

344

A plague doctor in a seventeenth-century German engraving published during a later outbreak of the dreaded disease. The doctor is fully covered, with a coat waxed smooth so that poisons just slide off. The beaked mask contains strong-smelling herbs, and the stick, beaten on the ground as he walks along, warns people away. (akg-images)

QUESTIONS FOR ANALYSIS

1. In the background of the plague doctor engraving, the artist shows a group of children running away as the plague doctor approaches. What aspects of his appearance or treatment methods contributed to this reaction?

2. Many people who lived through the plague reported that it created a sense of hopeless despair. Do these sources support this idea? Why?

Quotations from Rosemary Horrox, *The Black Death* (Manchester: Manchester University Press, 1994), p. 194.

bodies were all similarly carried away, and those best cared for died in the same manner as the poor."[1]

Across Europe the Black Death recurred intermittently from the 1360s to 1400. It reappeared from time to time over the following centuries, though never with the same virulence because Europeans now had some resistance. Improved standards of hygiene and strictly enforced quarantine measures also lessened the plague's toll, but only in 1721 did it make its last appearance in Europe, in the French port city of Marseilles. And only in 1947, six centuries after the arrival of the plague in Europe, did the American microbiologist Selman Waksman discover an effective treatment, streptomycin. Plague continues to infect rodent and human populations sporadically today.

> **❝ So incurable was the evil that neither any regularity of life, nor any bodily strength could resist it. Strong and weak bodies were all similarly carried away. ❞**
>
> —**EMPEROR JOHN VI KANTAKOUZENOS**

Care of the Sick

Fourteenth-century medical literature indicates that physicians tried many different things to prevent and treat the plague. They observed that crowded cities had high death rates, especially when the weather was warm and moist. We understand that warm, moist conditions make it easier for germs, viruses, and bacteria to grow and spread, but fourteenth-century people thought in terms of "poisons" in the air or "corrupted air" coming from swamps, unburied animals, or the positions of the stars, rather than germs. Their treatments thus focused on ridding the air and the body of these poisons, and on rebalancing bodily fluids to bring people back to health. (See "Living in the Past: Treating the Plague," at left.)

People tried anything they thought might help. Perhaps loud sounds like ringing church bells or firing the newly invented cannon would clean poisoned air. Medicines made from plants that were bumpy or that oozed liquid might work, keeping the more dangerous swelling and oozing of the plague away. Magical letter and number combinations, called cryptograms, were especially popular in Muslim areas. They were often the first letters of words in prayers or religious sayings, and they gave people a sense of order when faced with the randomness with which the plague seemed to strike.

> **❝ Almost no one cared for his neighbor . . . brother abandoned brother . . . and—even worse, almost unbelievable—fathers and mothers neglected to tend and care for their children. ❞**
>
> —GIOVANNI BOCCACCIO

It is noteworthy that, in an age of mounting criticism of clerical wealth (see page 356), the behavior of the clergy during the plague was often exemplary. Priests, monks, and nuns cared for the sick and buried the dead. In places like Venice, from which even physicians fled, priests remained to give what ministrations they could. Consequently, their mortality rate was phenomenally high. The German clergy especially suffered a severe decline in personnel in the years after 1350.

There were limits to care, however. The Italian writer Giovanni Boccaccio (1313–1375), describing the course of the disease in Florence in the preface to his book of

Picturing the Past

Patients in a Hospital Most victims of the plague died at home, but some went to special plague hospitals. This fifteenth-century painting shows what would have been a common scene, with female members of a religious order or Beguines caring for patients in a hospital. Here the women are also allegorical figures, judging the patients' worth as they take their pulse. At the right stands Justice holding scales, and at the left Prudence holding a rod. (Giraudon/The Bridgeman Art Library)

ANALYZING THE IMAGE What does this image suggest about the care for plague victims? Do the conditions shown at this hospital suggest that there is hope for these patients?

CONNECTIONS How does the allegorical depiction of the nuns shown here explain how medieval people understood the plague?

To complete this activity online, go to the Online Study Guide at **bedfordstmartins.com/mckaywest.**

tales, *The Decameron*, identified what many knew — that the disease passed from person to person:

> This pestilence was so powerful that it was transmitted to the healthy by contact with the sick, the way a fire close to dry or oily things will set them aflame. And the evil of the plague went even further: not only did talking to or being around the sick bring infection and a common death, but also touching the clothes of the sick or anything touched or used by them seemed to communicate this very disease to the person involved.[2]

To avoid contagion, wealthier people often fled cities for the countryside, though sometimes this simply spread the plague faster. Some cities tried shutting their gates to prevent infected people and animals from coming in, which worked in a few cities. They also walled up houses in which there was plague, trying to isolate those who were sick from those who were still healthy. In Boccaccio's words, "almost no one cared for his neighbor . . . brother abandoned brother . . . and — even worse, almost unbelievable — fathers and mothers neglected to tend and care for their children."[3]

Economic, Religious, and Cultural Effects

Economic historians and demographers sharply dispute the impact of the plague on the economy in the late fourteenth century. The traditional view that the plague had a disastrous effect has been greatly modified. The clearest evidence comes from England, where by the early fifteenth century most landlords enjoyed the highest revenues of the medieval period. Why? The answer appears to lie in the fact that England and many parts of Europe suffered from overpopulation in the early fourteenth century. Population losses caused by famines and the Black Death led to increased productivity by restoring a more efficient balance between labor, land, and capital.

What impact did visits of the plague have on urban populations? The rich evidence from a census of the city of Florence and its surrounding territory taken between 1427 and 1430 is fascinating. The region had suffered repeated epidemics since 1347. The census showed a high proportion of people who were age sixty or older, suggesting that the plague took the young rather than the mature. The high mortality rate of craftsmen between the ages of twenty and fifty-nine led Florentine guilds to recruit many new members, and also to develop new ways to organize production on a larger scale. Thus the post-plague years represent an age of "new men."

The Black Death brought on a general European inflation. High mortality produced a fall in production, shortages of goods, and a general rise in prices. The price of wheat in most of Europe increased, as did the costs of meat, sausage, and cheese. This inflation continued to the end of the fourteenth century. But labor shortages meant that workers could demand better wages, and the broad mass of people enjoyed a higher standard of living. The greater demand for labor also meant greater mobility for peasants in rural areas and for industrial workers in the towns and cities. Labor shortages caused by the Black Death throughout the Mediterranean region, from Constantinople to Spain, presented aggressive businessmen with a golden opportunity, and the price of slaves rose sharply.

The plague also had effects on religious practices. Despite Boccaccio's comments about family members' coldness, people were saddened by the loss of their loved ones, especially their children. It is not surprising that some people sought release from the devastating affliction in wild living, but more became more deeply pious. Rather than seeing the plague as a medical issue, they instead interpreted it as the result of an evil within themselves. God must be punishing them for terrible sins, they thought, so the best remedies were religious ones: asking for forgiveness, prayer, trust in God, making donations to churches, and trying to live better lives. John VI Kantakouzenos reported that in Constantinople, "many of the sick turned to better things in their minds . . . they abstained from all vice during that time and they lived virtuously; many divided their property among the poor, even before they were attacked by the disease."[4] In Muslim areas, religious leaders urged virtuous living in the face of death: give to the poor, reconcile with your enemies, free your slaves, and say a proper goodbye to your friends and family.

Some Christians turned to the severest forms of asceticism and frenzied religious fervor, joining groups of **flagellants** (FLA-juh-lunts), who whipped and scourged themselves as penance for their and society's sins in the belief that the Black Death was God's punishment for humanity's wickedness. Groups of flagellants traveled from town to town, often growing into unruly mobs. Officials worried that they would provoke violence and riots, and ordered groups to disband or forbade them to enter cities.

Along with seeing the plague as a call to reform their own behavior, however, people also searched for scapegoats, and savage cruelty sometimes resulted. Just as in the decades before the plague, many people believed that the Jews had poisoned the wells of Christian communities and thereby infected the drinking water. This charge led to the murder of thousands of Jews across Europe.

The literature and art of the late Middle Ages reveal a terribly morbid concern with death. One highly popular literary and artistic motif, the Dance of Death,

> **flagellants** People who believed that the plague was God's punishment for sin and sought to do penance by flagellating (whipping) themselves.

Flagellants In this manuscript illumination from 1349, shirtless flagellants scourge themselves with whips as they walk through the streets of the Flemish city of Tournai. The text notes that they are asking for God's grace to return to the city after it had been struck with the "most grave" illness. (HIP/Art Resource, NY)

depicted a dancing skeleton leading away living people, often in order of their rank. In the words of one early fifteenth-century English poem:

> Death spareth not low nor high degree
> Popes, Kings, nor worthy Emperors
> When they shine most in felicity
> He can abate the freshness of their flowers
> Eclipse their bright suns with his showers . . .
> Sir Emperor, lord of all the ground,
> Sovereign Prince, and highest of nobles
> You must forsake your round apples of gold
> Leave behind your treasure and riches
> And with others to my dance obey.[5]

Popular endowments of educational institutions multiplied. The years of the Black Death witnessed the foundation of new colleges at old universities and of entirely new universities. The foundation charters specifically mention the shortage of priests and the decay of learning. Whereas universities such as those at Bologna and Paris had international student bodies, new institutions established in the wake of the Black Death had more national or local constituencies. Thus the international character of medieval culture weakened, paving the way for schism (SKIH-zuhm) in the Catholic Church even before the Reformation.

As is often true with devastating events, the plague highlighted central qualities of medieval society: deep religious feeling, suspicion of those who were different, and a view of the world shaped largely by oral tradition, with a bit of classical knowledge mixed in among the educated elite.

The Hundred Years' War

What were the causes of the Hundred Years' War, and how did the war affect European politics, economics, and cultural life? ■

The plague ravaged populations in Asia, North Africa, and Europe; in western Europe a long international war added further misery to the frightful disasters of the plague. England and France had engaged in sporadic military hostilities from the time of the Norman Conquest in 1066, and in the middle of the fourteenth century these became more intense. From 1337 to 1453, the two countries intermittently fought one another in what was the longest war in European history, ultimately dubbed the Hundred Years' War, though it actually lasted 116 years.

Causes

The Hundred Years' War had both distant and immediate causes, including disagreements over rights to land, a dispute over the succession to the French throne, and economic conflicts. A distant cause was the duchy of

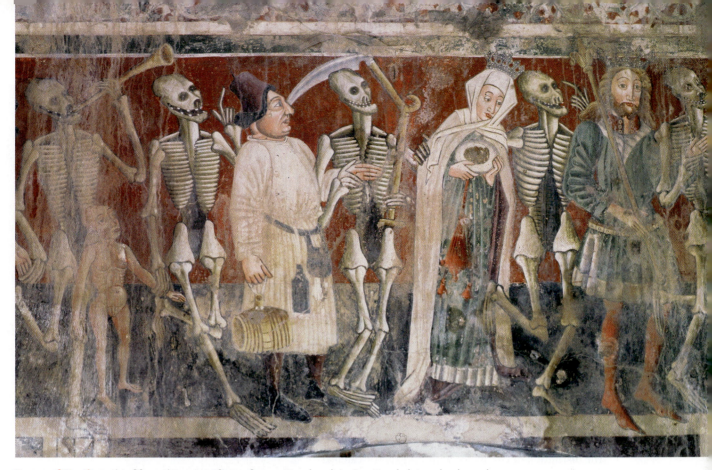

Dance of Death In this fifteenth-century fresco from a tiny church in Croatia, skeletons lead people from all social classes to their death. No one is spared, for the procession includes a king and queen, a pope, a bishop, and a little child. (Vladimir Bugarin, photographer)

Aquitaine, which became part of the holdings of the English crown when Eleanor of Aquitaine married King Henry II of England in 1152 (see Chapter 9; a duchy is a territory ruled by a duke). In 1259 Henry III of England had signed the Treaty of Paris with Louis IX of France, affirming English claims to Aquitaine in return for becoming a vassal of the French crown. French policy in the fourteenth century was strongly expansionist, however, and the French kings resolved to absorb the duchy into the kingdom of France. Aquitaine therefore became a disputed territory.

The immediate political cause of the war was a dispute over who would inherit the French throne after Charles IV of France, the last surviving son of Philip the Fair, died childless in 1328. With him ended the Capetian dynasty of France. Charles IV did have a sister — Isabella — and her son was Edward III, king of England. An assembly of French high nobles, meaning to exclude Isabella and Edward from the French throne, proclaimed that "no woman nor her son could succeed to the [French] monarchy." French lawyers defended the position with the claim that the exclusion of women from ruling or passing down the right to rule was part of Salic Law, a sixth-century law code of the Franks (see Chapter 7), and that Salic Law itself was part of the fundamental law of France. They used this invented tradition to argue that Edward should be barred from the French throne. (This notion became part of French legal tradition until the end of the monarchy in 1789.) The nobles passed the crown to Philip VI of Valois (r. 1328–1350), a nephew of Philip the Fair.

In 1329 Edward III paid homage to Philip VI for Aquitaine. In 1337 Philip, eager to exercise full French jurisdiction in Aquitaine, confiscated the duchy. Edward III interpreted this action as a gross violation of the treaty of 1259 and as a cause for war. Moreover, Edward argued, as the eldest directly surviving male descendant of Philip the Fair, he deserved the title of king of France. Edward III's dynastic argument upset the feudal order in France: to increase their independent power, French vassals of Philip VI used the excuse that they had to transfer their loyalty to a different overlord, Edward III. One reason the war lasted so long was that it became a French civil war, with some French nobles, most important the dukes of Burgundy, supporting English monarchs in order to thwart the centralizing goals of the French crown. On the other side, Scotland often allied with France; the French supported Scottish raids in northern England, and Scottish troops joined with French armies on the continent.

The governments of both England and France manipulated public opinion to support the war. The

English public was convinced that the war was waged for one reason: to secure for King Edward the French crown he had been unjustly denied. Edward III issued letters to the sheriffs describing the evil deeds of the French in graphic terms and listing royal needs. Kings in both countries instructed the clergy to deliver sermons filled with patriotic sentiment. Philip VI sent agents to warn communities about the dangers of invasion and to stress the French crown's revenue needs to meet the attack. The English were led to believe that King Philip intended to seize and slaughter all of England. Royal propaganda on both sides fostered a kind of early nationalism, and both sides developed a deep hatred of the other.

Economic factors involving the wool trade and the control of Flemish towns were linked to these long-term and immediate political issues. The wool trade between England and Flanders served as the cornerstone of both countries' economies; they were closely interdependent. Flanders was a fief of the French crown, and the Flemish aristocracy was highly sympathetic to the monarchy in Paris. But the wealth of Flemish merchants and cloth manufacturers depended on English wool, and Flemish burghers strongly supported the claims of Edward III. The disruption of commerce with England threatened their prosperity.

The war also presented opportunities for wealth and advancement. Poor knights and knights who were unemployed were promised regular wages. Criminals who enlisted were granted pardons. The great nobles expected to be rewarded with estates. Royal exhortations to the troops before battles repeatedly stressed that, if victorious, the men might keep whatever they seized. The French chronicler Jean Froissart (FROI-sahrt) wrote of one English invasion that some of the men of all ranks who flocked to the English king's banner came to acquire honor, but many came "to loot and pillage the fair and plenteous land of France."[6]

English Successes

The war began with a series of French sea raids on English coastal towns in 1337, but the French fleet was almost completely destroyed when it attempted to land soldiers on English soil, and from that point on the war was fought almost entirely in France and the Low Countries (Map 12.2). It consisted mainly of a series of random sieges and cavalry raids, fought in fits and starts, with treaties along the way to halt hostilities.

During the war's early stages, England was highly successful. At Crécy in northern France in 1346, English longbowmen scored a great victory over French knights and crossbowmen. Although the aim of the longbow was not very accurate, it allowed for rapid reloading, and an English archer could send off three arrows to the French crossbowman's one. The result was a blinding shower of arrows that unhorsed the French knights and caused mass confusion. The ring of cannon—probably the first use of artillery in the West—created further panic. Thereupon the English horsemen charged and butchered the French. This was not war according to the chivalric rules that Edward III would have preferred. Nevertheless, his son, Edward the Black Prince, used the same tactics ten years later to smash the French at Poitiers, where he captured the French king and held him for ransom. Edward was not able to take all of France, but the English held Aquitaine and other provinces, and allied themselves with many of France's feudal vassals. After a brief peace, the French fought back and recovered some territory, and a treaty again halted hostilities as both sides concentrated on conflicts over power at home.

War began again in 1415 when the able English soldier-king Henry V (r. 1413–1422) invaded. At **Agincourt** (AH-jihn-kort), Henry's army defeated a much larger French force, again primarily through the skill of English longbowmen. Henry followed up his triumph at Agincourt with the reconquest of Normandy, and by 1419 the English had advanced to the walls of Paris (see Map 12.2). Henry married the daughter of the French king, and a treaty made Henry and any sons the couple would have heir to the French throne. It appeared as if Henry would indeed rule both England and France, but he died unexpectedly in 1422, leaving an infant son as

Agincourt The location near Arras in Flanders where an English victory in 1415 led to the reconquest of Normandy.

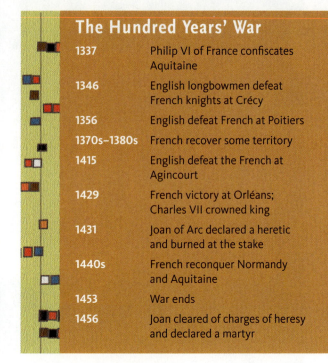

The Hundred Years' War

1337	Philip VI of France confiscates Aquitaine
1346	English longbowmen defeat French knights at Crécy
1356	English defeat French at Poitiers
1370s–1380s	French recover some territory
1415	English defeat the French at Agincourt
1429	French victory at Orléans; Charles VII crowned king
1431	Joan of Arc declared a heretic and burned at the stake
1440s	French reconquer Normandy and Aquitaine
1453	War ends
1456	Joan cleared of charges of heresy and declared a martyr

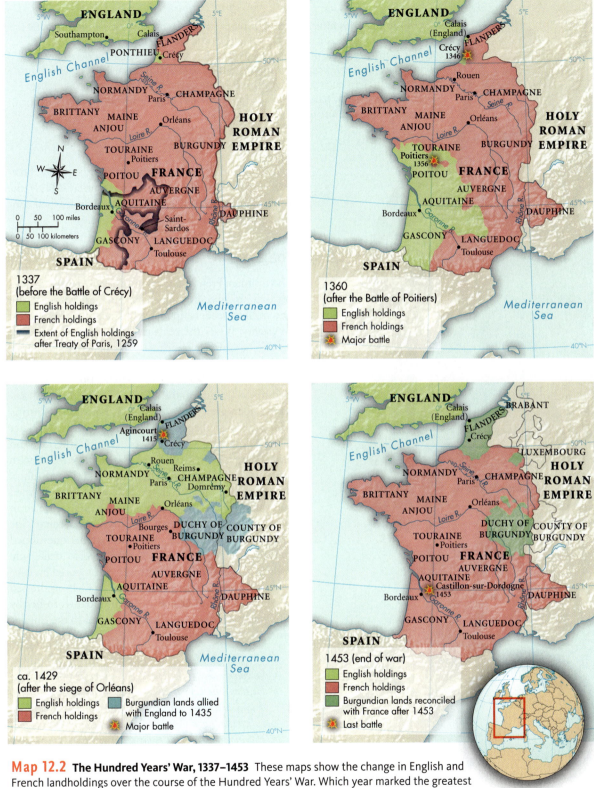

Map 12.2 The Hundred Years' War, 1337–1453 These maps show the change in English and French landholdings over the course of the Hundred Years' War. Which year marked the greatest extent of English holdings in France?

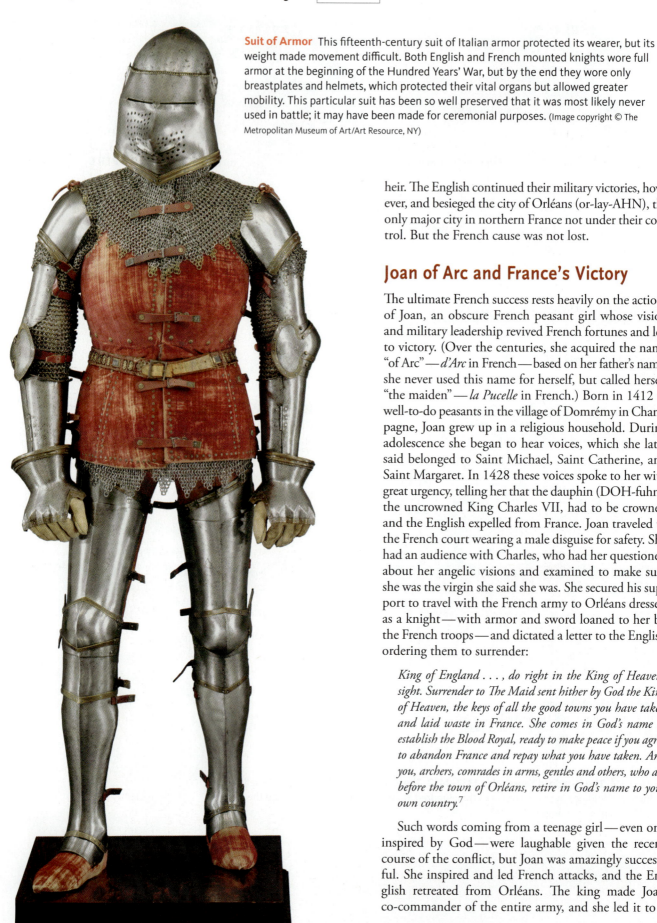

Suit of Armor This fifteenth-century suit of Italian armor protected its wearer, but its weight made movement difficult. Both English and French mounted knights wore full armor at the beginning of the Hundred Years' War, but by the end they wore only breastplates and helmets, which protected their vital organs but allowed greater mobility. This particular suit has been so well preserved that it was most likely never used in battle; it may have been made for ceremonial purposes. (Image copyright © The Metropolitan Museum of Art/Art Resource, NY)

heir. The English continued their military victories, however, and besieged the city of Orléans (or-lay-AHN), the only major city in northern France not under their control. But the French cause was not lost.

Joan of Arc and France's Victory

The ultimate French success rests heavily on the actions of Joan, an obscure French peasant girl whose vision and military leadership revived French fortunes and led to victory. (Over the centuries, she acquired the name "of Arc"—*d'Arc* in French—based on her father's name; she never used this name for herself, but called herself "the maiden"—*la Pucelle* in French.) Born in 1412 to well-to-do peasants in the village of Domrémy in Champagne, Joan grew up in a religious household. During adolescence she began to hear voices, which she later said belonged to Saint Michael, Saint Catherine, and Saint Margaret. In 1428 these voices spoke to her with great urgency, telling her that the dauphin (DOH-fuhn), the uncrowned King Charles VII, had to be crowned and the English expelled from France. Joan traveled to the French court wearing a male disguise for safety. She had an audience with Charles, who had her questioned about her angelic visions and examined to make sure she was the virgin she said she was. She secured his support to travel with the French army to Orléans dressed as a knight—with armor and sword loaned to her by the French troops—and dictated a letter to the English ordering them to surrender:

> *King of England . . . , do right in the King of Heaven's sight. Surrender to The Maid sent hither by God the King of Heaven, the keys of all the good towns you have taken and laid waste in France. She comes in God's name to establish the Blood Royal, ready to make peace if you agree to abandon France and repay what you have taken. And you, archers, comrades in arms, gentles and others, who are before the town of Orléans, retire in God's name to your own country.*[7]

Such words coming from a teenage girl—even one inspired by God—were laughable given the recent course of the conflict, but Joan was amazingly successful. She inspired and led French attacks, and the English retreated from Orléans. The king made Joan co-commander of the entire army, and she led it to a string of military victories; other cities simply surrendered without a fight and returned their allegiance to France. In July 1429, two months after Orléans, Charles VII was crowned king at Reims.

Joan and the French army continued their fight against the English and their Burgundian allies. In 1430 the Burgundians captured Joan. Charles refused to ransom her, and she was sold to the English. The English wanted Joan eliminated for obvious political reasons, but the primary charge against her was heresy, and the trial was conducted by church authorities. She was interrogated about the angelic voices and about why she wore men's clothing. The extensive trial transcript reveals that she apparently answered skillfully, but in 1431 the court condemned her as a heretic and burned her at the stake in the marketplace at Rouen.

The French army continued its victories without her. The Burgundians switched their allegiance to the French, who reconquered Normandy and, finally, ejected the English from Aquitaine. As the war dragged on, loss of life mounted, and money appeared to be flowing into a bottomless pit, demands for an end increased in England. Parliamentary opposition to additional war grants stiffened, fewer soldiers were sent, and more territory passed into French hands. At the war's end in 1453, only the town of Calais (KA-lay) remained in English hands.

What of Joan? A new trial in 1456 — requested by Charles VII, who either had second thoughts about his abandonment of Joan or did not wish to be associated with a condemned heretic — was held by the pope. This cleared her of all charges and declared her a martyr. She became a political symbol of France from that point on, and sometimes also a symbol of the Catholic Church in opposition to the government of France. In 1920, for example, she was canonized as a saint shortly after the French government declared separation of church and state in France. Similarly, Joan has been (and continues to be) a symbol of deep religious piety to some, of conservative nationalism to others, and of gender-bending cross-dressing to others. Beneath the pious and popular legends is a teenage girl who saved the French monarchy, which was the embodiment of France.

Siege of the Castle of Mortagne Medieval warfare usually consisted of small skirmishes and attacks on castles. This miniature shows the French besieging an English-held castle near Bordeaux in 1377 that held out for six months. Most of the soldiers use longbows, although at the left two men shoot primitive muskets above a pair of cannon. Painted in the late fifteenth century, the scene reflects military technology available at the time it was painted, not at the time of the actual siege. (© British Library Board, MS Royal 14 e. IV f. 23)

Aftermath

In France thousands of soldiers and civilians had been slaughtered and hundreds of thousands of acres of rich farmland were ruined, leaving the rural economy of many parts of France a shambles. The war had disrupted trade and the great fairs, resulting in the drastic reduction of French participation in international commerce. Defeat in battle and heavy taxation contributed to widespread dissatisfaction and aggravated peasant grievances.

The war had wreaked havoc in England as well, even though only the southern coastal ports saw battle. England spent the huge sum of over £5 million on the war effort, and despite the money raised by some victories, the net result was an enormous financial loss. The government attempted to finance the war by raising taxes on the wool crop, which priced wool out of the export market.

In both England and France, men of all social classes had volunteered to serve in the war in the hope of acquiring booty and becoming rich. Some were successful in the early years of the war, as one chronicler reported: "For the woman was of no account who did not possess something from the spoils of . . . cities overseas in clothing, furs, quilts, and utensils . . . tablecloths and jewels, bowls of murra [semiprecious stone] and silver, linen and linen cloths."[8] As time went on, however, most fortunes seem to have been squandered as fast as they were made. In addition, the social order was disrupted as the knights who ordinarily served as sheriffs, coroners, jurymen, and justices of the peace were abroad.

The war stimulated technological experimentation, especially with artillery. Cannon revolutionized warfare, making the stone castle no longer impregnable. Because only central governments, not private nobles, could afford cannon, they strengthened the military power of national states.

The long war also had a profound impact on the political and cultural lives of the two countries. Most notably, it stimulated the development of the English Parliament. Between 1250 and 1450, **representative assemblies** flourished in many European countries. In the English Parliament, German diets, and Spanish cortes, deliberative practices developed that laid the foundations for the representative institutions of modern democratic nations. While representative assemblies declined in most countries after the fifteenth century, the English Parliament endured. Edward III's constant need for money to pay for the war compelled him to summon not only the great barons and bishops, but knights of the shires and burgesses from the towns as well. Parliament met in thirty-seven of the fifty years of Edward's reign.

representative assemblies Deliberative meetings of lords and wealthy urban residents that flourished in many European countries between 1250 and 1450 and were the precursors to the English Parliament, German diets, and Spanish cortes.

The frequency of the meetings is significant. Representative assemblies were becoming a habit. Knights and wealthy urban residents—or the "Commons," as they came to be called—recognized their mutual interests and began to meet apart from the great lords. The Commons gradually realized that they held the country's purse strings, and a parliamentary statute of 1341 required parliamentary approval of all nonfeudal levies. By signing the law, Edward III acknowledged that the king of England could not tax without Parliament's consent. During the course of the war, money grants were increasingly tied to royal redress of grievances: to raise money, the government had to correct the wrongs its subjects protested.

In England, theoretical consent to taxation and legislation was given in one assembly for the entire country. France had no such single assembly; instead, there were many regional or provincial assemblies. Why did a national representative assembly fail to develop in France? Linguistic, geographical, economic, legal, and political differences were very strong. People tended to think of themselves as Breton, Norman, Burgundian, and so on, rather than French. Provincial assemblies, highly jealous of their independence, did not want a national assembly. The costs of sending delegates to it would be high, and the result was likely to be increased taxation. In addition, the initiative for convening assemblies rested with the king. But some monarchs lacked the power to call such assemblies, and others, including Charles VI, found the idea of representative assemblies thoroughly distasteful.

In both countries, however, the war did promote the growth of nationalism—the feeling of unity and identity that binds together a people. After victories, each country experienced a surge of pride in its military strength. Just as English patriotism ran strong after Crécy and Poitiers, so French national confidence rose after Orléans. French national feeling demanded the expulsion of the enemy not merely from Normandy and Aquitaine but from all French soil. Perhaps no one expressed this national consciousness better than Joan when she exulted that the enemy had been "driven out of *France*."

Challenges to the Church

What challenges faced the Christian church in the fourteenth century, and how did church leaders, intellectuals, and ordinary people respond?

In times of crisis or disaster, people of all faiths have sought the consolation of religion. In the fourteenth century, however, the official Christian church offered little solace. In fact, although many monks, nuns, and friars had committed their lives to helping the sick and the hungry, the leaders of the church added to the sorrow and misery of the times. In response to this lack of leadership, members of the clergy challenged the power of the pope, and laypeople challenged the authority of the church itself. Women and men increasingly relied on direct approaches to God, often through mystical encounters, rather than on the institutional church.

The Babylonian Captivity and Great Schism

Conflicts between the secular rulers of Europe and the popes were common throughout the High Middle Ages, and in the early fourteenth century the dispute between King Philip the Fair of France and Pope Boniface VIII became particularly bitter (see Chapter 11). With Boniface's death, in order to control the church and its policies, Philip pressured the new pope, Clement V, to settle permanently in Avignon in southeastern France, where the popes already had their summer residence. Clement, critically ill with cancer, lacked the will to resist Philip. The popes lived in Avignon from 1309 to 1376, a period in church history often called the **Babylonian Captivity** (referring to the seventy years the ancient Hebrews were held captive in Mesopotamian Babylon; see Chapter 3).

The Babylonian Captivity badly damaged papal prestige. The Avignon papacy reformed its financial administration and centralized its government. But the seven popes at Avignon concentrated on bureaucratic matters to the exclusion of spiritual objectives. Though some of the popes led austere lives, the general atmosphere was one of luxury and extravagance. The leadership of the church was cut off from its historic roots and the source of its ancient authority, the city of Rome. In 1377 Pope Gregory XI brought the papal court back to Rome. Unfortunately, he died shortly after the return. Between the time of Gregory's death and the opening of the conclave, Roman citizens put great pressure on the cardinals to elect an Italian. At the time, none of the cardinals protested this pressure, and they chose a distinguished administrator, the archbishop of Bari, Bartolomeo Prignano, who took the name Urban VI.

Urban VI (pontificate 1378–1389) had excellent intentions for church reform, but he went about it in a tactless and bullheaded manner. He attacked clerical luxury, denouncing individual cardinals by name, and even threatened to excommunicate certain of them. The cardinals slipped away from Rome and met at Anagni. They declared Urban's election invalid because it had come about under threats from the Roman mob, and they asserted that Urban himself was excommunicated. The cardinals then elected Cardinal Robert of Geneva, the cousin of King Charles V of France, as pope. Cardinal Robert took the name Clement VII. There were thus two popes in 1378 — Urban at Rome and Clement VII (pontificate 1378–1394), who set himself up at Avignon in opposition to Urban. So began the **Great Schism**, which divided Western Christendom until 1417.

The powers of Europe aligned themselves with Urban or Clement along strictly political lines. France naturally recognized the French pope, Clement. England, France's long-time enemy, recognized the Italian pope, Urban. Scotland, whose attacks on England were subsidized by France, followed the French and supported Clement. Aragon, Castile, and Portugal hesitated before deciding for Clement at Avignon. The German emperor, who bore ancient hostility to France, recognized Urban. At first the Italian city-states recognized Urban; when he alienated them with his attacks on luxury, they opted for Clement.

John of Spoleto, a professor at the law school at Bologna, eloquently summed up intellectual opinion of the schism: "The longer this schism lasts, the more it appears to be costing, and the more harm it does; scandal, massacres, ruination, agitations, troubles and disturbances."[9] The common people, wracked by inflation, wars, and plague, were thoroughly confused about which pope was legitimate. The schism weakened the religious faith of many Christians and brought church leadership into serious disrepute.

The Great Schism, 1378–1417
- Allegiance to Rome
- Allegiance to Avignon
- Official allegiance to Rome but with shifting local allegiances

Critiques, Divisions, and Councils

Criticism of the church during the Avignon papacy and the Great Schism often came from the ranks of highly learned clergy and lay professionals. One of these was William of Occam (1289?–1347?), a Franciscan friar and philosopher. Occam saw the papal court at Avignon firsthand and became convinced that the Avignon popes were heretics. He argued vigorously against the papacy and also wrote philosophical works in which he questioned the connection between reason and faith that had been developed by Thomas Aquinas (see Chapter 11). All governments should have limited powers and be accountable to those they govern, according to Occam, and church and state should be separate.

The Italian lawyer and university official Marsiglio of Padua (ca. 1275–1342)

Babylonian Captivity The period from 1309 to 1376 when the popes resided in Avignon rather than in Rome. The phrase refers to the seventy years when the Hebrews were held captive in Babylon.

Great Schism The division, or split, in church leadership from 1378 to 1417 when there were two, then three, popes.

Decorative Spoon Taking as his text a contemporary proverb, "When the fox preaches, beware your geese," the artist shows, in the bowl of this spoon from the southern Netherlands, a fox dressed as a monk or friar, preaching with three dead geese in his hood, while another fox grabs one of the congregation. The preaching fox reads from a scroll bearing the word *pax* (peace), implying the perceived hypocrisy of the clergy. The object from about 1430 suggests the widespread criticism of churchmen in the later Middle Ages. (Painted enamel and gilding on silver; 17.6 cm [6-7/8 in]. Museum of Fine Arts, Boston, Helen and Alice Coburn Fund, 51.2472)

agreed with Occam. In his *Defensor Pacis* (The Defender of the Peace), Marsiglio argued against the medieval idea of a society governed by both church and state, with church supreme. Instead, Marsiglio claimed, the state was the great unifying power in society, and the church should be subordinate to it. Church leadership should rest in a general council made up of laymen as well as priests, and superior to the pope. Marsiglio was excommunicated for these radical ideas, and his work was condemned as heresy—as was Occam's—but in the later fourteenth century many thinkers agreed with these two critics of the papacy. They believed that reform of the church could best be achieved through periodic assemblies, or councils, representing all the Christian people. Those who argued this position were called **conciliarists**. Some believed a council of clergy should share power with the papacy, while others believed that an elected council should be supreme and should even have the power to depose popes.

conciliarists People who believed that the authority in the Roman church should rest in a general council composed of clergy, theologians, and laypeople, rather than in the pope alone.

The English scholar and theologian John Wyclif (WIH-klihf) (ca. 1330–1384) went further than the conciliarists in his argument against medieval church structure. Wyclif wrote that Scripture alone should be the standard of Christian belief and practice, and papal claims of secular power had no foundation in the Scriptures. He urged that the church be stripped of its property. He wanted Christians to read the Bible for themselves and produced the first complete translation of the Bible into English. Although his ideas were condemned by church leaders, they were spread by humble clerics and enjoyed great popularity in the early fifteenth century.

Wyclif's followers, called Lollards by those who ridiculed them, from a Dutch word for "mumble," spread his ideas and made many copies of his Bible. Lollard teaching allowed women to preach, and women played a significant role in the movement. Lollards were persecuted in the fifteenth century; some were executed, some recanted, and others continued to meet secretly in houses, barns, and fields to read and discuss the Bible and other religious texts in English. Historians differ in their views on how widespread their beliefs were by the time Protestant ideas came into England in the sixteenth century, for Lollard records were intentionally hidden and thus are difficult to trace; however, the Lollard emphasis on biblical literacy certainly created groups of individuals who were open to Protestant views and practices.

Students returning from study at the University of Oxford around 1400 brought Wyclif's ideas with them to Prague, the capital of what was then Bohemia and is now the Czech Republic. There another university theologian, Jan Hus (ca. 1372–1415), built on them; he also denied papal authority, called for translations of the Bible into the local Czech language, and declared indulgences—papal offers of remission of penance—useless. Hus preached in Czech, first in Prague and, when he was forced to leave the city, throughout the countryside. He gained many followers, who linked his theological ideas with their opposition to the church's wealth and power and with a growing sense of Czech nationalism in opposition to the international power of the pope. Hus's followers were successful at defeating the combined armies of the pope and the emperor many times. In the 1430s the emperor finally agreed to recognize the Hussite church in Bohemia, which later merged with other Protestant churches.

Division of any type threatened the church, and in response to continued calls throughout Europe for a council, the cardinals of Rome and Avignon summoned a council at Pisa in 1409. That gathering of prelates and theologians deposed both popes and selected another. Neither the Avignon pope nor the Roman pope would resign, however, and the appalling result was the creation of a threefold schism.

Finally, under pressure from the German emperor Sigismund (SIH-guhs-muhnd), a great council met at the imperial city of Constance (1414–1418). It had three objectives: to end the schism, to reform the church "in head and members" (from top to bottom), and to wipe out heresy. The council moved first on the last point: despite being granted a safe-conduct to go to Constance by the emperor, Jan Hus was tried, condemned, and burned at the stake as a heretic in 1415. The council also eventually healed the schism. It deposed both the Roman pope and the successor of the pope chosen at Pisa, and it isolated the Avignon antipope. A conclave elected a new leader, the Roman cardinal Colonna, who took the name Martin V (pontificate 1417–1431).

Martin proceeded to dissolve the council. Nothing was done about reform, the third objective of the council. In the later fifteenth century the papacy concentrated on Italian problems to the exclusion of universal Christian interests. But the schism and the conciliar movement had exposed the crying need for ecclesiastical reform, thus laying the foundation for the great reform efforts of the sixteenth century.

The Hussite Revolution, 1415–1436

Lay Piety and Mysticism

The moral failings of the monks and parish clergy and the scandal of the Great Schism did much to weaken the spiritual mystique of the clergy in the popular mind. Thus during the fourteenth and fifteenth centuries laypeople began to develop their own forms of piety. They also exercised increasing control over parish affairs, taking responsibility for the management of parish lands and securing jurisdiction over the structure of the church building and its vestments, books, and furnishings.

Lay Christian men and women often formed **confraternities**, voluntary lay groups organized by occupation, devotional preference, neighborhood, or charitable activity. Confraternities expanded rapidly in larger cities and many villages with the growth of the mendicant orders in the thirteenth century. Some confraternities specialized in praying for souls in purgatory, either for specific individuals or for the anonymous mass of all souls. In England confraternities were generally associated with a parish and are called parish guilds, parish fraternities, or lights; by the late Middle Ages they held dances, church

> **confraternities** Voluntary lay groups organized by occupation, devotional preference, neighborhood, or charitable activity.

The Execution of Jan Hus
This fifteenth-century manuscript illustration shows workers placing logs on Hus's funeral pyre at the Council of Constance, while soldiers, officials, a priest, and a cardinal look on. Hus became an important symbol of Czech independence, and in 1990 the Czech Republic declared July 6, the date of his execution in 1415, a national holiday. (University Library, Prague/Gianni Dagli Orti/The Art Archive)

festivals, and collections to raise money to clean and repair church buildings and to supply churches with candles and other liturgical objects. Like craft guilds, most confraternities were groups of men, but separate women's confraternities were formed in some towns, often to oversee the production of vestments, altar cloths, and other items made of fabric. All confraternities carried out special devotional practices such as prayers or processions, often without the leadership of a priest.

In Holland beginning in the late fourteenth century, a group of pious laypeople called the Brethren and Sisters of the Common Life lived in stark simplicity while daily carrying out the Gospel teaching of feeding the hungry, clothing the naked, and visiting the sick. The Brethren also taught in local schools with the goal of preparing devout candidates for the priesthood. They sought to make religion a personal inner experience. The spirituality of the Brethren and Sisters of the Common Life found its finest expression in the classic *The Imitation of Christ* by the Dutch monk Thomas à Kempis (1380?–1471), which gained wide appeal among laypeople. It urges Christians to take Christ as their model, seek perfection in a simple way of life, and look to the Scriptures for guidance in living a spiritual life. In the mid-fifteenth century the movement had founded houses in the Netherlands, in central Germany, and in the Rhineland.

Most of this piety centered on prayer, pious actions, and charitable giving, but for some individuals, both laypeople and clerics, religious devotion included mystical experiences. (See "Individuals in Society: Meister Eckhart," at right.) Bridget of Sweden (1303–1373) was a noblewoman who journeyed to Rome after her husband's death. She began to see visions and gave advice based on these visions to both laypeople and church officials. Because she could not speak Latin, she dictated her visions in Swedish; these were later translated and eventually published in Latin. At the end of her life Bridget made a pilgrimage to Jerusalem, where she saw visions of the Virgin Mary, who described to her exactly how she was standing "with my knees bent" when she gave birth to Jesus, and how she "showed to the shepherds the nature and male sex of the child."[10] Bridget's visions convey her deep familiarity with biblical texts taught to her through sermons or stories, as there was no Bible available in Swedish. They also provide evidence of the ways in which laypeople used their own experiences to enhance their religious understanding; Bridget's own experiences of childbirth shaped the way she viewed the birth of Jesus, and she related to the Virgin Mary in part as one mother to another.

The confraternities and mystics were generally not considered heretical unless they began to challenge the authority of the papacy the way some conciliarists and Wyclif and Hus did. However, the movement of lay piety did alter many people's perceptions of their own spiritual power.

Jacquerie A massive uprising by French peasants in 1358 protesting heavy taxation.

Social Unrest in a Changing Society

How did economic and social tensions contribute to revolts, crime, violence, and a growing sense of ethnic and national distinctions?

At the beginning of the fourteenth century famine and disease profoundly affected the lives of European peoples. As the century wore on, decades of slaughter and destruction, punctuated by the decimating visits of the Black Death, added further woes. In many parts of France and the Low Countries, fields lay in ruin or untilled for lack of labor power. In England, as taxes increased, criticisms of government policy and mismanagement multiplied. Crime and new forms of business organization aggravated economic troubles, and throughout Europe the frustrations of the common people erupted into widespread revolts.

Peasant Revolts

Nobles and clergy lived on the produce of peasant labor, thinking little of adding taxes to the burden of peasant life. While peasants had endured centuries of exploitation, the difficult conditions of the fourteenth and fifteenth centuries spurred a wave of peasant revolts across Europe. Peasants were sometimes joined by their urban counterparts on the social ladder, resulting in a wider revolution of poor against rich.

The first large-scale rebellion was in Flanders in the 1320s (Map 12.3). In order to satisfy peace agreements, Flemish peasants were forced to pay taxes to the French, who claimed fiscal rights over the county of Flanders. Monasteries also pressed peasants for additional money above their customary tithes. In retaliation, peasants burned and pillaged castles and aristocratic country houses. A French army crushed peasant forces, and savage repression and the confiscation of peasant property followed in the 1330s.

In 1358, when French taxation for the Hundred Years' War fell heavily on the poor, the frustrations of the French peasantry exploded in a massive uprising called the **Jacquerie** (zhah-kuh-REE), after a mythical agricultural laborer, Jacques Bonhomme (Good Fellow). Peasants blamed the nobility for oppressive taxes, for the criminal banditry of the countryside, for losses on the battlefield, and for the general misery. Crowds swept through the countryside, slashing the throats of nobles,

INDIVIDUALS IN SOCIETY

Meister Eckhart

MYSTICISM — THE DIRECT EXPERIENCE OF THE DIVINE through sudden insight or intuition — is an aspect of many world religions and has been part of Christianity throughout its history. During the late Middle Ages, however, mysticism became an important part of the piety of many laypeople, especially in the Rhineland area of Germany, rather than a rare experience of only a few. In this they were guided by the sermons of the churchman generally known as Meister Eckhart. Born into a German noble family, Eckhart (1260–1329?) joined the Dominican order and studied theology at Paris and Cologne, attaining the academic title of "master" (*Meister* in German). The leaders of the Dominican order appointed him to a series of administrative and teaching positions, and he wrote learned treatises in Latin that reflected his scholastic training and deep understanding of classical philosophy.

He also began to preach in German, attracting many listeners through his beautiful language and mystical insights. God, he said, was "an oversoaring being and an overbeing nothingness," whose essence was beyond the ability of humans to express: "if the soul is to know God, it must know Him outside time and place, since God is neither in this or that, but One and above them." Only through "unknowing," emptying oneself, could one come to experience the divine. Yet God was also present in individual human souls, and to a degree in every creature, all of which God called into being before the beginning of time. Within each soul there was what Eckhart called a "little spark," an innermost essence that allows the soul—with God's grace and Christ's redemptive action—to come to God. "Our salvation depends upon our knowing and recognizing the Chief Good which is God Himself," preached Eckhart; "the Eye with which I see God is the same Eye with which God sees me." "I have a capacity in my soul for taking in God entirely," he went on, a capacity that was shared by all humans, not simply members of the clergy or those with special spiritual gifts. Although Eckhart did not reject church sacraments or the hierarchy, he frequently stressed that union with God was best accomplished through quiet detachment and simple prayer rather than pilgrimages, extensive fasts, or other activities: "If the only prayer you said in your whole life was 'thank you,' that would suffice."*

Eckhart's unusual teachings led to charges of heresy in 1327, which Eckhart denied. The pope—who was at this point in Avignon—presided over a trial condemning him, but Eckhart appears to have died during the course of the proceedings or shortly thereafter. His writings were ordered destroyed, but many survived, and his teachings continued to be spread by his followers.

In the last few decades, Meister Eckhart's ideas have been explored and utilized by philosophers and mystics in other religious traditions, including Buddhism, Hinduism, and neo-paganism, as well as by Christians. Books of his sermons sell widely for their spiritual insights, and quotations from them—including the one above about thank-you prayers—can be found on coffee mugs, tote bags, and T-shirts.

A sixteenth-century woodcut of Meister Eckhart teaching. (Visual Connection Archive)

QUESTIONS FOR ANALYSIS

1. Why might Meister Eckhart's preaching have been viewed as threatening by the leaders of the church?
2. Given the situation of the church in the late Middle Ages, why might mysticism have been attractive to pious Christians?

*Meister Eckhart's Sermons, trans. Claud Field (London: n.p., 1909).

burning their castles, raping their wives and daughters, and killing or maiming their horses and cattle. Artisans, small merchants, and parish priests joined the peasants. Urban and rural groups committed terrible destruction, and for several weeks the nobles were on the defensive. Then the upper class united to repress the revolt with merciless ferocity. Thousands of the "Jacques," innocent as well as guilty, were cut down. That forcible suppression of social rebellion, without any effort to alleviate its underlying causes, served to drive protest underground.

The 1381 **English Peasants' Revolt** involved thousands of people. Its causes were complex and varied from place to place. In general, though, the thirteenth century had witnessed the steady replacement of labor services by cash rents, and the Black Death had drastically cut the labor supply. As a result, peasants demanded higher wages and fewer manorial obligations. Their lords countered in 1351 with the Statute of Laborers, a law freezing wages and binding workers to their manors:

> *Whereas to curb the malice of servants who after the pestilence were idle and unwilling to serve without securing excessive wages, it was recently ordained . . . that such servants, both men and women, shall be bound to serve in return for salaries and wages that were customary . . . five or six years earlier.*[11]

This attempt to freeze wages and social mobility could not be enforced, but a huge gap remained between peasants and their lords, and the peasants sought release for their economic frustrations in revolt. Economic grievances combined with other factors. The south of England, where the revolt broke out, had been subjected to destructive French raids during the Hundred Years' War. The English government did little to protect the south, and villagers grew increasingly frightened and insecure. Moreover, decades of aristocratic violence against the

English Peasants' Revolt
Revolt by English peasants in 1381 in response to changing economic conditions.

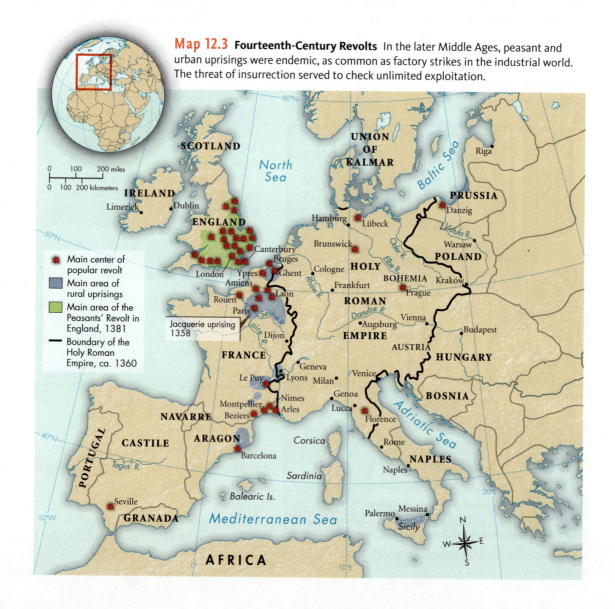

Map 12.3 Fourteenth-Century Revolts In the later Middle Ages, peasant and urban uprisings were endemic, as common as factory strikes in the industrial world. The threat of insurrection served to check unlimited exploitation.

weak peasantry had bred hostility and bitterness. Social and religious agitation by the popular preacher John Ball fanned the embers of discontent. Ball's famous couplet calling for a return to the social equality that had existed in the Garden of Eden — "When Adam delved and Eve span; / Who was then the gentleman?" — reflected real revolutionary sentiment.

The English revolt was ignited by the reimposition of a tax on all adult males. Despite widespread opposition to the tax in 1380, the royal council ordered the sheriffs to collect it again in 1381 on penalty of a huge fine. Beginning with assaults on the tax collectors, the uprising in England followed a course similar to that of the Jacquerie in France. Castles and manors were sacked. Manorial records were destroyed. Many nobles, including the archbishop of Canterbury who had ordered the collection of the tax, were murdered. The center of the revolt lay in the highly populated and economically advanced south and east, but sections of the north also witnessed rebellions (see Map 12.3).

The boy-king Richard II (r. 1377–1399) met the leaders of the revolt, agreed to charters ensuring peasants' freedom, tricked them with false promises, and then crushed the uprising with terrible ferocity. In the aftermath of the revolt, the nobility tried to restore the labor obligations of serfdom, but they were not successful, and the conversion to money rents continued. The English Peasants' Revolt did not bring social equality to England, but rural serfdom continued to decline, and it disappeared in England by 1550.

Urban Conflicts

In Flanders, France, and England, peasant revolts often blended with conflicts involving workers in cities. Unrest also occurred in Italian, Spanish, and German cities. The revolts typically flared in urban centers, where the conditions of work were changing for many people. In the thirteenth century craft guilds had organized the production of most goods, with masters, journeymen, and apprentices working side by side. In the fourteenth century a new system evolved to make products on a larger scale. Capitalist investors hired many households, with each household performing only one step of the process. Initially these investors were wealthy bankers and merchants, but eventually shop masters themselves embraced the system. This promoted a greater division within guilds between wealthier masters and the poorer masters and journeymen they hired. Some masters became so wealthy from the profits of their workers that they no longer had to work in a shop themselves, nor did their wives and family members, though they still generally belonged to the craft guild.

While capitalism provided opportunities for some artisans to become investors and entrepreneurs, especially in cloth production, for many it led to a decrease in income and status. Guilds sometimes responded to crises by opening up membership, as they did in some places immediately after the Black Death, but they more often responded to competition by limiting membership to existing guild families, which meant that journeymen who were not master's sons or who could not find a master's widow or daughter to marry could never become masters themselves. They remained journeymen their entire lives, losing their sense of solidarity with the masters of their craft. Resentment led to rebellion over economic issues.

Urban uprisings were also sparked by issues involving honor, such as employers' requiring workers to do tasks they regarded as beneath them. As their actual status and economic prospects declined and their work became basically wage labor, journeymen and poorer masters emphasized skill and honor as qualities that set them apart from less-skilled workers.

Guilds increasingly came to view the honor of their work as tied to an all-male workplace. When urban economies were expanding in the High Middle Ages, the master's wife and daughters worked alongside him, and female domestic servants also carried out productive tasks. (See "Listening to the Past: Christine de Pizan, Advice to the Wives of Artisans," page 362.) Masters' widows ran shops after the death of their husbands. But in the fourteenth century a woman's right to work slowly eroded. First, masters' widows were limited in the amount of time they could keep operating a shop or were prohibited from hiring journeymen; then female domestic servants were excluded from any productive tasks; then the number of daughters a master craftsman could employ was limited. When women were allowed to work, it was viewed as a substitute for charity.

Sex in the City

Peasant and urban revolts and riots had clear economic bases, but some historians have suggested that late medieval marital patterns may have also played a role in unrest. In northwestern Europe, people believed that couples should be economically independent before they married, so both spouses spent long periods as servants or workers in other households, saving money and learning skills, or they waited until their own parents had died and the family property was distributed.

The most unusual feature of this pattern was the late age of marriage for women. Unlike in earlier time periods and in most other parts of the world, a woman in late medieval northern and western Europe entered marriage as an adult and took charge of running a household immediately. She was thus not as dependent on her husband or mother-in-law as was a woman who married at a younger age. She had fewer pregnancies than

LISTENING TO THE PAST

Christine de Pizan, Advice to the Wives of Artisans

Christine de Pizan (1364?–1430) was the daughter and wife of highly educated men who held positions at the court of the king of France. She was widowed at twenty-five with young children and an elderly mother to support. Christine, who herself had received an excellent education, decided to support her family through writing, an unusual choice for anyone in this era and unheard of for a woman. She began to write prose works and poetry, sending them to wealthy individuals in the hope of receiving their support. Her works were well received, and Christine gained commissions to write specific works, including a biography of the French king Charles V, several histories, a long poem celebrating Joan of Arc's victory, and a book of military tactics. She became the first woman in Europe to make her living as a writer.

Among Christine's many works were several in which she considered women's nature and proper role in society, which had been a topic of debate since ancient times. The best known of these was The City of Ladies *(1404), in which she ponders why so many men have a negative view of women and provides examples of virtuous women to counter this view. A second book,* The Treasure of the City of Ladies *(1405, also called* The Book of Three Virtues*), provides moral suggestions and practical advice on behavior and household management for women of all social classes. Most of the book is directed toward princesses and court ladies (who would have been able to read it), but she also includes shorter sections for the wives of merchants and artisans, serving-women, female peasants, and even prostitutes. This is her advice to the wives of artisans, whose husbands were generally members of urban craft guilds, such as blacksmiths, bakers, or shoemakers.*

❝ All wives of artisans should be very painstaking and diligent if they wish to have the necessities of life. They should encourage their husbands or their workmen to get to work early in the morning and work until late, for mark our words, there is no trade so good that if you neglect your work you will not have difficulty putting bread on the table. And besides encouraging the others, the wife herself should be involved in the work to the extent that she knows all about it, so that she may know how to oversee his workers if her husband is absent, and to reprove them if they do not do well. She ought to oversee them to keep them from idleness, for through careless workers the master is sometimes ruined. And when customers come to her husband and try to drive a hard bargain, she ought to warn him solicitously to take care that he does not make a bad deal. She should advise him to be chary of giving too much credit if he does not know precisely where and to whom it is going, for in this way many come to poverty, although sometimes the greed to

Several manuscripts of Christine's works, such as this one, included illustrations showing her writing, which would have increased their appeal to the wealthy individuals who purchased them.
(© British Library Board, Harl. 79487, fol. 3r Det.)

362

earn more or to accept a tempting proposition makes them do it.

In addition, she ought to keep her husband's love as much as she can, to this end: that he will stay at home more willingly and that he may not have any reason to join the foolish crowds of other young men in taverns and indulge in unnecessary and extravagant expense, as many tradesmen do, especially in Paris. By treating him kindly she should protect him as well as she can from this. It is said that three things drive a man from his home: a quarrelsome wife, a smoking fireplace and a leaking roof. She too ought to stay at home gladly and not go every day traipsing hither and yon gossiping with the neighbours and visiting her chums to find out what everyone is doing. That is done by slovenly housewives roaming about the town in groups. Nor should she go off on these pilgrimages got up for no good reason and involving a lot of needless expense. Furthermore, she ought to remind her husband that they should live so frugally that their expenditure does not exceed their income, so that at the end of the year they do not find themselves in debt.

If she has children, she should have them instructed and taught first at school by educated people so that they may know how better to serve God. Afterwards they may be put to some trade by which they may earn a living, for whoever gives a trade or business training to her child gives a great possession. The children should be kept from wantonness and from voluptuousness above all else, for truly it is something that most shames the children of good towns and is a great sin of mothers and fathers, who ought to be the cause of the virtue and good behavior of their children, but they are sometimes the reason (because of bringing them up to be finicky and indulging them too much) for their wickedness and ruin.

Source: Christine de Pisan, *The Treasure of the City of Ladies*, translated with an Introduction by Sarah Lawson (Penguin Classics, 1985), pp. 167–168. This translation copyright © 1985 by Sarah Lawson. Used with permission of Penguin Group (UK). For more on Christine, see C. C. Willard, *Christine de Pisan: Her Life and Works* (1984), and S. Bell, *The Lost Tapestries of the City of Ladies: Christine de Pizan's Renaissance Legacy* (2004).

QUESTIONS FOR ANALYSIS

1. How would you describe Christine's view of the ideal artisan's wife?
2. The regulations of craft guilds often required that masters who ran workshops be married. What evidence does Christine's advice provide for why guilds would have stipulated this?
3. How are economic and moral virtues linked for Christine?

a woman who married earlier, though not necessarily fewer surviving children.

Men of all social groups were older when they married. In general, men were in their middle or late twenties at first marriage, with wealthier urban merchants often much older. Journeymen and apprentices were often explicitly prohibited from marrying, as were the students at universities, who were understood to be in "minor orders" and thus like clergy, even if they were not intending to have careers in the church.

The prohibitions on marriage for certain groups of men and the late age of marriage for most men meant that cities and villages were filled with large numbers of young adult men with no family responsibilities who often formed the core of riots and unrest. Not surprisingly, this situation also contributed to a steady market for sexual services outside of marriage, what in later centuries was termed prostitution. Research on the southern French province of Languedoc in the fourteenth and fifteenth centuries has revealed the establishment of legal houses of prostitution in many cities. Municipal authorities set up houses or red-light districts either outside the city walls or away from respectable neighborhoods. For example, authorities in Montpellier set aside Hot Street for prostitution, required public women to live there, and forbade anyone to molest them. Prostitution thus passed from being a private concern to a social matter requiring public supervision. The towns of Languedoc were not unique. Public authorities in Amiens, Dijon, Paris, Venice, Genoa, London, Florence, Rome, most of the larger German towns, and the English port of Sandwich set up brothels.

Young men associated visiting brothels with achieving manhood, though for the women themselves their activities were work. Some women had no choice, for they had been traded to the brothel manager by their parents or other people as payment for debt, or had quickly become indebted to the manager (most of whom were men) for the clothes and other finery regarded as essential to their occupation. The small amount they received from their customers did not equal what they had to pay for their upkeep in a brothel. Poor women—and men—also sold sex illegally outside of city brothels, combining this with other sorts of part-time work such as laundering or sewing. Prostitution was an urban phenomenon because only populous towns had large numbers of unmarried young men, communities of transient merchants, and a culture accustomed to a cash exchange.

Though selling sex for money was legal in the Middle Ages, the position of women who did so was always marginal. In the late fifteenth century cities began to limit brothel residents' freedom of movement and choice of clothing, requiring them to wear distinctive head coverings or bands on their clothing so that they would not be mistaken for "honorable" women. The cities also began to impose harsher penalties on women who did not

City Brothel In this rather fanciful scene of a medieval brothel, two couples share baths and wine, while a third is in bed in the back, and two nobles peer in from a window across the street. Most brothels were not this elaborate, although some did have baths. Many cities also had commercial bath houses where people paid a small fee to take a hot bath, a luxury otherwise unavailable. Bath houses did sometimes offer sex, but their main attraction was hot water. (Bibliothèque nationale de France)

live in the designated house or section of town. A few prostitutes did earn enough to donate money to charity or buy property, but most were very poor.

Along with buying sex, young men also took it by force. Unmarried women often found it difficult to avoid sexual contact. Many of them worked as domestic servants, where their employers or employers' sons or male relatives could easily coerce them, or they worked in proximity to men. Notions of female honor kept upper-class women secluded in their homes, particularly in southern and eastern Europe, but there was little attempt anywhere to protect female servants or day laborers from the risk of seduction or rape. Rape was a capital crime in many parts of Europe, but the actual sentences handed out were more likely to be fines and brief imprisonment, with the severity of the sentence dependent on the social status of the victim and the perpetrator.

According to laws regarding rape in most parts of Europe, the victim had to prove that she had cried out and had attempted to repel the attacker, and she had to bring the charge within a short period of time after the attack had happened. Women bringing rape charges were often more interested in getting their own honorable reputations back than in punishing the perpetrators, and for this reason they sometimes asked the judge to force their rapists to marry them.

Same-sex relations — what in the late nineteenth century would be termed "homosexuality" — were another feature of medieval urban life (and of village life, though there are very few sources relating to sexual relations of any type in the rural context). Same-sex relations were of relatively little concern to church or state authorities in the early Middle Ages, but this attitude changed beginning in the late twelfth century. By 1300 most areas had defined such actions as "crimes against nature," with authorities seeing them as particularly reprehensible because they thought they did not occur anywhere else in creation. Same-sex relations, usually termed "sodomy," became a capital crime in most of Europe, with adult offenders threatened with execution by fire. The Italian cities of Venice, Florence, and Lucca created special courts to deal with sodomy, which saw thousands of investigations.

How prevalent were same-sex relations? This is difficult to answer, even in modern society, but the city of Florence provides a provocative case study. In 1432 Florence set up a special board of adult men, the Office of the Night, to "root out . . . the abominable vice of sodomy."[12] Between 1432 and the abolition of the board in 1502, about seventeen thousand men came to its attention, which, even over a seventy-year period, represents a great number in a population of about forty thousand. The men came from all classes of society, but almost all cases involved an adult man and an adolescent boy; they ranged from sex exchanged for money or gifts to long-term affectionate relationships. Florentines believed in a generational model in which different roles were appropriate to different stages in life. In a socially and sexually hierarchical world, the boy in the passive role was identified as subordinate, dependent, and mercenary, words usually applied to women. Florentines, however, never described the dominant partner in feminine terms, for he had not compromised his masculine identity or violated a gender ideal; in fact, the adult partner might be married or have female sexual partners as well as male. Only if an adult male assumed the passive role was his masculinity jeopardized.

Thus in Florence, and no doubt elsewhere in Europe, sodomy was not a marginal practice, which may account for the fact that, despite harsh laws and special courts, actual executions for sodomy were rare. Same-sex relations often developed within the context of all-male environments, such as the army, the craft shop, and the artistic workshop, and were part of the collective male experience. Homoerotic relationships played important roles in defining stages of life, expressing distinctions of status, and shaping masculine gender identity. Same-sex relations involving women almost never came to the attention of legal authorities, so it is difficult to find out how common they were. However, female-female desire was expressed in songs, plays, and stories, as was male-male desire, offering evidence of the way people understood same-sex relations.

Same-Sex Relations This illustration, from a thirteenth-century French book of morals, interprets female and male same-sex relations as the work of devils. The illustration was painted at the time that religious and political authorities were increasingly criminalizing same-sex relations. (ONB/Vienna, Picture Archives, Cod. 2554, fol. 2r)

> **Men who come there ... should be judged on account of any crime ... according to Polish custom if they are Poles and according to German custom if they are Germans.**
>
> —Law on the Polish frontier

Fur-Collar Crime

The Hundred Years' War had provided employment and opportunity for thousands of idle and fortune-seeking knights. But during periods of truce and after the war finally ended, many nobles once again had little to do. Inflation hurt them. Although many were living on fixed incomes, their chivalric code demanded lavish generosity and an aristocratic lifestyle. Many nobles turned to crime as a way of raising money. The fourteenth and fifteenth centuries witnessed a great deal of "fur-collar crime," so called for the miniver fur nobles alone were allowed to wear on their collars.

Groups of noble bandits roamed the English countryside, stealing from both rich and poor. Operating like modern urban racketeers, knightly gangs demanded that peasants pay "protection money" or else have their hovels burned and their fields destroyed. They seized wealthy travelers and held them for ransom. When accused of wrongdoing, fur-collar criminals intimidated witnesses, threatened jurors, and used "pull" or cash to bribe judges. As a fourteenth-century English judge wrote to a young nobleman, "For the love of your father I have hindered charges being brought against you and have prevented execution of indictment actually made."[13] Criminal activity by nobles continued decade after decade because governments were too weak to stop it.

The ballads of Robin Hood, a collection of folk legends from late medieval England, describe the adventures of the outlaw hero and his merry men as they avenge the common people against fur-collar criminals—grasping landlords, wicked sheriffs, and mercenary churchmen. Robin Hood was a popular figure because he symbolized the deep resentment of aristocratic corruption and abuse; he represented the struggle against tyranny and oppression.

Ethnic Tensions and Restrictions

Large numbers of people in the twelfth and thirteenth centuries migrated from one part of Europe to another in search of food, work, and peace: the English into Scotland and Ireland; Germans, French, and Flemings into Poland, Bohemia, and Hungary; the French into Spain. The colonization of frontier regions meant that peoples of different ethnic backgrounds lived side by side. Everywhere in Europe, towns recruited people from the countryside (see Chapter 11). In frontier regions, townspeople were usually long-distance immigrants and, in eastern Europe, Ireland, and Scotland, ethnically different from the surrounding rural population. In eastern Europe, German was the language of the towns; in Irish towns, French, the tongue of Norman or English settlers, predominated.

In the early periods of conquest and colonization, and in all regions with extensive migrations, a legal dualism existed: native peoples remained subject to their traditional laws; newcomers brought and were subject to the laws of the countries from which they came. On the Prussian and Polish frontier, for example, the law was that "men who come there ... should be judged on account of any crime or contract engaged in there according to Polish custom if they are Poles and according to German custom if they are Germans."[14] Likewise, the conquered Muslim subjects of Christian kings in Spain had the right to be judged under Muslim law by Muslim judges.

The great exception to this broad pattern of legal pluralism was Ireland. From the start, the English practiced an extreme form of discrimination toward the native Irish. The English distinguished between the free and the unfree, and the entire Irish population, simply by the fact of Irish birth, was unfree. When English legal structures were established beginning in 1210, the Irish were denied access to the common-law courts. In civil (property) disputes, an English defendant need not respond to his Irish plaintiff; no Irish person could make a will. In criminal procedures, the murder of an Irishman was not considered a felony. This emphasis on blood descent provoked bitterness.

Other than in Ireland, although native peoples commonly held humbler positions, both immigrant and native townspeople prospered during the expanding economy of the thirteenth century. But with the economic turmoil of the fourteenth century, ethnic tensions multiplied.

The later Middle Ages witnessed a movement away from legal pluralism or dualism and toward legal homogeneity and an emphasis on blood descent. The dominant ethnic group in an area tried to bar others from positions of church leadership and guild membership. Marriage laws were instituted that attempted to maintain ethnic purity by prohibiting intermarriage, and some church leaders actively promoted ethnic discrimination. As Germans moved eastward, for example, German bishops refused to appoint non-Germans to any church office, while Czech bishops closed monasteries to Germans.

The most extensive attempt to prevent intermarriage and protect ethnic purity is embodied in Ireland's **Statute of Kilkenny** (1366), which states that "there were to be no marriages between those of immigrant and native stock; that the English inhabitants of Ireland must employ the English language and bear English names; that they must ride in the English way [that is, with saddles] and have English apparel; that no Irishmen were to be granted ecclesiastical benefices or admitted to monasteries in the English parts of Ireland."[15]

Late medieval chroniclers used words such as *gens* (race or clan) and *natio* (NAH-tee-oh; species, stock, or kind) to refer to different groups. They held that peoples differed according to language, traditions, customs, and laws. None of these were unchangeable, however, and commentators increasingly also described ethnic differences in terms of "blood"—"German blood," "English blood," and so on—which made ethnicity heritable. Religious beliefs also came to be conceptualized as blood, with people regarded as having Jewish blood, Muslim blood, or Christian blood. The most dramatic expression of this was in Spain, where "purity of blood"—having no Muslim or Jewish ancestors—became an obsession. Blood was also used as a way to talk about social differences, especially for nobles. Just as Irish and English were prohibited from marrying each other, those of "noble blood" were prohibited from marrying commoners in many parts of Europe. As Europeans increasingly came into contact with people from Africa and Asia, and particularly as they developed colonial empires, these notions of blood also became a way of conceptualizing racial categories.

Statute of Kilkenny Laws issued in 1366 that discriminated against the Irish, forbidding marriage between the English and the Irish, requiring the use of the English language, and denying the Irish access to ecclesiastical offices.

Literacy and Vernacular Literature

The development of ethnic identities had many negative consequences, but a more positive effect was the increasing use of the vernacular, that is, the local language that people actually spoke, rather than Latin. Two masterpieces of European culture, Dante's *Divine Comedy* (1310–1320) and Chaucer's *Canterbury Tales* (1387–1400), illustrate a sophisticated use of the rhythms and rhymes of the vernacular.

Chaucer's Wife of Bath Chaucer's *Canterbury Tales* were filled with memorable characters, including the often-married Wife of Bath, shown here in a fifteenth-century manuscript. In the prologue that details her life, she denies the value of virginity and criticizes her young and handsome fifth husband for reading a book about "wicked wives." "By God, if women had but written stories . . . ," she comments, "They would have written of men more wickedness, Than all the race of Adam could redress." (British Library/HIP/Art Resource, NY)

School Signboard Ambrosius Holbein, elder brother of the artist Hans Holbein, produced this signboard for the Swiss educator Myconius. It is an excellent example of what we would call commercial art — art used to advertise, in this case Myconius's profession. The German script above promised that all who enrolled, girls and boys, would learn to read and write. Most schools were for boys only, but a few offered instruction for girls as well. (Kunstmuseum Basel/Martin Buhler, photographer)

Dante Alighieri (DAHN-tay ah-luh-GYER-ee) (1265–1321) called his work a "comedy" because he wrote it in Italian and in a different style from the "tragic" Latin; a later generation added the adjective *divine*, referring both to its sacred subject and to Dante's artistry. The *Divine Comedy* is an epic poem of one hundred cantos (verses), each of whose three equal parts (1+33+33+33) describes one of the realms of the next world: Hell, Purgatory, and Paradise. The Roman poet Virgil, representing reason, leads Dante through Hell, where Dante observes the torments of the damned and denounces the disorders of his own time, especially ecclesiastical ambition and corruption. Passing up into Purgatory, Virgil shows the poet how souls are purified of their disordered inclinations. From Purgatory, Beatrice, a woman Dante once loved and the symbol of divine revelation in the poem, leads him to Paradise. In Paradise, home of the angels and saints, Saint Bernard — representing mystic contemplation — leads Dante to the Virgin Mary. Through her intercession, he at last attains a vision of God.

The *Divine Comedy* portrays contemporary and historical figures, comments on secular and ecclesiastical affairs, and draws on the Scholastic philosophy of uniting faith and reason. Within the framework of a symbolic pilgrimage to the City of God, the *Divine Comedy* embodies the psychological tensions of the age. A profoundly Christian poem, it also contains bitter criticism of some church authorities. In its symmetrical structure and use of figures from the ancient world such as Virgil, the poem perpetuates the classical tradition, but as the first major work of literature in the Italian vernacular, it is distinctly modern.

Geoffrey Chaucer (CHAW-suhr) (1342–1400) was an official in the administrations of the English kings Edward III and Richard II and wrote poetry as an avocation. Chaucer's *Canterbury Tales* is a collection of stories in lengthy rhymed narrative. On a pilgrimage to the shrine of Saint Thomas Becket at Canterbury (see Chapter 9), thirty people of various social backgrounds tell tales. For example, the gross Miller tells a vulgar story about a deceived husband; the earthy Wife of Bath, who has buried five husbands, sketches a fable about the selection of a spouse; and the elegant Prioress, who violates her vows by wearing jewelry, delivers a homily on the Virgin. In depicting the interests and behavior of all types of people, Chaucer presents a rich panorama of English social life in the fourteenth century. Like the *Divine Comedy*, the *Canterbury Tales* reflects the cultural tensions of the times. Ostensibly Christian, many of the pilgrims are also materialistic, sensual, and worldly, suggesting the ambivalence of the broader society's concern for the next world and frank enjoyment of this one.

Beginning in the fourteenth century, a variety of evidence attests to the increasing literacy of laypeople. Wills and inventories reveal that many people, not just nobles, possessed books—mainly devotional, but also romances, manuals on manners and etiquette, histories, and sometimes legal and philosophical texts. In England the number of schools in the diocese of York quadrupled between 1350 and 1500. Information from Flemish and German towns is similar: children were sent to schools and were taught the fundamentals of reading, writing, and arithmetic. Laymen increasingly served as managers or stewards of estates and as clerks to guilds and town governments; such positions obviously required the ability to keep administrative and financial records.

The penetration of laymen into the higher positions of governmental administration, long the preserve of clerics, also illustrates rising lay literacy. With growing frequency, the upper classes sent their daughters to convent schools, where, in addition to instruction in singing, religion, needlework, deportment, and household management, girls gained the rudiments of reading and sometimes writing.

The spread of literacy represents a response to the needs of an increasingly complex society. Trade, commerce, and expanding government bureaucracies required more and more literate people. Late medieval culture remained an oral culture in which most people received information by word of mouth. But by the fifteenth century the evolution toward a more literate culture was already perceptible, and craftsmen would develop the new technology of the printing press in response to the increased demand for reading materials.

LOOKING BACK LOOKING AHEAD

THE FOURTEENTH AND EARLY fifteenth centuries were certainly times of crisis in western Europe, meriting the label "calamitous" given to them by one prominent historian. Famine, disease, and war decimated the European population, and traditional institutions, including secular governments and the church, did little or nothing or, in some cases, made things worse. Trading connections that had been reinvigorated in the High Middle Ages spread the most deadly epidemic ever experienced through western Asia, North Africa, and almost all of Europe. No wonder survivors experienced a sort of shell shock and a fascination with death.

The plague did not destroy the prosperity of the medieval population, however, and it may in fact have indirectly improved the European economy. Wealthy merchants had plenty of money to spend on luxuries and talent. In the century after the plague, Italian artists began to create new styles of painting, writers new literary forms, educators new types of schools, and philosophers new ideas about the purpose of human life. These cultural changes eventually spread to the rest of Europe, following the same paths that the plague had traveled.

CHAPTER REVIEW

■ **What were the demographic, economic, and social, consequences of climate change? (p. 340)**

Colder climate and bad weather brought poor harvests, which contributed to widespread famine and disease. People abandoned homesteads, and the number of vagabonds and criminals increased. Political leaders attempted to find solutions but were unable to deal with the economic and social problems that resulted.

■ **How did the spread of the plague shape European society? (p. 341)**

In 1348 a new disease, most likely the bubonic plague, came to mainland Europe, carried from the Black Sea by ships. It spread quickly by land and sea and within two years may have killed as much as one-third of the European population. Medical explanations at the time linked the plague to poisoned air or water, and treatments were ineffective. Many people regarded the plague as a divine punishment and sought remedies in religious practices such as prayer, pilgrimages, or donations to churches. Art and literature showed an obsession with death. Population losses caused by the Black Death led to inflation but in the long run may have contributed to more opportunities for the peasants and urban workers who survived the disease.

■ **What were the causes of the Hundred Years' War, and how did the war affect European politics, economics, and cultural life? (p. 348)**

The Hundred Years' War, which was fought intermittently in France from 1337 to 1453, began as a dispute over the succession to the French crown, though economic factors also helped justify the war. Royal propaganda on both sides fostered a kind of early nationalism, and Joan of Arc became a powerful symbol in France. The war also served as a catalyst for the development of Parliament in England. While many people made fortunes during the war, most of this wealth was squandered. Both the French and English economies were devastated by the war, and the resulting taxation led to widespread discontent and peasant revolts.

■ **What challenges faced the Christian church in the fourteenth century, and how did church leaders, intellectuals, and ordinary people respond? (p. 354)**

Religious beliefs offered people solace through the difficult times of the later Middle Ages, but the Western Christian church was going through a particularly difficult period in the fourteenth and early fifteenth centuries. The papacy was pressured to move to Avignon in France, where it was dominated by the French monarchy. This eventually led some cardinals to elect a second, Roman, pope, a division in the church called the Great Schism. The Avignon papacy and the Great Schism weakened the prestige of the church and people's faith in papal authority. The conciliar movement, by denying the church's universal sovereignty, strengthened the claims of secular governments to jurisdiction over all their peoples. As members of the clergy challenged the power of the pope, laypeople challenged the authority of the church itself. Women and men increasingly relied on direct approaches to God, often through mystical encounters, rather than on the institutional church. Some, including John Wyclif and Jan Hus, questioned basic church doctrines.

■ **How did economic and social tensions contribute to revolts, crime, violence, and a growing sense of ethnic and national distinctions? (p. 358)**

The plague and the war both led to higher taxes and economic dislocations, which sparked peasant revolts in Flanders, France, and England. Peasant revolts often blended with conflicts involving workers in cities, where working conditions were changing, widening the gap between wealthy merchant-producers and poor workers. Unrest in the countryside and cities may have been further exacerbated by marriage patterns that left large numbers of young men unmarried and rootless. The pattern of late marriage for men contributed to a growth in prostitution. Along with peasant revolts and urban crime and unrest, violence perpetrated by nobles was a common part of late medieval life. The economic and demographic crises of the fourteenth century also contributed to increasing ethnic tensions in the many parts of Europe where migration had brought different population groups together. A growing sense of ethnic and national identity led to restrictions and occasionally to violence, but also to the increasing use of vernacular languages for works of literature. The increasing number of schools that led to the growth of lay literacy represents another positive achievement of the later Middle Ages.

Suggested Reading

Allmand, Christopher. *The Hundred Years War: England and France at War, ca 1300–1450*, rev. ed. 2005. Designed for students; examines the war from political, military, social, and economic perspectives and compares the way England and France reacted to the conflict.

Boswell, John. *Christianity, Social Tolerance, and Homosexuality: Gay People in Western Europe from the Beginning of the Christian Era to the Fourteenth Century*. 1981. Remains an important broad analysis of attitudes toward same-sex relations throughout the Middle Ages.

Dunn, Alastair. *The Peasants' Revolt: England's Failed Revolution of 1381.* 2004. Offers new interpretations of the causes and consequences of the English Peasants' Revolt.

Dyer, Christopher. *Standards of Living in the Later Middle Ages.* 1989. Examines economic realities and social conditions more generally.

Herlihy, David. *The Black Death and the Transformation of the West,* 2d ed. 1997. A fine treatment of the causes and cultural consequences of the disease that remains the best starting point for study of the great epidemic.

Holt, James Clarke. *Robin Hood.* 1982. A soundly researched and highly readable study of the famous outlaw.

Jordan, William Chester. *The Great Famine: Northern Europe in the Early Fourteenth Century.* 1996. Discusses catastrophic weather, soil exhaustion, and other factors that led to the Great Famine and the impact of the famine on community life.

Karras, Ruth M. *Sexuality in Medieval Europe: Doing unto Others.* 2005. A brief overview designed for undergraduates that incorporates the newest scholarship.

Kieckhefer, Richard. *Unquiet Souls: Fourteenth-Century Saints and Their Religious Milieu.* 1984. Sets the ideas of the mystics in their social and intellectual contexts.

Koch, H. W. *Medieval Warfare.* 1978. A beautifully illustrated book covering strategy, tactics, armaments, and costumes of war.

Lehfeldt, Elizabeth, ed. *The Black Death.* 2005. Includes excerpts from debates about many aspects of the Black Death.

Oakley, Frances. *The Western Church in the Later Middle Ages.* 1979. An excellent broad survey.

Robertson, D. W., Jr. *Chaucer's London.* 1968. Evokes the social setting of *Canterbury Tales* brilliantly.

Swanson, R. N. *Religion and Devotion in Europe, c. 1215–c. 1515.* 2004. Explores many aspects of spirituality.

Tuchman, Barbara. *A Distant Mirror: The Calamitous Fourteenth Century.* 1978. Written for a general audience, it remains a vivid description of this tumultuous time.

Notes

1. Christos S. Bartsocas, "Two Fourteenth Century Descriptions of the 'Black Death,'" *Journal of the History of Medicine,* October 1966, p. 395.
2. Giovanni Boccaccio, *The Decameron,* trans. Mark Musa and Peter Bondanella (New York: W.W. Norton, 1982), p. 7.
3. Ibid., p. 9.
4. Bartsocas, "Two Fourteenth Century Descriptions," p. 397.
5. Florence Warren, ed., *The Dance of Death* (Oxford: Early English Text Society, 1931), p. 8. Spelling modernized.
6. Quoted in J. Barnie, *War in Medieval English Society: Social Values and the Hundred Years' War* (Ithaca, N.Y.: Cornell University Press, 1974), p. 34.
7. W. P. Barrett, trans., *The Trial of Jeanne d'Arc* (London: George Routledge, 1931), pp. 165–166.
8. Quoted in Barnie, *War in Medieval English Society,* pp. 36–37.
9. Quoted in J. H. Smith, *The Great Schism, 1378: The Disintegration of the Medieval Papacy* (New York: Weybright & Talley, 1970), p. 15.
10. Quoted in Katharina M. Wilson, ed., *Medieval Women Writers* (Athens: University of Georgia Press, 1984), p. 245.
11. C. Stephenson and G. Marcham, eds., *Sources of English Constitutional History,* rev. ed. (New York: Harper & Row, 1972), p. 225.
12. Michael Rocke, *Forbidden Friendships: Homosexuality and Male Culture in Renaissance Florence* (New York: Oxford University Press, 1996), p. 45.
13. Quoted in Barbara A. Hanawalt, "Fur Collar Crime: The Pattern of Crime Among the Fourteenth-Century English Nobility," *Journal of Social History* 8 (Spring 1975): 7.
14. Quoted in R. Bartlett, *The Making of Europe: Conquest, Colonization and Cultural Change, 950–1350* (Princeton, N.J.: Princeton University Press, 1993), p. 205.
15. Quoted ibid., p. 239.

Key Terms

Great Famine (p. 340)
Black Death (p. 341)
flagellants (p. 347)
Agincourt (p. 350)
representative assemblies (p. 354)
Babylonian Captivity (p. 355)
Great Schism (p. 355)
conciliarists (p. 356)
confraternities (p. 357)
Jacquerie (p. 358)
English Peasants' Revolt (p. 360)
Statute of Kilkenny (p. 367)

For practice quizzes and other study tools, visit the Online Study Guide at **bedfordstmartins.com/mckaywest**.

For primary sources from this period, see **Sources of Western Society, Second Edition**.

For Web sites, images, and documents related to topics in this chapter, visit Make History at **bedfordstmartins.com/mckaywest**.

13

European Society in the Age of the Renaissance

1350–1550

While war gripped northern Europe, a new culture emerged in southern Europe. The fourteenth century witnessed remarkable changes in Italian intellectual, artistic, and cultural life. Artists and writers thought that they were living in a new golden age, but not until the sixteenth century was this change given the label we use today — the *Renaissance*, derived from the French word for "rebirth." That word was first used by art historian Giorgio Vasari (1511–1574) to describe the art of "rare men of genius" such as his contemporary Michelangelo. Through their works, Vasari judged, the glory of the classical past had been reborn after centuries of darkness. Over time, the word's meaning was broadened to include many aspects of life during that period. The new attitude had a slow diffusion out of Italy, so that the Renaissance "happened" at different times in different parts of Europe.

Later scholars increasingly saw the cultural and political changes of the Renaissance, along with the religious changes of the Reformation (see Chapter 14) and the European voyages of exploration (see Chapter 15), as ushering in the "modern" world. Some historians view the Renaissance as a bridge between the medieval and modern eras because it corresponded chronologically with the late medieval period and because there were many continuities along with the changes. Others have questioned whether the word *Renaissance* should be used at all to describe an era in which many social groups saw decline rather than advance. The debates remind us that these labels — medieval, Renaissance, modern — are intellectual constructs devised after the fact, and all contain value judgments. ■

Life in the Renaissance. In this detail from a fresco, Italian painter Lorenzo Lotto captures the mixing of social groups in a Renaissance Italian city. Wealthy merchants, soldiers, and boys intermingle, while at the right women sell vegetables and bread, a common sight at any city marketplace.

CHAPTER PREVIEW

Wealth and Power in Renaissance Italy
■ What economic and political developments in Italy provided the setting for the Renaissance?

Intellectual Change
■ What were the key ideas of the Renaissance, and how were they different for men and women and for southern and northern Europeans?

Art and the Artist
■ How did changes in art reflect new Renaissance ideals?

Social Hierarchies
■ What were the key social hierarchies in Renaissance Europe, and how did ideas about hierarchy shape people's lives?

Politics and the State in Western Europe, ca. 1450–1521
■ How did the nation-states of western Europe evolve in this period?

Wealth and Power in Renaissance Italy

What economic and political developments in Italy provided the setting for the Renaissance? ■

The magnificent art and new ways of thinking in the **Renaissance** rest on economic and political developments in the city-states of northern Italy. Economic growth laid the material basis for the Italian Renaissance, and ambitious merchants gained political power to match their economic power. They then used their money and power to buy luxuries and hire talent in a system of **patronage**, through which cities, groups, and individuals commissioned writers and artists to produce specific works. Political leaders in Italian cities admired the traditions and power of ancient Rome, and this esteem shaped their commissions. Thus, economics, politics, and culture were interconnected.

Renaissance A French word meaning "rebirth," first used by art historian and critic Giorgio Vasari to refer to the rebirth of the culture of classical antiquity.

patronage Financial support of writers and artists by cities, groups, and individuals, often to produce specific works or works in specific styles.

Trade and Prosperity

Northern Italian cities led the way in the great commercial revival of the eleventh century. By the middle of the twelfth century Venice, supported by a huge merchant marine, had grown enormously rich through overseas trade, as had Genoa and Milan. These cities made important strides in shipbuilding that allowed their ships to sail all year long at accelerated speeds and carrying ever more merchandise.

Another commercial leader, and the city where the Renaissance began, was Florence, situated on the fertile soil along the Arno River. Julius Caesar founded the city in the first century B.C.E. as a home for army veterans, rewarding them with land after their long years of service in the Roman army. The veterans worked hard, as did the settlers who came after them, and the city flourished. Its favorable location on the main road northward from Rome made Florence a commercial hub, and the city grew wealthy buying and selling all types of goods throughout Europe and the Mediterranean—grain, cloth, wool, weapons, armor, spices, glass, and wine.

Florentine merchants also loaned and invested money, and they acquired control of papal banking toward the end of the thirteenth century. Florentine mercantile

A Florentine Bank Scene Originally a "bank" was just a counter; moneychangers who sat behind the counter became "bankers," exchanging different currencies and holding deposits for merchants and business people. In this scene from fifteenth-century Florence, the bank is covered with an imported Ottoman geometric rug, one of many imported luxury items handled by Florentine merchants. Most cities issued their own coins, but the gold coins of Florence, known as "florins" (left), were accepted throughout Europe as a standard currency. (bank scene: Prato, San Francesco/Scala/Art Resource, NY; coins: Scala/Art Resource, NY)

families began to dominate European banking on both sides of the Alps, setting up offices in major European and North African cities. The profits from loans, investments, and money exchanges that poured back to Florence were pumped into urban industries, and by the early fourteenth century the city had about eighty thousand people, about twice the population of London at that time. Profits contributed to the city's economic vitality and allowed banking families to control the city's politics and culture.

By the first quarter of the fourteenth century, the economic foundations of Florence were so strong that even severe crises could not destroy the city. In 1344 King Edward III of England repudiated his huge debts to Florentine bankers, forcing some of them into bankruptcy. Florence suffered frightfully from the Black Death, losing at least half its population, and serious labor unrest shook the political establishment (see Chapter 12). Nevertheless, the basic Florentine economic structure remained stable. The Florentine merchant and historian Benedetto Dei (DAY-ee) boasted proudly of his city in a letter to an acquaintance from Venice:

> Our beautiful Florence contains within the city in this present year two hundred seventy shops belonging to the wool merchants' guild . . . eighty-three rich and splendid warehouses of the silk merchants' guild. . . . The number of banks amounts to thirty-three; the shops of the cabinet-makers, whose business is carving and inlaid work, to eighty-four . . . there are forty-four goldsmiths' and jewelers shops.[1]

In Florence and other cities, wealth allowed many people greater material pleasures, a more comfortable life, and leisure time to appreciate and patronize the arts. Merchants and bankers commissioned public and private buildings from architects, and hired sculptors and painters to decorate their homes and churches. The rich, social-climbing residents of Venice, Florence, Genoa, and Rome came to see life more as an opportunity to be enjoyed than as a painful pilgrimage to the City of God.

Communes and Republics of Northern Italy

The northern Italian cities were **communes**, sworn associations of free men who, like other town residents, began in the twelfth century to seek political and economic independence from local nobles. The merchant guilds that formed the communes built and maintained the city walls, regulated trade, collected taxes, and kept civil order. The local nobles frequently moved into the cities, marrying into rich commercial families and starting their own businesses. This merger of the northern Italian feudal nobility and the commercial elite created a powerful oligarchy, a small group that ruled the city and surrounding countryside. Yet because of rivalries among different powerful families within the ruling oligarchy, Italian communes were often politically unstable.

Unrest coming from below exacerbated the instability. Merchant elites made citizenship in the communes dependent on a property qualification, years of residence within the city, and social connections. Only a tiny percentage of the male population possessed these qualifications and thus could hold office in a commune's political councils. The common people, called the **popolo**, were disenfranchised and heavily taxed, and they bitterly resented their exclusion from power. Throughout most of the thirteenth century, in city after city, the popolo used armed force and violence to take over the city governments. Republican governments—in which political power theoretically resides in the people and is exercised by their chosen representatives—were established in Bologna, Siena, Parma, Florence, Genoa, and other cities. The victory of the popolo proved temporary, however, because they could not establish civil order within their cities. Merchant oligarchies reasserted their power and

Chronology

ca. 1350	Petrarch develops ideas of humanism
1434–1737	Medici family in power in Florence
1440s	Invention of movable metal type
1447–1514	Sforza family in power in Milan
1455–1471	Wars of the Roses in England
1469	Marriage of Isabella of Castile and Ferdinand of Aragon
1477	Louis XI conquers Burgundy
1478	Establishment of the Inquisition in Spain
1492	Spain conquers Granada, ending reconquista; practicing Jews expelled from Spain
1494	Invasion of Italy by Charles VIII of France
1508–1512	Michelangelo paints ceiling of Sistine Chapel
1513	Machiavelli, *The Prince*
1563	Establishment of first formal academy for artistic training in Florence

communes Sworn associations of free men in Italian cities led by merchant guilds that sought political and economic independence from local nobles.

popolo Disenfranchised common people in Italian cities who resented their exclusion from power.

Battle of San Romano Fascinated by perspective — the representation of spatial depth or distance on a flat surface — the Florentine artist Paolo Uccello (1397–1475) celebrated the 1432 Florentine victory over Siena in this painting. Though a minor battle, it started Florence on the road to domination over smaller nearby states. The painting hung in Lorenzo de' Medici's bedroom. (National Gallery, London/Erich Lessing/Art Resource, NY)

sometimes brought in powerful military leaders to establish order. These military leaders, called *condottieri* (kahn-duh-TYER-ee) (singular, *condottiero*), had their own mercenary armies, and in many cities they took over political power as well.

Many cities in Italy became **signori** (seen-YOHR-ee), in which one man ruled and handed down the right to rule to his son. Some signori (the word is plural in Italian and is used for both persons and forms of government) kept the institutions of communal government in place, but these had no actual power. Oligarchic regimes possessed constitutions and often boasted about how much more democratic their form of government was than the government in neighboring signori. In actuality, there wasn't much difference. Oligarchies maintained a façade of republican government, but the judicial, executive, and legislative functions of government were restricted to a small class of wealthy merchants.

In the fifteenth and sixteenth centuries the signori in many cities and the most powerful merchant oligarchs in others transformed their households into **courts**. Courtly culture afforded signori and oligarchs the opportunity to display and assert their wealth and power. They built magnificent palaces in the centers of cities and required all political business to be done there. The rulers of Florence, Milan, and other northern Italian cities became patrons of the arts, hiring architects to design and build private palaces and public city halls, artists to fill them with paintings and sculptures, and musicians and composers to fill them with music. They supported writers and philosophers, flaunting their patronage of learning and the arts. Ceremonies connected with family births, baptisms, marriages, and funerals offered occasions for magnificent pageantry and elaborate ritual. Cities welcomed rulers who were visiting with magnificent entrance parades that often included fireworks, colorful banners, mock naval battles, decorated wagons filled with people in costume, and temporary triumphal arches modeled on those of ancient Rome. Rulers of nation-states later copied and adapted all these aspects of Italian courts.

City-States and the Balance of Power

Renaissance Italians had a passionate attachment to their individual city-states: political loyalty and feeling centered on the local city. This intensity of local feeling perpetuated the dozens of small states and hindered the development of one unified state.

In the fifteenth century five powers dominated the Italian peninsula: Venice, Milan, Florence, the Papal States, and the kingdom of Naples (Map 13.1). Venice,

signori Government by one-man rule in Italian cities such as Milan.

courts Magnificent households and palaces where signori and other rulers lived, conducted business, and supported the arts.

with its enormous trade empire, ranked as an international power. Though Venice was a republic in name, an oligarchy of merchant-aristocrats actually ran the city. Milan was also called a republic, but the condottieri-turned-signori of the Sforza (SFORT-sah) family ruled harshly and dominated Milan and several smaller cities in the north from 1447 to 1535. Likewise, in Florence the form of government was republican, with authority vested in several councils of state. In reality, starting in 1434 the great Medici (MEH-duh-chee) banking family held power almost continually for centuries. Though not public officials, Cosimo (1434–1464) and Lorenzo (1469–1492) ruled from behind the scenes, and in the sixteenth century their descendants became the hereditary rulers of Florence and the surrounding area as the Grand Dukes of Tuscany, ruling until 1737. The Medici family produced three popes, and most other Renaissance popes were also members of powerful Italian families, selected for their political skills, not their piety. Pope Alexander VI (pontificate 1492–1503) was the most ruthless; aided militarily and politically by his illegitimate son Cesare Borgia, he reasserted papal authority in the papal lands. South of the Papal States, the kingdom of Naples was under the control of the king of Aragon.

The major Italian city-states controlled the smaller ones, such as Siena, Mantua, Ferrara, and Modena, and competed furiously among themselves for territory. The large cities used diplomacy, spies, paid informers, and any other available means to get information that could be used to advance their ambitions. While the states of northern Europe were moving toward centralization and consolidation, the world of Italian politics resembled a jungle where the powerful dominated the weak.

In one significant respect, however, the Italian city-states anticipated future relations among competing European states after 1500. Whenever one Italian state appeared to gain a predominant position within the peninsula, other states combined to establish a balance of power against the major threat. In the formation of these

MAP 13.1 **The Italian City-States, ca. 1494** In the fifteenth century the Italian city-states represented great wealth and cultural sophistication, though their many political divisions throughout the peninsula invited foreign intervention.

alliances, Renaissance Italians invented the machinery of modern diplomacy: permanent embassies with resident ambassadors in capitals where political relations and commercial ties needed continual monitoring. The resident ambassador was one of the great political achievements of the Italian Renaissance.

At the end of the fifteenth century Venice, Florence, Milan, and the papacy possessed great wealth and represented high cultural achievement. Wealthy and divided, however, they were also an inviting target for invasion. When Florence and Naples entered into an agreement to acquire Milanese territories, Milan called on France for support, and the French king Charles VIII (r. 1483–1498) invaded Italy in 1494.

In Florence, the French invasion was interpreted as the fulfillment of a prophecy by the Dominican friar Girolamo Savonarola (1452–1498). In a number of fiery sermons attended by large crowds, Savonarola had predicted that God would punish Italy for its moral vice and corrupt leadership. The Medici dynasty that ruled Florence fell after the French invasion, and Savonarola became the political and religious leader of the city. He reorganized the government and called on people to destroy anything that might lead them to sin: fancy clothing, cosmetics, pagan books, musical instruments, paintings, or poetry that celebrated human beauty. These were gathered together and burned on the main square of Florence in what became known as "bonfires of the vanities."

For a time Savonarola was wildly popular, but eventually people tired of his moral denunciations, and he was excommunicated by the pope, tortured, and burned at the very spot where he had overseen the bonfires. The Medici returned as the rulers of Florence. Savonarola's story has fascinated novelists and playwrights, but in the political history of Renaissance Italy he best serves as a reminder of the internal instability of Italian cities, an instability that invited foreign invasion.

The French invasion inaugurated a new period in Italian and European power politics. Italy became the focus of international ambitions and the battleground of foreign armies, particularly those of France and the Holy Roman Empire in a series of conflicts called the Habsburg-Valois wars (named for the German and French dynasties). The Italian cities suffered severely from continual warfare, especially in the frightful sack of Rome in 1527 by imperial forces under the emperor Charles V. Thus the failure of the city-states to form a federal system, to consolidate, or at least to establish a common foreign policy led to centuries of subjection by outside invaders. Italy was not to achieve unification until 1870.

humanism A program of study designed by Italians that emphasized the critical study of Latin and Greek literature with the goal of understanding human nature.

Intellectual Change

What were the key ideas of the Renaissance, and how were they different for men and women and for southern and northern Europeans?

The Renaissance was characterized by self-conscious awareness among educated Italians that they were living in a new era. Somewhat ironically, this idea rested on a deep interest in ancient Latin and Greek literature and philosophy. Through reflecting on the classics, Renaissance thinkers developed new notions of human nature, new plans for education, and new concepts of political rule. The advent of the printing press with movable type would greatly accelerate the spread of their ideas throughout Europe.

Humanism

Giorgio Vasari was the first to use the word *Renaissance* in print, but he was not the first to feel that something was being reborn. Two centuries earlier the Florentine poet and scholar Francesco Petrarch (1304–1374) spent long hours searching for classical Latin manuscripts in dusty monastery libraries and wandering around the many ruins of the Roman Empire remaining in Italy. He became obsessed with the classical past and felt that the writers and artists of ancient Rome had reached a level of perfection in their work that had never since been duplicated. Writers of his own day should follow these ancient models, thought Petrarch, and should ignore the thousand-year period between his own time and that of Rome, which he called the "dark ages" ushered in by the barbarian invasions. Petrarch believed that the recovery of classical texts would bring about a new golden age of intellectual achievement, an idea that many others came to share.

Petrarch clearly thought he was witnessing the dawning of a new era in which writers and artists would recapture the glory of the Roman republic. Around 1350 he proposed a new kind of education to help them do this, in which young men would study the works of ancient Latin and Greek authors, using them as models of how to write clearly, argue effectively, and speak persuasively. The study of Latin classics became known as the *studia humanitates* (STOO-dee-uh oo-mahn-ee-TAH-tayz), usually translated as "liberal studies" or the "liberal arts." People who advocated it were known as *humanists* and their program as **humanism**. Like all programs of study, humanism contained an implicit philosophy: that human nature and achievements, evident in the classics, were worthy of contemplation.

The glory of Rome had been brightest, in the opinion of the humanists, in the works of the Roman author and statesman Cicero (106 B.C.E.–43 B.C.E.). Cicero had lived during the turbulent era when Julius Caesar and other powerful generals transformed the Roman republic into an empire (see Chapter 5). In forceful and elegantly worded speeches, letters, and treatises, Cicero supported a return to republican government. Petrarch and other humanists admired Cicero's use of language, literary style, and political ideas. Many humanists saw Caesar's transformation of Rome as a betrayal of the great society, marking the beginning of a long period of decay that the barbarian migrations had simply sped up. In his history of Florence written in 1436, the humanist historian and Florentine city official Leonardo Bruni (1374–1444) closely linked the decline of the Latin language after the death of Cicero and the decline of the Roman republic: "After the liberty of the Roman people had been lost through the rule of the emperors . . . the flourishing condition of studies and of letters perished, together with the welfare of the city of Rome."[2] In this same book, Bruni was also very clear that by the time of his writing, the period of decay had ended and a new era had begun. He was the first to divide history into three eras—ancient, medieval, and modern—though another humanist historian actually invented the term "Middle Ages."

In the fifteenth century Florentine humanists became increasingly interested in Greek philosophy as well as Roman literature, especially in the ideas of Plato. Under the patronage of Cosimo de Medici (1389–1464), the most powerful man in Florence, the scholar Marsilio Ficino (1433–1499), who would eventually become an ordained priest, began to lecture to an informal group of Florence's cultural elite; his lectures became known as the Platonic Academy, but they were not really a school. Ficino regarded Plato as a divinely inspired precursor to Christ, and he translated Plato's dialogues into Latin, attempting to synthesize Christian and Platonic teachings. Plato's emphasis on the spiritual and eternal over the material and transient fit well with Christian teachings about the immortality of the soul. Platonic ideas about love, that the highest form of love was spiritual desire for pure, perfect beauty uncorrupted by bodily desires, could easily be interpreted as Christian desire for the perfection of God.

For Ficino and his most brilliant student, Giovanni Pico della Mirandola (1463–1494), both Christian and classical texts taught that the universe was a hierarchy of beings from God down through spiritual beings to material beings, with humanity the crucial link right in the middle, both material and spiritual. In a remarkable essay, *On the Dignity of Man* (1486), Pico stressed that man possesses great dignity because he was made as Adam in the image of God before the Fall and as Christ after the Resurrection. According to Pico, man is the one part of the created world that has no fixed place, but can freely choose whether to rise to the realm of the angels or descend to the realm of the animals; because of

Saltcellar of Francis I In gold and enamel, Benvenuto Cellini depicts on this precursor of the saltshaker from about 1540 the Roman sea god, Neptune, sitting beside a small boat-shaped container holding salt from the sea. Opposite him, a female figure personifying Earth guards the pepper. Portrayed on the base are the four seasons and the times of day, symbolizing seasonal festivities and daily meal schedules. Classical figures were common subjects in Renaissance art. (Kunsthistorisches Museum, Vienna/The Bridgeman Art Library)

the divine image planted in him, he is truly a "miraculous creature."

Man's miraculous nature meant there are no limits to what he can accomplish. Families, religious brotherhoods, neighborhoods, workers' organizations, and other groups continued to have meaning in peoples' lives, but Renaissance thinkers increasingly viewed these groups as springboards to far greater individual achievement. They were especially interested in individuals who had risen above their background to become brilliant, powerful, or unique. (See "Individuals in Society: Leonardo da Vinci," page 391.) Such individuals had the admirable quality of **virtù** (ver-TOO), which is not virtue in the sense of moral goodness, but the ability to shape the world around them according to their will. Bruni and other historians included biographies of individuals with virtù in their histories of cities and nations, describing ways in which they had affected the course of history. Through the quality of their works and their influence on others, artists could also exhibit virtù, an idea that Vasari captures in the title of his major work, "The Lives of the Most Excellent Painters, Sculptors and Architects." His subjects were not simply excellent, but had achieved the pinnacle of excellence.

> **virtù** The quality of being able to shape the world according to one's own will.

> **It is much safer for the prince to be feared than loved, but he ought to avoid making himself hated.**
> —Niccolò Machiavelli

The last artist included in Vasari's book is Vasari himself, for Renaissance thinkers did not exclude themselves when they searched for models of talent and achievement. Vasari begins his discussion of his own works with a bit of modesty, saying that these might "not lay claim to excellence and perfection" when compared with those of other artists, but he then goes on for more than thirty pages, clearly feeling he has achieved some level of excellence.

Leon Battista Alberti (1404–1472) had similar views of his own achievements. He had much to be proud of: he wrote novels, plays, legal treatises, a study of the family, and the first scientific analysis of perspective; he designed churches, palaces, and fortifications effective against cannon; he invented codes for sending messages secretly and a machine that could cipher and decipher them. In his autobiography—written late in his life, and in the third person, so that he calls himself "he" instead of "I"—Alberti described his personal qualities and accomplishments:

> *Assiduous in the science and skill of dealing with arms and horses and musical instruments, as well as in the pursuit of letters and the fine arts, he was devoted to the knowledge of the most strange and difficult things. . . . He played ball, hurled the javelin, ran, leaped, wrestled. . . . He learned music without teachers . . . and then turned to physics and the mathematical arts. . . . Ambition was alien to him. . . . When his favorite dog died he wrote a funeral oration for him.*[3]

His achievements in many fields did make Alberti a "Renaissance man," as we use the term, though it may be hard to believe his assertion that "ambition was alien to him."

Biographies and autobiographies presented individuals their humanist authors thought were worthy models, but sometimes people needed more direct instruction. The ancient Greek philosopher Plato, whom humanists greatly admired, taught that the best way to learn something was to think about its perfect, ideal form. If you wanted to learn about justice, for example, you should imagine what ideal justice would be, rather than look at actual examples of justice in the world around you, for these would never be perfect. Following Plato's ideas, Renaissance authors speculated about perfect examples of many things. Alberti wrote about the ideal country house, which was to be useful, convenient, and elegant, and the English humanist Thomas More described a perfect society, which he called Utopia (see page 385).

Education

Humanists thought that their recommended course of study in the classics would provide essential skills for future diplomats, lawyers, military leaders, businessmen, and politicians, as well as writers and artists. It would provide a much broader and more practical type of training than that offered at universities, which at the time focused on theology and philosophy or on theoretical training for lawyers and physicians. Humanists poured out treatises, often in the form of letters, on the structure and goals of education and the training of rulers and leaders. They taught that a life active in the world should be the aim of all educated individuals and that education was not simply for private or religious purposes, but benefited the public good.

Humanists put their ideas into practice. Beginning in the early fifteenth century, they opened schools and academies in Italian cities and courts in which pupils began with Latin grammar and rhetoric, went on to study Roman history and political philosophy, and then learned Greek in order to study Greek literature and philosophy. Gradually, humanist education became the basis for intermediate and advanced education for well-to-do urban boys and men. Humanist schools were established in Florence, Venice, and other Italian cities, and by the early sixteenth century across the Alps in Germany, France, and England.

Humanists disagreed about education for women. Many saw the value of exposing women to classical models of moral behavior and reasoning, but they also wondered whether a program of study that emphasized eloquence and action was proper for women, whose sphere was generally understood to be private and domestic. In his book on the family, Alberti stressed that a wife's role should be restricted to the orderliness of the household, food and the serving of meals, the education of children, and the supervision of servants. (Alberti never married, so he never put his ideas into practice in his own household.) Women themselves were more bold in their claims about the value of the new learning. Although humanist academies were not open to women, through tutors or programs of self-study a few women did become educated in the classics. They argued in letters and published writings that reason was not limited to men and that learning was compatible with virtue for women as well as men. (See "Listening to the Past: Perspectives on Humanist Learning and Women," page 382.)

No book on education had broader influence than Baldassare Castiglione's *The Courtier* (1528). This treatise sought to train, discipline, and fashion the young man into the courtly ideal, the gentleman. According to

Portrait of Baldassare Castiglione In this portrait by Raphael, the most sought-after portrait painter of the Renaissance, Castiglione is shown dressed exactly as he advised courtiers to dress, in elegant but subdued clothing that would enhance the splendor of the court, but never outshine the ruler. (Scala/Art Resource, NY)

Castiglione (kahs-teel-YOH-nay), who himself was a courtier serving several different rulers, the educated man should have a broad background in many academic subjects, and his spiritual and physical as well as intellectual capabilities should be trained. Castiglione envisioned a man who could compose a sonnet, wrestle, sing a song and accompany himself on an instrument, ride expertly, solve difficult mathematical problems, and, above all, speak and write eloquently. Castiglione also included discussion of the perfect court lady, who, like the courtier, was to be well educated and able to play a musical instrument, to paint, and to dance. Physical beauty, delicacy, affability, and modesty were also important qualities for court ladies.

In the sixteenth and seventeenth centuries, *The Courtier* was translated into every European language and widely read. It influenced the social mores and patterns of conduct of elite groups in Renaissance and early modern Europe and became a how-to manual for people seeking to improve themselves and rise in the social hierarchy as well. Echoes of its ideal for women have perhaps had an even longer life.

Political Thought

Ideal courtiers should preferably serve an ideal ruler, and biographies written by humanists often described rulers who were just, wise, pious, dignified, learned, brave, kind, and distinguished. For such flattering portraits of living rulers or their ancestors, authors sometimes received positions at court, or at least substantial payments. Particularly in Italian cities, however, which often were divided by political factions, taken over by homegrown or regional despots, and attacked by foreign armies, such ideal rulers were hard to find. Humanists thus looked to the classical past for their models. Some, such as Bruni, argued that republicanism was the best form of government. Others used the model of Plato's philosopher-king in the *Republic* to argue that rule by an enlightened single individual might be best. Both sides agreed that educated men should be active in the political affairs of their city, a position historians have since termed "civic humanism."

The most famous (or infamous) civic humanist, and ultimately the best-known political theorist of this era, was Niccolò Machiavelli (1469–1527). After the ouster of the Medici with the French invasion of 1494, Machiavelli was secretary to one of the governing bodies in the city of Florence, responsible for diplomatic missions and organizing a citizen army. Power struggles in Florence between rival factions brought the Medici family back to power, and Machiavelli was arrested, tortured, and imprisoned on suspicion of plotting against them. He was released but had no government position, and he spent the rest of his life writing — political theory, poetry, prose works, plays, and a multivolume history of Florence — and making fruitless attempts to regain employment.

The first work Machiavelli finished — though not the first to be published — is his most famous, *The Prince* (1513), which uses the examples of classical and contemporary rulers to argue that the function of a ruler (or any government) is to preserve order and security. Weakness would only lead to disorder, which might end in civil war or conquest by an outsider, clearly situations that were not conducive to any people's well-being. To preserve the state a ruler should use whatever means he needs — brutality, lying, manipulation — but should not do anything that would make the populace turn against him; stealing or cruel actions done for a ruler's own pleasure would lead to resentment and destroy the popular support needed for a strong, stable realm. "It is much safer

Perspectives on Humanist Learning and Women

LISTENING TO THE PAST

Italian humanists set out the type of education that they regarded as ideal and promoted its value to society and the individual. Several women from the bustling cities of northern Italy became excited by the new style of learning, and through tutors or programs of self-study became extremely well educated. Like male humanists, they wrote letters, orations, lectures, and dialogues demonstrating their learning on such topics as truth, virtue, knowledge, fame, and friendship, and circulated these to acquaintances and people whose good opinion they valued. Occasionally they presented orations and lectures orally in public settings or noble courts.

Some male humanists, including the influential Florentine official Leonardo Bruni, suggested that no woman who shared her ideas in public could possibly be virtuous, but by the middle of the fifteenth century other humanists celebrated the entrance of at least a few women into the largely male world of learning. The Venetian humanist nobleman Lauro Quirini (ca. 1420–ca. 1475), for example, had heard about the learned Isotta Nogarola (1418–1466) from her brother and from reading a collection of her letters. In this letter he praises her accomplishments and advises her on a plan of study.

Letter from Lauro Quirini to Isotta Nogarola, ca. 1450

" This letter asks of you nothing else than that you pursue in the most splendid way, until death, that same course of right living that you have followed since childhood.... Rightful therefore, should you also, famous Isotta, receive the highest praises, since you have, if I may so speak, overcome your own nature. For that true virtue that is proper to men you have pursued with remarkable zeal — not the mediocre virtue that many men seek, but that which would befit a man of the most flawless and perfect wisdom.... Therefore dissatisfied with the lesser studies, you have applied your noble mind to those highest disciplines, in which there is need for keenness of intelligence and mind. For you are engaged in the art of dialectic, which shows the way to learning the truth. Having mastered it, you may become engaged in a still more splendid and fertile field of philosophy [metaphysics]....

Read studiously, then, the glorious works of Boethius Severnius, unquestionably a most intelligent and abundantly learned man.* Read all the treatises he learnedly composed on the dialectic art.... After you have mastered dialectic, which is the method of knowing, you should read diligently and carefully the moral books of Aristotle, which he writes divinely, in which you may unfailingly recognize the essence of true and solid virtue.... Then, after you have also digested this part of philosophy, which is concerned with human matters, equipped with your nobility of the soul you should also set out for that ample and vast other part [divine matters].... Here you should begin especially with those disciplines that we call by the Greek term mathematics....

Diligently and carefully follow the Arabs, who very nearly approach the Greeks. You should constantly and assiduously read Averroes, admittedly a barbarous and uncultivated man, but otherwise an exceptional philosopher and rare judge of things.†... Read Thomas Aquinas often, who provides as it were an entryway to the understanding of Aristotle and Averroes.‡...

You should also make use of those studies, moreover, that you have splendidly embraced from your youth, and especially history, for history is as it were the teacher of life, which somehow makes the wisdom of the ancients ours and inflames us to imitate great men....

Take care of yourself so that you may be well, and study so that you may be wise.... For nothing is more lovely than philosophy, nothing more beautiful, nothing more lovable, as our Cicero said, to which I add, perhaps more truly, that there is nothing among human things more divine than philosophy. "

The Venetian Cassandra Fedele (1465–1558) applied advice such as Quirini's to her own studies and became the best-known female scholar in her time, corresponding with humanist writers, church officials, university professors, nobles, and even the rulers of Europe, including Isabella and Ferdinand of Spain, and becoming a positive example in the debate about women. She gave this oration in Latin at the University of Padua in honor of her (male) cousin's graduation.

---

for the prince to be feared than loved," Machiavelli advised, "but he ought to avoid making himself hated."[4]

Like the good humanist he was, Machiavelli knew that effective rulers exhibited the quality of virtù. He presented examples from the classical past of just the type of ruler he was describing, but also wrote about contemporary leaders. Cesare Borgia (1475?–1507), Machiavelli's primary example, was the son of Rodrigo Borgia, a Spanish nobleman who later became Pope Alexander VI. Cesare Borgia combined his father's power and his own ruthlessness to build up a city-state in central Italy. He made good use of new military equip-

In Praise of Letters

❝ I shall speak very briefly on the study of the liberal arts, which for humans is useful and honorable, pleasurable and enlightening since everyone, not only philosophers but also the most ignorant man, knows and admits that it is by reason that man is separated from beasts. For what is it that so greatly helps both the learned and the ignorant? What so enlarges and enlightens men's minds the way that an education in and knowledge of literature and the liberal arts do? . . . But erudite men who are filled with the knowledge of divine and human things turn all their thoughts and considerations toward reason as though toward a target, and free their minds from all pain, though plagued by many anxieties. These men are scarcely subjected to fortune's innumerable arrows and they prepare themselves to live well and in happiness. They follow reason as their leader in all things; nor do they consider themselves only, but they are also accustomed to assisting others with their energy and advice in matters public and private.

And so Plato, a man almost divine, wrote that those states would be fortunate in which the men who were heads of state were philosophers or in which philosophers took on the duty of administration. . . . The study of literature refines men's minds, forms and makes bright the power of reason, and washes away all stains from the mind, or at any rate, greatly cleanses it. It perfects the gifts and adds much beauty and elegance to the physical and material advantages that one has received by nature. States, however, and their princes who foster and cultivate these studies become more humane, more gracious, and more noble. For this reason, these studies have won for themselves the sweet appellation, "humanities." . . . Just as places that lie unused and uncultivated become fertile and rich in fruits and vegetables with men's labor and hard work and are always made beautiful, so are our natures cultivated, enhanced, and enlightened by the liberal arts. . . .

But enough on the utility of literature since it produces not only an outcome that is rich, precious, and sublime, but also provides one with advantages that are extremely pleasurable, fruitful, and lasting—benefits that I myself have enjoyed. And when I meditate on the idea of marching forth in life with the lowly and execrable weapons of the little woman—the needle and the distaff [the rod onto which yarn is wound after spinning]—even if the study of literature offers women no rewards or honors, I believe women must nonetheless pursue and embrace such studies alone for the pleasure and enjoyment they contain. ❞

Sources: Excerpt from *Nogarola, Complete Writings*, ed. and trans. Margaret L. King and Diana Robin, in *The Other Voices in Early Modern Europe*, pp. 108–113. Copyright © 2004 University of Chicago Press; excerpt from Cassandra Fedele, *Letters and Orations*, pp. 159–162, ed. and trans. Diana Robin. Copyright © 2000 University of Chicago Press. Used with permission of the publisher.

QUESTIONS FOR ANALYSIS

1. What do Quirini and Fedele view as the best course of study?
2. What do they see as the purposes of such study? Are these purposes different for men and women?
3. Quirini is male and Fedele female. Does the gender of the authors shape their ideas about humanist learning in general, or about its appropriateness for women?

*Boethius (ca. 480–524) was a philosopher and adviser to King Theoderic (see page 191); he translated Aristotle's works on logic from Greek into Latin.
†Averroes (1126–1198) was an Islamic philosopher from Spain who wrote commentaries on Aristotle.
‡Thomas Aquinas (1225–1274) was a scholastic theologian and philosopher who brought together Aristotelian philosophy and Christian teachings (see page 322).

Woodcut showing Isotta Nogarola with her books, from Jacopo Bergamo's *Of Many Renowned and Wicked Women* (1497), a listing of good and evil women. ([Ferrara: Laurentius de Rubeis de Valentia, 1497]. Photo: Visual Connection Archive)

ment and tactics, hiring Leonardo da Vinci (1452–1519) as a military engineer, and murdered his political enemies, including one of the husbands of his sister, Lucrezia. Despite Borgia's efforts, his state fell apart after his father's death, which Machiavelli ascribed not to weakness, but to the operations of fate (*fortuna*, for-TOO-nah, in Italian), whose power even the best-prepared and most merciless ruler could not fully escape, though he should try. Fortuna was personified and portrayed as a goddess in ancient Rome and Renaissance Italy, and Machiavelli's last words about fortune are expressed in gendered terms: "It is better to be impetuous than cautious, for fortune is a woman, and if one wishes to keep her down, it is necessary to beat her and knock her down."⁵

The Prince is often seen as the first modern guide to politics, though Machiavelli was denounced for writing it, and people later came to use the word *Machiavellian* to mean cunning and ruthless. Medieval political philosophers had debated the proper relation between church and state, but they regarded the standards by which all governments were to be judged as emanating from moral principles established by God. Machiavelli argued that governments should instead be judged by how well they provided security, order, and safety to their populace. A ruler's moral code in maintaining these was not the same as a private individual's, for a leader could—indeed, should—use any means necessary. Machiavelli put a new spin on the Renaissance search for perfection, arguing that ideals needed to be measured in the cold light of the real world. This more pragmatic view of the purposes of government, and Machiavelli's discussion of the role of force and cruelty, was unacceptable to many.

Even today, when Machiavelli's more secular view of the purposes of government is widely shared, scholars debate whether Machiavelli actually meant what he wrote. Most regard him as realistic or even cynical, but some suggest that he was being ironic or satirical, showing princely government in the worst possible light to contrast it with republicanism. He dedicated *The Prince* to the new Medici ruler of Florence, however, so any criticism was deeply buried within what was, in that era of patronage, essentially a job application.

Christian humanists Northern humanists who interpreted Italian ideas about and attitudes toward classical antiquity and humanism in terms of their own religious traditions.

Christian Humanism

In the last quarter of the fifteenth century, students from the Low Countries, France, Germany, and England flocked to Italy, absorbed the "new learning," and carried it back to their own countries. Northern humanists shared the ideas of Ficino and Pico about the wisdom of ancient texts, but they went beyond Italian efforts to synthesize the Christian and classical traditions to see humanist learning as a way to bring about reform of the church and deepen people's spiritual lives. These **Christian humanists**, as they were later called, thought that the best elements of classical and Christian cultures should be combined. For example, the classical ideals of calmness, stoical patience, and broad-mindedness should be joined in human conduct with the Christian virtues of love, faith, and hope.

The English humanist Thomas More (1478–1535) began life as a lawyer, studied the classics, and entered government service. This left him time to write, and he became most famous for his controversial dialogue

Procession of the Magi This segment of a huge fresco covering three walls of a chapel in the Medici Palace in Florence shows members of the Medici family and other contemporary individuals in a procession accompanying the biblical three wise men (*magi* in Italian) as they brought gifts to the infant Jesus. The painting was ordered in 1459 by Cosimo and Piero de' Medici, who had just finished building the family palace in the center of the city. Reflecting the self-confidence of his patrons, artist Bennozzo Gozzoli places the elderly Cosimo and Piero at the head of the procession, accompanied by their grooms. The group behind them includes Pope Pius II (in the last row in a red hat that ties under the chin) and the artist (in the second to the last row in a red hat with gold lettering). (Scala/Art Resource, NY)

Utopia (1516), a word More invented from the Greek words for "nowhere." *Utopia* describes a community on an island somewhere beyond Europe where all children receive a good education, primarily in the Greco-Roman classics, and adults divide their days between manual labor or business pursuits and intellectual activities. The problems that plagued More's fellow citizens, such as poverty and hunger, have been solved by a beneficent government. Because private property promoted inequality and greed, profits from business and property are held in common. There is religious toleration, and order and reason prevail. Because Utopian institutions are perfect, however, dissent and disagreement are not acceptable.

More's purposes in writing *Utopia* have been just as debated as have Machiavelli's in *The Prince*. Some view it as a revolutionary critique of More's own hierarchical and violent society, some as a call for an even firmer hierarchy, and others as part of the humanist tradition of satire. It was widely read by learned Europeans in the Latin in which More wrote it, and later in vernacular translations, and its title quickly became the standard word for any imaginary society.

Better known by contemporaries than Thomas More was the Dutch humanist Desiderius Erasmus (dez-ih-DARE-ee-us ih-RAZ-muhs) (1466?–1536) of Rotterdam. His fame rested largely on his exceptional knowledge of Greek and the Bible. Erasmus's long list of publications includes *The Education of a Christian Prince* (1504), a book combining idealistic and practical suggestions for the formation of a ruler's character through the careful study of Plutarch, Aristotle, Cicero, and Plato; *The Praise of Folly* (1509), a satire of worldly wisdom and a plea for the simple and spontaneous Christian faith of children; and, most important, a critical edition of the Greek New Testament (1516). In the preface to the New Testament, Erasmus explained the purpose of his great work: "I wish that even the weakest woman should read the Gospel—should read the epistles of Paul. And I wish these were translated into all languages, so that they might be read and understood, not only by Scots and Irishmen, but also by Turks and Saracens."[6]

Two fundamental themes run through all of Erasmus's work. First, education is the means to reform, the key to moral and intellectual improvement. The core of education ought to be study of the Bible and the classics. Second, the essence of Erasmus's thought is, in his own phrase, "the philosophy of Christ." By this Erasmus meant that Christianity is an inner attitude of the heart or spirit. Christianity is not formalism, special ceremonies, or law; Christianity is Christ—his life and what he said and did, not what theologians have written.

The Printed Word

The fourteenth-century humanist Petrarch and the sixteenth-century humanist Erasmus had similar ideas about many things, but the immediate impact of their ideas was very different because of one thing: the printing press with movable metal type. The ideas of Petrarch were spread slowly from person to person by hand copying. The ideas of Erasmus were spread quickly through print, in which hundreds or thousands of identical copies could be made in a short time.

Printing with movable metal type developed in Germany in the 1440s as a combination of existing technologies. Several metal-smiths, most prominently Johann Gutenberg, recognized that the metal stamps used to mark signs on jewelry could be covered with ink and used to mark symbols onto a surface, in the same way that other craftsmen were using carved wood stamps to print books. (This woodblock printing technique originated in China and Korea centuries earlier.) Gutenberg and his assistants made stamps—later called *type*—for every letter of the alphabet and built racks that held the type in rows. This type could be rearranged for every page and so used over and over.

Printing Press In this reproduction of Gutenberg's printing press, metal type sits in a frame ready to be placed in the bottom part of the press, with a leather-covered ink ball nearby for spreading ink on the type. Paper was then placed over the type, and a heavy metal plate brought down onto the paper with a firm pull of the large wooden handle, a technology adapted from wine presses. (Erich Lessing/Art Resource, NY)

Mapping the Past

Map 13.2 **The Growth of Printing in Europe, 1448–1551** The speed with which artisans spread printing technology across Europe provides strong evidence for the growing demand for reading material. Presses in the Ottoman Empire were first established by Jewish immigrants who printed works in Hebrew, Greek, and Spanish.

ANALYZING THE MAP What part of Europe had the greatest number of printing presses by 1550? What explains this?

CONNECTIONS Printing was developed in response to a market for reading materials. Use Maps 11.2 and 11.3 (pages 309 and 318) to help explain why printing spread the way it did.

To complete this activity online, go to the Online Study Guide at bedfordstmartins.com/mckaywest.

The printing revolution was also enabled by the ready availability of paper, which was also made using techniques that had originated in China and were brought into Europe through Muslim Spain. (See "Living in the Past: Muslim Technology: Advances in Papermaking," page 214.)

By the fifteenth century the increase in urban literacy, the development of primary schools, and the opening of more universities had created an expanding market for reading materials (see Chapter 12). When Gutenberg developed what he saw at first as a faster way to copy, professional copyists writing by hand and block-book makers, along with monks and nuns, were already churning out reading materials on paper as fast as they could for the growing number of people who could read.

Gutenberg's invention involved no special secret technology or materials, and he was not the only one to recognize the huge market for books. Other craftsmen made their own type, built their own presses, and bought their own paper, setting themselves up in business (Map 13.2). Historians estimate that, within a half century of the publication of Gutenberg's Bible in 1456, somewhere between 8 million and 20 million books were printed in Europe. Whatever the actual figure, the number is far greater than the number of books produced in all of Western history up to that point.

The effects of the invention of movable-type printing were not felt overnight. Nevertheless, movable type brought about radical changes, transforming both the private and the public lives of Europeans by the dawn of the sixteenth century. Print shops were gathering places for people interested in new ideas. Though printers were trained through apprenticeships just like blacksmiths or butchers, they had connections to the world of politics, art, and scholarship that other craftsmen did not.

Printing gave hundreds or even thousands of people identical books, so that they could more easily discuss the ideas that the books contained with one another in person or through letters. Printed materials reached an invisible public, allowing silent individuals to join causes and groups of individuals widely separated by geography to form a common identity; this new group consciousness could compete with older, localized loyalties.

Government and church leaders both used and worried about printing. They printed laws, declarations of war, battle accounts, and propaganda, and they also attempted to censor books and authors whose ideas they thought were wrong. Officials developed lists of prohibited books and authors, enforcing their prohibitions by confiscating books, arresting printers and booksellers, or destroying the presses of printers who disobeyed. None of this was very effective, and books were printed secretly, with fake title pages, authors, and places of publication, and smuggled all over Europe.

Printing also stimulated the literacy of laypeople and eventually came to have a deep effect on their private lives. Although most of the earliest books and pamphlets dealt with religious subjects, printers produced anything that would sell. They printed professional reference sets for lawyers, doctors, and students, and historical romances, biographies, and how-to manuals for the general public. They discovered that illustrations increased a book's sales, so they published books on a wide range of topics — from history to pornography — full of woodcuts and engravings. Single-page broadsides and flysheets allowed great public events and "wonders" such as comets and two-headed calves to be experienced vicariously by a stay-at-home readership. Since books and other printed materials were read aloud to illiterate listeners, print bridged the gap between the written and oral cultures.

Art and the Artist

How did changes in art reflect new Renaissance ideals?

No feature of the Renaissance evokes greater admiration than its artistic masterpieces. The 1400s (*quattrocento*) and 1500s (*cinquecento*) bore witness to dazzling creativity in painting, architecture, and sculpture. In all the arts, the city of Florence led the way. But Florence was not the only artistic center, for Rome and Venice also became important, and northern Europeans perfected their own styles.

Patronage and Power

As we saw earlier in this chapter, powerful urban groups often flaunted their wealth by commissioning works of art in early Renaissance Italy. The Florentine cloth merchants, for example, delegated Filippo Brunelleschi (fihl-EEP-oh broo-nayl-LAYS-kee) to build the magnificent dome on the cathedral of Florence and selected Lorenzo Ghiberti (law-REHN-tsoh gee-BEHR-tee) to design the bronze doors of the adjacent Baptistery, a separate building in which baptisms were performed. These works represented the merchants' dominant influence in the community.

Increasingly in the later fifteenth century, wealthy individuals and rulers, rather than corporate groups, sponsored works of art. Patrician merchants and bankers, popes, and princes spent vast sums on the arts as a means of glorifying themselves and their families. Writing in about 1470, Florentine ruler Lorenzo de' Medici declared that his family had spent hundreds of thousands of gold florins for artistic and architectural commissions, but commented, "I think it casts a brilliant light on our estate [public reputation] and it seems to me that the monies were well spent and I am very pleased with this."[7]

Patrons varied in their level of involvement as a work progressed; some simply ordered a specific subject or scene, while others oversaw the work of the artist or architect very closely, suggesting themes and styles and demanding changes while the work was in progress. For example, Pope Julius II (pontificate 1503–1513), who commissioned Michelangelo to paint the ceiling of the Vatican's Sistine Chapel in Rome in 1508, demanded that the artist work as fast as he could and frequently visited him at his work with suggestions and criticisms. Michelangelo, a Florentine who had spent his young adulthood at the court of Lorenzo de' Medici, complained in person and by letter about the pope's meddling, but his reputation did not match the power of the pope, and he kept working until the chapel was finished in 1512.

In addition to power, art reveals changing patterns of consumption among the nobility and wealthy merchants in Renaissance Italy. In the rural world of the Middle Ages, society had been organized for war, and men of wealth spent their money on military gear. As Italian nobles settled in towns (see Chapter 11), they adjusted to an urban culture. Rather than employing knights for warfare, cities hired mercenaries. Expenditures on military hardware declined. For the rich merchant or the noble recently arrived from the countryside, a grand urban palace represented the greatest outlay of cash. Wealthy individuals and families ordered gold

Michelangelo's David (1501–1504) and the Last Judgment (detail, 1537–1541)
Like all Renaissance artists, Michelangelo worked largely on commissions from patrons. Officials of the city of Florence contracted the young sculptor to produce a statue of the Old Testament hero David (left) to be displayed on the city's main square. Michelangelo portrayed David anticipating his fight against the giant Goliath, and the statue came to symbolize the republic of Florence standing up to its larger and more powerful enemies. More than thirty years later, Michelangelo was commissioned by the pope to paint a scene of the Last Judgment on the altar wall of the Sistine Chapel, where he had earlier spent four years covering the ceiling with magnificent frescoes. The massive work shows a powerful Christ standing in judgment, with souls ascending into Heaven while others are dragged by demons into Hell (above). The *David* captures ideals of human perfection and has come to be an iconic symbol of Renaissance artistic brilliance, while the dramatic and violent Last Judgment conveys both terror and divine power. (sculpture: Scala/Ministero per i Beni e le Attività Culturali/Art Resource, NY; painting: Alinari/The Bridgeman Art Library)

dishes, embroidered tablecloths, wall tapestries, paintings on canvas (an innovation), and sculptural decorations to adorn their homes. By the late sixteenth century the Strozzi banking family of Florence spent even more on household goods than they did on clothing, jewelry, or food, though these were increasingly elaborate as well.

After the palace itself, the private chapel within the palace symbolized the largest expenditure for the wealthy of the sixteenth century. Decorated with religious scenes and equipped with ecclesiastical furniture, the chapel served as the center of the household's religious life and its cult of remembrance of the dead.

Changing Artistic Styles

The content and style of Renaissance art were often different from those of the Middle Ages. Religious topics, such as the Annunciation of the Virgin and the Nativity, remained popular among both patrons and artists, but frequently the patron had himself and his family portrayed in the scene. As the fifteenth century advanced and humanist ideas spread more widely, classical themes and motifs, such as the lives and loves of pagan gods and goddesses, figured increasingly in painting and sculpture, with the facial features of the gods sometimes modeled on living people.

The individual portrait emerged as a distinct artistic genre. Rather than reflecting a spiritual ideal, as medieval painting and sculpture tended to do, Renaissance portraits showed human ideals, often portrayed in a more realistic style. The Florentine painter Giotto (JAH-toh) (1276–1337) led the way in the use of realism; his treatment of the human body and face replaced the formal stiffness and artificiality that had long characterized representation of the human body. Piero della Francesca (frahn-CHAY-skah) (1420–1492) and Andrea Mantegna (mahn-TEN-yuh) (1430/31–1506) seem to have pioneered perspective in painting, the linear representation of distance and space on a flat surface. The sculptor Donatello (1386–1466) revived the classical figure, with its balance and self-awareness. In architecture, Filippo Brunelleschi (1377–1446) looked to the classical past for inspiration, designing a hospital for orphans and foundlings in which all proportions—of the windows, height, floor plan, and covered walkway with a series of rounded arches—were carefully thought out to achieve a sense of balance and harmony.

Art produced in northern Europe in the fourteenth and fifteenth centuries tended to be more religious in orientation than that produced in Italy. Some Flemish painters, notably Rogier van der Weyden (1399/1400–1464) and Jan van Eyck (1366–1441), were considered the artistic equals of Italian painters and were much admired in Italy. Van Eyck was one of the earliest artists to use oil-based paints successfully, and his religious scenes and portraits all show great realism and remarkable attention to human personality. Northern architecture was little influenced by the classical revival so obvious in Renaissance Italy.

In the early sixteenth century the center of the new art shifted from Florence to Rome, where wealthy cardinals and popes wanted visual expression of the church's and their own families' power and piety. Renaissance popes expended enormous enthusiasm and huge sums of money to beautify the city. Pope Julius II tore down the

Descent from the Cross, ca. 1435 Taking as his subject the suffering and death of Jesus, a popular theme of Netherlandish piety, Rogier van der Weyden shows Christ's descent from the cross, surrounded by nine sorrowing figures. An appreciation of human anatomy, the rich fabrics of the clothes, and the pierced and bloody hands of Jesus were all intended to touch the viewers' emotions. (Museo del Prado/Scala/Art Resource, NY)

old Saint Peter's Basilica and began work on the present structure in 1506. Michelangelo went to Rome from Florence in about 1500 and began the series of statues, paintings, and architectural projects from which he gained an international reputation: the Pieta, Moses, the redesigning of the Capitoline Hill in central Rome, and, most famously, the dome for Saint Peter's and the ceiling and altar wall of the nearby Sistine Chapel.

Raphael Sanzio (1483–1520), another Florentine, got the commission for frescoes in the papal apartments, and in his relatively short life he painted hundreds of portraits and devotional images, becoming the most sought after artist in Europe. Raphael also oversaw a large workshop with many collaborators and apprentices — who assisted on the less difficult sections of some paintings — and wrote treatises on his philosophy of art in which he emphasized the importance of imitating nature and developing an orderly sequence of design and proportion.

Venice became another artistic center in the sixteenth century. Titian (TIH-shuhn) (1490–1576) produced portraits, religious subjects, and mythological scenes, developing techniques of painting in oil without doing elaborate drawings first, which speeded up the process and pleased patrons eager to display their acquisitions. Titian and other sixteenth-century painters developed an artistic style known in English as "mannerism" (from *maniera* or "style" in Italian) in which artists sometimes distorted figures, exaggerated musculature, and heightened color to express emotion and drama more intently. (A painting by Titian can be found on page 394; this is also the style in which Michelangelo painted the Last Judgment in the Sistine Chapel, shown on page 388.)

The Renaissance Artist

Some patrons rewarded certain artists very well, and some artists gained great public acclaim as, in Vasari's words, "rare men of genius." This adulation of the artist has led many historians to view the Renaissance as the beginning of the concept of the artist as having a special talent. In the Middle Ages people believed that only God created, albeit through individuals; the medieval conception recognized no particular value in artistic originality. Renaissance artists and humanists came to think that a work of art was the deliberate creation of a unique personality who transcended traditions, rules, and theories. A genius had a peculiar gift, which ordinary laws should not inhibit. Michelangelo and Leonardo da Vinci perhaps best embody the new concept of the Renaissance artist as genius. (See "Individuals in Society: Leonardo da Vinci," at right.)

It is important not to overemphasize the Renaissance notion of genius. As certain artists became popular and well known, they could assert their own artistic styles and pay less attention to the wishes of patrons, but even major artists like Raphael generally worked according to the patron's specific guidelines. Whether in Italy or northern Europe, most Renaissance artists trained in the workshops of older artists; Botticelli, Raphael, Titian, and at times even Michelangelo were known for their large, well-run, and prolific workshops. Though they might be men of genius, artists were still expected to be well trained in proper artistic techniques and stylistic conventions, for the notion that artistic genius could show up in the work of an untrained artist did not emerge until the twentieth century. Beginning artists spent years copying drawings and paintings, learning

Villa Capra Architecture as well as literature and art aimed to recreate classical styles. The Venetian architect Andrea Palladio modeled this country villa, constructed for a papal official in 1566, on the Pantheon of ancient Rome (see page 157). Surrounded by statues of classical deities, it is completely symmetrical, capturing humanist ideals of perfection and balance. This villa and others of Palladio's designs influenced later buildings all over the world, including the U.S. Capitol in Washington, D.C., and countless state capitol buildings. (age fotostock/Superstock)

Leonardo da Vinci

INDIVIDUALS IN SOCIETY

WHAT MAKES A GENIUS? A deep curiosity about an extensive variety of subjects? A divine spark that emerges in talents that far exceed the norm? Or is it just "one percent inspiration and ninety-nine percent perspiration," as Thomas Edison said? However it is defined, Leonardo da Vinci counts as a genius. In fact, Leonardo was one of the individuals whom the Renaissance label "genius" was designed to describe: a special kind of human being with exceptional creative powers. Leonardo (who, despite the title of a recent bestseller, is always called by his first name) was born in Vinci, near Florence, the illegitimate son of Caterina, a local peasant girl, and Ser Piero da Vinci, a notary public. Caterina later married another native of Vinci. When Ser Piero's marriage to Donna Albrussia produced no children, he and his wife took in Leonardo. Ser Piero secured Leonardo's apprenticeship with the painter and sculptor Andrea del Verrocchio in Florence. In 1472, when Leonardo was just twenty years old, he was listed as a master in Florence's "Company of Artists."

Leonardo's most famous portrait, *Mona Lisa*, shows a woman with an enigmatic smile that Giorgio Vasari described as "so pleasing that it seemed divine rather than human." The portrait, probably of the young wife of a rich Florentine merchant (her exact identity is hotly debated), may actually be the best known painting in the history of art. One of its competitors in that designation would be another work of Leonardo, *The Last Supper*, which has been called "the most revered painting in the world."

Leonardo's reputation as a genius does not rest simply on his paintings, however, which are actually few in number, but rather on the breadth of his abilities and interests. He is often understood to be the first "Renaissance man," a phrase we still use for a multitalented individual. He wanted to reproduce what the eye can see, and he drew everything he saw around him, including executed criminals hanging on gallows as well as the beauties of nature. Trying to understand how the human body worked, Leonardo studied live and dead bodies, doing autopsies and dissections to investigate muscles and circulation. He carefully analyzed the effects of light, and he experimented with perspective.

Leonardo used his drawings as the basis for his paintings and as a tool of scientific investigation. He drew plans for hundreds of inventions, many of which would become reality centuries later, such as the helicopter, tank, machine gun, and parachute. He was hired by one of the powerful new rulers in Italy, Duke Ludovico Sforza of Milan, to design weapons, fortresses, and water systems, as well as to produce works of art. Leonardo left Milan when Sforza was overthrown in war and spent the last years of his life painting, drawing, and designing for the pope and the French king.

Leonardo experimented with new materials for painting and sculpture, some of which worked and some of which did not. The experimental method he used to paint *The Last Supper* caused the picture to deteriorate rapidly, and it began to flake off the wall as soon as it was finished. Leonardo regarded it as never quite completed, for he could not find a model for the face of Christ who would evoke the spiritual depth he felt the figure deserved. His gigantic equestrian statue in honor of Ludovico's father, Duke Francesco Sforza, was never made, and the clay model collapsed. He planned to write books on many subjects but

Lady with an Ermine: The enigmatic smile and smoky quality of this portrait can be found in many of Leonardo's works.
(Czartoryski Museum, Krakow/The Bridgeman Art Library)

never finished any of them, leaving only notebooks. Leonardo once said that "a painter is not admirable unless he is universal." The patrons who supported him—and he was supported very well—perhaps wished that his inspirations would have been a bit less universal in scope, or at least accompanied by more perspiration.

Sources: Giorgio Vasari, *Lives of the Artists*, vol. 1, trans. G. Bull (London: Penguin Books, 1965); S. B. Nuland, *Leonardo da Vinci* (New York: Lipper/Viking, 2000).

QUESTIONS FOR ANALYSIS

1. In what ways do the notion of a "genius" and of a "Renaissance man" both support and contradict one another? Which better fits Leonardo?
2. Has the idea of artistic genius changed since the Renaissance? How?

Botticelli, *Primavera* (Spring), ca. 1482 Framed by a grove of orange trees, Venus, goddess of love, is flanked on the right by Flora, goddess of flowers and fertility, and on the left by the Three Graces, goddesses of banquets, dance, and social occasions. Above, Venus's son Cupid, the god of love, shoots darts of desire, while at the far right the wind god Zephyrus chases the nymph Chloris. The entire scene rests on classical mythology, though some art historians claim that Venus is an allegory for the Virgin Mary. Botticelli captured the ideal for female beauty in the Renaissance: slender, with pale skin, a high forehead, red-blond hair, and sloping shoulders. (Digital image © The Museum of Modern Art/Licensed by Scala/Art Resource, NY)

how to prepare paint and other artistic materials, and, by the sixteenth century, reading books about design and composition. Younger artists gathered together in the evenings for further drawing practice; by the later sixteenth century some of these informal groups had turned into more formal artistic "academies," the first of which was begun in 1563 in Florence by Vasari under the patronage of the Medicis.

As Vasari's phrase indicates, the notion of artistic genius that developed in the Renaissance was gendered. All the most famous and most prolific Renaissance artists were male; there are no female architects whose names are known and only one female sculptor. The types of art in which more women were active, such as textiles, needlework, and painting on porcelain, were not regarded as "major arts," but only as "minor" or "decorative" arts. (The division between "major" and "minor" arts begun in the Renaissance continues to influence the way museums and collections are organized today.) Like painting, embroidery changed in the Renaissance to become more classical in its subject matter, naturalistic, and visually complex. Embroiderers were not trained to view their work as products of individual genius, however, so they rarely included their names on the works, and there is no way to discover who they were.

Several women did become well known as painters in their day. Stylistically, their works are different from one another, but their careers show many similarities. The majority of female painters were the daughters of painters or of minor noblemen with ties to artistic circles. Many were eldest daughters or came from families in which there were no sons, so their fathers took unusual interest in their careers. Many women began their careers before they were twenty and produced far fewer paintings after they married, or stopped painting entirely. Women were not allowed to study the male nude, which was viewed as essential if one wanted to paint large history or biblical paintings with many figures. Women could also not learn the technique of fresco, in which colors are applied directly to wet plaster walls, because such works had to be done in public, which was judged inappropriate for women. Joining a group of male artists for informal practice was also seen as improper, and the artistic academies that were established were for men only. Like universities, humanist academies, and most craft guild shops, artistic workshops were male-only settings in which men of different ages came together for training and created bonds of friendship, influence, patronage, and sometimes intimacy.

Women were not alone in being excluded from the institutions of Renaissance culture. Though a few rare men of genius such as Leonardo and Michelangelo emerged from artisanal backgrounds, most scholars and artists came from families with at least some money. Renaissance culture did not influence the lives of most people in cities and did not affect life in the villages at all. A small, highly educated minority of literary humanists and artists created the culture of and for an exclusive elite. The Renaissance maintained, or indeed enhanced, a gulf between the learned minority and the uneducated multitude that has survived for many centuries.

Social Hierarchies

What were the key social hierarchies in Renaissance Europe, and how did ideas about hierarchy shape people's lives?

The division between educated and uneducated people was only one of many social hierarchies evident in the Renaissance. Every society has social hierarchies; in ancient Rome, for example, there were patricians and plebeians (see Chapter 5). Such hierarchies are to some degree descriptions of social reality, but they are also idealizations—that is, they describe how people imagined their society to be, without all the messy reality of social-climbing plebeians or groups that did not fit the standard categories. Social hierarchies in the Renaissance were built on the orders of the Middle Ages—those

Esther Before Ahasuerus, ca. 1630 In this oil painting, Artemisia Gentileschi (jehn-tuh-LEHS-kee) shows an Old Testament scene of the Jewish woman Esther who saved her people from being killed by her husband, King Ahasuerus. This deliverance is celebrated in the Jewish holiday of Purim. The elaborate clothes shown are of the type worn in Renaissance courts. Typical of a female painter, Artemisia Gentileschi was trained by her father. She mastered the dramatic style favored in the early seventeenth century and became known especially for her portraits of strong biblical and mythological heroines. (Image copyright © The Metropolitan Museum of Art/Art Resource, NY)

who fight, pray, and work—but they also developed new features that contributed to modern social hierarchies, such as those of race, class, and gender.

Race and Slavery

Renaissance people did not use the word *race* the way we do, but often used "race," "people," and "nation" interchangeably for ethnic, national, religious, or other groups—the French race, the Jewish nation, the Irish people, "the race of learned gentlemen," and so on. They did make distinctions based on skin color that provide some of the background for later conceptualizations of race, but these distinctions were interwoven with other characteristics when people thought about human differences.

Ever since the time of the Roman republic, a small number of black Africans had lived in western Europe. They had come, along with white slaves, as the spoils of war. Even after the collapse of the Roman Empire, Muslim and Christian merchants continued to import them. Unstable political conditions in many parts of Africa enabled enterprising merchants to seize people and sell them into slavery. Local authorities afforded them no protection. Long tradition, moreover, sanctioned the practice of slavery. The evidence of medieval art attests to the continued presence of Africans in Europe throughout the Middle Ages and to Europeans' awareness of them.

Beginning in the fifteenth century sizable numbers of black slaves entered Europe. Portuguese sailors brought perhaps a thousand Africans a year to the markets of Seville, Barcelona, Marseilles, and Genoa. In the late fifteenth century this flow increased, with thousands of people leaving the west coast of Africa. By 1530 between four thousand and five thousand were being sold to the Portuguese each year. By the mid-sixteenth century blacks, slave and free, constituted about 10 percent of the population of the Portuguese cities of Lisbon and Évora and roughly 3 percent of the Portuguese population overall. In the Iberian Peninsula African slaves intermingled with the people they lived among and sometimes intermarried. Cities such as Lisbon had significant numbers of people of mixed African and European descent.

Although blacks were concentrated in the Iberian Peninsula, there must have been some Africans in northern Europe as well. In the 1580s, for example, Queen Elizabeth I of England complained that there were too many "blackamoores" competing with needy English people for places as domestic servants. Black servants were much sought after; the medieval interest in curiosities, the exotic, and the marvelous continued in the Renaissance. Italian aristocrats had their portraits painted with their black pageboys to indicate their wealth (as in the painting on this page). Blacks were so greatly in demand at the Renaissance courts of northern Italy, in fact, that the Venetians defied papal threats of excommunication to secure them. In 1491 Isabella of Este, duchess of Mantua, instructed her agent to secure a black girl between four and eight years old, "shapely and as black as possible." She hoped the girl would become "the best buffoon in the world," noting that "we shall make her very happy and shall have great fun with her."[8] The girl would join musicians, acrobats, and

Laura de Dianti, 1523 The Venetian artist Titian shows a young Italian woman with a gorgeous blue dress and an elaborate pearl and feather headdress, accompanied by a young black page with a gold earring. Both the African page and the headdress connect the portrait's subject with the exotic, though slaves from Africa and the Ottoman Empire were actually common in wealthy Venetian households. (Courtesy, Heinz Kisters Collection)

Renaissance Fireplace, ca. 1458 This marble fireplace, carved for the palace of the Boni family in Florence, shows the family coat of arms in the center, with two heads on either side, possibly of ancestors. Wealthy people often had busts or painted portraits of their ancestors above the fireplaces around which they gathered in the evening for warmth and conversation. (V&A Images/Victoria and Albert Museum)

dancers as a source of entertainment, her status similar to that of the dwarves who could be found at many Renaissance courts.

Africans were not simply amusements at court. In Portugal, Spain, and Italy slaves supplemented the labor force in virtually all occupations — as servants, agricultural laborers, craftsmen, and seamen on ships going to Lisbon and Africa. Agriculture in Europe did not involve large plantations, so large-scale agricultural slavery did not develop there as it would in the late fifteenth century in the New World.

Until the voyages down the African coast in the late fifteenth century, Europeans had little concrete knowledge of Africans and their cultures. They perceived Africa as a remote place, the home of strange people isolated by heresy and Islam from superior European civilization. Africans' contact, even as slaves, with Christian Europeans could only "improve" the blacks, they thought. The expanding slave trade reinforced negative preconceptions about the inferiority of black Africans.

Wealth and the Nobility

The word *class* — working class, middle class, upper class — was not used in the Renaissance to describe social divisions, but by the thirteenth century, and even more so by the fifteenth, the idea of a hierarchy based on wealth was emerging alongside the medieval concept of orders (see Chapter 10). This was particularly true in towns. Most residents of towns were technically members of the "third order" — that is, "those who work" rather than "those who fight" and "those who pray." However, this group now included wealthy merchants who oversaw vast trading empires and lived in splendor that rivaled the richest nobles. As we saw earlier, in many cities these merchants had gained political power to match their economic might, becoming merchant oligarchs who ruled through city councils. This hierarchy of wealth was more changeable than the hierarchy of orders, allowing individuals and families to rise — and fall — within one generation.

The development of a hierarchy of wealth did not mean an end to the hierarchy of orders, however, and even poorer nobility still had higher status than wealthy commoners. If this had not been the case, wealthy Italian merchants would not have bothered to buy noble titles and country villas as they began doing in the fifteenth century, nor would wealthy English or Spanish merchants have been so eager to marry their daughters and sons into often-impoverished noble families. The nobility maintained its status in most parts of Europe not by maintaining rigid boundaries, but by taking in and integrating the new social elite of wealth.

Along with being tied to hierarchies of wealth and orders, social status was linked with considerations of honor. Among the nobility, for example, certain weapons and battle tactics were favored because they were viewed as more honorable. Among urban dwellers, certain occupations, such as city executioner or manager of the municipal brothel, might be well paid but were understood to be "dishonorable" and so of low status. In cities, sumptuary laws reflected both wealth and honor (see Chapter 11); merchants were specifically allowed fur and jewels, while prostitutes were ordered to wear yellow bands that would remind potential customers of the flames of Hell.

Gender Roles

Renaissance people would not have understood the word *gender* to refer to categories of people, but they would have easily grasped the concept. Toward the end of the fourteenth century, learned men (and a few women) began what was termed the **debate about women** (*querelle des femmes*), a debate about women's character and nature that would last for centuries. Misogynist (muh-SAH-juh-nihst) critiques of women from both clerical and secular authors denounced females as devious, domineering, and demanding. In answer, several authors compiled long lists of famous and praiseworthy women exemplary for their loyalty, bravery, and morality. Christine de Pizan was among the writers who were not only interested in defending women, but also in exploring the reasons behind women's secondary status—that is, why the great philosophers, statesmen, and poets had generally been men. In this they were anticipating discussions about the "social construction of gender" by six hundred years. (See "Listening to the Past: Christine de Pizan, Advice to the Wives of Artisans," page 362, and "Listening to the Past: Perspectives on Humanist Learning and Women," page 382.)

With the development of the printing press, popular interest in the debate about women grew, and works were translated, reprinted, and shared around Europe. Prints that juxtaposed female virtues and vices were also very popular, with the virtuous women depicted as those of the classical or biblical past and the vice-ridden dressed in contemporary clothes. The favorite metaphor for the virtuous wife was either the snail or the tortoise, both animals that never leave their "houses" and are totally silent, although such images were never as widespread as those depicting wives beating their husbands or hiding their lovers from them.

Beginning in the sixteenth century, the debate about women also became a debate about female rulers, sparked primarily by dynastic accidents in many countries, including Spain, England, France, and Scotland, which led to women serving as advisers to child kings or ruling in their own right. The questions were vigorously and at times viciously disputed. They directly concerned the social construction of gender: could a woman's being born into a royal family and educated to rule allow

debate about women Debate among writers and thinkers in the Renaissance about women's qualities and proper role in society.

Phyllis Riding Aristotle Among the many scenes that expressed the debate about women visually were woodcuts, engravings, paintings, and even cups and plates that showed the classical philosopher Aristotle as an old man being ridden by the young, beautiful Phyllis (shown here in a German woodcut). The origins of the story are uncertain, but in the Renaissance everyone knew the tale of how Aristotle's infatuation with Phyllis led to his ridicule. Male moralists used it as a warning about the power of women's sexual allure, though women may have interpreted it differently. (Réunion des Musées Nationaux/Art Resource, NY)

> **The employer ... may also give them soup and vegetables to eat in the morning—but no wine—milk and bread at midday, but nothing in the evening.**
>
> —SIXTEENTH-CENTURY WORKERS' REGULATION

her to overcome the limitations of her sex? Should it? Or stated another way: which was (or should be) the stronger determinant of character and social role, gender or rank? Despite a prevailing sentiment that women were not as fit to rule as men, there were no successful rebellions against female rulers simply because they were women, but in part this was because female rulers, especially Queen Elizabeth I of England, emphasized qualities regarded as masculine—physical bravery, stamina, wisdom, duty—whenever they appeared in public.

Ideas about women's and men's proper roles determined the actions of ordinary men and women even more forcefully. The dominant notion of the "true" man was that of the married head of household, so men whose social status and age would have normally conferred political power but who remained unmarried did not participate to the same level as their married brothers. Unmarried men in Venice, for example, could not be part of the ruling council. (See "Living in the Past: Male Clothing and Masculinity," page 398.)

Women were also understood as either "married or to be married," even if the actual marriage patterns in Europe left many women (and men) unmarried until quite late in life (see Chapter 12). This meant that women's work was not viewed as supporting a family—even if it did—and was valued less than men's. If they worked for wages, and many women did, women earned about half to two-thirds of what men did even for the same work. Regulations for vineyard workers in the early sixteenth century, for example, specified that

> *Men who work in the vineyards, doing work that is skilled, are to be paid 16 pence per day; in addition, they are to receive soup and wine in the morning, at midday beer, vegetables and meat, and in the evening soup, vegetables and wine. Young boys are to be paid 10 pence per day. Women who work as haymakers are to be given 6 pence a day. If the employer wants to have them doing other work, he may make an agreement with them to pay them 7 or 8 pence. He may also give them soup and vegetables to eat in the morning—but no wine—milk and bread at midday, but nothing in the evening.*[9]

The maintenance of appropriate power relationships between men and women, with men dominant and women subordinate, served as a symbol of the proper functioning of society as a whole. Disorder in the proper gender hierarchy was linked with social upheaval and was viewed as threatening. Of all the ways in which Renaissance society was hierarchically arranged—social rank, age, level of education, race, occupation—gender was regarded as the most "natural" and therefore the most important to defend.

Politics and the State in Western Europe, ca. 1450–1521

How did the nation-states of western Europe evolve in this period?

The High Middle Ages had witnessed the origins of many of the basic institutions of the modern state. Sheriffs, inquests, juries, circuit judges, professional bureaucracies, and representative assemblies all trace their origins to the twelfth and thirteenth centuries. The linchpin for the development of states, however, was strong monarchy, and during the period of the Hundred Years' War, no ruler in western Europe was able to provide effective leadership. The resurgent power of feudal nobilities weakened the centralizing work begun earlier.

Beginning in the fifteenth century rulers utilized aggressive methods to rebuild their governments. First in the regional states of Italy, then in the expanding monarchies of France, England, and Spain, rulers began the work of reducing violence, curbing unruly nobles, and establishing domestic order. They attempted to secure their borders and enhanced methods of raising revenue. The monarchs of western Europe emphasized royal majesty and royal sovereignty and insisted on the respect and loyalty of all subjects, including the nobility. In central Europe the Holy Roman emperors attempted to do the same, but they were not able to overcome the power of local interests to create a unified state (see Chapter 14).

France

The Black Death and the Hundred Years' War left France drastically depopulated, commercially ruined, and agriculturally weak. Nonetheless, the ruler whom Joan of Arc had seen crowned at Reims, Charles VII (r. 1422–1461), revived the monarchy and France. He seemed

Male Clothing and Masculinity

LIVING IN THE PAST

WEALTHY RENAISSANCE PEOPLE DISPLAYED THEIR POWER AND PROSPERITY on their bodies as well as in their houses and household furnishings. Expanded trade brought in silks, pearls, gemstones, feathers, dyestuffs, and furs, which tailors, goldsmiths, seamstresses, furriers, and hatmakers turned into magnificent clothing and jewelry. Nowhere was fashion more evident than on the men in Renaissance cities and courts. Young men favored multicolored garments that fit tightly, often topping the ensemble with a matching hat on carefully combed long hair. The close-cut garments emphasized the male form, which was further accentuated by tight hose stylishly split to reveal a brightly colored codpiece. Older men favored more subdued colors but with multiple padded shirts, vests, and coats that emphasized real or pretended upper-body strength and that allowed the display of many layers of expensive fabrics. Golden rings, earrings, pins, and necklaces provided additional glamour.

Padded leather jerkin embroidered with silk and metal thread from the late sixteenth century. There are eyelets for tying up hose inside. (Museo Stibbert, Florence)

Two young men, who are side figures in *The Adoration of the Magi*, by Luca Signorelli (1445–1523). (Scala/Art Resource, NY)

The Venetian painter Titian's portrait of Emperor Charles V with one of his hunting dogs. (Scala/Art Resource, NY)

QUESTIONS FOR ANALYSIS

1. Male clothing in any era communicates social values and ideas about masculinity. What does Renaissance fashion suggest about notions of manhood in this era?
2. In *The Prince*, Machiavelli used the word *effeminate* to describe the worst kind of ruler, though the word carried different connotations from what it does today. Strong heterosexual passion was not a sign of manliness but could make one "effeminate"—that is, dominated by as well as similar to a woman. Look at the portrait of Charles V here and at the other portraits in this chapter. How did male rulers visually symbolize their masculinity?

an unlikely person to do so. Frail, indecisive, and burdened with questions about his paternity (his father had been deranged; his mother, notoriously promiscuous), Charles VII nevertheless began France's long recovery.

Charles reconciled the Burgundians and Armagnacs (ahr-muhn-YAKZ), who had been waging civil war for thirty years. By 1453 French armies had expelled the English from French soil except in Calais. Charles reorganized the royal council, giving increased influence to lawyers and bankers, and strengthened royal finances through such taxes as the *gabelle* (guh-BEL) on salt and the *taille* (TA-yuh), a land tax. These taxes remained the Crown's chief sources of income until the Revolution of 1789.

By establishing regular companies of cavalry and archers—recruited, paid, and inspected by the state—Charles created the first permanent royal army. His son Louis XI (r. 1461–1483), called the "Spider King" because of his treacherous character, improved upon Charles's army and used it to control the nobles' separate militias and to curb urban independence. The army was also employed in 1477 when Louis conquered Burgundy upon the death of its ruler Charles the Bold. Three years later, the extinction of the house of Anjou (AN-joo) with the death of its last legitimate male heir brought Louis the counties of Anjou, Bar, Maine, and Provence.

Two further developments strengthened the French monarchy. The marriage of Louis XII (r. 1498–1515) and Anne of Brittany added the large western duchy of Brittany to the state. Then the French king Francis I and Pope Leo X reached a mutually satisfactory agreement about church and state powers in 1516. The new treaty, the Concordat of Bologna, approved the pope's right to receive the first year's income of new bishops and abbots. In return, Leo X recognized the French ruler's right to select French bishops and abbots. French kings thereafter effectively controlled the appointment and thus the policies of church officials in the kingdom.

The Expansion of France, 1475–1500

England

English society also suffered severely from the disorders of the fifteenth century. The aristocracy dominated the government of Henry IV (r. 1399–1413) and indulged in disruptive violence at the local level. Population continued to decline. Between 1455 and 1471 adherents of the ducal houses of York and Lancaster waged civil war, commonly called the Wars of the Roses because the symbol of the Yorkists was a white rose and that of the Lancastrians a red one. The chronic disorder hurt trade, agriculture, and domestic industry. Under the pious but mentally disturbed Henry VI (r. 1422–1461), the authority of the monarchy sank lower than it had been in centuries.

The Yorkist Edward IV (r. 1461–1483) began establishing domestic tranquility. He succeeded in defeating the Lancastrian forces and after 1471 began to reconstruct the monarchy. Edward, his brother Richard III (r. 1483–1485), and Henry VII (r. 1485–1509) of the Welsh house of Tudor worked to restore royal prestige, to crush the power of the nobility, and to establish order and law at the local level. All three rulers used methods that Machiavelli himself would have praised — ruthlessness, efficiency, and secrecy.

Edward IV and subsequently the Tudors, excepting Henry VIII, conducted foreign policy on the basis of diplomacy, avoiding expensive wars. Thus the English monarchy did not depend on Parliament for money, and the Crown undercut that source of aristocratic influence.

Henry VII did summon several meetings of Parliament in the early years of his reign, primarily to confirm laws, but the center of royal authority was the royal council, which governed at the national level. There Henry VII revealed his distrust of the nobility: though not completely excluded, very few great lords were among the king's closest advisers. Instead he chose men from among the smaller landowners and urban residents trained in law. The council conducted negotiations with foreign governments and secured international recognition of the Tudor dynasty through the marriage in 1501 of Henry VII's eldest son Arthur to Catherine of Aragon, the daughter of Ferdinand and Isabella of Spain. The council dealt with real or potential aristocratic threats through a judicial offshoot, the Court of Star Chamber, so called because of the stars painted on the ceiling of the room. The court applied methods that were sometimes terrifying: accused persons were not entitled to see evidence against them; sessions were secret; torture could be applied to extract confessions; and juries were not called. These procedures ran directly counter to English common-law precedents, but they effectively reduced aristocratic troublemaking.

When Henry VII died in 1509, he left a country at peace both domestically and internationally, a substantially augmented treasury, an expanding wool trade, and the dignity and role of the royal majesty much enhanced. He was greatly missed after he died "by all his subjects," wrote the historian Polydore Vergil, "who had been able to conduct their lives peaceably, far removed from the assaults and evildoings of scoundrels."[10]

Spain

While England and France laid the foundations of unified nation-states during the Middle Ages, Spain remained a conglomerate of independent kingdoms. By the middle of the fifteenth century, the kingdoms of Castile and Aragon dominated the weaker Navarre, Portugal, and Granada; and the Iberian Peninsula, with the exception of Granada, had been won for Christianity. But even the wedding in 1469 of the dynamic and aggressive Isabella of Castile and the crafty and persistent Ferdinand of Aragon did not bring about administrative unity. Rather, their marriage constituted a dynastic union of two royal houses, not the political union of two peoples. Although Ferdinand and Isabella (r. 1474–1516) pursued a common foreign policy, until about 1700 Spain existed as a loose confederation of separate kingdoms, each maintaining its own *cortes* (parliament), laws, courts, and systems of coinage and taxation (Map 13.3).

Ferdinand and Isabella were able to exert their authority in ways similar to the rulers of France and England, however. They curbed aristocratic power by excluding high nobles from the royal council, which had full executive, judicial, and legislative powers under the monarchy, instead appointing lesser landowners. The council and various government boards recruited men trained in Roman law, which exalted the power of the Crown. They also secured from the Spanish Borgia pope Alexander VI — Cesare Borgia's father — the right to appoint bishops in Spain and in the Hispanic territories in America, enabling them to establish the equivalent of a national church. With the revenues from ecclesiastical estates, they were able to expand their territories to include the remaining land held by Arabs in southern Spain. The victorious entry of Ferdinand and Isabella into Granada on January 6, 1492, signaled the conclusion of the reconquista (see Map 9.3 on page 248). Granada in the south was incorporated into the Spanish kingdom, and in 1512 Ferdinand conquered Navarre in the north.

There still remained a sizable and, in the view of the majority of the Spanish people, potentially dangerous minority, the Jews. When the kings of France and England had expelled the Jews from their kingdoms (see Chapter 9), many had sought refuge in Spain. During the long centuries of the reconquista, Christian kings had renewed Jewish rights and privileges; in fact, Jewish industry, intelligence, and money had supported royal power. While Christians borrowed from Jewish moneylenders and while all who could afford them sought Jewish physicians, a strong undercurrent of resentment of Jewish influence and wealth festered.

In the fourteenth century anti-Semitism in Spain was aggravated by fiery anti-Jewish preaching, by economic

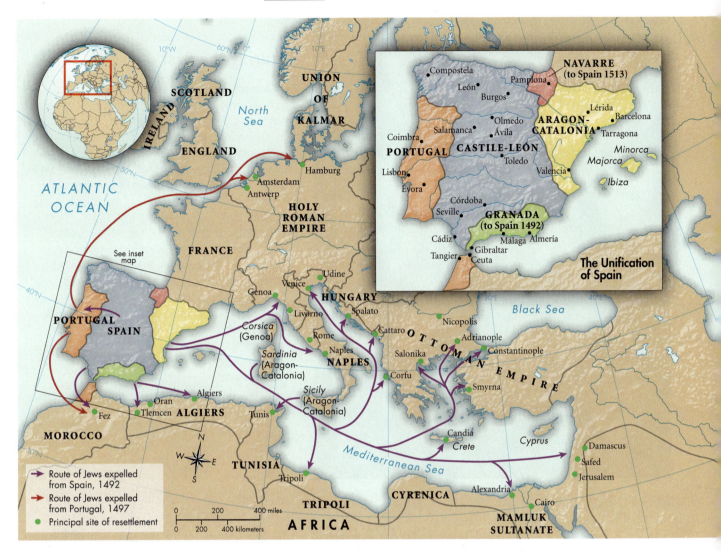

Map 13.3 **The Unification of Spain and the Expulsion of the Jews, Fifteenth Century** The marriage of Ferdinand of Aragon and Isabella of Castile in 1469 brought most of the Iberian Peninsula under one monarchy, although different parts of Spain retained distinct cultures, languages, and legal systems. In 1492 Ferdinand and Isabella conquered Granada, where most people were Muslim, and expelled the Jews from all of Spain. Spanish Jews resettled in cities of Europe and the Mediterranean that allowed them in, including many in Muslim states such as the Ottoman Empire. Muslims were also expelled from Spain over the course of the sixteenth and early seventeenth centuries.

dislocation, and by the search for a scapegoat during the Black Death. Anti-Semitic pogroms swept the towns of Spain, and perhaps 40 percent of the Jewish population was killed or forced to convert. Those converted were called *conversos* or **New Christians**. Conversos were often well educated and held prominent positions in government, the church, medicine, law, and business. Numbering perhaps two hundred thousand in a total Spanish population of about 7.5 million, New Christians and Jews in fifteenth-century Spain exercised influence disproportionate to their numbers.

Such successes bred resentment. Aristocratic grandees resented their financial dependence; the poor hated the converso tax collectors; and churchmen doubted the sincerity of their conversions. Queen Isabella shared these suspicions, and she and Ferdinand had received permission from Pope Sixtus IV in 1478 to establish their own Inquisition to "search out and punish converts from Judaism who had transgressed against Christianity by

New Christians A fourteenth-century term for Jews and Muslims who accepted Christianity; in many cases they included Christians whose families had converted centuries earlier.

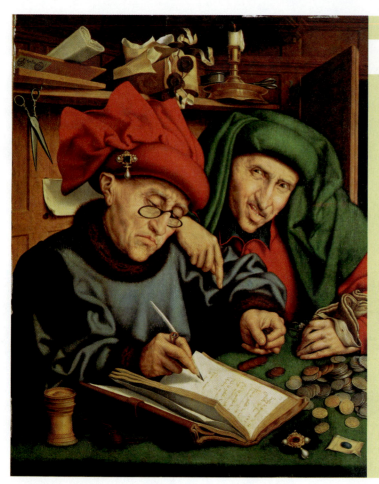

Picturing the Past

Tax Collectors New types of taxes, and more effective methods of tax collection, were essential to the growth of Renaissance states, but were often highly unpopular. In this painting from about 1540 the Dutch artist Marinus van Reymerswaele depicts two tax collectors as they count their take and record it in a ledger. Tax collectors were men of middling status, but here they are wearing clothing more appropriate for nobles. (Erich Lessing/Art Resource, NY)

ANALYZING THE IMAGE What elements of the men's clothing suggest wealth? How would you describe the expressions on their faces? What does the painting suggest about the artist's opinion of tax collectors?

CONNECTIONS In Spain converso tax collectors were widely resented. What were some of the reasons behind this resentment? What public event was an outgrowth of this hatred, and what were its aims?

To complete this activity online, go to the Online Study Guide at **bedfordstmartins.com/mckaywest**.

---

secretly adhering to Jewish beliefs and performing rites of the Jews."[11] Investigations and trials began immediately, as officials of the Inquisition looked for conversos who showed any sign of incomplete conversion, such as not eating pork.

Recent scholarship has carefully analyzed documents of the Inquisition. Most conversos identified themselves as sincere Christians; many came from families that had received baptism generations before. In response, officials of the Inquisition developed a new type of anti-Semitism. A person's status as a Jew, they argued, could not be changed by religious conversion, but was in the person's blood and was heritable, so Jews could never be true Christians. In what were known as "purity of blood" laws, having pure Christian blood became a requirement for noble status. Ideas about Jews developed in Spain were important components in European concepts of race, and discussions of "Jewish blood" later expanded into notions of the "Jewish race."

In 1492, shortly after the conquest of Granada, Isabella and Ferdinand issued an edict expelling all practicing Jews from Spain. Of the community of perhaps 200,000 Jews, 150,000 fled. Many Muslims in Granada were forcibly baptized and became another type of New Christian investigated by the Inquisition. Absolute religious orthodoxy and purity of blood served as the theoretical foundation of the Spanish national state.

The Spanish national state rested on marital politics as well as military victories and religious courts. In 1496 Ferdinand and Isabella married their second daughter Joanna, heiress to Castile, to the archduke Philip, heir to the Burgundian Netherlands and the Holy Roman Empire. Philip and Joanna's son, Charles V (r. 1519–1556), thus succeeded to a vast inheritance. When Charles's son Philip II joined Portugal to the Spanish crown in 1580, the Iberian Peninsula was at last politically united.

Saint Dominic Presiding over an Auto-da-Fe
In this 1495 painting the Spanish artist Pedro Berruguete shows an auto-da-fe, a public ritual of penance for those found guilty of religious crimes. In the foreground, the guilty wear tall hats with their crimes described on them, while above them two men are about to be burned at the stake. Technically execution did not happen at the auto-da-fe, but rather at a later secular execution, although the two events sometimes blended into one another. Berruguete portrays Saint Dominic, the founder of the Dominican order, as presiding over this trial, although autos-da-fe were not common until centuries after Dominic's death in 1221. (Museo del Prado, Madrid/Institut Amatller d'Art Hispànic)

LOOKING BACK LOOKING AHEAD THE ART HISTORIAN Giorgio Vasari, who first called this era the Renaissance, thought that his contemporaries had both revived the classical past and gone beyond it. Vasari's judgment was echoed for centuries, as the art, architecture, educational ideas, social structures, and attitude toward life of the Renaissance were set in sharp contrast with those of the Middle Ages: whereas the Middle Ages were corporate and religious, the Renaissance was individualistic and secular. More recently, historians and other scholars have stressed continuity as well as change. Families, kin networks, guilds, and other corporate groups remained important in the Renaissance, and religious belief remained firm. This re-evaluation changes our view of the relationship between the Middle Ages and the Renaissance. It may also change our view of the relationship between the Renaissance and the dramatic changes in religion that occurred in Europe in the sixteenth century. Those religious changes, the Reformation, used to be viewed as a rejection of the values of the Renaissance and a return to the intense concern with religion of the Middle Ages. This idea of the Reformation as a sort of counter-Renaissance may be true to some degree, but there are powerful continuities as well. Both movements looked back to a time they regarded as purer and better than their own, and both offered opportunities for strong individuals to shape their world in unexpected ways.

CHAPTER REVIEW

■ **What economic and political developments in Italy provided the setting for the Renaissance? (p. 374)**

In the commercial revival of the Middle Ages, ambitious merchants amassed great wealth, especially in the city-states of northern Italy. These city-states were communes in which all citizens shared power, but political instability led to their transformation into signori or oligarchies. As their riches and power grew, signori and oligarchs displayed their wealth in great public buildings as well as magnificent courts — palaces where they lived and conducted business. Political rulers, popes, and powerful families hired writers, artists, musicians, and architects through the system of patronage, which allowed for a great outpouring of culture.

■ **What were the key ideas of the Renaissance, and how were they different for men and women and for southern and northern Europeans? (p. 378)**

The Renaissance was characterized by self-conscious awareness among fourteenth- and fifteenth-century Italians, particularly scholars and writers known as humanists, that they were living in a new era. Key to this attitude was a serious interest in the Latin, and later the Greek, classics, especially the works of Cicero and Plato. Humanists also believed in striving for perfection, and they greatly admired individuals who exhibited the quality of virtù, the ability to shape the world around them to their will. These qualities are evident in political theory developed during the Renaissance, particularly that of Machiavelli. Humanists opened schools for boys and young men to train them for active lives of public service, but they had doubts about whether humanist education was appropriate for women. Some self-taught women did argue that study of the classics should not be limited to men. In northern Europe, religious concerns among humanists were more pronounced, and adherents came to be known as Christian humanists. Well-known writers such as Thomas More of England and Desiderius Erasmus of Rotterdam set out plans for the reform of church and society. Their ideas reached a much wider audience than those of early humanists because of the development of the printing press with movable metal type, which revolutionized communication.

■ **How did changes in art reflect new Renaissance ideals? (p. 387)**

Artistic patronage in the early Renaissance was primarily provided by groups such as guilds, but in the later Renaissance individuals increasingly supported the arts as a way of glorifying themselves and their families. At the same time, humanist interest in the classical past and in the individual shaped Renaissance art in terms of style and subject matter. Painting became more naturalistic, and the individual portrait emerged as a distinct artistic genre. Perspective was pioneered in painting, and balance and harmony became hallmarks of Italian architecture. Art in Italy became more secular and classical, with more works focused on pagan gods and goddesses. In northern Europe, where humanist thinking was more connected to Christian ideals, art retained a more religious tone. The style of mannerism evolved, which exaggerated the color and musculature of painted figures in order to provide more drama and emotion. Artists began to understand themselves as having a special creative genius, though they were still expected to undergo extensive technical training, and they continued to produce works on order for patrons, who often determined the content and form. Women were largely excluded from the major arts, as were most people from working families, and art itself was created for consumption mainly by an elite minority.

■ **What were the key social hierarchies in Renaissance Europe, and how did ideas about hierarchy shape people's lives? (p. 393)**

Social hierarchies in the Renaissance built on those of the Middle Ages, with the addition of new features that evolved into the modern social hierarchies of race, class, and gender. In the fifteenth century black slaves entered Europe in sizable numbers for the first time since the collapse of the Roman Empire. Europeans saw Africans as inferior, and they felt that contact with Christians would serve to improve the lives of blacks, even as slaves. The medieval hierarchy of orders based on function in society intermingled with a new hierarchy based on wealth, with new types of elites becoming more powerful through political and marital alliances. Noble families that were experiencing declining wealth could rebuild their fortunes by integrating with the newly rich. The Renaissance debate about women led to discussions of women's character and questioning of whether women could serve effectively as rulers. There was little debate, however, that among the nonruling classes, both men and women were expected to fit neatly into "natural" roles, with men as heads of households and women as subordinate; any deviation from this pattern was seen as a threat to societal order.

■ **How did the nation-states of western Europe evolve in this period? (p. 397)**

With taxes provided by business people, kings in western Europe established armies to maintain greater peace and order, both essential for trade, and feudal monarchies gradually evolved in the direction of nation-states. French kings benefited from opportunistic marriages and an alliance with the pope, and English kings used Machiavellian methods to crush the nobility. Spain used similar practices, though unification came more slowly, and Spanish rulers focused intently on expelling practicing Jews from their country.

Suggested Reading

Clark, Samuel. *State and Status: The Rise of the State and Aristocratic Power*. 1995. Discusses the relationship between centralizing states and the nobility.

Earle, T. F., and K. J. P. Lowe, eds. *Black Africans in Renaissance Europe*. 2005. Includes essays discussing many aspects of ideas about race and the experience of Africans in Europe.

Eisenstein, Elizabeth. *The Printing Press as an Agent of Change: Communications and Cultural Transformations in Early Modern Europe*. 1979. The definitive study of the impact of printing.

Ertman, Thomas. *The Birth of Leviathan: Building States and Regimes in Medieval and Early Modern Europe*. 1997. A good introduction to the creation of nation-states.

Grafton, Anthony, and Lisa Jardine. *From Humanism to the Humanities: Education and the Liberal Arts in Fifteenth and Sixteenth Century Europe*. 1986. Discusses humanist education and other developments in Renaissance learning.

Hale, J. R. *The Civilization of Europe in the Renaissance*. 1994. A comprehensive treatment of the period, arranged thematically.

Harbison, Craig. *The Mirror of the Artist: Northern Renaissance Art in Its Historical Context*. 1995. The best introduction to the art of northern Europe.

Hartt, Frederick, and David Wilkins. *History of Italian Renaissance Art*, 6th ed. 2008. Comprehensive survey of painting, sculpture, and architecture in Italy.

Holmes, George, ed. *Art and Politics in Renaissance Italy*. 1993. Treats the art of Florence and Rome against a political background.

Jardine, Lisa. *Worldly Goods: A New History of the Renaissance*. 1998. Discusses changing notions of social status, artistic patronage, and consumer goods.

Johnson, Geraldine. *Renaissance Art: A Very Short Introduction*. 2005. Excellent brief survey that includes male and female artists, and sets the art in its cultural and historical context.

King, Ross. *Machiavelli: Philosopher of Power*. 2006. Brief biography that explores Machiavelli's thought in its social and political context.

Lubkin, Gregory. *A Renaissance Court: Milan Under Galeazzo Maria Sforza*. 1994. A wonderful study of one of the most important Renaissance courts.

Man, John. *Gutenberg Revolution: The Story of a Genius and an Invention That Changed the World*. 2002. Presents a rather idealized view of Gutenberg, but has good discussions of his milieu and excellent illustrations.

McConica, James. *Erasmus*. 1991. A sensitive treatment of the leading northern humanist.

Nauert, Charles. *Humanism and the Culture of Renaissance Europe*, 2d ed. 2006. A thorough introduction to humanism throughout Europe.

Netanyahu, Benzion. *The Origins of the Inquisition in Fifteenth Century Spain*. 1995. An analysis of issues relating to the expulsion of the Jews.

Wiesner-Hanks, Merry E. *Women and Gender in Early Modern Europe*, 3d ed. 2008. Discusses all aspects of women's lives and ideas about gender.

Notes

1. In Gertrude R. B. Richards, *Florentine Merchants in the Age of the Medici* (Cambridge: Harvard University Press, 1932).
2. In James Bruce Ross and Mary Martin McLaughlin, *The Portable Renaissance Reader* (New York: Penguin, 1953), p. 27.
3. Ibid., pp. 480–481, 482, 492.
4. Niccolò Machiavelli, *The Prince*, trans. Leo Paul S. de Alvarez (Prospect Heights, Ill.: Waveland Press, 1980), p. 101.
5. Ibid., p. 149.
6. Quoted in F. Seebohm, *The Oxford Reformers* (London: J. M. Dent & Sons, 1867), p. 256.
7. Quoted in Lauro Martines, *Power and Imagination: City-States in Renaissance Italy* (New York: Vintage Books, 1980), p. 253.
8. Quoted in J. Devisse and M. Mollat, *The Image of the Black in Western Art*, vol. 2, trans. W. G. Ryan (New York: William Morrow, 1979), pt. 2, pp. 187–188.
9. Stuttgart, Württembergische Hauptstaatsarchiv, Generalreskripta, A38, Bü. 2, 1550; trans. Merry Wiesner-Hanks.
10. Denys Hay, ed. and trans., *The Anglia Historia of Polydore Vergil, AD 1485–1537*, book 74 (London: Camden Society, 1950), p. 147.
11. Quoted in Benzion Netanyahu, *The Origins of the Inquisition in Fifteenth Century Spain* (New York: Random House, 1995), p. 921.

Key Terms

Renaissance (p. 374)
patronage (p. 374)
communes (p. 375)
popolo (p. 375)
signori (p. 376)
courts (p. 376)
humanism (p. 378)
virtù (p. 379)
Christian humanists (p. 384)
debate about women (p. 396)
New Christians (p. 401)

For practice quizzes and other study tools, visit the Online Study Guide at **bedfordstmartins.com/mckaywest**.

For primary sources from this period, see **Sources of Western Society, Second Edition**.

For Web sites, images, and documents related to topics in this chapter, visit Make History at **bedfordstmartins.com/mckaywest**.

14
Reformations and Religious Wars

1500–1600

Calls for reform of the Christian church began very early in its history. Throughout the centuries, men and women believed that the early Christian church represented a golden age, akin to the golden age of the classical past celebrated by Renaissance humanists. When Christianity became the official religion of the Roman Empire in the fourth century, many believers thought that the church had abandoned its original mission, and they called for a return to a church that was not linked to the state. Throughout the Middle Ages individuals and groups argued that the church had become too wealthy and powerful and urged monasteries, convents, bishoprics, and the papacy to give up their property and focus on service to the poor. Some asserted that basic teachings of the church were not truly Christian and that changes were needed in theology as well as in institutional structures and practices. The Christian humanists of the late fifteenth and early sixteenth centuries urged reform, primarily through educational and social change. What was new in the sixteenth century was the breadth of acceptance and the ultimate impact of the calls for reform. This acceptance was due not only to religious issues and problems within the church, but also to political and social factors. In 1500 there was one Christian church in western Europe to which all Christians at least nominally belonged. One hundred years later there were many, a situation that continues today. ■

Religious Violence in Urban Life. This 1590 painting shows Catholic military forces, including friars in their robes, processing through one of the many towns affected by the French religious wars that followed the Reformation.

CHAPTER PREVIEW

The Early Reformation
■ What were the central ideas of the reformers, and why were they appealing to different social groups?

The Reformation and German Politics
■ How did the political situation in Germany shape the course of the Reformation?

The Spread of Protestant Ideas
■ How did Protestant ideas and institutions spread beyond German-speaking lands?

The Catholic Reformation
■ How did the Catholic Church respond to the new religious situation?

Religious Violence
■ What were the causes and consequences of religious violence, including riots, wars, and witch-hunts?

The Early Reformation

What were the central ideas of the reformers, and why were they appealing to different social groups?

In early sixteenth-century Europe a wide range of people had grievances with the church. Educated laypeople such as Christian humanists and urban residents, villagers and artisans, and church officials themselves called for reform. This widespread dissatisfaction helps explain why the ideas of an obscure professor from a new and not very prestigious German university found a ready audience. Within a decade of his first publishing his ideas (using the new technology of the printing press), much of central Europe and Scandinavia had broken with the Catholic Church, and even more radical concepts of the Christian message were being developed and linked to calls for social change.

anticlericalism Opposition to the clergy.

pluralism The clerical practice of holding more than one church benefice (or office) at the same time and enjoying the income from each.

The Christian Church in the Early Sixteenth Century

If external religious observances are an indication of conviction, Europeans in the early sixteenth century were deeply pious. Villagers participated in processions honoring the local saints. Merchants and guild members made pilgrimages to the great shrines, such as Saint Peter's in Rome, and paid for altars in local churches. Men and women continued to remember the church in their wills. People of all social groups devoted an enormous amount of their time and income to religious causes and foundations.

Despite — or perhaps because of — the depth of their piety, many people were also highly critical of the Roman Catholic Church and its clergy. The papal conflict with the German emperor Frederick II in the thirteenth century, followed by the Babylonian Captivity and the Great Schism, badly damaged the prestige of church leaders, and the fifteenth-century popes' concentration on artistic patronage and building up family power did not help matters. Papal tax collection methods were attacked orally and in print. Some criticized the papacy itself as an institution, and even the great wealth and powerful courts of the entire church hierarchy. Some groups and individuals argued that certain doctrines taught by the church, such as the veneration of saints and the centrality of the sacraments, were incorrect. They suggested measures to reform institutions, improve clerical education and behavior, and alter basic doctrines.

Occasionally these reform efforts had some success, and in at least one area, Bohemia (the modern-day Czech Republic), they led to the formation of a church independent of Rome a century before Luther (see Chapter 12).

In the early sixteenth century court records, bishops' visitations of parishes, and popular songs and printed images show widespread **anticlericalism**, or opposition to the clergy. The critics concentrated primarily on three problems: clerical immorality, clerical ignorance, and clerical **pluralism** (the practice of holding more than one church office at a time), with the related problem of absenteeism. Charges of clerical immorality were aimed at a number of priests who were drunkards, neglected the rule of celibacy, gambled, or indulged in fancy dress. Charges of clerical ignorance were motivated by barely literate priests who simply mumbled the Latin words of the Mass by rote without understanding their meaning. Many priests, monks, and nuns lived pious lives of devotion, learning, and service and had strong support from the laypeople in their areas, but everyone also knew (and repeated) stories about lecherous monks, lustful nuns, and greedy priests.

In regard to absenteeism and pluralism, many clerics held several benefices, or offices, simultaneously, but they seldom visited the benefices, let alone performed the spiritual responsibilities those offices entailed. Instead, they collected revenues from all of them and hired a poor priest, paying him just a fraction of the income to fulfill the spiritual duties of a particular local church. Many Italian officials in the papal curia, the pope's court in Rome, held benefices in England, Spain, and Germany. Revenues from those countries paid the Italian clerics' salaries, provoking not only charges of absenteeism but also nationalistic resentment aimed at the upper levels of the church hierarchy, which was increasingly viewed as foreign. This was particularly the case in Germany, where the lack of a strong central government to negotiate with the papacy meant that demands for revenue were especially high.

There was also local resentment of clerical privileges and immunities. Priests, monks, and nuns were exempt from civic responsibilities, such as defending the city and paying taxes. Yet religious orders frequently held large amounts of urban property, in some cities as much as one-third. City governments were increasingly determined to integrate the clergy into civic life by reducing their privileges and giving them public responsibilities. Urban leaders wanted some say in who would be appointed to high church offices, rather than having this decided far away in Rome. This brought city leaders into opposition with bishops and the papacy, which for centuries had stressed the independence of the church from lay control and the distinction between members of the clergy and laypeople.

Martin Luther

By itself, widespread criticism of the church did not lead to the dramatic changes of the sixteenth century. Those resulted from the personal religious struggle of a German university professor and priest, Martin Luther (1483–1546). Luther was born at Eisleben in Saxony. At considerable sacrifice, his father sent him to school and then to the University of Erfurt, where he earned a master's degree with distinction. Luther was to proceed to the study of law and a legal career, which for centuries had been the stepping-stone to public office and material success. Instead, however, a sense of religious calling led him to join the Augustinian friars, a religious order whose members often preached to, taught, and assisted the poor. (Religious orders were groups whose members took vows and followed a particular set of rules.) Luther was ordained a priest in 1507 and after additional study earned a doctorate of theology. From 1512 until his death in 1546, he served as professor of the Scriptures at the new University of Wittenberg. Throughout his life, he frequently cited his professorship as justification for his reforming work.

Martin Luther was a very conscientious friar, but his scrupulous observance of religious routine, frequent confessions, and fasting gave him only temporary relief from anxieties about sin and his ability to meet God's demands. Through his study of Saint Paul's letters in the New Testament, he gradually arrived at a new understanding of Christian doctrine. His understanding is often summarized as "faith alone, grace alone, Scripture alone." He believed that salvation and justification come through faith. Faith is a free gift of God's grace, not the result of human effort. God's word is revealed only in Scripture, not in the traditions of the church.

At the same time that Luther was engaged in scholarly reflections and professorial lecturing, Pope Leo X authorized the sale of a special Saint Peter's indulgence to finance his building plans in Rome. The archbishop who controlled the area in which Wittenberg was located, Albert of Mainz, was an enthusiastic promoter of this indulgence sale. For his efforts, he received a share of the profits in order to pay off a debt he had incurred in order to purchase a papal dispensation allowing him to become the bishop of several other territories as well.

Chronology

1517	Martin Luther, "Ninety-five Theses on the Power of Indulgences"
1521	Diet of Worms
1521–1559	Habsburg-Valois wars
1525	Peasants' War in Germany
1526	Turkish victory at Mohács, which allows spread of Protestantism in Hungary
1530s	Henry VIII ends the authority of the pope in England
1535	Angela Merici establishes the Ursulines as first women's teaching order
1536	John Calvin, *The Institutes of the Christian Religion*
1540	Papal approval of Society of Jesus (Jesuits)
1542	Pope Paul III establishes Supreme Sacred Congregation of the Roman and Universal Inquisition
1545–1563	Council of Trent
1553–1558	Reign of Mary Tudor and temporary restoration of Catholicism in England
1555	Peace of Augsburg, official recognition of Lutheranism
1558–1603	Reign of Elizabeth in England
1560–1660	Height of the European witch-hunt
1568–1578	Civil war in the Netherlands
1572	Saint Bartholomew's Day massacre
1588	England defeats Spanish Armada
1598	Edict of Nantes

What exactly was an **indulgence**? According to Catholic theology, individuals who sin could be reconciled to God by confessing their sins to a priest and by doing an assigned penance, such as praying or fasting. But beginning in the twelfth century learned theologians increasingly emphasized the idea of purgatory, a place where souls on their way to Heaven went to make further amends for their earthly sins. Both earthly penance and time in purgatory could be shortened by drawing on what was termed the "treasury of merits." This was a collection of all the virtuous acts that Christ, the apostles, and the saints had done during their lives. People thought of it as a sort of strongbox, like those in which merchants carried coins. An indulgence was a piece of parchment (later, paper), signed by the pope or another church official, that substituted a virtuous act from the treasury of merits for penance or time in purgatory. The papacy and bishops had given Crusaders such

> **indulgence** A document issued by the Catholic Church lessening penance or time in purgatory, widely believed to bring forgiveness of all sins.

Selling Indulgences A woodcut advertising Johann Tetzel's sale of indulgences in 1517, which shows him blessed by the Holy Spirit in the form of a dove, while people run to buy, as the rhyme here puts it, "grace and forgiveness for your sins, for you, your parents, wife, and child." Indulgences were often printed fill-in-the-blank forms. This indulgence (upper left), purchased in 1521, has space for the indulgence seller's name at the top, the buyer's name in the middle, and the date at the bottom. (woodcut: akg-images; indulgence: Visual Connection Archive)

indulgences, and by the later Middle Ages they were offered for making pilgrimages or other pious activities and also sold outright (see Chapter 10).

Albert's indulgence sale, run by a Dominican friar named Johann Tetzel who mounted an advertising blitz, promised that the purchase of indulgences would bring full forgiveness for one's own sins or release from purgatory for a loved one. One of the slogans—"As soon as coin in coffer rings, the soul from purgatory springs"—brought phenomenal success, and people traveled from miles around to buy indulgences.

Luther was severely troubled that many people believed they had no further need for repentance once they had purchased indulgences. In 1517 he wrote a letter to Archbishop Albert on the subject and enclosed in Latin his "Ninety-five Theses on the Power of Indulgences." His argument was that indulgences undermined the seriousness of the sacrament of penance, competed with the preaching of the Gospel, and downplayed the importance of charity in Christian life. After Luther's death, biographies reported that the theses were also nailed to the door of the church at Wittenberg Castle on October 31, 1517. Such an act would have been very strange—they were in Latin and written for those learned in theology, not for normal churchgoers—but it has become a standard part of Luther lore.

Whether the theses were posted or not, they were quickly printed, first in Latin and then in German translation. Luther was ordered to come to Rome, although because of the political situation in the empire, he was able instead to engage in formal scholarly debate with a representative of the church, Johann Eck, at Leipzig in 1519. He refused to take back his ideas and continued to develop his calls for reform, publicizing them in a series of pamphlets in which he moved further and further away from Catholic theology. Both popes and church councils could err, he wrote, and secular leaders should reform the church if the pope and clerical hierarchy did not. There was no distinction between clergy and laypeople, and requiring clergy to be celibate was a fruitless attempt to control a natural human drive. Luther clearly understood the power of the new medium of print, and so authorized the publication of his works.

The papacy responded with a letter condemning some of Luther's propositions, ordering that his books be burned, and giving him two months to recant or be excommunicated. Luther retaliated by publicly burning the letter. By 1521, when the excommunication was supposed to become final, Luther's theological issues had become interwoven with public controversies about the church's wealth, power, and basic structure. The papal legate wrote of the growing furor, "All Germany is in revolution. Nine-tenths shout 'Luther' as their war cry; and the other tenth cares nothing about Luther, and cries 'Death to the court of Rome.'"[1] In this highly charged atmosphere, the twenty-one-year-old emperor Charles V held his first diet (assembly of the nobility, clergy, and cities of the Holy Roman Empire) in the German city of Worms, and summoned Luther to appear. Luther refused to give in to demands that he take back his ideas. "Unless I am convinced by the evidence of Scripture or by plain reason," he said, "I cannot and will not recant anything, for it is neither safe nor right to go against conscience."[2] His appearance at the Diet of Worms in 1521 created an even broader audience for reform ideas, and throughout central Europe other individuals began to preach and publish against the existing doctrines and practices of the church, drawing on the long tradition of calls for change as well as on Luther.

Protestant Thought

The most important early reformer other than Luther was the Swiss humanist, priest, and admirer of Erasmus, Ulrich Zwingli (ZWIHN-glee) (1484–1531). Zwingli announced in 1519 that he would preach not from the church's prescribed readings but, relying on Erasmus's New Testament, go right through the New Testament "from A to Z," that is, from Matthew to Revelation. Zwingli was convinced that Christian life rested on the Scriptures, which were the pure words of God and the sole basis of religious truth. He went on

The Ten Commandments Lucas Cranach the Elder, the court painter for the elector of Saxony, painted this giant illustration of the Ten Commandments (more than 5 feet by 11 feet) for the city hall in Wittenberg in 1516, just at the point that Luther was beginning to question Catholic doctrine. Cranach was an early supporter of Luther, and many of his later works depict the reformer and his ideas. Paintings were used by both Protestants and Catholics to teach religious ideas. (Lutherhalle, Wittenberg/The Bridgeman Art Library)

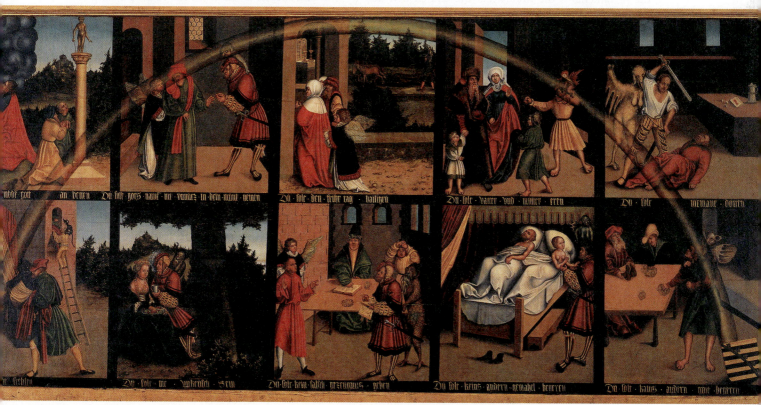

to attack indulgences, the Mass, the institution of monasticism, and clerical celibacy. In his gradual reform of the church in Zurich, he had the strong support of the city authorities, who had long resented the privileges of the clergy.

The followers of Luther, Zwingli, and others who called for a break with Rome came to be called Protestants. The word **Protestant** derives from the protest drawn up by a small group of reforming German princes at the Diet of Speyer in 1529. The princes "protested" the decisions of the Catholic majority, and the word gradually became a general term applied to all non-Catholic western European Christians.

Protestant The name originally given to Lutherans, which came to mean all non-Catholic Western Christian groups.

Luther, Zwingli, and other early Protestants agreed on many things. First, how is a person to be saved? Traditional Catholic teaching held that salvation is achieved by both faith and good works. Protestants held that salvation comes by faith alone, irrespective of good works or the sacraments. God, not people, initiates salvation. (See "Listening to the Past: Martin Luther, *On Christian Liberty*," page 414.) Second, where does religious authority reside? Christian doctrine had long maintained that authority rests both in the Bible and in the traditional teaching of the church. For Protestants, authority rested in the Bible alone. For a doctrine or issue to be valid, it had to have a scriptural basis. Because of this, most Protestants rejected Catholic teachings about the sacraments—the rituals that the church had defined as imparting God's benefits on the believer (see Chapter 10)—holding that only baptism and the Eucharist have scriptural support.

Third, what is the church? Protestants held that the church is a spiritual priesthood of all believers, an invisible fellowship not fixed in any place or person, which differed markedly from the Roman Catholic practice of a hierarchical clerical institution headed by the pope in Rome. Fourth, what is the highest form of Christian life? The medieval church had stressed the superiority of the monastic and religious life over the secular. Protestants disagreed and argued that every person should serve God in his or her individual calling.

Protestants did not agree on everything, and one important area of dispute was the ritual of the Eucharist (also called communion, the Lord's Supper, and, in Catholicism, the Mass). Catholicism holds the dogma of transubstantiation: by the consecrating words of the priest during the Mass, the bread and wine become the actual body and blood of Christ. In opposition, Luther believed that Christ is really present in the consecrated bread and wine, but this is the result of God's mystery, not the actions of a priest. Zwingli understood the Eucharist as a memorial in which Christ was present in spirit among the faithful, but not in the bread and wine. The Colloquy of Marburg, summoned in 1529 to unite Protestants, failed to resolve these differences, though Protestants reached agreement on almost everything else.

The Appeal of Protestant Ideas

Pulpits and printing presses spread the Protestant message all over Germany, and by the middle of the sixteenth century people of all social classes had rejected Catholic teachings and had become Protestant. What was the immense appeal of Luther's religious ideas and those of other Protestants?

Educated people and many humanists were much attracted by Luther's ideas. He advocated a simpler personal religion based on faith, a return to the spirit of the early church, the centrality of the Scriptures in the liturgy and in Christian life, and the abolition of elaborate ceremonies—precisely the reforms the Christian humanists had been calling for. The Protestant insistence that everyone should read and reflect on the Scriptures attracted literate and thoughtful city residents. This included many priests and monks who left the Catholic Church to become clergy in the new Protestant churches. In addition, townspeople who envied the church's wealth and resented paying for it were attracted by the notion that the clergy should also pay taxes and should not have special legal privileges. After Zurich became Protestant, the city council taxed the clergy and placed them under the jurisdiction of civil courts.

Scholars in many disciplines have attributed Luther's fame and success to the invention of the printing press, which rapidly reproduced and made known his ideas. Many printed works included woodcuts and other illustrations, so that even those who could not read could grasp the main ideas. (See "Living in the Past: Uses of Art in the Reformation," page 418.) Equally important was Luther's incredible skill with language, as seen in his two catechisms (compendiums of basic religious knowledge) and in hymns that he wrote for congregations to sing. Luther's linguistic skill, together with his translation of the New Testament into German in 1523, led to the acceptance of his dialect of German as the standard written version of the German language.

Both Luther and Zwingli recognized that for reforms to be permanent, political authorities as well as concerned individuals and religious leaders would have to accept them. Zwingli worked closely with the city council of Zurich, and city councils themselves took the lead in other cities and towns of Switzerland and south Germany. They appointed pastors whom they knew had accepted Protestant ideas, required them to swear an oath of loyalty to the council, and oversaw their preaching and teaching.

Luther lived in a territory ruled by a noble—the elector of Saxony—and he also worked closely with political authorities, viewing them as fully justified in as-

Picturing the Past

Domestic Scene The Protestant notion that the best form of Christian life was marriage and a family helps explain its appeal to middle-class urban men and women, such as those shown in this domestic scene. The engraving, titled "Concordia" (harmony), includes the biblical inscription of what Jesus called the greatest commandment — "You shall love the Lord your God with all your heart and all your soul and your neighbor as yourself" (Deuteronomy 6; Matthew 22) — on tablets at the back. The large covered bed at the back was both a standard piece of furniture in urban homes and a symbol of proper marital sexual relations. (Mary Evans Picture Library)

ANALYZING THE IMAGE What are the different family members doing? What elements of this image suggest that this is a pious, Christian family?

CONNECTIONS How do the various family roles shown here support the Protestant ideal of marriage and family?

To complete this activity online, go to the Online Study Guide at bedfordstmartins.com/mckaywest.

---

serting control over the church in their territories. Indeed, he demanded that German rulers reform the papacy and its institutions, and he instructed all Christians to obey their secular rulers, whom he saw as divinely ordained to maintain order. Individuals may have been convinced of the truth of Protestant teachings by hearing sermons, listening to hymns, or reading pamphlets, but a territory became Protestant when its ruler, whether a noble or a city council, brought in a reformer or two to reeducate the territory's clergy, sponsored public sermons, and confiscated church property. This happened in many of the states of the Holy Roman Empire during the 1520s.

The Radical Reformation and the German Peasants' War

While Luther and Zwingli worked with political authorities, some individuals and groups rejected the idea that church and state needed to be united. Beginning in the 1520s, they sought instead to create a voluntary

Martin Luther, *On Christian Liberty*

LISTENING TO THE PAST

The idea of liberty has played a powerful role in the history of Western society and culture, but the meaning and understanding of liberty has undergone continual change and interpretation. In the Roman world, where slavery was a basic institution, liberty meant the condition of being a free man, independent of obligations to a master. In the Middle Ages possessing liberty meant having special privileges or rights that other persons or institutions did not have. A lord or a monastery, for example, might speak of his or its liberties, and citizens in London were said to possess the "freedom of the city," which allowed them to practice trades and own property without interference.

The idea of liberty also has a religious dimension, and the reformer Martin Luther formulated a classic interpretation of liberty in his treatise *On Christian Liberty* (sometimes translated as *On the Freedom of a Christian*), arguably his finest piece. Written in Latin for the pope but translated immediately into German and published widely, it contains the main themes of Luther's theology: the importance of faith, the relationship of Christian faith and good works, the dual nature of human beings, and the fundamental importance of Scripture. Luther writes that Christians were freed from sin and death through Christ, not through their own actions.

" A Christian man is the most free lord of all, and subject to none; a Christian man is the most dutiful servant of all, and subject to everyone. Although these statements appear contradictory, yet, when they are found to agree together, they will do excellently for my purpose. They are both the statements of Paul himself, who says, "Though I be free from all men, yet have I made myself a servant unto all" (I Corinthians 9:19) and "Owe no man anything but to love one another" (Romans 13:8). Now love is by its own nature dutiful and obedient to the beloved object. Thus even Christ, though Lord of all things, was yet made of a woman; made under the law; at once free and a servant; at once in the form of God and in the form of a servant.

Let us examine the subject on a deeper and less simple principle. Man is composed of a twofold nature, a spiritual and a bodily. As regards the spiritual nature, which they name the soul, he is called the spiritual, inward, new man; as regards the bodily nature, which they name the flesh, he is called the fleshly, outward, old man. The Apostle speaks of this: "Though our outward man perish, yet the inward man is renewed day by day" (II Corinthians 4:16). The result of this diversity is that in the Scriptures opposing statements are made concerning the same man, the fact being that in the same man these two men are opposed to one another; the flesh lusting against the spirit, and the spirit against the flesh (Galatians 5:17).

We first approach the subject of the inward man, that we may see by what means a man becomes justified, free, and a true Christian; that is, a spiritual, new, and inward man. It is certain that absolutely none among outward things, under whatever name they may be reckoned, has any influence in producing Christian righteousness or liberty, nor, on the other hand, unrighteousness or slavery. This can be shown by an easy argument. What can it profit to the soul that the body should be in good condition, free, and full of life, that it should eat, drink, and act according to its pleasure, when even the most impious slaves of every kind of vice are prosperous in these matters? Again, what harm can ill health, bondage, hunger, thirst, or any other outward evil, do to the soul, when even the most pious of men, and the freest in the purity of their conscience, are harassed by these things? Neither of these states of things has to do with the liberty or the slavery of the soul.

And so it will profit nothing that the body should be adorned with sacred vestment, or dwell in holy places, or be occupied in sacred offices, or pray, fast, and abstain from certain meats, or do whatever works can be done through the body and in the body. Something widely different will be necessary for the justification and liberty of the soul, since the things I have spoken of can be done by an impious person, and only hypocrites are produced by devotion to these things. On the other hand, it will not at all injure the soul that the body should be clothed in profane raiment, should dwell in profane places, should eat and drink in the ordinary fashion, should not pray aloud, and should leave undone all the things above mentioned, which may be done by hypocrites.

. . . One thing, and one alone, is necessary for life, justification, and Christian liberty; and that is the most Holy Word of God, the Gospel of Christ, as He says, "I am the resurrection and the life; he that believeth in me shall not die eternally" (John 9:25), and also, "If the Son shall make you free, ye shall be free indeed" (John 8:36), and "Man shall not live by bread alone, but by every word that proceedeth out of the mouth of God" (Matthew 4:4).

Let us therefore hold it for certain and firmly established that the soul can do without everything except the Word of God, without which none at all of its wants is provided for. But, having the Word, it is rich and wants for nothing, since that is the Word of life, of truth, of light, of peace, of justification, of salvation,

On effective preaching, especially to the uneducated, Luther urged the minister "to keep it simple for the simple."
(Church of St. Marien, Wittenberg/The Bridgeman Art Library)

of joy, of liberty, of wisdom, of virtue, of grace, of glory, and of every good thing. . . .

But you will ask, "What is this Word, and by what means is it to be used, since there are so many words of God?" I answer, "The Apostle Paul (Romans 1) explains what it is, namely the Gospel of God, concerning His Son, incarnate, suffering, risen, and glorified through the Spirit, the Sanctifier." To preach Christ is to feed the soul, to justify it, to set it free, and to save it, if it believes the preaching. For faith alone, and the efficacious use of the Word of God, bring salvation. "If thou shalt confess with thy mouth the Lord Jesus, and shalt believe in thine heart that God hath raised Him from the dead, thou shalt be saved" (Romans 9:9); . . . and "The just shall live by faith" (Romans 1:17). . . .

But this faith cannot consist of all with works; that is, if you imagine that you can be justified by those works, whatever they are, along with it. . . . Therefore, when you begin to believe, you learn at the same time that all that is in you is utterly guilty, sinful, and damnable, according to that saying, "All have sinned, and come short of the glory of God" (Romans 3:23). . . . When you have learned this, you will know that Christ is necessary for you, since He has suffered and risen again for you, that, believing on Him, you might by this faith become another man, all your sins being remitted, and you being justified by the merits of another, namely Christ alone.

. . . [A]nd since it [faith] alone justifies, it is evident that by no outward work or labour can the inward man be at all justified, made free, and saved; and that no works whatever have any relation to him. . . . Therefore the first care of every Christian ought to be to lay aside all reliance on works, and strengthen his faith alone more and more, and by it grow in knowledge, not of works, but of Christ Jesus, who has suffered and risen again for him, as Peter teaches (I Peter 5).

QUESTIONS FOR ANALYSIS

1. What did Luther mean by liberty?
2. Why, for Luther, was Scripture basic to Christian life?

Source: *Luther's Primary Works*, ed. H. Wace and C. A. Buchheim (London: Holder and Stoughton, 1896). Reprinted in *The Portable Renaissance Reader*, ed. James Bruce Ross and Mary Martin McLaughlin (New York: Penguin Books, 1981), pp. 721–726.

> "Let everyone who can smite, slay, and stab [the peasants], secretly and openly, remembering that nothing can be more poisonous, hurtful or devilish than a rebel."
>
> —MARTIN LUTHER

community of believers separate from the state, as they understood it to have existed in New Testament times. In terms of theology and spiritual practices, these individuals and groups varied widely, though they are generally termed "radicals" for their insistence on a more extensive break with prevailing ideas. Some adopted the baptism of believers—for which they were given the title of "Anabaptists" or rebaptizers by their enemies—while others saw all outward sacraments or rituals as misguided. Some groups attempted communal ownership of property, living very simply and rejecting anything they thought unbiblical. Some reacted harshly to members who deviated, but others argued for complete religious toleration and individualism.

Religious radicals were often pacifists and refused to hold office or swear oaths, which marked them as societal outcasts and invited fanatical hatred and bitter persecution. Both Protestant and Catholic authorities felt threatened by the social, political, and economic implications of their religious ideas, and by their rejection of a state church, which the authorities saw as key to maintaining order. In Saxony, in Strasbourg, and in the Swiss cities, radicals were either banished or cruelly executed by burning, beating, or drowning. Their community spirit and heroism in the face of martyrdom, however, contributed to the survival of radical ideas. Later, the Quakers, with their pacifism; the Baptists, with their emphasis on inner spiritual light; the Congregationalists, with their democratic church organization; and in 1787 the authors of the U.S. Constitution, with their opposition to the "establishment of religion" (state churches), would all trace their origins, in part, to the radicals of the sixteenth century.

Radical reformers sometimes called for social as well as religious change, a message that German peasants heard. In the early sixteenth century the economic condition of the peasantry varied from place to place but was generally worse than it had been in the fifteenth century and was deteriorating. Crop failures in 1523 and 1524 aggravated an explosive situation. Nobles had aggrieved peasants by seizing village common lands, by imposing new rents and requiring additional services, and by taking the peasants' best horses or cows whenever a head of household died. The peasants made demands that they believed conformed to the Scriptures, and they cited radical thinkers as well as Luther as proof that they did.

Luther wanted to prevent rebellion. Initially he sided with the peasants, blasting the lords for robbing their subjects. But when rebellion broke out, peasants who expected Luther's support were soon disillusioned. Freedom for Luther meant independence from the authority of the Roman church; it did not mean opposition to legally established secular powers. As for biblical support for the peasants' demands, he maintained that Scripture had nothing to do with earthly justice or material gain, a position that Zwingli supported. Firmly convinced that rebellion would hasten the end of civilized society, Luther wrote the tract *Against the Murderous, Thieving Hordes of the Peasants*: "Let everyone who can smite, slay, and stab [the peasants], secretly and openly, remembering that nothing can be more poisonous, hurtful or devilish than a rebel."[3] The nobility ferociously crushed the revolt. Historians estimate that more than seventy-five thousand peasants were killed in 1525.

The German Peasants' War of 1525 greatly strengthened the authority of lay rulers. Not surprisingly, the Reformation lost much of its popular appeal after 1525, though peasants and urban rebels sometimes found a place for their social and religious ideas in radical groups. Peasants' economic conditions did moderately improve, however. For example, in many parts of Germany, enclosed fields, meadows, and forests were returned to common use.

Marriage and Sexuality

Luther and Zwingli both believed that a priest's or nun's vows of celibacy went against human nature and God's commandments, and that marriage brought spiritual advantages and so was the ideal state for nearly all human beings. Luther married a former nun, Katharina von Bora (1499–1532), and Zwingli married a Zurich widow, Anna Reinhart (1491–1538). Both women quickly had several children. Most other Protestant reformers also married, and their wives had to create a new and respectable role for themselves—pastor's wife—to overcome being viewed as simply a new type of priest's concubine. They were living demonstrations of their husband's convictions about the superiority of marriage to celibacy, and they were expected to be models of wifely obedience and Christian charity.

Though they denied that marriage was a sacrament, Protestant reformers stressed that it had been ordained by God when he presented Eve to Adam, served as a "remedy" for the unavoidable sin of lust, provided a site for the pious rearing of the next generation of God-fearing Christians, and offered husbands and wives companionship and consolation. A proper marriage was one that reflected both the spiritual equality of men and

Martin Luther and Katharina von Bora Lucas Cranach the Elder painted this double marriage portrait to celebrate Luther's wedding in 1525 to Katharina von Bora, a former nun. The artist was one of the witnesses at the wedding and, in fact, had presented Luther's marriage proposal to Katharina. Using a go-between for proposals was very common, as was having a double wedding portrait painted. This particular couple quickly became a model of the ideal marriage, and many churches wanted their portraits. More than sixty similar paintings, with slight variations, were produced by Cranach's workshop and hung in churches and wealthy homes. (Uffizi, Florence/Scala/Art Resource, NY)

women and the proper social hierarchy of husbandly authority and wifely obedience.

Protestants did not break with medieval scholastic theologians in their idea that women were to be subject to men. Women were advised to be cheerful rather than grudging in their obedience, for in doing so they demonstrated their willingness to follow God's plan. Men were urged to treat their wives kindly and considerately, but also to enforce their authority, through physical coercion if necessary. European marriage manuals used the metaphor of breaking a horse for teaching a wife obedience, though laws did set limits on the husband's power to do so. A few women took Luther's idea about the priesthood of all believers to heart. Argula von Grumbach, a German noblewoman, wrote religious pamphlets supporting Protestant ideas, asserting, "I am not unfamiliar with Paul's words that women should be silent in church but when I see that no man will or can speak, I am driven by the word of God when he said, he who confesses me on earth, him will I confess, and he who denies me, him will I deny."[4] No sixteenth-century Protestants officially allowed women to be members of the clergy, however, though monarchs such as Elizabeth I of England and female territorial rulers of the states of the Holy Roman Empire did determine religious policies just as male rulers did.

Protestants saw marriage as a contract in which each partner promised the other support, companionship, and the sharing of mutual goods. Because, in Protestant eyes, marriage was created by God as a remedy for human weakness, marriages in which spouses did not comfort or support one another physically, materially, or emotionally endangered their own souls and the surrounding community. The only solution might be divorce and remarriage, which most Protestants came to allow. Protestant allowance of divorce differed markedly from Catholic doctrine, which viewed marriage as a sacramental union that, if validly entered into, could not be dissolved (Catholic canon law allowed only separation with no remarriage). Although it was a dramatic legal change, divorce did not have a dramatic impact on newly Protestant areas. Because marriage was the cornerstone

Uses of Art in the Reformation

LIVING IN THE PAST

IN THE REFORMATION ERA, CONTROVERSY RAGED over the purpose and function of art. Protestants and Catholics disagreed, and Protestant groups disagreed with one another. Some Protestant leaders, including Ulrich Zwingli and John Calvin, stressed that "the Word of God" should be the only instrument used in the work of evangelization. Swiss Protestants and Calvinists in many parts of Europe stripped statues, images, and decoration out of many formerly Catholic churches or redesigned them with a stark, bare simplicity. Martin Luther, by contrast, believed that painting and sculpture had value in spreading the Gospel message because "children and simple folk are more apt to retain the divine stories when taught by pictures and parables than merely by words or instruction." He collaborated with artists such as Lucas Cranach the Elder (1472–1553), who conveyed Protestant ideas in woodcuts and paintings. (See Cranach's *The Ten Commandments*, page 411.)

Both Protestants and Catholics used pictures for propaganda purposes. In *The True and False Churches*, Lucas Cranach the Younger (1515–1586) shows Luther standing in a pulpit, preaching the word of God from an open Bible. At the right, a flaming open mouth symbolizing the jaws of Hell engulfs the pope, cardinals, and friars, one kind of "false church." At the left, Cranach shows a crucified Christ emerging out of the "lamb of God" on the altar as people are receiving communion. This image of the "true church" represents the Lutheran understanding of the Lord's Supper, in which Christ is really present in the bread and wine, in contrast to other Protestants such as Zwingli who saw the ceremony as a symbol or memorial.

The Catholic Church officially addressed the subject of art at the Council of Trent in 1563. The church declared that honor and veneration should be given to likenesses of Christ, the Virgin Mary, and the saints; that images should remind people of the saints' virtues in order to encourage imitation; and that pictorial art should promote piety and the love of God. Consider the anonymous painting *Jesuit Priest Distributing Holy Pictures*. Parish priests and Jesuits often distributed such pictures to laypeople, including children, to help educate them in matters of doc-

Lucas Cranach the Younger, *The True and False Churches*.
(Staatliche Kunstsammlungen Dresden)

418

of society socially and economically, divorce was a desperate last resort. In many Protestant jurisdictions the annual divorce rate hovered around 0.02 to 0.06 per thousand people. (By contrast, in 2007 the U.S. divorce rate was 3.6 per thousand people.)

As Protestants believed marriage was the only proper remedy for lust, they uniformly condemned prostitution. The licensed brothels that were a common feature of late medieval urban life (see Chapter 12) were closed in Protestant cities, and harsh punishments were set for prostitution. Many Catholic cities soon closed their brothels as well, although Italian cities favored stricter regulations rather than closure. Selling sex was couched in moral rather than economic terms, as simply one type of "whoredom," a term that also included premarital sex, adultery, and other unacceptable sexual activities. "Whore" was also a term that reformers used for their theological opponents; Protestants compared the pope to the biblical whore of Babylon, a symbol of the end of the world, while Catholics called Luther's wife a whore because she had first been married to Christ as a nun before her marriage to Luther. Closing brothels did not end the exchange of sex for money, of course, but simply reshaped it. Smaller illegal brothels were established, or women moved to areas right outside city walls.

The Protestant Reformation clearly had a positive impact on marriage, but its impact on women was more mixed. Many nuns were in convents because their parents placed them there and did not have a strong sense of religious calling, but convents nevertheless provided women of the upper classes with scope for their literary, artistic, medical, or administrative talents if they could not or would not marry. The Reformation generally brought the closing of monasteries and convents, and marriage became virtually the only occupation for upper-class Protestant women. Women in some convents recognized this and fought the Reformation, or argued that they could still be pious Protestants within convent walls. Most nuns left, however, and we do not know what happened to them. The Protestant emphasis on marriage made unmarried women (and men) suspect, for they did not belong to the type of household regarded as the cornerstone of a proper, godly society.

Jesuit Priest Distributing Holy Pictures. (From Pierre Chenu, *The Reformation* [New York: St. Martin's Press, 1986])

trine. Church leaders also sponsored the building of lavishly decorated churches that appealed to the senses and proclaimed the power of the reformed Catholic Church. (See Jesuit Church of the Gesù on page 430.)

QUESTIONS FOR ANALYSIS

1. What does Cranach's woodcut suggest about Protestants who had a different interpretation than Luther's about the Lord's Supper?
2. Cranach's woodcut could be easily reproduced through the technology of the printing press. How would this have enhanced its impact?
3. In what way does the artist of the Jesuit image suggest that people are eager for the Catholic message? How might this painting itself have aroused piety?

The Reformation and German Politics

How did the political situation in Germany shape the course of the Reformation? ■

Although criticism of the church was widespread in Europe in the early sixteenth century, reform movements could be more easily squelched by the strong central governments that had evolved in Spain and France.

England, too, had a strong monarchy, but the king broke from the Catholic Church for other reasons (see page 423). The Holy Roman Empire, in contrast, included hundreds of largely independent states. Against this background of decentralization and strong local power, Martin Luther had launched a movement to reform the church. Two years after he published the "Ninety-five Theses," the electors of the Holy Roman Empire chose as emperor a nineteen-year-old Habsburg prince who ruled as Charles V (r. 1519–1556). The course of the Reformation was shaped by this election and by the political relationships surrounding it.

The Rise of the Habsburg Dynasty

War and diplomacy were important ways that states increased their power in sixteenth-century Europe, but so was marriage. Royal and noble sons and daughters were important tools of state policy. The benefits of an advantageous marriage stretched across generations, a process that can be seen most dramatically with the Habsburgs. The Holy Roman emperor Frederick III, a Habsburg who was the ruler of most of Austria, acquired only a small amount of territory—but a great deal of money—with his marriage to Princess Eleonore of Portugal in 1452. He arranged for his son Maximilian to marry Europe's most prominent heiress, Mary of Burgundy, in 1477; she inherited the Netherlands, Luxembourg, and the County of Burgundy in what is now eastern France. Through this union with the rich and powerful duchy of Burgundy, the Austrian house of Habsburg, already the strongest ruling family in the empire, became an international power. The marriage of Maximilian and Mary angered the French, however, who considered Burgundy French territory, and inaugurated centuries of conflict between the Austrian house of Habsburg and the kings of France.

Maximilian learned the lesson of marital politics well, marrying his son and daughter to the children of Ferdinand and Isabella, the rulers of Spain, much of southern Italy, and eventually the Spanish New World empire. His grandson Charles V (1500–1558) fell heir to a vast and incredibly diverse collection of states and peoples, each governed in a different manner and held together only by the person of the emperor (Map 14.1). Charles's Italian adviser, the grand chancellor Gattinara, told the young ruler, "God has set you on the path toward world monarchy." Charles not only believed this but also was convinced that it was his duty to maintain the political and religious unity of Western Christendom.

Fresco of Pope Clement VII and the Emperor Charles V In this double portrait, artist Giorgio Vasari uses matching hand gestures to indicate agreement between the pope and the emperor, though the pope's red hat and cape make him the dominant figure. Charles V remained loyal to Catholicism, though the political situation and religious wars in Germany eventually required him to compromise with Protestants. (Palazzo Vecchio, Florence/Scala/Art Resource, NY)

Religious Wars in Switzerland and Germany

In the sixteenth century the practice of religion remained a public matter. The ruler determined the official form of religious practice in his (or occasionally her) jurisdiction. Almost everyone believed that the presence of a faith different from that of the majority represented a political threat to the security of the state, and few believed in religious liberty.

Luther's ideas appealed to German rulers for a variety of reasons. Though Germany was not a nation, people did have an understanding of being German because of their language and traditions. Luther frequently used the phrase "we Germans" in his attacks on the papacy. Luther's appeal to national feeling influenced many rulers otherwise confused by or indifferent to the complexities of the religious matters. Some German rulers were sincerely attracted to Lutheran ideas, but material considerations swayed many others to embrace the new faith. The rejection of Roman Catholicism and adoption of Protestantism would mean the legal confiscation of lush farmlands, rich monasteries, and wealthy shrines. Thus many political authorities in the empire used the religious issue to extend their financial and political power and to enhance their independence from the emperor.

Charles V was a vigorous defender of Catholicism, so it is not surprising that the Reformation led to religious wars. The first battleground was Switzerland, which was officially part of the Holy Roman Empire, though it was really a loose confederation of thirteen largely autonomous territories called "cantons." Some cantons remained Catholic, and some became Protestant, and in the late 1520s the two sides went to war. Zwingli was killed on the battlefield in 1531, and both sides quickly decided

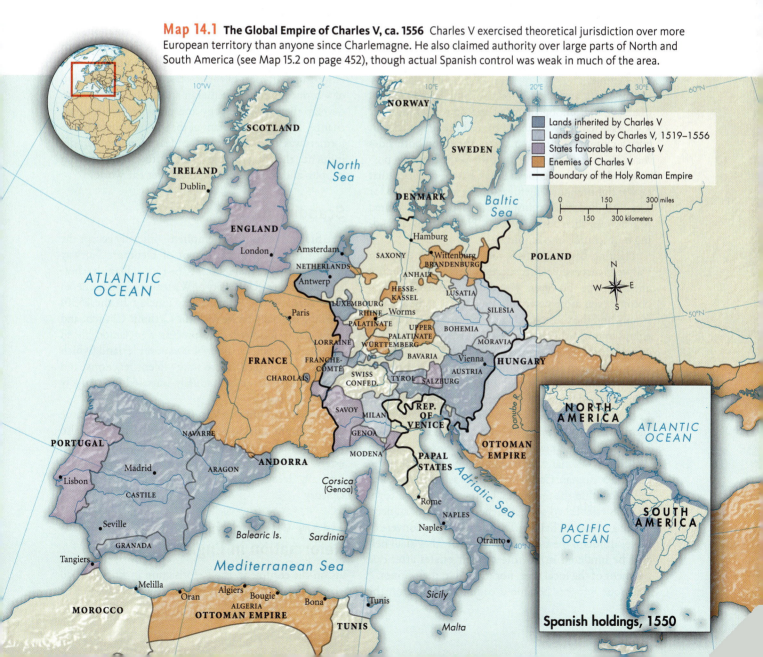

Map 14.1 **The Global Empire of Charles V, ca. 1556** Charles V exercised theoretical jurisdiction over more European territory than anyone since Charlemagne. He also claimed authority over large parts of North and South America (see Map 15.2 on page 452), though actual Spanish control was weak in much of the area.

that a treaty was preferable to further fighting. The treaty basically allowed each canton to determine its own religion and ordered each side to give up its foreign alliances, a policy of neutrality that has been characteristic of modern Switzerland.

Trying to halt the spread of religious division, Charles V called an Imperial Diet in 1530, to meet at Augsburg. The Lutherans developed a statement of faith, later called the Augsburg Confession, and the Protestant princes presented this to the emperor. (The Augsburg Confession remains an authoritative statement of belief for many Lutheran churches.) Charles refused to accept it and ordered all Protestants to return to the Catholic Church and give up any confiscated church property. This demand backfired, and Protestant territories in the empire—mostly northern German principalities and southern German cities—formed a military alliance. The emperor could not respond militarily, as he was in the midst of a series of wars with the French: the Habsburg-Valois wars (1521–1559), fought in Italy along the eastern and southern borders of France and eventually in Germany. The Ottoman Turks had also taken much of Hungary and in 1529 were besieging Vienna.

The 1530s and early 1540s saw complicated political maneuvering among many of the powers of Europe. Various attempts were made to heal the religious split with a church council, but stubbornness on both sides made it increasingly clear that this would not be possible and that war was inevitable. Charles V realized that he was fighting not only for religious unity, but also for a more unified state, against territorial rulers who wanted to maintain their independence. He was thus defending both church and empire.

Fighting began in 1546, and initially the emperor was very successful. This success alarmed both France and the pope, however, who did not want Charles to become even more powerful. The pope withdrew papal troops, and the Catholic king of France sent money and troops to the Lutheran princes. Finally, in 1555 Charles agreed to the Peace of Augsburg, which, "in order to bring peace into the holy empire," officially recognized Lutheranism. The political authority in each territory was permitted to decide whether the territory would be Catholic or Lutheran and was ordered to let other territories "enjoy their religious beliefs, liturgy, and ceremonies as well as their estates in peace." Most of northern and central Germany became Lutheran, while the south remained Roman Catholic. There was no freedom of religion within the territories, however. Princes or town councils established state churches to which all subjects of the area had to belong. Dissidents had to convert or leave, although the treaty did order that "they shall neither be hindered in the sale of their estates after due payment of the local taxes nor injured in their honor."[5] Religious refugees became a common feature on the roads of the empire, though rulers did not always let their subjects leave as easily as the treaty stipulated.

The Peace of Augsburg ended religious war in Germany for many decades. His hope of uniting his empire under a single church dashed, Charles V abdicated in 1556 and moved to a monastery, transferring power over his holdings in Spain and the Netherlands to his son Philip and his imperial power to his brother Ferdinand.

The Spread of Protestant Ideas

How did Protestant ideas and institutions spread beyond German-speaking lands?

States within the Holy Roman Empire were the earliest territories to accept the Protestant Reformation, but by the later 1520s and 1530s religious change came to Denmark-Norway, Sweden, England, France, and eastern Europe. In most of these areas, a second generation of reformers built on Lutheran and Zwinglian ideas to develop their own theology and plans for institutional change. The most important of the second-generation reformers was John Calvin, whose ideas would profoundly influence the social thought and attitudes of European peoples and their descendants all over the world.

Scandinavia

The first area outside the empire to officially accept the Reformation was the kingdom of Denmark-Norway under King Christian III (r. 1536–1559). Danish scholars studied at the University of Wittenberg, and Lutheran ideas spread into Denmark very quickly. In the 1530s the king officially broke with the Catholic Church, and most clergy followed. The process went smoothly in Denmark, but in northern Norway and Iceland (which Christian also ruled) there were violent reactions, and Lutheranism was only gradually imposed on a largely unwilling populace.

In Sweden, Gustavus Vasa (r. 1523–1560), who came to the throne during a civil war with Denmark, also took over control of church personnel and income. Protestant ideas spread, though the Swedish church did not officially accept Lutheran theology until later in the century.

Henry VIII and the Reformation in England

As on the continent, the Reformation in England had economic and political as well as religious causes. The

Allegory of the Tudor Dynasty The unknown creator of this work intended to glorify the virtues of the Protestant succession; the painting has no historical reality. Henry VIII (seated) hands the sword of justice to his Protestant son Edward VI. The Catholic Queen Mary and her husband Philip of Spain (left) are followed by Mars, god of war, signifying violence and civil disorder. At right the figures of Peace and Plenty accompany the Protestant Elizabeth I, symbolizing England's happy fate under her rule. (Yale Center for British Art, Paul Mellon Collection/The Bridgeman Art Library)

impetus for England's break with Rome was the desire of King Henry VIII (r. 1509–1547) for a new wife, though ultimately his own motives also combined personal, political, social, and economic elements.

Henry VIII was married to Catherine of Aragon, the daughter of Ferdinand and Isabella and widow of Henry's older brother Arthur. Marriage to a brother's widow went against canon law, and Henry had been required to obtain a special papal dispensation to marry Catherine. The marriage had produced only one living heir, a daughter, Mary. By 1527 Henry decided that God was showing his displeasure with the marriage by denying him a son, and he appealed to the pope to have the marriage annulled. He was also in love with a court lady-in-waiting, Anne Boleyn, and assumed that she would give him the son he wanted. Normally an annulment would not have been a problem, but the troops of Emperor Charles V were in Rome at that point, and Pope Clement VII was essentially their prisoner. Charles V was the nephew of Catherine of Aragon and thus was vigorously opposed to an annulment, which would have declared his aunt a fornicator and his cousin Mary a bastard. The pope stalled.

With Rome thwarting his matrimonial plans, Henry decided to remove the English church from papal jurisdiction. In a series of measures during the 1530s, Henry used Parliament to end the authority of the pope and make himself the supreme head of the church in England. Some opposed the king and were beheaded, among them Thomas More, the king's chancellor and author of *Utopia* (see Chapter 13). When Anne Boleyn failed twice to produce a male child, Henry VIII charged her with adulterous incest and in 1536 had her beheaded. His third wife, Jane Seymour, gave Henry the desired son, Edward, but she died in childbirth. Henry went on to three more wives.

Theologically, Henry was conservative, and the English church retained such traditional Catholic practices and doctrines as confession, clerical celibacy, and transubstantiation. Between 1535 and 1539, however, under the influence of his chief minister, Thomas Cromwell, Henry decided to dissolve the English monasteries because he wanted their wealth. Working through Parliament, the king ended nine hundred years of English monastic life, dispersing the monks and nuns and confiscating their lands. Their proceeds enriched the royal treasury, and hundreds of properties were sold to the middle and upper classes, the very groups represented in Parliament. The dissolution of the monasteries did not achieve a more equitable distribution of land and wealth; rather, the redistribution of land strengthened the upper classes and tied them to both the Tudor dynasty and the new Protestant church.

The nationalization of the church and the dissolution of the monasteries led to important changes in government administration. Vast tracts of formerly monastic land came temporarily under the Crown's jurisdiction, and new bureaucratic machinery had to be developed to manage those properties. Cromwell reformed and centralized the king's household, the council, the secretariats, and the Exchequer. New departments of state were set up. Surplus funds from all departments went into a liquid fund to be applied to areas where there were deficits. This balancing resulted in greater efficiency and economy, and Henry VIII's reign saw the growth of the modern centralized bureaucratic state.

Did the religious changes under Henry VIII have broad popular support? Some English people had been dissatisfied with the existing Christian church before Henry's measures, and Protestant literature circulated. Traditional Catholicism exerted an enormously strong and vigorous hold over the imagination and loyalty of the people, however. Most clergy and officials accepted Henry's moves, but all did not quietly acquiesce. In 1536 popular opposition in the north to the religious changes led to the Pilgrimage of Grace, a massive rebellion that proved the largest in English history. The "pilgrims" accepted a truce, but their leaders were arrested, tried, and executed. Recent scholarship points out that people rarely "converted" from Catholicism to Protestantism overnight. People responded to an action of the Crown that was played out in their own neighborhood — the closing of a monastery, the ending of Masses for the dead — with a combination of resistance, acceptance, and collaboration. Some enthusiastically changed to Protestant forms of prayer, for example, while others recited Protestant prayers in church while keeping pictures of the Catholic saints at home.

Loyalty to the Catholic Church was particularly strong in Ireland. Ireland had been claimed by English kings since the twelfth century, but in reality the English had firm control of only the area around Dublin, known as the Pale. In 1536, on orders from London, the Irish parliament, which represented only the English landlords and the people of the Pale, approved the English laws severing the church from Rome. The Church of Ireland was established on the English pattern, and the (English) ruling class adopted the new reformed faith. Most of the Irish people remained Roman Catholic, thus adding religious antagonism to the ethnic hostility that had been a feature of English policy toward Ireland for centuries (see Chapter 12). Irish armed opposition to the Reformation led to harsh repression by the English. Catholic property was confiscated and sold, and the profits were shipped to England. The Roman church was essentially driven underground, and the Catholic clergy acted as national as well as religious leaders.

Upholding Protestantism in England

In the short reign of Henry's sickly son, Edward VI (r. 1547–1553), Protestant ideas exerted a significant influence on the religious life of the country. Archbishop Thomas Cranmer simplified the liturgy, invited Protestant theologians to England, and prepared the first *Book of Common Prayer* (1549), which was later approved by Parliament. In stately and dignified English, the *Book of Common Prayer* included the order for all services and prayers of the Church of England.

The equally brief reign of Mary Tudor (r. 1553–1558) witnessed a sharp move back to Catholicism. The devoutly Catholic daughter of Catherine of Aragon, Mary rescinded the Reformation legislation of her father's reign and restored Roman Catholicism. Mary's marriage to her cousin Philip II of Spain, son of the emperor Charles V, proved highly unpopular in England, and her execution of several hundred Protestants further alienated her subjects. During her reign, about a thousand Protestants fled to the continent. Mary's death raised to the throne her sister Elizabeth, Henry's daughter with Anne Boleyn, who had been raised a Protestant. Her reign from 1558 to 1603 inaugurated the beginnings of religious stability.

At the start of Elizabeth's reign sharp differences existed in England. On the one hand, Catholics wanted a Roman Catholic ruler. On the other hand, a vocal number of returning exiles wanted all Catholic elements in the Church of England eliminated. The latter, because they wanted to "purify" the church, were called "Puritans."

Shrewdly, Elizabeth chose a middle course between Catholic and Puritan extremes. She referred to herself as the "supreme governor of the Church of England," using the term *governor* instead of the traditional *head* because this allowed Catholics to remain loyal to her without denying the pope. She required her subjects to attend services in the Church of England or risk a fine, but she did not interfere with their privately held beliefs. As she put it, she did not "want to make windows into men's souls." The Anglican Church, as the Church of England was called, moved in a moderately Protestant direction. Services were conducted in English, monasteries were not re-established, and clergymen were (grudgingly) allowed to marry. But the church remained hierarchical, with archbishops and bishops, and services continued to be elaborate, with the clergy in distinctive robes, in contrast to the simpler services favored by many continental Protestants.

Toward the end of the sixteenth century Elizabeth's reign was threatened by European powers attempting to re-establish Catholicism. Philip II of Spain had hoped that his marriage to Mary Tudor would reunite England with Catholic Europe, but Mary's death ended those plans. Another Mary—Mary, Queen of Scots—provided a new opportunity. Mary was Elizabeth's cousin, but she was Catholic. Mary was next in line to the English throne, and Elizabeth imprisoned her because she worried—quite rightly—that Mary would become the center of Catholic plots to overthrow her. In 1587 Mary became implicated in a plot to assassinate Elizabeth, a conspiracy that had Philip II's full backing. When the English executed Mary, the Catholic pope urged Philip to retaliate.

Philip prepared a vast fleet to sail from Lisbon to Flanders, where a large army of Spanish troops was stationed because of religious wars in the Netherlands (see page 435). The Spanish ships were to escort barges carrying some of the troops across the English Channel to attack England. On May 9, 1588, *la felicissima armada*—"the most fortunate fleet," as it was ironically called in official documents—composed of more than 130 vessels, sailed from Lisbon harbor. The **Spanish Armada** met an English fleet in the channel before it reached Flanders. The English ships were smaller, faster, and more maneuverable, and many of them had greater firing power than their Spanish counterparts. A combination of storms and squalls, spoiled food and rank water, inadequate Spanish ammunition, and, to a lesser extent, English fire ships that caused the Spanish to scatter gave England the victory. On the journey home many Spanish ships went down in the rough seas around Ireland; perhaps 65 ships managed to reach home ports.

The battle in the English Channel has frequently been described as one of the decisive battles in world history. In fact, it had mixed consequences. Spain soon rebuilt its navy, and after 1588 the quality of the Spanish fleet improved. The war between England and Spain dragged on for years. Yet the defeat of the Spanish Armada prevented Philip II from reimposing Catholicism on England by force. In England the victory contributed to a David and Goliath legend that enhanced English national sentiment.

The Route of the Spanish Armada, 1588

Spanish Armada The fleet sent by Philip II of Spain in 1588 against England as a religious crusade against Protestantism. Weather and the English fleet defeated it.

The Institutes of the Christian Religion Calvin's formulation of Christian doctrine, which became a systematic theology for Protestantism.

Calvinism

In 1509, while Luther was preparing for a doctorate at Wittenberg, John Calvin (1509–1564) was born in Noyon in northwestern France. As a young man he studied law, which had a decisive impact on his mind and later his thought. In 1533 he experienced a religious crisis, as a result of which he converted to Protestantism.

Calvin believed that God had specifically selected him to reform the church. Accordingly, he accepted an invitation to assist in the reformation of the city of Geneva. There, beginning in 1541, Calvin worked assiduously to establish a Christian society ruled by God through civil magistrates and reformed ministers. Geneva became the model of a Christian community for Protestant reformers.

To understand Calvin's Geneva, it is necessary to understand Calvin's ideas. These he embodied in **The Institutes of the Christian Religion**, published first in 1536 and in its final form in 1559. The cornerstone of Calvin's theology was his belief in the absolute sovereignty and omnipotence of God and the total weakness of humanity. Before the infinite power of God, he asserted, men and women are as insignificant as grains of sand.

Calvin did not ascribe free will to human beings because that would detract from the sovereignty of God. Men and women cannot actively work to achieve salvation; rather, God in his infinite wisdom decided at the beginning of time who would be saved and who damned. This viewpoint constitutes the theological principle called **predestination**. Calvin explained his view:

> Predestination we call the eternal decree of God, by which he has determined in himself, what he would have become of every individual.... For they are not all created with a similar destiny; but eternal life is foreordained for some, and eternal damnation for others.... To those whom he devotes to condemnation, the gate of life is closed by a just and irreprehensible, but incomprehensible, judgment. How exceedingly presumptuous it is only to inquire into the causes of the Divine will; which is in fact, and is justly entitled to be, the cause of everything that exists.... For the will of God is the highest justice; so that what he wills must be considered just, for this very reason, because he wills it.[6]

Many people consider the doctrine of predestination, which dates back to Saint Augustine and Saint Paul, to be a pessimistic view of the nature of God. But "this terrible decree," as even Calvin called it, did not lead to pessimism or fatalism. Rather, the Calvinist believed in the redemptive work of Christ and was confident that God had elected (saved) him or her. Predestination served as an energizing dynamic, giving a person the strength to undergo hardships in the constant struggle against evil.

predestination The teaching that God has determined the salvation or damnation of individuals based on his will and purpose, not on their merit or works.

In his reform of Geneva, Calvin had several remarkable assets, including complete mastery of the Scriptures and exceptional eloquence. He also understood the importance of institutions and established the Genevan Consistory, a body of laymen and pastors, "to keep watch over every man's life [and] to admonish amiably those whom they see leading a disorderly life" and provide "medicine to turn sinners to the Lord."[7]

Although all municipal governments in early modern Europe regulated citizens' conduct, none did so with the severity of Geneva's Consistory under Calvin's leadership. Absence from sermons, criticism of ministers, dancing, card playing, family quarrels, and heavy drinking were all investigated and punished by the Consistory.

Serious crimes and heresy were handled by the civil authorities, which, with the Consistory's approval, sometimes used torture to extract confessions. Between 1542 and 1546 alone seventy-six persons were banished from Geneva, and fifty-eight were executed for heresy, adultery, blasphemy, and witchcraft (see page 435). Among them was the Spanish humanist and refugee Michael Servetus, who was burned at the stake for denying the scriptural basis for the Trinity, rejecting child baptism, and insisting that a person under twenty cannot commit a mortal sin, all of which were viewed as threats to society.

Religious refugees from France, England, Spain, Scotland, and Italy visited Calvin's Geneva, and many of the most prominent exiles from Mary Tudor's England stayed. Subsequently, the church of Calvin—often termed "Reformed"—served as the model for the Presbyterian church in Scotland, the Huguenot church in France (see page 433), and the Puritan churches in England and New England.

Calvinism became the compelling force in international Protestantism. The Calvinist ethic of the "calling" dignified all work with a religious aspect. Hard work, well done, was pleasing to God. This doctrine encouraged an aggressive, vigorous activism, and Calvinism became the most dynamic force in sixteenth- and seventeenth-century Protestantism.

Calvinism spread on the continent of Europe, and also found a ready audience in Scotland. There as elsewhere,

Young John Calvin This oil painting of the reformer as a young man captures his spiritual intensity and determination, qualities that the artist clearly viewed as positive. (Bibliothèque de Genève, Département iconographique)

> "Predestination we call the eternal decree of God, by which he has determined in himself, what he would have become of every individual."

—JOHN CALVIN

political authority was the decisive influence in reform. The monarchy was weak, and factions of virtually independent nobles competed for power. King James V and his daughter Mary, Queen of Scots (r. 1560–1567), staunch Catholics and close allies of Catholic France, opposed reform, but the Scottish nobles supported it. One man, John Knox (1505?–1572), dominated the reform movement, which led to the establishment of a state church.

Knox was determined to structure the Scottish church after the model of Geneva, where he had studied and worked with Calvin. In 1560 Knox persuaded the Scottish parliament, which was dominated by reform-minded barons, to end papal authority and rule by bishops, substituting governance by presbyters, or councils of ministers. The Presbyterian Church of Scotland was strictly Calvinist in doctrine, adopted a simple and dignified service of worship, and laid great emphasis on preaching.

The Reformation in Eastern Europe

While political and economic issues determined the course of the Reformation in western and northern Europe, ethnic factors often proved decisive in eastern Europe, where people of diverse backgrounds had settled in the later Middle Ages. In Bohemia in the fifteenth century, a Czech majority was ruled by Germans. Most Czechs had adopted the ideas of Jan Hus, and the emperor had been forced to recognize a separate Hussite church (see Chapter 12). Yet Lutheranism appealed to Germans in Bohemia in the 1520s and 1530s, and the nobility embraced Lutheranism in opposition to the Catholic Habsburgs. The forces of the Catholic Reformation (see page 428) promoted a Catholic spiritual revival in Bohemia, and some areas reconverted. This complicated situation would be one of the causes of the Thirty Years' War in the early seventeenth century.

By 1500 Poland and the Grand Duchy of Lithuania were jointly governed by king, senate, and diet (parliament), but the two territories retained separate officials, judicial systems, armies, and forms of citizenship. The combined realms covered almost 500,000 square miles, making Poland-Lithuania the largest European polity. A population of only about 7.5 million people was very thinly scattered over that land.

The population of Poland-Lithuania was also very diverse; Germans, Italians, Tartars, and Jews lived with Poles and Lithuanians. Such peoples had come as merchants, invited by medieval rulers because of their wealth or to make agricultural improvements. Each group spoke its native language, though all educated people spoke Latin. Luther's ideas took root in Germanized towns but were opposed by King Sigismund I (r. 1506–1548) as well as by ordinary Poles, who held strong anti-German feeling. The Reformed tradition of John Calvin, with its stress on the power of church elders, appealed to the Polish nobility, however. The fact that Calvinism originated in France, not in Germany, also made it more attractive than Lutheranism. But doctrinal differences among Calvinists, Lutherans, and other groups prevented united opposition to Catholicism, and a Counter-Reformation gained momentum. By 1650, due to the efforts of Stanislaus Hosius (1505–1579) and those of the Jesuits (see page 431), Poland was again staunchly Roman Catholic.

Hungary's experience with the Reformation was even more complex. Lutheranism was spread by Hungarian students who had studied at Wittenberg, and sympathy for it developed at the royal court of King Louis II in Buda. But concern about "the German heresy" by the Catholic hierarchy and among the high nobles found expression in a decree of the Hungarian diet in 1523 that "all Lutherans and those favoring them . . . should have their property confiscated and themselves punished with death as heretics."[8]

Before such measures could be acted on, a military event on August 26, 1526, had profound consequences for both the Hungarian state and the Protestant Reformation there. On the plain of Mohács in southern Hungary, the Ottoman sultan Suleiman the Magnificent inflicted a crushing defeat on the Hungarians, killing King Louis II, many of the nobles, and more than sixteen thousand ordinary soldiers. The Hungarian kingdom was then divided into three parts: the Ottoman Turks absorbed the great plains, including the capital, Buda; the Habsburgs ruled the north and west; and Ottoman-supported Janos Zapolya held eastern Hungary and Transylvania.

The Turks were indifferent to the religious conflicts of Christians, whom they regarded as infidels. Christians of all types paid extra taxes to the sultan, but kept their faith. Many Magyar (Hungarian) nobles accepted Lutheranism; Lutheran schools and parishes headed by men educated at Wittenberg multiplied; and peasants

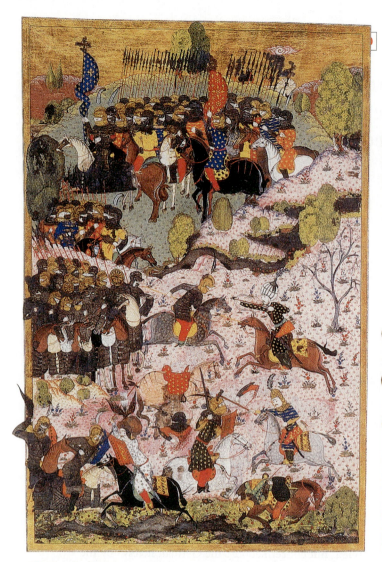 

The Battle of Mohács Massed armies on both sides confront each other in this Turkish illustration of the Battle of Mohács. In the right panel, Suleiman in a white turban sits on a black horse surrounded by his personal guard, while his soldiers fire muskets and large cannon at the enemy. In the left panel the Europeans are in disarray, and their weapons are clearly inferior. (Topkapi Saray Museum)

welcomed the new faith. The majority of people were Protestant until the late seventeenth century, when Hungarian nobles recognized Habsburg (Catholic) rule and Ottoman Turkish withdrawal in 1699 led to Catholic restoration.

The Catholic Reformation

How did the Catholic Church respond to the new religious situation?

Between 1517 and 1547 Protestantism made remarkable advances. Nevertheless, the Roman Catholic Church made a significant comeback. After about 1540 no new large areas of Europe, other than the Netherlands, accepted Protestant beliefs (Map 14.2). Many historians see the developments within the Catholic Church after the Protestant Reformation as two interrelated movements, one a drive for internal reform linked to earlier reform efforts, and the other a Counter-Reformation that opposed Protestants intellectually, politically, militarily, and institutionally. In both movements, the papacy, new religious orders, and the Council of Trent that met from 1545 to 1563 were important agents.

Papal Reform and the Council of Trent

Renaissance popes and their advisers were not blind to the need for church reforms, but they resisted calls for a general council representing the entire church, and feared that any transformation would mean a loss of power, revenue, and prestige. This changed beginning with Pope Paul III (pontificate 1534–1549), when the papal court became the center of the reform movement rather than its chief opponent. The lives of the pope and his reform-minded cardinals, abbots, and bishops were models of

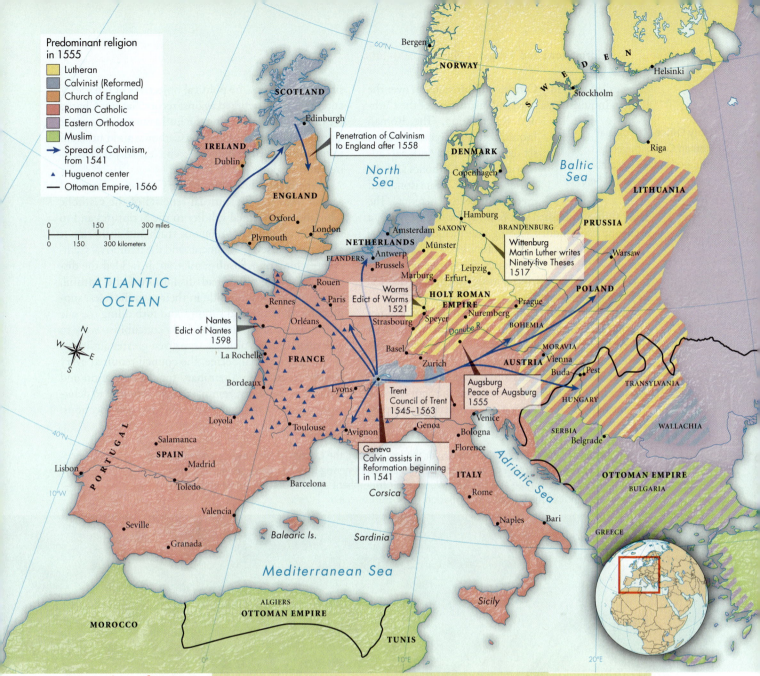

Mapping the Past

Map 14.2 Religious Divisions in Europe, ca. 1555 The Reformations shattered the religious unity of Western Christendom. The situation was even more complicated than a map of this scale can show. Many cities within the Holy Roman Empire, for example, accepted a different faith than the surrounding countryside; Augsburg, Basel, and Strasbourg were all Protestant, though surrounded by territory ruled by Catholic nobles.

ANALYZING THE MAP Which countries were the most religiously diverse in Europe? Which were the least diverse?

CONNECTIONS Where was the first arena of religious conflict in sixteenth-century Europe, and why did it develop there and not elsewhere? To what degree can nonreligious factors be used as an explanation for the religious divisions in sixteenth-century Europe?

To complete this activity online, go to the Online Study Guide at bedfordstmartins.com/mckaywest.

decorum and piety, in contrast to Renaissance popes who concentrated on building churches and enhancing the power of their own families. Paul III and his successors supported improvements in education for the clergy, the end of simony (the selling of church offices), and stricter control of clerical life.

In 1542 Pope Paul III established the Supreme Sacred Congregation of the Roman and Universal Inquisition, often called the **Holy Office**, with jurisdiction over the Roman Inquisition, a powerful instrument of the Catholic Reformation. The Roman Inquisition was a committee of six cardinals with judicial authority over all Catholics and the power to arrest, imprison, and execute suspected heretics. The Holy Office published the *Index of Prohibited Books*, a catalogue of forbidden reading that included works by Christian humanists such as Erasmus as well as by Protestants. Within the Papal States, the Inquisition effectively destroyed heresy, but outside the papal territories, its influence was slight.

Pope Paul III also called a general council, which met intermittently from 1545 to 1563 at Trent, an imperial city close to Italy. It was called not only to reform the Catholic Church but also to secure reconciliation with the Protestants. Lutherans and Calvinists were invited to participate, but their insistence that the Scriptures be the sole basis for discussion made reconciliation impossible. In addition, the political objectives of Charles V and France both worked against reconciliation: Charles wanted to avoid alienating the Lutheran nobility in the empire, and France wanted the Catholics and Lutherans to remain divided in order to keep Germany decentralized and weak.

Nonetheless, the decrees of the Council of Trent laid a solid basis for the spiritual renewal of the Catholic Church. It gave equal validity to the Scriptures and to tradition as sources of religious truth and authority. It reaffirmed the seven sacraments and the traditional Catholic teaching on transubstantiation. It tackled the disciplinary matters that had disillusioned the faithful, requiring bishops to reside in their own dioceses, suppressing pluralism and simony, and forbidding the sale of indulgences. Clerics who kept concubines were to give them up, and bishops were given greater authority. In a highly original decree, the council required every diocese to establish a seminary for the education and training of the clergy. Seminary professors were to determine whether candidates for ordination had vocations,

> **Holy Office** The official Roman Catholic agency founded in 1542 to combat international doctrinal heresy.

Church of the Gesù Begun in 1568 as the mother church for the Jesuit order, the Church of the Gesù conveyed a sense of drama, motion, and power through its lavish decorations and shimmering frescoes. Gesù served as a model for Catholic churches elsewhere in Europe and the New World, their triumphant and elaborate style reflecting the dynamic and proselytizing spirit of the Catholic Reformation. (The Art Archive/Corbis)

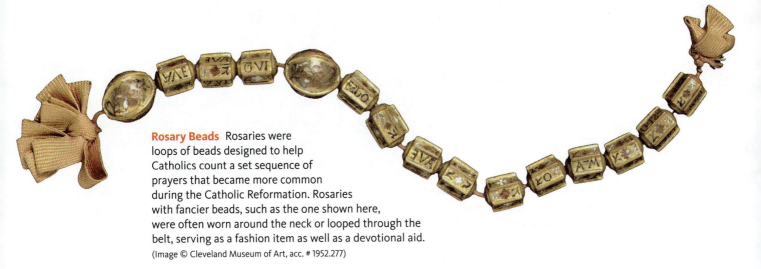

Rosary Beads Rosaries were loops of beads designed to help Catholics count a set sequence of prayers that became more common during the Catholic Reformation. Rosaries with fancier beads, such as the one shown here, were often worn around the neck or looped through the belt, serving as a fashion item as well as a devotional aid. (Image © Cleveland Museum of Art, acc. # 1952.277)

genuine callings to the priesthood. This was a novel idea, since from the time of the early church, parents had determined their sons' (and daughters') religious careers. For the first time, great emphasis was laid on preaching and instructing the laity, especially the uneducated.

One decision had especially important social consequences for laypeople. The Council of Trent stipulated that for a marriage to be valid, the marriage vows had to be made publicly before a priest and witnesses. Trent thereby ended the widespread practice of private marriages in Catholic countries, curtailing the number of denials and conflicts that inevitably resulted from marriages that took place in secret.

Although it did not achieve all of its goals, the Council of Trent composed decrees that laid a solid basis for the spiritual renewal of the church. The doctrinal and disciplinary legislation of Trent served as the basis for Roman Catholic faith, organization, and practice through the middle of the twentieth century.

New Religious Orders

The establishment of new religious orders within the church reveals a central feature of the Catholic Reformation. Most of these new orders developed in response to one crying need: to raise the moral and intellectual level of the clergy and people. (See "Individuals in Society: Teresa of Ávila," page 432.) Education was a major goal of the two most famous orders.

The Ursuline order of nuns, founded by Angela Merici (1474–1540), attained enormous prestige for the education of women. The daughter of a country gentleman, Angela Merici worked for many years among the poor, sick, and uneducated around her native Brescia in northern Italy. In 1535 she established the first women's religious order concentrating exclusively on teaching young girls, with the goal of re-Christianizing society by training future wives and mothers. After receiving papal approval in 1565, the Ursulines rapidly spread to France and the New World.

The Society of Jesus, or **Jesuits**, founded by Ignatius Loyola (1491–1556) played a powerful international role in strengthening Catholicism in Europe and spreading the faith around the world. While recuperating from a severe battle wound in his legs, Loyola studied books about Christ and the saints and decided to give up his military career and become a soldier of Christ. During a year spent in seclusion, prayer, and asceticism, he gained insights that went into his great classic, *Spiritual Exercises* (1548). This work, intended for study during a four-week period of retreat, set out a training program of structured meditation designed to develop spiritual discipline and allow one to meld one's will with that of God. Loyola introduces his program by noting:

> **Jesuits** Members of the Society of Jesus, founded by Ignatius Loyola, whose goal was the spread of the Roman Catholic faith.

> By the term "Spiritual Exercises" is meant every method of examination of conscience, of meditation, of contemplation, of vocal and mental prayer, and of other spiritual activities. For just as taking a walk, journeying on foot, and running are bodily exercises, so we call Spiritual Exercises every way of preparing and disposing the soul to rid itself of all inordinate attachments, and, after their removal, of seeking and finding the will of God in the disposition of our life for the salvation of our soul.[9]

Just as do today's physical trainers, Loyola provides daily exercises that build in intensity over the four weeks of the program, and charts on which the exerciser can track his progress.

Loyola was a man of considerable personal magnetism. After study at universities in Salamanca and Paris, he gathered a group of six companions and in 1540 secured papal approval of the new Society of Jesus. The first Jesuits, recruited primarily from wealthy merchant

Individuals in Society

Teresa of Ávila

HER FAMILY DERIVED FROM TOLEDO, center of the Moorish, Jewish, and Christian cultures in medieval Spain. Her grandfather, Juan Sanchez, made a fortune in the cloth trade. A New Christian (a convert from Judaism or Islam), he was accused of secretly practicing Judaism. He endured the humiliation of a public repentance and moved his family south to Ávila. Beginning again, he recouped his wealth and, perhaps hoping to hide his status as a convert, bought noble status. Juan's son Alzonzo Sanchez de Cepeda married a woman of thoroughly Christian background, giving his family an aura of impeccable orthodoxy. The third of their nine children, Teresa, became a saint and in 1970 was the first woman declared a Doctor of the Church, a title given to a theologian of outstanding merit.

At age twenty, inspired more by the fear of Hell than the love of God, Teresa (1515–1582) entered the Carmelite Convent of the Incarnation in Ávila. Most of the nuns were daughters of Ávila's leading citizens; they had entered the convent because of family decisions about which daughters would marry and which would become nuns. Their lives were much like those of female family members outside the convent walls, with good food, comfortable surroundings, and frequent visits from family and friends. Teresa was frequently ill, but she lived quietly in the convent for many years. In her late thirties, she began to read devotional literature intensely and had profound mystical experiences — visions and voices in which Christ chastised her for her frivolous life and friends. She described one such experience in 1560:

> It pleased the Lord that I should see an angel. . . . Short, and very beautiful, his face was so aflame that he appeared to be one of the highest types of angels. . . . In his hands I saw a long golden spear and at the end of an iron tip I seemed to see a point of fire. With this he seemed to pierce my heart several times so that it penetrated to my entrails. When he drew it out . . . he left me completely afire with the great love of God.*

Teresa responded with a new sense of purpose and resolved to found a reformed house. Four basic principles guided the new convent. First, poverty was to be fully observed, symbolized by the nuns' being barefoot, with charity and the nuns' own work supporting the community. Second, the convent must keep strict enclosure, with no visitors allowed, even if they were the convent's wealthy supporters. Third, the convent was to have an egalitarian atmosphere in which class distinctions were forbidden and all sisters, including those of aristocratic background, shared the manual chores. The discriminatory measures common in Spanish society that applied to New Christians were also not to be practiced. Fourth, like Ignatius Loyola and the Jesuits, Teresa placed great emphasis on obedience, especially to one's confessor.

Between 1562 and Teresa's death in 1582, she founded or reformed fourteen other houses of nuns, traveling widely to do so. Teresa thought of the new religious houses she founded as answers to the Protestant takeover of Catholic churches elsewhere in Europe. From her brother, who had obtained wealth in the Spanish colonies, she learned about conditions in Peru and instructed her nuns "to pray unceasingly for the missionaries working among the heathens." Through prayer, Teresa wrote, her nuns could share in the exciting tasks of evangelization and missionary work otherwise closed to women. Her books, along with her five hundred surviving letters, show her as a practical and down-to-earth woman as well as a mystic and a creative theologian.

Seventeenth-century cloisonné enamelwork illustrating Teresa of Ávila's famous vision of an angel piercing her heart. (By gracious permission of Catherine Hamilton Kappauf)

QUESTIONS FOR ANALYSIS

1. How did convent life in Ávila reflect the values of sixteenth-century society, and how did Teresa's reforms challenge these?
2. How is the life of Teresa of Ávila typical of developments in the Catholic Reformation? How is her life unusual?

*The Autobiography of St. Teresa of Ávila, trans. and ed. E. A. Peers (New York: Doubleday, 1960), pp. 273–274.

and professional families, saw the Reformation as a pastoral problem, its causes and cures related not to doctrinal issues but to people's spiritual condition. Reform of the church, as Luther and Calvin understood that term, played no role in the future the Jesuits planned for themselves. Their goal was "to help souls."

The Society of Jesus developed into a highly centralized, tightly knit organization. In addition to the traditional vows of poverty, chastity, and obedience, professed members vowed special obedience to the pope. Flexibility and the willingness to respond to the needs of time and circumstance formed the Jesuit tradition, which proved attractive to many young men. The Jesuits achieved phenomenal success for the papacy and the reformed Catholic Church, carrying Christianity to India and Japan before 1550 and to Brazil, North America, and the Congo in the seventeenth century. Within Europe the Jesuits brought southern Germany and much of eastern Europe back to Catholicism. Jesuit schools adopted the modern humanist curricula and methods, educating the sons of the nobility as well as the poor. As confessors and spiritual directors to kings, Jesuits exerted great political influence.

Religious Violence

What were the causes and consequences of religious violence, including riots, wars, and witch-hunts?

In 1559 France and Spain signed the Treaty of Cateau-Cambrésis (CAH-toh kam-BRAY-sees), which ended the long conflict known as the Habsburg-Valois wars. Spain was the victor. France, exhausted by the struggle, had to acknowledge Spanish dominance in Italy, where much of the fighting had taken place. However, true peace was elusive, and over the next century religious differences led to riots, civil wars, and international conflicts. Especially in France and the Netherlands, Protestants and Catholics used violent actions as well as preaching and teaching against each other, for each side regarded the other as a poison in the community that would provoke the wrath of God. Catholics continued to believe that Calvinists and Lutherans could be reconverted; Protestants persisted in thinking that the Roman church should be destroyed. Catholics and Protestants alike feared people of other faiths, whom they often saw as agents of Satan. Even more, they feared those who were explicitly identified with Satan: witches living in their midst. This era was the time of the most virulent witch persecutions in European history, as both Protestants and Catholics tried to make their cities and states more godly.

French Religious Wars

The costs of the Habsburg-Valois wars, waged intermittently through the first half of the sixteenth century, forced the French to increase taxes and borrow heavily. King Francis I (r. 1515–1547) also tried two new devices to raise revenue: the sale of public offices and a treaty with the papacy. The former proved to be only a temporary source of money: once a man bought an office he and his heirs were exempt from taxation. But the latter, known as the Concordat of Bologna (see page 399), gave the French crown the right to appoint all French bishops and abbots, ensuring a rich supplement of money and offices. Because French rulers possessed control over appointments and had a vested financial interest in Catholicism, they had no need to revolt against Rome.

Significant numbers of those ruled, however, were attracted to the Reformed religion of Calvinism. Initially, Calvinism drew converts from among reform-minded members of the Catholic clergy, industrious city dwellers, and artisan groups. Most French Calvinists (called **Huguenots**) lived in major cities, such as Paris, Lyons, and Rouen. When King Henry II (r. 1547–1559) died in 1559—accidentally shot in the face at a tournament celebrating the Treaty of Cateau-Cambrésis—perhaps one-tenth of the population had become Calvinist.

Huguenots French Calvinists.

The feebleness of the French monarchy was the seed from which the weeds of civil violence sprang. The three weak sons of Henry II who occupied the throne could not provide the necessary leadership, and they were often dominated by their mother, Catherine de' Medici. The French nobility took advantage of this monarchical weakness. Just as German princes in the Holy Roman Empire had adopted Lutheranism as a means of opposition to Emperor Charles V, so French nobles frequently adopted Protestantism as a religious cloak for their independence. Armed clashes between Catholic royalist lords and Calvinist antimonarchical lords occurred in many parts of France. Both Calvinists and Catholics believed that the others' books, services, and ministers polluted the community. Preachers incited violence, and religious ceremonies such as baptisms, marriages, and funerals triggered it.

Calvinist teachings called the power of sacred images into question, and mobs in many cities took down and smashed statues, stained-glass windows, and paintings, viewing this as a way to purify the church. Though it was often inspired by fiery Protestant sermons, this iconoclasm, or destruction of religious images, is an example of ordinary men and women carrying out the Reformation themselves. Catholic mobs responded by defending images, and crowds on both sides killed their opponents, often in gruesome ways.

A savage Catholic attack on Calvinists in Paris on Saint Bartholomew's Day, August 24, 1572, followed the usual pattern. The occasion was the marriage ceremony of the king's sister Margaret of Valois to the Protestant Henry of Navarre, which was intended to help reconcile Catholics and Huguenots. Instead, Huguenot wedding guests in Paris were massacred, and other Protestants were slaughtered by mobs. Religious violence spread to the provinces, where thousands were killed. This Saint Bartholomew's Day massacre led to a civil war that dragged on for fifteen years. Agriculture in many areas was destroyed; commercial life declined severely; and starvation and death haunted the land.

What ultimately saved France was a small group of moderates of both faiths, called **politiques**, who believed that only the restoration of strong monarchy could reverse the trend toward collapse. The politiques also favored accepting the Huguenots as an officially recognized and organized group. The death of Catherine de' Medici, followed by the assassination of King Henry III, paved the way for the accession of Henry of Navarre (the unfortunate bridegroom of the Saint Bartholomew's Day massacre), a politique who became Henry IV (r. 1589–1610).

Henry's willingness to sacrifice religious principles to political necessity saved France. He converted to Catholicism but also issued the **Edict of Nantes** in 1598, which granted liberty of conscience and liberty of public worship to Huguenots in 150 fortified towns. The reign of Henry IV and the Edict of Nantes prepared the way for French absolutism in the seventeenth century by helping restore internal peace in France.

The Netherlands Under Charles V

In the Netherlands, what began as a movement for the reformation of the church developed into a struggle for Dutch independence. Emperor Charles V had inherited the seventeen provinces that compose present-day Belgium and the Netherlands (see page 420). Each was self-governing and enjoyed the right to make its own laws and collect its own taxes. The provinces were united politically only in recognition of a common ruler, the emperor. The cities of the Netherlands made their living by trade and industry.

In the Low Countries as elsewhere, corruption in the Roman church and the critical spirit of the Renaissance provoked pressure for reform, and Lutheran ideas took root. Charles V had grown up in the Netherlands, however, and he was able to limit their impact. But Charles V abdicated in 1556 and transferred power over the Netherlands to his son Philip II, who had grown up in Spain. Protestant ideas spread.

By the 1560s Protestants in the Netherlands were primarily Calvinists. Calvinism's intellectual seriousness, moral gravity, and emphasis on any form of labor well done appealed to urban merchants, financiers, and artisans. Whereas Lutherans taught respect for the powers that be, Calvinism tended to encourage opposition to political authorities who were judged to be ungodly.

politiques Catholic and Protestant moderates who held that only a strong monarchy could save France from total collapse.

Edict of Nantes A document issued by Henry IV of France in 1598, granting liberty of conscience and of public worship to Calvinists, which helped restore peace in France.

Iconoclasm in the Netherlands Calvinist men and women break stained-glass windows, remove statues, and carry off devotional altarpieces. Iconoclasm, or the destruction of religious images, is often described as a "riot," but here the participants seem very purposeful. Calvinist Protestants regarded pictures and statues as sacrilegious and saw removing them as a way to purify the church. (The Fotomas Index/The Bridgeman Art Library)

When Spanish authorities attempted to suppress Calvinist worship and raised taxes in the 1560s, rioting ensued. Calvinists sacked thirty Catholic churches in Antwerp, destroying the religious images in them in a wave of iconoclasm. From Antwerp the destruction spread. Philip II sent twenty thousand Spanish troops under the duke of Alva to pacify the Low Countries. Alva interpreted "pacification" to mean ruthless extermination of religious and political dissidents. On top of the Inquisition, he opened his own tribunal, soon called the "Council of Blood." On March 3, 1568, fifteen hundred men were executed. To Calvinists, all this was clear indication that Spanish rule was ungodly and should be overthrown.

The Netherlands, 1609

Between 1568 and 1578 civil war raged in the Netherlands between Catholics and Protestants and between the seventeen provinces and Spain. Eventually the ten southern provinces, the Spanish Netherlands (the future Belgium), came under the control of the Spanish Habsburg forces. The seven northern provinces, led by Holland, formed the **Union of Utrecht** and in 1581 declared their independence from Spain. The north was Protestant; the south remained Catholic. Philip did not accept this, and war continued. England was even drawn into the conflict, supplying money and troops to the northern United Provinces. (Spain launched an unsuccessful invasion of England in response; see page 425.) Hostilities ended in 1609 when Spain agreed to a truce that recognized the independence of the United Provinces.

The Great European Witch-Hunt

The relationship between the Reformation and the upsurge in trials for witchcraft that occurred at roughly the same time is complex. Increasing persecution for witchcraft actually began before the Reformation in the 1480s, but it became especially common about 1560, and the mania continued until roughly 1660. Religious reformers' extreme notions of the Devil's powers and the insecurity created by the religious wars contributed to this increase. Both Protestants and Catholics tried and executed witches, with church officials and secular authorities acting together.

The heightened sense of God's power and divine wrath in the Reformation era was an important factor in the witch-hunts, but so was a change in the idea of what a witch was. Nearly all premodern societies believe in witchcraft and make some attempts to control witches, who are understood to be people who use magical forces. In the later Middle Ages, however, many educated Christian theologians, canon lawyers, and officials added a demonological component to this notion of what a witch was. For them, the essence of witchcraft was making a pact with the Devil. Witches were no longer simply people who used magical power to get what they wanted, but rather people used by the Devil to do what he wanted. Witches were thought to engage in wild sexual orgies with the Devil, fly through the night to meetings called sabbats that parodied Christian services, and steal communion wafers and unbaptized babies to use in their rituals. Some demonological theorists also claimed that witches were organized in an international conspiracy to overthrow Christianity. Witchcraft was thus spiritualized, and witches became the ultimate heretics, enemies of God.

Trials involving this new notion of witchcraft as diabolical heresy began in Switzerland and southern Germany in the late fifteenth century, became less numerous in the early decades of the Reformation when Protestants and Catholics were busy fighting each other, and then picked up again in about 1560. Scholars estimate that during the sixteenth and seventeenth centuries between 100,000 and 200,000 people were officially tried for witchcraft and between 40,000 and 60,000 were executed.

Union of Utrecht
The alliance of seven northern provinces (led by Holland) that declared its independence from Spain and formed the United Provinces of the Netherlands.

Though the gender balance varied widely in different parts of Europe, between 75 and 85 percent of those tried and executed were women. Ideas about women and the roles women actually played in society were thus important factors shaping the witch-hunts. Some demonologists expressed virulent misogyny, or hatred of women, and particularly emphasized women's powerful sexual desire, which could be satisfied only by a demonic lover. Most people viewed women as weaker and so more likely to give in to an offer by the Devil. In both classical and Christian traditions, women were associated with nature, disorder, and the body, all of which were linked with the demonic. Women's actual lack of power in society and gender norms about the use of violence meant that they were more likely to use scolding and cursing to get what they wanted instead of taking people to court or beating them up. Curses were generally expressed (as they often are today) in religious terms; "go to Hell" was calling on the powers of Satan. Women also had more contact with areas of life in which bad things happened unexpectedly, such as preparing food or caring for new mothers, children, and animals.

Legal changes also played a role in causing, or at least allowing for, massive witch trials. One of these was a change from an accusatorial legal procedure to an inquisitorial procedure. In the former, a suspect knew the accusers and the charges they had brought, and an accuser could in turn be liable for trial if the charges were not proven. In the latter, legal authorities themselves brought the case. This change made people much more willing to accuse others, for they never had to take personal responsibility for the accusation or face the accused person's relatives. Areas in Europe that did not make this legal change saw very few trials. Inquisitorial procedure involved intense questioning of the suspect, often with torture. Torture was also used to get the names of additional suspects, as most lawyers firmly believed that no witch could act alone.

The use of inquisitorial procedure did not always lead to witch-hunts. The most famous inquisitions in early modern Europe, those in Spain, Portugal, and Italy, were in fact very lenient in their treatment of people accused of witchcraft. The Inquisition in Spain executed only a handful of witches, the Portuguese Inquisition only one, and the Roman Inquisition none, though in each of these there were hundreds of cases. Inquisitors believed in the power of the Devil and were no less misogynist than other judges, but they doubted very much whether the people accused of witchcraft had actually made pacts with the Devil that gave them special powers. They viewed such people not as diabolical Devil-worshipers but as superstitious and ignorant peasants who should be educated

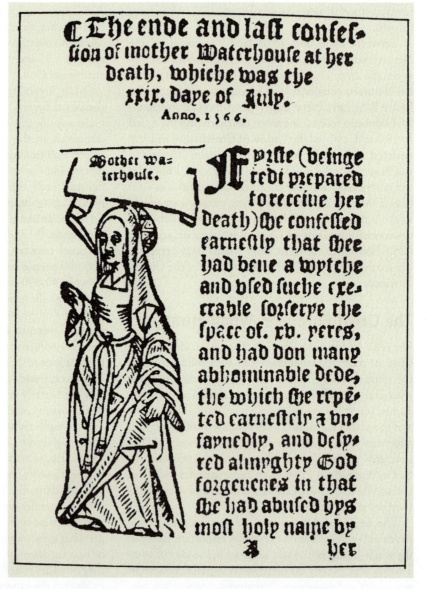

Witch Pamphlet This printed pamphlet presents the confession of "Mother Waterhouse," a woman convicted of witchcraft in England in 1566, who describes her "many abominable deeds" and "execrable sorcery" committed over fifteen years, and asks for forgiveness right before her execution. Enterprising printers often produced cheap, short pamphlets during witch trials, knowing they would sell, sometimes based on the actual trial proceedings and sometimes just made up. They both reflected and helped create stereotypes about what witches were and did. (The Granger Collection, New York)

rather than executed. Thus most people brought up before the Inquisition for witchcraft were sent home with a warning and a penance.

Most witch trials began with a single accusation in a village or town. Individuals accused someone they knew of using magic to spoil food, make children ill, kill animals, raise a hailstorm, or do other types of harm. Tensions within families, households, and neighborhoods often played a role in these accusations. Women number very prominently among accusers and witnesses as well as among those accused of witchcraft because the actions witches were initially charged with, such as harming children or curdling milk, were generally part of women's sphere. A woman also gained economic and social security by conforming to the standard of the good wife and mother and by confronting women who deviated from it.

Once a charge was made, the suspect was brought in for questioning. One German witch pamphlet from 1587 described a typical case:

> *Walpurga Hausmännin . . . upon kindly questioning and also torture . . . confessed . . . that the Evil One indulged in fornication with her . . . and made her many promises to help her in her poverty and need. . . . She promised herself body and soul to him and disowned God in heaven. . . . She destroyed a number of cattle, pigs, and geese . . . and dug up [the bodies] of one or two innocent children. With her devil-paramour and other playfellows she has eaten these and used their hair and their little bones for witchcraft.*

Confession was generally followed by execution. In this case, Hausmännin was "dispatched from life to death by burning at the stake . . . her body first to be torn five times with red-hot irons."[10]

Detailed records of witch trials survive for many parts of Europe. They have been used by historians to study many aspects of witchcraft, but they cannot directly answer what seems to us an important question: did people really practice witchcraft and think they were witches? They certainly confessed to evil deeds and demonic practices, sometimes without torture, but where would we draw the line between reality and fantasy? Clearly people were not riding through the air on pitchforks, but did they think they did? Did they actually invoke the Devil when they were angry at a neighbor, or was this simply in the minds of their accusers? Trial records cannot tell us, and historians have answered these questions very differently, often using insights from psychoanalysis or the study of more recent victims of torture in their explanations.

> ❝ Walpurga Hausmännin . . . dug up [the bodies] of one or two innocent children. With her devil-paramour and other playfellows she has eaten these and used their hair and their little bones for witchcraft. ❞
>
> —GERMAN WITCH PAMPHLET

After the initial suspect had been questioned, and particularly if he or she had been tortured, the people who had been implicated were brought in for questioning. This might lead to a small hunt, involving from five to ten suspects, and it sometimes grew into a much larger hunt, what historians have called a "witch panic." Panics were most common in the part of Europe that saw the most witch accusations in general: the Holy Roman Empire, Switzerland, and parts of France. Most of this area consisted of very small governmental units that were jealous of each other and, after the Reformation, were divided by religion. The rulers of these small territories often felt more threatened than did the monarchs of western Europe, and they saw persecuting witches as a way to demonstrate their piety and concern for order. Moreover, witch panics often occurred after some type of climatic disaster, such as an unusually cold and wet summer, and they came in waves.

In large-scale panics a wider variety of suspects were taken in — wealthier people, children, a greater proportion of men. Mass panics tended to end when it became clear to legal authorities, or to the community itself, that the people being questioned or executed were not what they understood witches to be, or that the scope of accusations was beyond belief. Some from their community might be in league with Satan, they thought, but not this type of person and not as many people as this.

As the seventeenth century ushered in new ideas about science and reason, many began to question whether witches could make pacts with the Devil or engage in the wild activities attributed to them. Doubts about whether secret denunciations were valid or torture would ever yield truthful confessions gradually spread among the same type of religious and legal authorities who had so vigorously persecuted witches. Prosecutions for witchcraft became less common and were gradually outlawed. The last official execution for witchcraft in England was in 1682, though the last one in the Holy Roman Empire was not until 1775.

LOOKING BACK LOOKING AHEAD

ALONG WITH THE RENAISSANCE, the Reformation is often seen as a key element in the creation of the "modern" world. This radical change contained many elements of continuity, however. Sixteenth-century reformers looked back to the early Christian church for their inspiration, and many of their reforming ideas had been advocated for centuries. Most Protestant reformers worked with political leaders to make religious changes, just as early church officials had worked with Emperor Constantine and his successors as Christianity became the official religion of the Roman Empire in the fourth century. The spread of Christianity and the spread of Protestantism were accomplished not only by preaching, persuasion, and teaching, but also by force and violence. The Catholic Reformation was carried out by activist popes, a church council, and new religious orders, just as earlier reforms of the church had been.

Just as they linked with earlier developments, the events of the Reformation were also closely connected with what is often seen as the third element in the "modern" world: European exploration and colonization. Only a week after Martin Luther stood in front of Charles V at the Diet of Worms declaring his independence in matters of religion, Ferdinand Magellan, a Portuguese sea captain with Spanish ships, was killed in a group of islands off the coast of Southeast Asia. Charles V had provided the backing for Magellan's voyage, the first to circumnavigate the globe. Magellan viewed the spread of Christianity as one of the purposes of his trip, and later in the sixteenth century institutions created as part of the Catholic Reformation, including the Jesuit order and the Inquisition, would operate in European colonies overseas as well as in Europe itself. The islands where Magellan was killed were later named the Philippines, in honor of Charles's son Philip, who sent the ill-fated Spanish Armada against England. Philip's opponent Queen Elizabeth was similarly honored when English explorers named a huge chunk of territory in North America "Virginia" as a tribute to their "Virgin Queen." The desire for wealth and power was an important motivation in the European voyages and colonial ventures, but so was religious zeal.

CHAPTER REVIEW

■ **What were the central ideas of the reformers, and why were they appealing to different social groups? (p. 408)**

By the early sixteenth century many lay Christians and members of the clergy had grown disillusioned with the church's wealth and certain practices, particularly its sale of indulgences and church offices. People were also critical of the immorality, ignorance, and absenteeism that they perceived among the clergy, and for centuries many individuals and groups had called for reform. Amid this background Luther and other Protestants developed a new understanding of Christian doctrine that emphasized faith, the power of God's grace, and the centrality of the Bible. Protestant ideas were attractive to educated people and urban residents, among whom anticlericalism had become widespread, and the new concepts spread rapidly among many groups through preaching, hymns, and the printing press. Most Protestant reformers worked with rulers to bring about religious change, but more radical thinkers and the German peasants wanted political and social, as well as religious, changes. Both radicals and the peasants were put down harshly. The Protestant reformers did not break with medieval ideas about the proper gender hierarchy, though they did elevate the status of marriage and viewed orderly households as the key building blocks of society.

■ **How did the political situation in Germany shape the course of the Reformation? (p. 419)**

Beginning in 1519 the Habsburg emperor Charles V ruled almost half of Europe along with Spain's overseas colonies. Within the empire his authority was limited, however, and local princes, nobles, and cities actually held most power. This decentralization allowed the Reformation to spread as local rulers assumed religious authority. Charles remained firmly Catholic, and in the late 1520s religious wars began in central Europe. The papacy and Catholic kings of France initially supported Charles V's cause, but they withdrew support when he began gaining too much ground. The wars were brought to an end with the Peace of Augsburg in 1555, which officially recognized Lutheranism and allowed rulers in each territory to choose whether their territory would be Catholic or Lutheran.

■ **How did Protestant ideas and institutions spread beyond German-speaking lands? (p. 422)**

Outside of Germany, Protestantism spread first to Scandinavia and then elsewhere in northern Europe. In England, Henry VIII's desire for an annulment triggered the split with Rome, and a Protestant church was established, first differing little from Catholicism in terms of theology and later, under Queen Elizabeth, breaking more firmly with Catholic practice. The printing press and increased literacy of European society, as well as the growing number of universities, allowed Protestant ideas to spread rapidly into France and eastern Europe. In all these areas, a second generation of reformers built on Lutheran and Zwinglian ideas to develop their own theology and plans for institutional change. The most important of the second-generation reformers was John Calvin, whose ideas would come to shape Christianity over a much wider area than did Luther's.

■ **How did the Catholic Church respond to the new religious situation? (p. 428)**

By the 1530s the papacy was leading a movement for reform within the church and countering Protestant challenges. Catholic doctrine was reaffirmed at the Council of Trent, and reform measures such as the opening of seminaries for priests, the insistence on morality for the clergy, and a ban on holding multiple church offices were introduced. New religious orders such as the Jesuits and the Ursulines spread Catholic ideas through teaching, and in the case of the Jesuits through missionary work.

■ **What were the causes and consequences of religious violence, including riots, wars, and witch-hunts? (p. 433)**

Religious differences led to riots, civil wars, and international conflicts in the later sixteenth century. In France and the Netherlands, Calvinist Protestants and Catholics used violent actions against one another, and religious differences mixed with political and economic grievances. Long civil wars resulted, with that in the Netherlands becoming an international conflict. War ended in France with the Edict of Nantes in which Protestants were given some civil rights, and in the Netherlands with a division of the country into a Protestant north and Catholic south. The era of religious wars was also a time of the most extensive witch persecutions in European history, as both Protestants and Catholics tried to rid their cities and states of people they regarded as linked to the Devil.

Suggested Reading

Bossy, John. *Christianity in the West, 1500–1700.* 1985. A lively brief overview.

Gordon, Bruce. *John Calvin.* 2009. Situates Calvin's theology and life within the context of his relationships and the historical events of his time.

Haigh, Christopher. *English Reformations: Religion, Politics, and Society under the Tudors.* 1998. Explores the religious views and practices of ordinary English people as well as of the political elite.

Hendrix, Scott. *Luther.* 2009. A brief introduction to his thought, in the Abingdon Pillars of Theology series.

Holt, Mack P. *The French Wars of Religion, 1562–1629.* 1995. A thorough survey designed for students.

Hsia, R. Po-Chia. *The World of Catholic Renewal, 1540–1770.* 1998. Situates the Catholic Reformation in a global context and provides coverage of colonial Catholicism.

Karant-Nunn, Susan C., and Merry E. Wiesner-Hanks, eds. and trans. *Luther on Women: A Sourcebook.* 2003. An extensive collection of Luther's writings on marriage, women, and sexuality.

Levack, Brian. *The Witchhunt in Early Modern Europe*, 3d ed. 2007. A good introduction to the witch-hunts, with helpful bibliographies of the vast literature on witchcraft.

Levi, Anthony. *Renaissance and Reformation: The Intellectual Genesis.* 2002. Surveys the ideas of major Reformation figures against the background of important political issues.

Lindbergh, Carter. *The European Reformations.* 1996. A thorough discussion of the Protestant Reformation and some discussion of Catholic issues.

Monter, William E. *Calvin's Geneva.* 1967. Shows the effect of Calvin's reforms on the social life of the Swiss city.

O'Malley, John W. *Trent and All That: Renaming Catholicism in the Early Modern Era.* 2000. Provides an excellent historiographical review of the literature, and explains why and how early modern Catholicism influenced early modern European history.

Roper, Lyndal. *The Holy Household: Women and Morals in Reformation Augsburg.* 1991. An important study in local religious history as well as the history of gender and the family.

Shagan, Ethan. *Popular Politics and the English Reformation.* 2003. Analyzes the process of the Reformation in local areas.

Wheatcroft, Andrew. *The Habsburgs: Embodying Empire.* 1995. A solid study of political developments surrounding the Reformation.

Key Terms

anticlericalism (p. 408)
pluralism (p. 408)
indulgence (p. 409)
Protestant (p. 412)
Spanish Armada (p. 425)
The Institutes of the Christian Religion (p. 425)
predestination (p. 426)
Holy Office (p. 430)
Jesuits (p. 431)
Huguenots (p. 433)
politiques (p. 434)
Edict of Nantes (p. 434)
Union of Utrecht (p. 435)

Notes

1. Quoted in Owen Chadwick, *The Reformation* (Baltimore: Penguin Books, 1976), p. 55.
2. Quoted in E. H. Harbison, *The Age of Reformation* (Ithaca, N.Y.: Cornell University Press, 1963), p. 52.
3. Quoted in S. E. Ozment, *The Age of Reform, 1250–1550: An Intellectual and Religious History of Late Medieval and Reformation Europe* (New Haven, Conn.: Yale University Press, 1980), p. 284.
4. Ludwig Rabus, *Historien der heyligen Außerwolten Gottes Zeugen, Bekennern und Martyrern* (n.p., 1557), fol. 41. Trans. Merry Wiesner-Hanks.
5. From Henry Bettenson, ed., *Documents of the Christian Church*, 2d ed. (London: Oxford University Press, 1963), pp. 301–302.
6. J. Allen, trans., *John Calvin: The Institutes of the Christian Religion* (Philadelphia: Westminster Press, 1930), bk. 3, chap. 21, para. 5, 7.
7. Quoted in E. William Monter, *Calvin's Geneva* (New York: John Wiley & Sons, 1967), p. 137.
8. Quoted in David P. Daniel, "Hungary," in *The Oxford Encyclopedia of the Reformation*, vol. 2, ed. H. J. Hillerbrand (New York: Oxford University Press, 1996), p. 273.
9. *The Spiritual Exercise of St. Ignatius of Loyola*, trans. Louis J. Puhl, S.J. (Chicago: Loyola University, 1951), p. 1.
10. From *the Fugger News-Letters*, ed. Victor von Klarwell, trans. P. de Chary (London: John Lane, The Boley Head Ltd., 1924), quoted in James Bruce Ross and Mary Martin McLaughlin, *The Portable Renaissance Reader* (New York: Penguin, 1968), pp. 258, 260, 262.

For practice quizzes and other study tools, visit the Online Study Guide at **bedfordstmartins.com/mckaywest**.

For primary sources from this period, see **Sources of Western Society, Second Edition**.

For Web sites, images, and documents related to topics in this chapter, visit Make History at **bedfordstmartins.com/mckaywest**.

15
European Exploration and Conquest
1450–1650

Before 1450 Europeans were relatively marginal players in a centuries-old trading system that linked Africa, Asia, and Europe. Elites everywhere prized Chinese porcelains and silks, while wealthy members of the Celestial Kingdom, as China called itself, wanted ivory and black slaves from Africa, and exotic goods and peacocks from India. African people wanted textiles from India and cowrie shells from the Maldives in the Indian Ocean. Europeans craved Asian silks and spices but they had few desirable goods to offer their trading partners.

The European search for better access to Asian trade led to a new overseas empire in the Indian Ocean and the accidental discovery of the Western Hemisphere. Within a few decades European colonies in South and North America would join this worldwide web. Europeans came to dominate trading networks and political empires of truly global proportions. The era of globalization had begun.

Global contacts created new forms of cultural exchange, assimilation, conversion, and resistance. Europeans struggled to comprehend the peoples and societies they found and sought to impose European cultural values on them. New forms of racial prejudice emerged, but so did new openness and curiosity about different ways of life. Together with the developments of the Renaissance and the Reformation, the Age of Discovery — as the period of European exploration and conquest from 1450 to 1650 is known — laid the foundations for the modern world. ■

the seventh through the fourteenth centuries, the volume of this trade steadily increased, declining only during the years of the Black Death.

Merchants congregated in a series of multicultural, cosmopolitan port cities strung around the Indian Ocean. Most of these cities had some form of autonomous self-government. Mutual self-interest had largely limited violence and attempts to monopolize trade. The most developed area of this commercial web was in the South China Sea. In the fifteenth century the port of Malacca (muh-LAH-kuh) became a great commercial entrepôt (AHN-truh-poh), a trading post to which goods were shipped for storage while awaiting redistribution to other places. To Malacca came Chinese porcelains, silks, and camphor (used in the manufacture of many medications); pepper, cloves, nutmeg, and raw materials such as sandalwood from the Moluccas; sugar from the Philippines; and Indian textiles, copper weapons, incense, dyes, and opium.

The Mongol emperors opened the doors of China to the West, encouraging Europeans like the Venetian trader and explorer Marco Polo to do business there. Marco Polo's tales of his travels from 1271 to 1295 and his encounter with the Great Khan fueled Western fantasies about the exotic Orient. After the Mongols fell to the Ming Dynasty in 1368, China entered a period of agricultural and commercial expansion, population growth, and urbanization. By the end of the dynasty in 1644, the Chinese population had tripled to between 150 million and 200 million. The city of Nanjing had one million inhabitants, making it the largest city in the world, while the new capital, Beijing, had more than six thousand inhabitants, larger than any European city. Historians agree that China had the most advanced economy in the world until at least the start of the eighteenth century.

China also took the lead in exploration, sending Admiral Zheng He's fleet along the trade web as far west as Egypt. From 1405 to 1433, each of his seven expeditions involved hundreds of ships and tens of thousands of men. In one voyage alone, Zheng He sailed more than 12,000 miles, compared to Columbus's 2,400 miles on his first voyage some sixty years later.[1] Court conflicts and the need to defend against renewed Mongol encroachment led to the abandonment of the expeditions after the deaths of Zheng He and the emperor. China's turning away from external trade opened new opportunities for European states to claim a decisive role in world trade.

Another center of trade in the Indian Ocean was India, the crucial link between the Persian Gulf and the Southeast Asian and East Asian trade networks. The subcontinent had ancient links with its neighbors to the northwest: trade between South Asia and Mesopotamia dates back to the origins of human civilization. Romans had acquired cotton textiles, exotic animals, and other luxury goods from India. Arab merchants who circumnavigated India on their way to trade in the South China Sea established trading posts along the southern coast of India, where the cities of Calicut and Quilon became thriving commercial centers. India was an important contributor of goods to the world trading system; much of the world's pepper was grown there, and Indian cotton textiles were highly prized.

The Trading States of Africa

Africa also played an important role in the world trade system before Columbus. By 1450 Africa had a few large and developed empires along with hundreds of smaller states. From 1250 until its defeat by the Ottomans in 1517, the Mamluk Egyptian empire was one of the most powerful on the continent. Its capital, Cairo, was a center of Islamic learning and religious authority as well as a hub for Indian Ocean trade goods. Sharing in Cairo's prosperity was the African highland state of Ethiopia, a Christian kingdom with scattered contacts with European rulers. On the east coast of Africa Swahili-speaking city-states engaged in the Indian Ocean trade, exchanging ivory, rhinoceros horn, tortoise shells, and slaves for textiles, spices, cowrie shells, porcelain, and other goods. Peopled by confident and urbane merchants, cities like Mogadishu and Mombasa were known for their prosperity and culture.

Another important African contribution to world trade was gold. In the fifteenth century most of the gold that reached Europe came from Sudan in West Africa and from the Akan (AH-kahn) peoples living near present-day Ghana (GAH-nuh). Transported across the Sahara by Arab and African traders on camels, the gold was sold in the ports of North Africa. Other trading routes led to the Egyptian cities of Alexandria and Cairo, where the Venetians held commercial privileges.

Chronology

1443	Portuguese establish first African trading post at Arguin
1492	Columbus lands in the Americas
1511	Portuguese capture Malacca from Muslims
1518	Spanish king authorizes slave trade to New World colonies
1519–1522	Magellan's expedition circumnavigates the world
1521	Cortés conquers the Mexica Empire
1533	Pizarro conquers the Inca Empire
1602	Dutch East India Company established

The Port of Banten in Western Java Influenced by Muslim traders and emerging in the early sixteenth century as a Muslim kingdom, Banten evolved into a thriving entrepôt. The city stood on the trade route to China and, as this Dutch engraving suggests, in the seventeenth century the Dutch East India Company used Banten as an important collection point for spices purchased for sale in Europe. (Archives Charmet/The Bridgeman Art Library)

Nations inland that sat astride the north-south caravan routes grew wealthy from this trade. In the mid-thirteenth century the kingdom of Mali emerged as an important player on the overland trade route. Malian ruler Mansa Musa reportedly discussed sending vessels to explore the Atlantic Ocean, which suggests that not only the Europeans envisaged westward naval exploration. In later centuries the diversion of gold away from the trans-Sahara routes would weaken the inland states of Africa politically and economically.

Gold was one important object of trade; slaves were another. Slavery was practiced in Africa, as virtually everywhere else in the world, before the arrival of Europeans. Arabic and African merchants took West African slaves to the Mediterranean to be sold in European, Egyptian, and Middle Eastern markets and also brought eastern Europeans—a major element of European slavery—to West Africa as slaves. In addition, Indian and Arabic merchants traded slaves in the coastal regions of East Africa.

Legends about Africa also played an important role in Europeans' imagination of the outside world. They long cherished the belief in a Christian nation in Africa ruled by a mythical king, Prester John, who was believed to be a descendant of one of the three kings who visited Jesus after his birth.

The Ottoman and Persian Empires

The Middle East served as an intermediary for trade between Europe, Africa, and Asia and was also an important supplier of goods for foreign exchange, especially silk and cotton. Two great rival empires, the Persian Safavids (sah-FAH-vidz) and the Turkish Ottomans, dominated the region. Persian merchants could be found in trading communities as far away as the Indian Ocean. Persia was also a major producer and exporter of silk.

The Persians' Shi'ite Muslim faith clashed with the Ottomans' adherence to Sunnism. Economically, the two competed for control over western trade routes to the East. Under Sultan Mohammed II (r. 1451–1481), the Ottomans captured Europe's largest city, Constantinople, in May 1453. Renamed Istanbul, the city became the capital of the Ottoman Empire. By the mid-sixteenth century the Ottomans controlled the sea trade in the eastern Mediterranean, Syria, Palestine, Egypt, and the rest of North Africa, and their power extended into Europe as far west as Vienna.

Ottoman expansion frightened Europeans. The Ottoman armies seemed nearly invincible and the empire's desire for expansion limitless. In France in the sixteenth century, twice as many books were printed about the Turkish threat as about the American discoveries. The strength of the Ottomans helps explain some of the missionary fervor Christians brought to new territories. It also raised economic concerns. With trade routes to the east in the hands of the Ottomans, Europeans needed to find new trade routes.

Genoese and Venetian Middlemen

Compared to the riches and vibrancy of the East, Europe constituted a minor outpost in the world trading system. European craftsmen produced few products to rival the fine wares and expensive spices of Asia. In the late Middle Ages, the Italian city-states of Venice and Genoa controlled the European luxury trade with the East.

In 1304 Venice established formal relations with the sultan of Mamluk Egypt, opening operations in Cairo, the gateway to Asian trade. Venetian merchants specialized in expensive luxury goods like spices, silks, and carpets, which they obtained from middlemen in the eastern Mediterranean and Asia Minor. A little went a long way. Venetians purchased no more than five hundred tons of spices a year around 1400, but with a profit of about 40 percent. The most important spice was pepper, grown in India and Indonesia, which composed 60 percent of the spices they purchased in 1400.[2]

The Venetians exchanged Eastern luxury goods for European products they could trade abroad, including Spanish and English wool, German metal goods, Flemish textiles, and silk cloth made in their own manufactures with imported raw materials. Eastern demand for such goods was low. To make up the difference, the Venetians earned currency in the shipping industry and through trade in firearms and slaves. At least half of what they traded with the East took the form of precious metal, much of it acquired in Egypt and North Africa. When the Portuguese arrived in Asia in the late fifteenth century, they found Venetian coins everywhere.

Venice's ancient rival was Genoa. In the wake of the Crusades, Genoa dominated the northern route to Asia through the Black Sea. Expansion in the thirteenth and fourteenth centuries took the Genoese as far as Persia and the Far East. In 1291 they sponsored an expedition into the Atlantic in search of India. The ships were lost,

The Taking of Constantinople by the Turks, April 22, 1453 The Ottoman conquest of the capital of the Byzantine Empire in 1453 sent shock and despair through Europe. Capitalizing on the city's strategic and commercial importance, the Ottomans made it the center of their empire. (Bibliothèque nationale de France)

and their exact destination and motivations remain unknown. This voyage reveals the long roots of Genoese interest in Atlantic exploration.

In the fifteenth century, with Venice claiming victory in the spice trade, the Genoese shifted focus from trade to finance and from the Black Sea to the western Mediterranean. Located on the northwestern coast of Italy, Genoa had always been active in the western Mediterranean, trading with North African ports, southern France, Spain, and even England and Flanders through the Strait of Gibraltar. When Spanish and Portuguese voyages began to expore the western Atlantic (see pages 451–456), Genoese merchants, navigators, and financiers provided their skills to the Iberian monarchs, whose own subjects had much less commercial experience. The Genoese, for example, ran many of the sugar plantations established on the Atlantic islands colonized by the Portuguese. Genoese merchants would eventually help finance Spanish colonization of the New World in return for a share in the profits.

A major element of both Venetian and Genoese trade was slavery. Merchants purchased slaves, many of whom were fellow Christians, in the Balkans. The men were sold to Egypt for the sultan's army or sent to work as agricultural laborers in the Mediterranean. Young girls, who made up the majority of the trade, were sold in western Mediterranean ports as servants or concubines. After the loss of the Black Sea — and thus the source of slaves — to the Ottomans, the Genoese sought new supplies of slaves in the West, taking the Guanches (indigenous peoples from the Canary Islands), Muslim prisoners and Jewish refugees from Spain, and by the early 1500s both black and Berber Africans. With the growth of Spanish colonies in the New World, Genoese and Venetian merchants would become important players in the Atlantic slave trade.

Italian experience in colonial administration, slaving, and international trade and finance served as a model for the Iberian states as they pushed European expansion to new heights. Mariners, merchants, and financiers from Venice and Genoa — most notably Christopher Columbus — played a crucial role in bringing the fruits of this experience to the Iberian Peninsula and to the New World.

The European Voyages of Discovery

How and why did Europeans undertake ambitious voyages of expansion?

As we have seen, Europe was by no means isolated before the voyages of exploration and its "discovery" of the New World. But because they did not produce many products desired by Eastern elites, Europeans were modest players in the Indian Ocean trading world. As Europe recovered after the Black Death, new European players entered the scene with new technology, eager to spread Christianity and to undo Italian and Ottoman domination of trade with the East. A century after the plague, Iberian explorers began the overseas voyages that helped create the modern world, with staggering consequences for their own continent and the rest of the planet.

Causes of European Expansion

European expansion had multiple causes. By the middle of the fifteenth century, Europe was experiencing a revival of population and economic activity after the lows of the Black Death. This revival created demands for luxury goods, especially spices, from the East. The fall of Constantinople and subsequent Ottoman control of trade routes created obstacles to fulfilling these demands. Europeans needed to find new sources of precious metal to trade with the Ottomans or trade routes that bypassed the Ottomans.

Why were spices so desirable? Introduced into western Europe by the Crusaders in the twelfth century, pepper, nutmeg, ginger, mace, cinnamon, and cloves added flavor and variety to the monotonous European diet. Spices evoked the scent of the Garden of Eden and of divinity itself; they seemed a marvel and a mystery. They were used not only as flavorings for food, but also for anointing oil and incense in religious rituals and as perfumes, medicines, and dyes in daily life. Take, for example, cloves, for which Europeans found many uses. If picked green and sugared, the buds could be transformed into jam; if salted and pickled, cloves became a flavoring for vinegar. Cloves sweetened the breath. When added to food or drink, they were thought to stimulate the appetite and clear the intestines and bladder. When crushed and powdered, they were a medicine rubbed on the forehead to relieve head colds and applied to the eyes to strengthen vision. Taken with milk, they were believed to enhance sexual pleasure.

Religious fervor was another important catalyst for expansion. The passion and energy ignited by the Christian reconquista (reconquest) of the Iberian Peninsula encouraged the Portuguese and Spanish to continue the Christian crusade. Just seven months separated the Spanish conquest of Granada, the last remaining Muslim state on the Iberian Peninsula, and Columbus's departure across the Atlantic. Overseas exploration was in some ways a transfer of religious zeal, enthusiasm for conquest, and certainty of God's blessing to new non-Christian territories. Since the remaining Muslim states, such as the mighty Ottoman Empire, were too strong to defeat, Iberians turned their attention elsewhere.

Combined with eagerness for profits and to spread Christianity was the desire for glory and the urge to chart new waters. Scholars have frequently described the European discoveries as a manifestation of Renaissance curiosity about the physical universe — the desire to know more about the geography and peoples of the world. The detailed journals kept by such voyagers as Christopher Columbus and Antonio Pigafetta (a survivor of Magellan's world circumnavigation) attest to their wonder and fascination with the new peoples and places they visited.

> **I have come to win gold, not to plow the fields like a peasant.**
>
> —HERNANDO CORTÉS

Individual explorers combined these motivations in unique ways. Christopher Columbus was a devout Christian who was increasingly haunted by messianic obsessions in the last years of his life. As Portuguese explorer Bartholomew Diaz put it, his own motives were "to serve God and His Majesty, to give light to those who were in darkness and to grow rich as all men desire to do." When the Portuguese explorer Vasco da Gama reached the port of Calicut, India, in 1498 and a native asked what he wanted, he replied, "Christians and spices."[3] The bluntest of the Spanish **conquistadors** (kahn-KEES-tuh-dorz), Hernando Cortés, announced as he prepared to conquer Mexico, "I have come to win gold, not to plow the fields like a peasant."[4]

Eagerness for exploration was heightened by a lack of opportunity at home. After the reconquista, young men of the Spanish upper classes found their economic and political opportunities greatly limited. The ambitious turned to the sea to seek their fortunes.

Whatever the reasons, the voyages were made possible by the growth of government power. The Spanish monarchy was stronger than before and in a position to support foreign ventures. In Portugal explorers also looked to the monarchy, to Prince Henry the Navigator in particular (page 451), for financial support and encouragement. Like voyagers, monarchs shared a mix of motivations, from the desire to please God to the desire to win glory and profit from trade. Competition among European monarchs was an important factor in encouraging the steady stream of expeditions that began in the late fifteenth century.

Ordinary sailors were ill paid, and life at sea meant danger, overcrowding, unbearable stench, and hunger. For months at a time, 100 to 120 people lived and worked in a space of 1,600 to 2,000 square feet. A lucky sailor would find enough space on deck to unroll his sleeping mat. Horses, cows, pigs, chickens, rats, and lice accompanied them on the voyages. As one scholar concluded, "traveling on a ship must have been one of the most uncomfortable and oppressive experiences in the world."[5]

conquistador Spanish for "conqueror"; Spanish soldier-explorers, such as Hernando Cortés and Francisco Pizarro, who sought to conquer the New World for the Spanish crown.

Men choose to join these miserable crews to escape poverty at home, to continue a family trade, to win a few crumbs of the great riches of empire, or to find better lives as illegal immigrants in the colonies. Many orphans and poor boys were placed on board as young pages and had little say in the decision. Women also paid a price for the voyages of exploration. Left alone for months or years at a time, and frequently widowed, sailors' wives struggled to feed their families. The widow of a sailor lost on Magellan's 1519 voyage had to wait until 1547 to collect her husband's salary from the Spanish crown.[6]

The people who stayed at home had a powerful impact on the process. Royal ministers and factions at court influenced monarchs to provide or deny support for exploration. The small number of people who could read served as a rapt audience for tales

The Travels of Sir John Mandeville The author of this tale claimed to be an English knight who traveled extensively in the Middle East and Asia from the 1320s to the 1350s. Although historians now consider the work a skillful fiction, it had a great influence on how Europeans understood the world at the time. This illustration, from an edition published around 1410, depicts Mandeville approaching a walled city on the first stage of his voyage to Constantinople. (© British Library Board)

caravel A small, maneuverable, three-mast sailing ship developed by the Portuguese in the fifteenth century that gave the Portuguese a distinct advantage in exploration and trade.

Ptolemy's *Geography* A second-century-C.E. work that synthesized the classical knowledge of geography and introduced the concepts of longitude and latitude. Reintroduced to Europeans in 1410 by Arab scholars, its ideas allowed cartographers to create more accurate maps.

of fantastic places and unknown peoples. Cosmography, natural history, and geography aroused enormous interest among educated people in the fifteenth and sixteenth centuries. One of the most popular books of the time was the fourteenth-century text *The Travels of Sir John Mandeville*, which purported to be a firsthand account of the author's travels in the Holy Land, Egypt, Ethiopia, the Middle East, and India and his service to the Mamluk sultan of Egypt and the Mongol Great Khan of China. Although we now know the stories were fictional, these fantastic tales of cannibals, one-eyed giants, men with the heads of dogs, and other marvels were believed for centuries and constituted the core of many Europeans' knowledge of such places. Christopher Columbus took a copy of Mandeville and the equally popular and more reliable *The Travels of Marco Polo* on his voyage in 1492.

Technology and the Rise of Exploration

Technological developments in shipbuilding, weaponry, and navigation provided another impetus for European expansion. Since ancient times, most seagoing vessels had been narrow, open boats called galleys, propelled largely by slaves or convicts manning the oars. Though well suited to the placid waters of the Mediterranean, galleys could not withstand the rough winds and uncharted shoals of the Atlantic. The need for sturdier craft, as well as population losses caused by the Black Death, forced the development of a new style of ship that would not require much manpower to sail. In the course of the fifteenth century, the Portuguese developed the **caravel**, a small, light, three-mast sailing ship. Though somewhat slower than the galley, the caravel held more cargo. Its triangular lateen sails and sternpost rudder also made the caravel a much more maneuverable vessel. When fitted with cannon, it could dominate larger vessels.

Great strides in cartography and navigational aids were also made during this period. Around 1410 Arab scholars reintroduced Europeans to **Ptolemy's *Geography***. Written in the second century C.E. by a Helle-

Ptolemy's *Geography* The recovery of Ptolemy's *Geography* in the early fifteenth century gave Europeans new access to ancient geographical knowledge. This 1486 world map, based on Ptolemy, is a great advance over medieval maps but contains errors with significant consequences for future exploration. It shows a single continent watered by a single ocean, with land covering three-quarters of the world's surface. Africa and Asia are joined with Europe, making the Indian Ocean a landlocked sea and rendering the circumnavigation of Africa impossible. The continent of Asia is stretched far to the east, greatly shortening the distance from Europe to Asia via the Atlantic. (Giraudon/Art Resource, NY)

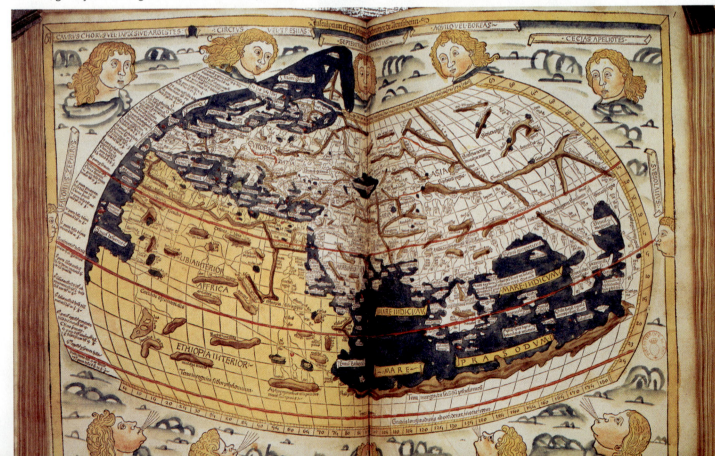

nized Egyptian, the work synthesized the geographical knowledge of the classical world. Ptolemy's work provided significant improvements over medieval cartography, showing the world as round and introducing the idea of latitude and longitude to plot position accurately. It also contained crucial errors. Unaware of the Americas, Ptolemy showed the world as much smaller than it is, so that Asia appeared not very distant from Europe to the west. Based on this work, cartographers fashioned new maps that combined classical knowledge with the latest information from mariners. First the Genoese and Venetians, and then the Portuguese and Spanish, took the lead in these advances.

The magnetic compass enabled sailors to determine their direction and position at sea. The astrolabe, an instrument invented by the ancient Greeks and perfected by Muslim navigators, was used to determine the altitude of the sun and other celestial bodies. It permitted mariners to plot their latitude, that is, their precise position north or south of the equator.

Like the astrolabe, much of the new technology that Europeans used on their voyages was borrowed from the East. Gunpowder, the compass, and the sternpost rudder were Chinese inventions. The lateen sail, which allowed European ships to tack against the wind, was a product of the Indian Ocean trade world and was brought to the Mediterranean on Arab ships. Advances in cartography also drew on the rich tradition of Judeo-Arabic mathematical and astronomical learning in Iberia. Sometimes assistance to Europeans came from humans rather than instruments. The famed explorer Vasco da Gama employed a local Indian pilot to guide his expedition from the East African coast to India. In exploring new territories, European sailors thus called on techniques and knowledge developed over centuries in China, the Muslim world, and the Indian Ocean.

The Portuguese Overseas Empire

For centuries Portugal was a small and poor nation on the margins of European life whose principal activities were fishing and subsistence farming. It would have been hard for a European to predict Portugal's phenomenal success overseas after 1450. Yet Portugal had a long history of seafaring and navigation. Blocked from access to western Europe by Spain, the Portuguese turned to the Atlantic and North Africa, whose waters they knew better than did other Europeans. Nature favored the Portuguese: winds blowing along their coast offered passage to Africa, its Atlantic islands, and, ultimately, Brazil.

In the early phases of Portuguese exploration, Prince Henry (1394–1460), a younger son of the king, played a leading role. A nineteenth-century scholar dubbed Henry "the Navigator" because of his support for the study of geography and navigation and for the annual expeditions he sponsored down the western coast of Africa. Although he never personally participated in voyages of exploration, Henry's involvement ensured that Portugal did not abandon the effort despite early disappointments.

The Portuguese Fleet Embarked for the Indies The image below shows a Portuguese trading fleet in the late fifteenth century bound for the riches of the Indies. Between 1500 and 1635 over nine hundred ships sailed from Portugal to ports on the Indian Ocean, in annual fleets composed of five to ten ships. Portuguese sailors used astrolabes, such as the one pictured at left, to accurately plot their position. (fleet: British Museum/HarperCollins Publishers/The Art Archive; astrolabe: Courtesy of the Trustees of the British Museum)

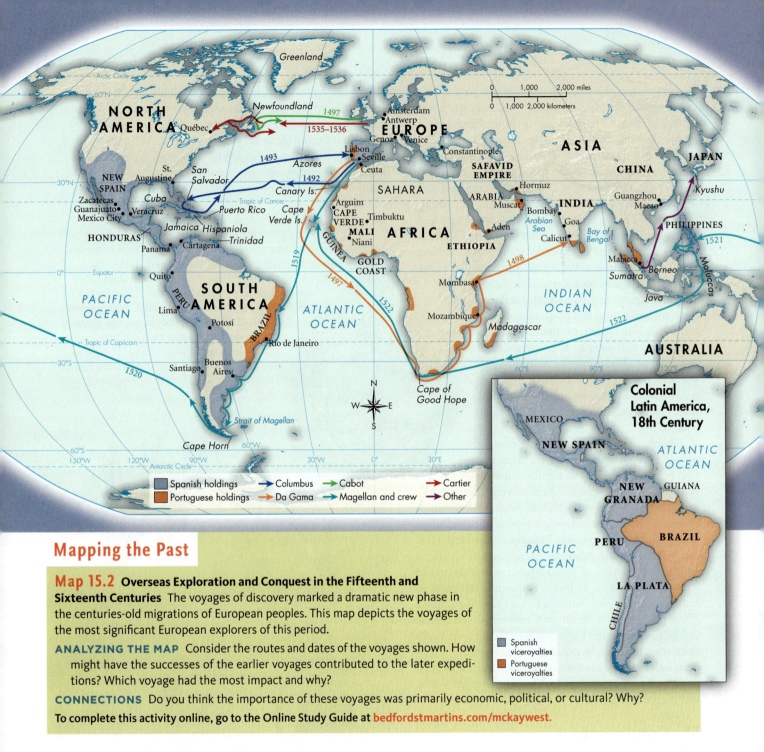

Mapping the Past

Map 15.2 Overseas Exploration and Conquest in the Fifteenth and Sixteenth Centuries The voyages of discovery marked a dramatic new phase in the centuries-old migrations of European peoples. This map depicts the voyages of the most significant European explorers of this period.

ANALYZING THE MAP Consider the routes and dates of the voyages shown. How might have the successes of the earlier voyages contributed to the later expeditions? Which voyage had the most impact and why?

CONNECTIONS Do you think the importance of these voyages was primarily economic, political, or cultural? Why?

To complete this activity online, go to the Online Study Guide at bedfordstmartins.com/mckaywest.

The objectives of Portuguese exploration policy included desires for military glory; crusades to Christianize Muslims and to locate a mythical Christian king of Africa, Prester John; and the quest to find gold, slaves, and an overseas route to the spice markets of India. Portugal's conquest of Ceuta, an Arab city in northern Morocco, in 1415 marked the beginning of European overseas expansion. In the 1420s, under Henry's direction, the Portuguese began to settle the Atlantic islands of Madeira (ca. 1420) and the Azores (1427). In 1443 they founded their first African commercial settlement at Arguin in North Africa. By the time of Henry's death in 1460, his support for exploration was vindicated by thriving sugar plantations on the Atlantic islands, the first arrival of enslaved Africans in Portugal (see page 465), and new access to African gold.

The Portuguese next established trading posts and forts on the gold-rich Guinea coast and penetrated into the African continent all the way to Timbuktu (Map 15.2). By 1500 Portugal controlled the flow of African gold to Europe. The golden century of Portuguese prosperity had begun.

The Portuguese then pushed farther south down the west coast of Africa. In 1487 Bartholomew Diaz rounded the Cape of Good Hope at the southern tip, but storms and a threatened mutiny forced him to turn back. A decade later Vasco da Gama succeeded in rounding the Cape while commanding a fleet of four ships in search of a sea route to India. With the help of an Indian guide, da Gama reached the port of Calicut in India. Overcoming local hostility, he returned to Lisbon loaded with spices and samples of Indian cloth. He had failed to forge any trading alliances with local powers, and Portuguese arrogance ensured the future hostility of Muslim merchants who dominated the trading system. Nonetheless, de Gama proved the possibility of lucrative trade with the East via the Cape route. Thereafter, a Portuguese convoy set out for passage around the Cape every March.

Lisbon became the entrance port for Asian goods into Europe, but this was not accomplished without a fight. Muslim-controlled port city-states had long controlled the rich spice trade of the Indian Ocean, and they did not surrender it willingly. Portuguese cannon blasted open the port of Malacca in 1511, followed by Calicut, Ormuz, and Goa. The bombardment of these cities laid the foundation for Portuguese imperialism in the sixteenth and seventeenth centuries.

In March 1493, between the voyages of Diaz and da Gama, Spanish ships under a triumphant Genoese mariner named Christopher Columbus (1451–1506), in the service of the Spanish crown, entered Lisbon harbor. Spain also had begun the quest for an empire.

The Problem of Christopher Columbus

Christopher Columbus is a controversial figure in history—glorified by some as the brave discoverer of America, vilified by others as a cruel exploiter of Native Americans. Rather than judging Columbus by debates and standards of our time, it is more important to understand him in the context of his own time. First, what kind of man was Columbus, and what forces or influences shaped him? Second, in sailing westward from Europe, what were his goals? Third, did he achieve his goals, and what did he make of his discoveries?

In his dream of a westward passage to the Indies, Columbus embodied a long-standing Genoese ambition to circumvent Venetian domination of eastward trade, which was now being claimed by the Portuguese. Columbus was very knowledgeable about the sea. He had worked as a mapmaker, and he was familiar with such fifteenth-century Portuguese navigational developments as *portolans*—written descriptions of the courses along which ships sailed—and the use of the compass as a nautical instrument. As he implied in his *Journal*, he had acquired not only theoretical but also practical experience: "I have spent twenty-three years at sea and have not left it for any length of time worth mentioning, and I have seen every thing from east to west [meaning he had been to England] and I have been to Guinea [North and West Africa]."[7] His successful thirty-three-day voyage to the Caribbean owed a great deal to his seamanship.

Columbus was also a deeply religious man. He began the *Journal* of his voyage to the Americas in the form of a letter to Ferdinand and Isabella of Spain:

> On 2 January in the year 1492, when your Highnesses had concluded their war with the Moors who reigned in Europe, I saw your Highnesses' banners victoriously raised on the towers of the Alhambra, the citadel of the city, and the Moorish king come out of the city gates and kiss the hands of your Highnesses and the prince, My Lord. And later in that same month, on the grounds of information I had given your Highnesses concerning the lands of India . . . your Highnesses decided to send me, Christopher Columbus, to see these parts of India and the princes and peoples of those lands and consider the best means for their conversion.

Columbus had witnessed the Spanish conquest of Granada and shared fully in the religious and nationalistic fervor surrounding that event. Like the Spanish rulers and most Europeans of his age, he understood Christianity as a missionary religion that should be carried to places where it did not exist. He viewed himself as a divine agent: "God made me the messenger of the new heaven and the new earth of which he spoke in the Apocalypse of St. John . . . and he showed me the post where to find it."[8]

What was the object of this first voyage? Columbus gave the answer in the very title of the expedition, "The Enterprise of the Indies." He wanted to find a direct ocean trading route to Asia. Rejected for funding by the Portuguese in 1483 and by Ferdinand and Isabella in 1486, the project finally won the backing of the Spanish monarchy in 1492. The Spanish crown named Columbus viceroy over any territory he might discover and gave him one-tenth of the material rewards of the journey. Inspired by the stories of Mandeville and Marco Polo, Columbus dreamed of reaching the court of the Mongol emperor, the Great Khan (not realizing that the Ming Dynasty had overthrown the Mongols in 1368). Based on Ptolemy's *Geography* and other texts, he expected to pass the islands of Japan and then land on the east coast of China.

How did Columbus interpret what he had found, and in his mind did he achieve what he had set out to do? Columbus's small fleet left Spain on August 3, 1492. He landed in the Bahamas, which he christened San Salvador, on October 12, 1492. Columbus believed he had found some small islands off the east coast of Japan. On encountering natives of the islands, he gave them some beads and "many other trifles of small value," pronouncing them delighted with these gifts and eager to trade. In a letter he wrote to Ferdinand and Isabella on his return to Spain, Columbus described the natives as handsome, peaceful, and primitive people whose body painting reminded him of the Canary Islands natives.

Columbus Describes His First Voyage

LISTENING TO THE PAST

On his return voyage to Spain in February 1493, Christopher Columbus composed a letter intended for wide circulation and had copies of it sent ahead to Isabella and Ferdinand. Because the letter sums up Columbus's understanding of his achievements, it is considered the most important document of his first voyage. Remember that his knowledge of Asia rested heavily on Marco Polo's Travels, published around 1298.

❝ Since I know that you will be pleased at the great success with which the Lord has crowned my voyage, I write to inform you how in thirty-three days I crossed from the Canary Islands to the Indies, with the fleet which our most illustrious sovereigns gave me. I found very many islands with large populations and took possession of them all for their Highnesses; this I did by proclamation and unfurled the royal standard. No opposition was offered.

I named the first island that I found "San Salvador," in honour of our Lord and Saviour who has granted me this miracle. . . . When I reached Cuba, I followed its north coast westwards, and found it so extensive that I thought this must be the mainland, the province of Cathay.* . . . From there I saw another island eighteen leagues eastwards which I then named "Hispaniola.". . .†

Hispaniola is a wonder. The mountains and hills, the plains and meadow lands are both fertile and beautiful. They are most suitable for planting crops and for raising cattle of all kinds, and there are good sites for building towns and villages. The harbours are incredibly fine and there are many great rivers with broad channels and the majority contain gold.‡ The trees, fruits and plants are very different from those of Cuba. In Hispaniola there are many spices and large mines of gold and other metals.§ . . .

The inhabitants of this island, and all the rest that I discovered or heard of, go naked, as their mothers bore them, men and women alike. A few of the women, however, cover a single place with a leaf of a plant or piece of cotton which they weave for the purpose. They have no iron or steel or arms and are not capable of using them, not because they are not strong and well built but because they are amazingly timid. All the weapons they have are canes cut at seeding time, at the end of which they fix a sharpened stick, but they have not the courage to make use of these, for very often when I have sent two or three men to a village to have conversation with them a great number of them have come out. But as soon as they saw my men all fled immediately, a father not even waiting for his son. And this is not because we have harmed any of them; on the contrary, wherever I have gone and been able to have conversation with them, I have given them some of the various things I had, a cloth and other articles, and received nothing in exchange. But they have still remained incurably timid.

True, when they have been reassured and lost their fear, they are so ingenuous and so liberal with all their possessions that no one who has not seen them would believe it. If one asks for anything they have they never say no. On the contrary, they offer a share to anyone with demonstrations of heartfelt affection, and they are immediately content with any small thing, valuable or valueless, that is given them. I forbade the men to give them bits of broken crockery, fragments of glass or tags of laces, though if they could get them they fancied them the finest jewels in the world. . . .

I hoped to win them to the love and service of their Highnesses and of the whole Spanish nation and to persuade them to collect and give us of the things which they possessed in abundance and which we needed. They have no religion and are not idolaters; but all believe that power and goodness dwell in the sky and they are firmly convinced that I have come from the sky with these ships and people. In this belief they gave me a good reception everywhere, once they had overcome their fear; and this is not because they are stupid—far from it, they are men of great intelligence, for they navigate all those seas, and give a marvellously good account of every thing—but because they have never before seen men clothed or ships like these. . . .

In all these islands the men are seemingly content with one woman, but their chief or king is allowed more than twenty. The women appear to work more than the men and I have not been able to find out if they have private property. As far as I could see whatever a man had was shared among all the rest and this particularly applies to food. . . . In another island, which I am told is larger than Hispaniola, the people have no hair. Here there is a vast quantity of gold, and from here and the other islands I bring Indians as evidence.

In conclusion, to speak only of the results of this very hasty voyage, their Highnesses can see that I will give them as much gold as they require, if they will render me some very slight assistance; also I will give them all the spices and cotton they want. . . . I will also bring them as much aloes as they ask and as many slaves, who will be taken from the idolaters. I believe

---

*Cathay is the old name for China. In the logbook and later in this letter, Columbus accepts the native story that Cuba is an island that can be circumnavigated in something more than twenty-one days, yet he insists here and during the second voyage that it is part of the Asiatic mainland.

†Hispaniola is the second largest island of the West Indies. Haiti occupies the western third of the island, the Dominican Republic the rest.

‡This did not prove to be true.

§These statements are also inaccurate.

Christopher Columbus, by Ridolpho Ghirlandio. Friend of Raphael and teacher of Michelangelo, Ghirlandio (1483–1561) enjoyed distinction as a portrait painter, and so we can assume that this is a good likeness of the older Columbus. (Scala/Art Resource, NY)

also that I have found rhubarb and cinnamon and there will be countless other things in addition....

So all Christendom will be delighted that our Redeemer has given victory to our most illustrious King and Queen and their renowned kingdoms, in this great matter. They should hold great celebrations and render solemn thanks to the Holy Trinity with many solemn prayers, for the great triumph which they will have, by the conversion of so many peoples to our holy faith and for the temporal benefits which will follow, for not only Spain, but all Christendom will receive encouragement and profit.

This is a brief account of the facts. Written in the caravel off the Canary Islands.**

15 February 1493

At your orders   THE ADMIRAL

QUESTIONS FOR ANALYSIS

1. How did Columbus explain the success of his voyage?
2. What was Columbus's view of the Native Americans he met?
3. Does he exaggerate about the Caribbean islands possessing gold, cotton, and spices?

Source: From *The Four Voyages of Christopher Columbus*, pp. 115–123, ed. and trans. J. M. Cohen (Penguin Classics, 1969). Copyright © J. M. Cohen, 1969. Used with permission of Penguin Group (UK).

**Actually, Columbus was off Santa Maria in the Azores.

Believing he was in the Indies, he called them "Indians," a name that was later applied to all inhabitants of the Americas. Columbus concluded that they would make good slaves and could quickly be converted to Christianity. (See "Listening to the Past: Columbus Describes His First Voyage," at left.)

Scholars have identified the inhabitants of the islands as the Taino people, speakers of the Arawak language, who inhabited Hispaniola (modern-day Haiti and Dominican Republic) and other islands in the Caribbean. Columbus received reassuring reports from Taino villagers — via hand gestures and mime — of the presence of gold and of a great king in the vicinity. From San Salvador, Columbus sailed southwest, believing that this course would take him to Japan or the coast of China. He landed instead on Cuba on October 28. Deciding that he must be on the mainland near the coastal city of Quinsay (now Hangzhou), he sent a small embassy inland with letters from Ferdinand and Isabella and instructions to locate the grand city.

The landing party found only small villages. Confronted with this disappointment, Columbus apparently gave up on his aim to meet the Great Khan. Instead, he focused on trying to find gold or other valuables among the peoples he had discovered. The sight of Taino people wearing gold ornaments on Hispaniola seemed to prove that gold was available in the region. In January, confident that its source would soon be found, he headed back to Spain to report on his discovery. News of his voyage spread rapidly across Europe.⁹

Columbus's First Voyage to the New World, 1492–1493

Over the next decades, the Spanish would follow a policy of conquest and colonization in the New World, rather than one of exchange with equals (as envisaged for the Mongol khan). On his second voyage, Columbus forcibly subjugated the island of Hispaniola and enslaved its indigenous peoples. On this and subsequent voyages, Columbus brought with him settlers for the new Spanish territories, along with agricultural seed and livestock. Columbus himself, however, had little interest in or capacity for governing. Revolt soon broke out against him and his brother on Hispaniola. A royal expedition sent to investigate returned the brothers to Spain in chains. Columbus was quickly cleared of wrongdoing, but he did not recover his authority over the territories. Instead, they came under royal control.

Columbus was very much a man of his times. To the end of his life in 1506, he believed that he had found small islands off the coast of Asia. He never realized the scope of his achievement: to have found a vast continent unknown to Europeans, except for a fleeting Viking presence centuries earlier. He could not know that the scale of his discoveries would revolutionize world power, raising issues of trade, settlement, government bureaucracy, and the rights of native and African peoples.

Later Explorers

The Florentine navigator Amerigo Vespucci (veh-SPOO-chee) (1454–1512) realized what Columbus had not. Writing about his discoveries on the coast of modern-day Venezuela, Vespucci stated: "Those new regions which we found and explored with the fleet . . . we may rightly call a New World." This letter, titled *Mundus Novus* (The New World), was the first document to describe America as a continent separate from Asia. In recognition of Amerigo's bold claim, the continent was named for him. (When later cartographers realized that Columbus had made the discovery first, it was too late to change the maps.)

To settle competing claims to the Atlantic discoveries, Spain and Portugal turned to Pope Alexander VI. The resulting **Treaty of Tordesillas** (tor-duh-SEE-yuhs) in 1494 gave Spain everything to the west of an imaginary line drawn down the Atlantic and Portugal everything to the east. This arbitrary division worked in Portugal's favor when in 1500 an expedition led by Pedro Alvares Cabral, en route to India, landed on the coast of Brazil, which Cabral claimed as Portuguese territory.

The search for profits determined the direction of Spanish exploration and expansion into South America. With insignificant profits from the Caribbean compared to the enormous riches that the Portuguese were reaping in Asia, Spain renewed the search for a western passage to Asia. In 1519 Charles V of Spain (and the Holy Roman Empire) sent the Portuguese mariner Ferdinand Magellan (1480–1521) to find a sea route to the spices of the Moluccas off the southeast coast of Asia. Magellan sailed southwest across the Atlantic to Brazil, and after a long search along the coast he located the treacherous straits that now bear his name (see Map 15.1). The new ocean he sailed into after a rough passage through the straits seemed so peaceful that Magellan dubbed it the Pacific, from the Latin word for peaceful. He was soon to realize his mistake. His fleet sailed north up the west coast of South America and then headed west into the immense expanse of the Pacific toward the Malay Archipelago.

Treaty of Tordesillas The 1494 agreement giving Spain everything to the west of an imaginary line drawn down the Atlantic and giving Portugal everything to the east.

World Map of Diogo Ribeiro, 1529 This map integrates the wealth of new information provided by European explorers in the decades after Columbus's 1492 voyage. Working on commission for the Spanish king Charles V, mapmaker Diogo Ribeiro incorporated new details on Africa, South America, India, the Malay Archipelago, and China. Note the inaccuracy in his placement of the Moluccas, or Spice Islands, which are much too far east. This "mistake" was intended to serve Spain's interests in trade negotiations with the Portuguese. (Biblioteca Apostolica Vaticana)

> **Those new regions which we found and explored with the fleet... we may rightly call a New World.**
>
> —AMERIGO VESPUCCI

Some of these islands were conquered in the 1560s and named the "Philippines" for Philip II of Spain.

Terrible storms, disease, starvation, and violence haunted the expedition. Magellan had set out with a fleet of five ships and around 270 men. Sailors on two of the ships attempted mutiny on the South American coast; one ship was lost, and another ship deserted and returned to Spain before even traversing the straits. The trip across the Pacific took ninety-eight days, and the men survived on rats and sawdust. Magellan himself was killed in a skirmish in the Philippines. The expedition had enough survivors to man only two ships, and one of them was captured by the Portuguese. One ship with only eighteen men returned to Spain from the east by way of the Indian Ocean, the Cape of Good Hope, and the Atlantic in 1522. The voyage—the first to circumnavigate the globe—had taken close to three years.

Despite the losses, this voyage revolutionized Europeans' understanding of the world by demonstrating the vastness of the Pacific. The earth was clearly much larger than Columbus had believed. Although the voyage made a small profit in spices, the westward passage to the Indies was too long and dangerous for commercial purposes. Spain soon abandoned the attempt to oust Portugal from the Eastern spice trade and concentrated on exploiting her New World territories.

The English and French also set sail across the Atlantic during the early days of exploration in search of a northwest passage to the Indies. In 1497 John Cabot, a Genoese merchant living in London, aimed for Brazil but discovered Newfoundland. The next year he returned and explored the New England coast. These forays proved futile, and the English established no permanent colonies in the territories they explored. One hundred years later, English efforts to find a passage to Asia focused on the extreme north. Between 1576 and 1578, Martin Frobisher made three voyages in and around the Canadian bay that now bears his name. Frobisher hopefully brought a quantity of ore back to England with him, but it proved to be worthless.

Early French exploration of the Atlantic was equally frustrating. Between 1534 and 1541 Frenchman Jacques Cartier made several voyages and explored the St. Lawrence region of Canada, searching for a passage to the wealth of Asia. His exploration of the St. Lawrence was halted at the great rapids west of the present-day island of Montreal; he named the rapids "La Chine" in the optimistic belief that China lay just beyond. When this hope proved vain, the French turned to a new source of profit within Canada itself: trade in beavers and other furs. As had the Portuguese in Asia, French traders bartered with local peoples, who maintained control over their trade goods. French fishermen also competed with Spanish and English for the teeming schools of cod they found in the Atlantic waters around Newfoundland. Fishing vessels salted the catch on board and brought it back to Europe, where a thriving market for fish was created by the Catholic prohibition of eating meat on Fridays and during Lent.

Spanish Conquest in the New World

In 1519, the year Magellan departed on his worldwide expedition, the Spanish sent an exploratory expedition from their post in Cuba to the mainland under the command of the brash and determined conquistador Hernando Cortés (1485–1547). Accompanied by six hundred men, sixteen horses, and ten cannon, Cortés was to launch the conquest of the **Mexica Empire**. Its people were later called the Aztecs, but now most scholars prefer to use the term *Mexica* to refer to them and their empire.

The Mexica Empire was ruled by Montezuma II (r. 1502–1520) from his capital at Tenochtitlán (tay-noch-teet-LAHN), now Mexico City. Larger than any European city of the time, it was the heart of a sophisticated civilization with advanced mathematics, astronomy, and engineering, with a complex social system, and with oral poetry and historical traditions.

Mexica Empire Also known as the Aztec Empire, a large and complex Native American civilization in modern Mexico and Central America that possessed advanced mathematical, astronomical, and engineering technology.

Cortés landed on the coast of the Gulf of Mexico on April 21, 1519. The Spanish camp was soon visited by delegations of unarmed Mexica leaders bearing gifts and news of their great emperor. Impressed by the wealth of the local people, Cortés decided to cut his ties with Spain. He founded the settlement of Vera Cruz and burned his ships to prevent any disloyal followers from returning to Cuba. Cortés soon began to realize that he could exploit internal dissension within the empire to his own advantage. The Mexica state religion necessitated constant warfare against neighboring peoples to secure captives for religious sacrifices and laborers for agricultural and building projects. Conquered peoples were required to pay products of their agriculture and craftsmanship as tribute to the Mexica state through their local chiefs.

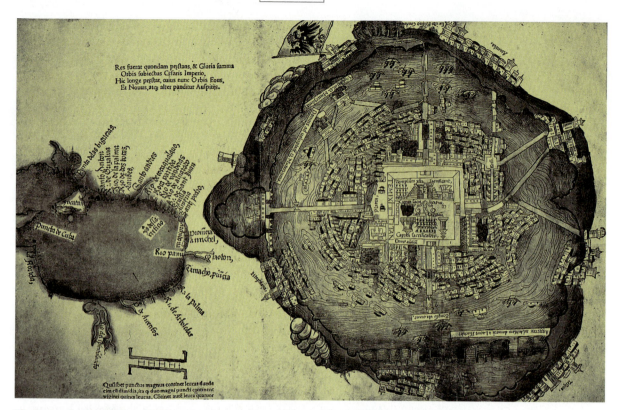

The Aztec Capital of Tenochtitlán Occupying a large island, Tenochtitlán was laid out in concentric circles. The administrative and religious buildings were at the heart of the city, which was surrounded by residential quarters. Cortés himself marveled at the city in his letters: "The city is as large as Seville or Cordoba. . . . There are bridges, very large, strong, and well constructed, so that, over many, ten horsemen can ride abreast. . . . The city has many squares where markets are held. . . . There is one square . . . where there are daily more than sixty thousand souls, buying and selling. In the service and manners of its people, their fashion of living was almost the same as in Spain, with just as much harmony and order." (The Newberry Library)

Cortés quickly forged an alliance with the Tlaxcalas and other subject kingdoms, which chafed under the tribute demanded by the Mexica. In October a combined Spanish-Tlaxcalan force occupied the city of Cholula, second largest in the empire and its religious capital, and massacred many thousands of inhabitants. Strengthened by this display of power, Cortés made alliances with other native kingdoms. In November 1519, with a few hundred Spanish men and some six thousand indigenous warriors, Cortés marched on Tenochtitlán.

Montezuma refrained from attacking the Spaniards as they advanced toward his capital and welcomed Cortés and his men into Tenochtitlán. Historians have often condemned the Mexica ruler for vacillation and weakness. Certainly other native leaders did attack the Spanish. But Montezuma relied on the advice of his state council, itself divided, and on the dubious loyalty of tributary communities. Historians have largely discredited one long-standing explanation, that he feared the Spaniards as living gods. This idea seems to have been a myth spread by Spanish missionaries and their converts after the fact, as a way of justifying and explaining the conquest. Montezuma's long hesitation proved disastrous. When Cortés—with incredible boldness—took Montezuma hostage, the emperor's influence over his people crumbled.

During the ensuing attacks and counterattacks, Montezuma was killed. The Spaniards and their allies escaped from the city and began gathering forces and making new alliances against the Mexica. In May 1520 Cortés led a second assault on

Invasion of Tenochtitlán, 1519–1521

Picturing the Past

Doña Marina Translating for Hernando Cortés During His Meeting with Montezuma In April 1519 Doña Marina (or La Malinche as she is known in Mexico) was among twenty women given to the Spanish as slaves. Fluent in Nahuatl (NAH-wha-tuhl) and Yucatec Mayan (spoken by a Spanish priest accompanying Cortés), she acted as an interpreter and diplomatic guide for the Spanish. She had a close relationship with Cortés and bore his son, Don Martín Cortés, in 1522. This image was created by Tlaxcalan artists shortly after the conquest of Mexico and represents one indigenous perspective on the events. (The Granger Collection, New York)

ANALYZING THE IMAGE What role does Doña Marina (far right) appear to be playing in this image? Does she appear to be subservient or equal to Cortés (right, seated)? How did the painter indicate her identity as non-Spanish?

CONNECTIONS How do you think the native rulers negotiating with Cortés might have viewed her? What about a Spanish viewer of this image? What does the absence of other women here suggest about the role of women in these societies?

To complete this activity online, go to the Online Study Guide at bedfordstmartins.com/mckaywest.

Tenochtitlán at the head of an army of approximately 1,000 Spanish and 75,000 native warriors.[10] Spanish victory in late summer 1521 was hard-won and greatly aided by the effects of smallpox, which had weakened and reduced the Mexica population. After the defeat of Tenochtitlán, Cortés and other conquistadors began the systematic conquest of Mexico. Over time, a series of indigenous kingdoms gradually fell under Spanish domination, although not without decades of resistance.

More surprising than the defeat of the Mexicas was the fall of the remote **Inca Empire**. Perched more than 9,800 feet above sea level, the Incas were isolated from other indigenous cultures and knew nothing of the Mexica civilization or its

Inca Empire The vast and sophisticated Peruvian empire centered at the capital city of Cuzco that was at its peak from 1438 until 1532.

collapse. Like the Mexica, the Incas had created a civilization that rivaled the Europeans in population and complexity. To unite their vast and well-fortified empire, the Incas built an extensive network of roads, along which traveled a highly efficient postal service. The imperial government taxed, fed, and protected its subjects.

At the time of the Spanish invasion the Inca Empire had been weakened by disease and warfare. An epidemic of disease, possibly smallpox, had begun spreading among the people. Even worse, the empire had been embroiled in a civil war over succession. Francisco Pizarro (ca. 1475–1541), a conquistador of modest Spanish origins, landed on the northern coast of Peru on May 13, 1532, the very day Atahualpa (ah-tuh-WAHL-puh) won control of the empire after five years of fighting. As Pizarro advanced across the steep Andes toward Cuzco, Atahualpa was proceeding to the capital for his coronation.

Like Montezuma in Mexico, Atahualpa was aware of the Spaniards' movements. He sent envoys to greet the Spanish and invite them to meet him in the provincial town of Cajamarca. His plan was to lure the Spaniards into a trap, seize their horses and ablest men for his army, and execute the rest. With a loyal army of some forty thousand men stationed nearby, Atahualpa felt he had little to fear. Instead, the Spaniards ambushed and captured him, collected an enormous ransom in gold, and then executed him in 1533 on trumped-up charges. The Spanish now marched on the capital of the empire itself, profiting once again from internal conflicts to form alliances with local peoples. When Cuzco fell in 1533, the Spanish plundered immense riches in gold and silver.

As with the Mexica, decades of violence and resistance followed the defeat of the Incan capital. Struggles also broke out among the Spanish for the spoils of empire. Nevertheless, Spanish conquest opened a new chapter in European relations with the New World. It was not long before rival European nations attempted to forge their own overseas empires.

Early French and English Settlement in the New World

For over a hundred years, the Spanish and the Portuguese dominated settlement in the New World. The first English colony was founded at Roanoke (in what is now North Carolina) in 1585. After a three-year loss of contact with England, the settlers were found to have disappeared; their fate remains a mystery. The colony of Virginia, founded at Jamestown in 1607, had better luck and gained a steady hold producing tobacco for a growing European market. While these colonies originated as bases for harassing Spanish shipping, settlement on the coast of New England was undertaken for different reasons. There, radical Protestants sought to escape Anglican repression in England and begin new lives. The small and struggling outpost of Plymouth (1620) was followed by Massachusetts (1630), which grew into a prosperous settlement. Religious disputes in Massachusetts itself led to the dispersion of settlers into the new communities of Providence, Connecticut, Rhode Island, and New Haven. Catholics acquired their own settlement in Maryland (1632) and Quakers in Pennsylvania (1681).

Where the Spanish conquered indigenous empires and established whole-scale dominance over Mexico and Peru, English settlements hugged the Atlantic coastline. This did not prevent conflict with the indigenous inhabitants over land and resources. The haphazard nature of English colonization also led to conflicts of authority within the colonies. As the English crown grew more interested in colonial expansion, efforts were made to acquire the territory between New England in the north and Virginia in the south. This would allow the English to unify their holdings and overcome French and Dutch competition on the North American mainland.

French navigator and explorer Samuel de Champlain founded the first permanent French settlement, at Quebec, in 1608, a year after the English founding of Jamestown. Ville-Marie, latter-day Montreal, was founded in 1642. Although the French population in New France was small compared to the English and Spanish colonies, the French were energetic and industrious traders and explorers. Following the waterways of the St. Lawrence, the Great Lakes, and the Mississippi, they ventured into much of modern-day Canada and at least thirty-five of the fifty states of the United States. In 1682 French explorer LaSalle descended the Mississippi to the Gulf of Mexico, opening the way for French occupation of Louisiana.

While establishing their foothold in the north, the French slowly acquired new territories in the West Indies. These included Cayenne (1604), St. Christophe (1625), Martinique, Guadeloupe, and Saint-Domingue (1697) on the western side of the island of Hispaniola. Originally used as bases for plundering Spanish shipping, these islands became centers of tobacco and then sugar production. French ambitions on the mainland and in the Caribbean sparked a century-long competition with the English that culminated in the Seven Years' War from 1756 to 1763. France lost Canada and Louisiana, but retained profitable colonies in the West Indies. France regained part of Louisiana by treaty in 1800 and sold it to the United States in 1803.

European involvement in the Americas led to profound transformation of pre-existing indigenous societies and the rise of a transatlantic slave trade. It also led to an acceleration of global trade and cultural exchange.

Over time, the combination of indigenous, European, and African cultures gave birth to new societies in the New World. In turn, the profits of trade and the impact of cultural exchange greatly influenced European society.

The Impact of Conquest

What was the impact of European conquest on the peoples and ecologies of the New World?

The growing European presence in the New World transformed its land and its peoples forever. Violence and disease wrought devastating losses, while surviving peoples encountered new political, social, and economic organizations imposed by Europeans. The Columbian exchange brought infectious diseases to the Americas, but also gave new crops to the Old World that altered consumption patterns in Europe and across the globe (see page 463).

Colonial Administration

Columbus, Cortés, and Pizarro had claimed the lands they had "discovered" for the Spanish crown. How were these lands governed? In the sixteenth century the Crown divided its New World territories into four **viceroyalties** or administrative divisions: New Spain, with the capital at Mexico City; Peru, with the capital at Lima; New Granada, with Bogotá as its administrative center; and La Plata, with Buenos Aires as the capital (see Map 15.2).

Within each territory, the viceroy, or imperial governor, exercised broad military and civil authority as the direct representative of Spain. The viceroy presided over the *audiencia* (ow-dee-EHN-see-ah), a board of twelve to fifteen judges that served as his advisory council and the highest judicial body. Later, the reform-minded Spanish king Charles III (r. 1759–1788) introduced the system of intendants to the New World territories. These royal officials possessed broad military, administrative, and financial authority within their intendancies and were responsible not to the viceroy but to the monarchy in Madrid. The intendant system was pioneered by the Bourbon kings of France and was used by the French in their overseas colonies.

The Portuguese governed their colony of Brazil in a similar manner. After the union of the crowns of Portugal and Spain in 1580, Spanish administrative forms were introduced. Local officials called *corregidores* (kuh-REH-gih-dawr-eez) held judicial and military powers. Royal policies placed severe restrictions on Brazilian industries that might compete with those of Portugal and Spain.

Impact of European Settlement on the Lives of Indigenous Peoples

Before Columbus's arrival, the Americas were inhabited by thousands of groups of indigenous peoples with different languages and cultures. Their patterns of life varied widely, from hunter-gatherer tribes organized into tribal confederations on the North American plains to large-scale agriculture-based empires connecting bustling cities and towns in modern-day Mexico and South America. Although historians continue to debate the numbers, the best estimate is that the peoples of the Americas numbered around 50 million in 1492.

Their lives were radically transformed by the arrival of Europeans. In the sixteenth century perhaps two hundred thousand Spaniards immigrated to the New World. After assisting in the conquest of the Mexica and the Incas, these men carved out vast estates called haciendas in temperate grazing areas and imported Spanish livestock for the kinds of ranching with which they were familiar. In coastal tropical areas, the Spanish erected huge plantations to supply sugar to the European market. Around 1550 silver was discovered in present-day Bolivia and Mexico. To work the cattle ranches, sugar plantations, and silver mines, the conquistadors first turned to the indigenous peoples.

The Spanish quickly established the **encomienda system**, in which the Crown granted the conquerors the right to employ groups of Native Americans as laborers or to demand tribute from them in exchange for providing food and shelter. Theoretically, the Spanish were forbidden to enslave the natives; in actuality, the encomiendas were a legalized form of slavery.

The new conditions and hardships imposed by conquest and colonization resulted in enormous native population losses. The major cause of death was disease. Having little or no resistance to diseases brought from the Old World, the inhabitants of the New World fell victim to smallpox, typhus, influenza, and other illnesses. Another factor was overwork. Unaccustomed to forced labor, especially in the blistering heat of tropical cane fields or in dank and dangerous mines, native workers died in staggering numbers. Moreover, forced labor diverted local people from agricultural work, leading to malnutrition, reduced fertility rates, and starvation. Women forced to work were separated from their infants, leading to high infant morality rates in a population with no livestock to supply alternatives to breast milk. Malnutrition and hunger in turn lowered resistance to disease. Finally,

> **viceroyalties** The name for the four administrative units of Spanish possessions in the Americas: New Spain, Peru, New Granada, and La Plata.
>
> **encomienda system** A system whereby the Spanish crown granted the conquerors the right to forcibly employ groups of Indians; it was a disguised form of slavery.

many indigenous peoples also died through outright violence in warfare.[11]

The Franciscan Bartolomé de Las Casas (1474–1566) was one of the most outspoken critics of Spanish brutality against indigenous peoples. Las Casas documented their treatment at the hands of the Spanish:

> *To these quiet Lambs . . . came the Spaniards like most c(r)uel Tygres, Wolves and Lions, enrag'd with a sharp and tedious hunger; for these forty years past, minding nothing else but the slaughter of these unfortunate wretches, whom with divers kinds of torments neither seen nor heard of before, they have so cruelly and inhumanely butchered, that of three millions of people which Hispaniola itself did contain, there are left remaining alive scarce three hundred persons.*[12]

Las Casas and other missionaries asserted that the Indians had human rights, and through their persistent pressure the Spanish emperor Charles V abolished the worst abuses of the encomienda system in 1531.

Franciscan, Dominican, and Jesuit missionaries who accompanied the conquistadors and other European settlers played an important role in converting indigenous peoples to Christianity, teaching them European methods of agriculture, and instilling loyalty to their colonial masters. In terms of numbers of people baptized, missionaries enjoyed phenomenal success, though the depth of the native peoples' adherence to Christianity remains debatable.

The pattern of devastating disease and population loss established in the Spanish colonies was repeated everywhere Europeans settled. Although precise figures are impossible to establish, the best estimate is that the native population declined from roughly 50 million in 1492 to around 9 million by 1700. It is important to note, however, that native populations and cultures did survive the conquest period, sometimes by blending with European incomers and sometimes by maintaining cultural autonomy.

For colonial administrators the main problem posed by the astronomically high death rate was the loss of a subjugated labor force to work the mines and sugar plantations. As early as 1511 King Ferdinand of Spain observed that the Indians seemed to be "very frail" and that

Mixed Races The unprecedented mixing of peoples in the Spanish New World colonies inspired great fascination. An elaborate terminology emerged to describe the many possible combinations of indigenous, African, and European blood, which were known collectively as *castas*. This painting belongs to a popular genre of the eighteenth century depicting couples composed of individuals of different ethnic origin and the children produced of their unions. (Schalkwijk/Art Resource, NY)

"one black could do the work of four Indians."[13] Thus was born an absurd myth and the new tragedy of the Atlantic slave trade (see page 468).

Life in the Colonies

Many factors helped to shape life in European colonies, including geographical location, religion, indigenous cultures and practices, patterns of European settlement, and the cultural attitudes and official policies of the European nations that claimed them as empire. Throughout the New World, Europeanized settlements were hedged by immense borderlands of European and non-European contact.

Women played a crucial role in the creation of new identities and the continuation of old ones. The first explorers formed unions with native women, through coercion or choice, and relied on them as translators and guides and to form alliances with indigenous powers. As settlement developed, the character of each colony was influenced by the presence or absence of European women. Where women and children accompanied men, as in the British colonies and the Spanish mainland colonies, new settlements took on European languages, religion, and ways of life that have endured, with input from local cultures, to this day. Where European women did not, as on the west coast of Africa and most European outposts in Asia, local populations largely retained their own cultures, to which male Europeans acclimatized themselves. The scarcity of women in all colonies, at least initially, opened up opportunities for those who did arrive, leading one cynic to comment that even "a whore, if handsome, makes a wife for some rich planter."[14]

It was not just the availability of Englishwomen that prevented Englishmen from forming unions with indigenous women. English cultural attitudes drew strict boundaries between civilized and savage, and even settlements of Christianized native peoples were segregated physically and socially from the English. This was in strong contrast with the situation in New France, where royal officials initially encouraged French traders to form ties with native peoples, including marrying local women. Assimilation of the native population was seen as one solution to the low levels of immigration from France.

Most women who crossed the Atlantic were Africans, constituting four-fifths of the female newcomers before 1800.[15] Wherever slavery existed, masters profited from their power to engage in sexual relations with enslaved women. One important difference among European colonies was in the status of children born from such unions. In some colonies, mostly those dominated by the Portuguese, Spanish, or French, substantial populations of free blacks descended from the freed children of such unions. In English colonies, masters were less likely to free children they fathered with female slaves.

The mixing of indigenous peoples with Europeans and Africans created whole new populations and ethnicities and complex self-identities. In Spanish America the word *mestizo*—*métis* in French—described people of mixed Native American and European descent. The blanket terms "mulatto" and "people of color" were used for those of mixed African and European origin. With its immense slave-based plantation agriculture system, large indigenous population, and relatively low Portuguese immigration, Brazil developed a particularly complex racial and ethnic mosaic.

The Columbian Exchange

The migration of peoples to the New World led to an exchange of animals, plants, and disease, a complex process known as the **Columbian exchange**. European immigrants to the Americas wanted the diet with which they were familiar, so they searched for climatic zones favorable to those crops. Columbus had brought sugar plants on his second voyage; Spaniards also introduced rice and bananas from the Canary Islands, and the Portuguese carried these items to Brazil. Everywhere they settled, the Spanish and Portuguese brought and raised wheat with labor provided by the encomienda system. By 1535 Mexico was exporting wheat. Grapes and olives brought over from Spain did well in parts of Peru and Chile. Not all plants arrived intentionally. In clumps of mud on shoes and in the folds of textiles came the seeds of immigrant grasses, including the common dandelion.

Apart from wild turkeys and game, Native Americans had no animals for food. Moreover, they did not domesticate animals for travel or use as beasts of burden,

> *To these quiet Lambs... came the Spaniards like most cruel Tygres, Wolves and Lions, enrag'd with a sharp and tedious hunger; for these forty years past, minding nothing else but the slaughter of these unfortunate wretches.*
> —**Bartolomé de Las Casas**

Columbian exchange The exchange of animals, plants, and diseases between the Old and the New Worlds.

except for alpacas and llamas in the Inca Empire. On his second voyage in 1493 Columbus introduced horses, cattle, sheep, dogs, pigs, chickens, and goats. The multiplication of these animals proved spectacular. The horse enabled the Spanish conquerors and native populations to travel faster and farther and to transport heavy loads. In turn, Europeans returned home with many food crops that became central elements of their diet. (See "Living in the Past: Foods of the Columbian Exchange," page 466.)

Disease was perhaps the most important form of exchange. The wave of catastrophic epidemic disease that swept the Western Hemisphere after 1492 can be seen as an extension of the swath of devastation wreaked by the Black Death in the 1300s, first on Asia and then on Europe. The world after Columbus was thus unified by disease as well as by trade and colonization. The old belief that syphilis originated in the New World and was brought to Europe by Columbus's sailors, however, has been challenged by the discovery of pre-Columbian skeletons in Europe that seem to bear signs of the disease.

Europe and the World After Columbus

How was the era of global contact shaped by new commodities, commercial empires, and forced migrations?

The centuries-old Afro-Eurasian trade world was forever changed by the European voyages of discovery and their aftermath. For the first time, a truly global economy emerged in the sixteenth and seventeenth centuries, and it forged new links among far-flung peoples, cultures, and societies. The ancient civilizations of Europe, Africa, the Americas, and Asia confronted one another in new and rapidly evolving ways. Those confrontations often led to conquest and exploitation, but they also contributed to cultural exchange and renewal.

Sugar and Slavery

Throughout the Middle Ages slavery was deeply entrenched in the Mediterranean, but it was not based on race; many slaves were white. How, then, did black African slavery enter the European picture and take root in South and then North America? In 1453 the Ottoman capture of Constantinople halted the flow of white slaves from the eastern Mediterranean. The successes of the

A New World Sugar Refinery, Brazil Sugar was the most important and most profitable plantation crop in the New World. This image shows the processing and refinement of sugar on a Brazilian plantation. Sugar cane was grown, harvested, and processed by African slaves who labored under brutal and ruthless conditions to generate enormous profits for plantation owners. (The Bridgeman Art Library/Getty Images)

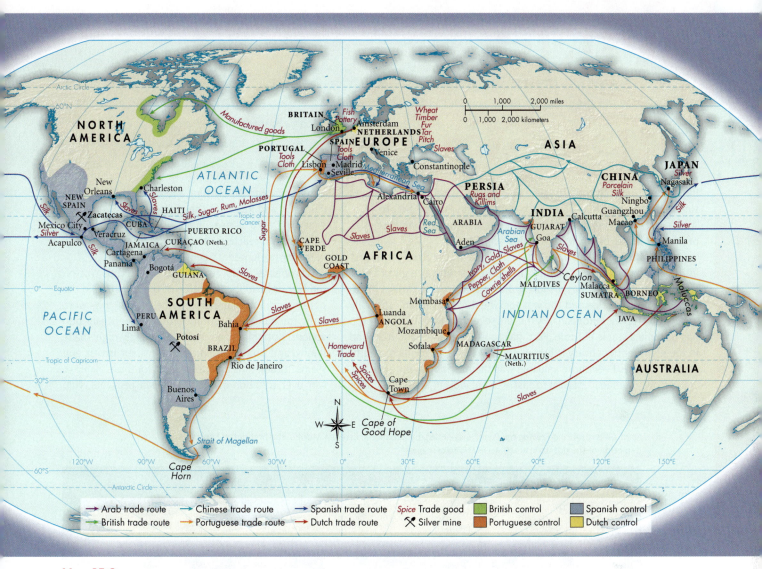

Map 15.3 Seaborne Trading Empires in the Sixteenth and Seventeenth Centuries By the mid-seventeenth century, trade linked all parts of the world except for Australia. Notice that trade in slaves was not confined to the Atlantic but involved almost all parts of the world.

Iberian reconquista also meant that the supply of Muslim captives had drastically diminished. Cut off from its traditional sources of slaves, Mediterranean Europe then turned to sub-Saharan Africa, which had a long history of slave trading. (See "Individuals in Society: Juan de Pareja," page 469.) As Portuguese explorers began their voyages along the western coast of Africa, one of the first commodities they sought was slaves. In 1444 the first ship returned to Lisbon with a cargo of enslaved Africans; the Crown was delighted, and more shipments followed.

While the first slaves were simply seized by small raiding parties, Portuguese merchants soon found that it was easier to trade with local leaders, who were accustomed to dealing in slaves captured through warfare with neighboring powers. From 1490 to 1530 Portuguese traders brought between three hundred and two thousand enslaved Africans to Lisbon each year (Map 15.3), where they performed most of the manual labor and constituted 10 percent of the city's population.

In this stage of European expansion, the history of slavery became intertwined with the history of sugar. Originally sugar was an expensive luxury that only the very affluent could afford, but population increases and monetary expansion in the fifteenth century led to increasing demand. Native to the South Pacific, sugar was taken in ancient times to India, where farmers learned to preserve cane juice as granules that could be stored and shipped. From there, sugar traveled to China and the Mediterranean, where islands like

Foods of the Columbian Exchange

LIVING IN THE PAST

MANY STUDENTS ARE AWARE of the devastating effects of European diseases on peoples of the New World and of the role of gunpowder and horses in the conquest of native civilizations. They may be less aware of how New World foodstuffs transformed Europeans' daily life. Prior to Christopher Columbus's voyages, many common elements of today's European diet were unknown in Europe. It's hard to imagine Italian pizza without tomato sauce or Irish stew without potatoes, yet tomatoes and potatoes were both unknown in Europe before 1492. Additional crops originating in the Americas included many varieties of beans, squash, pumpkins, avocados, and peppers.

One of the most important of such crops was maize (corn), first introduced to Europe by Columbus in 1493. Because maize gives a high yield per unit of land, has a short growing season, and thrives in climates too dry for rice and too wet for wheat, it proved an especially important crop for Europeans. By the late seventeenth century the crop had become a staple in Spain, Portugal, southern France, and Italy, and in the eighteenth century it became one of the chief foods of southeastern Europe. Even more valuable was the nutritious white potato, which slowly spread from west to east — to Ireland, England, and France in the seventeenth century, and to Germany, Poland, Hungary, and Russia in the eighteenth, contributing everywhere to a rise in population. Ironically, the white potato reached New England from old England in the early eighteenth century.

Europeans' initial reaction to these crops was often fear or hostility. Adoption of the tomato and the potato was long hampered by belief that they were unfit for human consumption and potentially poisonous. Both plants belong to the deadly nightshade family, and both contain poison in their leaves and stems. It took time and persuasion for these plants to win over tradition-minded European peasants, who

Saint Diego of Alcala Feeding the Poor (1645–1646), by Bartolome Esteban Murillo, the first dated European depiction of the potato in art. (Joseph Martin/akg-images)

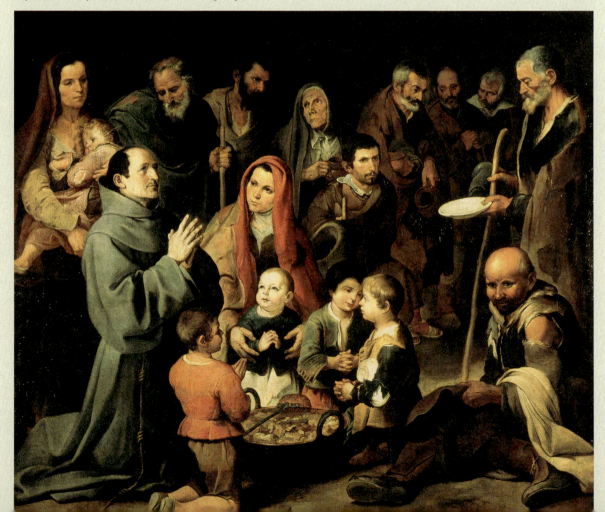

Incan women milking goats, from a collection of illustrations by a Spanish bishop that offers a valuable view of life in Peru in the 1780s. (Oronoz)

The first European scientific illustration of maize appeared in 1542, a half century after it was introduced to the continent. (The LuEsther T. Mertz Library, NYBG/Art Resource, NY)

used potatoes mostly as livestock feed. During the eighteenth-century Enlightenment, scientists and doctors played an important role in popularizing the nutritive benefits of the potato.

Columbus himself contributed to misconceptions about New World foods when he mistook the chili pepper for black pepper, one of the spices he had hoped to find in the Indies. The Portuguese quickly began exporting chili peppers from Brazil to Africa, India, and Southeast Asia along the trade routes they dominated. The chili pepper arrived in North America through its place in the diet of enslaved Africans.

European settlers introduced various foods to the native peoples of the New World, including rice, wheat, lettuce, and onions. Perhaps the most significant introduction to the diet of Native Americans came via the meat and milk of the livestock that the early conquistadors brought with them, including cattle, sheep, and goats.

The foods of the Columbian exchange traveled a truly global path. They provided important new sources of nutrition to people all over the world, as well as creating new and beloved culinary traditions. French fries with ketchup, anyone?

QUESTIONS FOR ANALYSIS

1. Why do you think it was so difficult for Europeans to accept new types of food, even when they were high in nutritional quality?
2. What do these illustrations suggest about the importance of the Columbian exchange?
3. List the foods you typically eat in a day. How many of them originated in the New World, and how many in the Old World? How does your own life exemplify the outcome of the Columbian exchange?

Crete, Sicily, and Cyprus had the warm and wet climate needed for growing sugar cane. When Genoese and other Italians colonized the Canary Islands and the Portuguese settled on the Madeira Islands, sugar plantations came to the Atlantic.

Sugar was a particularly difficult and demanding crop to produce for profit. Seed-stems were planted by hand, thousands to the acre. When mature, the cane had to be harvested and processed rapidly to avoid spoiling, forcing days and nights of work with little rest. Moreover, its growing season is virtually constant, meaning that there is no fallow period when workers could recuperate from the arduous labor. The demands of sugar production were only increased with the invention of roller mills to crush the cane more efficiently. Yields could be augmented, but only if a sufficient labor force was found to supply the mills. Europeans solved the labor problem by forcing first native islanders and then enslaved Africans to provide the backbreaking work.

Sugar gave New World slavery its distinctive shape. Columbus himself, who spent a decade in Madeira, brought sugar plants on his voyages to "the Indies." The transatlantic slave trade began in 1518 when Spanish king Charles I authorized traders to bring African slaves to New World colonies. The Portuguese brought the first slaves to Brazil around 1550; by 1600 four thousand were being imported annually. After its founding in 1621, the Dutch West India Company, with the full support of the United Provinces, transported thousands of Africans to Brazil and the Caribbean, mostly to work on sugar plantations. In the late seventeenth century, with the chartering of the Royal African Company, the English got involved.

European sailors found the Atlantic passage cramped and uncomfortable, but conditions for African slaves were lethal. Before 1700, when slavers decided it was better business to improve conditions, some 20 percent of slaves died on the voyage.[16] The most common cause of death was from dysentery induced by poor quality food and water, intense crowding, and lack of sanitation. Men were often kept in irons during the passage, while women and girls were considered fair game for sailors. To increase profits, slave traders packed several hundred captives on each ship. One slaver explained that he removed his boots before entering the slave hold because he had to crawl over the slaves' packed bodies.[17] On sugar plantations, death rates among slaves from illness and exhaustion were extremely high, leading to a constant stream of new shipments of slaves from Africa.

In total, scholars estimate that European traders embarked over 10 million African slaves across the Atlantic from 1518 to 1800 (of whom roughly 8.5 million disembarked), with the peak of the trade occurring in the eighteenth century.[18] By comparison, only 2 to 2.5 million Europeans migrated to the New World during the same period. Enslaved Africans worked in an infinite variety of occupations: as miners, soldiers, sailors, servants, and artisans and in the production of cotton, rum, indigo, tobacco, wheat, corn, and, most predominantly, sugar.

Spanish Silver and Its Economic Effects

The sixteenth century has often been called Spain's golden century, but silver mined in the Americas was the true source of Spain's incredible wealth. In 1545, at an altitude of fifteen thousand feet, the Spanish discovered an extraordinary source of silver at Potosí (poh-toh-SEE) (in present-day Bolivia) in territory conquered from the Inca Empire. The frigid place where nothing grew had been unsettled. A half century later 160,000 people lived there, making it about the size of the city of London. By 1550 Potosí yielded perhaps 60 percent of all the silver mined in the world. From Potosí and the mines at Zacatecas (za-kuh-TAY-kuhhs) and Guanajuato (gwah-nah-HWAH-toh) in Mexico, huge quantities of precious metals poured forth. To protect this treasure from French and English pirates, armed convoys transported it to Spain each year. Between 1503 and 1650, 35 million pounds of silver and over 600,000 pounds of gold entered Seville's port. Spanish predominance, however, proved temporary.

In the sixteenth century Spain experienced a steady population increase, creating a sharp rise in the demand for food and goods. Spanish colonies in the Americas also demanded consumer goods that were not produced in the colonies, such as cloth and luxury goods. Since Spain had expelled some of its best farmers and businessmen — the Muslims and Jews — in the fifteenth century, the Spanish economy was suffering and could not meet the new demands. The excess of demand over supply led to widespread inflation. The result was a rise in production costs and a further decline in Spain's productive capacity.

Did the flood of silver bullion from America cause the inflation? Prices rose most steeply before 1565, but bullion imports reached their peak between 1580 and 1620. Thus silver did not cause the initial inflation. It did, however, exacerbate the situation, and, along with the ensuing rise in population, the influx of silver significantly contributed to the upward spiral of prices. Inflation severely strained government budgets. Several times between 1557 and 1647, Spain's King Philip II and his successors wrote off the state debt, thereby undermining confidence in the government and leaving the economy in shambles. After 1600, when the population declined, prices gradually stabilized.

As Philip II paid his armies and foreign debts with silver bullion, Spanish inflation was transmitted to the rest of Europe. Between 1560 and 1600 much of Europe

Juan de Pareja

INDIVIDUALS IN SOCIETY

DURING THE LONG WARS OF THE RECONQUISTA, Muslims and Christians captured each other in battle and used the defeated as slaves. As the Muslims were gradually eliminated from Iberia in the fifteenth and sixteenth centuries, the Spanish and Portuguese turned to the west coast of Africa for a new supply of slaves. Most slaves worked as domestic servants, rather than in the fields. Some received specialized training as artisans.

Not all people of African descent were slaves, and some experienced both freedom and slavery in a single lifetime. The life and career of Juan de Pareja (pah-REH-huh) illustrates the complexities of the Iberian slave system and the heights of achievement possible for those who achieved freedom.

Pareja was born in Antequera, an agricultural region and the old center of Muslim culture near Seville in southern Spain. Of his parents we know nothing. Because a rare surviving document calls him a "mulatto," one of his parents must have been white and the other must have had some African blood. In 1630 Pareja applied to the mayor of Seville for permission to travel to Madrid to visit his brother and "to perfect his art." The document lists his occupation as "a painter in Seville." Since it mentions no other name, it is reasonable to assume that Pareja arrived in Madrid a free man. Sometime between 1630 and 1648, however, he came into the possession of the artist Diego Velázquez (1599–1660); Pareja became a slave.

How did Velázquez acquire Pareja? By purchase? As a gift? Had Pareja fallen into debt or committed some crime and thereby lost his freedom? We do not know. Velázquez, the greatest Spanish painter of the seventeenth century, had a large studio with many assistants. Pareja was set to grinding powders to make colors and to preparing canvases. He must have demonstrated ability because when Velázquez went to Rome in 1648, he chose Pareja to accompany him.

In 1650, as practice for a portrait of Pope Innocent X, Velázquez painted Pareja. The portrait shows Pareja dressed in fine clothing and gazing self-confidently at the viewer. Displayed in Rome in a public exhibition of Velázquez's work, the painting won acclaim from his contemporaries. That same year, Velázquez signed the document that gave Pareja his freedom, to become effective in 1654. Pareja lived out the rest of his life as an independent painter.

What does the public career of Pareja tell us about the man and his world? Pareja's career suggests that a person of African descent might fall into slavery and yet still acquire professional training and work alongside his master in a position of confidence. Moreover, if lucky enough to be freed, a former slave could exercise a profession and live his own life in Madrid. Pareja's experience was far from typical for a slave in the 1600s, but it reminds us of the myriad forms that slavery took in this period.

Velázquez, *Juan de Pareja*, 1650. (The Metropolitan Museum of Art, Fletcher Fund, Rogers Fund, and Bequest of Miss Adelaide Milton de Groot (1876–1967), by exchange, supplemented by gifts from friends of the Museum, 1971. [1971.86]. Image copyright © The Metropolitan Museum of Art)

QUESTIONS FOR ANALYSIS

1. Since slavery was an established institution in Spain, speculate on Velázquez's possible reasons for giving Pareja his freedom.
2. To what extent was Pareja a marginal person in Spanish society? Was he an insider or an outsider to Spanish society?

Sources: Jonathan Brown, *Velázquez: Painter and Courtier* (New Haven, Conn.: Yale University Press, 1986); *Grove Dictionary of Art* (New York: Macmillan, 2000); Sister Wendy Beckett, *Sister Wendy's American Collection* (New York: Harper Collins Publishers, 2000), p. 15.

In many ways, though, it was not Spain but China that controlled the world trade in silver. The Chinese demanded silver for their products and for the payment of imperial taxes. China was thus the main buyer of world silver, absorbing half the world's production. The silver market drove world trade, with New Spain and Japan being mainstays on the supply side and China dominating the demand side. The world trade in silver is one of the best examples of the new global economy that emerged in this period.

The Birth of the Global Economy

With the Europeans' discovery of the Americas and their exploration of the Pacific, the entire world was linked for the first time in history by seaborne trade. The opening of that trade brought into being three successive commercial empires: the Portuguese, the Spanish, and the Dutch.

The Portuguese were the first worldwide traders. In the sixteenth century they controlled the sea route to India (see Map 15.3). From their fortified bases at Goa on the Arabian Sea and at Malacca on the Malay Peninsula, ships carried goods to the Portuguese settlement at Macao in the South China Sea. From Macao Portuguese ships loaded with Chinese silks and porcelains sailed to the Japanese port of Nagasaki and to the Philippine port of Manila, where Chinese goods were exchanged for Spanish silver from New Spain. Throughout Asia the Portuguese traded in slaves — sub-Saharan Africans, Chinese, and Japanese. The Portuguese exported horses from Mesopotamia and copper from Arabia to India; from India they exported hawks and peacocks for the Chinese and Japanese markets. Back to Portugal they brought Asian spices that had been purchased with textiles produced in India and with gold and ivory from East Africa. They also shipped back sugar from their colony in Brazil, produced by enslaved Africans whom they had transported across the Atlantic.

Coming to empire a few decades later than the Portuguese, the Spanish were determined to claim their place in world trade. The Spanish Empire in the New World was basically a land empire, but across the Pacific the Spaniards built a seaborne empire centered at Manila in the Philippines. The city of Manila served as the transpacific bridge between Spanish America and China. In Manila, Spanish traders used silver from American mines to purchase Chinese silk for European markets. The European demand for silk was so huge that in 1597, for example, 12 million pesos of silver, almost the total value of the transatlantic trade, moved from Acapulco in New Spain to Manila (see Map 15.3). After 1640 the Spanish silk trade declined in the face of stiff competition from Dutch imports.

Philip II, ca. 1533 This portrait of Philip II as a young man and crown prince of Spain is by the celebrated artist Titian, court painter to Philip's father, Charles V. After taking the throne, Philip became another great patron of the artist. (Museo Nacional del Prado, Madrid)

experienced large price increases. Prices doubled and in some cases quadrupled. Spain suffered most severely, but all European countries were affected. Because money bought less, people who lived on fixed incomes, such as nobles, were badly hurt. Those who owed fixed sums of money, such as the middle class, prospered because in a time of rising prices, debts lessened in value each year. Food costs rose most sharply, and the poor fared worst of all.

In the seventeenth century the Dutch challenged the Spanish and Portuguese Empires. Drawing on their commercial wealth and long experience in European trade, the Dutch emerged by the end of the century as the most powerful worldwide seaborne trading power. The Dutch Empire was built on spices. In 1599 a Dutch fleet returned to Amsterdam carrying 600,000 pounds of pepper and 250,000 pounds of cloves and nutmeg. Those who had invested in the expedition received a 100 percent profit. The voyage led to the establishment in 1602 of the Dutch East India Company, founded with the stated intention of capturing the spice trade from the Portuguese.

The Dutch set their sights on gaining direct access to and control of the Indonesian sources of spices. The Dutch fleet, sailing from the Cape of Good Hope in

Goods from the Global Economy Spices from Southeast Asia were a driving force behind the new global economy, and among the most treasured European luxury goods. They were used not only for cooking but also as medicines and health tonics. This fresco (center) shows a fifteenth-century Italian pharmacist measuring out spices for a customer. After the discovery of the Americas, a wave of new items entered European markets, silver foremost among them. The incredibly rich silver mines at Potosí (modern-day Bolivia) were the source of this eight-reale coin (left) struck at the mine during the reign of Charles II. Such coins were the original "pieces of eight" prized by pirates and adventurers. Soon Asian and American goods were mixed together by enterprising tradesmen. The mid-seventeenth-century Chinese teapot (right) was made of porcelain with the traditional Chinese design prized in the West, but with a silver handle added to suit European tastes. (teapot: Private Collection/Paul Freeman/The Bridgeman Art Library; coin: Hoberman Collection/SuperStock; spice shop: Alfredo Dagli Orti/The Art Archive)

Africa and avoiding the Portuguese forts in India, steered directly for the Sunda Strait in Indonesia (see Map 15.3). In return for assisting Indonesian princes in local squabbles and disputes with the Portuguese, the Dutch won broad commercial concessions. Through agreements, seizures, and outright war, they gained control of the western access to the Indonesian archipelago in the first half of the seventeenth century. Gradually, they acquired political domination over the archipelago itself. By the 1660s the Dutch had managed to expel the Portuguese from Ceylon and other East Indian islands, thereby establishing control of the lucrative spice trade.

Not content with challenging the Portuguese in the Indian Ocean, the Dutch also aspired to a role in the Americas. Founded in 1621 in a period of war with Spain, the Dutch West India Company aggressively sought to open trade with North and South America and capture Spanish territories there. The company captured or destroyed hundreds of Spanish ships, seized the Spanish silver fleet in 1628, and captured portions of Brazil and the Caribbean. The Dutch also successfully interceded in the transatlantic slave trade, bringing much of the west coast of Africa under Dutch control. Ironically, the nation that was known throughout Europe as a bastion of tolerance and freedom came to be one of the principal operators of the slave trade starting in the 1640s.

Dutch efforts to colonize North America were less successful. The colony of New Netherland, governed from New Amsterdam (modern-day New York City), was hampered by lack of settlement and weak governance and was easily captured by the British in 1664.

Changing Attitudes and Beliefs

How did new ideas about race and the works of Montaigne and Shakespeare reflect the encounter with new peoples and places?

The age of overseas expansion heightened Europeans' contacts with the rest of the world. These contacts gave birth to new ideas about the inherent superiority or inferiority of different races, in part to justify European participation in the slave trade. Cultural encounters also inspired more positive views. The essays of Michel de Montaigne epitomized a new spirit of skepticism and cultural relativism, while the plays of William Shakespeare reflected the efforts of one great writer to come to terms with the cultural complexity of his day.

New Ideas About Race

At the beginning of the transatlantic slave trade, most Europeans would have thought of Africans, if they thought of them at all, as savages because of their eating habits, morals, clothing, and social customs and as barbarians because of their language and methods of war. Despite lingering belief in a Christian Ethiopia under the legendary Prester John, they grouped Africans into the despised categories of pagan heathens and Muslim infidels. Africans were certainly not the only peoples subject to such dehumanizing attitudes. Jews were also viewed as an alien group that was, like Africans, naturally given to sin and depravity. More generally, elite people across Europe were accustomed to viewing the peasant masses as a lower form of humanity. They scornfully compared rustic peasants to dogs, pigs, and donkeys and even reviled the dark skin color peasants acquired while laboring in the sun.[19]

As Europeans turned to Africa for new sources of slaves, they drew on and developed ideas about Africans' primitiveness and barbarity to defend slavery and even argue that enslavement benefited Africans by bringing the light of Christianity to heathen peoples. In 1444 an observer defended the enslavement of the first Africans by Portuguese explorers as necessary for their salvation "because they lived like beasts, without any of the customs of rational creatures, since they did not even know what were bread and wine, nor garments of cloth, nor life in the shelter of a house; and worse still was their ignorance, which deprived them of knowledge of good, and permitted them only a life of brutish idleness."[20] Compare this with an early seventeenth-century Englishman's complaint that the Irish "be so beastly that they are better like beasts than Christians."[21]

Over time, the institution of slavery fostered a new level of racial inequality. In contrast to peasants, Jews, and the Irish, Africans gradually became seen as utterly distinct from and wholly inferior to Europeans. From rather vague assumptions about non-Christian religious beliefs and a general lack of civilization, Europeans developed increasingly rigid ideas of racial superiority and inferiority to safeguard the growing profits gained from plantation slavery. Black skin became equated with slavery itself as Europeans at home and in the colonies convinced themselves that blacks were destined by God to serve them as slaves in perpetuity.

Support for this belief went back to the Greek philosopher Aristotle's argument that some people are naturally destined for slavery and to biblical associations between darkness and sin. A more explicit justification was found in the story of Noah's curse upon Canaan. According to the Bible, Ham defied his father's ban on sexual relations on the ark and further

> **They lived like beasts, without any of the customs of rational creatures, since they did not even know what were bread and wine, nor garments of cloth, nor life in the shelter of a house.**
>
> —EUROPEAN OBSERVER

enraged Noah by entering his tent and viewing his father unclothed. To punish Ham, Noah cursed Ham's son Canaan and all his descendants to be the "servant of servants." Biblical genealogies listing Ham's sons as those who peopled North Africa and Cush were read to mean that all inhabitants of those regions bore Noah's curse. From the sixteenth century onward, this story was often cited as justification for the enslavement of an entire race.

After 1700 the emergence of new methods of observing and describing nature led to the use of science to define race. From referring to a nation or an ethnic group, henceforth "race" would mean biologically distinct groups of people, whose physical differences produced differences in culture, character, and intelligence. Biblical justifications for inequality thereby gave way to supposedly scientific ones.

Michel de Montaigne and Cultural Curiosity

Racism was not the only possible reaction to the new worlds emerging in the sixteenth century. Decades of religious fanaticism, bringing civil anarchy and war, led both Catholics and Protestants to doubt that any one faith contained absolute truth. Added to these doubts was the discovery of peoples in the New World who had radically different ways of life. These shocks helped produce ideas of skepticism and cultural relativism in the sixteenth and seventeenth centuries. Skepticism is a school of thought founded on doubt that total certainty or definitive knowledge is ever attainable. The skeptic is cautious and critical and suspends judgment. Cultural relativism suggests that one culture is not necessarily superior to another, just different. Both notions found expression in the work of Frenchman Michel de Montaigne (duh mahn-TAYN) (1533–1592).

Montaigne developed a new literary genre, the essay—from the French *essayer*, meaning "to test or try"—to express his thoughts and ideas. Published in 1580, Montaigne's *Essays* consisted of short personal reflections drawing on his extensive reading in ancient texts, his experience as a government official, and his own moral judgment. Intended to be accessible to ordinary people, Montaigne wrote in French rather than Latin and in an engaging conversational style.

Montaigne's essay "Of Cannibals" reveals the impact of overseas discoveries on one thoughtful European's consciousness. In contrast to the prevailing views of the time, he rejected the notion that one culture is superior to another. Speaking of native Brazilians, he wrote:

> *I find that there is nothing barbarous and savage in this nation [Brazil], . . . except, that everyone gives the title of barbarism to everything that is not according to his usage; as, indeed, we have no other criterion of truth and reason, than the example and pattern of the opinions and customs of the place wherein we live. . . . They are savages in the same way that we say fruits are wild, which nature produces of herself and by her ordinary course; whereas, in truth, we ought rather to call those wild whose natures we have changed by our artifice and diverted from the common order.*[22]

In his own time and throughout the seventeenth century, few would have agreed with Montaigne's challenge to ideas of European superiority or his even more radical questioning of the superiority of humans over animals. The publication of his ideas, however, contributed to a basic shift in attitudes. Montaigne inaugurated an era of doubt. "Wonder," he said, "is the foundation of all philosophy, research is the means of all learning, and ignorance is the end."[23]

William Shakespeare and His Influence

In addition to the essay as a literary genre, the period fostered remarkable creativity in other branches of literature. England—especially in the latter part of Queen Elizabeth I's reign and in the first years of her successor, James I (r. 1603–1625)—witnessed remarkable literary expression. The terms *Elizabethan* and *Jacobean* (referring to the reign of James) are used to designate the English music, poetry, prose, and drama of this period.

The undisputed master of the period was the dramatist William Shakespeare, whose genius lay in the originality of his characterizations, the diversity of his plots,

Titus Andronicus With classical allusions, fifteen murders and executions, a Gothic queen who takes a black lover, and incredible violence, this early Shakespearean tragedy (1594) was a melodramatic thriller that enjoyed enormous popularity with the London audience. The shock value of a dark-skinned character on the English stage is clearly shown in this illustration. (Reproduced by permission of the Marquess of Bath, Longleat House, Warminster, Wilts)

his understanding of human psychology, and his unsurpassed gift for language. Born in 1564 to a successful glove manufacturer in Stratford-on-Avon, Shakespeare grew into a Renaissance man with a deep appreciation of classical culture, individualism, and humanism. Such plays as *Julius Caesar* and *Antony and Cleopatra* deal with classical subjects and figures. Several of his comedies have Italian Renaissance settings. His history plays, including *Richard III* and *Henry IV*, express English national consciousness. Shakespeare's later tragedies, including *Hamlet*, *Othello*, and *Macbeth*, explore an enormous range of human problems and are open to an almost infinite variety of interpretations.

Like Montaigne, Shakespeare's work reveals the impact of the new discoveries and contacts of his day. The title character of *Othello* is described as a "Moor of Venice." In Shakespeare's day, the term "moor" referred to Muslims of Moroccan or North African origin, including those who had migrated to the Iberian Peninsula. It could also be applied, though, to natives of the Iberian Peninsula who converted to Islam or to non-Muslim Berbers in North Africa. To complicate things even more, references in the play to Othello as "black" in skin color have led many to believe that Shakespeare intended him to be a sub-Saharan African, and he is usually depicted as such in modern performances. This confusion in the play reflects the uncertainty in Shakespeare's own day about racial and religious classifications.

The character of Othello is both vilified in racist terms by his enemies and depicted as a brave warrior, a key member of the city's military leadership, and a man capable of winning the heart of an aristocratic white woman. In contrast to the prevailing view of Moors as inferior, Shakespeare presents Othello as a complex human figure, whose only crime is to have "loved [his wife] not wisely, but too well." Shakespeare's play thus demonstrates both the intolerance of contemporary society and the possibility for some individuals to look beyond racial stereotypes.

Shakespeare's last play, *The Tempest*, displays a similar interest in race and race relations. The plot involves the stranding on an island of sorcerer Prospero and his daughter Miranda. There Prospero finds and raises Caliban, a native of the island, whom he instructs in his own language and religion. After Caliban's attempted rape of Miranda, Prospero enslaves him, earning the rage and resentment of his erstwhile pupil. Modern scholars often note the echoes between this play and the realities of imperial conquest and settlement in Shakespeare's day. It is no accident, they argue, that the poet portrayed Caliban as a monstrous dark-skinned island native who was best-suited for slavery. Shakespeare himself borrows words from Montaigne's essay "Of Cannibals," suggesting that he may have intended to criticize, rather than endorse, racial intolerance. Shakespeare's work shows us one of the finest minds of the age grasping to come to terms with the racial and religious complexities around him.

LOOKING BACK LOOKING AHEAD

JUST THREE YEARS SEPARATED the posting of Martin Luther's "Ninety-five Theses" in 1517 from Ferdinand Magellan's discovery of the Pacific Ocean in 1520. Within a few short years, the religious unity of western Europe and its notions of terrestrial geography were shattered. Old medieval certainties about Heaven and earth collapsed. In the ensuing decades, Europeans struggled to come to terms with religious difference at home and the multitudes of new peoples and places they encountered abroad. These processes were intertwined, as Puritans and Quakers fled religious persecution at home to colonize the New World and the new Jesuit order proved its devotion to the pope by seeking Catholic converts across the globe. While some Europeans were fascinated and inspired by this new diversity, too often the result was violence. Europeans endured decades of civil war between Protestants and Catholics, and indigenous peoples suffered massive population losses as a result of European warfare, disease, and exploitation. Tragically, both Catholic and Protestant religious leaders condoned the African slave trade that was to bring suffering and death to millions of Africans.

Even as the voyages of discovery contributed to the fragmentation of European culture, they also belonged to longer-term processes of state centralization and consolidation. The new monarchies of the Renaissance produced stronger and wealthier governments capable of financing the huge expenses of exploration and colonization. Competition to gain overseas colonies became an integral part of European politics. Spain's investment in conquest proved spectacularly profitable and yet, as we will see in Chapter 16, the ultimate result was a weakening of its power. Other European nations took longer to realize financial gain, yet over time the Netherlands, England, and France reaped tremendous profits from colonial trade, which helped them build modernized, centralized states. The path from medieval Christendom to modern nation-states led through religious warfare and global encounter.

CHAPTER REVIEW

■ **What was the Afro-Eurasian trading world before Columbus? (p. 444)**

Prior to Columbus's voyages, well-developed trade routes linked the peoples and products of Africa, Asia, and Europe. The Indian Ocean was the center of the Afro-Eurasian trade world, ringed by cosmopolitan commercial cities such as Mombasa in Africa, Calicut in India, and Malacca in Southeast Asia. Chinese silk and porcelain were desired by elites throughout the trading system. The Ottoman and Persian Empires produced textiles and other goods for the world market, while also serving as intermediaries for trade between East and West. Venetian and Genoese merchants brought spices, silks, and other luxury goods into western Europe from the East. Overall, Europeans played a minor role in the Afro-Eurasian trading world because they did not produce many products desired by Eastern elites.

■ **How and why did Europeans undertake ambitious voyages of expansion? (p. 448)**

In the sixteenth and seventeenth centuries Europeans gained access to large parts of the globe for the first time. A revival of populations and economies after the time of the Black Death created markets for spices and other goods from the East. In addition to searching for routes that would undo the Italian and Ottoman dominance of trade in the East, Europeans were motivated by intellectual curiosity, driving ambition, religious zeal, and a lack of opportunities at home. The revived monarchies of the sixteenth century now possessed sufficient resources to back ambitious seafarers like Christopher Columbus and Vasco da Gama. Technological developments such as the invention of the caravel and magnetic compass enabled Europeans to undertake ever more ambitious voyages.

■ **What was the impact of European conquest on the peoples and ecologies of the New World? (p. 461)**

In the aftermath of conquest, the Spanish established new forms of governance to dominate native peoples and exploit their labor. The arrival of Europeans also brought enormous population losses to native communities, primarily through the spread of infectious diseases. Women played an important role in creating new colonial societies, both through the union of native and African women with European men and through the migration of European women to the colonies. The Age of Discovery sparked a complex exchange of germs, flora, and fauna between the Old and New Worlds, which is known as the "Columbian exchange." Europeans brought familiar crops and livestock to the Americas, and brought home new ones, some of which became staples of the European diet.

■ **How was the era of global contact shaped by new commodities, commercial empires, and forced migrations? (p. 464)**

One of the most important consequences of the Age of Discovery was the creation of the first truly global economy in the sixteenth and seventeenth centuries. Tragically, a major component of global trade was the transatlantic slave trade, in which Europeans transported many millions of Africans to labor in horrific conditions in the mines and sugar plantations of the New World. The discovery of extraordinarily rich silver mines in New Spain brought enormous wealth to the Spanish crown, but little economic development. European nations vied for supremacy in global trade, with early Portuguese success in India and Asia being challenged first by the Spanish and then by the Dutch, who successfully imposed control of trade with the East in the mid-seventeenth century.

■ **How did new ideas about race and the works of Montaigne and Shakespeare reflect the encounter with new peoples and places? (p. 472)**

Increased contact with the outside world led Europeans to develop new ideas about cultural and racial difference. Europeans had long held negative attitudes toward Africans; as the slave trade grew, they began to express more rigid notions of racial inequality and to claim that Africans were inherently suited for slavery. Most Europeans shared such views, with some important exceptions. In his essays, Michel de Montaigne challenged the idea that natives of the Americas were inferior barbarians, while William Shakespeare's plays contain ambivalent attitudes toward complex non-European characters.

Suggested Reading

Crosby, Alfred W. *The Columbian Exchange: Biological and Cultural Consequences of 1492.* 30th anniversary ed. 2003. An innovative and highly influential account of the environmental impact of Columbus's voyages.

Elliot, J. H. *Empires of the Atlantic World: Britain and Spain in America, 1492–1830.* 2006. A masterful account of the differences and similarities between the British and Spanish Empires in the Americas.

Fernández-Armesto, Felip. *Columbus.* 1992. An excellent biography of Christopher Columbus.

Greenblatt, Stephen. *Marvelous Possessions: The Wonder of the New World.* 1991. Describes the cultural impact of New World discoveries on Europeans.

Menard, Russell. *Sweet Negotiations: Sugar, Slavery and Plantation Agriculture in Early Barbados.* 2006. Explores the intertwined history of sugar plantations and slavery in seventeenth-century Barbados.

Northrup, David, ed. *The Atlantic Slave Trade*. 1994. Collected essays by leading scholars on many different aspects of the slave trade.

Pérez-Mallaína, Pablo E. *Spain's Men of the Sea: Daily Life on the Indies Fleet in the Sixteenth Century*. 1998. A description of recruitment, daily life, and career paths of ordinary sailors and officers in the Spanish fleet.

Pomeranz, Kenneth, and Steven Topik. *The World That Trade Created: Society, Culture and the World Economy, 1400 to the Present*. 1999. The creation of a world market presented through rich and vivid stories of merchants, miners, slaves, and farmers.

Restall, Matthew. *Seven Myths of Spanish Conquest*. 2003. A re-examination of common ideas about why and how the Spanish conquered native civilizations in the New World.

Scammell, Geoffrey V. *The World Encompassed: The First European Maritime Empires, c. 800–1650*. 1981. A detailed overview of the first European empires, including the Italian city-states, Portugal, and Spain.

Schmidt, Benjamin. *Innocence Abroad: The Dutch Imagination and the New World, 1570–1670*. 2001. Examines changing Dutch attitudes toward the New World, from criticism of the cruelty of the Spanish conquest to eagerness for their own overseas empire.

Subrahamanyam, Sanjay. *The Career and Legend of Vasco da Gama*. 1998. A probing biography that places Vasco da Gama in the context of Portuguese politics and society.

Notes

1. Thomas Benjamin, *The Atlantic World: Europeans, Africans, Indians and Their Shared History, 1400–1900* (Cambridge, U.K.: Cambridge University Press, 2009), p. 56.
2. G. V. Scammell, *The World Encompassed: The First European Maritime Empires, c. 800–1650* (Berkeley: University of California Press, 1981), pp. 101, 104.
3. Quoted in C. M. Cipolla, *Guns, Sails, and Empires: Technological Innovation and the Early Phases of European Expansion, 1400–1700* (New York: Minerva Press, 1965), p. 132.
4. Quoted in F. H. Littell, *The Macmillan Atlas: History of Christianity* (New York: Macmillan, 1976), p. 75.
5. Pablo E. Pérez-Mallaína, *Spain's Men of the Sea: Daily Life on the Indies Fleet in the Sixteenth Century* (Baltimore: Johns Hopkins University Press, 1998), p. 133.
6. Ibid., p. 19.
7. Quoted in F. Maddison, "Tradition and Innovation: Columbus' First Voyage and Portuguese Navigation in the Fifteenth Century," in *Circa 1492: Art in the Age of Exploration*, ed. J. A. Levenson (Washington, D.C.: National Gallery of Art, 1991), p. 69.
8. Quoted in R. L. Kagan, "The Spain of Ferdinand and Isabella," in *Circa 1492: Art in the Age of Exploration*, ed. J. A. Levenson (Washington, D.C.: National Gallery of Art, 1991), p. 60.
9. Peter Hulme, *Colonial Encounters: Europe and the Native Caribbean, 1492–1797* (London and New York: Methuan, 1986), pp. 22–31.
10. Benjamin, *The Atlantic World*, p. 141.
11. Ibid., pp. 35–59.
12. Quoted in C. Gibson, ed., *The Black Legend: Anti-Spanish Attitudes in the Old World and the New* (New York: Knopf, 1971), pp. 74–75.
13. Quoted in L. B. Rout, Jr., *The African Experience in Spanish America* (New York: Cambridge University Press, 1976), p. 23.
14. Cited in Geoffrey Vaughn Scammell, *The First Imperial Age: European Overseas Expansion, c. 1400–1715* (London and New York: Routledge, 2002), p. 62.
15. Ibid., p. 432.
16. Herbert S. Klein, "Profits and the Causes of Mortality," in David Northrup, ed., *The Atlantic Slave Trade* (Lexington, Mass.: D. C. Heath and Co., 1994), p. 116.
17. Malcolm Cowley and Daniel P. Mannix, "The Middle Passage," in David Northrup, ed., *The Atlantic Slave Trade* (Lexington, Mass.: D. C. Heath and Co., 1994), p. 101.
18. Voyages: The Trans-Atlantic Slave Trade Database, http://www.slavevoyages.org/tast/assessment/estimates.faces (accessed May 9, 2009).
19. Paul Freedman, *Images of the Medieval Peasant* (Stanford, Calif.: Stanford University Press, 1999).
20. Quoted in James H. Sweet, "The Iberian Roots of American Racist Thought," *The William and Mary Quarterly*, Third Series, Vol. 54, No. 1 (Jan. 1997), p. 155.
21. Quoted in Sean J. Connolly, *Contested Island: Ireland, 1460–1630* (Oxford: Oxford University Press, 2007), p. 397.
22. C. Cotton, trans., *The Essays of Michel de Montaigne* (New York: A. L. Burt, 1893), pp. 207, 210.
23. Ibid., p. 523.

Key Terms

conquistador (p. 449)
caravel (p. 450)
Ptolemy's *Geography* (p. 450)
Treaty of Tordesillas (p. 456)
Mexica Empire (p. 457)
Inca Empire (p. 459)
viceroyalties (p. 461)
encomienda system (p. 461)
Columbian exchange (p. 463)

For practice quizzes and other study tools, visit the Online Study Guide at **bedfordstmartins.com/mckaywest**.

For primary sources from this period, see ***Sources of Western Society*, Second Edition**.

For Web sites, images, and documents related to topics in this chapter, visit Make History at **bedfordstmartins.com/mckaywest**.

16

Absolutism and Constitutionalism

ca. 1589–1725

The seventeenth century was a period of crisis and transformation in Europe. Agricultural and manufacturing slumps led to food shortages and shrinking population rates. Religious and dynastic conflicts led to almost constant war, visiting violence and destruction on ordinary people and reshaping European states. Armies grew larger than they had been since the time of the Roman Empire, resulting in new government bureaucracies and higher taxes. Despite these obstacles, European states succeeded in gathering more power, and by 1680 much of the unrest that originated with the Reformation was resolved.

These crises were not limited to western Europe. Central and eastern Europe experienced even more catastrophic dislocation, with German lands serving as the battleground of the Thirty Years' War and borders constantly vulnerable to attack from the east. In Prussia and in Habsburg Austria absolutist states emerged in the aftermath of this conflict. Russia and the Ottoman Turks also developed absolutist governments. The Russian and Ottoman Empires seemed foreign and exotic to western Europeans, who saw them as the antithesis of their political, religious, and cultural values. While absolutism emerged as the solution to crisis in many European states, a small minority adopted a different path, placing sovereignty in the hands of privileged groups rather than the Crown. Historians refer to states where power was limited by law as "constitutional." The two most important seventeenth-century constitutionalist states were England and the Dutch Republic. Constitutionalism should not be confused with democracy. The elite rulers of England and the Dutch Republic pursued familiar policies of increased taxation, government authority, and social control. Nonetheless, they served as influential models to onlookers across Europe as a form of government that checked the power of a single ruler. ■

Life in Absolutist France. King Louis XIV receives foreign ambassadors to celebrate a peace treaty. The king grandly occupied the center of his court, which in turn served as the pinnacle for the French people and, at the height of his glory, for all of Europe.

CHAPTER PREVIEW

Seventeenth-Century Crisis and Rebuilding
■ What were the common crises and achievements of seventeenth-century European states?

Absolutism in France and Spain
■ What factors led to the rise of the French absolutist state under Louis XIV, and why did absolutist Spain experience decline in the same period?

Absolutism in Austria and Prussia
■ How did the rulers of Austria and Prussia transform their nations into powerful absolutist monarchies?

The Development of Russia and the Ottoman Empire
■ What were the distinctive features of Russian and Ottoman absolutism?

Alternatives to Absolutism in England and the Dutch Republic
■ How and why did the constitutional state triumph in the Dutch Republic and England?

Baroque Art and Music
■ What was the baroque style in art and music, and where was it popular?

Seventeenth-Century Crisis and Rebuilding

What were the common crises and achievements of seventeenth-century European states?

Historians often refer to the seventeenth century as an "age of crisis." After the economic and demographic growth of the sixteenth century, Europe faltered into stagnation and retrenchment. This was partially due to climate changes beyond anyone's control, but it also resulted from bitter religious divides, increased governmental pressures, and war. Overburdened peasants and city-dwellers took action to defend themselves, sometimes profiting from conflicts to obtain relief. In the long run, however, governments proved increasingly able to impose their will on the populace. The period witnessed spectacular growth in army size as well as new forms of taxation, government bureaucracies, and increased state sovereignty.

Peasant Life in the Midst of Economic Crisis

In the seventeenth century most Europeans lived in the countryside. The hub of the rural world was the small peasant village centered on a church and a manor. Life was in many ways circumscribed by the village, although we should not underestimate the mobility induced by war, food shortage, fortune-seeking, and religious pilgrimage.

In western Europe, a small number of peasants in each village owned enough land to feed themselves and had the livestock and ploughs necessary to work their land. These independent farmers were leaders of the peasant village. They employed the landless poor, rented out livestock and tools, and served as agents for the noble lord. Below them were small landowners and tenant farmers who did not have enough land to be self-sufficient. These families sold their best produce on the market to earn cash for taxes, rent, and food. At the bottom were the rural workers who worked as dependent

An English Food Riot Nothing infuriated ordinary women and men more than the idea that merchants and landowners were withholding grain from the market in order to push high prices even higher. In this cartoon an angry crowd hands out rough justice to a rich farmer accused of hoarding. (Courtesy of the Trustees of the British Museum)

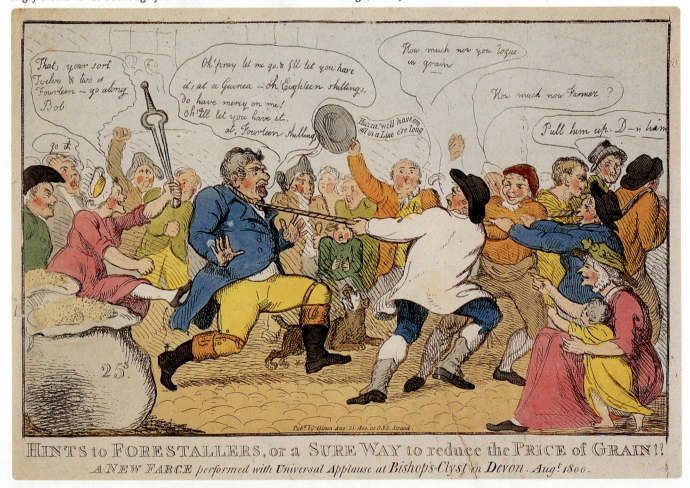

laborers and servants. In eastern Europe, the vast majority of peasants toiled as serfs for noble landowners and did not own land in their own right (see page 482).

Rich or poor, east or west, bread was the primary element of the diet. The richest ate a white loaf, leaving brown bread to those who could not afford better. Peasants paid stiff fees to the local miller for grinding grain into flour and sometimes to the lord for the right to bake bread in his oven. Bread was most often accompanied by a soup made of roots, herbs, beans, and perhaps a small piece of salt pork. An important annual festival in many villages was the killing of the family pig. The whole family gathered to help, sharing a rare abundance of meat with neighbors and carefully salting the extra and putting down the lard. In some areas, menstruating women were careful to stay away from the kitchen for fear they might cause the lard to spoil.

European rural society lived on the edge of subsistence. Because of the crude technology and low crop yield, peasants were constantly threatened by scarcity and famine. In the seventeenth century a period of colder and wetter climate throughout Europe, dubbed the "little ice age" by historians, meant a shorter farming season with lower yields. A bad harvest created food shortages; a series of bad harvests could lead to famine. Recurrent famines significantly reduced the population of early modern Europe. Most people did not die of outright starvation, but rather of diseases brought on by malnutrition and exhaustion. Facilitated by the weakened population, outbreaks of bubonic plague continued in Europe until the 1720s.

The Estates of Normandy, a provincial assembly, reported on the dire conditions in northern France during an outbreak of plague in which disease was compounded by the disruption of agriculture and a lack of food:

> *Of the 450 sick persons whom the inhabitants were unable to relieve, 200 were turned out, and these we saw die one by one as they lay on the roadside. A large number still remain, and to each of them it is only possible to dole out the least scrap of bread. We only give bread to those who would otherwise die. The staple dish here consists of mice, which the inhabitants hunt, so desperate are they from hunger. They devour roots which the animals cannot eat; one can, in fact, not put into words the things one sees. . . . We certify to having ourselves seen herds, not of cattle, but of men and women, wandering about the fields between Rheims and Rhétel, turning up the earth like pigs to find a few roots; and as they can only find rotten ones, and not half enough of them, they become so weak that they have not strength left to seek food.*[1]

Chronology

ca. 1500–1650	Consolidation of serfdom in eastern Europe
1533–1584	Reign of Ivan the Terrible in Russia
1589–1610	Reign of Henry IV in France
1598–1613	Time of Troubles in Russia
1620–1740	Growth of absolutism in Austria and Prussia
1642–1649	English civil war, which ends with execution of Charles I
1643–1715	Reign of Louis XIV in France
1653–1658	Military rule in England under Oliver Cromwell (the Protectorate)
1660	Restoration of English monarchy under Charles II
1665–1683	Jean-Baptiste Colbert applies mercantilism to France
1670	Charles II agrees to re-Catholicize England in secret agreement with Louis XIV
1670–1671	Cossack revolt led by Stenka Razin
ca. 1680–1750	Construction of baroque palaces
1682	Louis XIV moves court to Versailles
1682–1725	Reign of Peter the Great in Russia
1683–1718	Habsburgs push the Ottoman Turks from Hungary
1685	Edict of Nantes revoked
1688–1689	Glorious Revolution in England
1701–1713	War of the Spanish Succession

Given the harsh conditions of life, industry also suffered. The output of woolen textiles, one of the most important European manufactures, declined sharply in the first half of the seventeenth century. Food prices were high, wages stagnated, and unemployment soared. This economic crisis was not universal: it struck various regions at different times and to different degrees. In the middle decades of the century, Spain, France, Germany, and England all experienced great economic difficulties; but these years were the golden age of the Netherlands.

The urban poor and peasants were the hardest hit. When the price of bread rose beyond their capacity to pay, they frequently expressed their anger by rioting. In towns they invaded bakers' shops to seize bread and resell it at a "just price." In rural areas they attacked convoys taking grain to the cities. Women often led these actions, since their role as mothers gave them some impunity in authorities' eyes. Historians have labeled this vision of a world in which community needs predominate over competition and profit a **moral economy**.

The Return of Serfdom in the East

While economic and social hardship was common across Europe, important differences existed between east and west. In the west the demographic losses of the Black Death allowed peasants to escape from serfdom as they acquired enough land to feed themselves and the livestock and ploughs necessary to work their land. In eastern Europe seventeenth-century peasants had largely lost their ability to own land independently. Eastern lords dealt with the labor shortages caused by the Black Death by restricting the right of their peasants to move to take advantage of better opportunities elsewhere. In Prussian territories by 1500 the law required that runaway peasants be hunted down and returned to their lords. Moreover, lords steadily took more and more of their peasants' land and arbitrarily imposed heavier and heavier labor obligations. By the early 1500s lords in many eastern territories could command their peasants to work for them without pay for as many as six days a week.

The gradual erosion of the peasantry's economic position was bound up with manipulation of the legal system. The local lord was also the local prosecutor, judge, and jailer. There were no independent royal officials to provide justice or uphold the common law. The power of the lord reached far into serfs' everyday lives. Not only was their freedom of movement restricted, but they required permission to marry or could be forced to marry. Lords could reallocate the lands worked by their serfs at will or sell serfs apart from their families. These conditions applied even on lands owned by the church.

Between 1500 and 1650 the consolidation of serfdom in eastern Europe was accompanied by the growth of commercial agriculture, particularly in Poland and eastern Germany. As economic expansion and population growth resumed after 1500, eastern lords increased the production of their estates by squeezing sizable surpluses out of the impoverished peasants. They then sold these surpluses to foreign merchants, who exported them to the growing cities of wealthier western Europe. The Netherlands and England benefited the most from inexpensive grain from the east.

It was not only the peasants who suffered in eastern Europe. With the approval of kings, landlords systematically undermined the medieval privileges of the towns and the power of the urban classes. Instead of selling products to local merchants, landlords sold directly to foreigners, bypassing local towns. Eastern towns also lost their medieval right of refuge and were compelled to return runaways to their lords. The population of the towns and the urban middle classes declined greatly. This development both reflected and promoted the supremacy of noble landlords in most of eastern Europe in the sixteenth century.

The Thirty Years' War

In the first half of the seventeenth century, the fragile balance of life was violently upturned by the ravages of the Thirty Years' War (1618–1648). The Holy Roman Empire was a confederation of hundreds of principalities, in-

Estonian Serfs in the 1660s The Estonians were conquered by German military nobility in the Middle Ages and reduced to serfdom. The German-speaking nobles ruled the Estonian peasants with an iron hand, and Peter the Great reaffirmed their domination when Russia annexed Estonia. (Mansell Collection/Time Life Pictures/Getty Images)

Soldiers Pillage a Farmhouse Billeting troops among civilian populations during the Thirty Years' War caused untold hardships. In this late-seventeenth-century Dutch illustration, brawling soldiers take over a peasant's home, eat his food, steal his possessions, and insult his family. Peasant retaliation sometimes proved swift and bloody. (Rijksmuseum-Stichting Amsterdam)

dependent cities, duchies, and other polities loosely united under an elected emperor. The uneasy truce between Catholics and Protestants created by the Peace of Augsburg in 1555 deteriorated as the faiths of various areas shifted. Lutheran princes felt compelled to form the Protestant Union (1608), and Catholics retaliated with the Catholic League (1609). Each alliance was determined that the other should make no religious or territorial advance. Dynastic interests were also involved; the Spanish Habsburgs strongly supported the goals of their Austrian relatives: the unity of the empire and the preservation of Catholicism within it.

The war is traditionally divided into four phases. The first, or Bohemian, phase (1618–1625) was characterized by civil war in Bohemia between the Catholic League and the Protestant Union. In 1620 Catholic forces defeated Protestants at the Battle of the White Mountain. The second, or Danish, phase of the war (1625–1629) — so called because of the leadership of the Protestant king Christian IV of Denmark (r. 1588–1648) — witnessed additional Catholic victories. The Catholic imperial army led by Albert of Wallenstein swept through Silesia, north to the Baltic, and east into Pomerania, scoring smashing victories. Habsburg power peaked in 1629. The emperor issued the Edict of Restitution, whereby all Catholic properties lost to Protestantism since 1552 were restored, and only Catholics and Lutherans were allowed to practice their faiths.

The third, or Swedish, phase of the war (1630–1635) began with the arrival in Germany of the Swedish king Gustavus Adolphus (r. 1594–1632) and his army. The ablest administrator of his day and a devout Lutheran, he intervened to support the empire's Protestants. The French chief minister, Cardinal Richelieu, subsidized the Swedes, hoping to weaken Habsburg power in Europe. Gustavus Adolphus won two important battles but was fatally wounded in combat. The final, or French, phase of the war (1635–1648) was prompted by Richelieu's concern that the Habsburgs would rebound after the death of Gustavus Adolphus. Richelieu declared war on Spain and sent military as well as financial assistance. Finally, in October 1648 peace was achieved.

The 1648 **Peace of Westphalia** that ended the Thirty Years' War marked a turning point in European history. For the most part, conflicts fought over religious faith receded. The treaties recognized the independent authority of more than three hundred German princes (Map 16.1), reconfirming the emperor's severely limited authority. The Augsburg agreement of 1555 became permanent, adding Calvinism to Catholicism and Lutheranism as legally permissible creeds. The north German states remained Protestant; the south German states, Catholic.

Peace of Westphalia The name of a series of treaties that concluded the Thirty Years' War in 1648 and marked the end of large-scale religious violence in Europe.

The Thirty Years' War was probably the most destructive event for the central European economy and society prior to the world wars of the twentieth century. Perhaps one-third of urban residents and two-fifths of

Map 16.1 Europe After the Thirty Years' War This map shows the political division of Europe after the Treaty of Westphalia (1648) ended the war. Which country emerged from the Thirty Years' War as the strongest European power? What dynastic house was that country's major rival in the early modern period?

the rural population died, leaving entire areas depopulated. Trade in southern German cities, such as Augsburg, was virtually destroyed. Agricultural areas suffered catastrophically. Many small farmers lost their land, allowing nobles to enlarge their estates and consolidate their control.²

Achievements in State-Building

In this context of economic and demographic depression, monarchs began to make new demands on their people. Traditionally, historians have distinguished between the "absolutist" governments of France, Spain, central Europe, and Russia and the constitutionalist governments of England and the Dutch Republic. Whereas absolutist monarchs gathered all power under their personal control, English and Dutch rulers were obliged to respect laws passed by representative institutions. More recently, historians have emphasized commonalities among these powers. Despite their political differences, all these states shared common projects of protecting and expanding their frontiers, raising new taxes, consolidating central control, and competing for the new colonies opening up in the New and Old Worlds.

Rulers who wished to increase their authority encountered formidable obstacles. Some were purely material. Without paved roads, telephones, or other modern technology, it took weeks to convey orders from the central government to the provinces. Rulers also suffered from lack of information about their realms, making it impossible to police and tax the population effectively. Local power structures presented another serious obstacle. Nobles, the church, provincial and national assemblies, town councils, guilds, and other bodies held legal privileges, which could not easily be rescinded. In some kingdoms many people spoke a language different from the Crown's, further diminishing their willingness to obey its commands.

Nonetheless, over the course of the seventeenth century both absolutist and constitutional governments achieved new levels of central control. This increased authority focused in four areas in particular: greater taxation, growth in armed forces, larger and more efficient bureaucracies, and the increased ability to compel obedience from their subjects. Over time, centralized power added up to something close to sovereignty. A state may be termed sovereign when it possesses a monopoly over the instruments of justice and the use of force within clearly defined boundaries. In a sovereign state, no system of courts, such as ecclesiastical tribunals, competes with state courts in the dispensation of justice; and private armies, such as those of feudal lords, present no threat to central authority. While seventeenth-century states did not acquire total sovereignty, they made important strides toward that goal.

Warfare and the Growth of Army Size

The driving force of seventeenth-century state-building was warfare, characterized by dramatic changes in the size and style of armies. Medieval armies had been raised by feudal lords for particular wars or campaigns, after which the troops were disbanded. In the seventeenth century monarchs took command of recruiting and maintaining armies — in peacetime as well as wartime. Kings deployed their troops both inside and outside the country in the interests of the monarchy. Instead of serving their own interests, army officers were required to be loyal and obedient to the monarchs who commanded them. New techniques for training and deploying soldiers meant a rise in the professional standards of the army.

Along with professionalization came an explosive growth in army size. The French took the lead, with the army growing from roughly 125,000 men in the Thirty Years' War to 340,000 at the end of the seventeenth century.[3] This growth was caused in part by changes in the style of armies. Mustering a royal army took longer than simply hiring a mercenary band, giving enemies time to form coalitions. For example, the large coalitions Louis XIV confronted (see page 492) required him to fight on multiple fronts with huge armies. In turn, the relative size and wealth of France among European nations allowed Louis to field enormous armies and thereby to pursue the ambitious foreign policies

The Professionalization of the Swedish Army Swedish king Gustavus Adolphus, surrounded by his generals, gives thanks to God for the safe arrival of his troops in Germany during the Thirty Years' War. A renowned military leader, the king imposed constant training drills and rigorous discipline on his troops, which contributed to their remarkable success in the war. (Photo courtesy of The Army Museum, Stockholm)

that caused his alarmed neighbors to form coalitions against him.

The death toll during war for noble officers, who personally led their men in battle, was startlingly high. The paramount noble value of honor outshone concerns for safety or material benefit. Nobles had to purchase their positions in the army and supply horses, food, uniforms, and weapons for themselves and their troops. Royal stipends did not begin to cover these expenses. The only legacy an officer's widow received was the debt incurred to fund her husband's military career. It was not until the 1760s that the French government assumed the costs of equipping troops.

Other European powers were quick to follow the French example. The rise of absolutism in central and eastern Europe led to a vast expansion in the size of armies. Great Britain followed a similar, albeit distinctive pattern. Instead of building a land army, the British focused on naval forces and eventually built the largest navy in the world.

Popular Political Action

In the seventeenth century increased pressures of taxation and warfare turned neighborhood riots over the cost of bread into armed uprisings. Popular revolts were extremely common in England, France, Spain, Portugal, and Italy in the mid-seventeenth century. In 1640 Philip IV of Spain faced revolt in Catalonia, the economic center of his realm. At the same time he struggled to put down uprisings in Portugal and in the northern provinces of the Netherlands. In 1647 the city of Palermo, in Spanish-occupied Sicily, exploded in protest over food shortages caused by a series of bad harvests. Fearing public unrest, the city government subsidized the price of bread, attracting even more starving peasants from the countryside. When Madrid ordered an end to subsidies, municipal leaders decided to lighten the loaf rather than raise prices. Not fooled by this change, local women led a bread riot, shouting "Long live the king and down with the taxes and the bad government!" As riot transformed to armed revolt, insurgency spread to the rest of the island and eventually to Naples on the mainland. Apart from affordable food, rebels demanded the suppression of extraordinary taxes and participation in municipal government. Some dreamed of a republic in which noble tax exemptions would be abolished. Despite initial successes, the revolt lacked unity and strong leadership and could not withstand the forces of the state.

In France urban uprisings became a frequent aspect of the social and political landscape. Beginning in 1630 and continuing on and off through the early 1700s, major insurrections occurred at Dijon, Bordeaux (bor-DOH), Montpellier, Lyons, and Amiens. All were characterized by deep popular anger and violence directed at outside officials sent to collect taxes. These officials were sometimes seized, beaten, and hacked to death. For example, in 1673 Louis XIV's imposition of new taxes on legal transactions, tobacco, and pewter ware provoked an uprising in Bordeaux.

Municipal and royal authorities often struggled to overcome popular revolt. They feared that stern repressive measures, such as sending in troops to fire on crowds, would create martyrs and further inflame the situation, while forcible full-scale military occupation of a city would be very expensive. The limitations of royal authority gave some leverage to rebels. To quell riots, royal edicts were sometimes suspended, prisoners released, and discussions initiated.

By the beginning of the eighteenth century, this leverage had largely disappeared. Municipal governments were better integrated into the national structure, and local authorities had prompt military support from the central government. People who publicly opposed royal policies and taxes received swift and severe punishment.

Absolutism in France and Spain

What factors led to the rise of the French absolutist state under Louis XIV, and why did absolutist Spain experience decline in the same period?

In the Middle Ages jurists held that as a consequence of monarchs' coronation and anointment with sacred oil, they ruled "by the grace of God." Law was given by God; kings "found" the law and acknowledged that they must respect and obey it. Kings in absolutist states amplified these claims, asserting that, as they were chosen by God, they were responsible to God alone. They claimed exclusive power to make and enforce laws, denying any other institution or group the authority to check their power. In France the founder of the Bourbon monarchy, Henry IV, established foundations upon which his successors Louis XIII and Louis XIV built a stronger, more centralized French state. Louis XIV is often seen as the epitome of an "absolute" monarch, with his endless wars, increased taxes and economic regulation, and glorious palace at Versailles. In truth, his success relied on collaboration with nobles, and thus his example illustrates both the achievements and the compromises of absolutist rule.

As French power rose in the seventeenth century, the glory of Spain faded. Once the fabulous revenue from American silver declined, Spain's economic stagnation could no longer be disguised, and the country faltered under weak leadership.

The Foundations of Absolutism

Louis XIV's absolutism had long roots. In 1589 his grandfather Henry IV (r. 1589–1610), the founder of the Bourbon dynasty, acquired a devastated country. Civil wars between Protestants and Catholics had wracked France since 1561. Poor harvests had reduced peasants to starvation, and commercial activity had declined drastically. "Henri le Grand" (Henry the Great), as the king was called, promised "a chicken in every pot" and inaugurated a remarkable recovery.

He did so by keeping France at peace during most of his reign. Although he had converted to Catholicism, he issued the Edict of Nantes, allowing Protestants the right to worship in 150 traditionally Protestant towns throughout France. He sharply lowered taxes and instead charged royal officials an annual fee to guarantee the right to pass their positions down to their heirs. He also improved the infrastructure of the country, building new roads and canals and repairing the ravages of years of civil war. Despite his efforts at peace, Henry was murdered in 1610 by a Catholic zealot, setting off a national crisis.

After the death of Henry IV his wife, the queen-regent Marie de' Medici, headed the government for the nine-year-old Louis XIII (r. 1610–1643). In 1628 Armand Jean du Plessis—Cardinal Richelieu (1585–1642)—became first minister of the French crown. Richelieu's maneuvers allowed the monarchy to maintain power within Europe and within its own borders despite the turmoil of the Thirty Years' War.

Cardinal Richelieu's political genius is best reflected in the administrative system he established to strengthen royal control. He extended the use of intendants, commissioners for each of France's thirty-two districts who were appointed directly by the monarch, to whom they were solely responsible. They recruited men for the army, supervised the collection of taxes, presided over the administration of local law, checked up on the local nobility, and regulated economic activities in their districts. As the intendants' power increased under Richelieu, so did the power of the centralized French state.

Under Richelieu, the French monarchy also acted to repress Protestantism. Louis personally supervised the siege of La Rochelle, an important port city and a major commercial center with strong ties to Protestant Holland and England. After the city fell in October 1628, its municipal government was suppressed. Protestants retained the right of public worship, but the Catholic liturgy was restored. The fall of La Rochelle was one step in the removal of Protestantism as a strong force in French life.

Richelieu did not aim to wipe out Protestantism in the rest of Europe, however. His main foreign policy goal was to destroy the Catholic Habsburgs' grip on territories that surrounded France. Consequently, Richelieu supported Habsburg enemies, including Protestants. In 1631 he signed a treaty with the Lutheran king Gustavus Adolphus promising French support against the Habsburgs in the Thirty Years' War. For the French cardinal, interests of state outweighed religious considerations.

Richelieu's successor as chief minister for the next child-king, the four-year-old Louis XIV, was Cardinal Jules Mazarin (1602–1661). Along with the regent, Queen Mother Anne of Austria, Mazarin continued Richelieu's centralizing policies. His struggle to increase royal revenues to meet the costs of war led to the uprisings of 1648–1653 known as the **Fronde**. A *frondeur* was originally a street urchin who threw mud at the passing carriages of the rich, but the word came to be applied to the many individuals and groups who opposed the policies of the government. In Paris, magistrates of the Parlement of Paris, the nation's most important court, were outraged by the Crown's autocratic measures. These so-called robe nobles (named for the robes they wore in court) encouraged violent protest by the common people. During the first of several riots, the queen mother fled Paris with Louis XIV. As rebellion spread outside Paris and to the sword nobles (the traditional warrior nobility), civil order broke down completely. In 1651 Anne's regency ended with the declaration of Louis as king in his own right. Much of the rebellion died away, and its leaders came to terms with the government.

The violence of the Fronde had significant results for the future. The twin evils of noble rebellion and popular riots left the French wishing for peace and for a strong monarch to reimpose order. This was the legacy that Louis XIV inherited in 1661 when he assumed personal rule of the largest and most populous country in western Europe at the age of twenty-three. Humiliated by his flight from Paris, he was determined to avoid any recurrence of rebellion.

Louis XIV and Absolutism

In the reign of Louis XIV (r. 1643–1715), the longest in European history, the French monarchy reached the peak of absolutist development. In the magnificence of his court and the brilliance of the culture that he presided over, Louis dominated his age. Religion, Anne, and Mazarin all taught Louis the doctrine of the divine right of kings: God had established kings as his rulers on earth, and they were answerable ultimately to him alone. Kings were divinely anointed and shared in the sacred nature of divinity, but they could not simply do as they pleased. They had to obey God's laws and rule for the good of the people. To symbolize his central role in the divine order, when he was fifteen years old Louis danced at a court ballet dressed as the sun, thereby acquiring the title of the "Sun King."

In addition to parading his power before the court, Louis worked very hard at the business of governing. He ruled his realm through several councils of state and insisted on taking a personal role in many of the councils' decisions. He selected councilors from the recently ennobled or the upper middle class because he believed "that the public should know, from the rank of those whom I chose to serve me, that I had no intention of sharing power with them."[4] Despite increasing financial problems, Louis never called a meeting of the Estates General. The nobility, therefore, had no means of united expression or action. Nor did Louis have a

> **Fronde** A series of violent uprisings during the early reign of Louis XIV triggered by growing royal control and oppressive taxation.

Picturing the Past

Hyacinthe Rigaud, *Louis XIV, King of France and Navarre*, 1701 This was one of Louis XIV's favorite portraits of himself. He liked it so much that he had many copies of the portrait made, in full and half-size format. (Scala/Art Resource, NY)

ANALYZING THE IMAGE Why do you think the king liked the portrait so much? What image of the king does it present to the viewer? What details does the painter include, and what impression do they convey?

CONNECTIONS How does this representation of royal power compare with the images of Peter the Great (page 503) and Charles I (page 506)? Which do you find the most impressive, and why?

To complete this activity online, go to the Online Study Guide at **bedfordstmartins.com/mckaywest**.

---

first minister. In this way he kept himself free from worry about the inordinate power of a Richelieu.

Although personally tolerant, Louis hated division within the realm and insisted that religious unity was essential to his royal dignity and to the security of the state. He thus pursued the policy of Protestant repression launched by Richelieu. In 1685 Louis revoked the Edict of Nantes. The new law ordered the destruction of Huguenot churches, the closing of schools, the Catholic baptism of Huguenots, and the exile of Huguenot pastors who refused to renounce their faith. The result was the departure of some of his most loyal and industrially skilled subjects.

Despite his claims to absolute authority, there were multiple constraints on Louis's power. As a representative of divine power, he was obliged to rule in a way that seemed consistent with virtue and benevolent authority. He had to uphold the laws issued by his royal predecessors. Moreover, he also relied on the collaboration of nobles, who maintained tremendous prestige and authority in their ancestral lands. Without their cooperation, it would have been impossible to extend his power throughout France or wage his many foreign wars. Louis's need to elicit noble cooperation led him to revolutionize court life at his spectacular palace at Versailles.

Life at Versailles

Through most of the seventeenth century, the French court had no fixed home, following the monarch to his numerous palaces and country residences. In 1682 Louis moved his court and government to the newly renovated palace at Versailles, a former hunting lodge. The palace quickly became the center of political, social, and cultural life. The king required all great nobles to spend at least part of the year in attendance on him there, so he could keep an eye on their activities. Since he controlled the distribution of state power and wealth, nobles had no choice but to obey and compete with each other for his favor at Versailles.

The glorious palace, with its sumptuous interiors and extensive formal gardens, was a mirror to the world of French glory, soon copied by would-be absolutist monarchs across Europe. (See "Living in the Past: The Absolutist Palace," page 490.) The reality of daily life in the palace was less glamorous. Versailles served as government offices for royal bureaucrats, as living quarters for the royal family and nobles, and as a place of work for hundreds of domestic servants. It was also open to the public at certain hours of the day. As a result, it was crowded with three thousand to ten thousand people every day. Even high nobles had to put up with cramped living space, and many visitors complained of the noise, smell, and crowds.

Louis further revolutionized court life by establishing an elaborate set of etiquette rituals to mark every moment of his day, from waking up and dressing in the morning to removing his clothing and retiring at night. He required nobles to serve him in these rituals, and they vied for the honor of doing so, with the highest in rank claiming the privilege of handing the king his shirt. Endless squabbles broke out over what type of chair one could sit on at court and the order in which great nobles entered and were seated in the chapel for Mass.

These rituals may seem absurd, but they were far from meaningless or trivial. The king controlled immense resources and privileges; access to him meant favored treatment for government offices, military and religious posts, state pensions, honorary titles, and a host of other benefits. The Duke of Saint-Simon wrote of the king's power at court in his memoirs:

> No one understood better than Louis XIV the art of enhancing the value of a favour by his manner of bestowing it; he knew how to make the most of a word, a smile, even of a glance. If he addressed any one, were it but to ask a trifling question or make some commonplace remark, all eyes were turned on the person so honored; it was a mark of favour which always gave rise to comment.[5]

Courtiers sought these rewards for themselves and their family members and followers. A system of patronage—in which a higher-ranked individual protected a lower-ranked one in return for loyalty and services—flowed from the court to the provinces. Through this mechanism Louis gained cooperation from powerful nobles.

Although they were denied public offices and posts, women played a central role in the patronage system. At court the king's wife, mistresses, and other female relatives recommended individuals for honors, advocated policy decisions, and brokered alliances between noble factions. Noblewomen played a similar role among courtiers, bringing their family connections to marriage to form powerful social networks. Onlookers sometimes resented the influence of powerful women at court. The Duke of Saint-Simon said of Madame de Maintenon, Louis XIV's mistress and secret second wife, "Many people have been ruined by her, without having been able to discover the author of the ruin, search as they might."

Louis XIV was also an enthusiastic patron of the arts, having danced gracefully in court ballets in his youth. He commissioned many sculptures and paintings for Versailles as well as performances of dance and music. Scholars characterize the art and literature of the age of Louis XIV as French classicism. By this they mean that the artists and writers of the late seventeenth century imitated the subject matter and style of classical antiquity, that their work resembled that of Renaissance Italy, and that French art possessed the classical qualities of discipline, balance, and restraint. Louis XIV also loved the stage, and in the plays of Molière and Racine his court witnessed the finest achievements in the history of the French theater.

With Versailles as the center of European politics, French culture grew in international prestige. French became the language of polite society and international diplomacy, gradually replacing Latin as the language of scholarship and learning. The royal courts of Sweden, Russia, Poland, and Germany all spoke French. In the eighteenth century the great Russian aristocrats were more fluent in French than in Russian. In England George I spoke fluent French and only halting English. France inspired a cosmopolitan European culture in the late seventeenth century that looked to Versailles as its center.

French Financial Management Under Colbert

France's ability to build armies and fight wars depended on a strong economy. Fortunately for Louis, his controller general, Jean-Baptiste Colbert (1619–1683), proved to be a financial genius. Colbert's central principle was that the wealth and the economy of France should serve the state. To this end, from 1665 to his death in 1683, Colbert rigorously applied mercantilist policies to France.

Mercantilism is a collection of governmental policies for the regulation of economic activities by and for the state. It derives from the idea that a nation's international power is based on its wealth, specifically its supply of gold and silver. To accumulate wealth, a country always had to sell more goods abroad than it bought. To decrease the purchase of goods outside France, Colbert insisted that French industry should produce everything needed by the French people.

> **mercantilism** A system of economic regulations aimed at increasing the power of the state based on the belief that a nation's international power was based on its wealth, specifically its supply of gold and silver.

To increase exports, Colbert supported old industries and created new ones, focusing especially on textiles, which were the most important sector of the economy. Colbert enacted new production regulations, created guilds to boost quality standards, and encouraged foreign craftsmen to immigrate to France. To encourage the purchase of French goods, he abolished many domestic tariffs and raised tariffs on foreign products. In 1664 Colbert founded the Company of the East Indies with (unfulfilled) hopes of competing with the Dutch for Asian trade.

Colbert also hoped to make Canada—rich in untapped minerals and some of the best agricultural land in the world—part of a vast French empire. He sent four thousand colonists to Quebec, whose capital was founded in 1608 under Henry IV. Subsequently, the Jesuit Jacques Marquette and the merchant Louis Joliet

The Absolutist Palace

LIVING IN THE PAST

BY 1700 PALACE BUILDING HAD BECOME a veritable obsession for European rulers. Their dramatic palaces symbolized the age of absolutist power, just as soaring Gothic cathedrals had expressed the idealized spirit of the High Middle Ages. With its classically harmonious, symmetrical, and geometric design, Versailles served as the model for the wave of palace building that began in the last decade of the seventeenth century. Royal palaces like Versailles were intended to overawe the people and proclaim their owners' authority and power.

Located ten miles southwest of Paris, Versailles began as a modest hunting lodge built by Louis XIII in 1623. His son, Louis XIV, spent decades enlarging and decorating the original structure. Between 1668 and 1670, architect Louis Le Vau (luh VOH) enveloped the old building within a much larger one that still exists today. In 1682 the new palace became the official residence of the Sun King and his court, although construction continued until 1710, when the royal chapel was completed. At any one time, several thousand people occupied the bustling and crowded palace. The awesome splendor of the eighty-yard Hall of Mirrors, replete with floor-to-ceiling mirrors and ceiling murals illustrating the king's triumphs, contrasted with the strong odors from the courtiers who commonly relieved themselves in discreet corners.

In 1693 Charles XI of Sweden, having reduced the power of the aristocracy, ordered the construction of his Royal Palace, which domi-

View of the Chateau de Versailles, 1722. Right: Louis XIV leading a tour of the extensive grounds at Versailles. (below: Châteaux de Versailles et de Trianon, Versailles/Réunion des Musées Nationaux/Art Resource, NY; right: Erich Lessing/Art Resource)

Prince Eugene's Summer Palace in Vienna. (Erich Lessing/Art Resource, NY)

nates the center of Stockholm to this day. Another such palace was Schönbrunn, an enormous Viennese Versailles begun in 1695 by Emperor Leopold to celebrate Austrian military victories and Habsburg might. Shown at right is architect Joseph Bernhard Fischer von Erlach's ambitious plan for Schönbrunn palace. Fischer's plan emphasizes the palace's vast size and its role as a site for military demonstrations. Ultimately, financial constraints resulted in a more modest building.

In central and eastern Europe, the favorite noble servants of royalty became extremely rich and powerful, and they too built grandiose palaces in the capital cities. These palaces were in part an extension of the monarch, for they surpassed the buildings of less-favored nobles and showed all the high road to fame and fortune. Take, for example, the palaces of Prince Eugene of Savoy, a French nobleman who became Austria's most famous military hero. It was Eugene who led the Austrian army, smashed the Turks, fought Louis XIV to a standstill, and generally guided the triumph of absolutism in Austria. Rewarded with great wealth by his grateful king, Eugene called on the leading architects of the day, Fischer von Erlach and Johann Lukas von Hildebrandt, to consecrate his glory in stone and fresco. Fischer built Eugene's Winter (or Town) Palace in Vienna, and he and Hildebrandt collaborated on the prince's Summer Palace on the city's outskirts. The prince's summer residence featured two baroque gems, the Lower Belvedere and the Upper Belvedere, completed in 1722 and shown above. The building's interior is equally stunning, with crouching giants serving as pillars and a magnificent great staircase.

Plans for the Palace at Schönbrunn, ca. 1700. (ONB/Vienna, Picture Archive, L 8001-D)

QUESTIONS FOR ANALYSIS

1. Compare these images. What did concrete objects and the manipulation of space accomplish for these rulers that mere words could not?
2. What disadvantages might stem from using architecture in this way?
3. Is the use of space and monumental architecture still a political tool in today's world?

sailed down the Mississippi River, which they named Colbert in honor of their sponsor (the name soon reverted to the original Native American one). Marquette and Joliet claimed possession of the land on both sides of the river as far south as present-day Arkansas. In 1684 French explorers continued down the Mississippi to its mouth and claimed vast territories for Louis XIV. The area was called, naturally, "Louisiana."

During Colbert's tenure as controller general, Louis was able to pursue his goals without massive tax increases and without creating a stream of new offices. The constant pressure of warfare after Colbert's death, however, undid many of his economic achievements.

The Acquisitions of Louis XIV, 1668–1713

Louis XIV's Wars

Louis XIV wrote that "the character of a conqueror is regarded as the noblest and highest of titles." In pursuit of the title of conqueror, he kept France at war for thirty-three of the fifty-four years of his personal rule.

Peace of Utrecht A series of treaties, from 1713 to 1715, that ended the War of the Spanish Succession, ended French expansion in Europe, and marked the rise of the British Empire.

François le Tellier, Marquis de Louvois, Louis's secretary of state for war, equaled Colbert's achievements in the economic realm. Louvois created a professional army in which the French state, rather than private nobles, employed the soldiers. Uniforms and weapons were standardized, and a rational system of training and promotion was devised. Many historians believe that the new loyalty, professionalism, and growth of the French army represented the peak of Louis's success in reforming government. As in so many other matters, his model was followed across Europe.

Louis's goal was to expand France to what he considered its natural borders. His armies managed to extend French borders to include important commercial centers in the Spanish Netherlands and Flanders as well as the entire province of Franche-Comté between 1667 and 1678. In 1681 Louis seized the city of Strasbourg, and three years later he sent his armies into the province of Lorraine. At that moment the king seemed invincible. In fact, Louis had reached the limit of his expansion. The wars of the 1680s and 1690s brought no additional territories but placed unbearable strains on French resources. Colbert's successors resorted to desperate measures to finance these wars, including devaluation of the currency and new taxes.

Louis's last war was endured by a French people suffering high taxes, crop failure, and widespread malnutrition and death. In 1700 the childless Spanish king Charles II (r. 1665–1700) died, opening a struggle for control of Spain and its colonies. His will bequeathed the Spanish crown and its empire to Philip of Anjou, Louis XIV's grandson (Louis's wife, Maria-Theresa, had been Charles's sister). The will violated a prior treaty by which the European powers had agreed to divide the Spanish possessions between the king of France and the Holy Roman emperor, both brothers-in-law of Charles II. Claiming that he was following both Spanish and French interests, Louis broke with the treaty and accepted the will, thereby triggering the War of the Spanish Succession (1701–1713).

In 1701 the English, Dutch, Austrians, and Prussians formed the Grand Alliance against Louis XIV. War dragged on until 1713. The **Peace of Utrecht**, which ended the war, allowed Louis's grandson Philip to remain king of Spain on the understanding that the French and Spanish crowns would never be united. France surrendered Newfoundland, Nova Scotia, and the Hudson Bay territory to England, which also acquired Gibraltar, Minorca, and control of the African slave trade from Spain (Map 16.2).

The Peace of Utrecht represented the balance-of-power principle in operation, setting limits on the extent to which any one power — in this case, France — could expand. It also marked the end of French expansion. Thirty-five years of war had given France the rights to all of Alsace and some commercial centers in the north. But at what price? In 1714 an exhausted France hovered on the brink of bankruptcy. It is no wonder that when Louis XIV died on September 1, 1715, many subjects felt as much relief as they did sorrow.

The Decline of Absolutist Spain in the Seventeenth Century

At the beginning of the seventeenth century, France's position appeared extremely weak. Struggling to recover from decades of religious civil war that had destroyed its infrastructure and economy, France could not dare to compete with Spain's European and overseas empire or its mighty military. Yet by the end of the century their positions were reversed, and France had surpassed all expectations to attain European dominance.

By the early seventeenth century the seeds of Spanish disaster were sprouting. Between 1610 and 1650

Mapping the Past

Map 16.2 Europe After the Peace of Utrecht, 1715 The series of treaties commonly called the Peace of Utrecht ended the War of the Spanish Succession and redrew the map of Europe. A French Bourbon king succeeded to the Spanish throne. France surrendered the Spanish Netherlands (later Belgium), then in French hands, to Austria, and recognized the Hohenzollern rulers of Prussia. Spain ceded Gibraltar to Great Britain, for which it has been a strategic naval station ever since. Spain also granted Britain the *asiento*, the contract for supplying African slaves to the Americas.

ANALYZING THE MAP Identify the areas on the map that changed hands as a result of the Peace of Utrecht. How did these changes affect the balance of power in Europe?

CONNECTIONS How and why did so many European countries possess scattered or discontiguous territories? What does this suggest about European politics in this period? Does this map suggest potential for future conflict?

To complete this activity online, go to the Online Study Guide at **bedfordstmartins.com/mckaywest**.

Spanish trade with the colonies in the New World fell 60 percent due to competition from local industries in the colonies and from Dutch and English traders. At the same time, the native Indian and African slaves who toiled in the South American silver mines suffered frightful epidemics of disease. Ultimately, the mines that filled the empire's treasury started to run dry, and the quantity of metal produced steadily declined after 1620.

In Madrid, however, royal expenditures constantly exceeded income. To meet mountainous state debt, the Crown repeatedly devalued the coinage and declared bankruptcy, which resulted in the collapse of national credit. Meanwhile, manufacturing and commerce shrank. In contrast to the other countries of western Europe, Spain had a tiny middle class. The elite condemned moneymaking as vulgar and undignified. Thousands entered economically unproductive professions: there were said to be nine thousand monasteries in the province of Castile alone. To make matters worse, the Crown expelled some three hundred thousand *Moriscos*, or former Muslims, in 1609, significantly reducing the pool of skilled workers and merchants. Those working in the

Spanish Troops The long wars that Spain fought over Dutch independence, in support of Habsburg interests in Germany, and against France left the country militarily exhausted and financially drained by the mid-1600s. In this detail from a painting by Peeter Snayers, Spanish troops — thin, emaciated, and probably unpaid — straggle away from battle. (Museo Nacional del Prado, Madrid. Photo: José Baztan y Alberto Otero)

textile industry were forced out of business by steep inflation that pushed their production costs to the point where they could not compete in colonial and international markets.[6]

Spanish aristocrats, attempting to maintain an extravagant lifestyle they could no longer afford, increased the rents on their estates. High rents and heavy taxes in turn drove the peasants from the land, leading to a decline in agricultural productivity. In cities wages and production stagnated. Spain also ignored new scientific methods that might have improved agricultural or manufacturing techniques because they came from the heretical nations of Holland and England.

The Spanish crown had no solutions to these dire problems. Philip III, a melancholy and deeply pious man, handed the running of the government over to the duke of Lerma, who used it to advance his personal and familial wealth. Philip IV left the management of his several kingdoms to Gaspar de Guzmán, Count-Duke of Olivares. Olivares was an able administrator who has often been compared to Richelieu. He did not lack energy and ideas, and he succeeded in devising new sources of revenue. But he clung to the grandiose belief that the solution to Spain's difficulties rested in a return to the imperial tradition of the sixteenth century. Unfortunately, the imperial tradition demanded the revival of war with the Dutch at the expiration of a twelve-year truce in 1622 and a long war with France over Mantua (1628–1659). Spain thus became embroiled in the Thirty Years' War. These conflicts, on top of an empty treasury, brought disaster.

Spain's situation worsened with internal conflicts and fresh military defeats through the remainder of the seventeenth century. In 1640 Spain faced serious revolts in Catalonia and Portugal. In 1643 the French inflicted a crushing defeat on a Spanish army at Rocroi in what is now Belgium. By the Treaty of the Pyrenees of 1659, which ended the French-Spanish conflict, Spain was compelled to surrender extensive territories to France. In 1688 the Spanish crown reluctantly recognized the independence of Portugal, almost a century after the two crowns were joined. The era of Spanish dominance in Europe had ended.

Absolutism in Austria and Prussia

How did the rulers of Austria and Prussia transform their nations into powerful absolutist monarchies? ■

The rulers of eastern Europe also labored to build strong absolutist states in the seventeenth century. But they built on social and economic foundations far different from those in western Europe, namely serfdom and the strong nobility who benefited from it. The endless wars of the seventeenth century allowed monarchs to increase their power by building large armies, increasing taxation, and suppressing representative institutions. In exchange for their growing political authority, monarchs allowed nobles to remain as unchallenged masters of their peasants, a deal that appeased both king and nobility, but left serfs at the mercy of the lords. The most successful states were Austria and Prussia, which witnessed the rise of absolutism between 1620 and 1740.

The Austrian Habsburgs

Like all of central Europe, the Habsburgs emerged from the Thirty Years' War impoverished and exhausted. Their efforts to destroy Protestantism in the German lands and to turn the weak Holy Roman Empire into a real state had failed. Although the Habsburgs remained the hereditary emperors, real power lay in the hands of a bewildering variety of separate political jurisdictions. Defeat in central Europe encouraged the Habsburgs to turn away from a quest for imperial dominance and to focus inward and eastward in an attempt to unify their diverse holdings. If they could not impose Catholicism in the empire, at least they could do so in their own domains.

Habsburg victory over Bohemia during the Thirty Years' War was an important step in this direction. Ferdinand II (r. 1619–1637) drastically reduced the power of the Bohemian Estates, the largely Protestant representative assembly. He also confiscated the landholdings of Protestant nobles and gave them to loyal Catholic nobles and to the foreign aristocratic mercenaries who led his armies. After 1650 a large portion of the Bohemian nobility was of recent origin and owed its success to the Habsburgs.

With the support of this new nobility, the Habsburgs established direct rule over Bohemia. Under their rule the condition of the enserfed peasantry worsened substantially: three days per week of unpaid labor became the norm. Protestantism was also stamped out. These changes were important steps in creating absolutist rule in Bohemia.

Ferdinand III (r. 1637–1657) continued to build state power. He centralized the government in the empire's German-speaking provinces, which formed the core Habsburg holdings. For the first time, a permanent standing army was ready to put down any internal opposition.

The Habsburg monarchy then turned east toward the plains of Hungary, which had been divided between the Ottomans and the Habsburgs in the early sixteenth century. Between 1683 and 1699 the Habsburgs pushed the Ottomans from most of Hungary and Transylvania. The recovery of all the former kingdom of Hungary was completed in 1718.

The Hungarian nobility, despite its reduced strength, effectively thwarted the full development of Habsburg absolutism. Throughout the seventeenth century Hungarian nobles rose in revolt against attempts to impose absolute rule. They never triumphed decisively, but neither were they crushed the way the nobility in Bohemia had been in 1620. In 1703, with the Habsburgs bogged down in the War of the Spanish Succession, the Hungarians rose in one last patriotic rebellion under Prince Francis Rákóczy.

Rákóczy and his forces were eventually defeated, but the Habsburgs agreed to restore many of the traditional privileges of the aristocracy in return for Hungarian acceptance of hereditary Habsburg rule. Thus Hungary, unlike Austria and Bohemia, was never fully integrated into a centralized, absolute Habsburg state.

Despite checks on their ambitions in Hungary, the Habsburgs made significant achievements in state-building elsewhere by forging consensus with the church and the nobility. A sense of common identity and loyalty to the monarchy grew among elites in Habsburg lands, even to a certain extent in Hungary. German became the language of the state, and zealous Catholicism helped fuse a collective identity. Vienna became the political and cultural center of the empire. By 1700 it was a thriving city with a population of one hundred thousand and its own version of Versailles, the royal palace of Schönbrunn.

Prussia in the Seventeenth Century

In the fifteenth and sixteenth centuries, the Hohenzollern family had ruled parts of eastern Germany as the imperial electors of Brandenburg and the dukes of Prussia. The title of "elector" gave its holder the privilege of being one of only seven princes or archbishops entitled to elect the Holy Roman emperor, but the electors had little real power. When he came to power in 1640, the twenty-year-old Frederick William, later known as the "Great Elector," was determined to unify his three provinces and enlarge them by diplomacy and war. These provinces were Brandenburg; Prussia, inherited in 1618; and scattered holdings along the Rhine inherited in 1614 (Map 16.3). Each was inhabited by German-speakers, but each had its own estates. Although the estates had not met regularly during the chaotic Thirty Years' War, taxes could not be levied without their consent. The estates of Brandenburg and Prussia were dominated by the nobility and the landowning classes, known as the **Junkers**.

Frederick William profited from ongoing European war and the threat of invasion from Russia when he argued for the need for a permanent standing army. In 1660 he persuaded Junkers in the estates to accept taxation without consent in order to fund an army. They agreed to do so in exchange for reconfirmation of their own privileges, including authority over the serfs. Having won over

Junkers The nobility of Brandenburg and Prussia, they were reluctant allies of Frederick William in his consolidation of the Prussian state.

Map 16.3 **The Growth of Austria and Brandenburg-Prussia to 1748** Austria expanded to the southwest into Hungary and Transylvania at the expense of the Ottoman Empire. It was unable to hold the rich German province of Silesia, however, which was conquered by Brandenburg-Prussia.

the Junkers, the king crushed potential opposition to his power from the towns. One by one, Prussian cities were eliminated from the estates and subjected to new taxes on goods and services.

Thereafter, the estates' power declined rapidly, for the Great Elector had both financial independence and superior force. State revenue tripled during his reign, and the army expanded drastically. In 1688 a population of one million supported a peacetime standing army of thirty thousand. In 1701 the elector's son, Frederick I, received the elevated title of king of Prussia (instead of elector) as a reward for aiding the Holy Roman emperor in the War of the Spanish Succession.

The Consolidation of Prussian Absolutism

Frederick William I, "the Soldiers' King" (r. 1713–1740), completed his grandfather's work, eliminating the last traces of parliamentary estates and local self-government. It was he who truly established Prussian absolutism and transformed Prussia into a military state. Frederick William was intensely attached to military life. He always wore an army uniform, and he lived the highly disciplined life of the professional soldier. Years later he summed up his life's philosophy in his instructions to his son: "A formidable army and a war chest large enough to make this army mobile in times of need can create great respect for you in the world, so that you can speak a word like the other powers."[7]

Penny-pinching and hard-working, Frederick William achieved results. The king and his ministers built an exceptionally honest and conscientious bureaucracy to administer the country and foster economic development. Twelfth in Europe in population, Prussia had the fourth largest army by 1740. The Prussian army was the best in Europe, astonishing foreign observers with its precision, skill, and discipline. As one Western traveler put it: "There is no theatre in Berlin whatsoever, diversion is understood to be the handsome troops who parade daily. A special attraction is the great Potsdam Grenadier Regiment . . . when they practice drill, when they fire and when they parade up and down, it is as if they form a single body."[8]

A Prussian Giant Grenadier Frederick William I wanted tall, handsome soldiers. He dressed them in tight bright uniforms to distinguish them from the peasant population from which most soldiers came. He also ordered several portraits of his favorites, such as this one, from his court painter, J. C. Merk. Grenadiers (greh-nuh-DEERZ) wore the miter cap instead of an ordinary hat so that they could hurl their heavy grenades unimpeded by a broad brim. (The Royal Collection © 2010, Her Majesty Queen Elizabeth II)

> " A formidable army and a war chest large enough to make this army mobile in times of need can create great respect for you in the world, so that you can speak a word like the other powers. "
>
> —KING FREDERICK WILLIAM I

The Development of Russia and the Ottoman Empire

What were the distinctive features of Russian and Ottoman absolutism?

A favorite parlor game of nineteenth-century intellectuals was debating whether Russia was a Western (European) or non-Western (Asian) society. This question was particularly fascinating because it was unanswerable. To this day, Russia differs from the West in some fundamental ways, though its history has paralleled that of the West in other aspects.

There was no question in the mind of Europeans, however, that the Ottomans were outsiders. Even absolutist rulers disdained Ottoman sultans as cruel and tyrannical despots. Despite stereotypes, the Ottoman Empire was in many ways more tolerant than its Western counterparts, providing protection and security to other religions while steadfastly maintaining the Muslim faith. The Ottoman state combined the Byzantine heritage of the territory it had conquered with Persian and Arab traditions. Flexibility and openness to other ideas and practices were sources of strength for the empire.

The Mongol Yoke and the Rise of Moscow

The two-hundred-year period of rule by the Mongol khan (king) set the stage for the rise of absolutist Russia. The Mongols, a group of nomadic tribes from present-day Mongolia, established an empire that, at its height, stretched from Korea to eastern Europe. In the thirteenth century, the Mongols forced the Slavic princes

Nevertheless, Prussians paid a heavy and lasting price for the obsessions of their royal drillmaster. Army expansion was achieved in part through forced conscription, which was declared lifelong in 1713. Desperate draftees fled the country or injured themselves to avoid service. Finally, in 1733 Frederick William I ordered that all Prussian men would undergo military training and serve as reservists in the army, allowing him to preserve both agricultural production and army size. To appease the Junkers, the king enlisted them to lead his growing army. The proud nobility thus commanded the peasantry in the army as well as on the estates.

With all men harnessed to the war machine, Prussian civil society became rigid and highly disciplined. As a Prussian minister later summed up, "To keep quiet is the first civic duty."⁹ Thus the policies of Frederick William I, combined with harsh peasant bondage and Junker tyranny, laid the foundations for a highly militaristic country.

The Expansion of Russia to 1725

boyars The highest-ranking members of the Russian nobility.

Cossacks Free groups and outlaw armies originally comprising runaway peasants living on the borders of Russian territory from the fourteenth century onward. By the end of the sixteenth century they had formed an alliance with the Russian state.

to submit to their rule and to render payments of goods, money, and slaves. The princes of Moscow became particularly adept at serving the Mongols and were awarded the title of "great prince." Ivan III (r. 1462–1505), known as Ivan the Great, successfully expanded the principality of Moscow toward the Baltic Sea.

By 1480 Ivan III felt strong enough to stop acknowledging the khan as his supreme ruler and to cease paying tribute to the Mongols. To legitimize their new autonomy, the princes of Moscow modeled themselves on the Mongol khans. Like the khans, they declared themselves to be autocrats, meaning that they were the sole source of power. The Muscovite state also forced weaker Slavic principalities to render tribute previously paid to Mongols and borrowed Mongol institutions such as the tax system, postal routes, and census. Loyalty from the highest-ranking nobles, or **boyars**, helped the Muscovite princes consolidate their power.

Another source of legitimacy lay in Moscow's claim to the political and religious inheritance of the Byzantine Empire. After the fall of Constantinople to the Turks in 1453, the princes of Moscow saw themselves as the heirs of both the caesars (or emperors) and Orthodox Christianity. The title "tsar," first taken by Ivan IV in 1547, is in fact a contraction of *caesar*. The tsars considered themselves rightful and holy rulers, an idea promoted by Orthodox churchmen who spoke of "holy Russia" as the "Third Rome." The marriage of Ivan III to the daughter of the last Byzantine emperor further enhanced Moscow's claim to inherit imperial authority.

The Tsar and His People

Developments in Russia took a chaotic turn with the reign of Ivan IV (r. 1533–1584), the famous "Ivan the Terrible," who ascended to the throne at age three. His mother died, possibly poisoned, when he was eight, leaving Ivan to suffer insults and neglect from the boyars at court. At age sixteen he suddenly pushed aside his hated advisers, and in an awe-inspiring ceremony, complete with gold coins pouring down on his head, Ivan majestically crowned himself tsar.

Ivan's reign was successful in defeating the remnants of Mongol power, adding vast new territories to the realm, and laying the foundations for the huge, multi-ethnic Russian empire. After the sudden death of his beloved wife Anastasia Romanov, however, Ivan began a campaign of persecution against those he suspected of opposing him. Many were intimates of the court from leading boyar families, whom he had killed along with their families, friends, servants, and peasants. To further crush the power of the boyars, Ivan created a new service nobility, whose loyalty was guaranteed by their dependence on the state for noble titles and estates. Ivan portioned out the large estates seized from boyars to this new nobility, taking some of the land for his own personal domain.

Ivan also moved toward making all commoners servants of the tsar. As landlords demanded more from the serfs who survived the wars and persecutions, growing numbers of peasants fled toward wild, recently conquered territories to the east and south. There they joined free groups and warrior bands known as **Cossacks**. The solution to the problem of peasant flight was to tie peasants ever more firmly to the land and to the noble landholders, who in turn served the tsar.

Simultaneously, Ivan bound urban traders and artisans to their towns and jobs so that he could tax them more heavily. The urban classes had no security in their work or property, and even the wealthiest merchants were dependent agents of the tsar. These restrictions checked the growth of the Russian middle classes and stood in sharp contrast to developments in western Europe, where the middle classes were gaining security in their private property. From nobles down to merchants and peasants, all of the Russian people were thus brought into the tsar's service. Ivan even made use of Cossack armies in forays to the southeast, forging a new alliance between Moscow and the Cossacks.

After the death of Ivan and his successor, Russia entered a chaotic period known as the "Time of Troubles" (1598–1613). While Ivan's relatives struggled for power, ordinary people suffered drought, crop failure, and plague, leading to much suffering and death. The Cossacks and peasants rebelled against nobles and officials, demanding fairer treatment. This social explosion from below brought the nobles, big and small, together. They crushed the Cossack rebellion and elected Ivan's sixteen-year-old grandnephew, Michael Romanov, the new hereditary tsar (r. 1613–1645). Michael's election was represented as a restoration of tsarist autocracy. (See "Listening to the Past: A German Account of Russian Life," page 500.)

Russian Peasant An eighteenth-century French artist visiting Russia recorded his impressions of the daily life of the Russian people in this etching of a fish merchant pulling his wares through a snowy village on a sleigh. Two caviar vendors behind him make a sale to a young mother standing at her doorstep with her baby in her arms. (From Jean-Baptiste Le Prince's second set of Russian etchings, 1765. Private Collection/www.amis-paris-petersbourg.org)

Although the new tsar successfully reconsolidated central authority, he and his successors did not improve the lot of the common people. In 1649 a law extended serfdom to all peasants in the realm, giving lords unrestricted rights over their serfs and establishing penalties for harboring runaways. Social and religious uprisings among the poor and oppressed continued through the seventeenth century. One of the largest rebellions was led by the Cossack Stenka Razin, who in 1670 attracted a great army of urban poor and peasants, killing landlords and government officials and proclaiming freedom from oppression. In 1671 this rebellion was defeated.

Despite the turbulence of the period, the Romanov tsars, like their Western counterparts, made several important achievements during the second half of the seventeenth century. After a long war, Russia gained land in Ukraine from Poland in 1667 and completed the conquest of Siberia by the end of the century. Territorial expansion was accompanied by growth of the bureaucracy and the army. Foreign experts were employed to help build and reform the Russian army, and Cossack warriors were enlisted to fight Siberian campaigns. The great profits from Siberia's natural resources, especially furs, funded the Romanovs' bid for Great Power status. Thus, Russian imperialist expansion to the east paralleled the Western powers' exploration and conquest of the Atlantic world in the same period.

The Reforms of Peter the Great

Heir to Romanov efforts at state-building, Peter the Great (r. 1682–1725) embarked on a tremendous campaign to accelerate and complete these processes. A giant for his time at six feet seven inches, and possessing enormous energy and willpower, Peter was determined to build and improve the army and to continue the tsarist tradition of territorial expansion. After ruling as co-tsar with his half-brother and sister from 1682 to 1696, Peter reigned independently for thirty-six years. Only one of those years was peaceful.

Fascinated by weapons and foreign technology, the tsar led a group of 250 Russian officials and young nobles on an eighteen-month tour of western European capitals. Traveling unofficially to avoid lengthy diplomatic ceremonies, Peter worked with his hands at various crafts and met with foreign kings and experts. He

A German Account of Russian Life

LISTENING TO THE PAST

Seventeenth-century Russia remained a remote and mysterious land for western and even central Europeans, who had few direct contacts with the tsar's dominion. Westerners portrayed eastern Europe as more "barbaric" and less "civilized" than their homelands. Thus they expanded eastern Europe's undeniably harsher social and economic conditions to encompass a very debatable cultural and moral inferiority.

Knowledge of Russia came mainly from occasional travelers who had visited Muscovy and sometimes wrote accounts of what they saw. The most famous of these accounts was by the German Adam Olearius (ca. 1599–1671), who was sent to Moscow on three diplomatic missions in the 1630s. These missions ultimately proved unsuccessful, but they provided Olearius with a rich store of information for his *Travels in Muscovy*, from which the following excerpts are taken. Published in German in 1647 and soon translated into several languages (but not Russian), Olearius's unflattering but well-informed study played a major role in shaping European ideas about Russia.

❝ The government of the Russians is what political theorists call a "dominating and despotic monarchy," where the sovereign, that is, the tsar or the grand prince who has obtained the crown by right of succession, rules the entire land alone, and all the people are his subjects, and where the nobles and princes no less than the common folk — townspeople and peasants — are his serfs and slaves, whom he rules and treats as a master treats his servants. . . .

If the Russians be considered in respect to their character, customs, and way of life, they are justly to be counted among the barbarians. . . . The vice of drunkenness is so common in this nation, among people of every station, clergy and laity, high and low, men and women, old and young, that when they are seen now and then lying about in the streets, wallowing in the mud, no attention is paid to it, as something habitual. If a cart driver comes upon such a drunken pig whom he happens to know, he shoves him onto his cart and drives him home, where he is paid his fare. No one ever refuses an opportunity to drink and to get drunk, at any time and in any place, and usually it is done with vodka. . . .

The Russians being naturally tough and born, as it were, for slavery, they must be kept under a harsh and strict yoke and must be driven to do their work with clubs and whips, which they suffer without impatience, because such is their station, and they are accustomed to it. Young and

The brutality of serfdom is shown in this illustration from Olearius's *Travels in Muscovy*. (University of Illinois Library, Champaign)

was particularly impressed with the growing power of the Dutch and the English, and he considered how Russia could profit from their example.

Returning to Russia, Peter entered into a secret alliance with Denmark and Poland to wage a sudden war of aggression against Sweden with the goal of securing access to the Baltic Sea and opportunities for westward expansion. Peter and his allies believed that their combined forces could win easy victories because Sweden was in the hands of a new and inexperienced king.

Eighteen-year-old Charles XII of Sweden (1697–1718) surprised Peter. He defeated Denmark quickly in 1700, then turned on Russia. In a blinding snowstorm, his well-trained professional army attacked and routed unsuspecting Russians besieging the Swedish fortress of Narva on the Baltic coast. Peter and the survi-

half-grown fellows sometimes come together on certain days and train themselves in fisticuffs, to accustom themselves to receiving blows, and, since habit is second nature, this makes blows given as punishment easier to bear. Each and all, they are slaves and serfs....

Because of slavery and their rough and hard life, the Russians accept war readily and are well suited to it. On certain occasions, if need be, they reveal themselves as courageous and daring soldiers....

Although the Russians, especially the common populace, living as slaves under a harsh yoke, can bear and endure a great deal out of love for their masters, yet if the pressure is beyond measure, then it can be said of them: "Patience, often wounded, finally turned into fury." A dangerous indignation results, turned not so much against their sovereign as against the lower authorities, especially if the people have been much oppressed by them and by their supporters and have not been protected by the higher authorities. And once they are aroused and enraged, it is not easy to appease them. Then, disregarding all dangers that may ensue, they resort to every kind of violence and behave like madmen.... They own little; most of them have no feather beds; they lie on cushions, straw, mats, or their clothes; they sleep on benches and, in winter, like the non-Germans [natives] in Livonia, upon the oven, which serves them for cooking and is flat on the top; here husband, wife, children, servants, and maids huddle together. In some houses in the countryside we saw chickens and pigs under the benches and the ovens.... Russians are not used to delicate food and dainties; their daily food consists of porridge, turnips, cabbage, and cucumbers, fresh and pickled, and in Moscow mostly of big salt fish which stink badly, because of the thrifty use of salt, yet are eaten with relish....

The Russians can endure extreme heat. In the bathhouse they stretch out on benches and let themselves be beaten and rubbed with bunches of birch twigs and wisps of bast (which I could not stand); and when they are hot and red all over and so exhausted that they can bear it no longer in the bathhouse, men and women rush outdoors naked and pour cold water over their bodies; in winter they even wallow in the snow and rub their skin with it as if it were soap; then they go back into the hot bathhouse. And since bathhouses are usually near rivers and brooks, they can throw themselves straight from the hot into the cold bath....

Generally noble families, even the small nobility, rear their daughters in secluded chambers, keeping them hidden from outsiders; and a bridegroom is not allowed to have a look at his bride until he receives her in the bridal chamber. Therefore some happen to be deceived, being given a misshapen and sickly one instead of a fair one, and sometimes a kinswoman or even a maidservant instead of a daughter; of which there have been examples even among the highborn. No wonder therefore that often they live together like cats and dogs and that wife-beating is so common among Russians....

In the Kremlin and in the city there are a great many churches, chapels, and monasteries, both within and without the city walls, over two thousand in all. This is so because every nobleman who has some fortune has a chapel built for himself, and most of them are of stone. The stone churches are round and vaulted inside.... They allow neither organs nor any other musical instruments in their churches, saying: Instruments that have neither souls nor life cannot praise God....

In their churches there hang many bells, sometimes five or six, the largest not over two hundredweights. They ring these bells to summon people to church, and also when the priest during mass raises the chalice. In Moscow, because of the multitude of churches and chapels, there are several thousand bells, which during the divine service create such a clang and din that one unaccustomed to it listens in amazement. 〞

Source: "A Foreign Traveler in Russia" excerpt from pp. 249–251 in *A Source Book for Russian History from Early Times to 1917*, volume 1, *Early Times to the Late Seventeenth Century*, edited by George Vernadsky, Ralph T. Fisher, Jr., Alan D. Ferguson, Andrew Lossky, and Sergei Pushkarev, compiler. Copyright © 1972 by Yale University Press. Used with permission of the publisher.

QUESTIONS FOR ANALYSIS

1. How did Olearius characterize the Russians in general? What supporting evidence did he offer for his judgment?
2. How might Olearius's account help explain Stenka Razin's rebellion (page 499)?
3. On the basis of these representative passages, why do you think Olearius's book was so popular and influential in central and western Europe?

---

vors fled in panic to Moscow. It was, for the Russians, a grim beginning to the long and brutal Great Northern War, which lasted from 1700 to 1721.

Peter responded to this defeat with measures designed to increase state power, strengthen his armies, and gain victory. He required all nobles to serve in the army or in the civil administration—for life. Since a more modern army and government required skilled technicians and experts, Peter created schools and universities to produce them. One of his most hated reforms was requiring a five-year education away from home for every young nobleman. Peter established an interlocking military-civilian bureaucracy with fourteen ranks, and he decreed that all had to start at the bottom and work toward the top. The system allowed some people of non-noble origins to rise to high posi-

Saint Basil's Cathedral, Moscow With its sloping roofs and colorful onion-shaped domes, Saint Basil's is a striking example of powerful Byzantine influences on Russian culture. According to tradition, an enchanted Ivan the Terrible blinded the cathedral's architects to ensure that they would never duplicate their fantastic achievement, which still dazzles the beholder in today's Red Square. (George Holton/Photo Researchers)

tions, a rarity in Europe at the time. Drawing on his experience abroad, Peter sought talented foreigners and placed them in his service. These measures gradually combined to make the army and government more powerful and efficient.

Peter also greatly increased the service requirements of commoners. In the wake of the Narva disaster, he established a regular standing army of more than two hundred thousand peasant-soldiers commanded by officers from the nobility. In addition, one hundred thousand men were brought into the Russian army in special regiments of Cossacks and foreign mercenaries. The departure of a drafted peasant boy was celebrated by his family almost like a funeral, since the recruit was drafted for life. To fund the army, taxes on peasants increased threefold during Peter's reign. Serfs were also arbitrarily assigned to work in the growing number of factories and mines that supplied the military.

Peter's new war machine was able to crush the small army of Sweden in Ukraine at Poltava in 1709, one of the most significant battles in Russian history. Russia's victory against Sweden was conclusive in 1721, and Estonia and present-day Latvia came under Russian rule for the first time. The cost was high—warfare consumed 80 to 85 percent of all revenues. But Russia became the dominant power in the Baltic and very much a European Great Power.

After his victory at Poltava, Peter channeled enormous resources into building a new Western-style capital on the Baltic to rival the great cities of Europe. Originally a desolate and swampy Swedish outpost, the magnificent city of St. Petersburg was designed to reflect modern urban planning, with wide, straight avenues, buildings set in a uniform line, and large parks.

Peter the Great dictated that all in society realize his vision. Just as the government drafted the peasants for the armies, so it drafted twenty-five thousand to forty thousand men each summer to labor in St. Petersburg without pay. Many peasant construction workers died from hunger, sickness, and accidents. Nobles were ordered to build costly stone houses and palaces in St. Petersburg and to live in them most of the year. Merchants and artisans were also commanded to settle and build in the new capital. These nobles and merchants were then required to pay for the city's infrastructure. The building of St. Petersburg was, in truth, an enormous direct tax levied on the wealthy, with the peasantry forced to do the manual labor.

There were other important consequences of Peter's reign. For Peter, modernization meant westernization,

Peter the Great This compelling portrait by Grigory Musikiysky captures the strength and determination of the warrior-tsar in 1723, after more than three decades of personal rule. In his hand Peter holds the scepter, symbol of royal sovereignty, and across his breastplate is draped an ermine fur, a mark of honor. In the background are the battleships of Russia's new Baltic fleet and the famous St. Peter and St. Paul Fortress that Peter built in St. Petersburg. Peter the Great commissioned this magnificent new crown (left) for himself for his joint coronation in 1682 with his half-brother Ivan. (portrait: Kremlin Museums, Moscow/The Bridgeman Art Library; crown: Bildarchiv Preussischer Kulturbesitz/Art Resource, NY)

and both Westerners and Western ideas flowed into Russia for the first time. He required nobles to shave their heavy beards and wear Western clothing, previously banned in Russia. He required them to attend parties where young men and women would mix together and freely choose their own spouses. He forced a warrior elite to accept administrative service as an honorable occupation. From these efforts a new elite class of Western-oriented Russians began to emerge.

Peter's reforms were unpopular with many Russians. For nobles, one of Peter's most detested reforms was the imposition of unigeniture — inheritance of land by one son alone — cutting daughters and other sons from family property. For peasants, the reign of the tsar saw a significant increase in the bonds of serfdom, and the gulf between the enserfed peasantry and the educated nobility increased.

Peter's reforms were in some ways a continuation of Russia's distinctive history. He built on the service obligations of Ivan the Terrible and his successors, and his monarchical absolutism can be seen as the culmination of the long development of a unique Russian civilization.

Yet the creation of a more modern army and state introduced much that was new and Western to Russia. This development paved the way for Russia to move somewhat closer to the European mainstream in its thought and institutions during the Enlightenment, especially under Catherine the Great.

The Growth of the Ottoman Empire

Most Christian Europeans perceived the Ottomans as the antithesis of their own values and traditions and viewed the empire as driven by an insatiable lust for warfare and conquest. In their view the fall of Constantinople was a historic catastrophe and the taking of the Balkans a form of despotic imprisonment. To Ottoman eyes, the world looked very different. The siege of Constantinople liberated a glorious city from its long decline under the Byzantines. Rather than being a despoiled captive, the Balkans became a haven for refugees fleeing the growing intolerance of Western Christian powers. The Ottoman Empire provided Jews, Muslims,

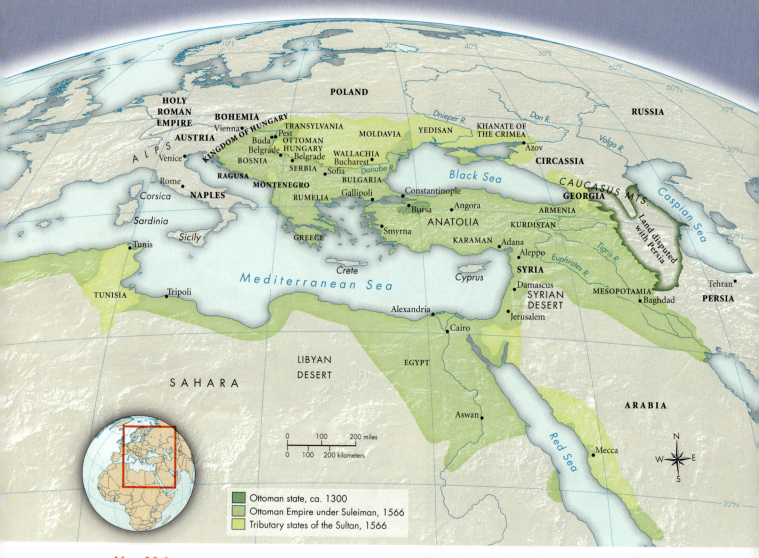

Map 16.4 The Ottoman Empire at Its Height, 1566 The Ottomans, like their great rivals the Hapsburgs, rose to rule a vast dynastic empire encompassing many different peoples and ethnic groups. The army and the bureaucracy served to unite the disparate territories into a single state under an absolutist ruler.

and even some Christians safety from the Inquisition and religious war.

The Ottomans came out of Central Asia as conquering warriors, settled in Anatolia (present-day Turkey), and, at their peak in the mid-sixteenth century, ruled one of the most powerful empires in the world (see Chapter 15). Their possessions stretched from western Persia across North Africa and into the heart of central Europe (Map 16.4).

The Ottoman Empire was originally built on a unique model of state and society. There was an almost complete absence of private landed property. Agricultural land was the personal hereditary property of the **sultan**, and peasants paid taxes to use the land. There was therefore no security of landholding and no hereditary nobility.

The Ottomans also employed a distinctive form of government administration. The top ranks of the bureaucracy were staffed by the sultan's slave corps. Because Muslim law prohibited enslaving other Muslims, the sultan's agents purchased slaves along the borders of the empire. Within the realm, the sultan levied a "tax" of one thousand to three thousand male children on the conquered Christian populations in the Balkans every year. These young slaves were raised in Turkey as Muslims and were trained to fight and to administer. Unlike the dire fate reserved for enslaved Africans in European colonies, the most talented Ottoman slaves rose to the top of the bureaucracy, where they might acquire wealth and power. The less fortunate formed the core of the sultan's army, the **janissary corps**. These highly organized and efficient troops gave the Ottomans a formidable advantage in war with western Europeans. By 1683 service in the janissary corps had become so prestigious that the sultan ceased recruitment by force, and it became a volunteer army open to Christians and Muslims.

sultan The ruler of the Ottoman Empire; he owned all the agricultural land of the empire and was served by an army and bureaucracy composed of highly trained slaves.

janissary corps The core of the sultan's army, composed of slave conscripts from non-Muslim parts of the empire; after 1683 it became a volunteer force.

The Ottomans divided their subjects into religious communities, and each *millet* (MIH-luht), or "nation," enjoyed autonomous self-government under its religious leaders. The Ottoman Empire recognized Orthodox Christians, Jews, Armenian Christians, and Muslims as distinct millets, but despite its tolerance, the empire was an explicitly Islamic state. The **millet system** created a powerful bond between the Ottoman ruling class and religious leaders, who supported the sultan's rule in return for extensive authority over their own communities. Each millet collected taxes for the state, regulated group behavior, and maintained law courts, schools, houses of worship, and hospitals for its people.

Istanbul (known outside the empire by its original name, Constantinople) was the capital of the empire. The "old palace" was for the sultan's female family members, who lived in isolation under the care of eunuchs, men who were castrated to prevent sexual relations with women. The newer Topkapi palace was where officials worked and young slaves trained for future administrative or military careers. Sultans married women of the highest social standing, while keeping many concubines of low rank. To prevent the elite families into which they married from acquiring influence over the government, sultans procreated only with their concubines and not with official wives. They also adopted a policy of allowing each concubine to produce only one male heir. At a young age, each son went to govern a province of the empire accompanied by his mother. These practices were intended to stabilize power and prevent a recurrence of the civil wars of the late fourteenth and early fifteenth centuries.

Sultan Suleiman undid these policies when he boldly married his concubine, a former slave of Polish origin named Hürrem, and had several children with her. He established a wing in the Topkapi palace for Hürrem, his other female family members, and his brothers' families. Starting with Suleiman, imperial wives began to take on more power. Marriages were arranged between sultans' daughters and high-ranking servants, creating powerful new members of the imperial household. Over time, the sultan's exclusive authority waned in favor of a more bureaucratic administration.

> **millet system** A system used by the Ottomans whereby subjects were divided into religious communities with each millet (nation) enjoying autonomous self-government under its religious leaders.

Hürrem and Her Ladies in the Harem In Muslim culture *harem* means a sacred place or a sanctuary. The term was applied to the part of the household occupied by women and children and forbidden to men outside the family. The most famous member of the Ottoman sultan's harem was Hürrem (1505–1585), wife of Suleiman the Magnificent. Captured, according to tradition, in modern-day Ukraine in a Tartar raid and brought to the harem as a slave-concubine, she quickly won the sultan's trust and affection. Suleiman's love for Hürrem led him to break all precedents and marry his concubine, a decision that shocked some courtiers. (Bibliothèque nationale de France)

Alternatives to Absolutism in England and the Dutch Republic

How and why did the constitutional state triumph in the Dutch Republic and England?

While France, Prussia, Russia, and Austria developed the absolutist state, England and Holland evolved toward **constitutionalism**, which is the limitation of government by law. Constitutionalism also implies a balance between the authority and power of the government, on the one hand, and the rights and liberties of the subjects, on the other. By definition, all constitutionalist governments have a constitution, be it written or unwritten. A nation's constitution may be embodied in one basic document and occasionally revised by amendment, like the Constitution of the United States. Or it may be only partly formalized and include parliamentary statutes, judicial decisions, and a body of traditional procedures and practices, like the English and Dutch constitutions.

Despite their common commitment to constitutional government, England and the Dutch Republic represented significantly different alternatives to absolute rule. After decades of civil war and an experiment with **republicanism**, the English opted for a constitutional monarchy in 1688. This settlement, which has endured to this day, retained a monarch as the titular head of government but vested sovereignty in an elected parliament. Upon gaining independence from Spain in 1648, the Dutch rejected monarchical rule, adopting a republican form of government in which elected estates held supreme power. Neither was democratic by any standard, but to other Europeans they were shining examples of the restraint of arbitrary power and the rule of law.

constitutionalism A form of government in which power is limited by law and balanced between the authority and power of the government on the one hand, and the rights and liberties of the subjects or citizens on the other hand; could include constitutional monarchies or republics.

republicanism A form of government in which there is no monarch and power rests in the hands of the people as exercised through elected representatives.

Van Dyck, *Charles I at the Hunt*, ca. 1635 Anthony Van Dyck was the greatest of Rubens's many students. In 1633 he became court painter to Charles I. This portrait of Charles just dismounted from a horse emphasizes the aristocratic bearing, elegance, and innate authority of the king. Van Dyck's success led to innumerable commissions by members of the court and aristocratic society. He had a profound influence on portraiture in England and beyond; some scholars believe that this portrait influenced Rigaud's 1701 portrayal of Louis XIV (see page 488). (Scala/Art Resource, NY)

Absolutist Claims in England

In 1588 Queen Elizabeth I of England exercised very great personal power; by 1689 the English monarchy was severely circumscribed. A rare female monarch, Elizabeth was able to maintain control over her realm in part by refusing to marry and submit to a husband. She was immensely popular with her people, but left no immediate heir to continue her legacy.

In 1603 Elizabeth's Scottish cousin James Stuart succeeded her as James I (r. 1603–1625). King James was well educated and had thirty-five years' experience as king of Scotland. But he was not as interested in displaying the majesty of monarchy as Elizabeth had been. Urged to wave at the crowds who waited to greet their new ruler, James complained that he was tired and threatened to drop his breeches "so they can cheer at my arse."[10]

James's greatest problem, however, stemmed from his absolutist belief that a monarch has a divine right to his authority and is responsible only to God. James went so far as to lecture the House of Commons: "There

are no privileges and immunities which can stand against a divinely appointed King." Such a view ran directly counter to the long-standing English idea that a person's property could not be taken away without due process of law. James I and his son Charles I considered such constraints intolerable and a threat to their divine-right prerogative. Consequently, at every Parliament between 1603 and 1640, bitter squabbles erupted between the Crown and the articulate and legally minded Commons. Charles I's attempt to govern without Parliament (1629–1640) and to finance his government by emergency taxes brought the country to a crisis.

Religious Divides and the English Civil War

Religious issues also embittered relations between the king and the House of Commons. In the early seventeenth century increasing numbers of English people felt dissatisfied with the Church of England established by Henry VIII and reformed by Elizabeth. Many **Puritans** believed that the Reformation had not gone far enough. They wanted to "purify" the Anglican Church of Roman Catholic elements—elaborate vestments and ceremonials, bishops, and even the giving and wearing of wedding rings.

James I responded to such ideas by declaring, "No bishop, no king." For James, bishops were among the chief supporters of the throne. His son and successor, Charles I, further antagonized religious sentiments. Not only did he marry a Catholic princess, but he also supported the heavy-handed policies of the Archbishop of Canterbury William Laud (1573–1645). In 1637

Puritans Members of a sixteenth- and seventeenth-century reform movement within the Church of England that advocated purifying it of Roman Catholic elements, such as bishops, elaborate ceremonials, and wedding rings.

Puritan Occupations These twelve engravings depict typical Puritan occupations and show that the Puritans came primarily from the artisan and lower middle classes. The governing classes and peasants made up a much smaller percentage of the Puritans and generally adhered to the traditions of the Church of England. (Visual Connection Archive)

Laud attempted to impose two new elements on church organization in Scotland: a new prayer book, modeled on the Anglican *Book of Common Prayer*, and bishoprics. The Presbyterian Scots rejected these elements and revolted. To finance an army to put down the Scots, King Charles was compelled to summon Parliament in November 1640.

Charles had ruled from 1629 to 1640 without Parliament, financing his government through extraordinary stopgap levies considered illegal by most English people. For example, the king revived a medieval law requiring coastal districts to help pay the cost of ships for defense, but he levied the tax, called "ship money," on inland as well as coastal counties. Most members of Parliament believed that such taxation without consent amounted to despotism. Consequently, they were not willing to trust the king with an army. Moreover, many supported the Scots' resistance to Charles's religious innovations. Accordingly, this Parliament, called the "Long Parliament" because it sat from 1640 to 1660, enacted legislation that limited the power of the monarch and made government without Parliament impossible.

In 1641 the Commons passed the Triennial Act, which compelled the king to summon Parliament every three years. The Commons impeached Archbishop Laud and then threatened to abolish bishops. King Charles, fearful of a Scottish invasion—the original reason for summoning Parliament—reluctantly accepted these measures.

The next act in the conflict was precipitated by the outbreak of rebellion in Ireland, where English governors and landlords had long exploited the people. In 1641 the Catholic gentry of Ireland led an uprising in response to a feared invasion by anti-Catholic forces of the British Long Parliament.

Without an army, Charles I could neither come to terms with the Scots nor respond to the Irish rebellion. After a failed attempt to arrest parliamentary leaders, Charles left London for the north of England. There, he recruited an army drawn from the nobility and its cavalry staff, the rural gentry, and mercenaries. In response, Parliament formed its own army, the New Model Army, composed of the militia of the city of London and country squires with business connections. During the spring of 1642 both sides prepared for war. In July a linen weaver became the first casualty of the civil war during a skirmish between royal and parliamentary forces in Manchester.

Protectorate The English military dictatorship (1653–1658) established by Oliver Cromwell following the execution of Charles I.

The English Civil War, 1642–1649

The English civil war (1642–1649) pitted the power of the king against that of the Parliament. After three years of fighting, Parliament's New Model Army defeated the king's armies at the Battles of Naseby and Langport in the summer of 1645. Charles, though, refused to concede defeat. Both sides jockeyed for position, waiting for a decisive event. This arrived in the form of the army under the leadership of Oliver Cromwell, a member of the House of Commons and a devout Puritan. In 1647 Cromwell's forces captured the king and dismissed members of the Parliament who opposed his actions. In 1649 the remaining representatives, known as the "Rump Parliament," put Charles on trial for high treason. Charles was found guilty and beheaded on January 30, 1649, an act that sent shock waves around Europe.

Cromwell and Puritanical Absolutism in England

With the execution of Charles, kingship was abolished. The question remained of how the country would be governed. One answer was provided by philosopher Thomas Hobbes (1588–1679). Hobbes held a pessimistic view of human nature and believed that, left to themselves, humans would compete violently for power and wealth. The only solution, as he outlined in his 1651 treatise *Leviathan*, was a social contract in which all members of society placed themselves under the absolute rule of a monarch, who would maintain peace and order. Hobbes imagined society as a human body in which the monarch served as head and individual subjects together made up the body. Just as the body cannot sever its own head, so Hobbes believed that society could not, having accepted the contract, rise up against its king. Deeply shocked by Charles's execution, he utterly denied the right of subjects to rebellion.

Hobbes's longing for a benevolent absolute monarch was not widely shared in England. Instead, a commonwealth, or republican government, was proclaimed. Theoretically, legislative power rested in the surviving members of Parliament, and executive power was lodged in a council of state. In fact, the army that had defeated the king controlled the government, and Oliver Cromwell controlled the army. Though called the **Protectorate**, the rule of Cromwell (1653–1658) constituted military dictatorship.

"The Royall Oake of Brittayne" The chopping down of this tree, as shown in this cartoon from 1649, signifies the end of royal authority, stability, and the rule of law. As pigs graze (representing the unconcerned common people), being fattened for slaughter, Oliver Cromwell, with his feet in Hell, quotes Scripture. This is a royalist view of the collapse of Charles I's government and the rule of Cromwell. (Courtesy of the Trustees of the British Museum)

The army prepared a constitution, the Instrument of Government (1653), that invested executive power in a lord protector (Cromwell) and a council of state. It provided for triennial parliaments and gave Parliament the sole power to raise taxes. But after repeated disputes, Cromwell dismissed Parliament in 1655, and the instrument was never formally endorsed. Cromwell continued the standing army and proclaimed quasi-martial law. He divided England into twelve military districts, each governed by a major general. Reflecting Puritan ideas of morality, Cromwell's state forbade sports, kept the theaters closed, and rigorously censored the press.

On the issue of religion, Cromwell favored some degree of toleration, and the Instrument of Government gave all Christians except Roman Catholics the right to practice their faith. Cromwell had long associated Catholicism in Ireland with sedition and heresy, and led an army there to reconquer the country in August 1649. One month later, his forces crushed a rebellion at Drogheda and massacred the garrison. After Cromwell's departure for England, atrocities worsened. The English banned Catholicism in Ireland, executed priests, and confiscated land from Catholics for English and Scottish settlers. These brutal acts left a legacy of Irish hatred for England.

Cromwell adopted mercantilist policies similar to those of absolutist France. He enforced a Navigation Act (1651) requiring that English goods be transported on English ships. The act was a great boost to the development of an English merchant marine and brought about a short but successful war with the commercially threatened Dutch. Cromwell also welcomed the immigration of Jews because of their skills, and they began to return to England after four centuries of absence.

The Protectorate collapsed when Cromwell died in 1658 and his ineffectual son succeeded him. Fed up with military rule, the English longed for a return to civilian government and, with it, common law and social stability. By 1660 they were ready to restore the monarchy.

The Restoration of the English Monarchy

The Restoration of 1660 brought to the throne Charles II (r. 1660–1685), eldest son of Charles I, who had been living on the continent. Both houses of Parliament were also restored, together with the established Anglican Church. The Restoration failed to resolve two serious problems, however. What was to be the attitude of the state toward Puritans, Catholics, and dissenters from the established church? And what was to be the relationship between the king and Parliament?

To answer the first question, Parliament enacted the **Test Act** of 1673 against those outside the Church of England, denying them the right to vote, hold public office, preach, teach, attend the universities, or even assemble for meetings. But these restrictions could not be enforced. When the Quaker William Penn held a meeting of his Friends and was arrested, the jury refused to convict him.

In politics Charles II was determined to avoid exile by working well with Parliament. This intention did not last, however. Finding that Parliament did not grant him an adequate income, in 1670 Charles entered into a secret agreement with his cousin Louis XIV. The French king would give Charles two hundred thousand pounds annually, and in return Charles would relax the laws against Catholics, gradually re-Catholicize England, and convert to Catholicism himself. When the details of this treaty leaked out, a great wave of anti-Catholic sentiment swept England.

When James II (r. 1685–1688) succeeded his brother, the worst English anti-Catholic fears were realized. In violation of the Test Act, James appointed Roman Catholics to positions in the army, the universities, and local government. When these actions were challenged in the courts, the judges, whom James had appointed, decided in favor of the king. The king was suspending the law at will and appeared to be reviving the absolutism of his father and grandfather. He went further. Attempting to broaden his base of support with Protestant dissenters and nonconformists, James granted religious freedom to all.

Seeking to prevent the return of Catholic absolutism, a group of eminent persons in Parliament and the Church of England offered the English throne to James's Protestant daughter Mary and her Dutch husband, Prince William of Orange. In December 1688 James II, his queen, and their infant son fled to France and became pensioners of Louis XIV. Early in 1689 William and Mary were crowned king and queen of England.

Constitutional Monarchy and Cabinet Government

The English call the events of 1688 and 1689 the "Glorious Revolution" because it replaced one king with another with a minimum of bloodshed. It also represented the destruction, once and for all, of the idea of divine-right monarchy. William and Mary accepted the English throne from Parliament and in so doing explicitly recognized the supremacy of Parliament. The revolution of 1688 established the principle that sovereignty, the ultimate power in the state, was divided between king and Parliament and that the king ruled with the consent of the governed.

The men who brought about the revolution framed their intentions in the Bill of Rights (1689), which was formulated in direct response to Stuart absolutism. Law was to be made in Parliament; once made, it could not be suspended by the Crown. Parliament had to be called at least once every three years. The independence of the judiciary was established, and there was to be no standing army in peacetime. Protestants could possess arms, but the Catholic minority could not. No Catholic could ever inherit the throne. Additional legislation granted freedom of worship to Protestant dissenters, but not to Catholics.

The Glorious Revolution and the concept of representative government found its best defense in political philosopher John Locke's *Second Treatise of Civil Government* (1690). Locke (1632–1704) maintained that a government that oversteps its proper function — protecting the natural rights of life, liberty, and property — becomes a tyranny. By "natural" rights Locke meant rights basic to all men because all have the ability to reason. (His idea that there are natural or universal rights equally valid for all peoples and societies was especially popular in colonial America.) Under a tyrannical government, the people have the natural right to rebellion. On the basis of this link, he justified limiting the vote to property owners. (American colonists also appreciated his arguments that Native Americans had no property rights since they did not cultivate the land and, by extension, no political rights because they possessed no property.)

The events of 1688 and 1689 did not constitute a democratic revolution. The revolution placed sovereignty in Parliament, and Parliament represented the upper classes. The age of aristocratic government lasted at least until 1832 and in many ways until 1928, when women received full voting rights.

In the course of the eighteenth century, the cabinet

Test Act Legislation, passed by the English parliament in 1673, to secure the position of the Anglican Church by stripping Puritans, Catholics, and other dissenters of the right to vote, preach, assemble, hold public office, and attend or teach at the universities.

system of government evolved. The term *cabinet* derives from the small private room in which English rulers consulted their chief ministers. In a cabinet system, the leading ministers, who must have seats in and the support of a majority of the House of Commons, formulate common policy and conduct the business of the country. During the administration of one royal minister, Sir Robert Walpole, who led the cabinet from 1721 to 1742, the idea developed that the cabinet was responsible to the House of Commons. The Hanoverian king George I (r. 1714–1727) normally presided at cabinet meetings throughout his reign, but his son and heir, George II (r. 1727–1760), discontinued the practice. The influence of the Crown in decision making accordingly declined. Walpole enjoyed the favor of the monarchy and of the House of Commons and came to be called the king's first, or "prime," minister. In the English cabinet system, both legislative power and executive power are held by the leading ministers, who form the government.

England's brief and chaotic experiment with republicanism under Oliver Cromwell convinced its people of the advantages of a monarchy, albeit with strong checks on royal authority. The eighteenth-century philosopher David Hume went so far as to declare that he would prefer England to be peaceful under an absolute monarch than in constant civil war as a republic. These sentiments would have found little sympathy among the proud burghers of the Dutch Republic.

The Dutch Republic in the Seventeenth Century

In the late sixteenth century the seven northern provinces of the Netherlands fought for and won their independence from Spain. The independence of the Republic of the United Provinces of the Netherlands was recognized in 1648 in the treaty that ended the Thirty Years' War. In this period, often called the "golden age of the Netherlands," Dutch ideas and attitudes played a profound role in shaping a new and modern worldview. At the same time, the United Provinces developed its own distinctive model of a constitutional state.

Jan Steen, *The Merry Family*, 1668 In this painting from the Dutch golden age, a happy family enjoys a boisterous song while seated around the dining table. Despite its carefree appearance, the painting was intended to teach a moral lesson. The children are shown drinking wine and smoking, bad habits they have learned from their parents. The inscription hanging over the mantelpiece (upper right) spells out the message clearly: "As the Old Sing, so Pipe the Young." (Gianni Dagli Orti/The Art Archive)

Glückel of Hameln

INDIVIDUALS IN SOCIETY

IN 1690 A JEWISH WIDOW IN THE SMALL GERMAN TOWN OF HAMELN in Lower Saxony sat down to write her autobiography. She wanted to distract her mind from the terrible grief she felt over the death of her husband and to provide her twelve children with a record "so you will know from what sort of people you have sprung, lest today or tomorrow your beloved children or grandchildren came and know naught of their family." Out of her pain and heightened consciousness, Glückel (1646–1724) produced an invaluable source for scholars.

She was born in Hamburg two years before the end of the Thirty Years' War. In 1649 the merchants of Hamburg expelled the Jews, who moved to nearby Altona, then under Danish rule. When the Swedes overran Altona in 1657–1658, the Jews returned to Hamburg "purely at the mercy of the Town Council." Glückel's narrative proceeds against a background of the constant harassment to which Jews were subjected — special papers, permits, bribes — and in Hameln she wrote, "And so it has been to this day and, I fear, will continue in like fashion."

When Glückel was "barely twelve," her father betrothed her to Chayim Hameln. She married at age fourteen. She describes him as "the perfect pattern of the pious Jew," a man who stopped his work every day for study and prayer, fasted, and was scrupulously honest in his business dealings. Only a few years older than Glückel, Chayim earned his living dealing in precious metals and in making small loans on pledges (pawned goods). This work required his constant travel to larger cities, markets, and fairs, often in bad weather, always over dangerous roads. Chayim consulted his wife about all his business dealings. As he lay dying, a friend asked if he had any last wishes. "None," he replied. "My wife knows everything. She shall do as she has always done." For thirty years Glückel had been his friend, full business partner, and wife. They had thirteen children, twelve of whom survived their father, eight then unmarried. As Chayim had foretold, Glückel succeeded in launching the boys in careers and in providing dowries for the girls.

Although no images of Glückel exist, Rembrandt's *The Jewish Bride* suggests the mutual devotion that Glückel and her husband felt for each other. (Rijksmuseum-Stichting Amsterdam)

Glückel's world was her family, the Jewish community of Hameln, and the Jewish communities into which her children married. Her social and business activities took her across Europe, from Amsterdam to Berlin, from Danzig to Vienna, so her world was not narrow or provincial. She took great pride that Prince Frederick of Cleves, later king of Prussia, danced at the wedding of her eldest daughter. The rising prosperity of Chayim's businesses allowed the couple to maintain up to six servants.

Glückel was deeply religious, and her culture was steeped in Jewish literature, legends, and mystical and secular works. Above all, she relied on the Bible. Her language, heavily sprinkled with scriptural references, testifies to a rare familiarity with the Scriptures.

Students who would learn about seventeenth-century business practices, the importance of the dowry in marriage, childbirth, Jewish life, birthrates, family celebrations, and even the meaning of life can gain a good deal from the memoirs of this extraordinary woman who was, in the words of one of her descendants, the poet Heinrich Heine, "the gift of a world to me."

Source: *The Memoirs of Glückel of Hameln* (New York: Schocken Books, 1977).

QUESTIONS FOR ANALYSIS

1. Consider the ways in which Glückel of Hameln was both an ordinary and an extraordinary woman of her times. Would you call her a marginal or a central person in her society?
2. How might Glückel's successes be attributed to the stabilizing force of absolutism in the seventeenth century?

Rejecting the rule of a monarch, the Dutch established a republic, a state in which power rested in the hands of the people and was exercised through elected representatives. Other examples of republics in early modern Europe included the Swiss Confederation and several autonomous city-states of Italy and the Holy Roman Empire. Among the Dutch, an oligarchy of wealthy businessmen called "regents" handled domestic affairs in each province's Estates (assemblies). The provincial Estates held virtually all the power. A federal assembly, or States General, handled foreign affairs and war, but it did not possess sovereign authority. All issues had to be referred back to the local Estates for approval, and each of the seven provinces could veto any proposed legislation. Holland, the province with the largest navy and the most wealth, usually dominated the republic and the States General.

In each province, the Estates appointed an executive officer, known as the **stadholder**, who carried out ceremonial functions and was responsible for military defense. Although in theory freely chosen by the Estates and answerable to them, in practice the reigning prince of Orange usually held the office of stadholder in several of the seven provinces of the Republic. This meant that tensions always lingered between supporters of the House of Orange and those of the staunchly republican Estates, who suspected the princes of harboring monarchical ambitions. When one of them, William III, took the English throne in 1688 with his wife, Mary, the republic simply continued without stadholders for several decades.

> **stadholder** The executive officer in each of the United Provinces of the Netherlands, a position often held by the princes of Orange.

The political success of the Dutch rested on their phenomenal commercial prosperity. The moral and ethical bases of that commercial wealth were thrift, frugality, and religious toleration. Although there is scattered evidence of anti-Semitism, Jews enjoyed a level of acceptance and assimilation in Dutch business and general culture unique in early modern Europe. (See "Individuals in Society: Glückel of Hameln," at left.) In the Dutch Republic, toleration paid off: it attracted a great deal of foreign capital and investment.

The Dutch came to dominate the shipping business by putting profits from their original industry — herring fishing — into shipbuilding. They boasted the lowest shipping rates and largest merchant marine in Europe, allowing them to undersell foreign competitors (see Chapter 15). Trade and commerce brought the Dutch the highest standard of living in Europe, perhaps in the world. Salaries were high, and all classes of society ate well. A scholar has described the Netherlands as "an island of plenty in a sea of want." Consequently, the Netherlands experienced very few of the food riots that characterized the rest of Europe.[11]

Baroque Art and Music

What was the baroque style in art and music, and where was it popular?

Throughout European history, the cultural tastes of one age have often seemed unsatisfactory to the next. So it was with the baroque. The term *baroque* may have come from the Portuguese word for an "odd-shaped, imperfect pearl" and was commonly used by late-eighteenth-century art critics as an expression of scorn for what they considered an overblown, unbalanced style. Specialists now agree that the baroque style marked one of the high points in the history of Western culture.

Rome and the revitalized Catholic Church of the later sixteenth century played an important role in the early development of the baroque. The papacy and the Jesuits encouraged the growth of an intensely emotional, exuberant art. These patrons wanted artists to go beyond the Renaissance focus on pleasing a small, wealthy cultural elite. They wanted artists to appeal to the senses and thereby touch the souls and kindle the faith of ordinary churchgoers while proclaiming the power and confidence of the reformed Catholic Church. In addition to this underlying religious emotionalism, the baroque drew its sense of drama, motion, and ceaseless striving from the Catholic Reformation. The interior of the famous Jesuit Church of Jesus in Rome—the Gesù—combined all these characteristics in its lavish, wildly active decorations and frescoes.

Taking definite shape in Italy after 1600, the baroque style in the visual arts developed with exceptional vigor in Catholic countries—in Spain and Latin America, Austria, southern Germany, and Poland. Yet baroque art was more than just "Catholic art" in the

Rubens, *Garden of Love*, 1633–1634 This painting is an outstanding example of the lavishness and richness of baroque art. Born and raised in northern Europe, Peter Paul Rubens trained as a painter in Italy. Upon his return to the Spanish Netherlands, he became a renowned and amazingly prolific artist, patronized by rulers across Europe. Rubens was a devout Catholic, and his work conveys the emotional fervor of the Catholic Reformation. (Scala/Art Resource, NY)

seventeenth century and the first half of the eighteenth. True, neither Protestant England nor the Netherlands ever came fully under the spell of the baroque, but neither did Catholic France. And Protestants accounted for some of the finest examples of baroque style, especially in music. The baroque style spread partly because its tension and bombast spoke to an agitated age that was experiencing great violence and controversy in politics and religion.

In painting, the baroque reached maturity early with Peter Paul Rubens (1577–1640), the most outstanding and most representative of baroque painters. Studying in his native Flanders and in Italy, where he was influenced by masters of the High Renaissance such as Michelangelo, Rubens developed his own rich, sensuous, colorful style, which was characterized by animated figures, melodramatic contrasts, and monumental size. Rubens excelled in glorifying monarchs such as Queen Mother Marie de' Medici of France. He was also a devout Catholic; nearly half of his pictures treat Christian subjects. Yet one of Rubens's trademarks was fleshy, sensual nudes who populate his canvases as Roman goddesses, water nymphs, and remarkably voluptuous saints and angels.

In music, the baroque style reached its culmination almost a century later in the dynamic, soaring lines of the endlessly inventive Johann Sebastian Bach (1685–1750). Organist and choirmaster of several Lutheran churches across Germany, Bach was equally at home writing secular concertos and sublime religious cantatas. Bach's organ music combined the baroque spirit of invention, tension, and emotion in an unforgettable striving toward the infinite. Unlike Rubens, Bach was not fully appreciated in his lifetime, but since the early nineteenth century his reputation has grown steadily.

LOOKING BACK LOOKING AHEAD

THE SEVENTEENTH CENTURY represented a difficult passage between two centuries of dynamism and growth. On one side lay the sixteenth century of religious enthusiasm and strife, overseas expansion, rising population, and vigorous commerce. On the other side stretched the eighteenth-century era of renewed population growth, economic development, and cultural flourishing. The first half of the seventeenth century was marked by the spread of religious and dynastic warfare across Europe, resulting in the death and dislocation of many millions. This catastrophe was compounded by recurrent episodes of crop failure, famine, and epidemic disease, all of which contributed to a stagnant economy and population loss. In the middle decades of the seventeenth century, the very survival of the European monarchies established in the Renaissance appeared in doubt.

With the re-establishment of order in the second half of the century, maintaining political and social stability appeared of paramount importance to European rulers and elites. In western and eastern Europe, a host of monarchs proclaimed their God-given and "absolute" authority to rule in the name of peace, unity, and good order. Rulers' ability to impose such claims in reality depended a great deal on compromise with local elites, who acquiesced to state power in exchange for privileges and payoffs. In this way, absolutism and constitutionalism did not always differ as much as they claimed. Both systems relied on political compromises forged from decades of strife.

The eighteenth century was to see this status quo thrown into question by new Enlightenment aspirations for human society, which themselves derived from the inquisitive and self-confident spirit of the scientific revolution. By the end of the century, demands for real popular sovereignty challenged the very bases of political order so painfully achieved in the seventeenth century.

CHAPTER REVIEW

■ What were the common crises and achievements of seventeenth-century European states? (p. 480)

Most parts of Europe experienced the seventeenth century as a period of severe economic, social, and military crisis. Across the continent, rulers faced popular rebellions from their desperate subjects, who were pushed to the brink by poor harvests, high taxes, and decades of war. Many forces, including powerful noblemen, the church, and regional and local loyalties, constrained the state's authority. Despite these obstacles, most European states emerged from the seventeenth century with increased powers and more centralized control. Whether they ruled through monarchical fiat or parliamentary negotiation, European governments strengthened their bureaucracies, raised more taxes, and significantly expanded their armies.

■ What factors led to the rise of the French absolutist state under Louis XIV, and why did absolutist Spain experience decline in the same period? (p. 486)

Under Louis XIV France witnessed the high point of monarchical ambitions in western Europe. Louis used the doctrine of the divine right of kings to justify his hold on power. Under his rule, France developed a centralized bureaucracy, a professional army, and a state-directed economy, all of which he personally supervised. Despite his claims to absolute power, Louis XIV ruled by securing the collaboration of high nobles. In exchange for confirmation of their ancient privileges, the nobles were willing to cooperate with the expansion of state power. In Spain, where monarchs made similar claims to absolute power, the seventeenth century witnessed economic catastrophe and a decline in royal capacities. This decline was due to a fall in colonial trade revenue, massive state debt, and a decline in manufacturing and agricultural productivity.

■ How did the rulers of Austria and Prussia transform their nations into powerful absolutist monarchies? (p. 494)

Within a framework of resurgent serfdom and entrenched nobility, Austrian and Prussian monarchs fashioned strong absolutist states in the seventeenth and early eighteenth centuries. These monarchs won absolutist control over standing armies, taxation, and representative bodies, but left intact the underlying social and economic relationships between the nobles and their peasants. In exchange for entrenched privileges over their peasants, nobles thus cooperated with the growth of state power.

■ What were the distinctive features of Russian and Ottoman absolutism? (p. 497)

In Russia, Mongol conquest and rule set the stage for absolutism, and a harsh tsarist autocracy was firmly in place by the reign of Ivan the Terrible in the sixteenth century. Ivan's brutal rule brought all segments of Russian society into state service, sparking resentment and revolt. The reign of Ivan and his successors saw a great expansion of Russian territory, laying the foundations for a huge, multiethnic empire. More than a century later Peter the Great succeeded in modernizing Russia's traditional absolutism by reforming the army and the bureaucracy. Farther to the east, the Ottoman sultans developed a distinctive political and economic system in which all land theoretically belonged to the sultan, who was served by a slave corps of administrators and soldiers. The Ottoman Empire was relatively tolerant on religious matters and served as a haven for Jews and other marginalized religious groups.

■ How and why did the constitutional state triumph in the Dutch Republic and England? (p. 506)

Holland and England defied the general trend toward absolute monarchy. Violently resisting Stuart kings' claims to absolute power, England descended into civil war and finally emerged with a constitutional monarchy. After the Glorious Revolution in 1688, English power was divided between king and Parliament, with Parliament enjoying the greater share. The Bill of Rights established parliamentary control of the legal system and dictated that Parliament had to be called at least once every three years. By contrast, the Dutch rejected monarchical rule after winning independence from Spain. Instead, the United Provinces of the Netherlands adopted a decentralized republican system in which local affairs were run by provincial Estates and the national States General handled foreign affairs and war.

■ What was the baroque style in art and music, and where was it popular? (p. 514)

The baroque style, practiced by artists such as Rubens and Bach, was intensely emotional and exuberant. It was inspired by the religious enthusiasm of the late-sixteenth-century Catholic Reformation, but appeared in both religious and secular themes. The baroque style in art and music thrived during the seventeenth century and was most popular in Catholic countries—Spain and Latin America, Austria, southern Germany, and Poland—though it never gained popularity in Catholic France and was practiced by Protestant artists.

Suggested Reading

Benedict, Philip, and Myron P. Gutmann, eds. *Early Modern Europe: From Crisis to Stability*. 2005. A helpful introduction to the many facets of the seventeenth-century crisis.

Burke, Peter. *The Fabrication of Louis XIV*. 1992. Explains the use of architecture, art, medals, and other symbols to promote the king's image.

Clark, Christopher. *Iron Kingdom: The Rise and Downfall of Prussia, 1600–1947*. 2006. A fascinating long-term account tracing Prussia's emergence as an international power and the impact of Prussian history on later political developments in Germany.

Collins, James B. *The State in Early Modern France*. 1995. A detailed and well-argued survey of French administration from Louis XIII to Louis XVI.

Elliott, John H. *Imperial Spain, 1469–1716*, 2d ed. 2002. An authoritative account of Spain's rise to imperial greatness and its slow decline.

Gaunt, Peter, ed. *The English Civil War: The Essential Readings*. 2000. A collection showcasing leading historians' interpretations of the civil war.

Hagen, William W. *Ordinary Prussians: Brandenburg Junkers and Villagers, 1500–1840*. 2002. Provides a fascinating encounter with the people of a Prussian estate.

Hughes, Lindsey, ed. *Peter the Great and the West: New Perspectives*. 2001. Essays by leading scholars on the reign of Peter the Great and his opening of Russia to the West.

Ingrao, Charles W. *The Habsburg Monarchy, 1618–1815*. 2d ed. 2000. An excellent synthesis of the political and social development of the Habsburg empire in the early modern period.

Parker, Geoffrey. *The Thirty Years War*, 2d ed. 1997. The standard account of the Thirty Years' War.

Roman, Rolf, ed. *Baroque: Architecture, Sculpture, Painting*. 2007. A beautifully illustrated presentation of multiple facets of the baroque across Europe.

Schama, Simon. *The Embarrassment of Riches: An Interpretation of Dutch Culture in the Golden Age*. 1987. A lengthy but vivid and highly readable account of Dutch culture in the seventeenth century, including a chapter on the mania for speculation on the tulip market.

Notes

1. Quoted in Cecile Hugon, *Social France in the XVIIe Century* (London: McMilland, 1911), p. 189.
2. H. Kamen, "The Economic and Social Consequences of the Thirty Years' War," *Past and Present* 39 (April 1968): 44–61.
3. John A. Lynn, "Recalculating French Army Growth," in *The Military Revolution Debate: Readings on the Military Transformation of Early Modern Europe*, ed. Clifford J. Rogers (Boulder, Colo.: Westview Press, 1995), p. 125.
4. Quoted in John A. Lynn, *Giant of the Grand Siècle: The French Army, 1610–1715* (Cambridge, U.K.: Cambridge University Press, 1997), p. 74.
5. F. Arkwright, ed., *The Memoirs of the Duke de Saint-Simon*, vol. 5 (New York: Brentano's, n.d.), p. 276.
6. J. H. Elliott, *Imperial Spain, 1469–1716* (New York: Mentor Books, 1963), pp. 306–308.
7. H. Rosenberg, *Bureaucracy, Aristocracy, and Autocracy: The Prussian Experience, 1660–1815* (Boston: Beacon Press, 1966), p. 43.
8. Cited in Giles MacDonogh, *Frederick the Great: A Life in Deed and Letters* (New York: St. Martin's, 2001), p. 23.
9. Rosenberg, *Bureaucracy, Aristocracy, and Autocracy*, p. 40.
10. For a revisionist interpretation, see J. Wormald, "James VI and I: Two Kings or One?" *History* 62 (June 1983): 187–209.
11. S. Schama, *The Embarrassment of Riches: An Interpretation of Dutch Culture in the Golden Age* (New York: Alfred A. Knopf, 1987), pp. 165–170; quotation is on p. 167.

Key Terms

Peace of Westphalia (p. 483)
Fronde (p. 487)
mercantilism (p. 489)
Peace of Utrecht (p. 492)
Junkers (p. 495)
boyars (p. 498)
Cossacks (p. 498)
sultan (p. 504)
janissary corps (p. 504)
millet system (p. 505)
constitutionalism (p. 506)
republicanism (p. 506)
Puritans (p. 507)
Protectorate (p. 508)
Test Act (p. 510)
stadholder (p. 513)

For practice quizzes and other study tools, visit the Online Study Guide at **bedfordstmartins.com/mckaywest**.

For primary sources from this period, see **Sources of Western Society, Second Edition**.

For Web sites, images, and documents related to topics in this chapter, visit Make History at **bedfordstmartins.com/mckaywest**.

17
Toward a New Worldview

1540–1789

The intellectual developments of the seventeenth and eighteenth centuries created the modern worldview that the West continues to hold — and debate — to this day. In the seventeenth century fundamentally new ways of understanding the natural world emerged. Those leading the changes saw themselves as philosophers and referred to their field of study as "natural philosophy." In the nineteenth century scholars hailed these achievements as a "scientific revolution" that produced modern science as we know it. The new science created in the seventeenth century entailed the search for precise knowledge of the physical world based on the union of experimental observations with sophisticated mathematics. Whereas medieval scholars looked to authoritative texts like the Bible or the classics, seventeenth-century natural philosophers performed experiments and relied on increasingly complex mathematical calculations. The resulting conception of the universe and its laws remained in force until Einstein's discoveries in the first half of the twentieth century.

In the eighteenth century philosophers extended the use of reason from the study of nature to the study of human society. They sought to bring the light of reason to bear on the darkness of prejudice, outmoded traditions, and ignorance. Self-proclaimed members of an "Enlightenment" movement, they wished to bring the same progress to human affairs as their predecessors had brought to the understanding of the natural world. While the scientific revolution ushered in modern science, the Enlightenment created concepts of human rights, equality, progress, universalism, and tolerance that still guide Western societies today. At the same time, some people used their new understanding of reason to explain their own superiority, thus rationalizing such attitudes as racism and male chauvinism. ■

Life During the Scientific Revolution. This 1768 painting by Joseph Wright captures the popularization of science and experimentation during the Enlightenment. Here, a scientist demonstrates the creation of a vacuum by withdrawing air from a flask, with the suffocating cockatoo serving as shocking proof of the experiment.

CHAPTER PREVIEW

The Scientific Revolution
■ What was revolutionary in the new attitudes toward the natural world?

The Enlightenment
■ How did the new worldview affect the way people thought about society and human relations?

Enlightened Absolutism
■ What impact did new ways of thinking have on political developments and monarchical absolutism?

The Scientific Revolution

What was revolutionary in the new attitudes toward the natural world?

The emergence of modern science was a development of tremendous long-term significance. A noted historian has said that the scientific revolution was "the real origin both of the modern world and the modern mentality."[1] With the scientific revolution, which lasted roughly from 1540 to 1690, Western society began to acquire its most distinctive traits.

Scientific Thought in 1500

The term "science" as we use it today only came into use in the nineteenth century. Prior to the scientific revolution, many different scholars and practitioners were involved in aspects of what came together to form science. One of the most important disciplines was **natural philosophy**, which focused on fundamental questions about the nature of the universe, its purpose, and how it functioned. In the early 1500s natural philosophy was still based primarily on the ideas of Aristotle, the great Greek philosopher of the fourth century B.C.E. Medieval theologians such as Thomas Aquinas brought Aristotelian philosophy into harmony with Christian doctrines. According to the revised Aristotelian view, a motionless earth was fixed at the center of the universe and was encompassed by ten separate concentric crystal spheres that revolved around it. In the first eight spheres were embedded, in turn, the moon, the sun, the five known planets, and the fixed stars. Then followed two spheres added during the Middle Ages to account for slight changes in the positions of the stars over the centuries. Beyond the tenth sphere was Heaven, with the throne of God and the souls of the saved. Angels kept the spheres moving in perfect circles.

Aristotle's cosmology made intellectual sense, but it could not account for the observed motions of the stars and planets and, in particular, provided no explanation for the apparent backward motion of the planets (which we now know occurs as planets closer to the sun periodically overtake the earth on their faster orbits). The great second-century Greek scholar Ptolemy (see Chapter 15) offered a cunning solution to this dilemma. According to Ptolemy, the planets moved in small circles,

natural philosophy An early modern term for the study of the nature of the universe, its purpose, and how it functioned; it encompassed what we would call "science" today.

The Aristotelian Universe as Imagined in the Sixteenth Century A round earth is at the center, surrounded by spheres of water, air, and fire. Beyond this small nucleus, the moon, the sun, and the five planets were embedded in their own rotating crystal spheres, with the stars sharing the surface of one enormous sphere. Beyond, the heavens were composed of unchanging ether. (Image Select/Art Resource, NY)

called epicycles, each of which moved in turn along a larger circle or deferent. Ptolemaic astronomy was less elegant than Aristotle's neat nested circles and required complex calculations, but it provided a surprisingly accurate model for predicting planetary motion.

Aristotle's views, revised by medieval philosophers, also dominated thinking about physics and motion on earth. Aristotle had distinguished sharply between the world of the celestial spheres and that of the earth—the sublunar world. The spheres consisted of a perfect, incorruptible "quintessence," or fifth essence. The sublunar world, however, was made up of four imperfect, changeable elements. The "light" elements (air and fire) naturally moved upward, while the "heavy" elements (water and earth) naturally moved downward. These natural directions of motion did not always prevail, however, for elements were often mixed together and could be affected by an outside force such as a human being. Aristotle and his followers also believed that a uniform force moved an object at a constant speed and that the object would stop as soon as that force was removed.

Aristotle's ideas about astronomy and physics were accepted, with revisions, for two thousand years, and with good reason. First, they offered an understandable, commonsense explanation for what the eye actually saw. Second, Aristotle's science as interpreted by Christian theologians fit neatly with Christian doctrines. It established a home for God and a place for Christian souls. It put human beings at the center of the universe and made them the critical link in a "great chain of being" that stretched from the throne of God to the lowliest insect on earth. This approach to the natural world was thus a branch of theology, and it reinforced religious thought.

Origins of the Scientific Revolution

Why did Aristotelian teachings give way to new views about the universe? The scientific revolution drew on long-term developments in European culture, as well as borrowings from Arabic scholars. The first important development was the medieval university. By the thirteenth century permanent universities with professors and large student bodies had been established in western Europe to train the lawyers, doctors, and church leaders society required. By 1300 philosophy had taken its place alongside law, medicine, and theology. Medieval philosophers developed a limited but real independence from theologians and a sense of free inquiry. They nobly pursued a body of knowledge and tried to arrange it meaningfully with abstract theories.

Chronology

ca. 1540–1690	Scientific revolution
ca. 1690–1789	Enlightenment
ca. 1700–1789	Growth of book publishing
1720–1780	Rococo style in art and decoration
1740–1748	War of Austrian Succession
1740–1780	Reign of the empress Maria Theresa
1740–1786	Reign of Frederick the Great of Prussia
ca. 1740–1789	French salons led by elite women
1756–1763	Seven Years' War
1762–1796	Reign of Catherine the Great of Russia
1765	Philosophes publish *Encyclopedia: The Rational Dictionary of the Sciences, the Arts, and the Crafts*
1780–1790	Reign of Joseph II of Austria
1791	Establishment of the Pale of Settlement

In the fourteenth and fifteenth centuries leading universities established new professorships of mathematics, astronomy, and physics (natural philosophy) within their faculties of philosophy. Although the prestige of the new fields was low, critical thinking was now applied to scientific problems by a permanent community of scholars.

The Renaissance also stimulated scientific progress. Many ancient works were recovered, often through Arabic translations of the original Greek and Latin that were then translated into European vernacular languages. In fields such as mathematics, the translations were accompanied by learned Arabic commentaries that went beyond ancient learning. Renaissance patrons played a role in funding scientific investigations, as they did for art and literature. In addition, Renaissance artists' turn toward realism and their use of geometry to convey three-dimensional perspective encouraged scholars to practice close observation and to use mathematics to describe the natural world. The rise of printing provided a faster and less expensive way to circulate knowledge across Europe.

The navigational problems of long sea voyages in the age of overseas expansion were another factor in the scientific revolution. As early as 1484 the king of Portugal appointed a commission of mathematicians to perfect tables to help seamen find their latitude. Navigational problems were also critical in the development of many new scientific instruments, such as the telescope, barometer, thermometer, pendulum clock, microscope, and air pump. Better instruments, which permitted more accurate observations, often led to important new knowledge.

Recent historical research has also focused on the contribution to the scientific revolution of practices now relegated far beyond the realm of science. For most of human history, interest in astronomy was inspired by belief that the changing relationships between planets and stars influenced events on earth. This was true in Europe up to and during the scientific revolution (and continues today). Many of the most celebrated astronomers were also astrologers and spent much time devising horoscopes for their patrons. Used as a diagnostic tool in medicine, astrology formed a regular part of the curriculum of medical schools.

Copernican hypothesis
The idea that the sun, not the earth, was the center of the universe.

Centuries-old practices of magic and alchemy also remained important traditions for participants in the scientific revolution. For many observers there was little to distinguish the conjuring tricks of magicians from the experiments and instruments of the emerging scientists, and, in fact, there was a great deal of crossover between the two. The idea that objects possessed hidden or "occult" qualities that allowed them to affect other objects was a particularly important legacy of the magical tradition. Belief in occult qualities—or numerology or cosmic harmony—was not antithetical to belief in God. On the contrary, adherents believed that only a divine creator could infuse the universe with such meaningful mystery.

The Copernican Hypothesis

The desire to explain and thereby glorify God's handiwork led to the first great departure from the medieval system. This departure was the work of the Polish cleric Nicolaus Copernicus (1473–1543). As a young man Copernicus was drawn to the intellectual and cultural vitality of the Italian Renaissance. After studies at the university of Kraków, he departed for Italy, where he studied astronomy, medicine, and church law at the famed universities of Bologna, Padua, and Ferrara. Copernicus noted how professional astronomers still depended for their most accurate calculations on the work of Ptolemy. Copernicus felt that Ptolemy's cumbersome and occasionally inaccurate rules detracted from the majesty of a perfect creator. He preferred an ancient Greek idea: that the sun, rather than the earth, was at the center of the universe.

Finishing his university studies and returning to a church position in East Prussia, Copernicus worked on his hypothesis from 1506 to 1530. Unlike other leaders of the scientific revolution, Copernicus was not a professional astronomer or a university professor and had limited instruments and free time for research. Without questioning the Aristotelian belief in crystal spheres or the idea that circular motion was divine, Copernicus theorized that the stars and planets, including the earth, revolved around a fixed sun. Fearing the ridicule of other astronomers, Copernicus did not publish his *On the Revolutions of the Heavenly Spheres* until 1543, the year of his death.

The **Copernican hypothesis** had enormous scientific and religious implications, many of which the conservative Copernicus did not anticipate. First, it put the stars at rest, their apparent nightly movement simply a result of the earth's rotation. Thus it destroyed the main reason for believing in crystal spheres capable of moving the stars around the earth. Second, Copernicus's theory suggested a universe of staggering size. If in the course of a year the earth moved around the sun and yet the stars appeared to remain in the same place, then the universe was unthinkably large. Finally, by characterizing the earth as just another planet, Copernicus destroyed the basic idea of Aristotelian physics—that the earthly world was quite different from the heavenly one. Where then were Heaven and the throne of God?

The Copernican hypothesis brought sharp attacks from religious leaders, especially Protestants, who objected to the idea that the earth moved but the sun did not. Protestant leaders John Calvin and Martin Luther condemned Copernicus. Luther noted that the theory was counter to the Bible: "as the Holy Scripture tells us, so did Joshua bid the sun stand still and not the earth."[2] Catholic reaction was milder at first. The Catholic Church had never held to literal interpretations of the Bible, and not until 1616 did it officially declare the Copernican hypothesis false.

Other events were almost as influential in creating doubts about traditional astronomical ideas. In 1572 a new star appeared and shone very brightly for almost two years. The new star, which was actually a distant exploding star, made an enormous impression on people. It seemed to contradict the idea that the heavenly spheres were unchanging and therefore perfect. In 1577 a new comet suddenly moved through the sky, cutting a straight path across the supposedly impenetrable crystal spheres. It was time, as a sixteenth-century scientific writer put it, for "the radical renovation of astronomy."[3]

Brahe, Kepler, and Galileo: Proving Copernicus Right

One astronomer who agreed with Copernicus was Tycho Brahe (TEE-koh BRAH-hee) (1546–1601). Born into a prominent Danish noble family, Brahe became passionately interested in astronomy as a young boy and spent many nights gazing at the skies. Completing his studies abroad and returning to Denmark, he established himself as Europe's leading astronomer with his de-

Hevelius and His Wife Portable sextants were used to chart a ship's position at sea by measuring the altitude of celestial bodies above the horizon. Astronomers used much larger sextants to measure the angular distances between two bodies. Here, Johannes Hevelius makes use of the great brass sextant at the Danzig observatory, with the help of his wife, Elisabetha. Six feet in radius, this instrument was closely modeled on the one used by Tycho Brahe. (Houghton Library, Harvard College Library)

tailed observations of the new star of 1572. Aided by generous grants from the king of Denmark, Brahe built the most sophisticated observatory of his day.

Upon the king's death, Brahe acquired a new patron in the Holy Roman emperor Rudolph II and built a new observatory in Prague. In return for the emperor's support, he pledged to create new and improved tables of planetary motions, dubbed the *Rudolfine Tables*. For twenty years Brahe meticulously observed the stars and planets with the naked eye, compiling much more complete and accurate data than ever before. His limited understanding of mathematics and his sudden death in 1601, however, prevented him from making much sense out of his mass of data. Part Ptolemaic, part Copernican, he believed that all the planets except the earth revolved around the sun and that the entire group of sun and planets revolved in turn around the earth-moon system.

It was left to Brahe's young assistant, Johannes Kepler (1571–1630), to rework Brahe's mountain of observations. From a minor German noble family, Kepler suffered a bout of smallpox as a small child, leaving him with permanently damaged hands and eyesight. A brilliant mathematician, Kepler was inspired by belief that the universe was built on mystical mathematical relationships and a musical harmony of the heavenly bodies.

Kepler's examination of his predecessor's meticulously recorded findings convinced him that they could not be explained by Ptolemy's astronomy. Abandoning the notion of epicycles and deferents—which even Copernicus had retained in part—Kepler developed three new and revolutionary laws of planetary motion. First, largely through observations of the planet Mars, he demonstrated that the orbits of the planets around the sun are elliptical rather than circular. Second, he demonstrated that the planets do not move at a uniform speed in their orbits. When a planet is close to the sun it moves more rapidly, and it slows as it moves farther away from the sun. Kepler published the first two laws in his 1609 book, *The New Astronomy*, which heralded the arrival of an entirely new theory of the cosmos. In 1619 Kepler put forth his third law: the time a planet takes to make its complete orbit is precisely related to its distance from the sun.

Kepler's contribution was monumental. Whereas Copernicus had speculated, Kepler proved mathematically the precise relations of a sun-centered (solar) system. He thus united for the first time the theoretical cosmology of natural philosophy with mathematics. His work demolished the old system of Aristotle and Ptolemy, and in his third law he came close to formulating the idea of universal gravitation (see page 526). In 1627 he also fulfilled Brahe's pledge by completing the Rudolfine Tables begun so many years earlier. These tables were used by astronomers for many years.

Kepler was a genius with many talents. Beyond his great contribution to astronomy, he pioneered the field of optics. He was the first to explain the role of refraction within the eye in creating vision, and he invented an improved telescope. He was also a great mathematician whose work furnished the basis for integral calculus and advances in geometry.

Kepler was not, however, the consummate modern scientist that these achievements suggest. His duties as court mathematician included casting horoscopes, and his own diary was based on astrological principles. He also wrote at length on cosmic harmonies and explained, for example, elliptical motion through ideas about the beautiful music created by the combined motion of the planets. Kepler's fictional account of travel to the moon, written partly to illustrate the idea of a non-earth-centered universe, caused controversy and may have contributed to the arrest and trial of his mother as a witch in 1620. Kepler also suffered deeply as a result of his unorthodox brand of Lutheranism, which led to his rejection by both Lutherans and Catholics. His career exemplifies the complex interweaving of ideas and beliefs in the emerging science of his day.

While Kepler was unraveling planetary motion, a young Florentine named Galileo Galilei (ga-luh-LEE-oh ga-luh-LAY) (1564–1642) was challenging all the old ideas about motion. Like Kepler and so many early scientists, Galileo was a poor nobleman first marked for a religious career. Instead, his fascination with mathematics led to a professorship in which he examined motion and mechanics in a new way. His great achievement was the elaboration and consolidation of the **experimental method**. That is, rather than speculate about what might or should happen, Galileo conducted controlled experiments to find out what actually did happen.

In some of his experiments Galileo measured the movement of a rolling ball across a surface that he constructed, repeating the action again and again to verify his results. In his famous acceleration experiment, he showed that a uniform force—in this case, gravity—produced a uniform acceleration. Through another experiment, he formulated the **law of inertia**. He found

experimental method
The approach, pioneered by Galileo, that the proper way to explore the workings of the universe was through repeatable experiments rather than speculation.

law of inertia A law formulated by Galileo that states that motion, not rest, is the natural state of an object, that an object continues in motion forever unless stopped by some external force.

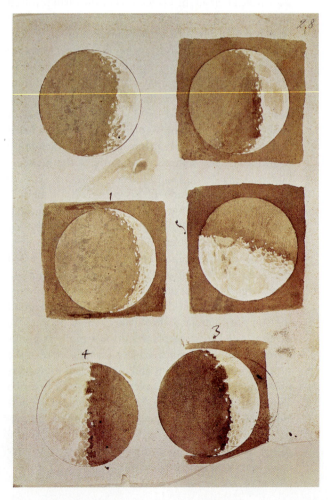

Galileo's Telescopic Observations of the Moon Among the many mechanical devices Galileo invented was a telescope that could magnify objects twenty times (other contemporary telescopes could magnify objects only three times). Using this telescope, he obtained the empirical evidence that proved the Copernican system. He sketched many illustrations of his observations, including the six phases of the moon shown here. (moons: Scala/Art Resource, NY; telescope: Museum of Science, Florence/Art Resource, NY)

that rest was not the natural state of objects. Rather, an object continues in motion forever unless stopped by some external force. His discoveries proved Aristotelian physics wrong.

Galileo also applied the experimental method to astronomy. On hearing details about the invention of the telescope in Holland, Galileo made one for himself and trained it on the heavens. He quickly discovered the first four moons of Jupiter, which clearly suggested that Jupiter could not possibly be embedded in any impenetrable crystal sphere as Aristotle and Ptolemy maintained. This discovery provided new evidence for the Copernican theory, in which Galileo already believed. Galileo then pointed his telescope at the moon. He wrote in 1610 in *Siderus Nuncius:*

> By the aid of a telescope anyone may behold [the Milky Way] in a manner which so distinctly appeals to the senses that all the disputes which have tormented philosophers through so many ages are exploded by the irrefutable evidence of our eyes, and we are freed from wordy disputes upon the subject. For the galaxy is nothing else but a mass of innumerable stars planted together in clusters.[4]

Reading these famous lines, one feels a crucial corner in Western civilization being turned. No longer should one rely on established authority. A new method of learning and investigating was being developed, one that proved useful in any field of inquiry. A historian investigating documents of the past, for example, is not so different from a Galileo studying stars and rolling balls.

As early as 1597, when Johannes Kepler sent Galileo an early publication defending Copernicus, Galileo wrote back agreeing with his position and confessing he lacked the courage to follow Kepler's example. Within the Catholic world, expressing public support for Copernicus was increasingly dangerous. In 1616 the Holy Office placed the works of Copernicus and his supporters, including Kepler, on a list of books Catholics were forbidden to read. The accompanying decree declared that belief in a heliocentric world was "foolish and absurd, philosophically false and formally heretical."[5]

Galileo was a devout Catholic who sincerely believed that his theories did not detract from the perfection of God. Out of caution he silenced his beliefs for several years, until in 1623 he saw new hope with the ascension of Pope Urban VIII, a man sympathetic to developments in the new science. However, Galileo's 1632 *Dialogue on the Two Chief Systems of the World* went too far. Published in Italian and widely read, this work openly lampooned the traditional views of Aristotle and Ptolemy and defended those of Copernicus. Galileo was tried for heresy by the papal Inquisition. Imprisoned and threatened with torture, the aging Galileo recanted, "renouncing and cursing" his Copernican errors. Like Kepler, his correspondent and fellow pioneer, Galileo suffered personal hardship through religious persecution.

Newton's Synthesis

Despite the efforts of the church, by about 1640 the work of Brahe, Kepler, and Galileo had been largely accepted by the scientific community. The old Aristotelian astronomy and physics were in ruins, and several fundamental breakthroughs had been made. But the new findings failed to explain what forces controlled the movement of the planets and objects on earth. That challenge was taken up by English scientist Isaac Newton (1642–1727).

Newton was born into the lower English gentry in 1642, the year of Galileo's death, and he enrolled at Cambridge University in 1661. A genius who spectacularly united the experimental and theoretical-mathematical sides of modern science, Newton was also fascinated by alchemy. He left behind thirty years' worth of encoded journals recording experiments to discover the elixir of life and a way to change base metals into gold and silver. Newton was also intensely religious. Like Kepler and other practitioners of the scientific revolution, he was far from being the perfect rationalist so glorified by writers in the eighteenth and nineteenth centuries.

Isaac Newton This portrait suggests the depth and complexity of Isaac Newton. Is the powerful mind behind those piercing eyes thinking of science or of religion, or perhaps of both? (Scala/Art Resource, NY)

> **I seem to have been only like a boy, playing on the seashore, and diverting myself, in now and then finding a smoother pebble or a prettier shell than ordinary, whilst the great ocean of truth lay all undiscovered before me.**
>
> —Isaac Newton

Newton arrived at some of his most basic ideas about physics between 1664 and 1666, during a break from studies at Cambridge caused by an outbreak of plague. During this period, he later claimed to have discovered his law of universal gravitation as well as the concepts of centripetal force and acceleration. Not realizing the significance of his findings, the young Newton did not publish them, and upon his return to Cambridge he took up the study of optics. It was in reference to his experiments in optics that Newton outlined his method of scientific inquiry most clearly, explaining the need for scientists "first to enquire diligently into the properties of things, and to establish these properties by experiment, and then to proceed more slowly to hypotheses for the explanation of them."[6]

In 1684 Newton returned to physics and the preparation of his ideas for publication. The result appeared three years later in *Philosophicae Naturalis Principia Mathematica* (Mathematical Principles of Natural Philosophy). Newton's towering accomplishment was a single explanatory system that could integrate the astronomy of Copernicus, as corrected by Kepler's laws, with the physics of Galileo and his predecessors. *Principia Mathematica* laid down Newton's three laws of motion, using a set of mathematical laws that explain motion and mechanics. These laws of dynamics are complex, and it took scientists and engineers two hundred years to work out all their implications.

The key feature of the Newtonian synthesis was the **law of universal gravitation**. According to this law, every body in the universe attracts every other body in the universe in a precise mathematical relationship, whereby the force of attraction is proportional to the quantity of matter of the objects and inversely proportional to the square of the distance between them. The whole universe—from Kepler's elliptical orbits to Galileo's rolling balls—was unified in one coherent system. The German mathematician Gottfried von Leibniz, with whom Newton contested the invention of calculus, was outraged by Newton's claim that the "occult" force of gravity could allow bodies to affect one another at great distances. Newton's religious faith, as well as his alchemical belief in the innate powers of certain objects, allowed him to dismiss such criticism.

Newton's synthesis of mathematics with physics and astronomy prevailed until the twentieth century and established him as one of the most important figures in the history of science. Yet, near the end of his life, this acclaimed figure declared: "I do not know what I may appear to the world; but to myself I seem to have been only like a boy, playing on the seashore, and diverting myself, in now and then finding a smoother pebble or a prettier shell than ordinary, whilst the great ocean of truth lay all undiscovered before me."[7]

Bacon, Descartes, and the Scientific Method

The creation of a new science was not accomplished by a handful of brilliant astronomers working alone. Scholars in many fields sought answers to long-standing problems, sharing their results in a community that spanned Europe. One of the keys to the achievement of a new worldview in the seventeenth century was the development of better ways of obtaining knowledge about the world. Two important thinkers, Francis Bacon (1561–1626) and René Descartes (day-KAHRT) (1596–1650), were influential in describing and advocating for improved scientific methods based, respectively, on experimentation and mathematical reasoning.

The English politician and writer Francis Bacon was the greatest early propagandist for the new experimental method. Rejecting the Aristotelian and medieval method of using speculative reasoning to build general theories, Bacon argued that new knowledge had to be pursued through empirical research. The researcher who wants to learn more about leaves or rocks, for example, should not speculate about the subject but should rather collect a multitude of specimens and then compare and analyze them to derive general principles. Bacon's contribution was to formalize the empirical method, which had already been used by Brahe and Galileo, into the general theory of inductive reasoning known as **empiricism**. Bacon's work, and his prestige as lord chancellor under James I, led to the widespread adoption of what was called the "experimental philosophy" in England after his death.

On the continent, more speculative methods retained support. The French philosopher René Descartes was a multitalented genius who made his first great discovery in mathematics. As a twenty-three-year-old

---

law of universal gravitation Newton's law that all objects are attracted to one another and that the force of attraction is proportional to the object's quantity of matter and inversely proportional to the square of the distance between them.

empiricism A theory of inductive reasoning that calls for acquiring evidence through observation and experimentation rather than reason and speculation.

soldier serving in the Thirty Years' War, he experienced a life-changing intellectual vision one night in 1619. Descartes saw that there was a perfect correspondence between geometry and algebra and that geometrical spatial figures could be expressed as algebraic equations and vice versa. A major step forward in the history of mathematics, Descartes's discovery of analytic geometry provided scientists with an important new tool.

Descartes used mathematics to elaborate a highly influential vision of the workings of the cosmos. Accepting Galileo's claim that all elements of the universe are composed of the same matter, Descartes began to investigate the basic nature of matter. Drawing on ancient Greek atomist philosophies, Descartes developed the idea that matter was made up of identical "corpuscles" that collided together in an endless series of motions. All occurrences in nature could be analyzed as matter in motion and, according to Descartes, the total "quantity of motion" in the universe was constant. Descartes's mechanistic view of the universe depended on the idea that a vacuum was impossible, so that every action had an equal reaction, continuing in an eternal chain reaction.

Although Descartes's hypothesis about the vacuum was proved wrong, his notion of a mechanistic universe intelligible through the physics of motion proved highly influential. Decades later, Newton rejected Descartes's idea of a full universe and several of his other ideas, but retained the notion of a mechanistic universe as a key element of his own system.

Descartes's greatest achievement was to develop his initial vision into a whole philosophy of knowledge and science. The Aristotelian cosmos was appealing in part because it corresponded with the evidence of the human senses. When the senses were proven to be wrong, Descartes decided it was necessary to doubt them and everything that could reasonably be doubted, and then, as in geometry, to use deductive reasoning from self-evident principles to ascertain scientific laws. Descartes's reasoning ultimately reduced all substances to "matter" and "mind" — that is, to the physical and the spiritual. The devout Descartes believed that God had endowed man with reason for a purpose and that rational speculation could provide a path to the truths of creation. His view of the world as consisting of two fundamental entities is known as **Cartesian dualism**. Descartes's thought was highly influential in France and the Netherlands, but less so in England, where experimental philosophy won the day.

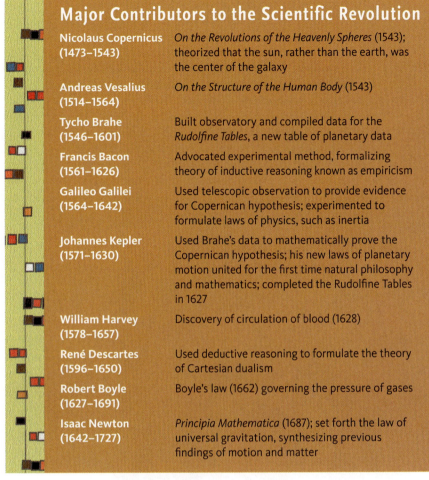

Major Contributors to the Scientific Revolution

Nicolaus Copernicus (1473–1543)	*On the Revolutions of the Heavenly Spheres* (1543); theorized that the sun, rather than the earth, was the center of the galaxy
Andreas Vesalius (1514–1564)	*On the Structure of the Human Body* (1543)
Tycho Brahe (1546–1601)	Built observatory and compiled data for the *Rudolfine Tables*, a new table of planetary data
Francis Bacon (1561–1626)	Advocated experimental method, formalizing theory of inductive reasoning known as empiricism
Galileo Galilei (1564–1642)	Used telescopic observation to provide evidence for Copernican hypothesis; experimented to formulate laws of physics, such as inertia
Johannes Kepler (1571–1630)	Used Brahe's data to mathematically prove the Copernican hypothesis; his new laws of planetary motion united for the first time natural philosophy and mathematics; completed the Rudolfine Tables in 1627
William Harvey (1578–1657)	Discovery of circulation of blood (1628)
René Descartes (1596–1650)	Used deductive reasoning to formulate the theory of Cartesian dualism
Robert Boyle (1627–1691)	Boyle's law (1662) governing the pressure of gases
Isaac Newton (1642–1727)	*Principia Mathematica* (1687); set forth the law of universal gravitation, synthesizing previous findings of motion and matter

Both Bacon's inductive experimentalism and Descartes's deductive mathematical reasoning had their faults. Bacon's inability to appreciate the importance of mathematics and his obsession with practical results clearly showed the limitations of antitheoretical empiricism. Likewise, some of Descartes's positions — he believed, for example, that it was possible to deduce the whole science of medicine from first principles — demonstrated the inadequacy of rigid, dogmatic rationalism. Although insufficient on their own, Bacon's and Descartes's extreme approaches are combined in the modern scientific method, which began to crystallize in the late seventeenth century.

Cartesian dualism Descartes's view that all of reality could ultimately be reduced to mind and matter.

Science and Society

The rise of modern science had many consequences, some of which are still unfolding. First, it went hand in hand with the rise of a new and expanding social group — the international scientific community. Members of this community were linked together by common interests and shared values as well as by journals and the learned scientific societies founded in many countries in the later seventeenth and the eighteenth centuries. The personal success of scientists and scholars depended on making new discoveries, and science became competitive. Second, as governments intervened to support and sometimes direct research, the new scientific community became closely tied to the state and its agendas. National academies of science were created under state sponsorship in London in 1662, Paris in 1666, Berlin in 1700, and later across Europe. At the same time, scientists developed a critical attitude toward established authority that would inspire thinkers to question traditions in other domains as well.

Metamorphoses of the Caterpillar and Moth Maria Sibylla Merian (1647–1717), the stepdaughter of a Dutch painter, became a celebrated scientific illustrator in her own right. Her finely observed pictures of insects in the South American colony of Surinam introduced many new species. For Merian, science was intimately tied with art: she not only painted but also bred caterpillars and performed experiments on them. Her two-year stay in Surinam, accompanied by a teenage daughter, was a daring feat for a seventeenth-century woman. (Bildarchiv Preussischer Kulturbesitz/Art Resource, NY)

Some things did not change in the scientific revolution. Scholars have recently analyzed representations of femininity and masculinity in the scientific revolution and have noted that nature was often depicted as a female, whose veil of secrecy needed to be stripped away and penetrated by male experts. New "rational" methods for approaching nature did not question traditional inequalities between the sexes—and may have worsened them in some ways. When Renaissance courts served as centers of learning, talented noblewomen could find niches in study and research. The rise of a professional scientific community raised barriers for women because the new academies that furnished professional credentials did not accept female members. (This continued for a long time. Marie Curie, the first person to win two Nobel prizes, was rejected by the French Academy of Science in 1911 because she was a woman.[8])

There were, however, a number of noteworthy exceptions. In Italy, universities and academies did offer posts to women, attracting some foreigners spurned by their own countries. Women across Europe were allowed to work as makers of wax anatomical models and as botanical and zoological illustrators. Women were also very much involved in informal scientific communities, attending salons, participating in scientific experiments, and writing learned treatises. Some female intellectuals were recognized as full-fledged members of the philosophical dialogue. In England, Margaret Cavendish, Anne Conway, and Mary Astell all contributed to debates about Descartes's mind-body dualism, among other issues. Descartes himself conducted an intellectual correspondence with the princess Elizabeth of Bohemia, of whom he stated: "I attach more weight to her judgment than to those messieurs the Doctors, who take for a rule of truth the opinions of Aristotle rather than the evidence of reason."[9]

The scientific revolution had few consequences for economic life and the living standards of the masses until the late eighteenth century. True, improvements in the techniques of navigation facilitated overseas trade and helped enrich states and merchant companies. But science had relatively few practical economic applications. Thus the scientific revolution of the seventeenth century was first and foremost an intellectual revolution. For more than a hundred years its greatest impact was on how people thought and believed.

Finally, there is the question of the role of religion in the development of science. Just as some historians have argued that Protestantism led to the rise of capitalism, others have concluded that Protestantism was a fundamental factor in the rise of modern science. According to this view, Protestantism, particularly in its Calvinist varieties, made scientific inquiry a question of individual conscience, not of religious doctrine. The Catholic Church, in contrast, supposedly suppressed scientific theories that conflicted with its teachings and thus discouraged scientific progress. The truth is more complicated. All Western religious authorities—Catholic, Protestant, and Jewish—opposed the Copernican system to a greater or lesser extent until about 1630, by which time the scientific revolution was definitely in progress. The Catholic Church was initially less hostile than Protestant and Jewish religious leaders, and Italian scientists played a crucial role in scientific progress right up to the trial of Galileo in 1633. Thereafter, the Counter-Reformation church became more hostile to science, a change that helped account for the decline of science in Italy (but not in Catholic France) after 1640. At the same time, Protestant countries such as the Netherlands and Denmark became quite "pro-science," especially countries that lacked a strong religious authority capable of imposing religious orthodoxy on scientific questions.

This was certainly the case with Protestant England after 1630. English religious conflicts became so intense that the authorities could not impose religious unity on anything, including science. The work of Bacon's many followers during Oliver Cromwell's commonwealth (see Chapter 16) helped solidify the independence of science. Bacon advocated the experimental approach precisely because it was open-minded and independent of preconceived religious and philosophical ideas. Neutral and useful, science became an accepted part of life and developed rapidly in England after about 1640.

Medicine, the Body, and Chemistry

The scientific revolution, which began with the study of the cosmos, soon inspired renewed study of the microcosm of the human body. For many centuries the ancient Greek physician Galen's explanation of the body carried the same authority as Aristotle's account of the universe. According to Galen, the body contained four humors: blood, phlegm, black bile, and yellow bile. Illness was believed to result from an imbalance of humors, which is why doctors frequently prescribed bloodletting to expell excess blood.

Swiss physician and alchemist Paracelsus (1493–1541) was an early proponent of the experimental method in medicine and pioneered the use of chemicals and drugs to address what he saw as chemical, rather than humoral, imbalances. Another experimentalist, Flemish physician Andreas Vesalius (1516–1564) studied anatomy by dissecting human bodies, often those of executed criminals. In 1543, the same year Copernicus published *On the Revolutions*, Vesalius issued his masterpiece, *On the Structure of the Human Body*. Its two hundred precise drawings revolutionized the understanding of human anatomy. The experimental approach also led English royal physician William Harvey (1578–1657) to discover the circulation of blood through the veins and arteries in 1628. Harvey was the first to explain that the heart worked like a pump and to explain the function of its muscles and valves.

Irishman Robert Boyle (1627–1691) founded the modern science of chemistry. Following Paracelsus's lead, he undertook experiments to discover the basic

Frontispiece to *De Humani Corporis Fabrica* (On the Structure of the Human Body) The frontispiece to Vesalius's pioneering work, published in 1543, shows him dissecting a corpse before a crowd of students. This was a revolutionary new hands-on approach for physicians, who usually worked from a theoretical, rather than a practical, understanding of the body. Based on direct observation, Vesalius replaced ancient ideas drawn from Greek philosophy with a much more accurate account of the structure and function of the body. (© SSPL/Science Museum/The Image Works)

elements of nature, which he believed was composed of infinitely small atoms. Boyle was the first to create a vacuum, thus disproving Descartes's belief that a vacuum could not exist in nature, and he discovered Boyle's law (1662), which states that the pressure of a gas varies inversely with volume.

The Enlightenment

How did the new worldview affect the way people thought about society and human relations?

The scientific revolution was the single most important factor in the creation of the new worldview of the eighteenth-century **Enlightenment**. This worldview, which has played a large role in shaping the modern mind, grew out of a rich mix of diverse and often conflicting ideas. For the writers who espoused them, these ideas competed vigorously for the attention of a growing public of well-educated but fickle readers, who remained a minority of the population.

Despite the diversity, three central concepts stand at the core of Enlightenment thinking. The most important and original idea was that the methods of natural science could and should be used to examine and understand all aspects of life. This was what intellectuals meant by *reason*, a favorite word of Enlightenment thinkers. Nothing was to be accepted on faith; everything was to be submitted to **rationalism**, a secular, critical way of thinking. A second important Enlightenment concept was that the scientific method was capable of discovering the laws of human society as well as those of nature. Thus was social science born. Its birth led to the third key idea, that of progress. Armed with the proper method of discovering the laws of human existence, Enlightenment thinkers believed, it was at least possible for human beings to create better societies and better people.

Enlightenment The influential intellectual and cultural movement of the late seventeenth and eighteenth centuries that introduced a new worldview based on the use of reason, the scientific method, and progress.

rationalism A secular, critical way of thinking in which nothing was to be accepted on faith, and everything was to be submitted to reason.

The Emergence of the Enlightenment

Loosely united by certain key ideas, the European Enlightenment (ca. 1690–1789) was a broad intellectual and cultural movement that gained strength gradually and did not reach its maturity until about 1750. Yet it was the generation that came of age between the publication of Newton's *Principia* in 1687 and the death of Louis XIV in 1715 that tied the crucial knot between the scientific revolution and a new outlook on life. Talented writers of that generation popularized hard-to-understand scientific achievements for the educated elite.

A new generation came to believe that the human mind itself is capable of making great progress. Medieval and Reformation thinkers had been concerned primarily with the abstract concepts of sin and salvation. The humanists of the Renaissance had emphasized worldly matters (especially art and literature), but their inspiration came from the classical past. Enlightenment thinkers came to believe that their era had gone far beyond antiquity and that intellectual progress was very possible.

The excitement of the scientific revolution also generated doubt and uncertainty, contributing to a widespread crisis in late-seventeenth-century European thought. In the wake of the devastation wrought by the Thirty Years' War, some people asked whether ideological conformity in religious matters was really necessary. Others skeptically asked if religious truth could ever be known with absolute certainty and concluded that it could not. This was a new development because many seventeenth-century scientists, Catholic and Protestant, believed that their work exalted God and helped explain his creation to fellow believers.

The most famous of these skeptics was Pierre Bayle (1647–1706), a French Huguenot who despised Louis XIV and found refuge in the Netherlands. Bayle critically examined the religious beliefs and persecutions of the past in his *Historical and Critical Dictionary* (1697). Demonstrating that human beliefs had been extremely varied and very often mistaken, he concluded that nothing can ever be known beyond all doubt, a view known as skepticism. His very influential *Dictionary* was reprinted frequently in the Netherlands and in England and was found in more private libraries of eighteenth-century France than any other book.

As they questioned religious teachings and traditions, some early Enlightenment philosophers became interested in Judaism. They read Jewish scripture mostly in the abstract to help define what true religion should be like. Some Jewish scholars participated in the early Enlightenment movement. The philosopher Baruch Spinoza (1632–1677) was excommunicated by the relatively large Jewish community of Amsterdam for his controversial religious ideas. Rejecting his youthful support for Descartes, Spinoza came to believe that mind and body are united in one substance and that God and nature were two names for the same thing. He envisioned a deterministic universe in which good and evil were merely relative values. Few of Spinoza's radical writings were published during his lifetime, but he is now recognized as among the most original thinkers of the early Enlightenment.

The rapidly growing travel literature on non-European lands and cultures was another cause of

Popularizing Science The frontispiece illustration of Fontenelle's *Conversations on the Plurality of Worlds* (1686) invites the reader to share the pleasures of astronomy with an elegant lady and an entertaining teacher. The drawing shows the planets revolving around the sun. (By permission of the Syndics of Cambridge University Library)

their ideas. Whereas Descartes based his deductive logic on the conviction that certain first premises, or innate ideas, are imbued in all humans by God, Locke insisted that all ideas are derived from experience. The human mind at birth is like a blank tablet, or tabula rasa on which the environment writes the individual's understanding and beliefs. Human development is therefore determined by education and social institutions, for good or for evil. Locke's essay contributed to the theory of sensationalism, the idea that all human ideas and thoughts are produced as a result of sensory impressions. With his emphasis on the role of perception in the acquisition of knowledge, Locke provided a systematic justification of Bacon's emphasis on the importance of observation and experimentation. The *Essay Concerning Human Understanding* passed through many editions and translations and, along with Newton's *Principia*, was one of the dominant intellectual inspirations of the Enlightenment.

The Influence of the Philosophes

By the time Louis XIV died in 1715, many of the ideas that would soon coalesce into the new worldview had been assembled. Yet Christian Europe was still strongly attached to its established political and social structures and its traditional spiritual beliefs. By 1775, however, a large portion of western Europe's educated elite had embraced many of the new ideas. This acceptance was the work of the **philosophes** (fee-luh-zawfz), a group of influential intellectuals who proudly proclaimed that they, at long last, were bringing the light of knowledge to their ignorant fellow creatures.

> **philosophes** A group of French intellectuals who proclaimed that they were bringing the light of knowledge to their fellow creatures in the Age of Enlightenment.

Philosophe is the French word for "philosopher," and it was in France that the Enlightenment reached its highest development. There were at least three reasons for this. First, French was the international language of the educated classes in the eighteenth century, and France was still the wealthiest and most populous country in Europe. Second, although French intellectuals were not free to openly criticize either church or state, they were not as strongly restrained as intellectuals in eastern and east-central Europe. Third, the French philosophes made it their goal to reach a larger audience of elites, many of whom were joined together in the eighteenth-century concept of the "republic of letters"—an imaginary transnational realm of the well-educated.

Knowing that published attacks on society and the church would probably be banned or burned, the philosophes circulated their most radical works in manuscript form. To appeal to the public and get around the censors, they wrote novels and plays, histories and philosophies, dictionaries and encyclopedias, all filled with

questioning among thinkers. In the wake of the great discoveries, Europeans were learning that the peoples of China, India, Africa, and the Americas all had their own very different beliefs and customs. Europeans shaved their faces and let their hair grow. Turks shaved their heads and let their beards grow. In Europe a man bowed before a woman to show respect. In Siam a man turned his back on a woman when he met her because it was disrespectful to look directly at her. Countless similar examples discussed in travel accounts helped change the perspective of educated Europeans. They began to look at truth and morality in relative, rather than absolute, terms. If anything was possible, who could say what was right or wrong?

Out of this period of intellectual turmoil came John Locke's *Essay Concerning Human Understanding* (1690), often viewed as the first major text of the Enlightenment. In this work Locke (1632–1704) brilliantly set forth a new theory about how human beings learn and form

Voltaire and Philosophes This painting belongs to a series commissioned by Catherine the Great to depict daily life at the philosopher's retreat at Ferney in Switzerland. It shows Voltaire seated at the dinner table surrounded by his followers, including *Encyclopedia* editors Diderot and d'Alembert. The scene is imaginary, for Diderot never visited Ferney. (Photo by permission of the Voltaire Foundation, University of Oxford)

satire and double meanings to spread their message to an eager audience.

One of the greatest philosophes, the baron de Montesquieu (mahn-tuhs-KYOO) (1689–1755), brilliantly pioneered this approach in *The Persian Letters*, an extremely influential social satire published in 1721. This work consisted of amusing letters supposedly written by two Persian travelers, Usbek and Rica, who as outsiders see European customs in unique ways and thereby allow Montesquieu a vantage point for criticizing existing practices and beliefs.

Like many Enlightenment philosophes, Montesquieu saw relations between men and women as highly representative of the overall social and political system. He used the oppression of women in the Persian harem, described in letters from Usbek's wives, to symbolize Eastern political tyranny. At the end of the book, the rebellion of Usbek's harem against the cruel eunuchs he left in charge demonstrates that despotism must ultimately fail. Montesquieu also used the Persians' observations of habitual infidelity among French wives and the strength of female power behind the throne to poke fun at European social and political customs. As Rica remarks:

The thing is that, for every man who has any post at court, in Paris, or in the country, there is a woman through whose hands pass all the favours and sometimes the injustices that he does. These women are all in touch with one another, and compose a sort of commonwealth whose members are always busy giving each other mutual help and support.[10]

Montesquieu was exaggerating, but he echoed other critics of the informal power women gained in an absolutist system, where royal mistresses and female courtiers could have more access to the king than government ministers (see Chapter 16). Having gained fame by using wit as a weapon against cruelty and superstition, Montesquieu settled down on his family estate to study history and politics. His interest was partly personal, for, like many members of the French robe nobility, he was disturbed by the growth in royal absolutism under Louis XIV. But Montesquieu was also inspired by the example of the physical sciences, and he set out to apply the critical method to the problem of government in *The Spirit of Laws* (1748). The result was a complex comparative study of republics, monarchies, and despotisms—a great pioneering inquiry in the emerging social sciences.

> **❝ The thing is that, for every man who has any post at court, in Paris, or in the country, there is a woman through whose hands pass all the favours and sometimes the injustices that he does. ❞**
>
> —MONTESQUIEU

Showing that forms of government were shaped by history, geography, and customs, Montesquieu focused on the conditions that would promote liberty and prevent tyranny. He argued for a separation of powers, with political power divided and shared by a variety of classes and legal estates holding unequal rights and privileges. Admiring greatly the English balance of power among the king, the houses of Parliament, and the independent courts, Montesquieu believed that in France the thirteen high courts—the *parlements*—were frontline defenders of liberty against royal despotism. Apprehensive about the uneducated poor, Montesquieu was clearly no democrat, but his theory of separation of powers had a great impact on the constitutions of the young United States in 1789 and of France in 1791.

The most famous and in many ways most representative philosophe was François Marie Arouet, who was known by the pen name Voltaire (vohl-TAIR) (1694–1778). In his long career, this son of a comfortable middle-class family wrote more than seventy witty volumes, hobnobbed with kings and queens, and died a millionaire because of shrewd business speculations. His early career, however, was turbulent, and he was arrested on two occasions for insulting noblemen. Voltaire moved to England for three years in order to avoid a longer prison term in France, and there he came to share Montesquieu's enthusiasm for English liberties and institutions.

Returning to France and soon threatened again with prison in Paris, Voltaire had the great fortune of meeting Gabrielle-Emilie Le Tonnelier de Breteuil, marquise du Châtelet (SHAH-tuh-lay) (1706–1749), a gifted woman from the high aristocracy with a passion for science. Inviting Voltaire to live in her country house at Cirey in Lorraine and becoming his long-time companion (under the eyes of her tolerant husband), Madame du Châtelet studied physics and mathematics and published scientific articles and translations, including the first—and only—translation of Newton's *Principia* into French. Excluded from the Royal Academy of Sciences because she was a woman, Madame du Châtelet had no doubt that women's limited role in science was due to their unequal education. She once wrote that if she were a ruler, "I would reform an abuse which cuts off, so to speak, half the human race. I would make women participate in all the rights of humankind, and above all in those of the intellect."[11]

While living at Cirey, Voltaire wrote various works praising England and popularizing English scientific progress. Newton, he wrote, was history's greatest man, for he had used his genius for the benefit of humanity. "It is," wrote Voltaire, "the man who sways our minds by the prevalence of reason and the native force of truth, not they who reduce mankind to a state of slavery by force and downright violence . . . that claims our reverence and admiration."[12] In the true style of the Enlightenment, Voltaire mixed the glorification of science and reason with an appeal for better individuals and institutions.

Yet, like almost all of the philosophes, Voltaire was a reformer, not a revolutionary, in social and political matters. He pessimistically concluded that the best one could hope for in the way of government was a good monarch, since human beings "are very rarely worthy to govern themselves." He lavishly praised Louis XIV

Madame du Châtelet The marquise du Châtelet was fascinated by the new world system of Isaac Newton. She helped spread Newton's ideas in France by translating his *Principia* and by influencing Voltaire, her companion for fifteen years until her death. (Giraudon/Art Resource, NY)

in a biography and conducted an enthusiastic correspondence with Prussian King Frederick the Great, whom he admired as an enlightened monarch. Nor did Voltaire believe in social and economic equality in human affairs. The idea of making servants equal to their masters was "absurd and impossible." The only realizable equality, Voltaire thought, was that "by which the citizen only depends on the laws which protect the freedom of the feeble against the ambitions of the strong."[13]

Voltaire's philosophical and religious positions were much more radical than his social and political beliefs. In the tradition of Bayle, his voluminous writings challenged, often indirectly, the Catholic Church and Christian theology at almost every point. Voltaire clearly believed in God, but his was a distant, deistic God. Drawing on Newton, he envisioned a mechanistic universe in which God acted like a great clockmaker who built an orderly system and then stepped aside and let it run. Above all, Voltaire and most of the philosophes hated all forms of religious intolerance, which they believed often led to fanaticism and savage, inhuman action. Simple piety and human kindness—as embodied in Christ's great commandments to "love God and your neighbor as yourself"—were religion enough, he believed.

The ultimate strength of the philosophes lay in their number, dedication, and organization. The philosophes felt keenly that they were engaged in a common undertaking that transcended individuals. Their greatest and most representative intellectual achievement was, quite fittingly, a group effort—the seventeen-volume *Encyclopedia: The Rational Dictionary of the Sciences, the Arts, and the Crafts*, edited by Denis Diderot (deh-nee DEE-duh-roh) (1713–1784) and Jean le Rond d'Alembert (dah-lum-BEHR) (1717–1783). From different circles and with different interests, the two men set out in 1751 to find coauthors who would examine the rapidly expanding whole of human knowledge. Even more fundamentally, they set out to teach people how to think critically and objectively about all matters. As Diderot said, he wanted the *Encyclopedia* to "change the general way of thinking."[14]

The *Encyclopedia* survived initial resistance from the French government and the Catholic Church. Completed in 1765, it contained seventy-two thousand articles by leading scientists, writers, skilled workers, and progressive priests, and it treated every aspect of life and knowledge. Not every article was daring or original, but the overall effect was little short of revolutionary. Science and the industrial arts were exalted, religion and immortality questioned. Intolerance, legal injustice, and out-of-date social institutions were openly criticized. The encyclopedists were convinced that greater knowledge would result in greater human happiness, for knowledge was useful and made possible economic, social, and political progress. Summing up the new worldview of the Enlightenment, the *Encyclopedia* was widely read, especially in less-expensive reprint editions, and it was extremely influential.

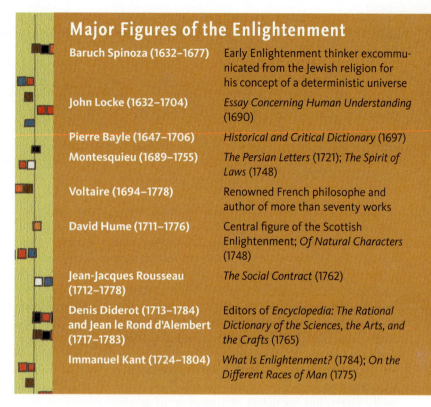

Major Figures of the Enlightenment

Baruch Spinoza (1632–1677)	Early Enlightenment thinker excommunicated from the Jewish religion for his concept of a deterministic universe
John Locke (1632–1704)	*Essay Concerning Human Understanding* (1690)
Pierre Bayle (1647–1706)	*Historical and Critical Dictionary* (1697)
Montesquieu (1689–1755)	*The Persian Letters* (1721); *The Spirit of Laws* (1748)
Voltaire (1694–1778)	Renowned French philosophe and author of more than seventy works
David Hume (1711–1776)	Central figure of the Scottish Enlightenment; *Of Natural Characters* (1748)
Jean-Jacques Rousseau (1712–1778)	*The Social Contract* (1762)
Denis Diderot (1713–1784) and Jean le Rond d'Alembert (1717–1783)	Editors of *Encyclopedia: The Rational Dictionary of the Sciences, the Arts, and the Crafts* (1765)
Immanuel Kant (1724–1804)	*What Is Enlightenment?* (1784); *On the Different Races of Man* (1775)

The Enlightenment Outside of France

Historians now recognize the existence of important strands of Enlightenment thought outside of France. They have identified distinctive Enlightenment movements in eighteenth-century Italy, Spain, Greece, the Balkans, Poland, Hungary, and Russia. Different areas developed different forms of Enlightenment thinking. In England and Germany, scholars have described a more conservative Enlightenment that tried to integrate the findings of the scientific revolution with religious faith. After the Act of Union with England and Ireland in 1707, Scotland was freed from political crisis to experience a vigorous period of intellectual growth. The Scottish Enlightenment, centered in Edinburgh, was marked by an emphasis on pragmatic and scientific reasoning. Intellectual revival there was stimulated by the creation of the first public educational system in Europe.

The most important figure in Edinburgh was David Hume (1711–1776), whose carefully argued religious skepticism had a powerful impact at home and abroad. Building on Locke's teachings on learning, Hume argued that the human mind is really nothing but a bundle of impressions. These impressions originate only in sense experiences and our habits of joining these experiences together. Since our ideas ultimately reflect only our sense experiences, our reason cannot tell us anything about questions that cannot be verified by sense experience (in the form of controlled experiments or mathematics), such as the origin of the universe or the existence of God. Paradoxically, Hume's rationalistic inquiry ended up undermining the Enlightenment's faith in the power of reason.

Urban Culture and Life in the Public Sphere

A series of new institutions and practices encouraged the spread of Enlightenment ideas in the late seventeenth and the eighteenth centuries. First, the European production and consumption of books grew significantly. In Germany, for example, the number of new titles appearing annually rose from roughly six hundred in 1700 to twenty-six hundred in 1780. Moreover, the types of books people read changed dramatically. The proportion of religious and devotional books published in Paris declined after 1750; history and law held constant; the arts and sciences surged.

Reading more books on many more subjects, the educated public in France and throughout Europe increasingly approached reading in a new way. The result was what some scholars have called a **reading revolution**. The old style of reading in Europe had been centered on a core of sacred texts that inspired reverence and taught earthly duty and obedience to God. Reading had been patriarchal and communal, with the father of the family slowly reading the text aloud and the audience savoring each word. Now reading involved a broader field of books that constantly changed. Reading became individual and silent, and texts could be questioned. Subtle but profound, the reading revolution ushered in new ways of relating to the written word.

Conversation, discussion, and debate also played a critical role in the Enlightenment. Paris set the example, and other French and European cities followed. In Paris from about 1740 to 1789, a number of talented, wealthy women presided over regular social gatherings

> **reading revolution** The transition in Europe from a society where literacy consisted of patriarchal and communal reading of religious texts to a society where literacy was commonplace and reading material was broad and diverse.

The French Book Trade Book consumption surged in the eighteenth century and, along with it, new bookstores. This appealing bookshop in France with its intriguing ads for the latest works offers to put customers "Under the Protection of Minerva," the Roman goddess of wisdom. Large packets of books sit ready for shipment to foreign countries. (Musée des Beaux-Arts, Dijon/Art Resource, NY)

salons Regular social gatherings held by talented and rich Parisian women in their homes, where philosophes and their followers met to discuss literature, science, and philosophy.

named after their elegant private drawing rooms, or **salons**. There they encouraged the exchange of witty, uncensored observations on literature, science, and philosophy with great aristocrats, wealthy middle-class financiers, high-ranking officials, and noteworthy foreigners. Talented hostesses, or *salonnières* (sah-lahn-ee-EHRZ), mediated the public's freewheeling examination of Enlightenment thought. As one philosophe described his Enlightenment hostess and her salon:

> She could unite the different types, even the most antagonistic, sustaining the conversation by a well-aimed phrase, animating and guiding it at will. . . . Politics, religion, philosophy, news: nothing was excluded. Her circle met daily from five to nine. There one found men of all ranks in the State, the Church, and the Court, soldiers and foreigners, and the leading writers of the day.[15]

As this passage suggests, the salons created a cultural realm free from religious dogma and political censorship. There a diverse but educated public could debate issues and form its own ideas. Through their invitation lists, salon hostesses brought together members of the intellectual, economic, and social elites. In such an atmosphere, the philosophes, the French nobility, and the prosperous middle classes intermingled and influenced one another. Thinking critically about almost any ques-

Picturing the Past

Enlightenment Culture An actor performs the first reading of a new play by Voltaire at the salon of Madame Geoffrin in this painting from 1755. Voltaire, then in exile, is represented by a bust statue. (Réunion des Musées Nationaux/Art Resource, NY)

ANALYZING THE IMAGE Which of these people do you think is the hostess, Madame Geoffrin, and why? Using details from the painting to support your answer, how would you describe the status of the people shown?

CONNECTIONS What does this image suggest about the reach of Enlightenment ideas to common people? To women? Does the painting of the bookstore on page 535 suggest a broader reach? Why?

To complete this activity online, go to the Online Study Guide at **bedfordstmartins.com/mckaywest**.

tion became fashionable and flourished alongside hopes for human progress through greater knowledge and enlightened public opinion.

Elite women also exercised great influence on artistic taste. Soft pastels, ornate interiors, sentimental portraits, and starry-eyed lovers protected by hovering cupids were all hallmarks of the style they favored. This style, known as **rococo** (ruh-KOH-koh), was popular throughout Europe in the period from 1720 to 1780. It has been argued that feminine influence in the drawing room went hand in hand with the emergence of polite society and the general attempt to civilize a rough military nobility. Similarly, some philosophes championed greater rights and expanded education for women, claiming that the position and treatment of women were the best indicators of a society's level of civilization and decency.[16] For these male philosophes, greater rights for women did not mean equal rights, and the philosophes were not particularly disturbed by the fact that elite women remained legally subordinate to men in economic and political affairs. Elite women lacked many rights, but so did the majority of European men, who were poor.

While membership at the salons was restricted to the well-born, the well-connected, and the exceptionally talented, a number of institutions emerged for the rest of society. Lending libraries served an important function for people who could not afford their own books. The coffeehouses that first appeared in the late seventeenth century became meccas of philosophical discussion. (See "Living in the Past: Coffeehouse Culture," page 538.) In addition to these institutions, book clubs, Masonic lodges (groups of Freemasons, a secret egalitarian society that existed across Europe), and journals all played roles in the creation of a new **public sphere** that celebrated open debate informed by critical reason. The public sphere was an idealized space where members of society came together as individuals to discuss issues relevant to the society, economics, and politics of the day.

What of the common people? Did they participate in the Enlightenment? Enlightenment philosophes did not direct their message to peasants or urban laborers. They believed that the masses had no time or talent for philosophical speculation and that elevating them would be a long, slow, potentially dangerous process. Deluded by superstitions and driven by violent passions, they thought, the people were like little children in need of firm parental guidance. D'Alembert characteristically made a sharp distinction between "the truly enlightened public" and "the blind and noisy multitude."[17]

There is some evidence, however, that the people were not immune to the words of the philosophes. At a time of rising literacy, book prices were dropping in cities and towns, and many philosophical ideas were popularized in cheap pamphlets. Moreover, even illiterate people had access to written material through the practice of public reading. Although they were barred from salons and academies, ordinary people were not immune to the new ideas in circulation.

Race and the Enlightenment

If philosophes did not believe the lower classes qualified for enlightenment, how did they regard individuals of different races? In recent years, historians have found in the scientific revolution and the Enlightenment a crucial turning point in European ideas about race. A primary catalyst for new ideas about race was the urge to classify nature unleashed by the scientific revolution's insistence on careful empirical observation. In *The System of Nature* (1735) Swedish botanist Carl von Linné argued that nature was organized into a God-given hierarchy. As scientists developed more elaborate taxonomies of plant and animal species, they also began to classify humans into hierarchically ordered "races" and to investigate the origins of race. The Comte de Buffon (komt duh buh-FOHN) argued that humans originated with one species that then developed into distinct races due largely to climatic conditions.

Enlightenment thinkers such as David Hume and Immanuel Kant (see page 541) helped popularize these ideas. In *Of Natural Characters* (1748), Hume wrote:

> *I am apt to suspect the negroes and in general all other species of men (for there are four or five different kinds) to be naturally inferior to the whites. There never was a civilized nation of any other complexion than white, nor even any individual eminent amongst them, no arts, no sciences. . . . Such a uniform and constant difference could not happen, in so many countries and ages if nature had not made an original distinction between these breeds of men.*[18]

Kant taught and wrote as much about "anthropology" and "geography" as he did about standard philosophical themes such as logic, metaphysics, and moral philosophy. He shared and elaborated Hume's views about race in *On the Different Races of Man* (1775), claiming that there were four human races, each of which had derived from a supposedly original race of "white brunette" people. According to Kant, the closest descendants of the original race were the white inhabitants of northern Germany. In deriving new physical characteristics, the other races had degenerated both physically and culturally from this origin. (Scientists now believe humans originated in Africa.)

rococo A popular style in Europe in the eighteenth century, known for its soft pastels, ornate interiors, sentimental portraits, and starry-eyed lovers protected by hovering cupids.

public sphere An idealized intellectual space that emerged in Europe during the Enlightenment, where the public came together to discuss important issues relating to society, economics, and politics.

Coffeehouse Culture

LIVING IN THE PAST

CUSTOMERS IN TODAY'S COFFEE SHOPS may be surprised to learn that they are participating in a centuries-old institution that has contributed a great deal to the idea of "modernity." Tradition has it that an Ethiopian goatherd first discovered coffee when he noticed that his goats became frisky and danced after consuming the berries. Botanists agree that coffee probably originated in Ethiopia and then spread to Yemen and across the Arabian peninsula by around 1000 C.E. In 1457, the first public coffeehouse opened in Istanbul, and from there coffeehouses became a popular institution throughout the Muslim world.

European travelers in Istanbul were astonished at its inhabitants' passion for coffee, which one described as "blacke as soote, and tasting not much unlike it."* However, Italian merchants introduced coffee to Europe around 1600, and the first European coffee shop opened in Venice in 1645, soon followed by shops in Oxford, England, in 1650, London in 1652, and Paris in 1672. By the 1730s, coffee shops had become so popular in London that one observer noted, "There are some people of moderate Fortunes, that lead their Lives mostly in Coffee-Houses, they eat, drink and sleep (in the Day-time) in them."†

Coffeehouses helped spread the ideas and values of the scientific revolution and the Enlightenment. They provided a new public space where urban Europeans could learn about and debate the issues of the day. Open to all social classes, they were a rare equalizing force in highly unequal societies. Within a few years, each political party, philosophical sect, scientific society, and literary circle had its own coffeehouse, which served as a central gathering point for

Seventeenth-century English coffeehouse. (The Granger Collection, NY)

---

*Quoted in Markman Ellis, *The Coffee-House: A Cultural History* (London: Phoenix, 2004), p. 8.
†Quoted ibid, p. 198.

its members and an informal recruiting site for new ones.

European coffeehouses also played a key role in the development of modern business, as their proprietors began to provide specialized business news to attract customers. Lloyd's of London, the famous insurance house, got its start in the shipping lists published by coffeehouse owner Edward Lloyd in the 1690s. The streets around London's stock exchange were crowded with coffeehouses where merchants and traders congregated to strike deals and hear the latest news.

Coffeehouses succeeded in Europe because they met a need common to politics, business, and intellectual life: the spread and sharing of information. In the late seventeenth century, newspapers were rare and expensive; there were no banks to guarantee credit; and politics was limited to a tiny elite. To break through these constraints, people needed reliable information. The coffeehouse was an ideal place to acquire it, along with a new kind of stimulant that provided the energy and attention to fuel a lively discussion.

QUESTIONS FOR ANALYSIS

1. What do these images suggest about the customers of eighteenth-century coffeehouses? Who frequented these establishments? Who was excluded?

2. What limitations on the exchange of information existed in early modern Europe? Why were coffeehouses so useful as sites for exchanging information?

3. What social role do coffeehouses play where you live? Do you see any continuities with the eighteenth-century coffeehouse?

Eighteenth-century Viennese coffeehouse. (Erich Lessing/Art Resource, NY)

Using the word *race* to designate biologically distinct groups of humans, akin to distinct animal species, was new. Previously, Europeans grouped other peoples into "nations" based on their historical, political, and cultural affiliations, rather than on supposedly innate physical differences. Unsurprisingly, when European thinkers drew up a hierarchical classification of human species, their own "race" was placed at the top. Europeans had long believed they were culturally superior to "barbaric" peoples in Africa and, since 1492, the New World. Now emerging ideas about racial difference taught them they were biologically superior as well. In turn, scientific racism helped legitimate and justify the tremendous growth of slavery that occurred during the eighteenth century. If one "race" of humans was fundamentally different and inferior, its members could be seen as particularly fit for enslavement and liable to benefit from tutelage by the superior race.

Racist ideas did not go unchallenged. *Encyclopedia* editor Denis Diderot penned a scathing critique of European arrogance and exploitation in the voice of Tahitian villagers. (See "Listening to the Past: Denis Diderot's 'Supplement to Bougainville's Voyage,'" page 542.) Scottish philosopher James Beattie (1735–1803) responded directly to claims of white superiority by pointing out that Europeans had started out as savage as nonwhites and that many non-European peoples in the Americas, Asia, and Africa had achieved high levels of civilization. German thinker Johann Gottfried von Herder (1744–1803) criticized Kant, arguing that humans could not be classified into races based on skin color and that each culture was as intrinsically worthy as any other. These challenges to ideas of racial inequality, however, were in the minority. Many other Enlightenment voices agreeing with Kant and Hume—Thomas Jefferson among them—may be found.

Scholars are only at the beginning of efforts to understand links between Enlightenment ideas about race and its notions of equality, progress, and reason. There are clear parallels, though, between the use of science to

Encyclopedia Image of the Cotton Industry This romanticized image of slavery in the West Indies cotton industry was published in Diderot and d'Alembert's *Encyclopedia*. It shows enslaved men, at right, gathering and picking over cotton bolls, while the woman at left mills the bolls to remove their seeds. The *Encyclopedia* presented mixed views on slavery; one article described it as "indispensable" to economic development, while others argued passionately for the natural right to freedom of all mankind. (Courtesy, Dover Publications)

propagate racial hierarchies and its use to defend social inequalities between men and women. French philosopher Jean-Jacques Rousseau used women's "natural" passivity to argue for their passive role in society, just as other thinkers used non-Europeans' "natural" inferiority to defend slavery and colonial domination. The new powers of science and reason were thus marshaled to imbue traditional stereotypes with the force of natural law.

Late Enlightenment

After about 1770 a number of thinkers and writers began to attack the Enlightenment's faith in reason, progress, and moderation. The most famous of these was the Swiss Jean-Jacques Rousseau (1712–1778), the son of a poor watchmaker who made his way into the world of Paris salons through his brilliant intellect. Appealing but neurotic, Rousseau came to believe that his philosophe friends and the women of the Parisian salons were plotting against him. In the mid-1750s he broke with them, living thereafter as a lonely outsider with his uneducated common-law wife and going in his own highly original direction.

Like other Enlightenment thinkers, Rousseau was passionately committed to individual freedom. Unlike them, however, he attacked rationalism and civilization as destroying, rather than liberating, the individual. Warm, spontaneous feeling had to complement and correct cold intellect. Moreover, the basic goodness of the individual and the unspoiled child had to be protected from the cruel refinements of civilization. Rousseau's ideals greatly influenced the early romantic movement, which rebelled against the culture of the Enlightenment in the late eighteenth century.

Echoing Montesquieu's critique of women's influence in public affairs, Rousseau called for a rigid division of gender roles. According to Rousseau, women and men were radically different beings. Destined by nature to assume a passive role in sexual relations, women should also be passive in social life. Women's love for displaying themselves in public, attending salons, and pulling the strings of power was unnatural and had a corrupting effect on both politics and society. Rousseau thus rejected the sophisticated way of life of Parisian elite women. His criticism led to broader calls for privileged women to renounce their frivolous ways and stay at home to care for their children.

Rousseau's contribution to political theory in *The Social Contract* (1762) drew less attention at first but proved to be highly significant. His contribution was based on two fundamental concepts: the general will and popular sovereignty. According to Rousseau, the general will is sacred and absolute, reflecting the common interests of all the people, who have displaced the monarch as the holder of sovereign power. The general will is not necessarily the will of the majority, however. At times the general will may be the authentic, long-term needs of the people as correctly interpreted by a farseeing minority. Little noticed before the French Revolution, Rousseau's concept of the general will appealed greatly to democrats and nationalists after 1789. (The concept has since been abused by dictators who have claimed that they, rather than some momentary majority of voters, represent the general will.) Rousseau was both one of the most influential voices of the Enlightenment and, in his rejection of rationalism and social discourse, a harbinger of reaction against Enlightenment ideas.

As the reading public developed, it joined forces with the philosophes to call for the autonomy of the printed word. Immanuel Kant (1724–1804), a professor in East Prussia and the greatest German philosopher of his day, posed the question of the age when he published a pamphlet in 1784 entitled *What Is Enlightenment?* Kant answered, "*Sapere Aude* (dare to know)! 'Have the courage to use your own understanding' is therefore the motto of enlightenment." He argued that if serious thinkers were granted the freedom to exercise their reason publicly in print, enlightenment would almost surely follow. Kant was no revolutionary; he also insisted that in their private lives, individuals must obey all laws, no matter how unreasonable, and should be punished for "impertinent" criticism. Kant thus tried to reconcile absolute monarchical authority with a critical public sphere. This balancing act characterized experiments with "enlightened absolutism" in the eighteenth century.

Enlightened Absolutism

What impact did new ways of thinking have on political developments and monarchical absolutism?

How did the Enlightenment influence political developments? To this important question there is no easy answer. Most Enlightenment thinkers outside of England and the Netherlands, especially in central and eastern Europe, believed that political change could best come from above—from the ruler—rather than from below. Royal absolutism was a fact of life, and the kings and queens of Europe's leading states clearly had no intention of giving up their great power. Therefore, the philosophes and their sympathizers realistically concluded that a benevolent absolutism offered the best opportunities for improving society.

Many government officials were interested in philosophical ideas. They were among the best-educated members of society, and their daily involvement in complex affairs of state made them naturally attracted to ideas for improving human society. Encouraged and instructed

Denis Diderot's "Supplement to Bougainville's Voyage"

LISTENING TO THE PAST

Denis Diderot (1713–1784) was born in a provincial town in eastern France and educated in Paris. Rejecting careers in the church and the law, he devoted himself to literature and philosophy. In 1749, sixty years before Charles Darwin's birth, Diderot was jailed by Parisian authorities for publishing an essay questioning God's role in the creation and suggesting the autonomous evolution of species. Following these difficult beginnings, Diderot's editorial work and writing on the Encyclopedia were the crowning intellectual achievements of his life and, according to some, of the Enlightenment itself.

Like other philosophes, Diderot employed numerous genres to disseminate Enlightenment thought, ranging from scholarly articles in the Encyclopedia to philosophical treatises, novels, plays, book reviews, and erotic stories. His "Supplement to Bougainville's Voyage" (1772) was a fictional account of a European voyage to Tahiti inspired by the writings of traveler Louis-Antoine de Bougainville. In this passage, Diderot expresses his own loathing of colonial conquest and exploitation through the voice of an elderly Tahitian man. The character's praise for his own culture allows Diderot to express his Enlightenment idealization of "natural man," free from the vices of civilized societies.

❝ He was the father of a numerous family. At the time of the Europeans' arrival, he cast upon them a look that was filled with scorn, though it revealed no surprise, no alarm and no curiosity. They approached him; he turned his back on them and retired into his hut. His thoughts were only too well revealed by his silence and his air of concern, for in the privacy of his thoughts he groaned inwardly over the happy days of his people, now gone forever. At the moment of Bougainville's departure, when all the natives ran swarming onto the beach, tugging at his clothing and throwing their arms around his companions and weeping, the old man stepped forward and solemnly spoke:

"Weep, wretched Tahitians, weep—but rather for the arrival than for the departure of these wicked and grasping men! The day will come when you will know them for what they are. Someday they will return, bearing in one hand that piece of wood you see suspended from this one's belt and in the other the piece of steel that hangs at the side of his companions. They will load you with chains, slit your throats and enslave you to their follies and vices. Someday you will be slaves to them, you will be as corrupt, as vile, as wretched as they are. . . ."

Then, turning to Bougainville, he went on: "And you, leader of these brigands who obey you, take your vessel swiftly from our shores. We are innocent and happy, and you can only spoil our happiness. We follow the pure instinct of nature, and you have tried to efface her imprint from our hearts. Here all things

This image depicts the meeting of French explorer Louis-Antoine de Bougainville with Tahitians in April 1768. Of his stay on the island, Bougainville wrote: "I felt as though I had been transported to the Garden of Eden. . . . Everywhere reigned hospitality, peace, joy, and every appearance of happiness." Diderot's philosophical tract was a fictional sequel to Bougainville's account. (Unknown artist, Tahitians presenting fruit to Bougainville attended by his officers. PIC T2996 NK5066 LOC7321, National Library of Australia)

are for all, and you have preached to us I know not what distinctions between mine and thine....

"... You are not slaves; you would suffer death rather than be enslaved, yet you want to make slaves of us! Do you believe, then, that the Tahitian does not know how to die in defense of his liberty? This Tahitian, whom you want to treat as a chattel, as a dumb animal—this Tahitian is your brother. You are both children of Nature—what right do you have over him that he does not have over you?

"You came; did we attack you? Did we plunder your vessel? Did we seize you and expose you to the arrows of our enemies? Did we force you to work in the fields alongside our beasts of burden? We respected our own image in you. Leave us our own customs, which are wiser and more decent than yours. We have no wish to barter what you call our ignorance for your useless knowledge. We possess already all that is good or necessary for our existence. Do we merit your scorn because we have not been able to create superfluous wants for ourselves? When we are hungry, we have something to eat; when we are cold, we have clothing to put on. You have been in our huts—what is lacking there, in your opinion? You are welcome to drive yourselves as hard as you please in pursuit of what you call the comforts of life, but allow sensible people to stop when they see they have nothing to gain but imaginary benefits from the continuation of their painful labors. If you persuade us to go beyond the bounds of strict necessity, when shall we come to the end of our labor? When shall we have time for enjoyment? We have reduced our daily and yearly labors to the least possible amount, because to us nothing seemed more desirable than leisure. Go and bestir yourselves in your own country; there you may torment yourselves as much as you like; but leave us in peace, and do not fill our heads with a hankering after your false needs and imaginary virtues."

Source: From Denis Diderot, *Supplement to Bougainville's Voyage*, edited by Jacques Barzun (Upper Saddle River, N.J.: Prentice-Hall, 1965. © 2010 by Jacques Barzun. All rights reserved, c/o Writers Representatives LLC, New York, NY, 10011, permissions@writersrep.com.

QUESTIONS FOR ANALYSIS

1. On what grounds does the speaker argue for the Tahitians' basic equality with the Europeans?
2. What is the good life according to the speaker, and how does it contrast with the European way of life? Which do you think is the better path?
3. In what ways could Diderot's thoughts here be seen as representative of Enlightenment ideas? Are there ways in which they are not?
4. How realistic do you think this account is? How might defenders of expansion respond?

by these officials, some absolutist rulers tried to reform their governments in accordance with Enlightenment ideals—what historians have often called the **enlightened absolutism** of the later eighteenth century. The most influential of the new-style monarchs were in Prussia, Russia, and Austria. Their example illustrates both the achievements and the great limitations of enlightened absolutism.

enlightened absolutism Term coined by historians to describe the rule of eighteenth-century monarchs who, without renouncing their own absolute authority, adopted Enlightenment ideals of rationalism, progress, and tolerance.

Frederick the Great of Prussia

Frederick II (r. 1740–1786), commonly known as Frederick the Great, built masterfully on the work of his father, Frederick William I (see Chapter 16). Although in his youth he embraced culture and literature rather than the crude life of the barracks championed by his father, by the time he came to the throne Frederick was determined to use the splendid army that his father had left him.

Therefore, when the young Maria Theresa of Austria inherited the Habsburg dominions upon the death of her father Charles VI, Frederick pounced. He invaded her rich, mainly German province of Silesia (sigh-LEE-zhuh), defying solemn Prussian promises to respect the Pragmatic Sanction, a diplomatic agreement that had guaranteed Maria Theresa's succession. In 1742, as other greedy powers vied for her lands in the European War of the Austrian Succession (1740–1748), Maria Theresa was forced to cede almost all of Silesia to Prussia. In one stroke Prussia had doubled its population to 6 million people. Now Prussia unquestionably towered above all the other German states and stood as a European Great Power.

Though successful in 1742, Frederick had to fight against great odds to save Prussia from total destruction after the ongoing competition between Britain and France for colonial empire brought another great conflict in 1756. Maria Theresa, seeking to regain Silesia, formed an alliance with the leaders of France and Russia. The aim of the alliance during the resulting Seven Years' War (1756–1763) was to conquer Prussia and divide

The War of the Austrian Succession, 1740–1748

> **I must enlighten my people, cultivate their manners and morals, and make them as happy as human beings can be, or as happy as the means at my disposal permit.**
>
> —FREDERICK THE GREAT

up its territory. Despite invasions from all sides, Frederick fought on with stoic courage. In the end he was miraculously saved: Peter III came to the Russian throne in 1762 and called off the attack against Frederick, whom he greatly admired.

The terrible struggle of the Seven Years' War tempered Frederick's interest in territorial expansion and brought him to consider how more humane policies for his subjects might also strengthen the state. Thus Frederick went beyond a superficial commitment to Enlightenment culture for himself and his circle. He tolerantly allowed his subjects to believe as they wished in religious and philosophical matters. He promoted the advancement of knowledge, improving his country's schools and permitting scholars to publish their findings. Moreover, Frederick tried to improve the lives of his subjects more directly. As he wrote his friend Voltaire, "I must enlighten my people, cultivate their manners and morals, and make them as happy as human beings can be, or as happy as the means at my disposal permit."

The legal system and the bureaucracy were Frederick's primary tools. Prussia's laws were simplified, torture of prisoners was abolished, and judges decided cases quickly and impartially. Prussian officials became famous for their hard work and honesty. After the Seven Years' War ended in 1763, Frederick's government energetically promoted the reconstruction of agriculture and industry in his war-torn country. Frederick himself set a good example. He worked hard and lived modestly, claiming that he was "only the first servant of the state." Thus Frederick justified monarchy in terms of practical results and said nothing of the divine right of kings.

Frederick's dedication to high-minded government went only so far, however. While he condemned serfdom in the abstract, he accepted it in practice and did not free the serfs on his own estates. He accepted and extended the privileges of the nobility, who remained the backbone of the army and the entire Prussian state.

In reforming Prussia's bureaucracy, Frederick drew on the principles of **cameralism**, the German science of public administration that emerged in the decades following the Thirty Years' War. Influential throughout the German lands, cameralism held that monarchy was the best of all forms of government, that all elements of society should be placed at the service of the state, and that, in turn, the state should make use of its resources and authority to improve society. Predating the Enlightenment, cameralist interest in the public good was usually inspired by the needs of war. Cameralism shared with the Enlightenment an emphasis on rationality, progress, and utilitarianism; in the eighteenth century, they overlapped a lot.

Catherine the Great of Russia

Catherine the Great of Russia (r. 1762–1796) was one of the most remarkable rulers of her age, and the French philosophes adored her. Catherine was a German princess from Anhalt-Zerbst, an insignificant principality sandwiched between Prussia and Saxony. Her father commanded a regiment of the Prussian army, but her mother was related to the Romanovs of Russia, and that proved to be Catherine's opening to power.

At the age of fifteen Catherine's Romanov connection made her a suitable bride for the heir to the Russian throne. It was a mismatch from the beginning, but her *Memoirs* made her ambitions clear: "I did not care about Peter, but I did care about the crown." When her husband Peter III came to power during the Seven Year's War, his decision to withdraw Russian troops from the coalition against Prussia alienated the army. Catherine profited from his unpopularity to form a conspiracy to depose her husband. In 1762 Catherine's lover Gregory Orlov and his three brothers, all army officers, murdered Peter, and the German princess became empress of Russia.

Catherine had drunk deeply at the Enlightenment well. Never questioning that absolute monarchy was the best form of government, she set out to rule in an enlightened manner. She had three main goals. First, she worked hard to continue Peter the Great's effort to bring the culture of western Europe to Russia (see Chapter 16). To do so, she imported Western architects, sculptors, musicians, and intellectuals. She bought masterpieces of Western art and patronized the philosophes. An enthusiastic letter writer, she corresponded extensively with Voltaire and praised him as the "champion of the human race." When the French government banned the *Encyclopedia*, she offered to publish it in St. Petersburg, and she sent money to Diderot when he needed it. With these actions, Catherine won good press in the West for herself and for her country. Moreover, this intellectual ruler, who wrote plays and loved good talk, set the tone for the entire Russian nobility. Peter the Great westernized Russian armies, but it was Catherine who westernized the imagination of the Russian nobility.

cameralism View that monarchy was the best form of government, that all elements of society should serve the monarch, and that, in turn, the state should use its resources and authority to increase the public good.

Catherine the Great Strongly influenced by the Enlightenment, Catherine the Great cultivated the French philosophes and instituted moderate reforms, only to reverse them in the aftermath of Pugachev's rebellion. This equestrian portrait now hangs above her throne in the palace throne room in St. Petersburg. (Musée des Beaux-Arts, Chartres/The Bridgeman Art Library)

Catherine's second goal was domestic reform, and she began her reign with sincere and ambitious projects. In 1767 she appointed a special legislative commission to prepare a new law code. This project was never completed, but Catherine did restrict the practice of torture and allowed limited religious toleration. She also tried to improve education and strengthen local government. The philosophes applauded these measures and hoped more would follow.

Such was not the case. In 1773 a common Cossack soldier named Emelian Pugachev sparked a gigantic uprising of serfs, very much as Stenka Razin had done a century earlier (see Chapter 16). Proclaiming himself the true tsar, Pugachev issued orders abolishing serfdom, taxes, and army service. Thousands joined his cause, slaughtering landlords and officials over a vast area of southwestern Russia. Pugachev's untrained forces eventually proved no match for Catherine's noble-led army. Betrayed by his own company, Pugachev was captured and savagely executed.

Pugachev's rebellion put an end to any intentions Catherine might have had about reforming the system. The peasants were clearly dangerous, and her empire rested on the support of the nobility. After 1775 Catherine gave the nobles absolute control of their serfs, and she extended serfdom into new areas, such as Ukraine. In 1785 she formalized the nobility's privileged position, freeing nobles forever from taxes and state service. Under Catherine the Russian nobility attained its most exalted position, and serfdom entered its most oppressive phase.

Catherine's third goal was territorial expansion, and in this respect she was extremely successful. Her armies subjugated the last descendants of the Mongols and the Crimean Tartars, and began the conquest of the Caucasus (KAW-kuh-suhs). Her greatest coup by far was the partition of Poland (Map 17.1). When, between 1768 and 1772, Catherine's armies scored unprecedented victories against the Turks and thereby threatened to disturb the balance of power between Russia and Austria in eastern Europe, Frederick of Prussia obligingly came forward with a deal. He proposed that Turkey be let off easily and that Prussia, Austria, and Russia each compensate itself by taking a gigantic slice of the weakly ruled Polish territory. Catherine jumped at the chance. The first partition of Poland took place in 1772. Subsequent

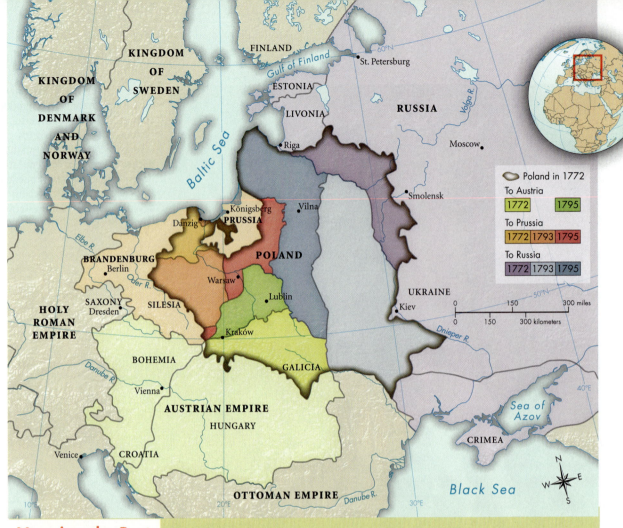

Mapping the Past

Map 17.1 **The Partition of Poland, 1772–1795** In 1772 war between Russia and Austria threatened over Russian gains from the Ottoman Empire. To satisfy desires for expansion without fighting, Prussia's Frederick the Great proposed that parts of Poland be divided among Austria, Prussia, and Russia. In 1793 and 1795 the three powers partitioned the remainder, and the ancient republic of Poland vanished from the map.

ANALYZING THE MAP Of the three powers that divided the kingdom of Poland, which benefited the most? How did the partition affect the geographical boundaries of each state, and what was the significance? What border with the former Poland remained unchanged? Why do you think this was the case?

CONNECTIONS Why was Poland vulnerable to partition in the latter half of the eighteenth century? What does it say about European politics at the time that a country could simply cease to exist on the map? Could that happen today?

To complete this activity online, go to the Online Study Guide at bedfordstmartins.com/mckaywest.

---

partitions in 1793 and 1795 gave away the rest of Polish territory, and the ancient republic of Poland vanished from the map.

The Austrian Habsburgs

Another female monarch, Maria Theresa (r. 1740–1780) of Austria, set out to reform her nation, although traditional power politics was a more important motivation for her than were Enlightenment teachings. A devout mother and wife who inherited power from her father, Charles VI, Maria Theresa was a remarkable but old-fashioned absolutist. Her more radical son, Joseph II (r. 1780–1790), drew on Enlightenment ideals, earning the title of "revolutionary emperor."

Emerging from the long War of the Austrian Succession in 1748 with the serious loss of Silesia, Maria Theresa was determined to introduce reforms that would make the state stronger and more efficient. First, she introduced measures aimed at limiting the papacy's political influence in her realm. Second, a whole series of administrative reforms strengthened the central

Maria Theresa The empress and her husband pose with twelve of their sixteen children at Schönbrunn palace in this family portrait by court painter Martin Meytens (1695–1770). Joseph, the heir to the throne, stands at the center of the star on the floor. Wealthy women often had very large families, in part because they, unlike poor women, seldom nursed their babies. (Réunion des Musées Nationaux/Art Resource, NY)

bureaucracy, smoothed out some provincial differences, and revamped the tax system, taxing even the lands of nobles, previously exempt from taxation. Third, the government sought to improve the lot of the agricultural population, cautiously reducing the power of lords over their hereditary serfs and their partially free peasant tenants.

Coregent with his mother from 1765 onward and a strong supporter of change, Joseph II moved forward rapidly when he came to the throne in 1780. Most notably, Joseph abolished serfdom in 1781, and in 1789 he decreed that peasants could pay landlords in cash rather than through compulsory labor on their land. This measure was violently rejected not only by the nobility but also by the peasants it was intended to help, because they lacked the necessary cash. When a disillusioned Joseph died prematurely at forty-nine, the entire Habsburg empire was in turmoil. His brother Leopold II (r. 1790–1792) canceled Joseph's radical edicts in order to re-establish order. Peasants once again were required to do forced labor for their lords.

Despite differences, Joseph II and the other eastern European absolutists of the later eighteenth century combined old-fashioned state-building with the culture and critical thinking of the Enlightenment. In doing so, they succeeded in expanding the role of the state in the life of society. They perfected bureaucratic machines that were to prove surprisingly adaptive and capable of enduring into the twentieth century. Their failure to implement policies we would recognize as humane and enlightened—such as abolishing serfdom—may reveal inherent limitations in Enlightenment

Individuals in Society

Moses Mendelssohn and the Jewish Enlightenment

IN 1743 A SMALL, HUMPBACKED JEWISH BOY with a stammer left his poor parents in Dessau (DE-sow) in central Germany and walked eighty miles to Berlin, the capital of Frederick the Great's Prussia. According to one story, when the boy reached the Rosenthaler (ROH-zuhn-taw-lehr) Gate, the only one through which Jews could pass, he told the inquiring watchman that his name was Moses and that he had come to Berlin "to learn." The watchman laughed and waved him through. "Go Moses, the sea has opened before you."*

In Berlin the young Mendelssohn studied Jewish law and eked out a living copying Hebrew manuscripts in a beautiful hand. But he was soon fascinated by an intellectual world that had been closed to him in the Dessau ghetto. There, like most Jews throughout central Europe, he had spoken Yiddish — a mixture of German, Polish, and Hebrew. Now, working mainly on his own, he mastered German; learned Latin, Greek, French, and English; and studied mathematics and Enlightenment philosophy. Word of his exceptional abilities spread in Berlin's Jewish community (the dwelling of 1,500 of the city's 100,000 inhabitants). He began tutoring the children of a wealthy Jewish silk merchant, and he soon became the merchant's clerk and later his partner. But his great passion remained the life of the mind and the spirit, which he avidly pursued in his off hours.

Gentle and unassuming in his personal life, Mendelssohn was a bold thinker. Reading eagerly in Western philosophy since antiquity, he was, as a pious Jew, soon convinced that Enlightenment teachings need not be opposed to Jewish thought and religion. He concluded that reason could complement and strengthen religion, although each would retain its integrity as a separate sphere.† Developing his idea in his first great work, "On the Immortality of the Soul" (1767), Mendelssohn used the neutral setting of a philosophical dialogue between Socrates and his followers in ancient Greece to argue that the human soul lived forever. In refusing to bring religion and critical thinking into conflict, he was strongly influenced by contemporary German philosophers who argued similarly on behalf of Christianity. He reflected the way the German Enlightenment generally supported established religion, in contrast to the French Enlightenment, which attacked it.

Mendelssohn's treatise on the human soul captivated the educated German public, which marveled that a Jew could have written a philosophical masterpiece. In the excitement, a Christian zealot named Lavater challenged Mendelssohn in a pamphlet to accept Christianity or to demonstrate how the Christian faith was not "reasonable." Replying politely but passionately, the Jewish philosopher affirmed that his studies had only strengthened him in his faith, although he did not seek to convert anyone not born into Judaism. Rather, he urged toleration in religious matters and spoke up courageously against Jewish oppression.

Orthodox Jew and German philosophe, Moses Mendelssohn serenely combined two very different worlds. He built a bridge from the ghetto to the dominant culture over which many Jews would pass, including his novelist daughter Dorothea and his famous grandson, the composer Felix Mendelssohn.

QUESTIONS FOR ANALYSIS

1. How did Mendelssohn seek to influence Jewish religious thought in his time?
2. How do Mendelssohn's ideas compare with those of the French Enlightenment?

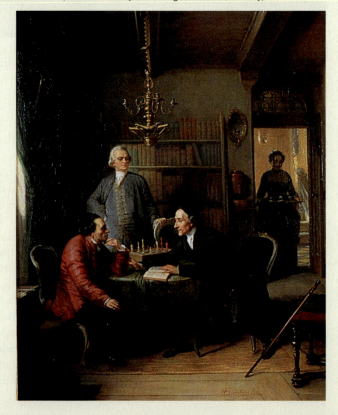

Lavater (right) attempts to convert Mendelssohn, in a painting of an imaginary encounter by Moritz Oppenheim. (Collection of the Judah L. Magnes Museum, Berkeley)

---

*H. Kupferberg, *The Mendelssohns: Three Generations of Genius* (New York: Charles Scribner's Sons, 1972), p. 3.
†D. Sorkin, *Moses Mendelssohn and the Religious Enlightenment* (Berkeley: University of California Press, 1996), pp. 8 ff.

thinking about equality and social justice, rather than in their execution of Enlightenment programs. The fact that leading philosophes supported rather than criticized eastern rulers' policies suggests some of the blinders of the era.

Jewish Life and the Limits of Enlightened Absolutism

Perhaps the best example of the limitations of enlightened absolutism are the debates surrounding the possible emancipation of the Jews. Europe's small Jewish populations lived under highly discriminatory laws. For the most part, Jews were confined to tiny, overcrowded ghettos, were excluded by law from most business and professional activities, and could be ordered out of a kingdom at a moment's notice. Still, a very few did manage to succeed and to obtain the right of permanent settlement, usually by performing some special service for the state. Many rulers relied on Jewish bankers for loans to raise armies and run their kingdoms. Because of their large and closely knit diaspora, Jewish merchants and traders were prominent in international trade.

In the eighteenth century, an Enlightenment movement known as the **Haskalah** emerged from within the European Jewish community, led by the Prussian philosopher Moses Mendelssohn (1729–1786). (See "Individuals in Society: Moses Mendelssohn and the Jewish Enlightenment," at left.) Christian and Jewish Enlightenment philosophers, including Mendelssohn, began to advocate for freedom and civil rights for European Jews. In an era of reason, tolerance, and universality, they argued, restrictions on religious grounds could not stand. The Haskalah accompanied a period of controversial social change within Jewish communities, in which rabbinic controls loosened and heightened interaction with Christians took place.

Arguments for tolerance won some ground. The British Parliament passed a law allowing naturalization of Jews in 1753, but later repealed the law due to public outrage. The most progressive reforms took place under Austrian emperor Joseph II. Among his liberal edicts of the 1780s were measures intended to integrate Jews more fully into society, including eligibility for military service, admission to higher education and artisanal trades, and removal of requirements for special clothing or emblems. Welcomed by many Jews, these reforms raised fears among traditionalists of assimilation into the general population.

Many monarchs refused to entertain the idea of emancipation. Although he permitted freedom of religion to his Christian subjects, Frederick the Great of Prussia firmly opposed any general emancipation for the Jews, as he did for the serfs. Catherine the Great, who acquired most of Poland's large Jewish population when she annexed part of that country in the late eighteenth century, similarly refused. In 1791 she established the Pale of Settlement, a territory including parts of modern-day Poland, Latvia, Lithuania, Ukraine, and Belorussia, in which most Jews were required to live. Jewish habitation was restricted to the Pale until the Russian Revolution in 1917.

The first European state to remove all restrictions on the Jews was France under the French Revolution. Over the next hundred years, Jews gradually won full legal and civil rights throughout the rest of western Europe. Emancipation in eastern Europe took even longer and aroused more conflict and violence.

Haskalah The Jewish Enlightenment of the second half of the eighteenth century, led by the Prussian philosopher Moses Mendelssohn.

The Pale of Settlement, 1791

LOOKING BACK LOOKING AHEAD

HAILED AS THE ORIGIN of modern thought, the scientific revolution must also be seen as a product of its past. Medieval universities gave rise to important new scholarship, and the ambition and wealth of Renaissance patrons nurtured intellectual curiosity. Religious faith also impacted the scientific revolution, inspiring thinkers to understand the glory of God's creation, while bringing censure and personal tragedy to others. Natural philosophers following Copernicus pioneered new methods of observing and explaining nature while drawing on centuries-old traditions of mysticism, astrology, alchemy, and magic.

The Enlightenment ideas of the eighteenth century were a similar blend of past and present; they could serve as much to bolster authoritarian regimes as to inspire revolutionaries to fight for individual rights and liberties. Although the Enlightenment fostered critical thinking about everything from science to religion, the majority of Europeans, including many prominent thinkers, remained devout Christians.

The achievements of the scientific revolution and the Enlightenment are undeniable. Key Western values of rationalism, human rights, and open-mindedness were born from these movements. With their new notions of progress and social improvement, Europeans would embark on important revolutions in industry and politics in the centuries that followed. Nonetheless, others have seen a darker side. For these critics, the mastery over nature permitted by the scientific revolution now threatens to overwhelm the earth's fragile equilibrium, and the Enlightenment belief in the universal application of reason can lead to arrogance and intolerance, particularly intolerance of other people's spiritual, cultural, and political values. Such vivid debate about the legacy of these intellectual and scientific developments testifies to their continuing importance in today's world.

CHAPTER REVIEW

■ **What was revolutionary in the new attitudes toward the natural world? (p. 520)**

Decisive breakthroughs in astronomy and physics in the seventeenth century demolished the medieval synthesis of Aristotelian philosophy and Christian theology. One of the most notable discoveries was that the sun, not the earth, was the center of the galaxy. Although the early scientists considered their ideas to be in line with religion, their discoveries ran counter to long-held beliefs about the design of the universe by the Creator; therefore, Copernicus, Kepler, Galileo, and others were branded as heretics. Meanwhile, Bacon promoted the experimental method that drew conclusions based on empirical evidence, and Descartes championed deductive reasoning that speculated truths based on known principles. These two important methods eventually combined to form the modern scientific method that relies on both experimentation and reason. Following these early innovators, Newton devised the law of universal gravitation, which for the first time synthesized the orbiting planets of the solar system with the motion of objects on earth. These scientific breakthroughs had only limited practical consequences at the time, but their impact on intellectual life was enormous, nurturing a new critical attitude in many disciplines. In addition, an international scientific community arose, and state-sponsored academies, which were typically closed to women, advanced scientific research.

■ **How did the new worldview affect the way people thought about society and human relations? (p. 530)**

Interpreting scientific findings and Newtonian laws in a manner that was both antitradition and antireligion, Enlightenment philosophes extolled the superiority of rational, critical thinking. This new method, they believed, promised not just increased knowledge but even the discovery of the fundamental laws of human society. Believing that all aspects of life were open to question and skepticism, Enlightenment thinkers opened the doors to religious tolerance, representative government, and general intellectual debate. One important downside of the new scientific method was that it led to the classification of human races, with white Europeans placing themselves at the top of a new racial hierarchy.

■ **What impact did new ways of thinking have on political developments and monarchical absolutism? (p. 541)**

The ideas of the Enlightenment were an inspiration for monarchs, particularly absolutist rulers in central and eastern Europe who saw in them important tools for reforming and rationalizing their governments. Their primary goal was to strengthen their states and increase the efficiency of their bureaucracies and armies. Enlightened absolutists believed that these reforms would ultimately improve the lot of ordinary people, but this was not their chief concern. With few exceptions, they did not question the institution of serfdom. The fact that leading philosophes supported rather than criticized Eastern rulers' policies suggests some of the limitations of the era. Christian and Jewish Enlightenment thinkers argued in favor of emancipating Europe's small Jewish population. Some reforms took place, but full emancipation did not take place until the nineteenth century in the West and even later in the East.

Suggested Reading

Alexander, John T. *Catherine the Great: Life and Legend*. 1989. The best biography of the famous Russian tsarina.

Beales, Derek. *Joseph II*. 1987. A fine biography of the reforming Habsburg ruler.

Delborgo, James, and Nicholas Dew, eds. *Science and Empire in the Atlantic World*. 2008. A collection of essays examining the relationship between the scientific revolution and the imperial expansion of European powers across the Atlantic.

Ellis, Markman. *The Coffee-House: A Cultural History*. 2004. An engaging study of the rise of the coffeehouse and its impact on European cultural and social life.

Eze, E. Chukwudi, ed. *Race and the Enlightenment: A Reader*. 1997. A pioneering source on the origins of modern racial thinking in the Enlightenment.

Goodman, Dena. *The Republic of Letters: A Cultural History of the Enlightenment*. 1994. An innovative study of the role of salons and salon hostesses in the rise of the Enlightenment.

MacDonogh, Giles. *Frederick the Great*. 2001. An outstanding biography of the Prussian king.

Osler, Margaret J., ed. *Rethinking the Scientific Revolution*. 2000. A collection of essays focusing on new historical approaches to the scientific revolution.

Outram, Dorinda. *The Enlightenment*, 2d ed. 2006. An outstanding and accessible introduction to Enlightenment debates that emphasizes the Enlightenment's social context and global reach.

Shapin, Steven. *The Scientific Revolution*. 2001. A concise and well-informed general introduction to the scientific revolution.

Sorkin, David. *Moses Mendelssohn and the Religious Enlightenment*. 1996. A brilliant study of the Jewish philosopher and of the role of religion in the Enlightenment.

Notes

1. H. Butterfield, *The Origins of Modern Science* (New York: Macmillan, 1951), p. viii.
2. Quoted in A. G. R. Smith, *Science and Society in the Sixteenth and Seventeenth Centuries* (New York: Harcourt Brace Jovanovich, 1972), p. 97.
3. Quoted in Butterfield, *The Origins of Modern Science*, p. 47.
4. Ibid., p. 120.
5. Quoted in John Freely, *Aladdin's Lamp: How Greek Science Came to Europe Through the Islamic World* (New York: Knopf, 2009), p. 206.
6. Ibid., p. 217.
7. Ibid., p. 225.
8. L. Schiebinger, *The Mind Has No Sex? Women in the Origins of Modern Science* (Cambridge, Mass.: Harvard University Press, 1989), p. 2.
9. Jacqueline Broad, *Women Philosophers of the Seventeenth Century* (Cambridge, U.K.: Cambridge University Press, 2003), p. 17.
10. Montesquieu, *Persian Letters*, trans. C. J. Betts (London: Penguin Books), 1993, p. 197.
11. Schiebinger, *The Mind Has No Sex?* p. 64.
12. Quoted in L. M. Marsak, ed., *The Enlightenment* (New York: John Wiley & Sons, 1972), p. 56.
13. Quoted in G. L. Mosse et al., eds., *Europe in Review* (Chicago: Rand McNally, 1964), p. 156.
14. Quoted in P. Gay, "The Unity of the Enlightenment," *History* 3 (1960): 25.
15. Quoted in G. P. Gooch, *Catherine the Great and Other Studies* (Hamden, Conn.: Archon Books, 1966), p. 149.
16. See E. Fox-Genovese, "Women in the Enlightenment," in *Becoming Visible: Women in European History*, 2d ed., ed. R. Bridenthal, C. Koonz, and S. Stuard (Boston: Houghton Mifflin, 1987), esp. pp. 252–259, 263–265.
17. Jean Le Rond d'Alembert, *Eloges lus dans les séances publiques de l'Académie française* (Paris, 1779), p. ix, quoted in Mona Ozouf, "'Public Opinion' at the End of the Old Regime," *The Journal of Modern History* 60, Supplement: Rethinking French Politics in 1788 (September 1988): S9.
18. Quoted in Emmanuel Chukwudi Eze, ed., *Race and the Enlightenment: A Reader* (Oxford: Blackwell, 1997), p. 33.

Key Terms

natural philosophy (p. 520)
Copernican hypothesis (p. 522)
experimental method (p. 524)
law of inertia (p. 524)
law of universal gravitation (p. 526)
empiricism (p. 526)
Cartesian dualism (p. 527)
Enlightenment (p. 530)
rationalism (p. 530)
philosophes (p. 531)
reading revolution (p. 535)
salons (p. 536)
rococo (p. 537)
public sphere (p. 537)
enlightened absolutism (p. 543)
cameralism (p. 544)
Haskalah (p. 549)

For practice quizzes and other study tools, visit the Online Study Guide at **bedfordstmartins.com/mckaywest**.

For primary sources from this period, see **Sources of Western Society, Second Edition**.

For Web sites, images, and documents related to topics in this chapter, visit Make History at **bedfordstmartins.com/mckaywest**.

18
The Expansion of Europe

1650–1800

Absolutism and aristocracy, a combination of raw power and elegant refinement, were a world apart from the common people. For most people in the eighteenth century, life remained a struggle with poverty and uncertainty, with the landlord and the tax collector. In 1700 peasants on the land and artisans in their shops lived little better than had their ancestors in the Middle Ages, primarily because European societies still could not produce very much as measured by modern standards. Despite the hard work of ordinary men and women, there was seldom enough good food, warm clothing, and decent housing. The idea of progress, of substantial improvement in the lives of great numbers of people, was still the dream of only a small elite in fashionable salons.

Yet the economic basis of European life was beginning to change. In the course of the eighteenth century, the European economy emerged from the long crisis of the seventeenth century, responded to challenges, and began to expand once again. Population resumed its growth, while colonial empires developed and colonial elites prospered. Some areas were more fortunate than others. The rising Atlantic powers — Holland, France, and above all England — and their colonies led the way. The expansion of agriculture, industry, trade, and population marked the beginning of a surge comparable to that of the eleventh- and twelfth-century springtime of European civilization. But this time, broadly based expansion was not cut short by plague and famine. This time the response to new challenges led toward one of the most influential developments in human history, the Industrial Revolution, considered in Chapter 21. ∎

Life in the Expanding Europe of the Eighteenth Century. The activities of the bustling cosmopolitan port of Marseilles were common to ports across Europe in the eighteenth century. Here a wealthy Frenchwoman greets a group of foreign merchants, while dockhands struggle to shift their heavy loads.

CHAPTER PREVIEW

Working the Land
■ What important developments led to the agricultural revolution, and how did these changes affect peasants?

The Beginning of the Population Explosion
■ Why did the European population rise dramatically in the eighteenth century?

The Growth of Rural Industry
■ How and why did rural industry intensify in the eighteenth century?

The Debate over Urban Guilds
■ What were guilds, and why did they become controversial in the eighteenth century?

Building the Global Economy
■ How did colonial markets boost Europe's economic and social development, and what conflicts and adversity did world trade entail?

Working the Land

What important developments led to the agricultural revolution, and how did these changes affect peasants? ■

At the end of the seventeenth century the economy of Europe was agrarian. With the possible exception of Holland, at least 80 percent of the people of all western European countries drew their livelihoods from agriculture. In eastern Europe the percentage was considerably higher. Men and women were tied to the land, plowing fields and sowing seed, reaping harvests and storing grain. Yet even in a rich agricultural region such as the Po Valley in northern Italy, every bushel of wheat seed sown yielded on average only five or six bushels of grain at harvest. By modern standards, output was distressingly low.

In most regions of Europe in the sixteenth and seventeenth centuries, climatic conditions produced poor or disastrous harvests every eight or nine years. Unbalanced and inadequate food in famine years made people extremely susceptible to illness. Eating material unfit for human consumption during times of crop failure, such as bark or grass, resulted in intestinal ailments of many kinds. Influenza and smallpox preyed on populations weakened by malnourishment. In famine years the number of deaths soared far above normal. A third of a village's population might disappear in a year or two. But new developments in agricultural technology and methods gradually brought an end to the ravages of hunger in western Europe.

The Legacy of the Open-Field System

Why, in the late seventeenth century, did Europeans produce barely enough food to survive? The answer lies in the pattern of farming that had developed in the Middle Ages, which sustained fairly large numbers of people, but did not produce material abundance. From the Middle Ages up to the seventeenth century, much of Europe was farmed through the open-field system. The land to be cultivated was divided into several large fields, which were in turn cut up into long, narrow strips. The fields were open, and the strips were not enclosed into small plots by fences or hedges. The whole peasant village followed the same pattern of plowing, sowing, and

Enclosure Mapmakers in Henlow, England This rare image shows the process of making new maps to document the enclosure of fields in England. Drawn on the enclosure map for Henlow, Bedfordshire, around 1795, the scene shows a surveyor and his assistants at work. (Bedfordshire and Luton Archives Service, Bedfordshire, U.K.)

harvesting in accordance with tradition and the village leaders.

The ever-present problem was soil exhaustion. Wheat planted year after year in a field will deplete nitrogen in the soil. Since the supply of manure for fertilizer was limited, the only way for the land to recover was to lie fallow for a period of time. Clover and other annual grasses that grew in unplanted fields restored nutrients to the soil and also provided food for livestock. In the early Middle Ages a year of fallow was alternated with a year of cropping; then three-year rotations were introduced, especially on more fertile lands. On each strip of land, a year of wheat or rye was followed by a year of oats or beans and only then by a year of fallow. Peasants staggered the rotation of crops, so some wheat, legumes, and pastureland were always available. The three-year system was an important achievement because cash crops could be grown two years out of three, rather than only one year in two.

Traditional village rights reinforced communal patterns of farming. In addition to rotating field crops in a uniform way, villages maintained open meadows for hay and natural pasture. After the harvest villagers also pastured their animals on the wheat or rye stubble. In many places such pasturing followed a brief period, also established by tradition, for the gleaning of grain. In this process, poor women would go through the fields picking up the few single grains that had fallen to the ground in the course of the harvest. Many villages were surrounded by woodlands, also held in common, which provided essential firewood, building materials, and nutritional roots and berries.

In the age of absolutism and nobility, the state and landlords continued to levy heavy taxes and high rents, thereby stripping peasants of much of their meager earnings. The level of exploitation varied. Generally speaking, the peasants of eastern Europe were worst off. As we saw in Chapter 16, they were serfs bound to their lords in hereditary service. In much of eastern Europe, working five or six days per week on the lord's land for no pay was not uncommon. Well into the nineteenth century, individual Russian serfs and serf families were regularly sold with and without land.

Social conditions were better in western Europe, where peasants were generally free from serfdom. In France, western Germany, England, and the Low Countries (modern-day Belgium and the Netherlands), they owned land and could pass it on to their children. Yet life in the village was unquestionably hard, and poverty was the great reality for most people. Owning only a portion of the land that they worked (the village lord typically owned as much as half), poor peasants were forced to seek wages in a variety of jobs in order to eke out a living. The privileges of Europe's ruling elites weighed heavily on the people of the land.

Chronology

1650–1850	Agricultural revolution
1651–1663	British Navigation Acts
1652–1674	Anglo-Dutch wars
1700–1790	Height of Atlantic slave trade; expansion of rural industry in Europe
1701–1763	British and French mercantilist wars of empire
1720–1722	Last outbreak of bubonic plague in Europe
1720–1789	Growth of European population
1756–1763	Seven Years' War
1760–1815	Height of parliamentary enclosure in England
1763	Treaty of Paris; France cedes its possessions in India and North America
1770	James Cook claims the east coast of Australia for England
1776	Smith, *Inquiry into the Nature and Causes of the Wealth of Nations*
1805	British takeover of India complete
1807	British slave trade abolished

The Agricultural Revolution

One way for European peasants to improve their difficult position was to revolt and take land from those who owned it but did no labor. Yet the social and political conditions that sustained the ruling elites were ancient and deeply rooted, and powerful forces stood ready to crush protest. Only with the coming of the French Revolution in 1789 were European peasants, mainly in France, able to improve their position by means of radical mass action. Technological progress offered another possibility. If peasants (and their noble landlords) could replace the idle fallow with crops, they could greatly increase the land under cultivation. So remarkable were the possibilities and the results that historians have often spoken of the progressive elimination of the fallow, which occurred gradually throughout Europe from about 1650 to 1850, as an **agricultural revolution**, a great milestone in human development.

agricultural revolution The period in Europe from the mid-seventeenth through the mid-nineteenth centuries during which great agricultural progress was made and the fallow, or idling of a field to replenish nutrients, was gradually eliminated.

Because grain crops exhaust the soil and make fallowing necessary, the secret to eliminating the fallow lies in alternating grain with nitrogen-storing crops. The most important of these land-reviving crops are peas and beans, root crops such as turnips and potatoes, and clovers and grasses. As the eighteenth century went on, the number of crops that were systematically rotated grew. New patterns of organization allowed some farmers to develop increasingly sophisticated patterns of crop rotation to suit different kinds of soils. For example, in the late eighteenth century farmers in French Flanders near Lille alternated a number of grain, root, and hay crops in a given field on a ten-year schedule. Continual experimentation, fueled by developments in the scientific revolution (see Chapter 17), led to more methodical farming.

Improvements in farming had multiple effects. The new crops made ideal feed for animals; with more fodder, hay, and root crops for the winter months, peasants and larger farmers could build up their herds of cattle and sheep. More animals meant more meat and better diets. More animals also meant more manure for fertilizer and therefore more grain for bread and porridge.

Advocates of the new crop rotations, who included an emerging group of experimental scientists, some government officials, and a few big landowners, believed that new methods were scarcely possible within the traditional framework of open fields and common rights. A farmer who wanted to experiment with new methods would have to get all the landholders in the village to agree to the plan. Advocates of improvement argued that innovating agriculturalists needed to enclose and consolidate their scattered holdings into compact, fenced-in fields in order to farm more effectively. In doing so, the innovators also needed to enclose their individual shares of a village's natural pastureland, the common. According to proponents of this movement, known as **enclosure**, a revolution in village life and organization was the necessary price of technical progress.

That price seemed too high to many poor rural people who had small, inadequate holdings or very little land at all. Traditional rights were precious to these poor peasants, who used commonly held pastureland to graze livestock, and marshlands or forest outside the village as a source for foraged goods that could make the difference between survival and famine in harsh times. Thus, when the small landholders and the village poor could effectively oppose the enclosure of the open fields and the common lands, they did so. In many countries they found allies among the larger, predominately noble landowners who were also wary of enclosure because it required large investments in purchasing and fencing land and thus posed risks for them as well.

The old system of unenclosed open fields and the new system of continuous rotation coexisted in Europe for a long time. Open fields could still be found in much of France and Germany as late as the nineteenth century because peasants there had successfully opposed eighteenth-century efforts to introduce the new techniques. Throughout the end of the eighteenth century, the new system of enclosure was extensively adopted only in the Low Countries and England.

The Leadership of the Low Countries and England

The new methods of the agricultural revolution originated in the Low Countries. Seventeenth-century republican Holland, already the most advanced country in Europe in many areas of human endeavor (see Chapter 16), led the way. By the middle of the seventeenth century intensive farming was well established, and the innovations of enclosed fields, continuous rotation, heavy manuring, and a wide variety of crops were all present. Agriculture was highly specialized and commercialized.

One reason for early Dutch leadership in farming was that the area was one of the most densely populated in Europe. In order to feed themselves and provide employment, the Dutch were forced at an early date to seek maximum yields from their land and to increase the cultivated area through the steady draining of marshes and swamps. The pressure of population was connected with the second cause: the growth of towns and cities. Stimulated by commerce and overseas trade, Amsterdam grew from thirty thousand to two hundred thousand inhabitants in its golden seventeenth century. The growing urban population provided Dutch peasants with markets for all they could produce and allowed each region to specialize in what it did best. Thus the Dutch could develop their potential, and the Low Countries became, as one historian wrote, "the Mecca of foreign agricultural experts who came . . . to see Flemish agriculture with their own eyes, to write about it and to propagate its methods in their home lands."[1]

The English were the best students. Drainage and water control were one subject in which they received instruction. Large parts of seventeenth-century Holland had once been sea and sea marsh, and the efforts of centuries had made the Dutch the world's leaders in drainage. In the first half of the seventeenth century Dutch experts made a great contribution to draining the extensive marshes, or fens, of wet and rainy England. The most famous of these Dutch engineers, Cornelius Vermuyden, directed one large drainage project in Yorkshire and another in Cambridgeshire. In the Cambridge fens, Vermuyden and his Dutch workers eventually reclaimed

enclosure The movement to fence in fields in order to farm more effectively, at the expense of poor peasants who relied on common fields for farming and pasture.

forty thousand acres, which were then farmed intensively in the Dutch manner. Swampy wilderness was converted into thousands of acres of some of the best land in England.

Jethro Tull (1674–1741), part crank and part genius, was an important English innovator. A true son of the early Enlightenment, Tull adopted a critical attitude toward accepted ideas about farming and tried to develop better methods through empirical research. He was especially enthusiastic about using horses, rather than slower-moving oxen, for plowing. He also advocated sowing seed with drilling equipment rather than scattering it by hand. Drilling distributed seed in an even manner and at the proper depth. There were also improvements in livestock, inspired in part by the earlier successes of English country gentlemen in breeding ever-faster horses for the races and fox hunts that were their passions. Selective breeding of ordinary livestock was a marked improvement over the haphazard breeding of the past.

By the mid-eighteenth century English agriculture was in the process of a long but radical transformation. The eventual result was that by 1870 English farmers were producing 300 percent more food than they had produced in 1700, even though the number of people working the land had increased by only 14 percent. This great surge of agricultural production provided food for England's rapidly growing urban population. Growth in production was achieved in part by land enclosures. About half the farmland in England was enclosed through private initiatives prior to 1700; Parliament completed this work in the eighteenth century. From the 1760s to the end of the Napoleonic era in 1815, a series of acts of Parliament enclosed most of the remaining common land.

By eliminating common rights and greatly reducing the access of poor men and women to the land, the eighteenth-century enclosure movement marked the completion of two major historical developments in England — the rise of market-oriented estate agriculture and the emergence of a landless rural proletariat. By the early nineteenth century a tiny minority of wealthy English and Scottish landowners held most of the land and pursued profits aggressively, leasing their holdings through agents at competitive prices to middle-size farmers, who relied on landless laborers for their workforce.

The Vegetable Market, 1662 The wealth and well-being of the industrious, capitalistic Dutch shine forth in this winsome market scene by Dutch artist Hendrick Sorgh. The market woman's baskets are filled with delicious fresh produce that ordinary citizens can afford — eloquent testimony to the responsive, enterprising character of Dutch agriculture. (Rijksmuseum, Amsterdam)

These landless laborers worked very long hours, usually following a dawn-to-dusk schedule six days a week all year long. Not only was the small landholder deprived of his land, but fewer laborers were needed to work the large farms, and unemployment spread throughout the countryside. As one sympathetic observer commented:

> It is no uncommon thing for four or five wealthy graziers to engross a large inclosed lordship, which was before in the hands of twenty or thirty farmers, and as many smaller tenants or proprietors. All these are thereby thrown out of their livings, and many other families, who were chiefly employed and supported by them, such as blacksmiths, carpenters, wheelwrights and other artificers and tradesmen, besides their own labourers and servants.[2]

In no other European country had this **proletarianization** (proh-luh-tair-ee-uh-nuh-ZAY-shun)—this transformation of large numbers of small peasant farmers into landless rural wage earners—gone so far. England's village poor found the cost of change heavy and unjust.

proletarianization The transformation of large numbers of small peasant farmers into landless rural wage earners.

The Beginning of the Population Explosion

Why did the European population rise dramatically in the eighteenth century?

Another factor that affected the existing order of life and forced economic changes in the eighteenth century was the beginning of the population explosion. Explosive growth continued in Europe until the twentieth century, by which time it was affecting nonwestern areas of the globe. In this section we examine the causes of the population growth; the following section considers how the challenge of more mouths to feed and more hands to employ affected the European economy.

Long-standing Obstacles to Population Growth

Until 1700 the total population of Europe grew slowly much of the time, and it followed an irregular cyclical pattern (Figure 18.1). This cyclical pattern had a great influence on many aspects of social and economic life. The terrible ravages of the Black Death caused a sharp drop in population and food prices after 1350 and also created a labor shortage throughout Europe. Some economic historians calculate that for those common people in western Europe who managed to steer clear of warfare and of power struggles within the ruling class, the later Middle Ages was an era of exceptional well-being.

But this well-being eroded in the course of the sixteenth century. The second great surge of population growth outstripped the growth of agricultural production after about 1500. There was less food per person, and food prices rose more rapidly than wages, a development intensified by the inflow of precious metals from the Americas (see Chapter 15) and a general, if uneven, European price revolution. The result was a substantial decline in living standards throughout Europe. By 1600 the pressure of population on resources was severe in much of Europe, and widespread poverty was an undeniable reality.

For this reason, population growth slowed and stopped in seventeenth-century Europe. Births and deaths, fertility and mortality, were in a crude but effective balance. The population grew modestly in normal years at a rate of perhaps 0.5 to 1 percent, or enough to double the population in 70 to 140 years. This is, of course, a generalization encompassing many different patterns. In areas such as Russia and colonial New England, where there was a great deal of frontier to be settled, the annual rate of natural increase, not counting in-migration, might well have exceeded 1 percent. In a country such as France, where the land had long been densely settled, the rate of increase might have been less than 0.5 percent.

Although population growth of even 1 percent per year seems fairly modest, it will produce a very large increase over a long period: in three hundred years it will result in sixteen times as many people. Yet such gigantic increases did not occur in agrarian Europe. In certain abnormal years and tragic periods—the Black Death was only the most extreme example—many more people died than were born, and total population fell sharply, even catastrophically. A number of years of

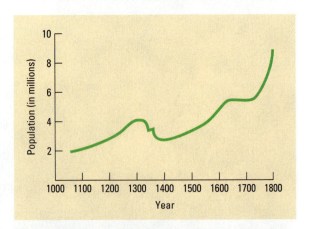

Figure 18.1 **The Growth of Population in England, 1000–1800** England is a good example of both the uneven increase of European population before 1700 and the third great surge of growth that began in the eighteenth century.
(Source: Adapted from E. A. Wrigley, *Population and History*. Copyright © 1969 by E. A. Wrigley. Reprinted with permission of Weidenfeld & Nicolson, an imprint of The Orion Publishing Group, London.)

modest growth would then be necessary to make up for those who had died in an abnormal year. Such savage increases in deaths occurred periodically in the seventeenth century on a local and regional scale, and these demographic crises combined to check the growth of population until after 1700.

The grim reapers of demographic crisis were famine, epidemic disease, and war. Famine, the inevitable result of low yields and periodic crop failures, was particularly murderous because it was accompanied by disease. With a brutal one-two punch, famine stunned and weakened a population, and disease finished it off. Disease, as the example of the Black Death illustrates, could also ravage the population independently of famine.

War was another scourge, and its indirect effects were even more harmful than the organized killing. Soldiers and camp followers passed all manner of contagious diseases throughout the countryside. Armies also requisitioned scarce food supplies and disrupted the agricultural cycle while battles destroyed precious crops and farmlands. The Thirty Years' War witnessed all possible combinations of distress. The number of inhabitants in the German states alone declined by more than two-thirds in some large areas and by at least one-third almost everywhere else.

The New Pattern of the Eighteenth Century

In the eighteenth century the population of Europe began to grow markedly. This increase in numbers occurred in all regions of Europe. The size of the European population grew steadily from 1720 to 1789, with especially dramatic increases after about 1750 (Figure 18.2).

What caused this population growth? In some areas women had more babies than before because new opportunities for employment in rural industry (see page 560) allowed them to marry at an earlier age. But the basic cause of European population increase as a whole was a decline in mortality—fewer deaths.

One of the primary reasons behind this decline was the mysterious disappearance of the bubonic plague. Following the Black Death in the fourteenth century, plagues had remained part of the European experience, striking again and again with savage force, particularly in towns. In 1720 a ship from Syria and the Levant brought the disease to Marseilles. As a contemporary account described it, "The Porters employ'd in unloading the Vessel, were immediately seiz'd with violent Pains in the Head . . . soon after they broke out in Blotches and Buboes, and died in three Days."[3] Plague quickly spread within and beyond Marseilles, killing up to one hundred thousand. By 1722 the epidemic had passed, and that was the last time plague fell on western and central Europe. Exactly why plague disappeared is unknown. Stricter measures of quarantine in Mediterra-

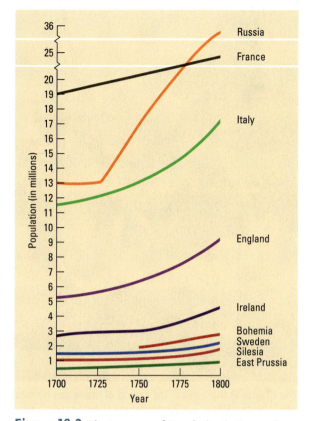

FIGURE 18.2 The Increase of Population in Europe in the Eighteenth Century Population grew across Europe in the eighteenth century, though the most dramatic increases occurred after 1750. Russia experienced the largest increase and emerged as Europe's most populous state as natural increase was complemented by growth from territorial expansion.

nean ports and along the Austrian border with Turkey helped by carefully isolating human carriers of plague. Chance and plain good luck were probably just as important.

Advances in medical knowledge did not contribute much to reducing the death rate in the eighteenth century. The most important advance in preventive medicine in this period was inoculation against smallpox, and this great improvement was long confined mainly to England, probably doing little to reduce deaths throughout Europe until the latter part of the century. However, improvements in the water supply and sewage, which were frequently promoted by strong absolutist monarchies, resulted in somewhat better public health and helped reduce such diseases as typhoid and typhus in some urban areas of western Europe. Improvements in water supply and the drainage of swamps also reduced Europe's large insect population. Flies and mosquitoes played a major role in spreading diseases, especially those striking children and young adults. Thus early public health measures helped the decline in mortality that

The Plague at Marseilles The bishop of Marseilles blesses victims of the plague that overwhelmed Marseilles in 1720. Some one hundred thousand people died in the outbreak, which was the last great episode of plague in western Europe. (Louvre/Réunion des Musée Nationaux/Art Resource, NY)

began with the disappearance of plague and continued into the early nineteenth century.

Human beings also became more successful in their efforts to safeguard the supply of food. The eighteenth century was a time of considerable canal and road building in western Europe. These advances in transportation, which were also among the more positive aspects of strong absolutist states, lessened the impact of local crop failure and famine. Emergency supplies could be brought in, and localized starvation became less frequent. Wars became less destructive than in the seventeenth century and spread fewer epidemics. Nutritious new foods, particularly the potato from South America, were introduced. In short, population grew in the eighteenth century primarily because years of higher than average death rates were less catastrophic. Famines, epidemics, and wars continued to occur and to affect population growth, but their severity moderated.

Renewed population growth in the eighteenth century intensified the imbalance between the number of people and the economic opportunities available to them. At a time of rapidly rising population, improvements in agricultural efficiency lessened the need for rural laborers. The rural poor were forced to look for new ways to make a living.

cottage industry A stage of industrial development in which rural workers used hand tools in their homes to manufacture goods on a large scale for sale in a market.

The Growth of Rural Industry

How and why did rural industry intensify in the eighteenth century?

The growth of population increased the number of rural workers with little or no land, and this in turn contributed to the development of industry in rural areas. The poor in the countryside increasingly needed to supplement their agricultural earnings with other types of work, and urban capitalists were eager to employ them, often at lower wages than urban workers received. **Cottage industry**, which consisted of manufacturing with hand tools in peasant cottages and work sheds, grew markedly in the eighteenth century and became a crucial feature of the European economy.

To be sure, peasant communities had always made clothing, processed food, and constructed housing for their own use. But medieval peasants did not produce manufactured goods on a large scale for sale in a market. By the eighteenth century, however, the pressures of rural poverty led many poor villagers to seek additional work, and far-reaching changes for daily rural life were set in motion.

The Putting-Out System

Cottage industry was often organized through the **putting-out system**. The two main participants in the putting-out system were the merchant capitalist and the rural worker. In this system, the merchant loaned, or "put out," raw materials to cottage workers, who processed the raw materials in their own homes and returned the finished products to the merchant. There were endless variations on this basic relationship. Sometimes rural workers bought their own raw materials and worked as independent producers before they sold to the merchant. Sometimes whole families were involved in domestic industry; at other times the tasks were closely associated with one gender. Sometimes several workers toiled together to perform a complicated process in a workshop outside the home. The relative importance of earnings from the land and from industry varied greatly for handicraft workers, although industrial wages usually became more important for a given family with time.

As industries grew in scale and complexity, production was often broken into many stages. For example, a merchant would provide raw wool to one group of workers for spinning into thread. He would then pass the thread to another group of workers to be bleached, to another for dyeing, and to another for weaving into cloth. The merchant paid outworkers by the piece and proceeded to sell the finished product to regional, national, or international markets.

The putting-out system grew because it had competitive advantages. Underemployed labor was abundant, and poor peasants and landless laborers would work for low wages. Since production in the countryside was unregulated, workers and merchants could change procedures and experiment as they saw fit. Because workers did not need to meet rigid guild standards, cottage industry became capable of producing many kinds of goods. Textiles; all manner of knives, forks, and housewares; buttons and gloves; and clocks could be produced quite satisfactorily in the countryside. Although luxury goods for the rich, such as exquisite tapestries and fine porcelain, demanded special training, close supervision, and centralized workshops, the limited skills of rural industry were sufficient for everyday articles.

Rural manufacturing did not spread across Europe at an even rate. It developed most successfully in England, particularly for the spinning and weaving of woolen cloth. By 1500 half of England's textiles were being produced in the countryside. By 1700 English industry was generally more rural than urban and heavily reliant on the putting-out system. Most continental countries, with the exception of Flanders and the Netherlands, developed rural industry more slowly. The latter part of the eighteenth century witnessed a remarkable expansion of rural industry in certain densely populated regions of continental Europe (Map 18.1).

> **putting-out system** The eighteenth-century system of rural industry in which a merchant loaned raw materials to cottage workers, who processed them and returned the finished products to the merchant.

The Lives of Rural Textile Workers

Until the nineteenth century, the industry that employed the most people in Europe was textiles. The making of linen, woolen, and eventually cotton cloth was the typical activity of cottage workers engaged in the putting-out system. A look inside the cottage of the English weaver illustrates a way of life as well as an economic system. The rural worker lived in a small cottage with tiny windows and little space. The cottage was often a

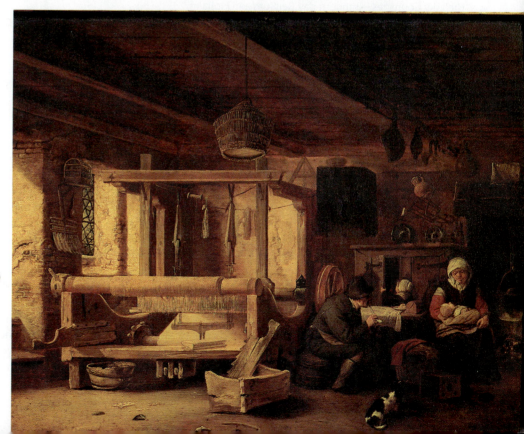

The Weaver's Repose This painting by Decker Cornelis Gerritz (1594–1637) captures the pleasure of release from long hours of toil in cottage industry. The loom realistically dominates the cramped living space and the family's modest possessions. (Musées Royaux des Beaux-Arts, Brussels. Copyright A.C.I.)

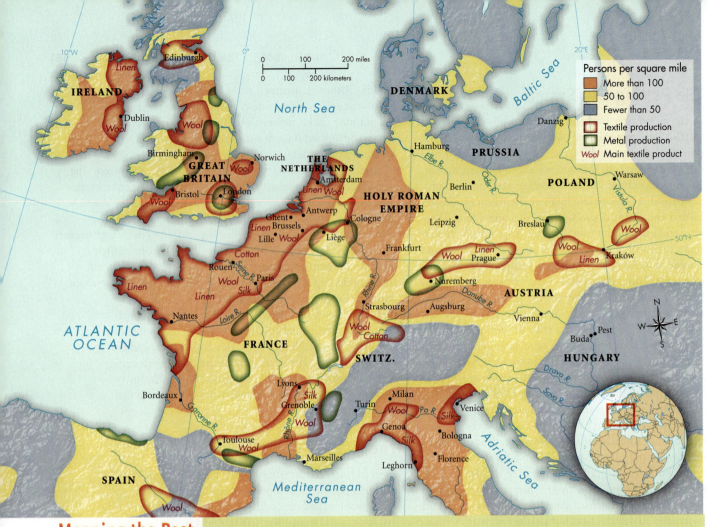

Mapping the Past

Map 18.1 Industry and Population in Eighteenth-Century Europe The growth of cottage manufacturing in rural areas helped country people increase their income and contributed to population growth. The putting-out system began in England, and much of the work was in the textile industry. Cottage industry was also strong in the Low Countries — modern-day Belgium and Holland.

ANALYZING THE MAP What does this map suggest about the relationship between population density and the growth of textile production? What geographical characteristics seem to have played a role in encouraging this industry?

CONNECTIONS How would you account for the distribution of each type of cloth across Europe? Did metal production draw on different demographic and geographical conditions? Why do you think this was the case?

To complete this activity online, go to the Online Study Guide at **bedfordstmartins.com/mckaywest**.

---

single room that served as workshop, kitchen, and bedroom. There were only a few pieces of furniture, of which the weaver's loom was by far the largest and most important. That loom had changed somewhat in the early eighteenth century when John Kay's invention of the flying shuttle enabled the weaver to throw the shuttle back and forth between the threads with one hand. Aside from that improvement, however, the loom was as it had been for much of history and as it would remain until the arrival of mechanized looms in the first decades of the nineteenth century.

Handloom weaving was a family enterprise. All members of the family helped in the work, so that "every person from seven to eighty (who retained their sight and who could move their hands) could earn their bread," as one eighteenth-century English observer put it.[4] Operating the loom was considered a man's job, reserved for the male head of the family. Women and children worked at auxiliary tasks; they prepared the warp (vertical) threads and mounted them on the loom, wound threads on bobbins for the weft (horizontal) threads, and sometimes operated the warp frame while the father passed the shuttle.

The work of four or five spinners was needed to keep one weaver steadily employed. Since the weaver's family usually could not produce enough thread, alternate sources of labor were needed. Merchants turned to the wives and daughters of agricultural workers, who took on spinning work in their spare time. In England, many widows and single women also became "spinsters," so many in fact that the word became a synonym for an unmarried woman. In parts of Germany, spinning employed whole families and was not reserved for women. As the industry expanded and merchants covered ever greater distances in search of workers, they sometimes turned to local shopkeepers to manage the spinners in their villages.

Relations between workers and employers were often marked by sharp conflict. (See "Listening to the Past: Contrasting Views on the Effects of Rural Industry," page 564.) There were constant disputes over the weights of materials and the quality of finished work. Merchants accused workers of stealing raw materials, and weavers complained that merchants delivered underweight bales. Suspicion abounded.

Conditions were particularly hard for female workers. While men could earn decent wages through long hours of arduous labor, women's wages were always terribly low. In England's Yorkshire wool industry, a male wool comber earned a good wage of twelve shillings or more a week, while a spinner could hope for only three-and-a-half shillings.[5] A single or widowed spinner faced a desperate struggle with poverty. Any period of illness or unemployment could spell disaster for her and her children. In 1788 one English writer condemned the low wages of spinners in Norwich: "The suffering of thousands of wretched individuals, willing to work, but starving from their ill requited labour; of whole families of honest industrious children offering their little hands to the wheel, and asking bread of the helpless mother, unable through this well regulated manufacture to give it to them."[6]

From the merchant capitalist's point of view, the problem was not low wages but the control of rural labor. Scattered across the countryside, cottage workers were difficult to supervise and direct. Moreover, the pace of their work depended on the agricultural calendar. In spring and late summer planting and haymaking occupied all hands in the rural village, leading to shortages in the supply of thread. Merchants, whose livelihood depended on their ability to meet orders on time, bitterly resented their lack of control over rural labor. They accused workers — especially female spinners — of laziness, drunkenness, and immorality. If workers failed to produce enough thread, they reasoned, it must be because their wages were too high and they had little incentive to work.

Merchants thus insisted on maintaining the lowest possible wages to force the "idle" poor into productive labor. They also lobbied for, and obtained, new police powers over workers. Imprisonment and public whipping became common punishments for pilfering small amounts of yarn or cloth. For poor workers, their right to hold on to the bits and pieces left over in the production process was akin to the traditional peasant right of gleaning in common lands. With progress came the loss of traditional safeguards for the poor.

The Linen Industry in Ireland Many steps went into making textiles. Here the women are beating away the woody part of the flax plant so that the man can comb out the soft part. The combed fibers will then be spun into thread and woven into cloth by this family enterprise. The increased labor of women and girls from the late seventeenth century helped produce an industrious revolution. (Victoria & Albert Museum, London/Eileen Tweedy/The Art Archive)

Contrasting Views on the Effects of Rural Industry

LISTENING TO THE PAST

English commentators quickly noted the effects of rural industry on families and daily life. Some were greatly impressed by the rise in living standards made possible by the putting-out system, while others noted the rising economic inequality between merchant and workers and the power the former acquired over the latter. In the first excerpt, novelist and economic writer Daniel Defoe enthusiastically praises cottage industry.

He notes that the labor of women and children in spinning and weaving brought in as much as or more income than the man's agricultural work, allowing the family to eat well and be warmly clothed. It is interesting to note that Defoe assumes a rural world in which the process of enclosure is complete; poor men do not own their own land, but toil as wage laborers on the land of others. He also offers one explanation for the increasing use of Africans as slaves in British colonies: reliable wages from cottage industry meant that the English poor did not have to "sell themselves to the Plantations," thus leading plantation owners to seek other sources of labor.

The second source is a popular song written around 1700. Couched in the voice of the ruthless cloth merchant, it expresses the bitterness and resentment textile workers felt against the employers. One can imagine a group of weavers gathered together at the local tavern singing their protest on a rare break from work.

Daniel Defoe, *A Plan of the English Commerce*

❝ *Being a compleat prospect of the trade of this nation, as well the home trade as the foreign*, 1728

[A] poor labouring man that goes abroad to his Day Work, and Husbandry, Hedging, Ditching, Threshing, Carting, &c. and brings home his Week's Wages, suppose at eight Pence to twelve Pence a Day, or in some Counties less; if he has a Wife and three or four Children to feed, and who get little or nothing for themselves, must fare hard, and live poorly; 'tis easy to suppose it must be so.

But if this Man's Wife and Children can at the same Time get Employment, if at next Door, or at the next Village there lives a Clothier, or a Bay Maker, or a stuff or Drugget Weaver;* the Manufacturer sends the poor Woman combed Wool, or carded Wool every Week to spin, and she gets eight Pence or nine Pence a day at home; the Weaver sends for her two little Children, and they work by the Loom, winding, filling quills, &c. and the two bigger Girls spin at home with their Mother, and these earn three Pence or four Pence a Day each: So that put it together, the Family at Home gets as much as the Father gets Abroad, and generally more.

This alters the Case extremely, the Family feels it, they all feed better, are cloth'd warmer, and do not so easily nor so often fall into Misery and Distress; the Father gets them Food, and the Mother gets them Clothes; and as they grow, they do not run away to be Footmen and Soldiers, Thieves and Beggars or sell themselves to the Plantations to avoid the Goal and the Gallows, but have a Trade at their Hands, and every one can get their Bread.

N.B. I once went through a large populous manufacturing Town in England, and observ'd, that an Officer planted there, with a Serjeant and two Drums, had been beating up a long Time and could get no Recruits, except two or three Sots . . . Enquiring the Reason of it, an honest Clothier of the Town answered me effectually thus, *The Case is plain*, says he, thus there is at this Time a brisk Demand for Goods, we have 1100 Looms, *added he*, in this Town and the Villages about it and not one of them want Work; and there is not a poor Child in the Town of above four Years old, but can earn his Bread; besides, there being so good a Trade at this Time, causes us to advance Wages a little and the Weaver and the Spinner get more than they used to do; and while it is so, they may beat the Heads of their Drums out, if they will, they'll get no Soldiers here. ❞

Anonymous, *The Clothier's Delight*

❝ *Or the rich Men's Joy, and the poor Men's Sorrow, wherein is exprest the Craftiness and Subtility of many Clothiers in England, by beating down their Workmen's Wages*, ca. 1700

Of all sorts of callings that in England be
There is none that liveth so gallant as we;
Our trading maintains us as brave as a knight,
We live at our pleasure and take our delight;
We heapeth up richest treasure great store
Which we get by griping and grinding the poor.
   And this is a way for to fill up our purse
   Although we do get it with many a curse.

Throughout the whole kingdom, in country and town,
There is no danger of our trade going down,
So long as the Comber can work with his comb,
And also the Weaver weave with his lomb;
The Tucker and Spinner that spins all the year,
We will make them to earn their wages full dear.
   And this is a way, etc.

And first for the Combers, we will bring them down,
From eight groats a score until half a crown;

---

*Bay, stuff, and drugget were types of coarse woolen cloth typical of the inexpensive products of rural weaving.

If at all they murmur and say 'tis too small
We bid them choose whether they will work at all.
We'll make them believe that trading is bad
We care not a pin, though they are n'er so sad.
   And this is a way, etc.

We'll make the poor Weavers work at a low rate,
We'll find fault where there's no fault, and so we
   will bate;
If trading grows dead, we will presently show it,
But if it grows good, they shall never know it;
We'll tell them that cloth beyond sea will not go,
We care not whether we keep clothing or no.
   And this is a way, etc.

Then next for the Spinners we shall ensue;
We'll make them spin three pound instead
   of two;
When they bring home their work unto
   us, they complain
And say that their wages will not them
   maintain;
But that if an ounce of weight they do
   lack,
Then for to bate threepence we will not
   be slack.
   And this is a way, etc.

But if it holds weight, then their wages they
   crave,
We have got no money, and what's that you'd
   have?
We have bread and bacon and butter that's good,
With oatmeal and salt that is wholesome for food;
We have soap and candles whereby to give light,
That you may work by them so long as you have
   sight.
   And this is a way, etc.

. . .

And thus, we do gain our wealth and estate
By many poor men that work early and late;
If it were not for those that labour so hard,
We might go and hang ourselves without regard;
The combers, the weavers, the tuckers also,
With the spinners that work for wages full low,
By these people's labour we fill up our purse,
Although we do get it with many a curse. 〞

Sources: Daniel Defoe, *A Plan of the English Commerce. Being a compleat prospect of the trade of this nation, as well the home trade as the foreign*. London, 1728, pp. 90–91; Paul Mantoux and Marjorie Vernon, eds., *The Industrial Revolution in the Eighteenth Century: An Outline of the Beginnings of the Modern Factory System in England* (1928; Taylor and Francis, 2006), pp. 76–77.

QUESTIONS FOR ANALYSIS

1. What division of labor in the textile industry does Defoe describe? How does this division of labor resemble or differ from the household in which you grew up?

2. On what basis are wages paid, and what strategies do merchants use to keep wages down, according to *The Clothier's Delight*? How are they able to impose such strategies on workers?

3. How do you reconcile the difference of opinion between the two sources? Was one right and the other wrong, or could a more complex analysis be true?

This spinning wheel was powered by the spinner's foot by means of the treadle, which was connected to the wheel by a rod and crankshaft. Purchasing a spinning wheel, which cost a few days of a laborer's wage, allowed rural women and children to generate precious supplemental income in the off-season. The work was relatively slow, however, and thread from four or five wheels was required to supply one weaver.
(Science and Society Picture Library/SuperStock)

The Industrious Revolution

One scholar has used the term **industrious revolution** to summarize the social and economic changes taking place in Europe in the late seventeenth and early eighteenth centuries.[7] This occurred as households in northwestern Europe reduced leisure time, stepped up the pace of work, and, most important, redirected the labor of women and children away from the production of goods for household consumption and toward wage work. In the countryside, the spread of cottage industry can be seen as one manifestation of the industrious revolution, while in the cities there was a rise in female employment outside the home (see page 568). By working harder and increasing the number of wageworkers, rural and urban households could purchase more goods, even in a time of stagnant or falling wages.

The effect of these changes is still debated. While some scholars lament the encroachment of longer work hours and stricter discipline, others insist that poor families made decisions based on their own self-interests. With more finished goods becoming available at lower prices, households sought cash income to participate in an emerging consumer economy.

The role of women and girls in this new economy is particularly controversial. When women entered the labor market, they almost always worked at menial, tedious jobs for very low wages. Yet when women earned their own wages, they also seem to have taken on a proportionately greater role in household decision making. Most of their scant earnings went for household necessities, items they could no longer produce now that they worked full-time, but there were sometimes a few shillings left for a few ribbons or a new pair of stockings. Women's use of their surplus income thus helped spur the rapid growth of the textile industries in which they labored so hard.

These new sources and patterns of labor established important foundations for the Industrial Revolution of the late eighteenth and nineteenth centuries. They created households in which all members worked for wages rather than in a united family business and in which consumption relied on market-produced rather than homemade goods. It was not until the mid-nineteenth century, with rising industrial wages, that a new model emerged in which the male "breadwinner" was expected to earn enough to support the whole family and women and children were relegated back to the domestic sphere. With women estimated to compose 39 percent of the global workforce, today's world is experiencing a second industrious revolution in a similar climate of stagnant wages and increased demand for consumer goods.[8]

industrious revolution The shift that occurred as families in northwestern Europe focused on earning wages instead of producing goods for household consumption; this reduced their economic self-sufficiency but increased their ability to purchase consumer goods.

guild system The organization of artisanal production into trade-based associations, or guilds, each of which received a monopoly over its trade and the right to train apprentices and hire workers.

The Debate over Urban Guilds

What were guilds, and why did they become controversial in the eighteenth century?

One consequence of the growth of rural industry was an undermining of the traditional **guild system** that protected urban artisans. Guilds continued to dominate production in towns and cities, providing their masters with economic privileges as well as a proud social identity, but they increasingly struggled against competition from rural workers. Meanwhile, those excluded from guild membership—women, day laborers, Jews, and foreigners—worked on the margins of the urban economy.

In the second half of the eighteenth century, critics attacked the guilds as outmoded institutions that obstructed technical progress and innovation. Until recently, most historians repeated that view. An ongoing reassessment of guilds now emphasizes their ability to adapt to changing economic circumstances.

Urban Guilds

Originating around 1200 during the economic boom of the Middle Ages, the guild system reached its peak in most of Europe in the seventeenth and eighteenth centuries. During this period, urban guilds grew dramatically in number in cities and towns across Europe. In Louis XIV's France, for example, finance minister Jean-Baptiste Colbert revived the urban guilds and used them to encourage high-quality production and to collect taxes (see Chapter 16). In this period, the number of guilds in the city of Paris grew from 60 in 1672 to 129 in 1691.

Guild masters in Paris occupied the summit of the world of work. Each guild received a detailed set of privileges from the French crown, including exclusive rights to produce and sell certain goods, access to restricted markets in raw materials, and the rights to train apprentices, hire workers, and open shops. Any individual who violated these monopolies could be prosecuted. Guilds also served social and religious functions, providing a locus of sociability and group identity to the middling classes of European cities.

Guild Procession in Seventeenth-Century Brussels Guilds played an important role in the civic life of the early modern city. They collected taxes from their members, imposed quality standards and order on the trades, and represented the interests of commerce and industry to the government. In return, they claimed exclusive monopolies over their trades and the right to govern their own affairs. Guilds marched in processions, like the one shown here, at important city events, proudly displaying their corporate insignia. (Victoria & Albert Museum, London/Art Resource, NY)

To ensure there was enough work to go around, guilds jealously restricted their membership to local men who were good Christians, had several years of work experience, paid stiff membership fees, and completed a masterpiece. They also favored family connections. Masters' sons enjoyed automatic access to their fathers' guilds, while outsiders were often barred from entering. In the 1720s Parisian guild masters numbered only about thirty-five thousand in a population of five hundred thousand. Most urban men and women worked in non-guild trades as domestic servants, as manual laborers, and as vendors of food, used clothing, and other goods.

The guilds' ability to enforce their rigid barriers varied a great deal across Europe. In England, national regulations superseded guild regulations, sapping their importance. In France, the Crown developed an ambiguous attitude toward guilds, relying on them for taxes and enforcement of quality standards, yet allowing non-guild production to flourish in the countryside in the 1760s, and even in some urban neighborhoods. The Faubourg Saint-Antoine, an eastern suburb of Paris, maintained freedom from guild privileges through an old legal loophole, acting as a haven for the "false-workers" bitterly denounced by masters. The German guilds were perhaps the most powerful in Europe, and the most conservative. Journeymen in German cities, with their masters' support, violently protested the encroachment of non-guild workers.

At the same time that cottage industry began to infringe on the livelihoods of urban artisans, new Enlightenment ideals called into question the very existence of the guild system. Eighteenth-century critics of guilds derided them as outmoded and exclusionary institutions that obstructed technical innovation and progress. Reform minister Anne-Robert-Jacques Turgot's 1776 law that abolished French guilds embodied the sentiments of many enlightened government officials.

> We wish to abolish these arbitrary institutions, which do not allow the poor man to earn his living; which reject a sex whose weakness has given it more needs and fewer resources . . . ; which destroy emulation and industry and nullify the talents of those whose circumstances have excluded them from membership of a corporation; which deprive the state and the arts of all the knowledge brought to them by foreigners; which retard the progress of these arts . . . ; [and which] burden industry with an oppressive tax, which bears heavily on the people.[9]

Although many historians have repeated Turgot's charges, more recent scholarship has emphasized the flexibility and adaptability of the guild system and its vitality through the eighteenth century. Guild masters

> **" No society can surely be flourishing and happy, of which the far greater part of the members are poor and miserable. "**
>
> **—Adam Smith**

adopted new technologies and found creative ways to circumvent impractical rules. Instead of reviling non-guild workers, some masters gave them piecework or even formed partnerships with them. For many merchants and artisans, economic regulation did not hinder commerce but instead fostered the confidence necessary to stimulate it. In an economy with few banks or credit institutions, knowing that a guild had examined a master's qualifications and regularly inspected his shop helped potential buyers trust the goods they purchased.

Contrary to Turgot's statement, some guilds were accessible to women in Paris and a handful of other European cities. Most involved needlework and textiles, occupations that were considered appropriate for women. In 1675 seamstresses gained a new all-female guild in Paris, and soon seamstresses joined tailors' guilds in parts of France, England, and the Netherlands. In the same period new vocational training programs were established for poor girls in many European cities. By the mid-eighteenth century male masters began to hire more female workers, often in defiance of their own guild statutes. One eighteenth-century observer of this phenomenon blamed the decline of the London button trade on women's involvement in it:

economic liberalism
A belief in free trade and competition based on Adam Smith's argument that the invisible hand of free competition would benefit all individuals, rich and poor.

> [Button-making] requires no great Strength, and is follow'd by Women as well as Men, which has reduced the Trade to small Profits, and a small Share of Reputation; the Women are generally Gin-Drinkers, and consequently bad Wives; this makes them poor, and to get something to keep Soul and Body together, work for a mere Trifle, and hawk their Work about to the Trade at an Under-Price. . . . This has reduced the Craft to a very low Ebb.[10]

Whatever the complaints, urban women, like their counterparts in the countryside, were entering the paid labor market in greater numbers. Some attempts were made to redress the discrimination they faced. When Turgot's anti-guild law was repealed and French guilds received new statutes in 1777, the government formally opened all of them to women. But the guilds' abolition in the French Revolution in 1791 makes it impossible to know how this experiment in sexual equality would have fared.

Adam Smith and Economic Liberalism

The impact of new patterns of labor inspired comment and controversy. One of the best-known critics of government regulation of trade or industry was Adam Smith (1723–1790), a professor of philosophy and a leading figure of the Scottish Enlightenment. Smith developed the general idea of freedom of enterprise and established the basis for modern economics in his groundbreaking work, *Inquiry into the Nature and Causes of the Wealth of Nations* (1776). Like Turgot, Smith criticized guilds, or corporations, for their stifling and outmoded restrictions, a critique he extended to all state-approved monopolies and privileged companies. Far preferable was free competition, which would best protect consumers from price gouging and give all citizens a fair and equal right to do what they did best.

In keeping with his deep-seated fear of political oppression and with the "system of natural liberty" that he advocated, Smith argued that government should limit itself to "only three duties": it should provide a defense against foreign invasion, maintain civil order with courts and police protection, and sponsor certain indispensable public works and institutions that could never adequately profit private investors. He believed that the pursuit of self-interest in a competitive market would be sufficient to improve the living conditions of citizens, a view that quickly emerged as the classic argument for **economic liberalism**.

Many artisans welcomed the eighteenth-century economic liberalization that came with Smith, the Enlightenment, and the French Revolution, but some continued to uphold the ideals of the guilds. In parts of Germany guilds persisted until the second half of the nineteenth century. Clandestine journeymen's associations in France also survived into the nineteenth century. Skilled artisans across Europe espoused the values of hand craftsmanship and limited competition in contrast to the proletarianization and loss of skills they endured in mechanized production. Nevertheless, by the middle of the nineteenth century economic deregulation was championed by most European governments and elites.

In the nineteenth and twentieth centuries Smith was often seen as an advocate of unbridled capitalism, but his ideas were considerably more complex. In his own mind, Smith spoke for truth, not for special interests. Unlike many disgruntled merchant capitalists, he applauded the modest rise in real wages of British workers in the eighteenth century and went on to say that "No society can surely be flourishing and happy, of which the far greater part of the members are poor and miserable." Quite realistically, Smith concluded that employers were "always and everywhere in a sort of tacit, but constant and uniform combination, not to raise the wages of labour above their actual rate" and sometimes entered "into particular combinations to sink the wages even below this rate." He also deplored the deadening effects of the division of labor and called for government intervention to raise workers' living standards.[11] Smith's provocative work had a great international impact, going through eight editions in English and being translated into several languages within twenty years. His ideas inspired not only domestic reformers, but also independent merchants around the globe who campaigned against the monopolies of colonial empires and called for free trade.

Building the Global Economy

How did colonial markets boost Europe's economic and social development, and what conflicts and adversity did world trade entail?

In addition to agricultural improvement, population pressure, and growing cottage industry, the expansion of Europe in the eighteenth century was characterized by the increase of world trade. Adam Smith himself declared that "the discovery of America and that of a passage to the East Indies by the Cape of Good Hope, are the two greatest and most important events recorded in the history of mankind."[12] In the eighteenth century Spain and Portugal revitalized their empires and began drawing more wealth from renewed colonial development. Yet once again the countries of northwestern Europe—the Netherlands, France, and above all Great Britain—benefited most.

The Atlantic economy that these countries developed from 1650 to 1790 would prove crucial in the building of a global economy. Great Britain, which was formed in 1707 by the union of England and Scotland into a single kingdom, gradually became the leading maritime power. Thus the British played the critical role in building a fairly unified Atlantic economy that provided remarkable opportunities for them and their colonists. They also competed ruthlessly with France and the Netherlands for trade and territory in Asia.

Mercantilism and Colonial Wars

Britain's commercial leadership in the eighteenth century had its origins in the mercantilism of the seventeenth century (see Chapter 16). Eventually eliciting criticism from Enlightenment thinker Adam Smith and other proponents of free trade in the late eighteenth century, European mercantilism was a system of economic regulations aimed at increasing the power of the state. As practiced by a leading advocate such as Colbert under Louis XIV, mercantilism aimed particularly at creating a favorable balance of foreign trade in order to increase a country's stock of gold. A country's gold holdings served as an all-important treasure chest that could be opened periodically to pay for war in a violent age.

In England the desire to increase both military power and private wealth resulted in the mercantile system of the **Navigation Acts**. Oliver Cromwell established the first of these laws in 1651, and the restored monarchy of Charles II extended them in 1660 and 1663. The acts required that most goods imported from Europe into England and Scotland (Great Britain after 1707) be carried on British-owned ships with British crews or on ships of the country producing the article. Moreover, these laws gave British merchants and shipowners a virtual monopoly on trade with British colonies. The colonists were required to ship their products on British (or American) ships and to buy almost all European goods from Britain. It was believed that these economic regulations would eliminate foreign competition, thereby helping British merchants and workers as well as colonial plantation owners and farmers. It was hoped, too, that the emerging British Empire would develop a shipping industry with a large number of experienced seamen who could serve when necessary in the Royal Navy.

> **Navigation Acts** A series of English laws that controlled the import of goods to Britain and British colonies.

The Navigation Acts were a form of economic warfare. Their initial target was the Dutch, who were far ahead of the English in shipping and foreign trade in the mid-seventeenth century (see Chapter 16). In conjunction with three Anglo-Dutch wars between 1652 and 1674, the Navigation Acts seriously damaged Dutch shipping and commerce. The British seized the thriving Dutch colony of New Amsterdam in 1664 and renamed it New York. By the late seventeenth century the Netherlands was falling behind England in shipping, trade, and colonies. Thereafter France stood clearly as England's most serious rival in the competition for overseas empire. Rich in natural resources, with a population three or four times that of England, and allied with Spain, continental Europe's leading military power, was already building a powerful fleet and a worldwide system of rigidly monopolized colonial trade. Thus from 1701 to 1763 Britain and France were locked in a series of wars to decide, in part, which nation would become the leading maritime power and claim the profits of Europe's overseas expansion (Map 18.2).

The first round was the War of the Spanish Succession (see Chapter 16), which started in 1701 when Louis XIV accepted the Spanish crown willed to his grandson. Besides upsetting the continental balance of power, a union of France and Spain threatened to encircle and destroy the British colonies in North America (see Map 18.2). Defeated by a great coalition of states

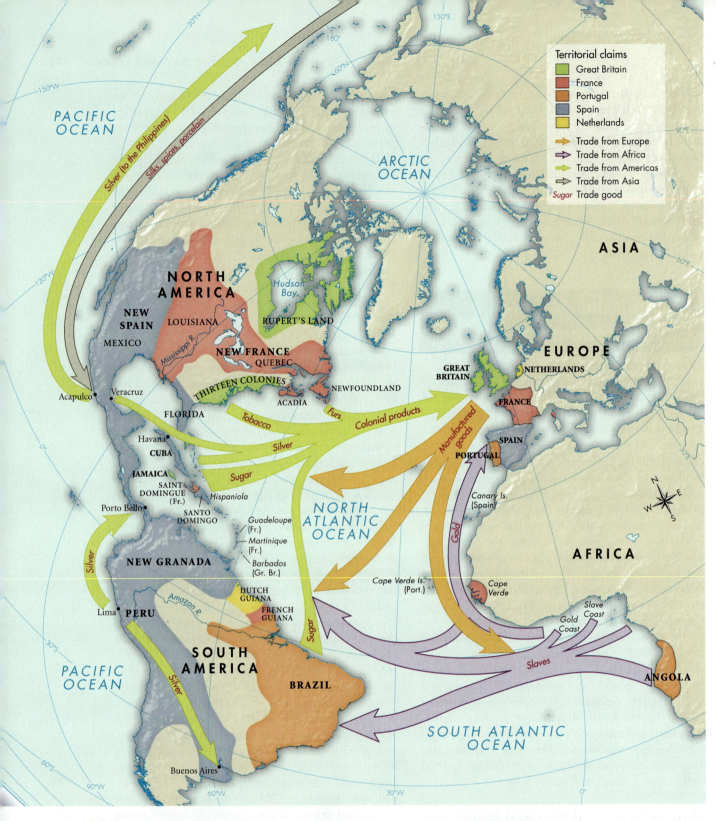

Map 18.2 The Atlantic Economy in 1701 The growth of trade encouraged both economic development and military conflict in the Atlantic basin. Four continents were linked together by the exchange of goods and slaves.

after twelve years of fighting, Louis XIV was forced in the Peace of Utrecht (YOO-trehkt) in 1713 to cede its North American holdings in Newfoundland, Nova Scotia, and the Hudson Bay territory to Britain. Spain was compelled to give Britain control of its West African slave trade—the so-called *asiento* (ah-SYEN-toh)—and to let Britain send one ship of merchandise into the Spanish colonies annually.

Conflict continued among the European powers over both domestic and colonial affairs. The War of the Austrian Succession (1740–1748), which started when Frederick the Great of Prussia seized Silesia from Austria's Maria Theresa (see Chapter 17), gradually became a world war that included Anglo-French conflicts in India and North America. The war ended with no change in the territorial situation in North America. This inconclusive standoff helped set the stage for the Seven Years' War (1756–1763). In central Europe, Austria's Maria Theresa sought to win back Silesia and crush Prussia, thereby re-establishing the Habsburgs' traditional leadership in German affairs. She almost succeeded in her goals, but Prussia survived with its boundaries intact.

Inconclusive in Europe, the Seven Years' War was the decisive round in the Franco-British competition for colonial empire. The fighting began in North America. The population of New France was centered in Quebec and along the St. Lawrence River, but French soldiers and Canadian fur traders had also built forts and trading posts along the Great Lakes, through the Ohio country, and down the Mississippi to New Orleans (Map 18.3). Allied with many Native American tribes, the French built more forts in 1753 in what is now western Pennsylvania to protect their claims. The following year a Virginia force attacked a small group of French soldiers, and soon the war to conquer Canada was on.

Although the inhabitants of New France were greatly outnumbered—Canada counted fifty-five thousand inhabitants, as opposed to 1.2 million in the thirteen English colonies—French and Canadian forces under the experienced marquis de Montcalm fought well and scored major victories until 1758. Then, led by their new chief minister, William Pitt, whose grandfather had made a fortune in India, the British diverted men and money from the war in Europe, using superior sea power to destroy the French fleet and choke off French commerce around the world. In 1759 a combined British naval and land force laid siege to Quebec for four long months, defeating Montcalm's army in a dramatic battle that sealed the fate of France in North America.

British victory on all colonial fronts was ratified in the 1763 **Treaty of Paris**. France lost its remaining possessions on mainland North America. Canada and all French territory east of the Mississippi River passed to Britain, and France ceded Louisiana to Spain as compensation for Spain's loss of Florida to Britain. France also gave up most of its holdings in India, opening the way to British dominance on the subcontinent. By 1763 British naval power, built in large part on the rapid growth of the British shipping industry after the passage of the Navigation Acts, had triumphed decisively: Britain had realized its goal of monopolizing a vast trading and colonial empire.

Eighteenth-Century Colonial Trade

In the eighteenth century, stimulated by trade and empire building, London grew into the West's largest and richest city. (See "Living in the Past: The Remaking of

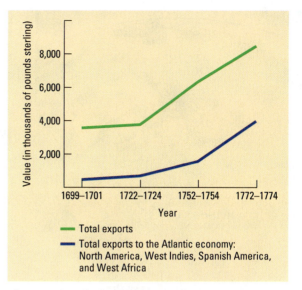

Figure 18.3 **Exports of English Manufactured Goods, 1700–1774** While trade between England and Europe stagnated after 1700, English exports to Africa and the Americas boomed and greatly stimulated English economic development.
(Source: Data from R. Davis, "English Foreign Trade, 1700–1774," *Economic History Review*, 2d ser., 15 [1962]: 302–303.)

London," page 574.) Above all, the rapidly growing and increasingly wealthy agricultural populations of the mainland colonies provided an expanding market for English manufactured goods. This situation was extremely fortunate, for England in the eighteenth century was gradually losing, or only slowly expanding, its sales to many of its traditional European markets.

English exports of manufactured goods to the Atlantic economy came to the rescue. Sales to the mainland colonies of North America and the West Indian sugar islands—with an important assist from West Africa and Latin America—soared from £500,000 to £4.0 million (Figure 18.3). Exports to England's other colonies in Ireland and India also rose substantially in the eighteenth century. English exports also became more balanced and diversified. To America and Africa went large quantities of metal items—axes to frontier settlers, firearms and chains to slave owners. There were also clocks and coaches, buttons and saddles, china and furniture, musical instruments and scientific equipment, and a host of other things. Foreign trade became the bread and butter of some industries; for example, by 1750 half the nails made in England were going to the colonies. Thus, the mercantilist system achieved remarkable success for England in the eighteenth century, and by the 1770s England stood on the threshold of the epoch-making

Treaty of Paris The treaty that ended the Seven Years' War in Europe and the colonies in 1763 and ratified British victory on all colonial fronts.

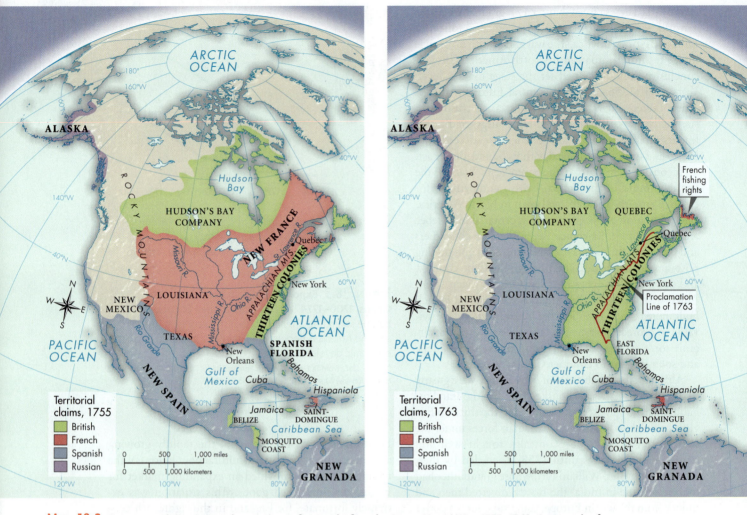

Map 18.3 **European Claims in North America Before and After the Seven Years' War, 1755–1763** As a result of the war, France lost its vast territories. In an effort to avoid costly conflicts with Native Americans living in the newly conquered territory, the British government in 1763 prohibited colonists from settling west of the Appalachian Mountains. One of the few remaining French colonies in the Americas, Saint-Domingue (on the island of Hispaniola) was the most profitable plantation colony in the New World.

industrial changes that would become known as the Industrial Revolution.

Although they lost many possessions to the English, the French still profited enormously from colonial trade. The colonies of Saint-Domingue (modern-day Haiti) and Martinique and Guadeloupe remained in French hands and provided immense fortunes in plantation agriculture and slave trading during the second half of the eighteenth century. By 1789 the population of Saint-Domingue included five hundred thousand slaves whose labor had allowed the colony to become the world's leading producer of coffee and sugar and the most profitable plantation colony in the New World.[13] The wealth generated from colonial trade fostered the confidence of the merchant classes in Paris, Bordeaux, and other large cities, and merchants soon joined other elite groups clamoring for more political power.

The third major player in the Atlantic economy, Spain, also saw its colonial fortunes improve during the eighteenth century. Not only did it gain Louisiana from France in 1763, but its influence expanded westward all the way to northern California through the efforts of Spanish missionaries and ranchers. Its mercantilist goals were boosted by a recovery in silver production, which had dropped significantly in the seventeenth century.

Silver mining also stimulated food production for the mining camps, and wealthy Spanish landowners developed a system of **debt peonage** to keep indigenous workers on their estates. Under this system, which was

debt peonage A form of serfdom that allowed a planter or rancher to keep his workers or slaves in perpetual debt bondage by periodically advancing food, shelter, and a little money.

Atlantic slave trade The forced migration of Africans across the Atlantic for slave labor on plantations and in other industries; the trade reached its peak in the eighteenth century and ultimately involved more than twelve million Africans.

similar to serfdom, a planter or rancher would keep workers in perpetual debt bondage by advancing them food, shelter, and a little money.

The Atlantic Slave Trade

As the volume of transatlantic trade increased, the four continents bordering the ocean were increasingly drawn into an integrated economic system. At the core of this Atlantic world were the misery and profit of the **Atlantic slave trade**. The forced migration of millions of Africans—cruel, unjust, and tragic—was a key element in the Atlantic system and western European economic expansion throughout the eighteenth century. The brutal practice intensified dramatically after 1700 and especially after 1750 with the growth of trade and demand for slave-produced goods like sugar and cotton. According to the most authoritative source, European traders purchased and shipped 6.5 million African slaves across the Atlantic between 1701 and 1800—more than half of the estimated total of 12.5 million Africans transported between 1450 and 1900, of whom 15 percent died in procurement and transit.[14] By the peak decade of the 1780s, shipments averaged about eighty thousand individuals per year in an attempt to satisfy the constantly rising demand for labor power—and also for slave owners' profits—in the Americas.

The rise of plantation agriculture was responsible for the tremendous growth of the slave trade. Among all European colonies, the plantations of Portuguese Brazil received by far the largest number of enslaved Africans over the entire period of the slave trade—45 percent of the total. Another 45 percent were divided among the many

Plantation Zones, ca. 1700

The Atlantic Slave Trade This engraving from 1814 shows traders leading a group of slaves to the West African coast, where they will board ships to cross the Atlantic. Many slaves died en route or arrived greatly weakened and ill. The newspaper advertisement of the sale of a ship's cargo of slaves in Charleston, South Carolina, promises "fine, healthy negroes," testifying to the dangers of the crossing and to the frequency of epidemic diseases like smallpox. (engraving: Bibliothèque de l'Arsenal, Paris/Archives Charmet/The Bridgeman Art Library; advertisement: The Granger Collection, New York)

The Remaking of London

LIVING IN THE PAST

THE IMPERIAL CAPITAL OF LONDON dominated Britain and astonished the visitor. Equal in population to Paris with four hundred thousand inhabitants in 1650, London grew to nine hundred thousand by 1800, while second-place Paris had six hundred thousand. And as London grew, its citizens created a new urban landscape and style of living.

In 1666 the Great Fire of London destroyed about 80 percent of the old, predominately wooden central city. Reconstruction proceeded quickly, with brick structures made mandatory to prevent fires. As London rebuilt and kept growing, noble landowners sought to increase their incomes by setting up residential developments on their estates west of the city. A landowner would lay out a square with streets and building lots and lease the lots to speculative builders who put up fine houses for sale or rent. Soho Square, first laid out in the 1670s and shown here as it appeared in 1731, was fairly typical. The spacious square with its gated park is surrounded by three-story row houses on deep, narrow lots. Set in the country but close to the city, a square like Soho was a kind of elegant village with restrictive building codes that catered to aristocrats, officials, and successful professionals who were served by the artisans and shopkeepers living in side streets. The classy new area, known as the West End, contrasted sharply with the shoddy rentals and makeshift shacks of laborers and sailors in the mushrooming East End, which artists rarely painted. Residential segregation by income level increased substantially in eighteenth-century London and became a key feature of the modern city.

As the suburban villages grew and gradually merged, the West End increasingly attracted the well-to-do from all over England. Rural landowners and provincial notables came for the social season from October to May. The picture at right of Bloomsbury Square in 1787 and the original country mansion of the enterprising noble developer provides a glimpse into this well-born culture.

London before the Great Fire. (Hulton Archive/Getty Images)

Caribbean colonies. The colonies of mainland North America took only 3 percent of slaves arriving from Africa, a little under four hundred thousand, relying mostly on natural growth of the enslaved population.

Eighteenth-century intensification of the slave trade resulted in fundamental changes in its organization. After 1700, as Britain became the undisputed leader in shipping slaves across the Atlantic, European governments and ship captains cut back on fighting among themselves and concentrated on commerce. They generally adopted the shore method of trading, which was less expensive than maintaining fortified trading posts. Under this system, European ships sent boats ashore or invited African dealers to bring traders and slaves out to their ships. This method allowed ships to move easily along the coast from market to market and to depart more quickly for the Americas.

Some African merchants and rulers who controlled exports profited from the greater demand for slaves. With their newfound wealth, some Africans gained access to European and colonial goods, including firearms. But generally such economic returns did not spread very far, and the negative consequences of the expanding slave trade predominated. Wars among African states to obtain salable captives increased, and leaders used slave profits to purchase more arms than textiles and consumer goods. While the populations of Europe and Asia grew substantially in the eighteenth century, the population of Africa stagnated or possibly declined. As one contemporary critic observed:

Soho Square, 1731. (Private Collection/The Stapleton Collection/The Bridgeman Art Library)

Bloomsbury Square, 1787. (HarperCollins Publishers/The Art Archive)

QUESTIONS FOR ANALYSIS
1. Examining the picture shown at left, how would you characterize pre-Fire London?
2. Compare the paintings of Soho and Bloomsbury Squares. How are they complementary? Why did the artist choose to include a milkmaid and her cows in the illustration of Bloomsbury Square?

I do not know if coffee and sugar are essential to the happiness of Europe, but I know that these two products have accounted for the unhappiness of two great regions of the world: America has been depopulated so as to have land on which to plant them; Africa has been depopulated so as to have the people to cultivate them.[15]

Most Europeans did not personally witness the horrors of the slave trade between Africa and the Americas, and until the early part of the eighteenth century, they considered the African slave trade a legitimate business. But as details of the plight of slaves became known, a campaign to abolish slavery developed in Britain. In the late 1780s the abolition campaign grew into a mass movement of public opinion, the first in British history. British women were prominent in this movement, denouncing the immorality of human bondage and stressing the cruel and sadistic treatment of female slaves and slave families. These attacks put the defenders of slavery on the defensive. In 1807 Parliament abolished the British slave trade, although slavery continued in British colonies and the Americas for decades.

Identities and Communities of the Atlantic World

Not only slaves and commodities but also free people and ideas circulated through the eighteenth-century Atlantic world. As contacts among the Atlantic coasts of the Americas, Africa, and Europe became more

Slaves Harvesting Sugar Cane In this 1828 print a long line of hard-working slaves systematically harvests the ripe cane on the island of Antigua, while on the right more slaves load cut cane into wagons for refining at the plantation's central crushing mill. The manager on horseback may be ordering the overseer to quicken the work pace, always brutal and unrelenting at harvest time. Slave labor made high-intensity capitalist production of sugar possible in the Americas. (John Carter Brown Library at Brown University)

> “ A turn of mind peculiar to the planter, occasioned by a physical difference of constitution, climate, customs, and education, tends . . . to repress the remains of his former attachment to his native soil. ”
>
> —European observer

frequent, and as European settlements grew into well-established colonies, new identities and communities emerged.

The term *Creole* referred to people of Spanish ancestry born in the Americas. Wealthy Creoles and their counterparts throughout the Atlantic colonies prided themselves on following European ways of life. In addition to their lavish plantation estates, they maintained townhouses in colonial cities built on the European model, with theaters, central squares, churches, and coffeehouses. They purchased luxury goods made in Europe, and their children were often sent to be educated in the home country. Over time, however, the colonial elite came to feel that their circumstances gave them different interests and characteristics from those of their home population. As one observer explained, "a turn of mind peculiar to the planter, occasioned by a physical difference of constitution, climate, customs, and education, tends . . . to repress the remains of his former attachment to his native soil."[16] Creole traders and planters increasingly resented the regulations and taxes imposed by colonial bureaucrats.

Not all Europeans in the colonies were wealthy. Numerous poor or middling whites worked as clerks, shopkeepers, craftsmen, and plantation managers. Whether rich or poor, however, white Europeans usually made up a small proportion of the population. Since most European migrants were men, much of the population of the Atlantic world descended from unions — forced or through choice — of European men and indigenous or African women (see Chapter 15). Colonial attempts to classify and systematize racial categories greatly influenced developing Enlightenment thought on racial difference (see Chapter 16).

Mixed-race populations sometimes rose to the colonial elite. The Spanish conquistadores often consolidated their power through marriage to the daughters of local rulers, and their descendants were among the most powerful inhabitants of Spanish America. In the Spanish and French Caribbean, as in Brazil, many masters acknowledged and freed their mixed-race children, leading to sizable populations of free people of color. Advantaged by their fathers, some became wealthy land and slave owners in their own right. In the second half of the eighteenth century, the prosperity of some free people of color brought a backlash from the white population of Saint-Domingue in the form of new race laws prohibiting nonwhites from marrying whites and forcing them to adopt distinctive attire. In the British colonies of the Caribbean and the southern mainland, by contrast,

Picturing the Past

Mulatto Painting The caption in the upper left-hand corner of this mid-eighteenth-century painting identifies the family as being composed of a Spanish father and a black mother, whose child is described as "mulato." The painting was number six in a series of sixteen images by the painter Jose de Alcibar, each showing a different racial and ethnic combination. The series belonged to a popular genre in the Spanish Americas known as *castas* paintings, which commonly depicted sixteen different forms of racial mixing. (Attrib. Jose de Alcibar, 6, *De Espanol y Negra, Mulato*, ca. 1760–1770. Denver Art Museum: Collection of Frederick and Jan Mayer. Photography provided by the Denver Art Museum)

ANALYZING THE IMAGE How would you characterize the relations among mother, father, and child as shown in this painting? Does the painter suggest power relations within the family? What attitude does the painter seem to have toward the family?

CONNECTIONS Why do you think such paintings were so popular? Who do you think the audience might have been, and why would viewers be fascinated by such images?

To complete this activity online, go to the Online Study Guide at **bedfordstmartins.com/mckaywest.**

masters tended to leave their mixed-race progeny in slavery, maintaining a stark discrepancy between free whites and enslaved people of color.[17] British colonial law forbade marriage between English men and women and Africans or Native Americans.

The identities inspired by racial and ethnic mixing were equally complex. Colonial elites became "Americanized" by adopting native foods, like chocolate and potatoes, and sought relief from tropical disease in native remedies. Some mixed-race people sought to enter Creole society and obtain its many official and unofficial privileges by passing as white. Where they existed in any number, though, free people of color established their own proud social hierarchies based on wealth, family connections, occupation, and skin color. Olaudah Equiano, who traveled throughout the Atlantic as a slave and later as a free man, was an eloquent spokesman for the mixing of African and European cultures in his own life experience. (See "Individuals in Society: Olaudah Equiano," at right.)

Converting indigenous people to Christianity was a key ambition for all European powers in the New World. Galvanized by the Protestant Reformation and the perceived need to protect and spread Catholicism, Catholic powers actively sponsored missionary efforts. Jesuits, Franciscans, Dominicans, and other religious orders established missions throughout Spanish, Portuguese, and French colonies. Rather than a straightforward imposition of Christianity, conversion entailed a complex process of cultural exchange. Catholic friars were among the first Europeans to seek understanding of native cultures and languages as part of their effort to render Christianity comprehensible to indigenous people. In turn, Christian ideas and practices in the New World took on a distinctive character. For example, a sixteenth-century apparition of the Virgin Mary in Mexico City, known as the Virgin of Guadalupe, became a central icon of Spanish-American Catholicism.

Missionaries' success in the New World varied over time and space. In Central and South America, large-scale conversion forged enduring Catholic cultures in Portuguese and Spanish colonies. For example, it is estimated that missionaries baptized up to 10 million indigenous people in New Spain in the first two decades of Spanish rule.[18] Conversion efforts in North America were less effective due to the scattered nature of settlement and the lesser integration of native people into the colonial community. On the whole, Protestants were less active as missionaries in this period, although some dissenters, like Quakers and Methodists, did seek converts among native people.

The practice of slavery reveals important limitations on efforts to spread Christianity. Slave owners often refused to baptize their slaves in case baptism would confer additional rights upon them. In some areas, particularly among the mostly African-born slaves of the Caribbean, elements of African religious belief and practice endured, often incorporated with Christian traditions.

Restricted from owning land and holding many occupations in Europe, Jews were eager participants in the new Atlantic economy and established a network of mercantile communities along its trade routes. As in the Old World, Jews in European colonies faced discrimination; for example, restrictions existed on the number of slaves they could own in Barbados in the early eighteenth century.[19] Jews were considered to be white Europeans and thus ineligible to be slaves, but they did not enjoy equal status with Christians. The status of Jews adds one more element to the complexity of Atlantic identities.

Trade and Empire in Asia and the Pacific

As the Atlantic economy took shape, Europeans continued to vie for dominance in the Asian trade. Between 1500 and 1600 the Portuguese had become major players in the Indian Ocean trading world, eliminating Venice as Europe's chief supplier of spices and other Asian luxury goods. The Portuguese dominated but did not fundamentally alter the age-old pattern of Indian Ocean trade, which involved merchants from many areas as more or less autonomous players. This situation changed radically with the intervention of the Dutch and then the English (see Chapter 15).

Formed in 1602, the Dutch East India Company had taken control of the Portuguese spice trade in the Indian Ocean, with the port of Batavia (Jakarta) in Java as its center of operations. Within a few decades they had expelled the Portuguese from Ceylon and other East Indian islands. Unlike the Portuguese, the Dutch transformed the Indian Ocean trading world. Whereas East Indian states and peoples maintained independence under the Portuguese, who treated them as autonomous business partners, the Dutch established outright control and reduced them to dependents.

After these successes, the Dutch hold in Asia faltered in the eighteenth century due to the company's failure to diversify to meet changing consumption patterns. Spices continued to compose much of its shipping, despite their declining importance in the European diet, probably due to changing fashions in food and luxury consumption. Fierce competition from its main rival, the English East India Company (established 1600), also severely undercut Dutch trade.

Britain initially struggled for a foothold in Asia. With the Dutch monopolizing the Indian Ocean, the British turned to India, the source of lucrative trade in silks, textiles, and pepper. Throughout the seventeenth century the English East India Company relied on trade concessions from the powerful Mughal emperor, who granted only piecemeal access to the subcontinent. Finally, in

Olaudah Equiano

INDIVIDUALS IN SOCIETY

THE SLAVE TRADE WAS A MASS MIGRATION involving millions of human beings. It was also the sum of individual lives spent partly or entirely in slavery. Although most of the individuals remain hidden to us, Olaudah Equiano (1745–1797) is an important exception. According to his autobiography, Equiano was born in Benin (modern Nigeria) of Ibo ethnicity. His father, one of the village elders (or chieftains), presided over a large household that included "many slaves," prisoners captured in local wars. All people, slave and free, shared in the cultivation of family lands. One day when all the adults were in the fields, two strange men and a woman broke into the family compound, kidnapped the eleven-year-old boy and his sister, tied them up, and dragged them into the woods. Brother and sister were separated, and Olaudah was sold several times to various dealers before reaching the coast. As it took six months to walk there, his home must have been far inland.

The slave ship and the strange appearance of the white crew terrified the boy. Much worse was the long voyage from Benin to Barbados in the Caribbean, as Equiano later recounted. "The stench of the [ship's] hold . . . became absolutely pestilential . . . [and] brought on a sickness among the slaves, of which many died. . . . The shrieks of the women and the groans of the dying rendered the whole a scene of horror almost inconceivable." Placed on deck with the sick and dying, Equiano saw two and then three of his "enchained countrymen" escape somehow through the nettings and jump into the sea, "preferring death to such a life of misery."*

Equiano's new owner, an officer in the Royal Navy, took him to England and saw that the lad received some education. Engaged in bloody action in Europe for almost four years as a captain's boy in the Seven Years' War, Equiano hoped that his loyal service and Christian baptism would help secure his freedom. He also knew that slavery was generally illegal in England. But his master deceived him. Docking in London, the slave owner and his accomplices forced a protesting and heartbroken Equiano onto a ship bound for the Caribbean.

There he was sold to Robert King, a Quaker merchant from Philadelphia who dealt in sugar and rum. Equiano developed his mathematical skills, worked hard to please as a clerk in King's warehouse, and became first mate on one of King's ships. Allowed to trade on the side for his own profit, Equiano amassed capital, repaid King his original purchase price, and received his deed of manumission, authorizing his freedom, at the age of twenty-one. King urged his talented former slave to stay on as a business partner, but Equiano hated the limitations and dangers of black freedom in the colonies — he was almost kidnapped back into slavery while loading a ship in Georgia — and could think only of England. Settling in London, Equiano studied, worked as a hairdresser, and went to sea periodically as a merchant seaman. He developed his ardent Christian faith and became a leading member of London's sizable black community.

Equiano loathed the brutal slavery and the vicious exploitation that he saw in the West Indies and Britain's mainland colonies. A complex and sophisticated man, he also respected the integrity of Robert King and admired British navigational and industrial technologies. He encountered white oppressors and made white friends. He once described himself as "almost an Englishman." In the 1780s he joined with white and black activists in the antislavery campaign and wrote *The Interesting Narrative of the Life of Olaudah Equiano Written by Himself*, a well-documented autobiographical indictment of slavery. Above all, he urged Christians to live by the principles they professed and to treat Africans equally as free human beings and children of God. With the success of his widely read book, he carried his message to large audiences across Britain and Ireland and inspired the growing movement to abolish slavery.

Recently, scholars have unearthed contemporary documents in which Equiano gave an American, rather than African, birthplace.† This discovery has raised controversy about the authenticity of parts of his autobiography; whatever his place of birth, Equiano's account of the Middle Passage was certainly based on discussions with many fellow slaves even if not on his own experience.

QUESTIONS FOR ANALYSIS

1. What aspects of Olaudah Equiano's life as a slave were typical? What aspects were atypical?
2. Describe Equiano's culture and personality. What aspects are most striking? Why?

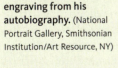

Olaudah Equiano, in an engraving from his autobiography. (National Portrait Gallery, Smithsonian Institution/Art Resource, NY)

*Olaudah Equiano, *The Interesting Narrative of the Life of Olaudah Equiano Written by Himself*, ed. with an introduction by Robert J. Allison (Boston: Bedford Books, 1995), pp. 56–57. Recent scholarship has re-examined Equiano's life and thrown some details of his identity into question.

†Vincent Carretta, "Olaudah Equiano or Gustavus Vassa? New Light on an Eighteenth-Century Question of Identity," *Slavery and Abolition* 20, 3 (December 1999): 96–105.

579

The British in India, ca. 1785 This Indian miniature shows the wife (center) of a British officer attended by many Indian servants. A British merchant (left) awaits her attention. The picture reflects the luxurious lifestyle of the British elite in India, many members of which returned home with colossal fortunes. (Scala/Art Resource, NY)

1716 the Mughals conceded empire-wide trading privileges. To further their economic interests, British East India Company agents increasingly intervened in local affairs and made alliances or waged war against Indian princes.

Britain's great rival for influence in India was France. During the War of the Austrian Succession, British and French forces in India supported opposing rulers in local power struggles. Their rivalry was finally resolved by the Treaty of Paris, which granted all of France's possessions in India to the British with the exception of Pondicherry, an Indian Ocean port city. With the elimination of their rival, British ascendancy in India accelerated. In 1764 company forces defeated the Mughal emperor, leaving him on the throne as a ruler in title only. Robert Clive, a company agent who had led its forces in battle, became the first British governor general of Bengal, in northeast India, with direct authority over the province. By about 1805 the British had overcome vigorous Indian resistance to gain economic and political dominance of much of the subcontinent, and India was lauded as the "jewel" in the British Empire in the nineteenth century.

The late eighteenth century also witnessed the beginning of British settlement of the continent of Australia. The continent was first sighted by Europeans in the early seventeenth century, and thereafter parts of the coast were charted by European ships. Captain James Cook claimed the east coast of Australia for England in 1770, naming it New South Wales. The first colony was established there in the late 1780s, relying on the labor of convicted prisoners forcibly transported from Britain. Settlement of the western portion of the continent followed in the 1790s. The first colonies struggled for survival and, after an initial period of friendly relations, soon aroused the hostility and resistance of aboriginal peoples. Cook himself was killed by islanders in Hawaii in 1779, having charted much of the Pacific Ocean for the first time.

The rising economic and political power of Europeans in this period drew on the connections they established between the Asian and Atlantic trade worlds. An outstanding example is the trade in cowry shells. These seashells, originating in the Maldive Islands in the Indian Ocean, were used as a form of currency in West Africa. European traders obtained them in Asia, packing them alongside porcelains, spices, and silks for the journey home. The cowries were then brought from European ports to the West African coast to be traded for slaves. Indian textiles were also prized in Africa and played a similar role in exchange. Thus, the trade of the Atlantic was inseparable from Asian commerce, and Europeans were increasingly found dominating commerce in both worlds.

India, 1805

LOOKING BACK LOOKING AHEAD

BY THE TURN of the eighteenth century, western Europe had begun to shake off the effects of long decades of famine, disease, warfare, economic depression, and demographic stagnation. The eighteenth century witnessed a breakthrough in agricultural production that, along with improved infrastructure and the retreat of epidemic disease, contributed to a substantial increase in population. One crucial catalyst for agricultural innovation was the scientific revolution, which provided new tools of empirical observation and experimentation. The Enlightenment as well, with its emphasis on progress and public welfare, convinced government officials, scientists, and informed landowners to seek better solutions to old problems. By the end of the century, industry and trade also attracted enlightened commentators who advocated free markets and less government control. Modern political economy is thus one more legacy of the Enlightenment.

As the era of European exploration and conquest gave way to colonial empire-building, the eighteenth century witnessed increased consolidation of global markets and bitter competition among Europeans for the spoils of empire. From its slow inception in the mid-fifteenth century, the African slave trade reached brutal heights in the second half of the eighteenth century. The eighteenth-century Atlantic world thus tied the shores of Europe, the Americas, and Africa in a web of commercial and human exchange that also had strong ties with the Pacific and the Indian Ocean.

The new dynamics of the eighteenth century prepared the way for world-shaking changes. Population growth and rural industry began to undermine long-standing traditions of daily life in western Europe. The transformed families of the industrious revolution developed not only new habits of work, but also a new sense of confidence in their abilities. By the 1770s England was approaching an economic breakthrough as fully significant as the great political upheaval destined to develop shortly in neighboring France. In the same period, the first wave of resistance to European domination rose up in the colonies. The great revolutions of the late eighteenth century would change the world forever.

CHAPTER REVIEW

■ **What important developments led to the agricultural revolution, and how did these changes affect the peasants? (p. 554)**

The agricultural revolution consisted of new techniques of working the land and new crops, which together greatly improved agricultural production. It began in the Low Countries and then England, where farmers drained wetlands to create more farmland, introduced new crops, and intensified crop rotation. Better breeding of horses for farm work and improved seed-sowing methods also increased crop yields. These innovations, inspired in part by the experimentation of the scientific revolution and the reform ideals of the Enlightenment, created new food sources for people and livestock. Along with new techniques came the enclosure of the open fields that had characterized much of European agriculture. Enclosure permitted reform-minded landowners to experiment with new techniques, but it also allowed wealthy landowners to enlarge their own holdings. Thus, increased production came at a high cost to poor farmers, who lost access to common village land that had provided pasture and food and were often forced to sell their small holdings to the rich. The landless poor became wage laborers, a transformation known as proletarianization.

■ **Why did the European population rise dramatically in the eighteenth century? (p. 558)**

The decrease in mortality from famine, disease, and war all contributed to the eighteenth-century population explosion. The agricultural revolution led to increased food production, and better storage and transportation systems meant that more food reached hungry populations. Also, for reasons historians do not yet understand, the recurring curse of bubonic plague disappeared, and improved public health and sanitation generally cut down on other diseases as well. In addition, wars became more gentlemanly, wreaking less havoc on farmlands and resulting in fewer overall deaths. As a result of all these factors, the European population recovered from the stagnation and losses of the seventeenth century to reach unprecedented new levels in the eighteenth century.

■ **How and why did rural industry intensify in the eighteenth century? (p. 560)**

The combination of the enclosure movement and population increases led to growth in the number of people in the countryside with little or no land. Peasant households set up industrial production within their cottages, allocating family members' labor during the slack seasons of agriculture or, in some cases, abandoning farming altogether for a new life of weaving or spinning. Merchant capitalists distributed such work among rural laborers in order to escape the constraints of the urban guilds. Although they profited from the low wages paid to rural workers, merchants complained about their lack of control over them. The spread of cottage industry was one sign of an industrious revolution that helped pave the path of the Industrial Revolution of the late eighteenth century. The labor of women and children was crucial to the spread of cottage industry.

■ **What were guilds, and why did they become controversial in the eighteenth century? (p. 566)**

Guilds were associations of master craftsmen in the towns and cities. Each guild received a monopoly over its trade from the state and was responsible for ensuring high-quality standards among workers. In most cases, guilds were restricted to Christian men, although some female guilds existed, mostly in needlework and textiles. Critics like Adam Smith attacked guilds in the second half of the eighteenth century as part of a larger call for free trade and an end to government economic regulation. With the growth of liberal political and economic views, most of Europe's guilds disappeared by the mid-nineteenth century.

■ **How did colonial markets boost Europe's economic and social development, and what conflicts and adversity did world trade entail? (p. 569)**

During the eighteenth century Europeans continued their overseas expansion, fighting for empire and profit and, in particular, consolidating their hold on the Americas. Britain's Navigation Acts imposed a form of economic warfare, which allowed it to profit mightily from overseas trade and expand its global empire. France and Spain continued to profit from their own colonial trade, but England and its empire proved most successful. The Atlantic slave trade grew enormously as colonial plantations used slaves to produce commodities for trade. Although public outcry at slavery's horrors led Britain to abolish slavery in 1807, the practice continued throughout the European colonies. The movement of people and ideas across the Atlantic in the eighteenth century led to new ethnic identities as inhabitants of the colonies developed customs and attitudes apart from those of their homeland.

Suggested Reading

Allen, Robert, et al., eds. *Living Standards in the Past: New Perspectives on Well-Being in Asia and Europe.* 2004. Offers rich comparative perspectives on population growth and living standards among common people.

Bell, Dean Philip. *Jews in the Early Modern World.* 2008. A broad examination of Jewish life and relations with non-Jews in the early modern period.

Carpenter, Roger M. *The Renewed, the Destroyed, and the Remade: The Three Thought Worlds of the Iroquois and the Huron, 1609–1650.* 2004. Explores the culture and beliefs of two Native American peoples in the period of European colonization.

De Vries, Jan, and Ad van der Woude. *The First Modern Economy: Success, Failure, and Perseverance of the Dutch Economy, 1500–1815*. 1997. Examines the early success of the Dutch economy and the challenges it faced in the eighteenth century.

Epstein, S. R., and Maarten Prak, eds. *Guilds, Innovation and the European Economy, 1400–1800*. 2008. A recent contribution to the debate on European guilds that emphasizes their adaptability and responsiveness to economic change.

Farr, James R. *Artisans in Europe, 1300–1914*. 2000. Provides an overview of guilds and artisanal labor in early modern Europe.

Gullickson, Gary L. *Spinners and Weavers of Auffay: Rural Industry and the Sexual Division of Labor in a French Village, 1750–1850*. 1986. Examines women's labor in cottage industry in northern France.

Harms, Robert W. *The Diligent: A Voyage Through the Worlds of the Slave Trade*. 2002. A deeply moving account of a French slave ship and its victims.

Klein, Herbert S. *The Atlantic Slave Trade*. 1999. An excellent short synthesis on slavery in the Atlantic world.

Liebersohn, Harry. *The Traveler's World: Europe to the Pacific*. 2006. Imaginatively recounts European explorations and imaginations of the Pacific.

Morgan, Jennifer Lyle. *Laboring Women: Reproduction and Gender in New World Slavery*. 2004. Focuses on the role of women's labor in the evolution of slavery in Britain's North American colonies.

Ormrod, David. *The Rise of Commercial Empires: England and the Netherlands in the Age of Mercantilism, 1650–1770*. 2003. Examines the battle for commercial and maritime supremacy in the North Sea.

Overton, Mark. *Agricultural Revolution in England*. 1996. Charts the path of agricultural progress in England.

Porter, Roy. *London: A Social History*. 1994. A sparkling combination of fine scholarship and exciting popular history.

Prak, Maarten, ed. *Early Modern Capitalism: Economic and Social Change in Europe, 1400–1800*. 2001. Collected essays on economic and social developments in early modern Europe.

Rothschild, Emma. *Economic Sentiments: Adam Smith, Condorcet, and the Enlightenment*. 2001. A fascinating reconsideration of Smith and the birth of modern economic thought.

Notes

1. B. H. Slicher van Bath, *The Agrarian History of Western Europe, A.D. 500–1850* (New York: St. Martin's Press, 1963), p. 240.
2. Cited in Paul Mantoux, *The Industrial Revolution in the Eighteenth Century: An Outline of the Beginnings of the Modern Factory System* (1961; Abingdon, U.K.: Routledge, 2005), p. 175.
3. Thomas Salmon, *Modern History: Or the Present State of All Nations* (London, 1730), p. 406.
4. Quoted in I. Pinchbeck, *Women Workers and the Industrial Revolution, 1750–1850* (New York: F. S. Crofts, 1930), p. 113.
5. Richard J. Soderlund, "'Intended as a Terror to the Idle and Profligate': Embezzlement and the Origins of Policing in the Yorkshire Worsted Industry, c. 1750–1777," *Journal of Social History* 31 (Spring 1998): 658.
6. Cited in Maxine Berg, *The Age of Manufactures, 1700–1820: Industry, Innovation, and Work in Britain* (London: Routledge, 1994), p. 124.
7. Jan de Vries, *The Industrious Revolution: Consumer Behavior and the Household Economy, 1650 to the Present* (Cambridge, U.K.: Cambridge University Press, 2008).
8. Jan de Vries, "The Industrial Revolution and the Industrious Revolution," *The Journal of Economic History* 54, 2 (June 1994): 249–270, discusses the industrious revolution of the second half of the twentieth century.
9. S. Pollard and C. Holmes, eds., *Documents of European Economic History*, vol. 1: The Process of Industrialization, 1750–1870 (New York: St. Martin's Press, 1968), p. 53.
10. R. Campbell, *The London Tradesman* (London, 1757), p. 152.
11. R. Heilbroner, *The Essential Adam Smith* (New York: W. W. Norton, 1986), p. 196.
12. Ibid., p. 281.
13. Laurent Dubois and John D. Garrigus, *Slave Revolution in the Caribbean, 1789–1904* (New York: Palgrave, 2006), p. 8.
14. Figures obtained from Voyages: The Trans-Atlantic Slave Trade Database, http://www.slavevoyages.org/tast/assessment/estimates.faces (accessed June 11, 2009).
15. Cited in Thomas Benjamin, *The Atlantic World: Europeans, Africans, Indians and Their Shared History, 1400–1900* (Cambridge, U.K.: Cambridge University Press, 2009), p. 211.
16. Pierre Marie François Paget, *Travels Round the World in the Years 1767, 1768, 1769, 1770, 1771* (London, 1793), vol. 1, p. 262.
17. Orlando Patterson, *Slavery and Social Death* (Cambridge, Mass.: Harvard University Press, 1982), p. 255.
18. Mark A. Noll, *The Old Religion in a New World: The History of North American Christianity* (Grand Rapids, Mich.: Wm. B. Eerdmans, 2002), pp. 28–29.
19. Erik R. Seeman, "Jews in the Early Modern Atlantic: Crossing Boundaries, Keeping Faith," in *The Atlantic in Global History, 1500–2000*, ed. Jorge Cañizares-Esguerra and Erik R. Seeman (Upper Saddle River, N.J.: Pearson Prentice Hall, 2007), p. 43.

Key Terms

agricultural revolution (p. 555)
enclosure (p. 556)
proletarianization (p. 558)
cottage industry (p. 560)
putting-out system (p. 561)
industrious revolution (p. 566)
guild system (p. 566)
economic liberalism (p. 568)
Navigation Acts (p. 569)
Treaty of Paris (p. 571)
debt peonage (p. 572)
Atlantic slave trade (p. 573)

For practice quizzes and other study tools, visit the Online Study Guide at **bedfordstmartins.com/mckaywest**.

For primary sources from this period, see **Sources of Western Society, Second Edition**.

For Web sites, images, and documents related to topics in this chapter, visit Make History at **bedfordstmartins.com/mckaywest**.

19

The Changing Life of the People

1700–1800

The discussion of agriculture and industry in the last chapter showed the common people at work, straining to make ends meet within the larger context of population growth, gradual economic expansion, and ferocious political competition at home and overseas. This chapter shows us how that world of work was embedded in a rich complex of family organization, community practices, everyday experiences, and collective attitudes. As with the economy, traditional habits and practices of daily life changed considerably over the eighteenth century. Change was particularly dramatic in the growing cities of northwestern Europe, where traditional social controls were undermined by the anonymity and increased social interaction of the urban setting.

Historians have intensively studied many aspects of popular life, including marriage patterns and family size, childhood and education, nutrition, health care, and religious worship. Uncovering the life of the common people has been a formidable challenge because they left few written records and regional variations abounded. Yet imaginative research has resulted in major findings and much greater knowledge. It is now possible to follow the common people into their homes, workshops, churches, and taverns and to ask, "What were the everyday experiences of ordinary people, and how did they change over the eighteenth century?" ■

Life in the Eighteenth Century. The huge fresh-food market known as Les Halles was the pulsing heart of eighteenth-century Paris. Here, peddlers offer food and drink to the men and women of the market, many of whom had arrived in the predawn hours to set up their stalls.

CHAPTER PREVIEW

Marriage and the Family
■ What changes occurred in marriage and the family in the course of the eighteenth century?

Children and Education
■ What was life like for children, and how did attitudes toward childhood evolve?

Popular Culture and Consumerism
■ How did increasing literacy and new patterns of consumption affect people's lives?

Religious Authority and Beliefs
■ What were the patterns of popular religion, and how did they interact with the worldview of the educated public and their Enlightenment ideals?

Medical Practice
■ How did the practice of medicine evolve in the eighteenth century?

Marriage and the Family

What changes occurred in marriage and the family in the course of the eighteenth century?

The basic unit of social organization is the family. Within the structure of the family human beings love, mate, and reproduce. It is primarily the family that teaches the child, imparting values and customs that condition an individual's behavior for a lifetime. The family is also an institution woven into the web of history. It evolves and changes, assuming different forms in different times and places. The eighteenth century witnessed such an evolution, as patterns of marriage shifted and individuals adapted and conformed to the new and changing realities of the family unit.

Late Marriage and Nuclear Families

Because census data before the modern period are rare, historians have turned to parish registers of births, deaths, and marriages to uncover details of European family life before the nineteenth century. These registers reveal that the three-generation extended family was a rarity in western and central Europe by 1700. Indeed, the extended family may never have been common in Europe, although it is hard to know about the early Middle Ages because very few records survive. When young European couples married, they normally established their own households and lived apart from their parents, much like the nuclear families (a family group consisting of parents and their children with no other relatives) common in America today. If a three-generation household came

Young Serving Girl Increased migration to urban areas in the eighteenth century contributed to a loosening of traditional morals and soaring illegitimacy rates. Young women who worked as servants or shopgirls could not be supervised as closely as those who lived at home. The themes of seduction, fallen virtue, and familial conflict were popular in eighteenth-century art, such as in this painting by Pietro Longhi (1702–1785). (Cameraphoto Arte, Venice/Art Resource, NY)

into existence, it was usually because a widowed parent moved into the home of a married child.

Most people did not marry young in the seventeenth and eighteenth centuries. The average person married surprisingly late, many years after reaching adulthood and many more after beginning to work. Studies of England and France in the seventeenth and eighteenth centuries show that both men and women married for the first time at an average age of twenty-five to twenty-seven. Ten to 20 percent of men and women never married at all.

Why was marriage delayed? The main reason was that couples normally did not marry until they could start an independent household and support themselves and their future children. Peasants often needed to wait until the father's death to inherit land and marry. In the towns, men and women worked to accumulate enough savings to start a small business and establish their own home. Laws and tradition also stemmed the tide of early marriage. In some areas couples needed the legal permission or tacit approval of the local lord or landowner in order to marry. Poor couples had particular difficulty securing the approval of local officials, who believed that freedom to marry for the lower classes would result in more landless paupers, more abandoned children, and more money for welfare. Village elders often agreed.

The custom of late marriage combined with the nuclear-family household distinguished European society from other areas of the world. It seems likely that the economic advantage early modern Europe acquired relative to other world regions derived in large part from this marriage pattern. Late marriage joined a mature man and a mature woman — two adults who had already accumulated social and economic capital and could transmit self-reliance and skills to the next generation. This marriage pattern also favored a greater degree of equality between husband and wife.

Work Away from Home

Many young people worked within their families until they could start their own households. Boys plowed and wove; girls spun and tended the cows. Many others left home to work elsewhere. In the trades, a lad would enter apprenticeship around age sixteen and finish in his late teens or early twenties. During that time he would not be permitted to marry. An apprentice from a rural village would typically move to a city or town to learn a trade, earning little and working hard. If he was lucky and had connections, he might eventually be admitted to

Chronology

1717	Elementary school attendance mandatory in Prussia
1750–1790	John Wesley preaches revival in England
1750–1850	Illegitimacy explosion
1757	Madame du Coudray, *Manual on the Art of Childbirth*
1762	Jean-Jacques Rousseau advocates more attentive child care in *Emile*
1763	Louis XV orders Jesuits out of France
1774	Elementary school attendance mandatory in Austria
1776	Thomas Paine, *Common Sense*
1796	Jenner performs first smallpox vaccination

a guild and establish his economic independence. Many poor families could not afford apprenticeships for their sons. Without craft skills, these youths drifted from one tough job to another: hired hand for a small farmer, wage laborer on a new road, carrier of water or domestic servant in a nearby town. They were always subject to economic fluctuations and unemployment.

Many adolescent girls also left their families to work. The range of opportunities open to them was more limited, however. Apprenticeship was sometimes available with mistresses in traditionally female occupations like seamstress, linen draper, or midwife. With the growth in production of finished goods for the emerging consumer economy during the eighteenth century (see Chapter 18), demand rose for skilled female labor and, with it, greater opportunities for women. Even male guildsmen hired girls and women, despite guild restrictions.

Service in another family's household was by far the most common job for girls, and even middle-class families often sent their daughters into service. The legions of young servant girls worked hard but had little independence. Sometimes the employer paid the girl's wages directly to her parents. Constantly under the eye of her mistress, the servant girl had many tasks — cleaning, shopping, cooking, child care. Often the work was endless, for there were few laws to limit exploitation. Court records are full of servant girls' complaints of physical mistreatment by their mistresses. There were many like the fifteen-year-old English girl in the early eighteenth century who told the judge that her mistress had not only called her "very opprobrious names, as Bitch, Whore and the like," but also "beat her without provocation and beyond measure."[1]

Male apprentices told similar tales of abuse, but they were far less vulnerable to the sexual harassment and assault that threatened female servants. In theory, domestic service offered a young girl protection and security in a new family. But in practice she was often the easy prey of a lecherous master or his sons or friends. If the girl became pregnant, she could be fired without notice and thrown out in disgrace. Many families could not or would not accept such a girl back into the home. Forced to make their own way, they had no choice but to turn to a harsh life of prostitution and petty thievery (see page 590). "What are we?" exclaimed a bitter Parisian prostitute. "Most of us are unfortunate women, without origins, without education, servants and maids for the most part."[2]

Premarital Sex and Community Controls

Ten years between puberty and marriage was a long time for sexually mature young people to wait. Many unmarried couples satisfied their sexual desires with fondling and petting. Others went further and engaged in premarital intercourse. Those who did so risked pregnancy and the stigma of illegitimate birth. Birth control was not unknown in Europe before the nineteenth century, but it was primitive and unreliable. Condoms, made from sheep intestines, became available in the mid-seventeenth century, replacing uncomfortable earlier versions made from cloth. They were expensive and mainly used by aristocratic libertines and by prostitutes. The most common method of contraception was coitus interruptus—withdrawal by the male before ejaculation. The French, who were early leaders in contraception, were using this method extensively by the end of the eighteenth century.

community controls A pattern of cooperation and common action in a traditional village that sought to uphold the economic, social, and moral stability of the closely knit community.

Did the combination of sexual activity and lack of reliable contraception mean that late marriage in preindustrial Europe went hand in hand with many illegitimate children? For most of western and central Europe until at least 1750, the answer is no. English parish registers seldom listed more than one illegitimate child out of every twenty children baptized. Some French parishes in the seventeenth century had extraordinarily low rates of illegitimacy, with less than 1 percent of babies born out of wedlock. Illegitimate babies were apparently a rarity, at least as far as the official church records are concerned.

Where collective control over sexual behavior among youths failed, community pressure to marry often prevailed. A study of seven representative parishes in seventeenth-century England shows that around 20 percent of children were conceived before the couple was married, while only 2 percent were born out of wedlock.[3] Figures for the French village of Auffay in Normandy in the eighteenth century were remarkably similar. No doubt many of these French and English couples were already engaged, or at least in a committed relationship, before they entered into intimate relations, and pregnancy simply set the marriage date once and for all.

The combination of low rates of illegitimate birth with large numbers of pregnant brides reflects the powerful **community controls** of the traditional village, particularly the open-field village, with its pattern of cooperation and common action. That spirit of common action was rapidly mobilized by the prospect of an unwed mother with an illegitimate child, a condition inevitably viewed as a grave threat to the economic, social, and moral stability of the community. Irate parents, anxious village elders, indignant priests, and stern landlords all combined to pressure young people who wavered about marriage in the face of unexpected pregnancies. In the countryside these controls meant that premarital sex was not entered into lightly and that it was generally limited to those contemplating marriage.

The concerns of the village and the family weighed heavily on couples' lives after marriage as well. Whereas uninvolved individuals today try to stay out of the domestic disputes of their neighbors, the people in peasant communities gave such affairs loud and unfavorable publicity either at the time or during the carnival season (see page 597). Relying on degrading public rituals, the young men of the village would typically gang up on their victim and force him or her to sit astride a donkey facing backward and holding up the donkey's tail. They would parade the overly brutal spouse-beater or the adulterous couple around the village, loudly proclaiming the offenders' misdeeds. The donkey ride and other colorful humiliations ranging from rotten vegetables splattered on the doorstep to obscene and insulting midnight serenades were common punishments throughout much of Europe. They epitomized the community's effort to police personal behavior and maintain moral standards.

New Patterns of Marriage and Illegitimacy

In the second half of the eighteenth century, longstanding patterns of marriage and illegitimacy shifted dramatically. One important change was a rise in young people's ability to choose partners for themselves, rather than following the economic or social interests of their families. This change occurred because social and economic transformations made it harder for families and communities to supervise their behavior. More youths in the countryside worked for their own wages, rather than on a family farm, and their economic autonomy translated into increased freedom of action. Moreover, many youths joined the flood of migrants to the cities, either with their families or in search of work on their own. Urban life provided young people with more social contacts and less social control.

The Village Wedding The spirited merrymaking of a peasant wedding was a popular theme of European artists in the eighteenth century. Given the harsh conditions of life, a wedding provided a treasured moment of feasting, dancing, and revelry. With the future of the village at stake, the celebration of marriage was a public event. (Private Collection/The Bridgeman Art Library)

One less positive outcome of loosening social control was an **illegitimacy explosion**. In Frankfurt, Germany, for example, births out of wedlock rose steadily from about 2 percent of all births in the early 1700s to a peak of about 25 percent around 1850. In Bordeaux, France, 36 percent of all babies were being born out of wedlock by 1840. Small towns and villages experienced less startling climbs, but between 1750 and 1850, increases from a range of 1 to 3 percent initially and then 10 to 20 percent were commonplace. The rise in numbers did not alter social disapproval of single mothers and their offspring, leaving them in desperate circumstances.

Why did the number of illegitimate births skyrocket? One reason was a rise in sexual activity among young people. The loosened social controls that gave young people more choice in marriage also provided them with more opportunities to yield to the attraction of the opposite sex. As in previous generations, many of the young couples who engaged in sexual activity intended to marry. In one medium-size French city in 1787–1788, the great majority of unwed mothers stated that sexual intimacy had followed promises of marriage. Their sisters in rural Normandy reported again and again that they had been "seduced in anticipation of marriage."[4]

The problem for young women who became pregnant was that fewer men followed through on their promises. The second half of the eighteenth century witnessed sharply rising prices for food, homes, and other necessities of life. Wages rose too, but not enough to offset price increases. Many soldiers, day laborers, and male servants were no doubt sincere in their proposals, but their lives were insecure, and they hesitated to take on the burden of a wife and child.

Other men profited from the eased social controls to make false promises. For seduced women, there was little recourse against a deceitful suitor, especially since recrimination meant revealing their sexual activity. In 1788 a female servant in London pressed charges of rape against a man whom she said had forced her into

> **illegitimacy explosion**
> The sharp increase in out-of-wedlock births that occurred in Europe between 1750 and 1850, caused by low wages and the breakdown of community controls.

> "Most of us are unfortunate women, without origins, without education, servants and maids for the most part."
>
> —Parisian prostitute

sexual relations under pretense of courtship. According to her statement in court, after the act:

> He began talking to me, and said, if I would not say any thing about it, he would marry me, he did not go away out of the room, but he quitted me; he said, if I would not mention it to my master or mistress, or any body, he would be married to me, that was the most of his discourse, and then afterwards he went away.

The judge did not believe the charge of rape, perhaps because the woman admitted to subsequent sexual relations apparently without physical coercion. Nevertheless, he told the accused: "The seduction of these young women, under pretense of marrying, is not a crime of much less criminality than that which you have been tried for; and you will some time or another get your neck into the halter, if you do not leave off these practices." For the seduced woman who had been forced to recount each detail of the encounters in a public courtroom, this scolding provided little comfort.[5]

Thus, while some happy couples benefited from matches of love rather than convenience, in many cases the intended marriage did not take place. The romantic, yet practical dreams and aspirations of young people were frustrated by low wages, inequality, and changing economic and social conditions. Old patterns of marriage and family were breaking down. Only in the late nineteenth century would more stable patterns reappear.

Sex on the Margins of Society

Not all sex acts took place between men and women hopeful of marriage. Prostitution offered both single and married men an outlet for sexual desire. After a long period of relative tolerance, prostitutes encountered increasingly harsh and repressive laws in the sixteenth and early seventeenth centuries as officials across Europe began to close licensed brothels and declare prostitution illegal.

Despite this repression, prostitution continued to flourish in the eighteenth century. Most prostitutes were working women who turned to the sex trade when confronted with unemployment or seasonal shortages of work. Such women did not become social pariahs, but retained ties with the communities of laboring poor to which they belonged. If caught by the police, however, they were liable to imprisonment or banishment. Venereal disease was also a constant threat. Prostitutes were often subjected to humiliating police examinations for disease, although medical treatments were at best rudimentary. Farther up the social scale were courtesans whose wealthy protectors provided apartments, servants, fashionable clothing, and cash allowances. After a brilliant, but brief, career, an aging courtesan faced with the loss of her wealthy client could descend once more to streetwalking.

Relations between individuals of the same sex attracted even more condemnation than prostitution, since they defied the Bible's limitation of sex to the purposes of procreation. Male same-sex relations, described as "sodomy" or "buggery," were prohibited by law in most European states, under pain of death. Such laws, however, were enforced unevenly, most strictly in Spain and far less so in the Scandinavian countries and Russia.[6]

Protected by their status, nobles and royals sometimes openly indulged their same-sex passions, which were accepted as long as they married and produced legitimate heirs. It was common knowledge that King James I, sponsor of the first translation of the Bible into English, had male lovers, but such relations did not prevent him from having seven children with his wife, Anne of Denmark. The duchess of Orléans, sister-in-law of French king Louis XIV, repeated rumors in her letters about the homosexual inclinations of King William of England, hero of the Glorious Revolution (see Chapter 16). She was hardly shocked by the news, given the fortune and favor her own husband lavished on his many *mignons*, as they were called.

In the late seventeenth century new homosexual subcultures began to emerge in Paris, Amsterdam, and London, with their own slang, meeting places, and styles of dress. Unlike the relations described above, which involved men who took both wives and male lovers, these groups included men exclusively oriented toward other men. In London they called themselves "mollies," a term originally applied to prostitutes, and some began to wear women's clothing and act in effeminate ways. A new self-identity began to form among homosexual men: a belief that their same-sex desire made them fundamentally different from other men. As a character in one late eighteenth-century fiction explained, he was in "a category of men different from the other, a class Nature has created in order to diminish or minimize propagation."[7]

Same-sex relations existed among women as well, but they attracted less anxiety and condemnation than those among men. Some women were prosecuted for "unnatural" relations; others attempted to escape the narrow confines imposed on them by dressing as men.

Cross-dressing women occasionally snuck into the armed forces, such as Ulrika Elenora Stålhammar, who served as a man in the Swedish army for thirteen years and married a woman. After confessing her transgressions, she was sentenced to a lenient one-month imprisonment.[8] The beginnings of a distinctive lesbian subculture appeared in London at the end of the eighteenth century.

Across the early modern period, traditional tolerance for sexual activities outside of heterosexual marriage — be they sex with prostitutes or same-sex relations among male courtiers — began to fade. This process accelerated in the eighteenth century, as Enlightenment critics attacked court immorality and preached virtue and morality for middle-class men, who should prove their worthiness to take over the reins of power.

Children and Education

What was life like for children, and how did attitudes toward childhood evolve?

On the whole, European women married late, but then began bearing children rapidly. If a woman married before she was thirty, and if both she and her husband lived to fifty, she would most likely give birth to six or more children. Infant mortality was extremely high by modern standards, and many women died in childbirth due to limited medical knowledge and techniques.

For those children who did survive, new Enlightenment ideals in the latter half of the century stressed the importance of parental nurturing. New worldviews also led to an increase in elementary schools throughout Europe, but despite the efforts of enlightened absolutists and religious institutions, formal education played only a modest role in the lives of ordinary children.

Child Care and Nursing

Newborns entered a dangerous world. They were vulnerable to infectious diseases, and many babies died of dehydration brought about by bad bouts of ordinary diarrhea. Of those who survived infancy, many more died in childhood. Even in a rich family, little could be done for an ailing child. Childbirth was also dangerous. Women who bore six children faced a cumulative risk of dying in childbirth of 5 to 10 percent, a thousand times as great as the risk in Europe today.[9] They died from blood loss and shock during delivery and from infections caused by unsanitary conditions. The joy of pregnancy was thus shadowed by fear of loss of the mother or her child. The creation of life in early modern families was always accompanied by suffering and death.

In the countryside, women of the lower classes generally breast-fed their infants for two years or more. Although not a foolproof means of birth control, breast-feeding decreases the likelihood of pregnancy by delaying the resumption of ovulation. By nursing their babies, women limited their fertility and spaced their children two or three years apart. Nursing also saved lives: breast-fed infants received precious immunity-producing substances and were more likely to survive than those who were fed other food.

Women of the aristocracy and upper middle class seldom nursed their own children. The upper-class woman felt that breast-feeding was undignified and interfered with her social responsibilities. Instead, she hired a live-in wet nurse to suckle her child (which usually meant sending the nurse's own infant away to be nursed by someone else). Working women in the cities also relied on wet nurses because they needed to earn a living. Unable to afford live-in wet nurses, they often turned to the cheaper services of women in the countryside. Rural **wet-nursing** was a widespread business in the eighteenth century, conducted within the framework of the putting-out system. The traffic was in babies rather than in yarn or cloth, and two or three years often passed before the wet-nurse worker in the countryside finished her task.

> **wet-nursing** A widespread and flourishing business in the eighteenth century in which women were paid to breast-feed other women's babies.

Wet-nursing was particularly common in northern France. Whereas the trend was toward more maternal nursing in other parts of Europe, wet-nursing grew substantially in Paris and other northern cities over the eighteenth century. Toward the end of the century roughly twenty thousand babies were born in Paris each year. Almost half were placed with rural wet nurses through a government-supervised distribution network; 20 to 25 percent were placed in the homes of Parisian nurses personally selected by their parents; and another 20 to 25 percent were abandoned to foundling hospitals, which would send them to wet nurses in the countryside. The remainder (perhaps 10 percent) were nursed at home by their mothers or live-in nurses.[10]

Reliance on wet nurses contributed to the high levels of infant mortality due to the dangers of travel, the lack of supervision of conditions in wet nurses' homes, and the need to share milk between a wet nurse's own baby and the one or more babies she was hired to feed. A study of parish registers in northern France during the late seventeenth and early eighteenth centuries reveals that 35 percent of babies died before their first birthdays, and another 20 percent before age ten.[11] In England, where more mothers nursed, only some 30 percent of children did not reach their tenth birthdays.

Why did Frenchwomen send their babies to wet-nurses, given these high mortality rates? Historians have offered several explanations, including parental indifference to the babies' survival. The likeliest explanation appears to be a combination of cultural, socioeconomic,

Arrival of the Wet Nurses Wet-nursing was big business in eighteenth-century France, particularly in Paris and the north. Here, rural wet nurses bring their charges back to the city to be reunited with their families after around two years of care. These children were lucky survivors of a system that produced high mortality rates. (Réunion des Musées Nationaux/Art Resource, NY)

and biological factors. Wet-nursing was a centuries-old tradition in France, so families were merely following well-established patterns. Moreover, in this period migration to the cities, high prices, and stagnant wages pushed more women into the workforce, often into jobs outside the home where it was impossible to nurse their own babies. A third factor was that few alternatives to breast milk existed. In an era before germ theory and sterilization, artificial feeding methods were known to be dangerous to the newborn. By turning to wet nurses, mothers who could not nurse sought the safest affordable alternative.

In the second half of the eighteenth century critics mounted a harsh attack against wet-nursing. Enlightenment thinkers proclaimed that wet-nursing was robbing European society of reaching its full potential. They were convinced, incorrectly, that the population was declining (in fact it was rising, but they lacked accurate population data) and blamed this decline on women's failure to nurture their children properly. Some also railed against practices of contraception and masturbation, which they believed were robbing their nations of potential children. Despite these complaints, many women had no choice but to rely on wet nurses until the late-nineteenth-century introduction of sterilized cows' milk and artificial nipples.

Foundlings and Infanticide

The young woman who could not provide for an unwanted child had few choices, especially if she had no prospect of marriage. Abortions were illegal, dangerous, and apparently rare. In desperation, some women, particularly in the countryside, hid unwanted pregnancies, delivered in secret, and smothered their newborn infants. If discovered, infanticide was punishable by death.

Women in cities had more choices to dispose of babies they could not support. Foundling homes (orphanages) first took hold in Italy, Spain, and Portugal in the sixteenth century, spreading to France in 1670 and the rest of Europe in the following decades. In eighteenth-century England the government acted on a petition calling for a foundling hospital "to prevent the frequent murders of poor, miserable infants at birth" and "to suppress the inhuman custom of exposing newborn children to perish in the streets." As new homes were established and old ones expanded, the number of foundlings being cared for surged. By the end of the century European foundling hospitals were admitting annually about one hundred thousand abandoned children, nearly all of them infants. Across Europe, foundling homes emerged as a favorite charity of the rich and powerful. At their best, eighteenth-century foundling homes were a good example of Christian charity and social concern in an age of great poverty and inequality. Yet the foundling home was no panacea. By the 1770s one-third of all babies born in Paris were being immediately abandoned to foundling homes by their mothers. Many were the offspring of single women, the result of the illegitimacy explosion of the second half of the eighteenth century. But fully one-third of all the foundlings were abandoned by married couples too poor to feed another child.[12]

Great numbers of babies entered foundling homes, but few left. Even in the best of these homes, 50 percent of the babies normally died within a year. In the worst, fully 90 percent did not survive.[13] They succumbed to long journeys over rough roads, neglect by their wet nurses, and customary childhood illnesses. So great were the losses that some contemporaries called the foundling hospitals "legalized infanticide."

Attitudes Toward Children

What were the typical circumstances of children's lives? The topic of parental attitudes toward children in the early modern period remains controversial. Some scholars have claimed that parents did not risk forming emotional attachments to young children because of high mortality rates. With a reasonable expectation that a child might die, some scholars believe, parents maintained an attitude of indifference, if not downright negligence.

Contemporaries were well aware of the dangers of childhood and of the high mortality rates. The great eighteenth-century English historian Edward Gibbon (1737–1794) wrote, with some exaggeration, that "the death of a new born child before that of its parents may seem unnatural but it is a strictly probable event, since of any given number the greater part are extinguished before the ninth year, before they possess the faculties of the mind and the body." Gibbon's father named all his boys Edward after himself, hoping that at least one of them would survive to carry his name. His prudence was not misplaced. Edward the future historian and eldest survived. Five brothers and sisters who followed him all died in infancy.

> **The death of a new born child before that of its parents may seem unnatural but it is a strictly probable event, since of any given number the greater part are extinguished before the ninth year, before they possess the faculties of the mind and the body.**
> —Edward Gibbon

Emotional prudence could lead to emotional distance. The French essayist Michel de Montaigne, who lost five of his six daughters in infancy, wrote, "I cannot abide that passion for caressing new-born children, which have neither mental activities nor recognisable bodily shape by which to make themselves loveable and I have never willingly suffered them to be fed in my presence."[14] In contrast to this harsh picture, however, historians have drawn ample evidence from diaries, letters, and family portraits that many parents did cherish their children and suffered greatly when they died. The English poet Ben Jonson wrote movingly in "On My First Son" of the death of his six-year-old son Benjamin, which occurred during a London plague outbreak in 1603:

Farewell, thou child of my right hand, and joy;
My sin was too much hope of thee, loved boy.
Seven years thou wert lent to me, and I thee pay,
Exacted by thy fate, on the just day.

In a society characterized by much violence and brutality, discipline of children was often severe. The axiom "Spare the rod and spoil the child" seems to have been coined in the mid-seventeenth century. Susannah Wesley (1669–1742), mother of John Wesley, the founder of Methodism (see page 607), agreed. According to her, the first task of a parent toward her children was "to conquer the will, and bring them to an obedient temper." She reported that her babies were "taught to fear the rod, and to cry softly; by which means they escaped the abundance of correction they might otherwise have had, and that most odious noise of the crying of children was rarely heard in the house."[15]

The Enlightenment produced an enthusiastic new discourse about childhood and child rearing. Starting around 1760 critics called for greater tenderness toward children and proposed imaginative new teaching methods. In addition to supporting foundling

The First Step of Childhood This tender snapshot of a baby's first steps toward an adoring mother exemplifies new attitudes toward children and raising them ushered in by the Enlightenment. Authors like Jean-Jacques Rousseau encouraged elite mothers like the one pictured here to take a more personal interest in raising their children, instead of leaving them in the hands of indifferent wet nurses and nannies. Many women responded eagerly to this call, and the period saw a more sentimentalized view of childhood and family life. (Erich Lessing/Art Resource, NY)

homes and urging women to nurse their babies, these new voices ridiculed the practice of swaddling babies and using rigid whale-boned corsets to mold children's bones. Instead of dressing children in miniature versions of adult clothing, critics called for loose and comfortable clothing to allow freedom of movement. These voices belonged to the overall Enlightenment celebration of nature and the natural laws that should guide human behavior. For Enlightenment thinkers, the best hopes for creating a new society, untrammeled by the prejudices of the past, lay in a radical reform of child-rearing techniques.

One of the century's most influential works on child rearing was Jean-Jacques Rousseau's *Emile or On Education* (1762), which fervently advocated breast-feeding and natural dress. Rousseau argued that boys' education should include plenty of fresh air and exercise and that they should be taught practical craft skills in addition to book learning. Reacting to what he perceived as the vanity and frivolity of upper-class Parisian women,

Rousseau insisted that girls' education focus on their future domestic responsibilities. For Rousseau, women's "nature" destined them solely for a life of marriage and child rearing. The ideas of Rousseau and other reformers were enthusiastically adopted by elite women, who did not adopt universal nursing but did at least begin to supervise their wet nurses more carefully.

For all his influence, Rousseau also reveals the occasional hypocrisy of Enlightenment thinkers. With regard to the child-rearing techniques he believed would create a better society, Rousseau had extremely high expectations; when it came to the five children he fathered with his common-law wife, however, he abandoned them all in foundling hospitals despite their mother's protests. None are known to have survived. For Rousseau, the idea of creating a natural man was more important than raising real children.

The Spread of Elementary Schools

The availability of education outside the home gradually increased over the early modern period. The wealthy led the way in the sixteenth century with special colleges, often run by Jesuits in Catholic areas. Schools charged specifically with educating children of the common people began to appear in the second half of the seventeenth century. Such schools specialized in teaching six- to twelve-year-old children basic literacy, religion, and perhaps some arithmetic for the boys and needlework for the girls. The number of such schools expanded in the eighteenth century, although they were never sufficient to educate the mass of the population.

Religious faith played an important role in the spread of education. From the middle of the seventeenth century, Presbyterian Scotland was convinced that the path to salvation lay in careful study of the Scriptures, and it established an effective network of parish schools for rich and poor alike. The Church of England and the dissenting congregations—Puritans, Presbyterians, Quakers, and so on—established "charity schools" to instruct poor children. The first proponents of universal education, in Prussia, were inspired by the Protestant idea that every believer should be able to read the Bible and by the new idea of a population capable of effectively serving the state. As early as 1717 Prussia made attendance at elementary schools compulsory for boys and girls, albeit only in areas where schools already existed.[16] More Protestant German states, such as Saxony and Württemberg (VUHR-tuhm-burg), followed suit in the eighteenth century.

Catholic states pursued their own programs of popular education. In the 1660s France began setting up charity schools to teach poor children their catechism and prayers as well as reading and writing. These were run by parish priests or by new teaching orders created for this purpose. One of the most famous orders was Jean-Baptiste de la Salle's Brothers of the Christian Schools. Founded in 1684 and still in existence today, the schools had thirty-five thousand students across France by the 1780s. Enthusiasm for popular education was even greater in the Habsburg empire, inspired by the expansion of schools in rival German states. In 1774 Maria Theresa issued her own compulsory education edict, imposing five hours of school, five days a week, for all children aged six to twelve.[17] Across Europe some elementary education was becoming a reality, and schools were of growing significance in the life of the child.

Popular Culture and Consumerism

How did increasing literacy and new patterns of consumption affect people's lives?

Because of the new efforts in education, basic literacy was growing among the popular classes, whose reading habits centered primarily on religious material, but who also began to incorporate more practical and entertaining literature. In addition to reading, people of all classes enjoyed a range of leisure activities including storytelling, fairs, festivals, and sports.

One of the most important developments in European society in the eighteenth century was the emergence of a fledgling consumer culture. Much of the expansion took place among the upper and upper-middle classes, but a boom in cheap reproductions of luxury items also permitted people of modest means to participate. From food to ribbons and from coal stoves to umbrellas, the material worlds of city dwellers grew richer and more diverse. This "consumer revolution," as it has been called, created new expectations for comfort, hygiene, and self-expression in daily life, thus dramatically changing European life in the eighteenth century.

Popular Literature

The surge in childhood education in the eighteenth century led to a remarkable growth in basic literacy between 1600 and 1800. Whereas in 1600 only one male in six was barely literate in France and Scotland, and one in four in England, by 1800 almost nine out of ten Scottish males, two out of three French males (Map 19.1), and more than half of English males were literate. In all three countries, the bulk of the jump occurred in the eighteenth century. Women were also increasingly literate, although they lagged behind men.

The growth in literacy promoted growth in reading, and historians have carefully examined what the common people read. While the Bible remained the overwhelming favorite, especially in Protestant countries, short pamphlets known as chapbooks were the staple of popular literature. Printed on the cheapest paper, many chapbooks featured Bible stories, prayers, devotions, and the lives of saints and exemplary Christians. This pious literature gave believers moral teachings and a confidence in God that helped them endure the struggles of daily living.

Entertaining, often humorous stories formed a second element of popular literature. Fairy tales, medieval romances, true crime stories, and fantastic adventures were some of the delights that filled the peddler's pack as he approached a village. These tales presented a world of danger and magic, of supernatural powers, fairy godmothers, and evil trolls, that provided a temporary flight from harsh everyday reality. They also contained nuggets of ancient folk wisdom, counseling prudence in a world full of danger and injustice, where wolves dress like grandmothers and eat Little Red Riding Hoods.

Finally, some popular literature was highly practical, dealing with rural crafts, household repairs, useful plants, and similar matters. Much lore was stored in almanacs, where calendars listing secular, religious, and astrological events were mixed with agricultural schedules, arcane facts, and jokes. The almanac was universal, was not controversial, and was highly appreciated even by many in the comfortable classes. In this way, elites still shared some elements of a common culture with the masses.

While it is safe to say that the vast majority of ordinary people—particularly peasants in isolated villages—did not read the great works of the Enlightenment, that does not mean they were immune to the ideas. Urban working people were exposed to new ideas through the rumors and gossip that spread across city streets, workshops, markets, cafés, and taverns. They also had access to cheap pamphlets that helped translate Enlightenment critiques into ordinary language. Servants, who usually came from rural areas and traveled home periodically, were well situated to transmit ideas from educated employers to the village.

Certainly some ordinary people did assimilate Enlightenment ideals. Thomas Paine, author of some of the most influential texts of the American Revolution, was an English corset-maker's son who left school at age twelve and carried on his father's trade before emigrating to the colonies. His 1776 pamphlet *Common Sense* attacked the weight of custom and the evils of govern-

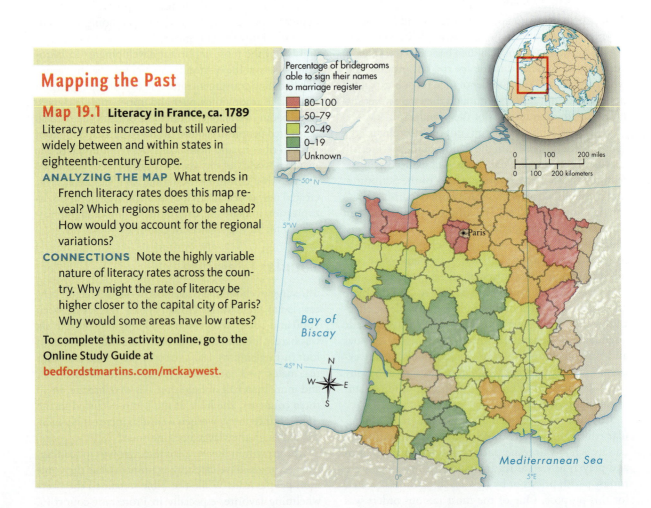

Mapping the Past

Map 19.1 Literacy in France, ca. 1789
Literacy rates increased but still varied widely between and within states in eighteenth-century Europe.

ANALYZING THE MAP What trends in French literacy rates does this map reveal? Which regions seem to be ahead? How would you account for the regional variations?

CONNECTIONS Note the highly variable nature of literacy rates across the country. Why might the rate of literacy be higher closer to the capital city of Paris? Why would some areas have low rates?

To complete this activity online, go to the Online Study Guide at bedfordstmartins.com/mckaywest.

Young Woman Reading a Letter Literacy rates for men and women rose substantially during the eighteenth century. The novel also emerged as a new literary genre in this period. With its focus on emotions, love, and family melodrama, the novel was seen as a particularly feminine genre, and it allowed women writers more access to publication. Writing and reading letters were also associated with women. Some contemporaries worried that women's growing access to reading and writing would excite their imaginations and desires, leading to moral dissolution. (Réunion des Musées Nationaux/Art Resource, NY)

ment against the natural society of men. This text, which sold 120,000 copies in its first months of publication and was soon translated into French and German, is vivid proof of working people's ability to receive Enlightenment ideas. Paine's stirring mastery of them was perhaps unique, but his access to them was certainly not.

Leisure and Recreation

Despite the spread of literacy, the culture of the village remained largely oral rather than written. In the cold, dark winter months, peasant families gathered around the fireplace to talk, sing, tell stories, do craftwork, and keep warm. In some parts of Europe, women would gather together in someone's cottage to chat, sew, spin, and laugh. Sometimes a few young men would be invited so that the daughters (and mothers) could size up potential suitors in a supervised atmosphere. A favorite recreation of men was drinking and talking with buddies in public places, and it was a sorry village that had no tavern. In addition to old favorites such as beer and wine, the common people turned with gusto to cheap and potent hard liquor, which fell in price because of improved techniques for distilling grain in the eighteenth century.

Towns and cities offered a wider range of amusements, including pleasure gardens, theaters, and lending libraries. Urban fairs featured prepared foods, acrobats, freak shows, and conjuring acts. Leisure activities were another form of consumption marked by growing commercialization. For example, commercial, profit-oriented spectator sports emerged in this period, such as horse races, boxing matches, and bullfights. Modern sports heroes, such as brain-bashing heavyweight champions and haughty bull-fighting matadors, made their appearance on the historical scene.

Blood sports, such as bull-baiting and cockfighting, also remained popular with the masses. In bull-baiting, the bull, usually staked on a chain in the courtyard of an inn, was attacked by ferocious dogs for the amusement of the innkeeper's clients. Eventually the maimed and tortured animal was slaughtered by a butcher and sold as meat. In cockfighting, two roosters, carefully trained by their owners and armed with razor-sharp steel spurs, slashed and clawed each other in a small ring until the victor won—and the loser died. An added attraction of cockfighting was that the screaming spectators could bet on the lightning-fast combat and its uncertain outcome.

Popular recreation merged with religious celebration in a variety of festivals and processions throughout the year. The most striking display of these religiously inspired events was **carnival**, a time of reveling and excess in Catholic Europe, especially in Mediterranean countries. Carnival preceded Lent—the forty days of fasting and penitence before Easter—and for a few exceptional days in February or March, a wild

---

blood sports Popular with the eighteenth-century European masses, events such as bull-baiting and cockfighting that involved inflicting violence and bloodshed on animals.

carnival The few days of revelry in Catholic countries that preceded Lent and that included drinking, masquerading, dancing, and rowdy spectacles that turned the established order upside down.

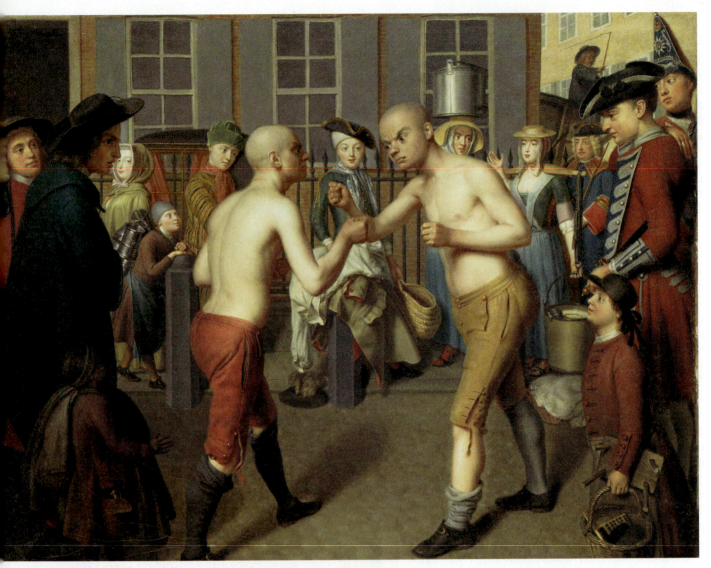

A Boxing Match The eighteenth century witnessed a rise in commercial sporting events and other leisure activities. Here two men spar in a boxing match staged in London for the entertainment of the gathered crowd. The popularity of boxing rose among wealthy spectators in the eighteenth century as bear-baiting and bull-baiting were increasingly condemned as excessively brutal. In the early years, female boxers were as popular as men. (Bildarchiv Preussischer Kulturbesitz/Art Resource, NY)

release of drinking, masquerading, and dancing reigned. Moreover, a combination of plays, processions, and raucous spectacles turned the established order upside down. Peasants dressed as nobles and men as women, and rich masters waited on their servants at the table. This annual holiday gave people a much appreciated chance to release their pent-up frustrations and aggressions before life returned to the usual pattern of hierarchy and hard work.

In trying to place the vibrant popular culture of the common people in broad perspective, historians have stressed the growing criticism levied against it by the educated elites in the second half of the eighteenth century. These elites, which had previously shared the popular enthusiasm for religious festivals, carnival, drinking in taverns, blood sports, and the like, now tended to see superstition, sin, disorder, and vulgarity.[18] The resulting attack on popular culture, which was tied to the clergy's efforts to eliminate paganism and superstition, was intensified as an educated public embraced the critical worldview of the Enlightenment.

New Foods and Appetites

At the beginning of the eighteenth century, ordinary men and women depended on grain as fully as they had in the past. Bread was quite literally the staff of life. Peasants in the Beauvais region of France ate two pounds of bread a day, washing it down with water, wine, or beer. Their dark bread was made from roughly ground wheat and rye — the standard flour of the common people. Even peasants normally needed to buy some grain for food, and, in full accord with landless laborers and urban workers, they believed in the moral economy and the **just price**. That is, they believed that prices should be "fair," protecting both consumers and producers, and that just prices should be imposed by government decree if necessary. When prices rose above this level, they often took action in the form of bread riots (see Chapter 16).

The rural poor also ate a fair quantity of vegetables. Peas and beans were probably the most common. Grown as field crops in much of Europe since the Middle Ages, they were eaten fresh in late spring and summer. Dried, they became the basic ingredients in the soups and stews of the long winter months. In most regions other vegetables appeared on the tables of the poor in season, primarily cabbages, carrots, and wild greens. Fruit was mostly limited to the summer months. Too precious to drink, milk was used to make cheese and butter, which peasants sold in the market to earn cash for taxes and land rents.

The common people of Europe ate less meat in 1700 than in 1500 because their general standard of living had declined and meat was more expensive. Moreover, harsh laws in most European countries reserved the right to hunt and eat game, such as rabbits, deer, and partridges, to nobles and large landowners. Few laws were more bitterly resented — or more frequently broken — by ordinary people than those governing hunting.

The diet of small traders and artisans — the people of the towns and cities — was less monotonous than that of the peasantry. Bustling markets provided a substantial variety of meats, vegetables, and fruits, although bread and beans still formed the bulk of such families' diets. Not surprisingly, the diet of the rich was quite different from that of the poor. The upper classes were rapacious carnivores, and a truly elegant dinner consisted of an abundance of rich meat and fish dishes laced with piquant sauces and complemented with sweets, cheeses, and nuts of all kinds. During such dinners, it was common to spend five or more hours at table, eating and drinking and enjoying the witty banter of polite society.

Patterns of food consumption changed markedly as the century progressed. Because of a growth of market gardening, a greater variety of vegetables appeared in towns and cities. This was particularly the case in the Low Countries and England, which pioneered new methods of farming. Introduced into Europe from the Americas — along with corn, squash, tomatoes, and many other useful plants — the humble potato provided an excellent new food source. Containing a good supply of carbohydrates, calories, and vitamins A and C, the potato offset the lack of vitamins from unavailable green vegetables in the poor person's winter and early-spring diet, and it provided a much higher caloric yield

> **just price** The idea that prices should be fair, protecting both consumers and producers, and that they should be imposed by government decree if necessary.

Chocolate Drinking These Spanish tiles from 1710 illustrates the new practice of preparing and drinking hot chocolate. Originating in the New World, chocolate was one of the many new foods imported to Europe in the wake of the voyages of discovery. The first Spanish chocolate mills opened in the mid-seventeenth century, and consumption of chocolate rapidly increased. The inclusion of this tile in the decoration of a nobleman's house testifies to public interest in the new drink. (Courtesy, Museu de Ceramica. Photo: Guillem Fernandez-Huerta)

Rose Bertin, "Minister of Fashion"

INDIVIDUALS IN SOCIETY

ONE DAY IN 1779, AS THE FRENCH ROYAL FAMILY RODE in a carriage through the streets of Paris, Queen Marie-Antoinette noticed her fashion merchant, Rose Bertin, observing the royal procession. "Ah! there is mademoiselle Bertin," the queen exclaimed, waving her hand. Bertin responded with a curtsey. The king then stood and greeted Bertin, followed by the royal family and their entourage.* The incident shocked the public, for no common merchant had ever received such homage from royalty.

Bertin had come a long way from her humble beginnings. Born in 1747 to a poor family in northern France, she moved to Paris in the 1760s to work as a shop assistant. Bertin eventually opened her own boutique on the fashionable rue Saint-Honoré. In 1775 Bertin received the highest honor of her profession when she was selected by Marie-Antoinette as one of her official purveyors.

Based on the queen's patronage, and riding the wave of the new consumer revolution, Bertin became one of the most successful entrepreneurs in Europe. Bertin established not only a large clientele, but also a reputation for arrogance. She refused to work for non-noble customers, claiming that the orders of the queen and her court claimed all her attention. She astounded courtiers by referring to her "work" with the queen, as though the two were collaborators rather than absolute monarch and lowly subject. Bertin's close relationship with Marie Antoinette and the fortune the queen spent on her wardrobe hurt the royal family's image. One journalist derided Bertin as a "minister of fashion," whose influence outstripped that of all the others in royal government.

In January 1787 rumors spread through Paris that Bertin had filed for bankruptcy with debts of 2 to 3 million livres (a garment worker's annual salary was around 200 livres). Despite her notoriously high prices and rich clients, this news did not shock Parisians, because the nobility's reluctance to pay its debts was equally well-known. Bertin somehow held on to her business. Some said she had spread the bankruptcy rumors herself to shame the court into paying her bills.

Bertin remained loyal to the Crown during the tumult of the French Revolution and sent dresses to the queen even after the arrest of the royal family. Fearing for her life, she left France for Germany in 1792 and continued to ply her profession in exile. She returned to France in 1800 and died in 1813, one year before the restoration of the Bourbon monarchy might have renewed her acclaim.†

Rose Bertin scandalized public opinion with her self-aggrandizement and ambition, yet history was on her side. She was the first celebrity fashion stylist and one of the first self-made career women to rise from obscurity to fame and fortune based on her talent, taste, and hard work. Her legacy remains in the exalted status of today's top fashion designers and in the dreams of small-town girls to make it in the big city.

This portrait of Rose Bertin was painted at the height of her popularity in 1780. (Jean-Francois Janinet, French, 1752–1814, *Mademoiselle Bertin*, n.d., engraving on paper, 155 x 135 mm (image/plate); 120 x 105 mm (primary support); 280 x 215 mm (secondary support), Celia Culver Gilbert Memorial Collection, 1924.1309, The Art Institute of Chicago. Photography © The Art Institute of Chicago)

QUESTIONS FOR ANALYSIS

1. Why was the relationship between Queen Marie Antoinette and Rose Bertin so troubling to public opinion? Why would relations between a queen and a fashion merchant have political implications?
2. Why would someone who sold fashionable clothing and accessories rise to such a prominent position in business and society? What makes fashion so important in the social world?

*Mémoires secrets pour servir à l'histoire de la république des lettres en France, vol. 13, 299, 5 mars 1779 (London: John Adamson, 1785).

†On Rose Bertin, see Clare Haru Crowston, "The Queen and Her 'Minister of Fashion': Gender, Credit and Politics in Pre-Revolutionary France," *Gender and History* 14, 1 (April 2002): 92–116.

than grain for a given piece of land. After initial resistance, the potato became an important dietary supplement in much of Europe by the end of the century. In the course of the eighteenth century the large towns and cities of maritime Europe also began to receive semitropical fruits, such as oranges and lemons, from Portugal and the West Indies, but they remained expensive.

The most remarkable dietary change in the eighteenth century was in the consumption of sugar and tea. No other commodities grew so quickly in popularity. Previously expensive and rare luxury items, they became dietary staples for people of all social classes. This was possible because of the steady drop in prices created by the expansion of colonial slave labor in the New World. Other colonial goods also became important items of daily consumption in this period, including coffee, tobacco, and chocolate.

Why were colonial products so popular? Part of the motivation for consuming these products was a desire to emulate the luxurious lifestyles of the elite. Having seen pictures of or read about the fine lady's habit of "tea time" or the gentleman's appreciation for a pipe, common Europeans sought to experience these pleasures for themselves. Moreover, the quickened pace of work in the eighteenth century created new needs for stimulants among working people. (See "Listening to the Past: Louis-Sébastien Mercier, a Day in the Life of Paris," page 604.) Whereas the gentry took tea as a leisurely and genteel ritual, the lower classes usually drank tea at work to fight monotony or fatigue. With the widespread adoption of these products (which turned out to be mildly to extremely addictive), working people in Europe became increasingly dependent on faraway colonial economies and slave labor. Their understanding of daily necessities and how to procure those necessities shifted definitively, linking them to global trade networks beyond their ability to shape or control.

Toward a Consumer Society

Along with foodstuffs, all manner of other goods increased in variety and number in the eighteenth century. This proliferation led to a growth in consumption and new attitudes toward consumer goods so wide-ranging that some historians have referred to an eighteenth-century **consumer revolution**.[19] The result of this revolution was the birth of a new type of society in which people derived their self-identity as much from their consuming practices as from their working lives and place in the production process. As people were provided the opportunity to pick and choose among a new variety of consumer goods, new notions of individuality and self-expression developed. A shopgirl could stand out from her peers by her choice of a striped jacket, a colored parasol, or simply a new ribbon for her hair. The full emergence of a consumer society did not take place until much later, but its roots lie in the eighteenth century.

Increased demand for consumer goods was not merely an innate response to increased supply. Eighteenth-century merchants cleverly pioneered new techniques to incite demand: they initiated marketing campaigns, opened fancy boutiques with large windows, and advertised the patronage of royal princes and princesses. By diversifying their product lines and greatly accelerating the turnover of styles, they seized the reins of fashion from the courtiers who had earlier controlled it. Instead of setting new styles, duchesses and marquises now bowed to the dictates of fashion merchants. (See "Individuals in Society: Rose Bertin, 'Minister of Fashion,'" at left.) Fashion also extended beyond court circles to touch many more items and social groups.

Clothing was one of the chief indicators of the growth of consumerism. Shrewd entrepreneurs made fashionable clothing seem more desirable, while legions of women entering the textile and needle trades made it ever cheaper. As a result, eighteenth-century western Europe witnessed a dramatic rise in the consumption of clothing, particularly in large cities. One historian has documented an enormous growth in the size and value of Parisians' wardrobes from 1700 to 1789, as well as a new level of diversity in garments and accessories, colors, and fabrics.[20] Colonial economies again played an important role lowering the cost of materials, such as cotton and vegetable dyes, largely due to the unpaid toil of enslaved Africans. Cheaper copies of elite styles made it possible for working people to aspire to follow fashion for the first time. Elite onlookers were bemused by the sight of lower-class people in fashionable dress. In 1784 Mrs. Fanny Cradock described encountering her milkman during an evening stroll "dressed in a fashionable suit, with an embroidered waistcoat, silk knee-breeches and lace cuffs."[21]

Mrs. Cradock's milkman notwithstanding, the spread of fashion was primarily a female phenomenon. Parisian women significantly out-consumed men, acquiring larger and more expensive wardrobes than those of their husbands, brothers, and fathers. This was true across the social spectrum; in ribbons, shoes, gloves, and lace, European working women reaped in the consumer revolution what they had sown in the industrious revolution (see Chapter 18). There were also new gender distinctions in dress. Previously, noblemen vied with noblewomen in the magnificence and ostentation of their apparel; by the end of the eighteenth century men had renounced brilliant colors and voluptuous

consumer revolution The wide-ranging growth in consumption and new attitudes toward consumer goods that emerged in the cities of northwestern Europe in the second half of the eighteenth century.

Picturing the Past

The Fashion Merchant Well-to-do women spent their mornings preparing their toilettes and receiving visits from close friends and purveyors of various goods and services. In this 1746 painting by François Boucher, a leisured lady has just been coiffed by her hairdresser. Wearing the cape she donned to protect her clothing from the hair powder, she receives a fashion merchant, who displays an array of ribbons and other baubles. (Photos12.com—ARJ)

ANALYZING THE IMAGE In this painting, which woman is the fashion merchant and which is her client? What are they doing at the moment the picture is painted? How would you characterize the relationship between the two women in this painting?

CONNECTIONS In what ways does the fashion merchant's attire provide evidence of the consumer revolution of the eighteenth century? Compare this image to the painting of the serving girl (page 586). What contrasting images of the working woman do these two images present?

To complete this activity online, go to the Online Study Guide at **bedfordstmartins.com/mckaywest.**

---

fabrics to don early versions of the plain dark suit that remains standard male formal wear in the West. This was one more aspect of the increasingly rigid differences drawn between appropriate male and female behavior.

Changes in outward appearances were reflected in inner spaces as new attitudes about privacy and intimate life also emerged. Historians have used notaries' after-death inventories to peer into ordinary people's homes. In 1700 the cramped home of a modest family consisted of a few rooms, each of which had multiple functions. The same room was used for sleeping, receiving friends, and working. In the eighteenth century rents rose sharply, making it impossible to gain more space, but families began attributing specific functions to specific rooms. They also began to erect inner barriers within the home to provide small niches in which individuals could seek privacy.

New levels of comfort and convenience accompanied this trend toward more individualized ways of life. In 1700 a meal might be served in a common dish, with each person dipping his or her spoon into the pot. By the end of the eighteenth century even humble households contained a much greater variety of cutlery and dishes, making it possible for each person to eat from his or her own plate. More books and prints, which also proliferated at lower prices, decorated the shelves and walls. Improvements in glass-making provided more transparent

The Consumer Revolution From the mid-eighteenth century on, the cities of western Europe witnessed a new proliferation of consumer goods. Items once limited to the wealthy few — such as fans (lower right), watches, snuffboxes, umbrellas, ornamental containers (right), and teapots — were now reproduced in cheaper versions for middling and ordinary people. The fashion for wide hoopskirts was so popular that the armrests on the chairs of the day, known as Louis XV chairs (left), were specially designed to accommodate them. (fan: Scala/White Images/Art Resource, NY; jar: Victoria & Albert Museum, London/The Bridgeman Art Library; chair: Louvre/Réunion des Musées Nationaux/Art Resource, NY)

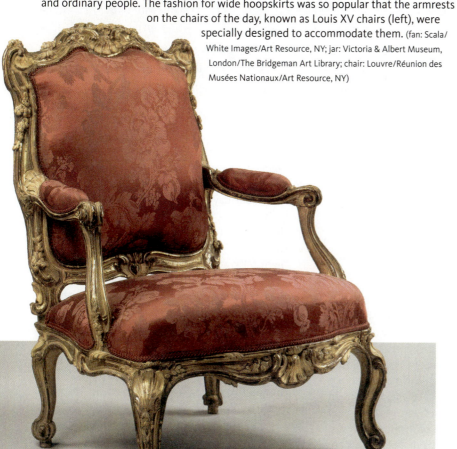

glass, which allowed daylight to penetrate into gloomy rooms. Cold and smoky hearths were increasingly replaced by more efficient and cleaner coal stoves, which also eliminated the backache of cooking over an open fire. Rooms were warmer, better lit, more comfortable, and more personalized.

The scope of the new consumer economy should not be exaggerated. These developments were concentrated in large cities in northwestern Europe and in the colonial cities of North America. Even in these centers the elite benefited the most from new modes of life. This was not yet the society of mass consumption that emerged toward the end of the nineteenth century with the full expansion of the Industrial Revolution. The eighteenth century did, however, lay the foundations for one of the most distinctive features of modern Western life: societies based on the consumption of goods and services obtained through the market in which individuals form their identities and self-worth through the goods they consume.

Louis-Sébastien Mercier, a Day in the Life of Paris

LISTENING TO THE PAST

Louis-Sébastien Mercier (1740–1814) was the best chronicler of everyday life in eighteenth-century Paris. His masterpiece was the Tableau de Paris (1781–1788), a multivolume work composed of 1,049 chapters that covered subjects ranging from convents to cafés, bankruptcy to booksellers, the latest fashions to royal laws. As this excerpt demonstrates, he aimed to convey the infinite diversity of people, places, and things he saw around him, and in so doing he left future generations a precious record of the changing dynamics of Parisian society in the second half of the eighteenth century.

Mercier's family belonged to the respectable artisan classes. This middling position ideally suited Mercier for observing the extremes of wealth and poverty around him. Although these volumes contain many wonderful glimpses of daily life, they should not be taken for an objective account. Mercier brought his own moral and political sensibilities, influenced by Jean-Jacques Rousseau, to the task.

Chapter 39: How the Day Goes

❝ It is curious to see how, amid what seems perpetual life and movement, certain hours keep their own characteristics, whether of bustle or of leisure. Every round of the clock-hand sets another scene in motion, each different from the last, though all about equal in length. Seven o'clock in the morning sees all the gardeners, mounted on their nags and with their baskets empty, heading back out of town again. No carriages are about, and not a presentable soul, except a few neat clerks hurrying to their offices. Nine o'clock sets all the barbers in motion, covered from head to foot with flour — hence their soubriquet of "whitings"* — wig in one hand, tongs in the other. Waiters from the lemonade-shops are busy with trays of coffee and rolls, breakfast for those who live in furnished rooms.... An hour later the Law comes into action; a black cloud of legal practitioners and hangers-on descend upon the Châtelet,† and the other courts; a procession of wigs and gowns and briefbags, with plaintiffs and defendants at their heels. Midday is the stockbrokers' hour, and the idlers'; the former hurry off to the Exchange, the latter to the Palais-Royal.‡ The Saint-Honoré§ quarter, where all the financiers live, is at its busiest now, its streets are crowded with the customers and clients of the great.

At two o'clock those who have invitations to dine set out, dressed in their best, powdered, adjusted, and walking on tiptoe not to soil their stockings. All the cabs are engaged, not one is to be found on the rank; there is a good deal of competition for these vehicles, and you may see two would-be passengers jumping into a cab together from different sides, and furiously disputing which was first....

Three o'clock and the streets are not so full; everyone is at dinner; there is a momentary calm, soon to be broken, for at five fifteen the din is as though the gates of hell were opened, the streets are impassable with traffic going all ways at once, towards the playhouses or the public gardens. Cafés are at their busiest.

Towards seven the din dies down, everywhere and all at once. You can hear the cab-horses' hoofs pawing the stones as they wait — in vain. It is as though the whole town were gagged and bound, suddenly, by an invisible hand. This is the most dangerous time of the whole day for thieves and such, especially towards autumn when the days begin to draw in; for the watch is not yet about, and violence takes its opportunity.

Night falls; and, while scene-shifters set to work at the play-houses, swarms of other workmen, carpenters, masons and the like, make their way towards the poorer quarters. They leave white footprints from the plaster on their shoes, a trail that any eye can follow. They are off home, and to bed, at the hour which finds elegant ladies sitting down to their dressing-tables to prepare for the business of the night.

At nine this begins; they all set off for the play. Houses tremble as the coaches rattle by, but soon the noise ceases; all the fine ladies are making their evening visits, short ones, before supper. Now the prostitutes begin their night parade, breasts uncovered, heads tossing, colour high on their cheeks, and eyes as bold as their hands. These creatures, careless of the light from shop-windows and street lamps, follow and accost you, trailing through the mud in their silk stockings and low shoes, with words and gestures well matched for obscenity....

By eleven, renewed silence. People are at supper, private people, that is; for the cafés begin at this hour to turn out their patrons, and to send the various idlers and workless and poets back to their garrets for the night. A few prostitutes still linger, but they have to use more circumspection, for the watch is about, patrolling the streets, and this is the hour when they "gather 'em in"; that is the traditional expression.

A quarter after midnight, a few carriages make their way home, taking the non–card players back to bed. These lend the town a sort of transitory life; the tradesman wakes out of his first sleep at the sound of them, and turns to his wife, by no means unwilling. More than one young Parisian must owe his existence to this sudden passing rattle of wheels....

---

* Small fish typically rolled in flour and fried.

† The main criminal court of Paris.

‡ A garden surrounded by arcades with shops and cafés.

§ A fashionable quarter for the wealthy.

In this Parisian street scene, a milk seller doubles as a provider of news, reading a hand-printed news sheet to a small gathering. Gossip, rumor, and formal or informal newspapers, like the one pictured here, ensured that information traversed the city at astonishing speeds. (Musée de la Ville de Paris, Musée Carnavalet, Paris/Lauros/Giraudon/The Bridgeman Art Library)

At one in the morning six thousand peasants arrive, bringing the town's provision of vegetables and fruits and flowers, and make straight for the Halles**; . . . As for the market itself, it never sleeps. . . . Perpetual noise, perpetual motion, the curtain never rings down on the enormous stage; first come the fishmongers, and after these the egg-dealers, and after these the retail buyers; for the Halles keep all the other markets of Paris going; they are the warehouses whence these draw their supplies. The food of the whole city is shifted and sorted in high-piled baskets; you may see eggs, pyramids of eggs, moved here and there, up steps and down, in and out of the throngs, miraculous; not one is ever broken. . . .

This impenetrable din contrasts oddly with the sleeping streets, for at that hour none but thieves and poets are awake.

Twice a week, at six, those distributors of the staff of life, the bakers of Gonesse,†† bring in an enormous quantity of loaves to the town, and may take none back through the barriers. And at this same hour workmen take up their tools, and trudge off to their day's labour. Coffee with milk is, unbelievably, the favoured drink among these stalwarts nowadays. . . .

So coffee-drinking has become a habit, and one so deep-rooted that the working classes will start the day on nothing else. It is not costly, and has more flavour to it, and more nourishment too, than anything else they can afford to drink; so they consume immense quantities, and say that if a man can only have coffee for breakfast it will keep him going till nightfall.

Source: Excerpt from *Panorama of Paris: Selections from "Le Tableau de Paris,"* by Louis Sébastien Mercier, based on the translation by Helen Simpson, edited with a new preface and translations by Jeremy D. Popkin. Copyright © 1999 The Pennsylvania State University. Reprinted by permission of Penn State Press.

QUESTIONS FOR ANALYSIS

1. What different social groups does Mercier describe? Does he approve or disapprove of Parisian society as he describes it?
2. How do the social classes described by Mercier differ in their use of time, and why? Do you think the same distinctions exist today?
3. What evidence of the consumer revolution can you find in Mercier's account? How do the goods used by eighteenth-century Parisians compare to the ones you use in your life today?

** The city's central wholesale food market.
†† A suburb of Paris, famous for the excellent bread baked there.

Religious Authority and Beliefs

What were the patterns of popular religion, and how did they interact with the worldview of the educated public and their Enlightenment ideals? ■

Though the critical spirit of the Enlightenment made great inroads in the eighteenth century, the majority of ordinary men and women, especially those in rural areas, remained committed Christians. Religious faith promised salvation, and it gave comfort in the face of sorrow and death. Religion also remained strong because it was embedded in local traditions and everyday social experience.

Yet the popular religion of village Europe was also enmeshed in a larger world of church hierarchies and state power. These powerful outside forces sought to regulate religious life at the local level. Their efforts created tensions that helped set the scene for vigorous religious revivals in Protestant Germany and England as well as in Catholic France. Tensions arose between authorities and the people as powerful elites began to criticize many popular religious practices that their increasingly rationalistic minds deemed foolish and superstitious.

Church Hierarchy

As in the Middle Ages, the local parish church remained the focal point of religious devotion and community cohesion. Congregants gossiped and swapped stories after services, and neighbors came together in church for baptisms, marriages, funerals, and special events. Priests and parsons kept the community records of births, deaths, and marriages; distributed charity; looked after orphans; and provided primary education to the common people. Thus the parish church was woven into the very fabric of community life.

While the parish church remained central to the community, it was also subject to greater control from the state. In Protestant areas princes and monarchs headed the official church, and they regulated their "territorial churches" strictly, selecting personnel and imposing detailed rules. By the eighteenth century the radical ideas of the Reformation had resulted in another version of church bureaucracy.

Catholic monarchs in this period also took greater control of religious matters in their kingdoms, weakening papal authority. Spain, a deeply Catholic country with devout rulers, took firm control of ecclesiastical appointments. Papal proclamations could not even be read in Spanish churches without prior approval from the government. Spain also asserted state control over the Spanish Inquisition, which pursued heresy as an independent agency under Rome's direction and went far toward creating a "national" Catholic Church, as France had done earlier.

A more striking indication of state power and papal weakness was the fate of the Society of Jesus, or Jesuits. The well-educated Jesuits were extraordinary teachers, missionaries, and agents of the papacy. In many Catholic countries they exercised tremendous political influence, holding high government positions and educating the nobility in their colleges. Yet by playing politics so effectively, the Jesuits eventually elicited a broad coalition of enemies. Bitter controversies led Louis XV to order the Jesuits out of France in 1763 and to confiscate their property. France and Spain then pressured Rome to dissolve the Jesuits completely. In 1773 a reluctant pope caved in, although the order was revived after the French Revolution.

Some Catholic rulers also believed that the clergy in monasteries and convents should make a more practical contribution to social and religious life. Austria, a leader in controlling the church (see Chapter 17) and promoting primary education, showed how far the process could go. Maria Theresa began by sharply restricting entry into "unproductive" orders. In his Edict on Idle Institutions, her successor, Joseph II, abolished contemplative orders, henceforth permitting only orders that were engaged in teaching, nursing, or other practical work. The state expropriated the dissolved monasteries and used their wealth for charitable purposes and higher salaries for ordinary priests. Joseph II also issued edicts of religious tolerance, including for Jews, making Austria one of the first European states to lift centuries-old restrictions on its Jewish population.

Protestant Revival

By the late seventeenth century the vast reforms of the Protestant Reformation were complete and had been widely adopted in most Protestant churches. Medieval practices of idolatry, saint worship, and pageantry were abolished; stained-glass windows were smashed and murals whitewashed. Yet many official Protestant churches had settled into a smug complacency. This, along with the growth of state power and bureaucracy in local parishes, threatened to eclipse one of the Reformation's main goals — to bring all believers closer to God.

In the Reformation heartland, one concerned German minister wrote that the Lutheran church "had become paralyzed in forms of dead doctrinal conformity" and badly needed a return to its original inspiration.[22] His voice was one of many that prepared and then guided a powerful Protestant revival that succeeded because it answered the intense but increasingly unsatisfied needs of common people.

Religious Authority and Beliefs

The Protestant revival began in Germany in the late seventeenth century. It was known as **Pietism** (PIGH-uh-tih-zum), and three aspects helped explain its powerful appeal. First, Pietism called for a warm, emotional religion that everyone could experience. Enthusiasm—in prayer, in worship, in preaching, in life itself—was the key concept. "Just as a drunkard becomes full of wine, so must the congregation become filled with spirit," declared one exuberant writer. Another said simply, "The heart must burn."[23]

Second, Pietism reasserted the earlier radical stress on the priesthood of all believers, thereby reducing the gulf between official clergy and Lutheran laity. Bible reading and study were enthusiastically extended to all classes, and this provided a powerful spur for popular literacy as well as individual religious development (see page 595). Pietists were largely responsible for the educational reforms implemented by Prussia in the early eighteenth century. Finally, Pietists believed in the practical power of Christian rebirth in everyday affairs. Reborn Christians were expected to lead good, moral lives and to come from all social classes.

Pietism soon spread through the German-speaking lands and to Scandinavia. It also had a major impact on John Wesley (1703–1791), who served as the catalyst for popular religious revival in England. Wesley came from a long line of ministers, and when he went to Oxford University to prepare for the clergy, he mapped a fanatically earnest "scheme of religion." After becoming a teaching fellow at Oxford, Wesley organized a Holy Club for similarly minded students, who were soon known contemptuously as **Methodists** because they were so methodical in their devotion. Yet like the young Martin Luther, Wesley remained intensely troubled about his own salvation even after his ordination as an Anglican priest in 1728.

Wesley's anxieties related to grave problems of the faith in England. The government shamelessly used the Church of England to provide favorites with high-paying jobs. Both church and state officials failed to respond to the spiritual needs of the people, abandoning the construction of new churches while the population grew, and in many parishes there was a shortage of pews. Services and sermons had settled into an uninspiring routine. The separation of religion from local customs and social life was symbolized by church doors that were customarily locked on weekdays. Moreover, Enlightenment skepticism was making inroads among the educated classes, and deism—a belief in God but not in organized religion—was becoming popular. Some bishops and church leaders seemed to believe that doctrines such as the virgin birth were little more than elegant superstitions.

Pietism A Protestant revival movement in early-eighteenth-century Germany and Scandinavia that emphasized a warm and emotional religion, the priesthood of all believers, and the power of Christian rebirth in everyday affairs.

Methodists Members of a Protestant revival movement started by John Wesley, so called because they were so methodical in their devotion.

Hogarth's Satirical View of the Church William Hogarth (1697–1764) was one of the foremost satirical artists of his day. This image mocks a London Methodist meeting, where the congregation swoons in enthusiasm over the preacher's sermon. The woman in the foreground giving birth to rabbits refers to a hoax perpetrated in 1726 by a servant named Mary Tofts; the gullibility of those who believed Tofts is likened to that of the Methodist congregation. (HIP/Art Resource, NY)

Spiritual counseling from a sympathetic Pietist minister from Germany prepared Wesley for a mystical, emotional "conversion" in 1738. He described this critical turning point in his *Journal*:

> *In the evening I went to a [Christian] society in Aldersgate Street where one was reading Luther's preface to the Epistle to the Romans. About a quarter before nine, while he was describing the change which God works in the heart through faith in Christ, I felt my heart strangely warmed. I felt I did trust in Christ, Christ alone for salvation; and an assurance was given me that he had taken away my sins, even mine, and saved me from the law of sin and death.*[24]

Wesley's emotional experience resolved his intellectual doubts. Moreover, he was convinced that any person, no matter how poor or uneducated, might have a similarly heartfelt conversion and gain the same blessed assurance. He took the good news to the people, traveling some 225,000 miles by horseback and preaching more than forty thousand sermons between 1750 and 1790. Since existing churches were often overcrowded and the church-state establishment was hostile, Wesley preached in open fields. People came in large numbers. Of critical importance was Wesley's rejection of Calvinist predestination—the doctrine of salvation granted to only a select few. Instead, he preached that all men and women who earnestly sought salvation might be saved. It was a message of hope and joy, of free will and universal salvation.

Jansenism A sect of Catholicism originating with Cornelius Jansen that emphasized the heavy weight of original sin and accepted the doctrine of predestination; it was outlawed as heresy by the pope.

Wesley's ministry won converts, formed Methodist cells, and eventually resulted in a new denomination. And just as Wesley had been inspired by the Pietist revival in Germany, so evangelicals in the Church of England and the old dissenting groups now followed Wesley's example of preaching to all people, giving impetus to an even broader awakening among the lower classes. Thus, in Protestant countries religion continued to be a vital force in the lives of the people.

Catholic Piety

Religion also flourished in Catholic Europe around 1700, but there were important differences from Protestant practice. First, the visual contrast was striking; baroque art still lavished rich and emotionally exhilarating figures and images on Catholic churches, just as most Protestants had removed theirs during the Reformation. Moreover, people in Catholic Europe on the whole participated more actively in formal worship than did Protestants. More than 95 percent of the population probably attended church for Easter communion, the climax of the religious year.

The tremendous popular strength of religion in Catholic countries can in part be explained by the church's integral role in community life and popular culture. Thus, although Catholics reluctantly confessed their sins to priests, they enthusiastically joined together in religious festivals to celebrate the passage of the liturgical year. In addition to the great processional days—such as Palm Sunday, the joyful reenactment of Jesus' triumphal entry into Jerusalem—each parish had its own saints' days, processions, and pilgrimages. Led by its priest, a congregation might march around the village or across the countryside to a local shrine. Before each procession or feast day, the priest explained its religious significance to kindle group piety. Processions were also folklore and tradition, an escape from work, and a form of recreation. The Reformation had largely eliminated such festivities in Protestant areas.

Catholicism had its own version of the Pietist revivals that shook Protestant Europe. **Jansenism** has been described by one historian as the "illegitimate off-spring of the Protestant Reformation and the Catholic Counter-Reformation."[25] It originated with Cornelius Jansen (1585–1638), bishop of Ypres in the Spanish Netherlands, who called for a return to the austere early Christianity of Saint Augustine. In contrast to the worldly Jesuits, Jansen emphasized the heavy weight of original sin and accepted the doctrine of predestination. Although outlawed by papal and royal edicts as Calvinist heresy, Jansenism attracted Catholic followers eager for religious renewal, particularly among the French. Many members of France's urban elite, especially judicial nobles and some parish priests, became known for their Jansenist piety and spiritual devotion. Such stern religious values encouraged the judiciary's increasing opposition to the French monarchy in the second half of the eighteenth century.

Among the urban poor, a different strain of Jansenism took hold. Prayer meetings brought men and women together in ecstatic worship, and some participants fell into convulsions and spoke in tongues. The police of Paris posted spies to report on such gatherings and conducted mass raids and arrests.

Marginal Beliefs and Practices

In the countryside, many peasants continued to hold religious beliefs that were marginal to the Christian faith altogether, often of obscure or even pagan origin. On the Feast of Saint Anthony, for example, priests were expected to bless salt and bread for farm animals to protect them from disease. Catholics believed that saints' relics could bring fortune or attract lovers, and there were healing springs for many ailments. In 1796 the Lutheran villagers of Beutelsbach incurred the ire of local officials when they buried a live bull at a crossroads to ward off an epidemic of hoof and mouth disease.[26]

Procession of Nuns at Port-Royal des Champs The convent of Port-Royal, located twenty miles southwest of Paris, was a center of Jansenist activity throughout the seventeenth century. Angered by the nuns' defiance, Louis XIV ordered them forcibly relocated in 1709. To generate support, the artist Magdelaine Horthemels painted a series of images depicting the pious and placid religious life at the convent. The convent was nonetheless destroyed by Louis's forces in 1710. This image is one of many copies of Horthemels's work made by Jansenists in the eighteenth century. (Réunion des Musées Nationaux/Art Resource, NY)

The ordinary person combined strong Christian faith with a wealth of time-honored superstitions.

Inspired initially by the fervor of the Reformation era, then by the critical rationalism of the Enlightenment, religious and secular authorities sought increasingly to "purify" popular spirituality. Thus one parish priest in France lashed out at his parishioners, claiming that they were "more superstitious than devout . . . and sometimes appear as baptized idolators."[27] French priests particularly denounced the "various remnants of paganism" found in popular bonfire ceremonies during Lent, in which young men, "yelling and screaming like madmen," tried to jump over the bonfires in order to help the crops grow and protect themselves from illness. One priest saw rational Christians regressing into pagan animals—"the triumph of Hell and the shame of Christianity."[28]

The severity of the attack on popular belief varied widely by country and region. Where authorities pursued purification vigorously, as in Austria under Joseph II, pious peasants saw only an incomprehensible attack on age-old faith and drew back in anger. Their reaction dramatized the growing tension between the attitudes of educated elites and the common people.

It was in this era of growing intellectual disdain for popular beliefs that the persecution of witches slowly came to an end across Europe. Common people in the countryside continued to fear the Devil and his helpers, but the elite increasingly dismissed such fears and refused to prosecute suspected witches. The last witch was executed in England in 1682, the same year France prohibited witchcraft trials. By the late eighteenth century most European states and their colonies had followed suit.

Medical Practice

How did the practice of medicine evolve in the eighteenth century?

Although significant breakthroughs in medical science would not come until the middle and late nineteenth century, the Enlightenment's growing focus on discovering the laws of nature and on human problems did give rise to a great deal of research and experimentation in the 1700s. Medical practitioners greatly increased in number, although their techniques did not differ much from those of previous generations. Care of the sick in this era was the domain of several competing groups: faith healers, apothecaries (pharmacists), physicians, surgeons, and midwives. From the Middle Ages through the seventeenth century, both men and women were medical practitioners. However, since women were

An Eighteenth-Century Pharmacy In this lively painting a woman consults an apothecary (in the elegant red suit) while his assistants assemble drugs for new prescriptions. By 1700 apothecaries had emerged as a separate group of state-licensed medical professionals. They drew on published lists and books describing the properties and dosages of their concoctions, but there were many different "recipes" and trade secrets. (Civico Museo Bibliograco Musicale, Bologna, Italy/The Bridgeman Art Library)

generally denied admission to medical colleges and lacked the diplomas necessary to practice, the range of medical activities open to them was restricted. In the eighteenth century women's traditional roles as midwives and healers eroded even further.

Faith Healing and General Practice

In the course of the eighteenth century, faith healers remained active. They and their patients believed that evil spirits caused illness by lodging in people and that the proper treatment was to exorcise, or drive out, the offending devil. This demonic view of disease was strongest in the countryside, where popular belief placed great faith in the healing power of religious relics, prayer, and the laying on of hands.

In the larger towns and cities, apothecaries sold a vast number of herbs, drugs, and patent medicines for every conceivable "temperament and distemper." Some of the drugs and herbs undoubtedly worked. For example, strong laxatives were given to the rich for their constipated bowels, and regular purging of the bowels was considered essential for good health and the treatment of illness. Like all varieties of medical practitioners, apothecaries advertised their wares, their high-class customers, and their miraculous cures in newspapers and commercial circulars. Medicine, like food and fashionable clothing, thus joined the era's new commercial culture.

Physicians, who were invariably men, were apprenticed in their teens to practicing physicians for several years of on-the-job training. This training was then rounded out with hospital work or some university courses. Because such prolonged training was expensive, physicians came mainly from prosperous families, and they usually concentrated on urban patients from similar social backgrounds. They had little contact with urban workers and less with peasants.

Physicians in the eighteenth century were increasingly willing to experiment with new methods, but time-honored practices lay heavily on them. Like apothecaries, they laid great stress on purging, and bloodletting was still considered a medical cure-all. It was the way "bad blood," the cause of illness, was removed and the balance of humors necessary for good health was restored.

Hospitals and Surgery

Long considered to be craftsmen comparable to butchers and barbers, surgeons began studying anatomy seriously and improved their art in the eighteenth century. With endless opportunities to practice, army surgeons on gory battlefields led the way. They learned that a soldier with an extensive wound, such as a shattered leg or arm, could perhaps be saved if the surgeon could obtain a flat surface above the wound that could be cauterized with fire. Thus if a soldier (or a civilian) had a broken limb and the bone stuck out, the surgeon amputated so that the remaining stump could be cauterized and the likelihood of death reduced.

The eighteenth-century surgeon (and patient) labored in the face of incredible difficulties. Almost all operations were performed without painkillers, for the anesthesia of the day was hard to control and too dangerous for general use. Many patients died from the agony and shock of such operations. Surgery was also performed in utterly unsanitary conditions, for there was no knowledge of bacteriology and the nature of infection. The simplest wound treated by a surgeon could fester and lead to death.

Midwifery

Midwives continued to deliver the overwhelming majority of babies throughout the eighteenth century. Trained initially by another woman practitioner — and regulated by a guild in many cities — the midwife primarily assisted in labor and delivering babies. She also treated female problems, such as irregular menstrual cycles, breast-feeding difficulties, infertility, and venereal disease, and ministered to small children.

The midwife orchestrated labor and birth in a woman's world, where friends and relatives assisted the pregnant woman in the familiar surroundings of her own home. The male surgeon (and the husband) rarely entered this female world, because most births, then as now, were normal and spontaneous. After the invention of forceps became publicized in 1734, surgeon-physicians used their monopoly over this and other instruments to seek lucrative new business. Attacking midwives as ignorant and dangerous, they sought to undermine faith in midwives and persuaded growing numbers of wealthy women of the superiority of their services.

Research suggests that women practitioners successfully defended much but not all of their practice in the eighteenth century. One enterprising French midwife, Madame du Coudray, wrote a widely used textbook, *Manual on the Art of Childbirth* (1757). She then secured royal financing for her campaign to teach better birthing techniques to village midwives. Du Coudray traveled all over France using a life-size model of the female torso and fetus to help teach illiterate women. (See "Living in the Past: Improvements in Childbirth," page 612.) It appears that midwives generally lost no more babies than did male doctors, who were still summoned to treat nonelite women only when life-threatening situations required surgery.

The Conquest of Smallpox

Experimentation and the intensified search for solutions to human problems led to some real advances in medicine after 1750. The eighteenth century's greatest medical triumph was the eradication of smallpox. With the progressive decline of bubonic plague, smallpox became the most terrible of the infectious diseases, and it is estimated that 60 million Europeans died of it in the eighteenth century. Fully 80 percent of the population was stricken at some point in life.

The first step in the conquest of this killer in Europe came in the early eighteenth century. An English aristocrat whose beauty had been marred by the pox, Lady Mary Wortley Montagu, learned about the

"The Wonderful Effects of the New Inoculation!" The talented caricaturist James Gillray satirized widespread anxieties about the smallpox vaccination in this lively image. The discoveries of Edward Jenner a few years prior to Gillray's caricature had led to the adoption of a safer vaccine derived from cowpox. The artist mocks this breakthrough by showing cows bursting from the boils supposedly brought on by the vaccine. (Private Collection/The Bridgeman Art Library)

Improvements in Childbirth

LIVING IN THE PAST

MOST WOMEN IN EIGHTEENTH-CENTURY EUROPE gave birth to five or six children over their lifetimes. They were assisted in the arduous, often dangerous process of childbirth by friends, relatives, and, in many cases, professional midwives. Birth took place at home, sometimes with the aid of a birthing chair, such as the folding chair from Sicily shown here.

The training and competency of midwives was often rudimentary, especially in the countryside. Enlightenment interest in education and public health helped inspire a movement across Europe to raise standards. One of its pioneers was Madame Angelique Marguerite Le Boursier du Coudray. Du Coudray herself had undergone a rigorous three-year apprenticeship and was a member of the Parisian surgeons' guild. She set off on a mission to teach rural midwives in the French province of Auvergne.

Du Coudray saw that her unlettered pupils learned through the senses, not through books. Thus she made, possibly for the first time in history, a life-size obstetrical model—a "machine"—out of fabric and stuffing for use in her classes. "I had ... the students maneuver in front of me on a machine ... which represented the pelvis of a woman, the womb, its opening, its ligaments, the conduit called the vagina, the bladder, and *rectum intestine*. I added [an artificial] child of natural size, whose joints were flexible enough to be able to be put in different positions."* Now du Coudray could demonstrate the problems of childbirth, and each student could practice on the model in the "lab session."

As her reputation grew, du Coudray sought to reach a national audience. In 1757 she published her *Manual on the Art of Childbirth*. The *Manual* incorporated her hands-on teaching method and served as a reference for students and graduates. In 1759 the government autho-

Eighteenth-century birthing chair from Sicily. (Science & Society Picture Library)

Du Coudray's life-size model for simulating childbirth. (Musée Flaubert d'histoire de la médecine, Rouen)

*Quotes are from Nina Gelbart, *The King's Midwife: A History and Mystery of Madame du Coudray* (Berkeley: University of California Press, 1998), pp. 60–61.

the age of ten. Infant mortality was particularly high in France, where wet-nursing was commonly practiced. Treatment of children could be harsh in an early modern society that was characterized by much higher levels of violence and brutality than are Western societies today. The second half of the eighteenth century witnessed a new concern with methods of child rearing inspired by Enlightenment efforts to reform human society, and schools for nonelite children spread across Europe.

How did increasing literacy and new patterns of consumption affect people's lives? (p. 595)

Increasing literacy rates allowed many more commoners to read the large numbers of texts that were becoming available: religious pamphlets, how-to manuals, and escapist fantasies. But the oral tradition continued, as did the many fairs, festivals, and sports that had existed for centuries. The urban populace benefited from the surge in agricultural and industrial production. People found a greater variety of food products at the market, including new stimulants produced in the colonies that soon became staples of elite and popular consumption. New foods, especially the potato, provided appealing new flavors and important vitamins. Within homes, standards of comfort and hygiene increased, and the emerging consumer society offered new possibilities for self-expression and individuality.

What were the patterns of popular religion, and how did they interact with the worldview of the educated public and their Enlightenment ideals? (p. 606)

As the Enlightenment swept through the circles of the intellectual elite, many long-standing beliefs and practices remained strong forces and sustained continuity in popular life. Protestant religious revival sought to reaffirm Martin Luther's original mission and carried the promise of salvation to the common people. Through Jansenism, which found a particularly willing audience in France, Catholicism also experienced a type of revival that emphasized original sin and predestination. Obscure and pagan beliefs persisted in rural areas, where they were roundly criticized by secular officials and increasingly rational religious authorities.

How did the practice of medicine evolve in the eighteenth century? (p. 609)

Although the number of medical practitioners—faith healers, apothecaries, physicians, surgeons, and midwives—grew, methods of healing the sick continued to be crude and primitive. Women began to lose prominence in midwifery beginning with the introduction of forceps in the mid-eighteenth century, and their lack of access to medical schools eroded their ability to compete with male physicians. In 1796 Edward Jenner devised a vaccine for smallpox, the most deadly disease in Europe since the disappearance of the plague earlier in the century.

Suggested Reading

Bongie, Laurence L. *From Rogue to Everyman: A Foundling's Journey to the Bastille.* 2005. The life story of an eighteenth-century foundling and, through his eyes, the Parisian underworld of gamblers, prostitutes, and police spies.

Brewer, John, and Roy Porter, eds. *Consumption and the World of Goods.* 1993. Pioneering essays from leading scholars on the consumer revolution of eighteenth-century Europe.

Burke, Peter. *Popular Culture in Early Modern Europe*, 3d ed. 2009. A thoroughly updated version of a classic introduction to everyday life, mentalities, and leisure pursuits.

Carrell, Jennifer. *The Speckled Monster: A Historical Tale of Battling Smallpox.* 2003. A lively popular account of the spread of inoculation.

Crawford, Katherine. *European Sexualities, 1400–1800.* 2007. A broad survey of cultural and social aspects of sex and sexuality in early modern Europe.

Gawthrop, Richard. *Pietism and the Making of Eighteenth-Century Prussia.* 2006. An examination of the importance of Pietist morality and institutions in the making of the Prussian state.

Gelbart, Nina. *The King's Midwife: A History and Mystery of Madame du Coudray.* 2002. A vivid and accessible biography of the most famous midwife of eighteenth-century France.

Hartman, Mary S. *The Household and the Making of History.* 2004. A bold study of the economic and social ramifications of the European pattern of late marriage.

Immel, Andrea, and Michael Witmore. *Childhood and Children's Books in Early Modern Europe, 1550–1800.* 2005. A collection of essays describing the experience of childhood and the rise of children's literature, mostly in Britain.

Kertzer, David I., and Marzio Barbagli, eds. *Family Life in Early Modern Times, 1500–1789.* 2001. A rich collection of essays on the history of the family, women, and children in early modern Europe.

Lindeman, Mary. *Health and Healing in Eighteenth-Century Germany.* 2001. A study of the day-to-day activities of German medical practitioners — doctors, surgeons, faith healers, quacks — and their patients.

Mintz, Sidney W. *Sweetness and Power: The Place of Sugar in Modern History.* 1985. A fascinating exploration of the shifting cultural significance of sugar and its transformation from elite luxury good to everyday staple.

Sussman, George D. *Selling Mother's Milk: The Wet-Nursing Business in France, 1715–1914.* 1982. An engrossing account of the large-scale organization of wet-nursing in eighteenth-century France.

Key Terms

community controls (p. 588)
illegitimacy explosion (p. 589)
wet-nursing (p. 591)
blood sports (p. 597)
carnival (p. 597)
just price (p. 599)
consumer revolution (p. 601)
Pietism (p. 607)
Methodists (p. 607)
Jansenism (p. 608)

Notes

1. Quoted in J. M. Beattie, "The Criminality of Women in Eighteenth-Century England," *Journal of Social History* 8 (Summer 1975): 86.
2. Quoted in R. Cobb, *The Police and the People: French Popular Protest, 1789–1820* (Oxford, U.K.: Clarendon Press, 1970), p. 238.
3. Peter Laslett, *Family Life and Illicit Love: Essays in Historical Sociology* (Cambridge, U.K.: Cambridge University Press, 1977).
4. G. Gullickson, *Spinners and Weavers of Auffay: Rural Industry and the Sexual Division of Labor in a French Village, 1750–1850* (Cambridge, U.K.: Cambridge University Press, 1986), p. 186.
5. Trial of Barton Dorrington, *Old Bailey Proceedings Online*, September 10, 1788, www.oldbaileyonline.org, October 9, 2009, t17880910-46.
6. Louis Crompton, *Homosexuality and Civilization* (Cambridge, Mass.: Belknap Press, 2003), p. 321.
7. D. S. Neff, "Bitches, Mollies, and Tommies: Byron, Masculinity and the History of Sexualities," in *Journal of the History of Sexuality* 11, 3 (July 2002): 404.
8. George E. Haggerty, ed., *Encyclopedia of Gay Histories and Cultures* (New York: Garland Publishing, 2000), pp. 1311–1312.
9. Pier Paolo Viazzo, "Mortality, Fertility, and Family," in *Family Life in Early Modern Times, 1500–1789*, ed. David I. Kertzer and Marzio Barbagli (New Haven, Conn.: Yale University Press, 2001), p. 180.
10. George Sussman, *Selling Mother's Milk: The Wet-Nursing Business in France, 1715–1914* (Urbana: University of Illinois Press, 1982), p. 22.
11. Robert Woods, "Did Montaigne Love His Children? Demography and the Hypothesis of Parental Indifference," *Journal of Interdisciplinary History* 33, 3 (2003): 426.
12. P. Viazzo, "Mortality, Fertility, and Family," in *The History of the European Family*, vol. 1, ed. D. Kertzer and M. Barbagli (New Haven, Conn.: Yale University Press, 2001), pp. 176–178.
13. Alysa Levene, "The Estimation of Mortality at the London Foundling Hospital, 1741–99," *Population Studies* 59, 1 (2005): 87–97.
14. Cited in Woods, "Did Montaigne Love His Children?" p. 421.
15. Ibid., pp. 13, 16.
16. James Van Horn Melton, *Absolutism and the Eighteenth-Century Origins of Compulsory Schooling in Prussia and Austria* (Cambridge, U.K.: Cambridge University Press, 2003), p. 46.
17. James Van Horn Melton, "The Theresian School Reform of 1774," in *Early Modern Europe*, ed. James B. Collins and Karen L. Taylor (Oxford, U.K.: Blackwell, 2006).
18. I. Woloch, *Eighteenth-Century Europe: Tradition and Progress, 1715–1789* (New York: W. W. Norton, 1982), pp. 220–221.
19. Neil McKendrik, John Brewer, and J. H. Plumb, *The Birth of a Consumer Society: The Commercialization of Eighteenth-Century England* (Bloomington: Indiana University Press, 1982).
20. Daniel Roche, *The Culture of Clothing: Dress and Fashion in the Ancien Regime*, trans. Jean Birrell (Cambridge, U.K.: Cambridge University Press, 1996).
21. Quoted in Cissie Fairchilds, "The Production and Marketing of Populuxe Goods in Eighteenth-Century Paris," in *Consumption and the World of Goods*, ed. John Brewer and Roy Porter (London: Routledge, 1993), p. 228.
22. Quoted in K. Pinson, *Pietism as a Factor in the Rise of German Nationalism* (New York: Columbia University Press, 1934), p. 13.
23. Ibid., pp. 43–44.
24. Quoted in S. Andrews, *Methodism and Society* (London: Longmans, Green, 1970), p. 327.
25. Dale Van Kley, "The Rejuvenation and Rejection of Jansenism in History and Historiography," *French Historical Studies* 29 (Fall 2006): 649–684.
26. David Sabean, *The Power in the Blood: Popular Culture and Village Discourse in Early Modern Germany* (Cambridge, U.K.: Cambridge University Press, 1984), p. 174.
27. Quoted in Woloch, *Eighteenth-Century Europe*, p. 292.
28. Quoted in T. Tackett, *Priest and Parish in Eighteenth-Century France* (Princeton, N.J.: Princeton University Press, 1977), p. 214.

For practice quizzes and other study tools, visit the Online Study Guide at **bedfordstmartins.com/mckaywest**.

For primary sources from this period, see **Sources of Western Society, Second Edition**.

For Web sites, images, and documents related to topics in this chapter, visit Make History at **bedfordstmartins.com/mckaywest**.

20

The Revolution in Politics

1775–1815

The last years of the eighteenth century were a time of great upheaval as a series of revolutions and wars challenged the old order of monarchs and aristocrats. The ideas of freedom and equality, ideas that have not stopped shaping the world since that era, flourished and spread. The revolutionary era began in North America in 1775. Then in 1789 France, the most populous country in western Europe and a center of culture and intellectual life, became the leading revolutionary nation. It established first a constitutional monarchy, then a radical republic, and finally a new empire under Napoleon that would last until 1815. During this period of constant domestic turmoil, French armies violently exported revolution beyond the nation's borders, eager to establish new governments throughout much of Europe. Inspired both by the ideals of the Revolution on the continent and by internal colonial conditions, the slaves of Saint-Domingue rose up in 1791. Their rebellion would eventually lead to the creation of the new independent nation of Haiti in 1804. In Europe and its colonies abroad, the world of modern politics was born. ■

Life in Revolutionary France. On the eve of the French Revolution, angry crowds like this one gathered in Paris to protest the high-handed actions of the royal government. Throughout the Revolution, decisive events took place in the street as much as in the chambers of the National Assembly.

CHAPTER PREVIEW

Background to Revolution
■ What social, political, and economic factors formed the background to the French Revolution?

Politics and the People, 1789–1791
■ How did the events of 1789 result in a constitutional monarchy in France, and how did the new constitution affect the various members of French society at home and in the colony of Saint-Domingue?

World War and Republican France, 1791–1799
■ How and why did the Revolution take a radical turn at home and in the colonies?

The Napoleonic Era, 1799–1815
■ Why did Napoleon Bonaparte assume control of France, and what factors led to his downfall? How did the new republic of Haiti gain independence from France?

Background to Revolution

What social, political, and economic factors formed the background to the French Revolution?

The origin of the French Revolution has been one of the most debated topics in history. In order to understand the path to revolution, numerous interrelated factors must be taken into account. These include deep social changes in France, a long-term political crisis that eroded monarchical legitimacy, the practical and ideological effects of the American Revolution, the impact of new political ideas derived from the Enlightenment, and, perhaps most important, a financial crisis created by France's participation in expensive overseas wars.

estates The three legal categories, or orders, of France's inhabitants: the clergy, the nobility, and everyone else.

Legal Orders and Social Reality

As in the Middle Ages, France's 25 million inhabitants were still legally divided into three orders, or **estates**— the clergy, the nobility, and everyone else. As the nation's first estate, the clergy numbered about one hundred thousand and had important privileges. It owned about 10 percent of the land and paid only a "voluntary gift," rather than regular taxes, to the government every five years. Moreover, the church levied a property tax (tithe) on landowners.

The second estate consisted of some four hundred thousand nobles, the descendants of "those who fought" in the Middle Ages. Nobles owned about 25 percent of the land in France outright, and they too were lightly taxed. Moreover, nobles continued to enjoy certain manorial rights, or privileges of lordship, that dated back to medieval times. These included exclusive rights to hunt and fish, village monopolies on baking bread and pressing grapes for wine, fees for justice, and a host of other entitlements. In addition, nobles had "honorific privileges" such as the right to precedence on public occasions and the right to wear swords. These rights conspicuously proclaimed the nobility's legal superiority and exalted social position.

Everyone else—nearly 98 percent of the population—was a commoner, legally a member of the third estate. A few commoners—prosperous merchants, lawyers, and officials—were well educated and rich, and they might have purchased manorial rights as a way of obtaining profit and social honor. Yet the vast majority of the third estate consisted of peasants, rural agricultural workers, urban artisans, and unskilled day laborers. Thus the third estate was a conglomeration of very different social groups united only by their shared legal status.

In discussing the origins of the French Revolution, historians long focused on growing tensions between the nobility and the comfortable members of the third estate, the bourgeoisie (boorzh-wah-ZEE), or upper middle class. Increasing in size, wealth, culture, and self-confidence, this rising bourgeoisie became progressively exasperated by feudal laws restraining the economy and by the pretensions of a nobility that was closing ranks against middle-class aspirations. As a result, the French bourgeoisie eventually rose up to lead the entire third estate in a great social revolution that destroyed feudal privileges and established a capitalist order based on individualism and a market economy.

The Three Estates In this political cartoon from 1789 a peasant of the third estate struggles under the weight of a happy clergyman and a plumed nobleman. The caption—"Let's hope this game ends soon"—sets forth a program of reform that any peasant could understand. (Réunion des Musées Nationaux/Art Resource, NY)

In the last thirty years, the French Revolution's origins have been subject to what historians refer to as revisionism, or new interpretations. A flood of research uncovered in the late twentieth century challenged the long-accepted view and led to revised theories. Above all, revisionist historians have questioned the existence of growing social conflict between a progressive capitalistic bourgeoisie and a reactionary feudal nobility in eighteenth-century France. Instead, they see both bourgeoisie and nobility as highly fragmented, riddled with internal rivalries. The ancient sword nobility, for example, made up of people who descended from the oldest noble families, was separated by differences in wealth, education, and worldview from the newer robe nobility, people who acquired noble titles through service in the royal administration and judiciary. Differences within the bourgeoisie—between wealthy financiers and local lawyers, for example—were no less profound. Rather than standing as unified blocs against each other, nobility and bourgeoisie formed two parallel social ladders increasingly linked together at the top by wealth, marriage, and Enlightenment culture.

Revisionist historians note that the nobility and the bourgeoisie were not really at odds in the economic sphere. Investment in land and government service were the preferred activities of both groups, and the ideal of the merchant capitalist was to gain enough wealth to retire from trade, purchase an estate, and live nobly as a large landowner. Wealthy members of the third estate could even move into the second estate by serving the government and purchasing noble positions. At the same time, wealthy nobles often acted as aggressive capitalists, investing especially in mining, metallurgy, and foreign trade. In addition, until the Revolution actually began, key sections of the nobility were liberal and generally joined the bourgeoisie in opposition to the government.

Revisionists have clearly shaken the belief that the bourgeoisie and the nobility were inevitably locked in growing conflict before the Revolution. Yet they also make clear that the Old Regime had ceased to correspond with social reality by the 1780s. Legally, society was still based on rigid orders inherited from the Middle Ages, but in reality those distinctions were often blurred.

An upper echelon of aristocratic and bourgeois notables saw itself as an educated elite that stood well above the common masses. Although wealthy and influential, society's upper crust was frustrated by a bureaucratic monarchy that continued to claim the right to absolute power. Meanwhile, for France's laboring poor—the vast majority of the population—traditions remained strong and life itself remained a struggle.

Chronology

1773	Boston Tea Party
1775–1783	American Revolution
1786–1789	Height of French monarchy's financial crisis
1789	Feudalism abolished in France; ratification of U.S. Constitution; storming of the Bastille
1789–1799	French Revolution
1790	Burke, *Reflections on the Revolution in France*
1791	Slave insurrection in Saint-Domingue
1792	Wollstonecraft, *A Vindication of the Rights of Woman*
1793	Execution of Louis XVI
1793–1794	Robespierre's Reign of Terror
1794	Robespierre deposed and executed; France abolishes slavery in all territories
1794–1799	Thermidorian reaction
1799–1815	Napoleonic era
1804	Haitian republic declares independence
1812	Napoleon invades Russia
1814–1815	Napoleon defeated and exiled

The Crisis of Political Legitimacy

Overlying these social changes was a structural deadlock in France's tax system and the century-long political and fiscal struggle between the monarchy and its opponents sparked by the expenses of a series of foreign wars. When the Sun King, Louis XIV, finally died in 1715 and was succeeded by his five-year-old great-grandson, Louis XV (r. 1715–1774), the system of absolutist rule was challenged. Under the young monarch's regent, the duke of Orléans (1674–1723), a number of institutions retrieved powers they had lost under the Sun King. Most important, the high courts of France—the parlements—regained their ancient right to evaluate royal decrees publicly in writing before they were registered and given the force of law. The restoration of this right, which had been suspended under Louis XIV, was a fateful step. The magistrates of the parlements were leaders of the robe nobility who passed their judicial offices from father to son. By allowing a well-entrenched and highly articulate branch of the nobility to evaluate the king's decrees before they became law, the duke of Orléans sanctioned a counterweight to absolute power.

These implications became clear when the heavy expenses of war in the eighteenth century proved unbearable for the state treasury. Because many privileged groups escaped direct taxes and indirect taxes were relatively low, revenue from taxation could not meet the costs of war. The War of the Austrian Succession (see Chapter 17) plunged France into financial crisis and pushed the state to attempt a reform of the tax system. In 1748 Louis XV's finance minister decreed a 5 percent income tax on every individual regardless of social status. The result was a vigorous protest from those previously exempt from taxation — the nobility, the clergy, towns, and some wealthy bourgeoisie — led by the influential Parlement of Paris. The monarchy retreated; the new tax was dropped.

Following the disastrously expensive Seven Years' War (see Chapter 18), the conflict re-emerged. The government tried to maintain emergency taxes after the war ended; the Parlement of Paris protested and even challenged the basis of royal authority, claiming that the king's power had to be limited to protect liberty. Once again the government caved in and withdrew the taxes. The judicial opposition then asserted that the king could not levy taxes without the consent of the Parlement of Paris.

After years of attempted compromise, Louis XV finally roused himself to defend his absolutist inheritance. "The magistrates," he angrily told the Parlement of Paris in a famous face-to-face confrontation, "are my officers. . . . In my person only does the sovereign power rest."[1] In 1768 Louis appointed a tough career official named René de Maupeou (moh-POO) as chancellor and ordered him to crush the judicial opposition. Maupeou abolished the existing parlements and exiled the vociferous members of the Parlement of Paris to the provinces. He created new and docile parlements of royal officials, known as the Maupeou parlements, and he began once again to tax the privileged groups. Public opinion as a whole sided with the old parlements, however, and there was widespread criticism of "royal despotism."

Learned dissent was accompanied by scandalous libels. Known as Louis *le bien-aimé* (beloved Louis) in his youth, the king found his people turning against him for moral as well as political reasons. Kings had always maintained mistresses, who were invariably chosen from the court nobility. Louis XV broke that pattern with Madame de Pompadour, daughter of a disgraced bourgeois financier. As the king's favorite mistress from 1745 to 1750, Pompadour exercised tremendous influence over literature, art, and the decorative arts, using her patronage to support Voltaire and promote the rococo style (see Chapter 17). Even after their love affair ended, Pompadour wielded considerable influence over the king, helping bring about the alliance with Austria that resulted in the Seven Years' War. Pompadour's low birth and hidden political influence generated a stream of resentful and illegal pamphleteering.

After Pompadour, the king appeared to sink ever lower in immorality, and the stream of scandalmongering became a torrent. Lurid and pornographic depictions of the court ate away at the foundations of royal authority, especially among the common people. The king was being stripped of the sacred aura of God's anointed on earth (a process called *desacralization*) and was being reinvented in the popular imagination as a degenerate.

Despite the progressive desacralization (dee-SAY-kruh-ligh-ZAY-shun) of the monarchy, its power was still great enough to overcome opposition; Louis XV would probably have prevailed had he lived to a ripe old age, but he died in 1774. The new king, Louis XVI (r. 1774–1792), was a shy twenty-year-old with good intentions. Taking the throne, he is reported to have said, "What I should like most is to be loved."[2] The eager-to-please monarch yielded in the face of vehement opposition from France's educated elite. He dismissed chancellor Maupeou and repudiated the strong-willed minister's work. Louis also waffled on the economy, dismissing controller-general Turgot when his attempts to liberalize the economy drew fire (see Chapter 18). A weakened but unreformed monarchy now faced a judicial opposition that claimed to speak for the entire French nation.

The American Revolution and Its Impact

Coinciding with the first years of Louis XVI's reign, the American Revolution had an enormous impact on France in both practical and ideological terms. French expenses to support the colonists bankrupted the Crown, while the ideals of liberty and equality provided heady inspiration for political reform.

Like the French Revolution, the American Revolution had its immediate origin in struggles over increased taxes. The high cost of the Seven Years' War — fought with little financial contribution from the colonies — doubled the British national debt. When the government tried to recoup some of the losses by increasing taxes in the colonies in 1765, the colonists reacted with anger. The key questions were political rather than economic. To what extent could the home government assert its power while limiting the authority of colonial legislatures and their elected representatives? Accordingly, who should represent the colonies, and who had the right to make laws for Americans? The British government replied that Americans were represented in Parliament, albeit indirectly (like most British people themselves), and that the absolute supremacy of Parliament throughout the empire could not be questioned. Many Americans felt otherwise.

In 1773 the dispute over taxes and representation flared up again after the British government awarded a monopoly on Chinese tea to the East India Company, suddenly excluding colonial merchants from a lucrative business. In response, Boston men disguised as Indians held a rowdy "tea party" and threw the company's tea into the harbor. This led to extreme measures. The so-called Coercive Acts closed the port of Boston, curtailed local elections, and greatly expanded the royal governor's power. County conventions in Massachusetts protested vehemently and urged that the acts be "rejected as the attempts of a wicked administration to enslave America."

Other colonial assemblies joined in the denunciations. In September 1774 the First Continental Congress met in Philadelphia, where the more radical members argued successfully against concessions to the Crown. Compromise was also rejected by the British Parliament, and in April 1775 fighting began at Lexington and Concord. The uncompromising attitude of the British government and its use of German mercenaries dissolved long-standing loyalties to the home country and rivalries among the separate colonies. Some colonists remained loyal to the Crown; large numbers of these Loyalists emigrated to the northern colonies of Canada.

On July 4, 1776, the Second Continental Congress adopted the Declaration of Independence. Written by Thomas Jefferson, it boldly listed the tyrannical acts committed by George III (r. 1760–1820) and confidently proclaimed the natural rights of mankind and the sovereignty of the American states. The Declaration of Independence in effect universalized the traditional rights of English people and made them the rights of all mankind. It stated that "all men are created equal. . . . They are endowed by their Creator with certain unalienable rights. . . . Among these are life, liberty, and the pursuit of happiness."

The European powers closely followed the course of the American Revolution. The French wanted revenge

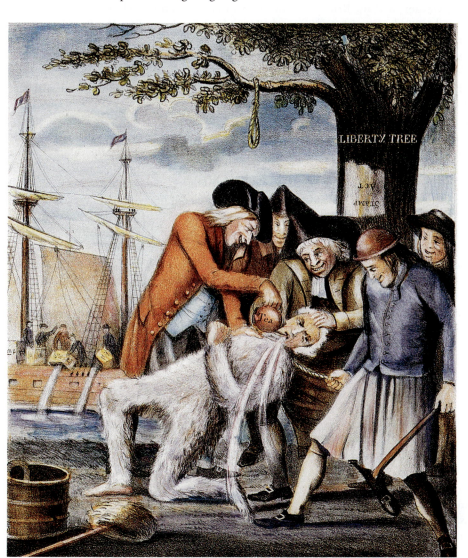

Toward Revolution in Boston
The Boston Tea Party was only one of many angry confrontations between British officials and Boston patriots. On January 27, 1774, an angry crowd seized a British customs collector and tarred and feathered him. This English cartoon from 1774 satirizes the event. What does the noose in the "liberty tree" suggest about the cartoonist's view of these events? (The Granger Collection, New York)

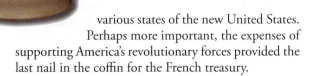

Commemorative Teapot
Manufacturers were quick to bring products to the market celebrating weighty political events, like this British teapot heralding "Stamp Act Repeal'd." By purchasing such items, ordinary people could champion political causes of the day and bring public affairs into their private lives. (Peabody Essex Museum, Salem, Massachusetts)

for the humiliating defeats of the Seven Years' War. They sympathized with the rebels and supplied guns and gunpowder. By 1777 French volunteers were arriving in Virginia, and a dashing young nobleman, the marquis de Lafayette (1757–1834), quickly became one of George Washington's most trusted generals. In 1778 the French government offered a formal alliance to the American ambassador in Paris, Benjamin Franklin, and in 1779 and 1780 the Spanish and Dutch declared war on Britain, their rival in transatlantic trade. Catherine the Great of Russia helped organize the League of Armed Neutrality in order to protect neutral shipping rights, which Britain refused to recognize.

Thus by 1780 Great Britain was engaged in an imperial war against most of Europe as well as against the thirteen colonies. In these circumstances, and in the face of severe reverses, a new British government decided to cut its losses and offered peace on extremely generous terms. By the Treaty of Paris in 1783, Britain recognized the independence of the thirteen colonies and ceded all its territory between the Allegheny Mountains and the Mississippi River to the Americans. Out of the bitter rivalries of the Old World, the Americans snatched dominion over a vast territory.

Europeans who dreamed of a new era were fascinated by the political lessons of the American Revolution. The Americans had begun with a revolutionary defense against tyrannical oppression, and they had been victorious. They had then shown how rational beings could assemble to exercise sovereignty and write a permanent constitution—a new social contract. All this gave greater reality to the concepts of individual liberty and representative government and reinforced one of the primary ideas of the Enlightenment: that a better world was possible.

No country felt the consequences of the American Revolution more directly than France. Hundreds of French officers served in America and were inspired by the experience, the marquis de Lafayette chief among them. French intellectuals and publicists engaged in passionate analysis of the new federal Constitution—ratified in 1789—as well as the constitutions of the various states of the new United States.

Perhaps more important, the expenses of supporting America's revolutionary forces provided the last nail in the coffin for the French treasury.

Financial Crisis

The French Revolution thus had its immediate origins in the king's financial difficulties. Thwarted by the Parlement of Paris in its efforts to raise revenues by reforming the tax system, the government was forced to finance all of its enormous expenditures during the American war with borrowed money. As a result, the national debt and the annual budget deficit soared.

By the 1780s fully 50 percent of France's annual budget went for interest payments on the debt. Another 25 percent went to maintain the military, while 6 percent was absorbed by the king and his court at Versailles. Less than 20 percent of the entire national budget was available for the productive functions of the state, such as transportation and general administration. This was an impossible financial situation.

The king was too weak to take the drastic measure of declaring partial bankruptcy and forcing his creditors to accept greatly reduced payments, as previous monarchs had done. Nor could the king and his ministers print money and create inflation to cover their deficits. Unlike England and Holland, which had far larger national debts relative to their populations, France had no central bank, no paper currency, and no means of creating credit. Faced with imminent financial disaster in 1786, the royal government had no alternative but to try to increase taxes. Since France's tax system was unfair and out-of-date, increased revenues were possible only through fundamental reform.

In 1787 Louis XVI's minister of finance revived old proposals to impose a general tax on all landed property as well as to form provincial assemblies to help administer the tax, and he convinced the king to call an Assembly of Notables to gain support for the idea. The notables, who were mainly important noblemen and high-ranking clergy, insisted that such sweeping tax changes required the approval of the **Estates General**, the representative body of all three estates, which had not met since 1614.

In an attempt to reassert his authority, the king dismissed the notables and established new taxes by decree. In stirring language, the judges of the Parlement of Paris promptly declared the royal initiative null and void. When the king tried to exile the judges, a tremendous wave of protest swept the country. Frightened investors also refused to advance more loans to the state. Finally, in July 1788, Louis XVI bowed to public opinion and called for a spring session of the Estates General.

Politics and the People, 1789–1791

How did the events of 1789 result in a constitutional monarchy in France, and how did the new constitution affect the various members of French society at home and in the colony of Saint-Domingue? ■

The calling of the Estates General opened a Pandora's box of social and political demands across the country. The process of electing delegates and formulating grievances politicized the French as no event in their prior history had done. As delegates at Versailles struggled over who truly represented the nation, the common people of France took matters into their own hands, rising up against noble lords and even reaching out to the royal family in their demands for change. Meanwhile, the complex slave society of colonial Saint-Domingue was rocked by conflicting political aspirations inspired by events in Paris.

The Formation of the National Assembly

Once Louis had agreed to hold the Estates General, the three orders — clergy, nobility, and commoners — separately elected delegates in each electoral district and prepared their own lists of grievances. The process of drafting their complaints unleashed a flood of debate and discussion across France, helping to galvanize public opinion and demands for reform.

Results of the elections reveal the political loyalties and mindsets of each estate on the eve of the Revolution. The local assemblies of the clergy elected mostly parish priests rather than church leaders, demonstrating their dissatisfaction with the church hierarchy. The nobility voted in a majority of conservatives, primarily from the provinces, where nobles were less wealthy and more numerous. Despite this conservative showing, fully one-third of noble representatives were liberals committed to major changes. The third estate experienced great popular participation in the elections. Almost all male commoners over age twenty-four had the right to vote, and they elected primarily lawyers and government officials to represent them, with few delegates representing business or the poor.

Although the elected representatives displayed a range of differing political viewpoints, the petitions for change coming from the three estates showed a surprising degree of consensus about the issues at stake. There was general agreement that royal absolutism should give way to a constitutional monarchy in which laws and taxes would require the consent of the Estates General in regular meetings. All agreed that individual liberties would have to be guaranteed by law and that economic regulations should be loosened. The striking similarities in the grievance petitions of the clergy, nobility, and third estate reflected a shared commitment to a basic reform platform among the educated elite.

On May 5, 1789, the twelve hundred delegates of the three estates paraded in medieval pageantry through the streets of Versailles to an opening session resplendent with feudal magnificence. Hopes were high throughout France for serious reform of state finance and politics in cooperation with the king. For the moment, there was no talk of revolution, only reform, and cries of "long live the king" interrupted his opening speech to the Estates General.

Despite these high hopes, the Estates General was almost immediately deadlocked due to arguments about voting procedures. Controversy had begun during the electoral process, when the government confirmed that, following precedent, each estate should meet and vote separately. During the lead-up to the Estates General, critics denounced this situation and demanded a single assembly dominated by the third estate to ensure fundamental reforms. In his famous pamphlet "What Is the Third Estate?" the abbé Emmanuel Joseph Sieyès (himself a member of the first estate) argued that the nobility was a tiny overprivileged minority and that the neglected third estate constituted the true strength of the French nation. (See "Listening to the Past: Abbé de Sieyès, 'What Is the Third Estate?'" page 626.) The government conceded that the third estate should have as many delegates as the clergy and the nobility combined, but then rendered this act meaningless by upholding voting by separate order. Reform-minded critics saw fresh evidence of an aristocratic conspiracy.

The issue came to a head in June 1789 when the delegates of the third estate refused to transact any business until the king ordered the clergy and nobility

> **Estates General** A legislative body in prerevolutionary France made up of representatives of each of the three classes, or estates; it was called into session in 1789 for the first time since 1614.

Abbé de Sieyès, "What Is the Third Estate?"

LISTENING TO THE PAST

In the flood of pamphlets that appeared after Louis XVI's call for a meeting of the Estates General, the most influential was written in 1789 by a Catholic priest named Emmanuel Joseph Sieyès. In "What is the Third Estate?" the abbé Sieyès vigorously condemned the system of privilege that lay at the heart of French society. The term "privilege" combined the Latin words for "private" and "law." In Old Regime France, no one set of laws applied to all; over time, the monarchy had issued a series of particular laws, or privileges, that enshrined special rights and entitlements for select individuals and groups. Noble privileges were among the weightiest.

Sieyès rejected this entire system of legal and social inequality. Deriding the nobility as a foreign parasite, he argued that the common people of the third estate, who did most of the work and paid most of the taxes, constituted the true nation. His pamphlet galvanized public opinion and played an important role in convincing representatives of the third estate to proclaim themselves a "National Assembly" in June 1789. Sieyès later helped bring Napoleon Bonaparte to power, abandoning the radicalism of 1789 for an authoritarian regime.

> 1. What is the Third Estate? Everything.
> 2. What has it been until now in the political order? Nothing.
> 3. What does it want? To become something.
>
> ... What is a Nation? A body of associates living under a *common* law and represented by the same *legislature*.
>
> Is it not more than certain that the noble order has privileges, exemptions, and even rights that are distinct from the rights of the great body of citizens? Because of this, it [the noble order] does not belong to the common order, it is not covered by the law common to the rest. Thus its civil rights already make it a people apart inside the great Nation. It is truly *imperium in imperio* [a law unto itself].
>
> As for its *political* rights, the nobility also exercises them separately. It has its own representatives who have no mandate from the people. Its deputies sit separately, and even when they assemble in the same room with the deputies of the ordinary citizens, the nobility's representation still remains essentially distinct and separate: it is foreign to the Nation by its very principle, for its mission does not emanate from the people, and by its purpose, since it consists in defending, not the general interest, but the private interests of the nobility.
>
> The Third Estate therefore contains everything that pertains to the Nation and nobody outside of the Third Estate can claim to be part of the Nation. What is the Third Estate? EVERYTHING....
>
> By Third Estate is meant the collectivity of citizens who belong to the common order. Anybody who holds a legal privilege of any kind leaves that common order, stands as an exception to the common law, and in consequence does not belong to the Third Estate.... It is certain that the moment a citizen acquires privileges contrary to common law, he no longer belongs to the common order. His new interest is opposed to the general interest; he has no right to vote in the name of the people....
>
> In vain can anyone's eyes be closed to the revolution that time and the force of things have brought to pass; it is none the less real. Once upon a time the Third Estate was in bondage and the noble order was everything that mattered. Today the Third is everything and nobility but a word. Yet under the cover of this word a new and intolerable aristocracy has slipped in, and the people has every reason to no longer want aristocrats....
>
> What is the will of a Nation? It is the result of individual wills, just as the Nation is the aggregate of the individuals who compose it. It is impossible to conceive of a legitimate association that does not have for its goal the common security, the common liberty, in short, the public good. No doubt each individual also has his own personal aims. He says to himself, "protected by the common security, I will be able to peacefully pursue my own personal projects, I will seek my happiness where I will, assured of encountering only those legal obstacles that society will prescribe

This bust, by the sculptor Pierre Jean David d'Angers, shows an aged and contemplative Sieyès reflecting, perhaps, on his key role in the outbreak and unfolding of the Revolution. (Erich Lessing/Art Resource, NY)

for the common interest, in which I have a part, and with which my own personal interest is so usefully allied.". . .

Advantages which differentiate citizens from one another lie outside the purview of citizenship. Inequalities of wealth or ability are like the inequalities of age, sex, size, etc. In no way do they detract from the *equality* of citizenship. These individual advantages no doubt benefit from the protection of the law; but it is not the legislator's task to create them, to give privileges to some and refuse them to others. The law grants nothing; it protects what already exists until such time that what exists begins to harm the common interest. These are the only limits on individual freedom. I imagine the law as being at the center of a large globe; we the citizens without exception, stand equidistant from it on the surface and occupy equal places; all are equally dependent on the law, all present it with their liberty and their property to be protected; and this is what I call the *common rights* of citizens, by which they are all alike. All these individuals communicate with each other, enter into contracts, negotiate, always under the common guarantee of the law. If in this general activity somebody wishes to get control over the person of his neighbor or usurp his property, the common law goes into action to repress this criminal attempt and puts everyone back in their place at the same distance from the law. . . .

It is impossible to say what place the two privileged orders [the clergy and the nobility] ought to occupy in the social order: this is the equivalent of asking what place one wishes to assign to a malignant tumor that torments and undermines the strength of the body of a sick person. It must be *neutralized*. We must re-establish the health and working of all organs so thoroughly that they are no longer susceptible to these fatal schemes that are capable of sapping the most essential principles of vitality.

Source: Excerpt from pp. 65–70 in *The French Revolution and Human Rights: A Brief Documentary History*, edited, translated and with an introduction by Lynn Hunt. Copyright © 1996 by Bedford Books of St. Martin's Press. Used by permission of Bedford/St. Martin's.

QUESTIONS FOR ANALYSIS

1. What criticism of noble privileges does Sieyès offer? Why does he believe nobles are "foreign" to the nation?
2. How does Sieyès define the nation, and why does he believe that the third estate constitutes the nation?
3. What relationship between citizens and the law does Sieyès envision? What limitations on the law does he propose?

to sit with them in a single body. Finally, after a six-week war of nerves, a few parish priests began to go over to the third estate, which on June 17 voted to call itself the **National Assembly**. On June 20 the delegates of the third estate, excluded from their hall because of "repairs," moved to a large indoor tennis court where they swore the famous Oath of the Tennis Court, declaring:

> *The National Assembly, considering that it has been called to establish the constitution of the realm, to bring about the regeneration of public order, and to maintain the true principles of the monarchy, nothing may prevent it from continuing its deliberations in any place it is forced to establish itself and, finally, the National Assembly exists wherever its members are gathered.*

Taking the first step toward revolution, the members of the National Assembly pledged not to disband until they had written a new constitution.

The king's response to this crucial challenge to his authority was disastrously ambivalent. On June 23 he made a conciliatory speech to a joint session in which he urged reforms, and four days later he ordered the three estates to meet together. At the same time, the vacillating and indecisive monarch apparently followed the advice of relatives and court nobles who urged him to dissolve the National Assembly by force. Belatedly asserting his divine right to rule, the king called an army of eighteen thousand troops toward the capital, and on July 11 he dismissed his finance minister and other more liberal ministers. It appeared that the monarchy was prepared to renege on its promises for reform and to use violence to restore its control.

National Assembly The first French revolutionary legislature, made up primarily of representatives of the third estate and a few from the nobility and clergy, in session from 1789 to 1791.

The Storming of the Bastille

While delegates at Versailles were pressing for political rights, economic hardship gripped the common people. A poor grain harvest in 1788 had caused the price of bread to soar, unleashing a classic economic depression of the preindustrial age. With food so expensive and with so much uncertainty, the demand for manufactured goods collapsed. Thousands of artisans and small traders were thrown out of work. Bread riots broke out in Paris and the surrounding area in late April and May. In Paris perhaps 150,000 of the city's 600,000 people were without work by July 1789.

Against this background of poverty and ongoing political crisis, the people of Paris entered decisively onto the revolutionary stage. They believed that they should

The Tennis Court Oath, June 20, 1789 Painted two years after the event shown, this dramatic painting by Jacques-Louis David depicts a crucial turning point in the early days of the Revolution. On June 20 delegates of the third estate arrived at their meeting hall in the Versailles palace to find the doors closed and guarded. Fearing the king was about to dissolve their meeting by force, the deputies reassembled at a nearby indoor tennis court and swore a solemn oath not to disperse until they had been recognized as the National Assembly. (Musée de la Ville de Paris, Musée Carnavalet, Paris/Lauros/Giraudon, The Bridgeman Art Library)

have steady work and enough bread at fair prices to survive. They also feared that the dismissal of the king's moderate finance minister would put them at the mercy of aristocratic landowners and grain speculators. At the beginning of July, knowledge spread of the massing of troops near Paris, and it seemed that the royal government was prepared to use violence to impose order. Angry crowds formed, and passionate voices urged action. On July 13, 1789, the people began to seize arms for the defense of the city, and on July 14 several hundred people marched to the Bastille (in English ba-STEEL) to search for weapons and gunpowder.

The Bastille, once a medieval fortress, was a royal prison guarded by eighty retired soldiers and thirty Swiss mercenaries. The governor of the fortress-prison refused to hand over the powder, panicked, and ordered his men to resist; the guards killed ninety-eight people attempting to enter. Cannon were brought to batter the main gate, and fighting continued until the prison surrendered. The governor of the prison was later hacked to death, and his head was stuck on a pike and paraded through the streets. The next day a committee of citizens appointed the marquis de Lafayette commander of the city's armed forces.

The popular uprising forestalled the king's attempt to reassert his authority. On July 17 Louis announced the reinstatement of his liberal finance minister and the withdrawal of troops from Paris. The National Assembly was now free to continue its work without the threat of royal military intervention.

Peasant Revolt and the Rights of Man

Just as the laboring poor of Paris had been roused to a revolutionary fervor, the struggling French peasantry had also reached its boiling point, and in the summer of 1789 the countryside sent the delegates at

> **" Free expression of thoughts and opinions is one of the most precious rights of mankind: every citizen may therefore speak, write, and publish freely. "**
>
> —Declaration of the Rights of Man and of the Citizen

Versailles a radical and unmistakable message. Throughout France peasants began to rise in insurrection against their lords, ransacking manor houses and burning feudal documents that recorded their obligations. In some areas peasants reinstated traditional village practices, undoing recent enclosures and reoccupying old common lands. They seized forests, and taxes went unpaid. Fear of marauders and vagabonds hired by vengeful landlords—called the **Great Fear** by contemporaries—seized the rural poor and fanned the flames of rebellion.

Faced with chaos, yet afraid to call on the king to restore order, some liberal nobles and middle-class delegates at Versailles responded to peasant demands with a surprise maneuver on the night of August 4, 1789. The duke of Aiguillon, a powerful noble landowner, declared that the peasantry was seeking "to throw off at last a yoke that has for many centuries weighted it down."[3] He urged equality in taxation and the elimination of feudal dues. In the end, all the old noble privileges—peasant serfdom where it still existed, exclusive hunting rights, fees for justice, village monopolies, the right to make peasants work on the roads, and a host of other dues—were abolished along with the tithes paid to the church. Thus the French peasantry achieved an unprecedented victory in the early days of revolutionary upheaval. Henceforth, French peasants would seek mainly to protect and consolidate their triumph.

Having granted new rights to the peasantry, the National Assembly moved forward with its mission of reform. On August 27, 1789, it issued the Declaration of the Rights of Man and of the Citizen, which stated, "Men are born and remain free and equal in rights." The declaration also maintained that mankind's natural rights are "liberty, property, security,

The Figure of Liberty In this painting, the figure of Liberty bears a copy of the Declaration of the Rights of Man and of the Citizen in one hand and a pike to defend them in the other. The painting, by female artist and ardent revolutionary Nanine Vallain, hung in the Jacobin club until its fall from power. (Musée de la Revolution Française, Vizille/The Bridgeman Art Library)

The Great Fear, 1789

and resistance to oppression" and that "every man is presumed innocent until he is proven guilty." As for law, "it is an expression of the general will; all citizens have the right to concur personally or through their representatives in its formation. . . . Free expression of thoughts and opinions is one of the most precious rights of mankind: every citizen may therefore speak, write, and publish freely." In short, this call of the liberal revolutionary ideal guaranteed equality before the law, representative government for a sovereign people, and individual freedom. This revolutionary credo, only two pages long, was disseminated throughout France and Europe and around the world.

> **Great Fear** The fear of noble reprisals against peasant uprisings that seized the French countryside and led to further revolt.

Parisian Women March on Versailles

While high-minded in principle, the National Assembly's declaration had little practical effect for the poor and hungry people of Paris, where a revolutionary spirit continued to smolder. The economic crisis in the city worsened after the fall of the Bastille, as aristocrats fled the country and the luxury market collapsed. Foreign markets also shrank in the aftermath of the crisis, and unemployment among the urban working class grew. In addition, women — the traditional managers of food and resources in poor homes — could no longer look to the church, which had been stripped of its tithes, for aid.

On October 5 some seven thousand desperate women marched the twelve miles from Paris to Versailles to demand action. This great crowd, "armed with scythes, sticks and pikes," invaded the National Assembly. Interrupting a delegate's speech, a tough old woman defiantly shouted into the debate, "Who's that talking down there? Make the chatterbox shut up. That's not the point: the point is that we want bread."[4] Hers was the genuine voice of the people, essential to any understanding of the French Revolution.

The women invaded the royal apartments, killed some of the royal bodyguards, and furiously searched for the queen, Marie Antoinette, who was widely despised for her frivolous and supposedly immoral behavior. "We are going to cut off her head, tear out her heart, fry her liver, and that won't be the end of it," they shouted, surging through the palace. It seems likely that only the intervention of Lafayette and the National Guard saved the royal family. But the only way to calm the disorder was for the king to live closer to his people in Paris, as the crowd demanded.

A Constitutional Monarchy and Its Challenges

The day after the women's march on Versailles, the National Assembly followed the king to Paris, and the next two years, until September 1791, saw the consolidation of the liberal revolution. Under middle-class leadership, the National Assembly abolished the French nobility as a legal order and pushed forward with the creation of a **constitutional monarchy**, which Louis XVI reluctantly agreed to accept in July 1790. In the final constitution, the king remained the head of state, but all lawmaking power now resided in the National Assembly, elected by the wealthiest half of French males. New laws broadened women's rights to seek divorce, to inherit

constitutional monarchy
A form of government in which the king retains his position as head of state, while the authority to tax and make new laws resides in an elected body.

The Women of Paris March to Versailles On October 5, 1789, a large group of poor Parisian women marched to Versailles to protest the price of bread. For the people of Paris, the king was the baker of last resort, responsible for feeding his people during times of scarcity. The angry women forced the royal family to return with them and to live in Paris, rather than remain isolated from their subjects at court. (Erich Lessing/Art Resource, NY)

Village Festival in Honor of Old Age, 1795 The French Revolution inaugurated many new civic festivals in an attempt to erase memories of the Catholic holidays and feast days of the prerevolutionary era. As in bygone days, the new festivals, like this one honoring village elders, included dancing, drinking, and courting among the young couples of the village. Many people, however, especially in rural France, missed the religious tenor of prerevolutionary holidays. (Bibliothèque nationale de France/Archives Charmet/The Bridgeman Art Library)

property, and to obtain financial support for illegitimate children from fathers, but women were not allowed to hold political office or even vote.

This decision was attacked by a small number of men and women who believed that the rights of man should be extended to all French citizens. The liberal marquis de Condorcet accused the legislators of having "violated the principle of equality of rights by quietly depriving half of mankind of the right to participate in the formation of the laws."[5] Olympe de Gouges (1748–1793), a self-taught writer and woman of the people, took up her pen to protest the evils of slavery as well as the injustices done to women. In September 1791 she published her "Declaration of the Rights of Woman," a direct challenge to revolutionaries to respect the ideals of the great 1789 declaration. De Gouges's pamphlet echoed its famous predecessor, proclaiming, "Woman is born free and remains equal to man in rights." She further demanded that both sexes be "equally admissible to all public dignities, offices, and employments, according to their ability, and with no other distinction than their virtues and talents."

Such arguments found little sympathy among leaders of the Revolution. The editor of one revolutionary journal offered a public response to complaints he had received from women about their exclusion from politics. He agreed that they should be allowed to speak in assemblies, but not to vote or serve as representatives. As he explained, "a household should never remain deserted for a single instant. When the father of a family leaves to defend or lay claim to the rights of property, security, equality, or liberty in a public assembly, the mother of the family, focused on her domestic duties, must make order and cleanliness, ease and peace reign at home."[6] His sentiments represented the opinions of the vast majority of legislators and ordinary Frenchmen.

In addition to ruling on women's rights, the National Assembly replaced the complicated patchwork of historic provinces with eighty-three departments of approximately equal size. Monopolies, guilds, and workers' associations were prohibited, and barriers to trade within France were abolished in the name of economic liberty.

Thus the National Assembly applied the spirit of the Enlightenment in a thorough reform of France's laws and institutions.

The National Assembly also imposed a radical reorganization on the country's religious life. It granted religious freedom to the small minority of French Jews and Protestants. In November 1789 it nationalized the Catholic Church's property and abolished monasteries as useless relics of a distant past. The government used all former church property as collateral to guarantee a new paper currency, the assignats (A-sihg-nat), and then sold the property in an attempt to put the state's finances on a solid footing. Although the land was sold in large blocks, peasants eventually purchased much when it was subdivided. These purchases strengthened their attachment to the new revolutionary order in the countryside.

Imbued with the rationalism and skepticism of the eighteenth-century philosophes (see Chapter 17), many delegates distrusted popular piety and "superstitious religion." Thus in July 1790, with the Civil Constitution of the Clergy, they established a national church with priests chosen by voters. The National Assembly then forced the Catholic clergy to take a loyalty oath to the new government. The pope formally condemned this attempt to subjugate the church, and only half the priests of France swore the oath. Many sincere Christians, especially those in the countryside, were upset by these changes in the religious order. The attempt to remake the Catholic Church, like the abolition of guilds and workers' associations, sharpened the conflict between the educated classes and the common people that had been emerging in the eighteenth century.

Revolutionary Aspirations in Saint-Domingue

The French Revolution radically transformed not only the territorial nation of France but its overseas colonies as well. On the eve of the Revolution, Saint-Domingue — the most profitable of all Caribbean colonies — was even more rife with social tensions than France itself. The island was inhabited by a variety of social groups who resented and mistrusted one another. The European population included French colonial officials, wealthy plantation owners and merchants, and poor immigrants. Greatly outnumbering the white population were the

Saint-Domingue Slave Life Although the brutal conditions of plantation slavery left little time or energy for leisure, slaves on Saint-Domingue took advantage of their day of rest on Sunday to engage in social and religious activities. The law officially prohibited slaves of different masters from mingling together, but such gatherings were often tolerated if they remained peaceful. This image depicts a fight between two slaves, precisely the type of unrest and violence feared by authorities. (Musée du Nouveau Monde, La Rochelle/Photos12.com — ARJ)

colony's five hundred thousand slaves, along with a sizable population of free people of African and mixed African and European descent. Members of this last group referred to themselves as "free coloreds" or free people of color.

The 1685 *Code Noir* (Black Code) that set the parameters of slavery had granted free people of color the same legal status as whites: they could own property, live where they wished, and pursue any education or career they desired. From the 1760s on, however, colonial administrators began rescinding these rights, and by the time of the Revolution, myriad aspects of free coloreds' lives—from the professions they could practice, to the names they could adopt, to the clothes they could wear—were ruled by discriminatory laws. White planters eagerly welcomed these laws, convinced that the best defense of slavery was a rigid color line.

The political and intellectual turmoil of the 1780s, with its growing rhetoric of liberty, equality, and fraternity, raised new challenges and possibilities for each of these groups. For slaves, news of abolitionist movements in France and the royal government's own attempts to rein in the worst abuses of slavery led to hopes that the mother country might grant them freedom. Free people of color found in such rhetoric the principles on which to shore up their eroded legal and political rights. They looked to reforms in Paris as a means of gaining political enfranchisement and reasserting equal status with whites. The white elite, not surprisingly, saw matters very differently. Infuriated by talk of abolition and determined to protect their way of life, they looked to revolutionary ideals of representative government for the chance to gain control of their own affairs, as had the American colonists before them. The meeting of the Estates General and the Declaration of the Rights of Man and of the Citizen raised these conflicting colonial aspirations to new levels.

The National Assembly frustrated the hopes of all these groups. Cowed by colonial representatives who claimed that support for free people of color would result in slave insurrection and independence, the Assembly refused to extend French constitutional safeguards to the colonies. Instead, it ruled that each colony would draft its own constitution, with free rein over decisions on slavery and the enfranchisement of free people of color. After dealing this blow to the aspirations of slaves and free coloreds, the committee also reaffirmed French monopolies over colonial trade, thereby angering planters as well.

In July 1790 Vincent Ogé (aw-ZHAY), a free man of color, returned to Saint-Domingue from Paris determined to redress these issues. He raised an army of several hundred and sent letters to the new Provincial Assembly of Saint-Domingue demanding political rights for all free citizens, a statute already passed in France. After initial victories, his army was defeated, and Ogé himself was tortured and executed by colonial officials. In May 1791, in an attempt to respond to what it perceived as partly justified grievances, the National Assembly granted political rights to free people of color born to two free parents who possessed sufficient property. When news of this legislation arrived in Saint-Domingue, the white elite was furious, and the colonial governor refused to enact it. Violence now erupted between groups of whites and free coloreds in parts of the colony. The liberal revolution had failed to satisfy the contradictory ambitions in the colonies.

World War and Republican France, 1791–1799

How and why did the Revolution take a radical turn at home and in the colonies?

When Louis XVI accepted the final version of the National Assembly's constitution in September 1791, a young and still obscure provincial lawyer and delegate named Maximilien Robespierre (1758–1794) concluded that "The Revolution is over." Robespierre (ROHBZ-pee-air) was right in the sense that the most constructive and lasting reforms were in place; no substantial reforms in the way of liberty would be gained in the next generation. Yet he was wrong in the sense that a much more radical stage lay ahead. New heroes and new ideologies were to emerge in revolutionary wars and international conflict in which Robespierre himself would play a central role.

Foreign Reactions to the Revolution

The outbreak and progress of revolution in France produced great excitement and a sharp division of opinion in Europe and the United States. Liberals and radicals saw a mighty triumph of liberty over despotism. In Great Britain, especially, they hoped that the French example would lead to a fundamental reordering of Parliament, which was in the hands of the aristocracy and a few wealthy merchants. On the other hand, conservative leaders such as British statesman Edmund Burke (1729–1797) were deeply troubled by the aroused spirit of reform. In 1790 Burke published *Reflections on the Revolution in France*, in which he defended inherited privileges in general and those of the English monarchy and aristocracy in particular. He glorified the unrepresentative Parliament and predicted that reform like that occurring in France would lead only to chaos and tyranny. Burke's work sparked much debate.

One passionate rebuttal came from a young writer in London, Mary Wollstonecraft (1759–1797). Determined to be independent in a society that expected women of her class to become obedient wives, Wollstonecraft (WOOL-stuhn-kraft) struggled for years to earn her living as a governess and a teacher — practically the only acceptable careers for single educated women — before attaining success as a translator and author. Incensed by Burke's book, she immediately wrote a blistering, widely read attack, *A Vindication of the Rights of Man* (1790). Two years later, she published her masterpiece, *A Vindication of the Rights of Woman* (1792). Like de Gouges one year before her, Wollstonecraft demanded equal rights for women. She advocated rigorous coeducation, which would make women better wives and mothers, good citizens, and economically independent. Women could manage businesses and enter politics if only men would give them the chance. Wollstonecraft's analysis testifies to the power of the Revolution to excite and inspire outside of France. The controversial book was quickly reissued in French and American editions. It became a classic of the early feminist movement.

The kings and nobles of continental Europe, who had at first welcomed the revolution in France as weakening a competing power, began to feel as threatened by its message, as did conservatives such as Burke. In June 1791 Louis XVI and Marie Antoinette were arrested and returned to Paris after trying unsuccessfully to slip out of France. For supporters of the Revolution, the attempted flight was proof that the king's professed acceptance of the constitution was a sham and that he was a traitor intent on procuring foreign support for an invasion of France. The shock of the arrest of a crowned head of state led the monarchs of Austria and Prussia to issue the Declaration of Pillnitz two months later. The Declaration professed the rulers' willingness to intervene in France to restore Louis XVI's monarchical rule if necessary. It was expected to have a sobering effect on revolutionary France without causing war.

But the crowned heads of Europe misjudged the revolutionary spirit in France. The new representative body that convened in Paris in October 1791, called the Legislative Assembly, had completely new delegates and a different character. The great majority of the legislators were still prosperous, well-educated middle-class men, but they were younger and less cautious than their predecessors. Many of the deputies belonged to the political **Jacobin club**, named after the former monastery in which they held their meetings. Such clubs had proliferated in Parisian neighborhoods since the beginning of the Revolution, drawing men and women to debate the burning political questions of the day.

The Outbreak of War

The new representatives to the Assembly whipped themselves into a patriotic fury against the Declaration of

Jacobin club A political club in revolutionary France whose members were well-educated radical republicans.

The Capture of Louis XVI, June 1791 This painting commemorates the midnight arrest of Louis XVI and the royal family as they tried to flee France in disguise and reach counter-revolutionaries in the Austrian Netherlands. Recognized and stopped at Varennes, just forty miles from the border, the king still nearly succeeded, telling municipal officers that dangerous mobs controlled Paris and securing promises of safe passage. But within hours the local leaders reversed themselves, and by morning Louis XVI was headed back to Paris. (Bibliothèque nationale de France)

Pillnitz. If the kings of Europe were attempting to incite war against France, then "we will incite a war of people against kings. . . . Ten million Frenchmen, kindled by the fire of liberty, armed with the sword, with reason, with eloquence would be able to change the face of the world and make the tyrants tremble on their thrones."⁷ Only Robespierre and a very few others argued that people would not welcome liberation at the point of a gun. Such warnings were brushed aside. France would "rise to the full height of her mission," as one deputy urged. In April 1792 France declared war on Francis II, the Habsburg monarch.

France's crusade against tyranny went poorly at first. Prussian forces joined Austria against the French, who broke and fled at their first military encounter with this First Coalition. The road to Paris lay open, and it is possible that only conflict between the Eastern monarchs over the division of Poland (see Chapter 17) saved France from an early and total defeat.

The Assembly declared the country in danger, and volunteers rallied to the capital. In this supercharged wartime atmosphere, rumors of treason by the king and queen spread in Paris. On August 10, 1792, a revolutionary crowd attacked the royal palace at the Tuileries (TWEE-luh-reez), while the king and his family fled for their lives to the nearby Legislative Assembly. Rather than offering refuge, the Assembly suspended the king from all his functions, imprisoned him, and called for a new National Convention to be elected by universal male suffrage. Monarchy in France was on its deathbed, mortally wounded by war and popular upheaval.

The Second Revolution

The fall of the monarchy marked a rapid radicalization of the Revolution, a phase that historians often call the **second revolution**. Louis's imprisonment was followed by the September Massacres. Wild stories that imprisoned counter-revolutionary aristocrats and priests were plotting with the allied invaders seized the city. As a result, angry crowds invaded the prisons of Paris and slaughtered half the men and women they found. In late September 1792 the new, popularly elected National Convention proclaimed France a republic, a nation in which the people, instead of a monarch, held sovereign power.

All the members of the National Convention were republicans, and at the beginning almost all belonged to the Jacobin (JA-kuh-bihn) club of Paris. But the Jacobins themselves were increasingly divided into two bitterly competitive groups—the **Girondists** (juh-RAHN-dihsts), named after a department in southwestern France that was home to several of their leaders, and **the Mountain**, led by Robespierre and another young lawyer, Georges Jacques Danton. The Mountain was so called because its members sat on the uppermost benches on the left side of the assembly hall. A majority of the indecisive Convention members, seated in the "Plain" below, floated back and forth between the rival factions.

This division emerged clearly after the National Convention overwhelmingly convicted Louis XVI of treason. The Girondists accepted his guilt but did not wish to put the king to death. By a narrow majority, the Mountain carried the day, and Louis was executed on January 21, 1793, on the newly invented guillotine. One of his last statements was "I am innocent and shall die without fear. I would that my death might bring happiness to the French, and ward off the dangers which I foresee."⁸ But both the Girondists and the Mountain were determined to continue the "war against tyranny." The Prussians had been stopped at the Battle of Valmy on September 20, 1792, one day before the republic was proclaimed. French armies then invaded Savoy and captured Nice, moved into the German Rhineland, and by November 1792 were occupying the entire Austrian Netherlands (modern Belgium).

> **second revolution** From 1792 to 1795, the second phase of the French Revolution, during which the fall of the French monarchy introduced a rapid radicalization of politics.
>
> **Girondists** A moderate group that fought for control of the French National Convention in 1793.
>
> **the Mountain** Led by Robespierre, the French National Convention's radical faction, which seized legislative power in 1793.

Everywhere they went, French armies of occupation chased the princes, abolished feudalism, and found support among some peasants and middle-class people. But the French armies also lived off the land, requisitioning food and supplies and plundering local treasures. The liberators looked increasingly like foreign invaders. International tensions mounted. In February 1793 the National Convention, at war with Austria and Prussia, declared war on Britain, Holland, and Spain as well. Republican France was now at war with almost all of Europe, a great war that would last almost without interruption until 1815.

Groups within France added to the turmoil. Peasants in western France revolted against being drafted into the army, with the Vendée region of Brittany emerging as the epicenter of revolt. Devout Catholics, royalists, and foreign agents encouraged their rebellion, and the counter-revolutionaries recruited veritable armies to fight for their cause.

In March 1793 the National Convention was locked in a life-and-death political

Areas of Insurrection, 1793

struggle between members of the Mountain and the more moderate Girondists, with the radicals accusing the Girondists of inciting sedition in the provinces. With the middle-class delegates so bitterly divided, the laboring poor of Paris once again emerged as the decisive political factor. The laboring poor and the petty traders were often known as the **sans-culottes** (sanz-koo-LAHT, "without breeches") because their men wore trousers instead of the knee breeches of the aristocracy and the solid middle class. They demanded radical political action to guarantee them their daily bread. The Mountain, sensing an opportunity to outmaneuver the Girondists, joined with sans-culottes activists in the city government to engineer a popular uprising. On June 2, 1793, armed sans-culottes invaded the Convention and forced deputies to arrest twenty-nine Girondist deputies for treason. All power passed to the Mountain.

The Convention also formed the Committee of Public Safety in April 1793 to deal with the threats from within and outside France. The committee, which Robespierre led, was given dictatorial power to deal with the national emergency. Moderates in the leading provincial cities of Caen, Bordeaux, Lyon, and Marseilles revolted against the committee's power and demanded a decentralized government. Counter-revolutionary forces in the Vendée won significant victories, and the repub-

sans-culottes The laboring poor of Paris, so called because the men wore trousers instead of the knee breeches of the aristocracy and middle class; the word came to refer to the militant radicals of the city.

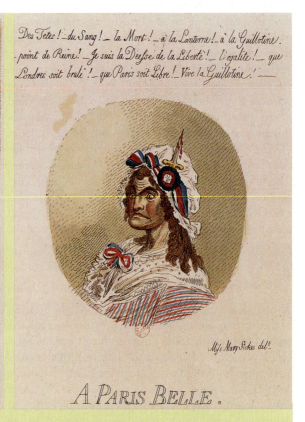

Picturing the Past

Contrasting Visions of the Sans-Culottes These two images offer profoundly different representations of a sans-culotte woman. The image on the left was created by a French artist, while the image on the right is English. The French words above the image on the right read in part, "Heads! Blood! Death! . . . I am the Goddess of Liberty! . . . Long Live the Guillotine!" (Bibliothèque nationale de France)

ANALYZING THE IMAGE How would you describe the woman on the left? What qualities does the artist seem to ascribe to her, and how do you think these qualities relate to the sans-culottes and the Revolution? How would you characterize the facial expression and attire of the woman on the right? How does the inclusion of the text contribute to your impressions of her?

CONNECTIONS What does the contrast between these two images suggest about differences between French and English perceptions of the sans-culottes and of the French Revolution? Why do you think the artists have chosen to depict women?

To complete this activity online, go to the Online Study Guide at **bedfordstmartins.com/mckaywest.**

lic's armies were driven back on all fronts. By July 1793 only the areas around Paris and on the eastern frontier were firmly held by the central government. Defeat seemed imminent.

Total War and the Terror

A year later, in July 1794, the central government had reasserted control over the provinces. In addition, the Austrian Netherlands and the Rhineland were once again in the hands of conquering French armies, and the First Coalition was falling apart. This remarkable change of fortune was due to the revolutionary government's success in harnessing, for perhaps the first time in history, the explosive forces of a planned economy, revolutionary terror, and modern nationalism in a total war effort.

Robespierre and the Committee of Public Safety advanced with implacable resolution on several fronts in 1793 and 1794. Claiming they alone could speak for the "general will" of the French people, they sought to impose republican unity across the nation, on pain of death if necessary. First, they collaborated with the fiercely patriotic and democratic sans-culottes, who retained the common people's faith in fair prices and a moral economic order and who distrusted most wealthy capitalists and all aristocrats. Thus in September 1793 Robespierre and his coworkers established, as best they could, a planned economy with egalitarian social overtones. Rather than let supply and demand determine prices, the government set maximum allowable prices for key products. Though the state was too weak to enforce all its price regulations, it did fix the price of bread in Paris at levels the poor could afford. Rationing was introduced, and bakers were permitted to make only the "bread of equality"—a brown bread made of a mixture of all available flours. White bread and pastries were outlawed as luxuries. The poor of Paris may not have eaten well, but at least they ate.

The people also worked, mainly to produce arms and munitions for the war effort. The government told craftsmen what to produce, nationalized many small workshops, and requisitioned raw materials and grain. The second revolution and the ascendancy of the sans-culottes had produced an embryonic emergency socialism, which thoroughly frightened Europe's propertied classes and greatly influenced the subsequent development of socialist ideology.

Second, while radical economic measures supplied the poor with bread and the armies with weapons, the **Reign of Terror** (1793–1794) solidified the home front. Special revolutionary courts responsible only to Robespierre's Committee of Public Safety tried "enemies of the nation" for political crimes. Some forty thousand French men and women were executed or died in prison. Another three hundred thousand suspects were arrested. Robespierre's Reign of Terror is one of the most controversial phases of the French Revolution. Presented as a necessary measure to save the republic, the Terror was a political weapon directed against all suspected of opposing the revolutionary government. As Robespierre himself put it, "Terror is nothing more than prompt, severe inflexible justice."[9] For many Europeans of the time, however, the Reign of Terror represented a frightening perversion of the generous ideals of 1789, strengthening the belief that France

Reign of Terror The period from 1793 to 1794 during which Robespierre's Committee of Public Safety tried and executed thousands suspected of treason and a new revolutionary culture was imposed.

> ❝ Terror is nothing more than prompt, severe inflexible justice. ❞
> — ROBESPIERRE

The Guillotine Prior to the French Revolution, methods of execution included hanging and being broken at the wheel. Only nobles enjoyed the privilege of a relatively swift and painless death by decapitation, delivered by an executioner's ax. The guillotine, a model of which is shown here, was devised by French revolutionaries as a humane and egalitarian form of execution. Ironically, due to the mass executions under the Terror, it is now seen instead as a symbol of revolutionary cruelty. (Musée de la Ville de Paris, Musée Carnavalet, Paris/Lauros/Giraudon, The Bridgeman Art Library)

had foolishly replaced a weak king with a bloody dictatorship.

In their efforts to impose unity, the Jacobins took actions to suppress women's participation in political debate, which they perceived as disorderly and a distraction from women's proper place in the home. On October 30, 1793, the National Convention declared that "The clubs and popular societies of women, under whatever denomination are prohibited." Included in the ban were such groups as the Society of Revolutionary Republican Women, a club of militant women that had called for the creation of female armies to combat counter-revolution.[10] Among those convicted of sedition was writer Olympe de Gouges, who was sent to the guillotine in November 1793.

Beyond imposing political unity by force, the program of the Terror also included efforts to transform French citizens into true republican patriots by bringing the Revolution into all aspects of everyday life. The government sponsored revolutionary art and songs as well as a new series of secular holidays and open-air festivals to celebrate republican virtue and a love of nation. They attempted to rationalize French daily life by adopting the decimal system for weights and measures and a new calendar based on ten-day weeks. (See "Living in the Past: A Revolution of Culture and Daily Life," page 640.) An important element of this cultural revolution was the campaign of **dechristianization**, which aimed to eliminate Catholic symbols and beliefs. Many churches were sold, clerics were humiliated and persecuted, and religious images and statues were destroyed. Fearful of the hostility aroused in rural France, Robespierre called for a halt to dechristianization measures in mid-1794.

The third and perhaps most decisive element in the French republic's victory over the First Coalition was its ability to draw on the explosive power of patriotic dedication to a national state and a national mission. An essential part of modern nationalism, which would fully emerge

dechristianization
Campaign to eliminate Christian faith and practice in France undertaken by the revolutionary government.

The French Revolution

▪ National Assembly (1789–1791)

May 5, 1789	Estates General meets at Versailles
June 17, 1789	Third estate declares itself the National Assembly
June 20, 1789	Oath of the Tennis Court
July 14, 1789	Storming of the Bastille
July–August 1789	Great Fear
August 4, 1789	Abolishment of feudal privileges
August 27, 1789	Declaration of the Rights of Man and of the Citizen
October 5, 1789	Women march on Versailles; royal family returns to Paris
November 1789	National Assembly confiscates church land
July 1790	Civil Constitution of the Clergy establishes a national church; Louis XVI agrees to constitutional monarchy
June 1791	Royal family arrested while fleeing France
August 1791	Declaration of Pillnitz; slave insurrections in Saint-Domingue

▪ Legislative Assembly (1791–1792)

April 1792	France declares war on Austria; enfranchisement of free people of color
August 1792	Mob attacks the palace, and Legislative Assembly takes Louis XVI prisoner

▪ National Convention (1792–1795)

September 1792	September Massacres; National Convention abolishes monarchy and declares France a republic
January 1793	Louis XVI executed
February 1793	France declares war on Britain, Holland, and Spain; revolts take place in some provinces
March 1793	Struggle between Girondists and the Mountain
April 1793	Creation of the Committee of Public Safety
June 1793	Arrest of Girondist leaders
September 1793	Price controls instituted; British troops invade Saint-Domingue
October 1793	National Convention bans women's political societies
1793–1794	Reign of Terror
February 1794	Abolishment of slavery in all French territories
Spring 1794	French armies victorious on all fronts
July 1794	Robespierre executed; Thermidorian reaction begins

▪ The Directory (1795–1799)

1795	Economic controls abolished; suppression of the sans-culottes begins
1796	France regains control of Saint-Domingue under Toussaint L'Ouverture
1799	Napoleon seizes power

throughout Europe in the nineteenth century, this commitment was something new in history. With a common language and a common tradition newly reinforced by the ideas of popular sovereignty and democracy, large numbers of French people were stirred by a common loyalty. They developed an intense emotional commitment to the defense of the nation, and they saw the war as a life-and-death struggle between good and evil.

Everyone had to participate in the national effort. According to a famous decree of August 23, 1793:

> *The young men shall go to battle and the married men shall forge arms. The women shall make tents and clothes, and shall serve in the hospitals; children shall tear rags into lint. The old men will be guided to the public places of the cities to kindle the courage of the young warriors and to preach the unity of the Republic and the hatred of kings.*

The all-out mobilization of French resources under the Terror combined with the fervor of modern nationalism to create an awesome fighting machine. After August 1793 all unmarried young men were subject to the draft, and by January 1794 the French had about eight hundred thousand soldiers on active duty in fourteen armies. A force of this size was unprecedented in the history of European warfare; French armed forces outnumbered their enemies almost four to one.[11] The revolutionary government deployed this awesome force to combat internal as well as external enemies. Bitter resistance from the Vendée rebels could not withstand the ruthless forces of the republic, resulting in some one hundred thousand deaths among the opposition forces.

Well-trained, well-equipped, and constantly indoctrinated, the enormous armies of the republic were led by young, impetuous generals. These generals often had risen from the ranks, and they personified the opportunities the Revolution offered gifted sons of the people. Following orders from Paris to attack relentlessly, French generals used mass assaults at bayonet point to overwhelm the enemy. "No maneuvering, nothing elaborate," declared the fearless General Hoche. "Just cold steel, passion and patriotism."[12] By spring 1794 French armies were victorious on all fronts. The republic was saved.

Revolution in Saint-Domingue

Just as the sans-culottes had been instrumental in pushing forward more radical reforms in France, the second stage of revolution in Saint-Domingue also resulted from decisive action from below. In August 1791 slaves, who had been witnesses to the confrontation between whites and free coloreds for over a year, took events into their own hands. Groups of slaves held a series of nighttime meetings to plan a mass insurrection. These meetings reportedly included religious ceremonies in which participants made ritual offerings and swore a sacred oath

Slave Revolt on Saint-Domingue Starting in August 1791 the slaves of Saint-Domingue rose in revolt, an event captured vividly by this engraving. (Giraudon/Art Resource, NY)

A Revolution of Culture and Daily Life

LIVING IN THE PAST

THE FRENCH REVOLUTION BROUGHT SWEEPING POLITICAL AND SOCIAL CHANGE to France, removing one of the oldest monarchies in Europe in favor of broad-based representative government and eliminating age-old distinctions between nobles and commoners. Revolutionaries feared, however, that these measures were not enough to transform the nation. They therefore undertook a parallel revolution of culture intended to purify and regenerate the French people and turn former royal subjects into patriotic citizens capable of realizing the dream of liberty, equality, and fraternity.

To bring about cultural revolution, officials of the new republic targeted the most fundamental elements of daily life: the experience of space and time. Prior to the Revolution, regions of France had their own systems of measurement, meaning that the length of an inch or the weight of a pound differed substantially across the realm. Disgusted with the inefficiency of this state of affairs and determined to impose national unity, the government adopted the decimal-based metric system first proposed in 1670. The length of the meter was scientifically set at one ten-millionth of the distance from the pole to the equator. Henceforth, all French citizens would inhabit spaces that were measured and divided in the same way.

The government attempted a similar rationalization of the calendar. Instead of twelve months of varying lengths, each of the twelve months on the new revolutionary calendar was made up of three ten-day weeks, with a five- or six-day interval at the end of each year. To mark the total rebirth of time, the new calendar began at Year 1 on the day of the foundation of the French Republic (September 22, 1792). A series of festivals with patriotic themes replaced the traditional Catholic feast days. There was even a short-lived attempt to put the clock on a decimal system.

Cultural revolution also took on more concrete forms. Every citizen was required to wear a cockade on his or her hat, like the one shown on this plate celebrating the festival of the Supreme Being (a form of deism promoted by Robespierre as the state religion), to symbolize loyalty to the republic. Enterprising merchants sold a plethora of everyday goods with revolutionary themes. One could eat from revolutionary plates, drink from revolutionary mugs, waft revolutionary fans, and even decorate the home with revolutionary wallpaper. Living the French Revolution meant entering a whole new world of sense and experience.

Plate showing a festival of the Cult of the Supreme Being. (Erich Lessing/Art Resource, NY)

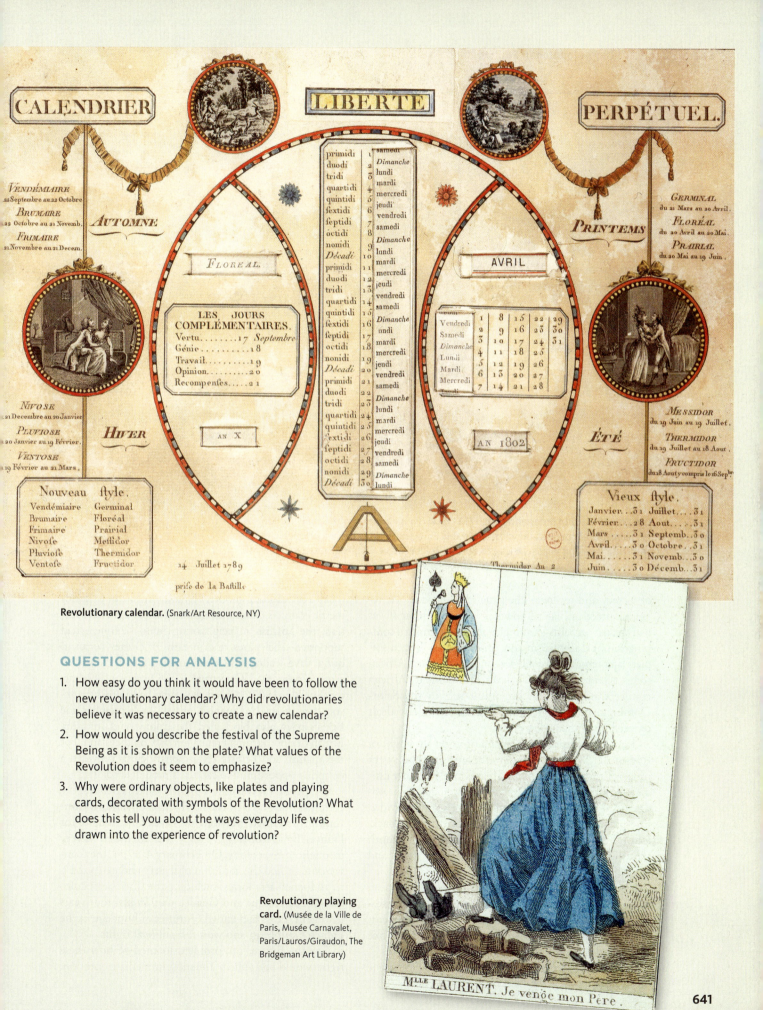

Revolutionary calendar. (Snark/Art Resource, NY)

QUESTIONS FOR ANALYSIS

1. How easy do you think it would have been to follow the new revolutionary calendar? Why did revolutionaries believe it was necessary to create a new calendar?
2. How would you describe the festival of the Supreme Being as it is shown on the plate? What values of the Revolution does it seem to emphasize?
3. Why were ordinary objects, like plates and playing cards, decorated with symbols of the Revolution? What does this tell you about the ways everyday life was drawn into the experience of revolution?

Revolutionary playing card. (Musée de la Ville de Paris, Musée Carnavalet, Paris/Lauros/Giraudon, The Bridgeman Art Library)

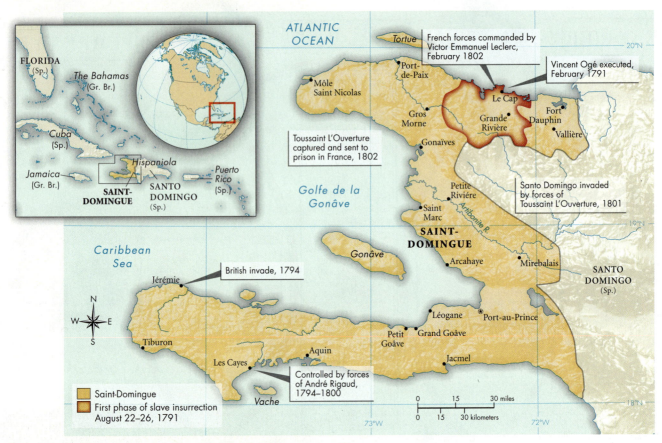

Map 20.1 The War of Haitian Independence, 1791–1804 Neighbored by the Spanish colony of Santo Domingo, Saint-Domingue was the most profitable European colony in the Caribbean. In 1770 the French transferred the capital from Le Cap to Port-au-Prince. Slave revolts erupted in the north near Le Cap in 1791. Port-au-Prince became capital of the newly independent Haiti in 1804.

of secrecy and revenge. The rituals belonged to the religious practices, later known as "voodoo," that slaves had created on Saint-Domingue plantations from a combination of Catholicism and African cults. French soldiers later reported that religious incantations and African songs accompanied rebel slaves into combat. African culture thus played an important role in the Saint-Domingue revolution, alongside Enlightenment ideals of freedom and equality.

Revolts began on a few plantations on the night of August 22. Within a few days the uprising had swept much of the northern plain, creating a slave army estimated at around 2,000 individuals. By August 27 it was described by one observer as "10,000 strong, divided into 3 armies, of whom 700 or 800 are on horseback, and tolerably well-armed."[13] During the next month slaves attacked and destroyed hundreds of sugar and coffee plantations.

On April 4, 1792, as war loomed with the European states, the National Assembly issued a decree enfranchising all free blacks and free people of color. The Assembly hoped this measure would win the loyalty of free blacks and their aid in defeating the slave rebellion.

Warfare in Europe soon spread to Saint-Domingue (Map 20.1), adding another complicating factor to its domestic conflicts. Since the beginning of the slave insurrection, the Spanish in neighboring Santo Domingo had supported rebel slaves, and in early 1793 they began to bring slave leaders and their soldiers into the Spanish army. Toussaint L'Ouverture (TOO-sahn LOO-vair-toor) (1743–1803), a freed slave who had joined the revolt, was named a Spanish officer. In September the British navy also blockaded the colony, and invading British troops captured French territory on the island. For the Spanish and British, revolutionary chaos provided a tempting opportunity to capture a profitable colony.

Desperate for forces to oppose France's enemies, the commissioners sent by the newly elected National Convention promised freedom to slaves who fought for France. By October 1793 they had abolished slavery throughout the colony. On February 4, 1794, the Convention ratified the abolition of slavery and extended it to all French territories, including the Caribbean colonies of Martinique and Guadeloupe. In just four years insurgent slaves had ended centuries of bondage in the French Caribbean and won full political rights.

For the future, the problem loomed of how these rights would be applied. The most immediate question, however, was whether France would be able to retain the colony, which was still under attack by Spanish and British forces. The tide began to turn when Toussaint L'Ouverture switched sides, bringing his military and political skills, along with four thousand well-trained soldiers, to support the French war effort.

By 1796 the French had gradually regained control of the colony, and L'Ouverture had emerged as the key leader of the combined slave and free colored forces. In May 1796 he was named commander of the western province of Saint-Domingue (see Map 20.1). The increasingly conservative nature of the French government during the Thermidorian reaction, however, threatened to undo the gains made by former slaves and free people of color. As exiled planters gained a stronger voice in French policymaking, L'Ouverture and other local leaders grew ever more wary of what the future might hold.

The Thermidorian Reaction and the Directory

The success of the French armies led Robespierre and the Committee of Public Safety to relax the emergency economic controls, but they extended the political Reign of Terror. In March 1794, to the horror of many sans-culottes, Robespierre's Terror wiped out many of his critics. Two weeks later, Robespierre sent long-standing collaborators, including the famous orator Danton, up the steps to the guillotine. A group of radicals and moderates in the Convention, knowing that they might be next, organized a conspiracy. They howled down Robespierre when he tried to speak to the National Convention on July 27, 1794 — a date known as "9 Thermidor" according to France's newly adopted republican calendar. The next day it was Robespierre's turn to be shaved by the revolutionary razor.

As Robespierre's closest supporters followed their leader to the guillotine, France unexpectedly experienced a thorough reaction to the despotism of the Reign of Terror. In a general way, this **Thermidorian reaction** recalled the early days of the Revolution. The respectable middle-class lawyers and professionals who had led the liberal Revolution of 1789 reasserted their authority, drawing support from their own class,

the provincial cities, and the better-off peasants. In 1795 the National Convention abolished many economic controls, let prices rise sharply, and severely restricted the local political organizations in which the sans-culottes had their strength.

The collapse of economic controls, coupled with runaway inflation, hit the working poor very hard. After the Convention used the army to suppress the sans-culottes' protests, the urban poor lost their revolutionary fervor. Excluded and disillusioned, they would have little interest in and influence on politics until 1830. The poor of the countryside turned toward religion as a relief from earthly cares. Rural women, especially, brought back the Catholic Church and the open worship of God as the government began to soften its antireligious revolutionary stance.

> **Thermidorian reaction** A reaction to the violence of the Reign of Terror in 1794, resulting in the execution of Robespierre and the loosening of economic controls.

As for the middle-class members of the National Convention, in 1795 they wrote yet another constitution that they believed would guarantee their economic position and political supremacy. As in previous elections, the mass of the population voted only

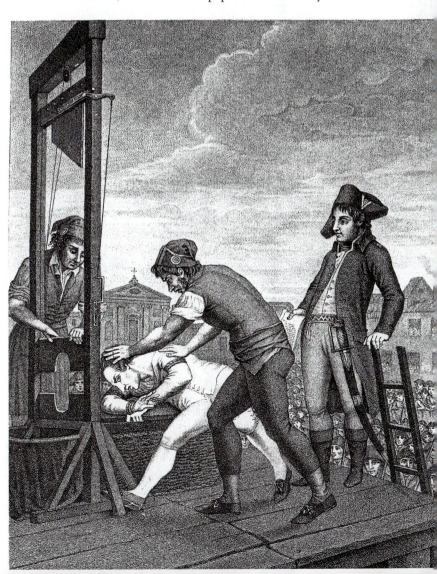

The Execution of Robespierre Completely wooden except for the heavy iron blade, the guillotine was painted red for Robespierre's execution, a detail not captured in this black-and-white engraving of the 1794 event. Large crowds witnessed the execution in a majestic public square in central Paris, then known as the Place de la Revolution and now called the Place de la Concorde (Harmony Square). (Snark/Art Resource, NY)

for electors, whose number was cut back to men of substantial means. Electors then elected the members of a reorganized legislative assembly as well as key officials throughout France. The new assembly also chose a five-man executive called the Directory.

The Directory continued to support French military expansion abroad. War was no longer so much a crusade as a means to meet ever-present, ever-unsolved economic problems. Large, victorious French armies reduced unemployment at home and were able to live off the territories they conquered and plundered. Yet the French people felt a widespread disgust with war and food rationing, and they quickly grew weary of the unprincipled actions of the Directory. This general dissatisfaction revealed itself clearly in the national elections of 1797, which returned a large number of conservative and even monarchist deputies who favored peace at almost any price. The members of the Directory, fearing for their skins, used the army to nullify the elections and began to govern dictatorially. Two years later Napoleon Bonaparte ended the Directory in a coup d'état (koo day-TAH) and substituted a strong dictatorship for a weak one. The effort to establish stable representative government had failed.

> May they learn from you that the God of peace is also the God of armies, and that He fights alongside those who defend the independence and liberty of France.

— NAPOLEON BONAPARTE

The Napoleonic Era, 1799–1815

Why did Napoleon Bonaparte assume control of France, and what factors led to his downfall? How did the new republic of Haiti gain independence from France?

For almost fifteen years, from 1799 to 1814, France was in the hands of a keen-minded military dictator of exceptional ability. One of history's most fascinating leaders, Napoleon Bonaparte (1769–1821) realized the need to put an end to civil strife in France in order to create unity and consolidate his rule. And he did. But Napoleon saw himself as a man of destiny, and the glory of war and the dream of universal empire proved irresistible. For years he spiraled from victory to victory, but in the end he was destroyed by a mighty coalition united in fear of his restless ambition.

Napoleonic Code French civil code promulgated in 1804 that reasserted the 1789 principles of the equality of all male citizens before the law and the absolute security of wealth and private property as well as restricting rights accorded to women by previous revolutionary laws.

Napoleon's Rule of France

Born in Corsica into an impoverished noble family in 1769, Napoleon left home and became a lieutenant in the French artillery in 1785. After a brief and unsuccessful adventure fighting for Corsican independence in 1789, he returned to France as a French patriot and a dedicated revolutionary. Rising rapidly in the new army, Napoleon was placed in command of French forces in Italy and won brilliant victories there in 1796 and 1797. His next campaign, in Egypt, was a failure, but Napoleon returned to France before the fiasco was generally known, and his reputation remained intact.

Napoleon soon learned that some prominent members of the legislature were plotting against the Directory. The dissatisfaction of these plotters stemmed not so much from the fact that the Directory was a dictatorship as from the fact that it was a weak dictatorship. Ten years of upheaval and uncertainty had made firm rule much more appealing than liberty and popular politics to these disillusioned revolutionaries. The abbé Sieyès personified this evolution in thinking. In 1789 he had written that the nobility was grossly overprivileged and that the entire people should rule the French nation. Now Sieyès's motto was "Confidence from below, authority from above."

Like the other members of his group, Sieyès wanted a strong military ruler. The flamboyant thirty-year-old Napoleon, nationally revered for his heroism, was ideal. Thus the conspirators and Napoleon organized a takeover. On November 9, 1799, they ousted the Directors, and the following day soldiers disbanded the legislature at bayonet point. Napoleon was named first consul of the republic, and a new constitution consolidating his position was overwhelmingly approved in a plebiscite in December 1799. Republican appearances were maintained, but Napoleon became the real ruler of France.

The essence of Napoleon's domestic policy was to use his popularity and charisma to maintain order and end civil strife. He did so by working out unwritten agreements with powerful groups in France whereby the groups received favors in return for loyal service. Napoleon's bargain with the solid middle class was codified in the famous Civil Code of March 1804, also known as the **Napoleonic Code**, which reasserted two

The Coronation of Napoleon, 1804 In this detail from a grandiose painting by Jacques-Louis David, Napoleon, instead of the pope, prepares to crown his wife, Josephine, in an elaborate ceremony in Notre Dame Cathedral. Napoleon, the ultimate upstart, also crowned himself. Pope Pius VII, seated glumly behind the emperor, is reduced to being a spectator. (Louvre/Réunion des Musées Nationaux/Art Resource, NY)

of the fundamental principles of the Revolution of 1789: equality of all male citizens before the law, and absolute security of wealth and private property. Napoleon and the leading bankers of Paris established the privately owned Bank of France in 1800, which loyally served the interests of both the state and the financial oligarchy. Peasants were appeased when Napoleon defended the gains in land and status they had claimed during the Revolution.

At the same time, Napoleon built on the bureaucracy inherited from the Revolution and the Old Regime to create a thoroughly centralized state. He consolidated his rule by recruiting disillusioned revolutionaries for the network of ministers, prefects, and centrally appointed mayors that depended on him and came to serve him well. Only former revolutionaries who leaned too far to the left or to the right were pushed to the sidelines.[14] Nor were members of the old nobility slighted. In 1800 and again in 1802 Napoleon granted amnesty to one hundred thousand émigrés on the condition that they return to France and take a loyalty oath. Members of this returning elite soon ably occupied many high posts in the expanding centralized state. Napoleon also created a new imperial nobility in order to reward his most talented generals and officials.

Napoleon applied his diplomatic skills to healing the Catholic Church in France so that it could serve as a bulwark of social stability. After arduous negotiations, Napoleon and Pope Pius VII (pontificate 1800–1823) signed the Concordat (kuhn-KOHR-dat) of 1801. The pope gained the precious right for French Catholics to practice their religion freely, but Napoleon gained political power: his government now nominated bishops, paid the clergy, and exerted great influence over the church in France. In an 1802 proclamation, he called on priests to help instill patriotism for the "fatherland":

> *Exert for it all the force and ascendancy of spirit that your ministry gives you; that your lessons and examples may form in young citizens the love of our institutions, respect for and attachment to the tutelary authorities which have been created to protect them; may they learn from you that the God of peace is also the God of armies, and that He fights alongside those who defend the independence and liberty of France.*

The domestic reforms of Napoleon's early years were his greatest achievement. Much of his legal and administrative reorganization has survived in France to this day. More generally, Napoleon's domestic initiatives gave the great majority of French people a welcome sense of stability and national unity.

Order and unity had a price: authoritarian rule. Women, who had often participated in revolutionary politics without having legal equality, lost many of the gains they made in the 1790s. Under the new Napoleonic Code, women were dependents of either their fathers or their husbands, and they could not make contracts or have bank accounts in their own names. Napoleon and his advisers aimed at re-establishing a family monarchy, where the power of the husband and father was as absolute over the wife and the children as that of Napoleon was over his subjects.

Free speech and freedom of the press were continually violated. By 1811 only four newspapers were left, and they were little more than organs of government propaganda. The occasional elections were a farce. Later laws prescribed harsh penalties for political offenses, and people were watched carefully under an efficient spy system. People suspected of subversive activities were arbitrarily detained, placed under house arrest, or consigned to insane asylums. After 1810 political suspects were held in state prisons, as they had been during the Terror. There were about twenty-five hundred such political prisoners in 1814.

Napoleon's Expansion in Europe

Napoleon was above all a great military man. After coming to power in 1799 he sent peace feelers to Austria and Great Britain, the two remaining members of the Second Coalition that had been formed against France in 1798. When these overtures were rejected, French armies led by Napoleon decisively defeated the Austrians. In the Treaty of Lunéville (1801), Austria accepted the loss of almost all its Italian possessions, and German territory on the west bank of the Rhine was incorporated into France. The British agreed to the Treaty of Amiens in 1802, allowing France to remain in control of Holland, the Austrian Netherlands, the west bank of the Rhine, and most of the Italian peninsula. The Treaty of Amiens was clearly a diplomatic triumph for Napoleon, and peace with honor and profit increased his popularity at home.

In 1802 Napoleon was secure but driven to expand his power. Aggressively redrawing the map of Germany so as to weaken Austria and encourage the secondary states of southwestern Germany to side with France, Napoleon tried to restrict British trade with all of Europe. He then plotted to attack Great Britain, but his Mediterranean fleet was destroyed by Lord Nelson at the Battle of Trafalgar on October 21, 1805. Invasion of England was henceforth impossible. Renewed fighting had its advantages, however, for the first consul used the wartime atmosphere to have himself proclaimed emperor in late 1804.

Austria, Russia, and Sweden joined with Britain to form the Third Coalition against France shortly before the Battle of Trafalgar. Actions such as Napoleon's assumption of the Italian crown had convinced both Alexander I of Russia and Francis II of Austria that Napoleon was a threat to their interests and to the European balance of power. Yet the Austrians and the Russians were no match for Napoleon, who scored a brilliant victory over them at the Battle of Austerlitz in December 1805. Alexander I decided to pull back, and Austria accepted large territorial losses in return for peace as the Third Coalition collapsed.

German Confederation of the Rhine, 1806

Napoleon then proceeded to reorganize the German states to his liking. In 1806 he abolished many of the tiny German states as well as the ancient Holy Roman Empire and established by decree the German Confederation of the Rhine, a union of fifteen German states minus Austria, Prussia, and Saxony. Naming himself "protector" of the confederation, Napoleon firmly controlled western Germany.

Napoleon's intervention in German affairs alarmed the Prussians, who mobilized their armies after more than a decade of peace with France. Napoleon attacked and won two more brilliant victories in October 1806 at Jena and Auerstädt, where the Prussians were outnumbered two to one. The war with Prussia, now joined by Russia, continued into the following spring. After Napoleon's larger armies won another victory, Alexander I of Russia was ready to negotiate the peace. In the subsequent treaties of Tilsit in 1807, Prussia lost half of its population, while Russia accepted Napoleon's reorganization of western and central Europe and promised to enforce Napoleon's economic blockade against British goods.

The War of Haitian Independence

In the midst of these victories, Napoleon was forced to accept defeat overseas. With Toussaint L'Ouverture acting increasingly as an independent ruler of the western province of Saint-Domingue, another general, André

Rigaud, set up his own government in the southern peninsula, which had long been more isolated from France than the rest of the colony. Both leaders maintained policies, initially established by the French, of requiring former slaves to continue to work on their plantations. They believed that reconstructing the plantation economy was crucial to maintaining their military and political victories, and thus harshly suppressed resistance from former slaves.

Tensions mounted, however, between L'Ouverture and Rigaud. While L'Ouverture was a freed slave of African descent, Rigaud belonged to the free colored elite. This elite resented the growing power of former slaves like L'Ouverture, who in turn accused them of adopting the racism of white settlers. Civil war broke out between the two sides in 1799 when L'Ouverture's forces, led by his lieutenant Jean Jacques Dessalines (deh-suh-LEEN), invaded the south. Victory over Rigaud gave L'Ouverture control of the entire colony. (See "Individuals in Society: Toussaint L'Ouverture," page 648.)

This victory was soon challenged by Napoleon, who had his own plans for using profits from Caribbean plantations as a basis for expanding French power. His new constitution of 1799 opened the way for a re-establishment of slavery much feared in the colony. When the colonial assembly of Saint-Domingue, under L'Ouverture's direction, drafted its own constitution—which reaffirmed the abolition of slavery and granted L'Ouverture governorship for life—Napoleon viewed it as a seditious act. He ordered his brother-in-law, General Charles-Victor-Emmanuel Leclerc, to lead an expedition to the island to crush the new regime. Napoleon placed a high premium on bringing the colony to heel, writing to Leclerc: "Once the blacks have been disarmed and the principal generals sent to France, you will have done more for the commerce and civilization of Europe than we have done in our most brilliant campaigns." An officer sent to serve in the colony had a more cynical interpretation, writing that he was being sent to "fight with the Negroes for their own sugar."[15]

In 1802 Leclerc landed in Saint-Domingue. Although Toussaint L'Ouverture cooperated with the French and turned his army over to them, he was arrested and deported to France, along with his family, where he died in 1803. Jean Jacques Dessalines united the resistance under his command and led it to a crushing victory over the French forces. Of the fifty-eight thousand French soldiers, fifty thousand were lost in combat and to disease. On January 1, 1804, Dessalines formally declared the independence of Saint-Domingue and the creation of the new sovereign nation of Haiti, the name used by the pre-Columbian inhabitants of the island. The Haitian constitution was ratified in 1805.

Haiti, the second independent state in the Americas and the first in Latin America, was thus born from the first successful large-scale slave revolt in history. Fearing the spread of slave rebellion to the United States, President Thomas Jefferson refused to recognize Haiti. Both the American and the French Revolutions thus exposed their limits by acting to protect economic interests at the expense of revolutionary ideals of freedom and equality. Yet Haitian independence had fundamental repercussions for world history, helping spread the idea that liberty, equality, and fraternity must apply to all people.

The Napoleonic Era

November 1799	Napoleon overthrows the Directory
December 1799	Napoleon's new constitution approved
1800	Foundation of the Bank of France
1801	France defeats Austria and acquires Italian and German territories in the Treaty of Lunéville; Napoleon signs papal Concordat
1802	Treaty of Amiens
1803	Death of Toussaint L'Ouverture in France
January 1804	Declaration of Haitian independence
March 1804	Napoleonic Code
December 1804	Napoleon crowned emperor
May 1805	First Haitian constitution
October 1805	Britain defeats the French fleet at the Battle of Trafalgar
December 1805	Napoleon defeats Austria and Russia at the Battle of Austerlitz
1807	Napoleon redraws map of Europe in the treaties of Tilsit
1808	Spanish revolt against French occupation
1810	Height of the Grand Empire
June 1812	Napoleon invades Russia
Fall–Winter 1812	Napoleon makes a disastrous retreat from Russia
March 1814	Russia, Prussia, Austria, and Britain sign the Treaty of Chaumont, pledging alliance to defeat Napoleon
April 1814	Napoleon abdicates and is exiled to Elba; Louis XVIII restored to constitutional monarchy
February–June 1815	Napoleon escapes from Elba but is defeated at the Battle of Waterloo; Louis XVIII restored to throne for second time

Toussaint L'Ouverture

INDIVIDUALS IN SOCIETY

LITTLE IS KNOWN OF THE EARLY LIFE of Saint-Domingue's brilliant military and political leader Toussaint L'Ouverture. He was born in 1743 on a plantation outside Le Cap owned by the Count de Bréda. According to tradition, L'Ouverture was the eldest son of a captured African prince from modern-day Benin. Toussaint Bréda, as he was then called, occupied a privileged position among slaves. Instead of performing backbreaking labor in the fields, he served his master as a coachman and livestock keeper. He also learned to read and write French and some Latin, but he was always more comfortable with the Creole dialect.

During the 1770s the plantation manager emancipated L'Ouverture, who subsequently leased his own small coffee plantation, worked by slaves. He married Suzanne Simone, who already had one son, and the couple had another son during their marriage. In 1791 he joined the slave uprisings that swept Saint-Domingue, and he took on the *nom de guerre* ("war name") "L'Ouverture," meaning "the opening." L'Ouverture rose to prominence among rebel slaves allied with Spain and by early 1794 controlled his own army. A devout Catholic who led a frugal and ascetic life, L'Ouverture impressed others with his enormous physical energy, intellectual acumen, and air of mystery. In 1794 he defected to the French side and led his troops to a series of victories against the Spanish. In 1795 the National Convention promoted L'Ouverture to brigadier general.

Over the next three years L'Ouverture successively eliminated rivals for authority on the island. First he freed himself of the French commissioners sent to govern the colony. With a firm grip on power in the northern province, L'Ouverture defeated General André Rigaud in 1800 to gain control in the south. His army then marched on the capital of Spanish Santo Domingo on the eastern half of the island, meeting little resistance. The entire island of Hispaniola was now under his command.

With control of Saint-Domingue in his hands, L'Ouverture was confronted with the challenge of building a post-emancipation society, the first of its kind. The task was made even more difficult by the chaos wreaked by war, the destruction of plantations, and bitter social and racial tensions. For L'Ouverture the most pressing concern was to reestablish the plantation economy. Without revenue to pay his army, the gains of the rebellion could be lost. He therefore encouraged white planters to return and reclaim their property. He also adopted harsh policies toward former slaves, forcing them back to their plantations and restricting their ability to acquire land. When they resisted, he sent troops across the island to enforce submission. L'Ouverture's 1801 constitution reaffirmed his draconian labor policies and named L'Ouverture governor for life, leaving Saint-Domingue as a colony in name alone. In June 1802 French forces arrested L'Ouverture and jailed him at Fort de Joux in France's Jura Mountains near the Swiss border. L'Ouverture died of pneumonia on April 7, 1803. It was left to his lieutenant, Jean Jacques Dessalines, to win independence for the new Haitian nation.

QUESTIONS FOR ANALYSIS

1. Toussaint L'Ouverture was both slave and slave owner. How did each experience shape his life and actions?
2. What did Toussaint L'Ouverture and Napoleon Bonaparte have in common? How did they differ?

Equestrian portrait of Toussaint L'Ouverture.
(Réunion des Musées Nationaux/Art Resource, NY)

The Grand Empire and Its End

Napoleon resigned himself to the loss of Saint-Domingue, but he still maintained imperial ambitions in Europe. Increasingly, he saw himself as the emperor of Europe, not just of France. The so-called **Grand Empire** he built had three parts. The core, or first part, was an ever-expanding France, which by 1810 included Belgium, Holland, parts of northern Italy, and much German territory on the east bank of the Rhine. The second part consisted of a number of dependent satellite kingdoms, on the thrones of which Napoleon placed (and replaced) the members of his large family. The third part comprised the independent but allied states of Austria, Prussia, and Russia. After 1806 both satellites and allies were expected to support Napoleon's **Continental System**, a blockade in which no ship coming from Britain or her colonies was allowed to dock at any port controlled by the French. It was intended to halt all trade between Britain and continental Europe, thereby destroying the British economy and its military force.

The impact of the Grand Empire on the peoples of Europe was considerable. In the areas incorporated into France and in the satellites (Map 20.2), Napoleon abolished feudal dues and serfdom. Some of the peasants and middle class benefited from these reforms. Yet Napoleon had to put the prosperity and special interests of France first in order to safeguard his power base. Levying heavy taxes in money and men for his armies, he came to be regarded more as a conquering tyrant than as an enlightened liberator. Thus French rule sparked patriotic upheavals and encouraged the growth of reactive nationalism, for individuals in different lands learned to identify emotionally with their own embattled national families as the French had done earlier.

The first great revolt occurred in Spain. In 1808 a coalition of Catholics, monarchists, and patriots rebelled against Napoleon's attempts to make Spain a French satellite. French armies occupied Madrid, but the foes of Napoleon fled to the hills and waged uncompromising guerrilla warfare. Spain was a clear warning: resistance to French imperialism was growing.

Yet Napoleon pushed on, determined to hold his complex and far-flung empire together. In 1810, when

> **Grand Empire** The empire over which Napoleon and his allies ruled, encompassing virtually all of Europe except Great Britain and Russia.
>
> **Continental System** A blockade imposed by Napoleon to halt all trade between continental Europe and Britain, thereby weakening the British economy and military.

Francisco Goya, *The Third of May 1808* Spanish master Francisco Goya created a passionate and moving indictment of the brutality of war in this painting from 1814, which depicts the close-range execution of Spanish rebels by Napoleon's forces in May 1808. Goya's painting evoked the bitterness and despair of many Europeans who suffered through Napoleon's invasions. (Erich Lessing/Art Resource, NY)

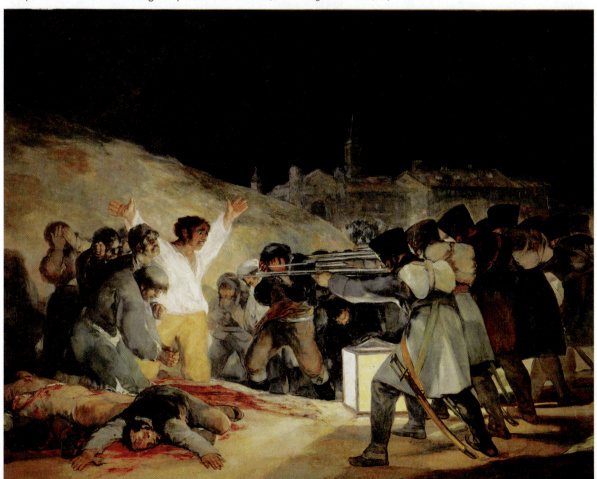

Mapping the Past

Map 20.2 Napoleonic Europe in 1812 Only Great Britain remained at war with Napoleon at the height of the Grand Empire. Many British goods were smuggled through Helgoland, a tiny but strategic British possession off the German coast. Compare this map with Map 16.2 (page 493), which shows the division of Europe in 1715.

ANALYZING THE MAP How had the balance of power shifted in Europe from 1715 to 1812? What changed, and what remained the same? What was the impact of Napoleon's wars on Germany and the Italian peninsula?

CONNECTIONS Why did Napoleon succeed in achieving vast territorial gains where Louis XIV did not?

To complete this activity online, go to the Online Study Guide at **bedfordstmartins.com/mckaywest**.

the Grand Empire was at its height, Britain still remained at war with France, helping the guerrillas in Spain and Portugal. The Continental System, expected to force the British "nation of shopkeepers" to its knees, was a failure. Instead, it was France that suffered from Britain's counter-blockade, which created hard times for French artisans and the middle class. Perhaps looking for a scapegoat, Napoleon turned on Alexander I of Russia, who in 1811 openly repudiated Napoleon's war of prohibitions against British goods.

Napoleon's invasion of Russia began in June 1812 with a force that eventually numbered 600,000, probably the largest force yet assembled in a single army. Only one-third of this Great Army was French, however; nationals of all the satellites and allies were drafted into the operation. Originally planning to winter in the Russian city of Smolensk if Alexander did not sue for peace, Napoleon reached Smolensk and recklessly pressed on toward Moscow. The great Battle of Borodino that followed was a draw, and the Russians retreated in good order. Alexander ordered the evacuation of Moscow, which the Russians then burned in part, and he refused to negotiate. Finally, after five weeks in the scorched and abandoned city, Napoleon ordered a retreat. That retreat was one of the greatest military disasters in history. The Russian army, the Russian winter, and starvation cut Napoleon's army to pieces. When the frozen remnants staggered into Poland and Prussia in December, 370,000 men had died and another 200,000 had been taken prisoner.[16]

Leaving his troops to their fate, Napoleon raced to Paris to raise yet another army. Possibly he might still have saved his throne if he had been willing to accept a France reduced to its historical size—the proposal offered by Austria's foreign minister, Prince Klemens von Metternich. But Napoleon refused. Austria and Prussia deserted Napoleon and joined Russia and Great Britain in the Treaty of Chaumont in March 1814, by which the four powers pledged allegiance to defeat the French emperor.

All across Europe patriots called for a "war of liberation" against Napoleon's oppression. Less than a month later, on April 4, 1814, a defeated Napoleon abdicated his throne. After this unconditional abdication, the victorious allies granted Napoleon the island of Elba off the coast of Italy as his own tiny state. Napoleon was allowed to keep his imperial title, and France was required to pay him a yearly income of 2 million francs.

The allies also agreed to the restoration of the Bourbon dynasty under Louis XVIII (r. 1814–1824) and promised to treat France with leniency in a peace settlement. The new monarch tried to consolidate support among the people by issuing the Constitutional Charter, which accepted many of France's revolutionary changes and guaranteed civil liberties.

Yet Louis XVIII—old, ugly, and crippled by gout—lacked the magnetism of Napoleon. Hearing of political unrest in France and diplomatic tensions in Vienna, Napoleon staged a daring escape from Elba in February 1815. Landing in France, he issued appeals for support and marched on Paris with a small band of followers. French officers and soldiers who had fought so long for their emperor responded to the call. Louis XVIII fled, and once more Napoleon took command. But Napoleon's gamble was a desperate long shot, for the allies were united against him. At the end of a frantic period known as the Hundred Days, they crushed his forces at Waterloo on June 18, 1815, and imprisoned him on the rocky island of St. Helena, far off the western coast of Africa. Louis XVIII returned to the throne, and the allies dealt more harshly with the apparently incorrigible French. As for Napoleon, he took revenge by writing his memoirs, nurturing the myth that he had been Europe's revolutionary liberator, a romantic hero whose lofty work had been undone by oppressive reactionaries.

LOOKING BACK LOOKING AHEAD

UNTIL 1789 the medieval ordering of French society into three estates remained in force, and the king, claiming to embody the nation in his person by the grace of God, continued to rule absolutely. Yet monumental changes had occurred over the eighteenth century as population grew, urbanization spread, and literacy increased. Enlightenment ideals influenced members of all three estates, who increasingly questioned the power of the monarchy and the rigid structure of society. As the sacred aura of the monarchy diminished, the royal government became increasingly incapable of resolving the urgent financial and political crises of the Old Regime. Exactly who should have the power, however, and how France should be governed, were questions that had many conflicting answers and resulted in decades of war and instability.

The age of revolution both drew on and affected European colonies in the Americas. The high stakes of colonial empire had heightened competition among European states, leading to a series of wars that generated crushing costs for overburdened treasuries. As was the case for the British in their North American colonies, the desperate need for new taxes weakened the French state and opened the door to revolution. In turn, the ideals of the French Revolution inspired slaves and free people of color in Saint-Domingue, thus opening the promise of liberty, equality, and fraternity to people of all races.

As complex as its origins are the long legacies of this period of revolution. Nineteenth- and early-twentieth-century Europe experienced periodic convulsions of revolution as successive generations struggled over political rights first proclaimed by the generation of 1789. Meanwhile, as dramatic events unfolded in France, a parallel revolution had gathered steam across the Channel. This was the British Industrial Revolution, originating around 1750 and accelerating through the end of the eighteenth century. After 1815 the twin forces of industrialization and democratization would combine to create the modern nation-states of Europe.

CHAPTER REVIEW

■ What social, political, and economic factors formed the background to the French Revolution? (p. 620)

An earlier generation of historians believed that the origins of the French Revolution lay in a single cause: class struggle between the nobility and the rising bourgeoisie. It is now clear that there were multiple causes of the Revolution. One was the growing ties — rather than conflict — between nobles and the wealthy bourgeoisie, who had grown economically and culturally closer over the course of the eighteenth century. The upper echelon's frustration with absolute rule emerged in political struggles between the monarchy and its officers, particularly in the high law courts. Public opinion turned against the monarchy as a rising torrent of political theory, cheap pamphlets, and gossip offered scathing and even pornographic depictions of the king and his court. With their sacred royal aura severely tarnished, Louis XV and his successor Louis XVI were unable to respond to the financial crises generated by French involvement in the Seven Years' War and the American Revolution. French support of the American colonists' fight for independence from Britain, moreover, inspired many to embrace the real possibility of political freedom. Louis XVI's half-hearted efforts to redress the situation were quickly overwhelmed by elite and popular demands for fundamental reform.

■ How did the events of 1789 result in a constitutional monarchy in France, and how did the new constitution affect the various members of French society at home and in the colony of Saint-Domingue? (p. 625)

When the Estates General gathered in 1789, delegates from the third estate refused to accept the old system of one vote per estate. Instead, they proclaimed that they alone constituted a "National Assembly" and refused to disband. Popular revolts prevented the king from intervening, and he was forced to accept the situation. Pushed forward by calls for freedom and equality from the streets of Paris to the faraway countryside, the National Assembly established a constitutional monarchy in 1791. The new constitution abolished the second estate and ended feudalism, thereby eliminating Old Regime privileges. Only men were given the right to vote for the new Assembly, however, and even among men, those in the lower economic stratum were disenfranchised. In the spirit of economic freedom, guilds and workers' associations were outlawed, which benefited merchants but threatened the livelihoods of master artisans and prevented workers from defending their rights. To the horror of the pope and devout French Catholics, the government seized church property and imposed an oath of loyalty on priests. The new constitution waffled in regard to the French colony of Saint-Domingue. By allowing the colonies to make their own laws regarding slavery and voting rights, it disheartened the slaves and free coloreds. And by reaffirming French trade monopolies, it angered the white planters.

■ How and why did the Revolution take a radical turn at home and in the colonies? (p. 633)

Support for constitutional monarchy ended with the royal family's attempted flight in June 1791. The new Legislative Assembly, comprising younger and more radical delegates led by members of the Jacobin club, declared war on Austria and proclaimed France a republic. With the execution of the royal couple and the declaration of terror as the order of the day, the French Revolution took an increasingly radical turn from the end of 1792.

After initial military defeats, France was largely victorious, mostly because of the total war effort undertaken by the Jacobin leadership. To defend the Revolution against its perceived internal enemies, Jacobins eliminated political opponents and then factions within their own party. They also attempted to bring about a cultural revolution, in part by attacking Christianity and substituting secular republican festivals. The Directory government that took power after the fall of Robespierre restored political equilibrium at the cost of the radical platform of social equality he had pursued. In Saint-Domingue, Spain and England profited from revolutionary conflict to invade the colony. To gain military support, the National Assembly agreed to enfranchise free people of color and to free any slave who fought on their side.

■ Why did Napoleon Bonaparte assume control of France, and what factors led to his downfall? How did the new republic of Haiti gain independence from France? (p. 644)

Wearied by the weaknesses of the Directory, a group of conspirators gave Napoleon Bonaparte control of France. His reputation as a brilliant military leader and his charisma and determination made him seem ideal to lead France to victory over its enemies. However, Napoleon's relentless ambitions ultimately led to his downfall. Not satisfied with his successes throughout Europe, and struggling to maintain his hold on Spain and Portugal, Napoleon made the fatal mistake of attempting to invade Russia in the summer of 1812. After a disastrous retreat from Moscow, he was eventually forced to abdicate the throne in 1814. His story is paralleled by that of Toussaint L'Ouverture, another soldier who emerged into the political limelight from the chaos of revolution, only to endure exile and defeat. Unlike Napoleon, L'Ouverture's cause ultimately prevailed. After his exile, war between the French forces and the armies he had led and inspired resulted in French defeat and independence for Saint-Domingue.

Suggested Reading

Bell, David A. *The Cult of the Nation in France: Inventing Nationalism, 1680–1800*. 2001. Traces early French nationalism through its revolutionary culmination.

Blanning, T. C. W. *The French Revolutionary Wars (1787–1802)*. 1996. A masterful account of the revolutionary wars that also places the French Revolution in its European context.

Broers, Michael. *Europe Under Napoleon*. 2002. Probes Napoleon's impact on the territories he conquered.

Connelly, Owen. *The French Revolution and Napoleonic Era*. 1991. An excellent introduction to the French Revolution and Napoleon.

Desan, Suzanne. *The Family on Trial in Revolutionary France*. 2004. Studies the effects of revolutionary law on the family, including the legalization of divorce.

Dubois, Laurent. *Avengers of the New World: The Story of the Haitian Revolution*. 2004. An excellent and highly readable account of the revolution that transformed the French colony of Saint-Domingue into the independent state of Haiti.

Englund, Steven. *Napoleon: A Political Life*. 2004. A good biography of the French emperor.

Hunt, Lynn. *Politics, Culture and Class in the French Revolution*, 2d ed. 2004. A pioneering examination of the French Revolution as a cultural phenomenon that generated new festivals, clothing, and songs, and even a new calendar.

Landes, John B. *Visualizing the Nation: Gender, Representation, and Revolution in Eighteenth-Century France*. 2001. Analyzes images of gender and the body in revolutionary politics.

Schechter, Ronald. *Obstinate Hebrews: Representations of Jews in France, 1715–1815*. 2003. An illuminating study of Jews and attitudes toward them in France from Enlightenment to emancipation.

Sutherland, Donald. *France, 1789–1815*. 1986. An overview of the French Revolution that emphasizes its many opponents, as well as its supporters.

Tackett, Timothy. *When the King Took Flight*. 2003. An exciting re-creation of the royal family's doomed effort to escape from Paris.

Notes

1. Quoted in R. R. Palmer, *The Age of Democratic Revolution*, vol. 1 (Princeton, N.J.: Princeton University Press, 1959), pp. 95–96.
2. Quoted in G. Wright, *France in Modern Times*, 4th ed. (New York: W. W. Norton, 1987), p. 34.
3. P. H. Beik, ed., *The French Revolution* (New York: Walker, 1970), p. 89.
4. G. Pernoud and S. Flaisser, eds., *The French Revolution* (Greenwich, Conn.: Fawcett, 1960), p. 61.
5. Quoted in Lynn Hunt, ed., *The French Revolution and Human Rights: A Brief Documentary History* (Boston/New York: Bedford/St. Martin's, 1996), p. 119.
6. Louis-Marie Prudhomme, *Revolutions of Paris*, quoted in Hunt, *The French Revolution and Human Rights*, p. 130.
7. Quoted in L. Gershoy, *The Era of the French Revolution, 1789–1799* (New York: Van Nostrand, 1957), p. 150.
8. Pernoud and Flaisser, *The French Revolution*, pp. 193–194.
9. Cited in Wim Klooster, *Revolutions in the Atlantic World: A Comprehensive History* (New York and London: New York University Press, 2009), p. 74.
10. Quotation from Hunt, *The French Revolution and Human Rights*, p. 138.
11. T. Blanning, *The French Revolutionary Wars, 1787–1802* (London: Arnold, 1996), pp. 116–128.
12. Quoted ibid., p. 123.
13. Quoted in Laurent Dubois, *Avengers of the New World: The Story of the Haitian Revolution* (Cambridge, Mass.: Harvard University Press, 2004), p. 97.
14. I. Woloch, *Napoleon and His Collaborators: The Making of a Dictatorship* (New York: W. W. Norton, 2001), pp. 36–65.
15. Quoted in Dubois, *Avengers of the New World*, pp. 255–256.
16. D. Sutherland, *France, 1789–1815: Revolution and Counterrevolution* (New York: Oxford University Press, 1986), p. 420.

Key Terms

estates (p. 620)
Estates General (p. 625)
National Assembly (p. 627)
Great Fear (p. 629)
constitutional monarchy (p. 630)
Jacobin club (p. 634)
second revolution (p. 635)
Girondists (p. 635)
the Mountain (p. 635)
sans-culottes (p. 636)
Reign of Terror (p. 637)
dechristianization (p. 638)
Thermidorian reaction (p. 643)
Napoleonic Code (p. 644)
Grand Empire (p. 649)
Continental System (p. 649)

For practice quizzes and other study tools, visit the Online Study Guide at **bedfordstmartins.com/mckaywest**.

For primary sources from this period, see *Sources of Western Society*, **Second Edition**.

For Web sites, images, and documents related to topics in this chapter, visit Make History at **bedfordstmartins.com/mckaywest**.

Glossary

Agincourt The location near Arras in Flanders where an English victory in 1415 led to the reconquest of Normandy. (p. 350)

agricultural revolution The period in Europe from the mid-seventeenth through the mid-nineteenth centuries during which great agricultural progress was made and the fallow, or idling of a field to replenish nutrients, was gradually eliminated. (p. 555)

anticlericalism Opposition to the clergy. (p. 408)

Atlantic slave trade The forced migration of Africans across the Atlantic for slave labor on plantations and in other industries; the trade reached its peak in the eighteenth century and ultimately involved more than twelve million Africans. (p. 573)

Babylonian Captivity Period from 587 to 538 B.C.E. during which the survivors of a Babylonian attack on the southern kingdom of Judah were exiled in Babylonia. The term was later used to refer to the period from 1309 to 1376 when the popes resided in Avignon rather than in Rome. (p. 355)

Black Death Plague that first struck Europe in 1347 and killed perhaps one-third of the population. (p. 341)

blood sports Popular with the eighteenth-century European masses, events such as bull-baiting and cockfighting that involved inflicting violence and bloodshed on animals. (p. 597)

boyars The highest-ranking members of the Russian nobility. (p. 498)

cameralism View that monarchy was the best form of government, that all elements of society should serve the monarch, and that, in turn, the state should use its resources and authority to increase the public good. (p. 544)

caravel A small, maneuverable, three-mast sailing ship developed by the Portuguese in the fifteenth century that gave the Portuguese a distinct advantage in exploration and trade. (p. 450)

carnival The few days of revelry in Catholic countries that preceded Lent and that included drinking, masquerading, dancing, and rowdy spectacles that turned the established order upside down. (p. 597)

Cartesian dualism Descartes's view that all of reality could ultimately be reduced to mind and matter. (p. 527)

Christian humanists Northern humanists who interpreted Italian ideas about and attitudes toward classical antiquity and humanism in terms of their own religious traditions. (p. 384)

Columbian exchange The exchange of animals, plants, and diseases between the Old and the New Worlds. (p. 463)

communes Sworn associations of free men in Italian cities led by merchant guilds that sought political and economic independence from local nobles. (p. 375)

community controls A pattern of cooperation and common action in a traditional village that sought to uphold the economic, social, and moral stability of the closely knit community. (p. 588)

conciliarists People who believed that the authority in the Roman church should rest in a general council composed of clergy, theologians, and laypeople, rather than in the pope alone. (p. 356)

confraternities Voluntary lay groups organized by occupation, devotional preference, neighborhood, or charitable activity. (p. 357)

conquistador Spanish for "conqueror"; Spanish soldier-explorers, such as Hernando Cortés and Francisco Pizarro, who sought to conquer the New World for the Spanish crown. (p. 449)

constitutionalism A form of government in which power is limited by law and balanced between the authority and power of the government on the one hand and the rights and liberties of the subject or citizen on the other hand; could include constitutional monarchies or republics. (p. 506)

constitutional monarchy A form of government in which the king retains his position as head of state, while the authority to tax and make new laws resides in an elected body. (p. 630)

consumer revolution The wide-ranging growth in consumption and new attitudes toward consumer goods that emerged in the cities of northwestern Europe in the second half of the eighteenth century. (p. 601)

Continental System A blockade imposed by Napoleon to halt all trade between continental Europe and Britain, thereby weakening the British economy and military. (p. 649)

Copernican hypothesis The idea that the sun, not the earth, was the center of the universe. (p. 522)

Cossacks Free groups and outlaw armies originally comprising runaway peasants living on the borders of Russian territory from the fourteenth century onward. By the end of the sixteenth century they had formed an alliance with the Russian state. (p. 498)

cottage industry A stage of industrial development in which rural workers used hand tools in their homes to manufacture goods on a large scale for sale in a market. (p. 560)

courts Magnificent households and palaces where the signori and the most powerful merchant oligarchs required political business to be conducted. (p. 376)

debate about women Debate among writers and thinkers in the Renaissance about women's qualities and proper role in society. (p. 396)

debt peonage A form of serfdom that allowed a planter or rancher to keep his workers or slaves in perpetual debt bondage by periodically advancing food, shelter, and a little money. (p. 572)

dechristianization Campaign to eliminate Christian faith and practice in France undertaken by the revolutionary government. (p. 638)

economic liberalism A belief in free trade and competition based on Adam Smith's argument that the invisible hand of free competition would benefit all individuals, rich and poor. (p. 568)

Edict of Nantes A document issued by Henry IV of France in 1598, granting liberty of conscience and of public worship to Calvinists, which helped restore peace in France. (p. 434)

empiricism A theory of inductive reasoning that calls for acquiring evidence through observation and experimentation rather than reason and speculation. (p. 526)

enclosure The movement to fence in fields in order to farm more effectively, at the expense of poor peasants who relied on common fields for farming and pasture. (p. 556)

encomienda system A system whereby the Spanish crown granted the conquerors the right to forcibly employ groups of Indians; it was a disguised form of slavery. (p. 461)

English Peasants' Revolt Revolt by English peasants in 1381 in response to changing economic conditions. (p. 360)

enlightened absolutism Term coined by historians to describe the rule of eighteenth-century monarchs who, without renouncing their own absolute authority, adopted Enlightenment ideals of rationalism, progress, and tolerance. (p. 543)

Enlightenment The influential intellectual and cultural movement of the late seventeenth and eighteenth centuries that introduced a new worldview based on the use of reason, the scientific method, and progress. (p. 530)

estates The three legal categories, or orders, of France's inhabitants: the clergy, the nobility, and everyone else. (p. 620)

Estates General A legislative body in prerevolutionary France made up of representatives of each of the three classes, or estates; it was called into session in 1789 for the first time since 1614. (p. 625)

experimental method The approach, pioneered by Galileo, that the proper way to explore the workings of the universe was through repeatable experiments rather than speculation. (p. 524)

flagellants People who believed that the plague was God's punishment for sin and sought to do penance by flagellating (whipping) themselves. (p. 347)

Fronde A series of violent uprisings during the early reign of Louis XIV triggered by growing royal control and oppressive taxation. (p. 487)

Girondists A moderate group that fought for control of the French National Convention in 1793. (p. 635)

Grand Empire The empire over which Napoleon and his allies ruled, encompassing virtually all of Europe except Great Britain and Russia. (p. 649)

Great Famine A terrible famine in 1315–1322 that hit much of Europe after a period of climate change. (p. 340)

Great Fear The fear of noble reprisals against peasant uprisings that seized the French countryside and led to further revolt. (p. 629)

Great Schism The division, or split, in church leadership from 1378 to 1417 when there were two, then three, popes. (p. 355)

guild system The organization of artisanal production into trade-based associations, or guilds, each of which received a monopoly over its trade and the right to train apprentices and hire workers. (p. 566)

Haskalah The Jewish Enlightenment of the second half of the eighteenth century, led by the Prussian philosopher Moses Mendelssohn. (p. 549)

Holy Office The official Roman Catholic agency founded in 1542 to combat international doctrinal heresy. (p. 430)

Huguenots French Calvinists. (p. 433)

humanism A program of study designed by Italians that emphasized the critical study of Latin and Greek literature with the goal of understanding human nature. (p. 378)

illegitimacy explosion The sharp increase in out-of-wedlock births that occurred in Europe between 1750 and 1850, caused by low wages and the breakdown of community controls. (p. 589)

Inca Empire The vast and sophisticated Peruvian empire centered at the capital city of Cuzco that was at its peak from 1438 until 1532. (p. 459)

indulgence A document issued by the Catholic Church lessening penance or time in purgatory, widely believed to bring forgiveness of all sins. (p. 409)

industrious revolution The shift that occurred as families in northwestern Europe focused on earning wages instead of producing goods for household consumption; this reduced their economic self-sufficiency but increased their ability to purchase consumer goods. (p. 566)

Institutes of the Christian Religion, The Calvin's formulation of Christian doctrine, which became a systematic theology for Protestantism. (p. 425)

Jacobin club A political club in revolutionary France whose members were well-educated radical republicans. (p. 634)

Jacquerie A massive uprising by French peasants in 1358 protesting heavy taxation. (p. 358)

janissary corps The core of the sultan's army, composed of slave conscripts from non-Muslim parts of the empire; after 1683 it became a volunteer force. (p. 504)

Jansenism A sect of Catholicism originating with Cornelius Jansen that emphasized the heavy weight of original sin and accepted the doctrine of predestination; it was outlawed as heresy by the pope. (p. 608)

Jesuits Members of the Society of Jesus, founded by Ignatius Loyola, whose goal was the spread of the Roman Catholic faith. (p. 431)

Junkers The nobility of Brandenburg and Prussia, they were reluctant allies of Frederick William in his consolidation of the Prussian state. (p. 495)

just price The idea that prices should be fair, protecting both consumers and producers, and that they should be imposed by government decree if necessary. (p. 599)

law of inertia A law formulated by Galileo that states that motion, not rest, is the natural state of an object, that an object continues in motion forever unless stopped by some external force. (p. 524)

law of universal gravitation Newton's law that all objects are attracted to one another and that the force of attraction is proportional to the object's quantity of matter and inversely proportional to the square of the distance between them. (p. 526)

mercantilism A system of economic regulations aimed at increasing the power of the state based on the belief that a nation's international power was based on its wealth, specifically its supply of gold and silver. (p. 489)

Methodists Members of a Protestant revival movement started by John Wesley, so called because they were so methodical in their devotion. (p. 607)

Mexica Empire Also known as the Aztec Empire, a large and complex Native American civilization in modern Mexico and Central America that possessed advanced mathematical, astronomical, and engineering technology. (p. 457)

millet system A system used by the Ottomans whereby subjects were divided into religious communities with each millet (nation) enjoying autonomous self-government under its religious leaders. (p. 505)

Mountain, the Led by Robespierre, the French National Convention's radical faction, which seized legislative power in 1793. (p. 635)

Napoleonic Code French civil code promulgated in 1804 that reasserted the 1789 principles of the equality of all male citizens before the law and the absolute security of wealth and private property as well as restricting rights accorded to women by previous revolutionary laws. (p. 644)

National Assembly The first French revolutionary legislature, made up primarily of representatives of the third estate and a few from the nobility and clergy, in session from 1789 to 1791. (p. 627)

natural philosophy An early modern term for the study of the nature of the universe, its purpose, and how it functioned; it encompassed what we would call "science" today. (p. 520)

Navigation Acts A series of English laws that controlled the import of goods to Britain and British colonies. (p. 569)

New Christians A fourteenth-century term for Jews and Muslims who accepted Christianity; in many cases they included Christians whose families had converted centuries earlier. (p. 401)

patronage Financial support of writers and artists by cities, groups, and individuals, often to produce specific works or works in specific styles. (p. 374)

Peace of Utrecht A series of treaties, from 1713 to 1715, that ended the War of the Spanish Succession, ended French expansion in Europe, and marked the rise of the British Empire. (p. 492)

Peace of Westphalia The name of a series of treaties that concluded the Thirty Years' War in 1648 and marked the end of large-scale religious violence in Europe. (p. 483)

philosophes A group of French intellectuals who proclaimed that they were bringing the light of knowledge to their fellow creatures in the Age of Enlightenment. (p. 531)

Pietism A Protestant revival movement in early-eighteenth-century Germany and Scandinavia that emphasized a warm and emotional religion, the priesthood of all believers, and the power of Christian rebirth in everyday affairs. (p. 607)

pluralism The clerical practice of holding more than one church benefice (or office) at the same time and enjoying the income from each. (p. 408)

politiques Catholic and Protestant moderates who held that only a strong monarchy could save France from total collapse. (p. 434)

popolo Disenfranchised common people in Italian cities who resented their exclusion from power. (p. 375)

predestination The teaching that God has determined the salvation or damnation of individuals based on his will and purpose, not on their merit or works. (p. 426)

proletarianization The transformation of large numbers of small peasant farmers into landless rural wage earners. (p. 558)

Protectorate The English military dictatorship (1653–1658) established by Oliver Cromwell following the execution of Charles I. (p. 508)

Protestant The name originally given to Lutherans, which came to mean all non-Catholic Western Christian groups. (p. 412)

Ptolemy's *Geography* A second-century-C.E. work that synthesized the classical knowledge of geography and introduced the concepts of longitude and latitude. Reintroduced to Europeans in 1410 by Arab scholars, its ideas allowed cartographers to create more accurate maps. (p. 450)

public sphere An idealized intellectual space that emerged in Europe during the Enlightenment, where the public came together to discuss important issues relating to society, economics, and politics. (p. 537)

Puritans Members of a sixteenth- and seventeenth-century reform movement within the Church of England that advocated purifying it of Roman Catholic elements, such as bishops, elaborate ceremonials, and wedding rings. (p. 507)

putting-out system The eighteenth-century system of rural industry in which a merchant loaned raw materials to cottage workers, who processed them and returned the finished products to the merchant. (p. 561)

rationalism A secular, critical way of thinking in which nothing was to be accepted on faith, and everything was to be submitted to reason. (p. 530)

reading revolution The transition in Europe from a society where literacy consisted of patriarchal and communal reading of religious texts to a society where literacy was commonplace and reading material was broad and diverse. (p. 535)

Reign of Terror The period from 1793 to 1794 during which Robespierre's Committee of Public Safety tried and executed thousands suspected of treason and a new revolutionary culture was imposed. (p. 637)

Renaissance A French word meaning "rebirth," first used by art historian and critic Giorgio Vasari to refer to the rebirth of the culture of classical antiquity. (p. 374)

representative assemblies Deliberative meetings of lords and wealthy urban residents that flourished in many European countries between 1250 and 1450 and were the precursors to the English parliament, German diets, and Spanish cortes. (p. 354)

republicanism A form of government in which there is no monarch and power rests in the hands of the people as exercised through elected representatives. (p. 506)

rococo A popular style in Europe in the eighteenth century, known for its soft pastels, ornate interiors, sentimental portraits, and starry-eyed lovers protected by hovering cupids. (p. 537)

salons Regular social gatherings held by talented and rich Parisian women in their homes, where philosophes and their followers met to discuss literature, science, and philosophy. (p. 536)

sans-culottes The laboring poor of Paris, so called because the men wore trousers instead of the knee breeches of the aristocracy and middle class; the word came to refer to the militant radicals of the city. (p. 636)

second revolution From 1792 to 1795, the second phase of the French Revolution, during which the fall of the French monarchy introduced a rapid radicalization of politics. (p. 635)

signori Government by one-man rule in Italian cities such as Milan. (p. 376)

Spanish Armada The fleet sent by Philip II of Spain in 1588 against England as a religious crusade against Protestantism. Weather and the English fleet defeated it. (p. 425)

stadholder The executive officer in each of the United Provinces of the Netherlands, a position often held by the princes of Orange. (p. 513)

Statute of Kilkenny Laws issued in 1366 that discriminated against the Irish, forbidding marriage between the English and the Irish, requiring the use of the English language, and denying the Irish access to ecclesiastical offices. (p. 367)

sultan The ruler of the Ottoman Empire; he owned all the agricultural land of the empire and was served by an army and bureaucracy composed of highly trained slaves. (p. 504)

Test Act Legislation passed by the English parliament in 1673 to secure the position of the Anglican Church by stripping Puritans, Catholics, and other dissenters of the right to vote, preach, assemble, hold public office, and attend or teach at the universities. (p. 510)

Thermidorian reaction A reaction to the violence of the Reign of Terror in 1794, resulting in the execution of Robespierre and the loosening of economic controls. (p. 643)

Treaty of Paris The treaty that ended the Seven Years' War in Europe and the colonies in 1763 and ratified British victory on all colonial fronts. (p. 571)

Treaty of Tordesillas The 1494 agreement giving Spain everything to the west of an imaginary line drawn down the Atlantic and giving Portugal everything to the east. (p. 456)

Union of Utrecht The alliance of seven northern provinces (led by Holland) that declared its independence from Spain and formed the United Provinces of the Netherlands. (p. 435)

viceroyalties The name for the four administrative units of Spanish possessions in the Americas: New Spain, Peru, New Granada, and La Plata. (p. 461)

virtù The quality of being able to shape the world according to one's own will. (p. 379)

wet-nursing A widespread and flourishing business in the eighteenth century in which women were paid to breast-feed other women's babies. (p. 591)

Index

A Note about the Index: Names of individuals appear in boldface. Letters in parentheses following page numbers refer to:
- *(i)* illustrations, including photographs and artifacts
- *(f)* figures, including charts and graphs
- *(m)* maps
- *(b)* boxed features

Abolition of slavery
   in France and French territories, 642
   slave trade and, 575
Aboriginal peoples (Australia), 581
Abortion, 592
Absenteeism, clerical, 408
Absolute monarchy and absolutism, 478, 479(i), 486–505
   in Austria, 494–495
   England and, 506–511
   enlightened, 541–549
   in France, 434, 486–492
   in Ottoman Empire, 503–505
   palaces and, 490–491(b), 490(i), 491(i)
   in Prussia, 495–497, 497(i)
   in Russia, 497
   in Spain, 492–494
   state-building and, 484–485
Academies
   artistic, 392, 393
   scientific, 528
Administration. *See* Government
Adoration of the Magi, The (Signorelli), 398(i)
Adultery, Protestants on, 419
Africa. *See also* North Africa
   English exports to, 571
   gold from, 452
   human origins in, 537
   slavery and, 446, 452, 492
   trade and, 581
   trading states of, 445–446
   voodoo and, 642
Africans
   as American settlers, 463
   in Europe, 394
   as freed slaves, 469(b)
   racial ideas about, 472–473
   as slaves, 448, 464–468, 464(i), 573–575, 573(i)
   as slave traders, 574
Against the Murderous, Thieving Hordes of the Peasants (Luther), 416
Age of crisis, 17th century as, 480
Age of Discovery, 442, 443(i), 448–461
Age of exploration. *See* Age of Discovery; Exploration
Agincourt, battle at, 350–352
Agricultural revolution, 554–558
Agriculture. *See also* Farms and farming; Peasant(s)
   commercial, 482
   estate, 557
   population and, 558
Akan peoples, gold from, 445
Alberti, Leon Battista, 380
Albert of Mainz, 409–410
Albert of Wallenstein, 483
Alcibar, Jose de, 577(i)
Alexander I (Russia), 646, 650, 651
Alexander VI (Pope), 377, 382, 400, 456

Algebra, 527
Allegory of the Tudor Dynasty, 423(i)
Alliance(s). *See also* specific alliances
   in Seven Years' War, 543–544
Almanacs, 596
Alpacas, 464
Alsace, France and, 492
Alva, duke of, 435
American Indians, 571
   Columbus and, 455
   rights of, 510
American Revolution, 623–624
Americas. *See also* New World
   colonial settlement in, 455, 461–470
   Dutch and, 472
   potato from, 560
   silver from, 471(i)
   Spanish holdings in, 421(m)
Amiens
   revolt in, 486
   Treaty of, 646
Anabaptists, 416
Anagni, papacy and, 355
Anastasia Romanov (wife of Ivan IV), 498
Andes region, 460
Anesthesia, in 18th century, 611
Anglican Church, 423, 425
   education and, 595
   Puritans and, 507–508, 510
   Wesley and, 607
Anglo-Dutch wars, 569
Animals
   in Columbian exchange, 463–464
   crops for, 556
Anjou, house of, 399
Anne of Austria, 487
Anne of Brittany, 399
Anne of Denmark, 590
Anthropology, Kant on, 537
Anticlericalism, 408
Antigua, 576(i)
Antipope, 357
Anti-Semitism. *See also* Jews and Judaism
   in Spain, 400–401
Antwerp, 435
Apothecaries, 609, 610(i)
Apprenticeships, in 18th century, 587
Aquinas. *See* Thomas Aquinas
Aquitaine, 348–349, 350
Arabic language, scientific translations in, 521
Arabs and Arab world. *See also* Islam
   Spain and, 400
Aragon, 400
Arawak language, 455
Architecture, in Renaissance, 390(i)
Arguin, North Africa, 452
Aristocracy. *See also* Nobility
   languages spoken by, 489
   Spanish, 494
Aristotle, on universe, 520, 520(i), 522
Armagnacs (France), 399
Armed forces. *See also* Military; Navy; Soldiers
   in England, 508
   French, 399, 492
   in French Revolution, 639
   Habsburg, 495
   Ottoman janissaries and, 504

professionalization of, 485, 485(i)
   in Prussia, 496–497, 543–544
   in Russia, 499, 502
   size of, 485–486
   Spanish, 494(i)
Armor, 352(i)
Arouet, François Marie. *See* Voltaire
Art(s). *See also* Architecture; Literature; Painting; specific arts and artists
   baroque, 514–515
   commercial, 368(i)
   in Reformation, 418–419(b), 418(i), 419(i)
   in Renaissance, 376, 387–393
   rococo style in, 537
Arthur (England), 400, 423
Artillery. *See also* Weapons
   in Hundred Years' War, 354
Artisans, 568. *See also* Labor; Workers
Asia
   Dutch in, 578
   European empires and, 578–581
   Portuguese slave trade and, 470
   sea routes to, 453–457
Asiento, 570
Assemblies. *See also* Estates (assemblies); National assembly (France)
   representative, 354
Assembly of Notables (France), 624–625
Assimilation, in New France, 463
Astell, Mary, 528
Astrolabe (instrument), 451
Astronomy. *See also* Scientific revolution; Universe
   Aristotle and, 520, 520(i), 521
   Brahe and, 522–523
   Copernicus and, 522
   exploration and, 451
   Galileo and, 525
   Newton and, 525–526
   Ptolemaic, 520–521
   scientific revolution and, 522
   sextants and, 523(i)
Atahualpa (Inca), 460
Athletics. *See* Sports
Atlantic Ocean region. *See also* Exploration
   economy in, 569–571, 570(m)
   Genoese exploration in, 447, 448
   identities and communities of, 575–578
   powers of, 552
Atomist theory, Descartes and, 527
Audiencia, 460
Auerstädt, battle at, 646
Augsburg Confession, 422
Augustinian friars, 409
Austerlitz, Battle of, 646
Australia, British settlement of, 581
Austria
   absolutism in, 494–495
   education in, 595
   France and, 420, 634, 635
   growth to 1748, 496(m)
   Habsburgs and, 420, 483, 495, 546–549
   Jews in, 549, 606
   Napoleon and, 646
Austrian Netherlands. *See also* Belgium
   France and, 635, 637, 646
Authority. *See* Power (authority)
Autobiography, in Renaissance, 380

I-1

I-2 Index

Autocracy, in Russia, 498
Auto-da-fe, 403(i)
Avignon, pope in, 355–357
Azores, 452
Aztecs, 457–459

Babylonian Captivity
 of Catholic Church, 355, 408
 of Hebrews, 355
Bach, Johann Sebastian, 515
Bacon, Francis, 526, 527, 529
Bacteria. *See* Disease
Bahamas, 453
Balance of power
 in Italian Renaissance, 376–378
 Peace of Utrecht and, 492
Balkan region
 Ottomans and, 503–504
 slaves from, 448
Ball, John, 361
Baltic region
 Black Death and, 342
 Russia and, 502
 in Thirty Years' War, 483
Banking, in Florence, 374–375
Bank of France, 645
Bankruptcy, in Florence, 375
Banten, Java, 446(i)
Baptism, of Jews, 401–402
Baptistery (Florence), doors of, 387
Baptists, 416
Barbados, Jews in, 578
Barbarians, race and, 540
Barcelona, 394
Baroque period, arts of, 514–515
Bastille (Paris), storming of, 627–628
Batavia (Jakarta), 578
Bath houses, 364(i)
Battles. *See* specific battles and wars
Bayle, Pierre, 530, 534
Beattie, James, 540
Beaver trade, 457
Beijing (Peking), China, 445
Belarus (Belorussia), 549
Belgium. *See also* Austrian Netherlands; Netherlands
 Charles V and, 434
 Spanish Netherlands as, 434
Benefices (offices), 408
Berbers, 448
Berruguete, Pedro, 403
Bertin, Rose, 600(b), 600(i)
Beutelsbach, peasant beliefs in, 608
Beverages, 601
Bible. *See also* New Testament
 Copernican hypothesis and, 522
 darkness, sin, and, 472–473
 in English, 356
 Gutenberg, 386
 Protestants and, 412
 reading of, 595–596
Biographies, in Renaissance, 380
Birth control, in 18th century, 588, 592
Births and birthrate
 in 18th century, 559
 illegitimacy and, 589–590
 in 17th century, 558
Black, skin color, slavery, and, 472–473
Black Code, in Saint-Domingue, 633
Black Death, 341–348, 343(m). *See also* Plague
 population after, 558
 treatment of, 344(b), 344(i), 345, 345(i)
Black people. *See also* Africans; Slaves and slavery
 in Europe, 394
Black Prince. *See* Edward (Black Prince, England)

Black Sea region
 Black Death in, 342
 Genoese trade and, 447
Blockade(s), by Napoleon, 646, 650
Blood
 circulation of, 529
 ethnic differences by, 367, 402
Blood descent, 366–367
Blood sports, 597
Bloomsbury Square (London), 574, 575(i)
Boats. *See* Ships and shipping
Boccaccio, Giovanni, 346–347
Body. *See also* Medicine
 scientific revolution and, 529–530
Bogotá, 461
Bohemia
 Black Death and, 343
 Christianity in, 408
 Habsburgs in, 495
 Reformation in, 427
 Thirty Years' War and, 483, 495
 Wyclif's ideas in, 356
Bohemian Phase, of Thirty Years' War, 483
Boleyn, Anne, 423, 424
Bolivia, 461, 468, 471
Bologna
 Concordat of, 399, 433
 republic in, 375
Bonhomme, Jacques, 358–359
Boniface VIII (Pope), 355
Boni family (Florence), 395(i)
Book of Common Prayer (England), 424, 508
Book of Revelation, 338
Books. *See also* Literature
 in Enlightenment, 535, 535(i)
Bora, Katharina von, 416, 417(i)
Bordeaux, revolt in, 486
Borgia family
 Cesare, 377, 382–383
 Rodrigo (Pope Alexander VI), 382, 400
Borodino, Battle of, 651
Boston Tea Party, 623(i)
Botticelli, Sandro, 390, 392(i)
Boucher, François, 602(i)
Bougainville, Louis-Antoine de, 542–543(b), 542(i)
Bourbon dynasty, 461, 486, 493(m)
 restoration of, 651
Bourgeoisie, in France, 620, 621
Boxing, 597, 598(i)
Boyars, 498
Boyle, Robert, 529–530
Boyle's law, 530
Boys. *See also* Children; Men
 work opportunities for, 587
Brahe, Tycho, 522–523, 523(i)
Brandenburg, 495
Brandenburg-Prussia, 496(m)
Brazil
 Dutch and, 472
 plantation slavery in, 573–574
 Portugal and, 456, 461
 sugar and, 464(i), 470
Bread, 598–599
 in France, 627
 in peasant diet, 481
Breast-feeding, 591–592
Bréda, Count de, 648(b)
Brethren and Sisters of the Common Life, 358
Britain. *See* England (Britain)
British East India Company. *See* English East India Company
British Empire. *See also* Colonies and colonization
 in 19th century, 581

Brittany, 399
Brothels, 363–364, 364(i), 419
Brothers of the Christian Schools, 595
Brunelleschi, Filippo, 387, 389
Bruni, Leonardo, 379, 382(b)
Brussels, 567(i)
 guilds in, 567(i)
Bubonic plague, 342, 481, 559. *See also* Black Death
Buda, 427
Buenos Aires, 461
Buffon, Comte de, 537
Buildings. *See* Architecture
Bullfights, 597
Bullion, silver, 468–470
Bureaucracy
 in Austria, 547
 Ottoman, 504, 505
 in Prussia, 544
Burgundians (France), 353, 399
Burgundy, 399
 dukes of, 349
Burials, medieval, 340(i)
Burke, Edmund, 633
Business. *See also* Trade
 coffeehouses and, 539(b)
Byzantine Empire
 Black Death and, 343
 Ottomans and, 447, 447(i)
 Russia and, 498, 502(i)
Byzantium. *See* Constantinople

Cabinet system, in England, 510
Cabot, John, 457
Cabral, Pedro Alvares, 456, 456(i)
Caesar, Julius, humanists on, 379
Cairo, 445
Calais, 353, 399
Calculus, 524, 526
Calendar, in France, 640, 641(i)
Calicut, India, 445, 453
California, Spain and, 572
Calvin, John, and Calvinism, 425–427, 426(i)
 Copernicus and, 522
 France and, 433
 in Netherlands, 434–435
 religious art and, 418(b)
 Wesley and, 608
Cameralism, in Prussia, 544
Canada
 European exploration of, 457
 France and, 460, 489–492
 Franco-British competition over, 571
Canary Islands, 448, 453, 468
Cannon, in Hundred Years' War, 354
Canon law, marriage and, 417
Canterbury Tales (Chaucer), 367, 367(i), 368–369
Cantons (Switzerland), religion in, 421–422
Cape of Good Hope, 452–453, 472
Capetian dynasty (France), 349
Capitalism
 in France, 620
 urban conflicts and, 361
Capitoline Hill (Rome), 390
Caravan trade, 446
Caravel, 450
Caribbean region, 456. *See also* West Indies
 Christianity in, 578
 Dutch and, 472
 mixed-race people in, 577
Carmelite nuns, 432
Carnival, 597–598
Cartesian dualism, 527, 528
Cartier, Jacques, 457
Cartography, 450, 451

Castas, 462
   paintings, 577*(i)*
Castiglione, Baldassare, 380–381, 381*(i)*
Castile, 400. *See also* Ferdinand and Isabella (Spain); Spain
Castles, of Mortagne, 353*(i)*
Catalonia, 486, 494
Cateau-Cambrésis, Treaty of, 433
Catherine de' Medici, 433
Catherine of Aragon, 400, 423
Catherine the Great (Russia), 544–546, 624
Catholic Church. *See also* Christianity; Councils (Christian); Counter-Reformation; Protestantism
   in Austria, 495
   Babylonian Captivity of, 355
   baroque art and, 514–515
   in Bohemia, 427
   conversion by, 578
   Copernican hypothesis and, 525
   criticisms of, 408
   in England, 510
   in France, 433–434, 486–487, 638
   in French Revolution, 632
   in Germany, 421, 422
   hierarchy of, 606
   in Hungary, 495
   in Ireland, 424, 509
   Jansenism and, 608
   in Later Middle Ages, 354–358
   lay piety and, 357–358
   marriage in, 417
   in Maryland, 460
   in Poland, 427
   reforms in, 406
   on religious art, 418–419
   in Scandinavia, 422
   schism in, 348
   science and, 528–529
   in Spain, 400
   Voltaire on, 534
Catholic League, 483
Catholic Reformation, 428–433
Caucasus region, 545
Cavendish, Margaret, 528
Cayenne, 460
Celibacy, Luther and Zwingli on, 416
Cellini, Benvenuto, 379*(i)*
Central Europe
   armies in, 486
   Black Death in, 343
   Ottomans and, 504
   Thirty Years' War and, 483–484
Central Middle Ages. *See* High Middle Ages
Ceuta, Morocco, 452
Ceylon, 578
Champlain, Samuel de, 460
Chapbooks, 596
Charity
   foundlings and, 593
   schools, 595
Charles I (England), 506*(i)*, 507, 508
Charles I at the Hunt (Van Dyck), 506*(i)*
Charles II (England), 510
Charles II (Spain), 492
Charles III (Spain), 461
Charles IV (France), 349
Charles V (France), 355
Charles V (Holy Roman Empire), 399*(i)*, 402, 420, 420*(i)*, 456, 462
   abdication by, 422
   empire of, 421*(m)*
   Luther and, 411, 420
   Netherlands under, 434–435

   papacy and, 430
   religion and, 421–422
Charles VI (Austria), 543, 546
Charles VI (France), 354
Charles VII (France), 352, 353, 397–399
Charles VIII (France), 378
Charles XI (Sweden), 490–491*(b)*
Charles XII (Sweden), 500–501
Charles the Bold (Burgundy), 399
Châtelet, marquise de, 533, 533*(i)*
Chaucer, Geoffrey, 367, 367*(i)*, 368–369
Chaumont, Treaty of, 651
Childbirth. *See also* Midwives
   in 18th century, 591, 611, 612–613*(b)*, 612*(i)*, 613*(i)*
Childhood, in 18th century, 593–594
Children. *See also* Illegitimacy
   in 18th century, 591–595
   in Spanish colonies, 463
   voyages of exploration and, 449
Chili peppers, 467
China
   Black Death in, 342
   Mongol emperors in, 445
   trade and, 470
Chivalry, 350
Chocolate, 599*(i)*, 601
Chollolan, 458
Christian III (Denmark), 422
Christian IV (Denmark), 483
Christian church. *See* Christianity; Protestant Reformation; Reformation
Christian humanism, 384–385
Christianity. *See also* Orthodox Christianity; Reformation; Saint(s)
   astronomy and, 521
   in Balkan region, 503–504
   conversion to, 578
   conversos and, 401–402
   exploration and, 448, 452
   in France, 632
   heathens and, 472
   plague and, 347
   Reformation and, 408–419
Christine de Pizan, 362–363*(b)*, 362*(i)*, 396
Church(es). *See also* Religion
   Reformation politics and, 419–422
   reforms of, 408–419
   and state in France, 353, 399
Church councils. *See* Councils
Church of England. *See* Anglican Church
Church of Ireland, 424
Church of Scotland. *See* Presbyterians
Church of the Gesù, 430*(i)*, 514
Cicero, Marcus Tullius, humanists on, 378–379
Circumnavigation of earth, Magellan and, 448, 457
Cities and towns. *See also* City-states; Villages
   leisure and recreation in, 597–598
   Renaissance arts in, 376
City of Ladies, The (Christine de Pizan), 362
City-states
   in Italian Renaissance, 376–378, 377*(m)*
   in Italy, 513
Civil Code (France, 1804), 644–645, 646
Civil service. *See* Bureaucracy
Class. *See also* Hierarchy; Orders
   diet and, 599
   Junkers as, 495
   in Ottoman Empire, 505
   in Russia, 503
   use of term, 395
Classical culture, Renaissance and, 378
Classicism, 489
Classification (scientific), race and, 537, 540

Clement VII (Pope), 355, 420*(i)*, 423
Clergy. *See also* Friars; Monks and monasteries; Pope(s); Priests and priestesses
   Conciliarists and, 356
   criticisms of, 408
   in 18th century, 606
   in England, 424
   as French estate, 620, 625
   hypocrisy of, 356*(i)*
   plague and, 346
   Protestant, 412
   reforms of, 430–431
   wealth of, 346
   women in, 417
Climate
   in 14th century, 340
   in 16th and 17th centuries, 554
Clive, Robert, 580
Cloth and cloth industry. *See also* Textile industry
   from India, 453
   in Later Middle Ages, 341
Clothier's Delight, The, 564–565
Clothing. *See also* Cloth and cloth industry; Fashion; Textile industry
   consumerism and, 601–602
   in French Revolution, 640
   male, 398*(b)*, 398*(i)*
Clover, 555, 556
Cloves, 471
Coalitions
   against France, 646
   against Napoleon (1808), 649
Cockfighting, 597
Code Napoleon. *See* Civil Code (France, 1804)
Code noir (Black Code), in Saint-Domingue, 633
Codes of law. *See* Law codes
Coercive Acts, 623
Coffee, 575, 601
Coffeehouses, 537, 538–539*(b)*, 538*(i)*, 539*(i)*
Coins
   silver, 471
   in Spain, 493
Colbert, Jean-Baptiste, 489–492, 566
Colleges. *See* Universities
Colloquy of Marburg, 412
Colonies and colonization. *See also* Imperialism
   American, 510
   American Revolution and, 622–623
   costs of goods from, 601
   Diderot and, 542–543*(b)*
   Dutch, 472
   English, 460, 578–581
   ethnic tensions and, 366
   Franco-British competition for, 571
   notions of "blood" and, 367
   Prussia and, 543–544
   Spanish, 461–464, 492, 493
   trade in, 571–573
   women and children in, 463
Color. *See* Skin color
Columbian exchange, 463–464, 466–467*(b)*, 466*(i)*, 467*(i)*
Columbus, Christopher, 444, 455*(i)*
   description of first voyage, 454–455*(b)*
   exploration by, 449, 450, 452*(m)*, 453–456, 455*(m)*
   journal of, 448, 453
Commerce. *See* Economy; Trade
Commercial art, 368*(i)*
Commercialization, 597
Committee of Public Safety (France), 636, 637, 643
Common people
   education for, 595
   in 18th century, 584, 585*(i)*

Common people (*continued*)
  in Enlightenment, 537
  as French estate, 620, 625
  lifestyle of, 552
Commons, in England, 354, 507
Common Sense (Paine), 596–597
Communes, in northern Italian cities, 375
Community controls, in 18th century, 588
Company of the East Indies (France), 489
Compass, 451
Compulsory education, 595
Conciliarists, 356
Concord, American Revolution and, 623
Concordat of Bologna, 399, 433
Concordat of 1801, 645
Concubines, Ottoman, 505
Condorcet, marquis de, 631
Condottieri, 376, 377
Confraternities, 357–358
Congregationalists, 416
Connecticut, 460
Conquistadors, 449, 457, 459, 461, 467
Consistory (Geneva), 426
Constance, Council of, 357
Constantinople (Istanbul). *See also* Byzantine Empire
  as Istanbul, 505
  Ottoman Turks in, 447, 447(i), 498, 503
Constitution
  in Haiti, 647
  in United States, 624
Constitutional monarchies, 478, 484, 485
  in England, 510–511
  in France, 630–632
  in Holland, 506, 511
Consumer goods. *See also* Goods and services
  in 18th century, 600–605, 603(i)
Consumer revolution, in 18th century, 601–605
Consumption
  in 18th century, 598–605
  food, 599–600
Contagious disease. *See* Disease
Continental System, of Napoleon, 649, 650
Contraception. *See* Birth control
Conversations on the Plurality of Worlds (Fontenelle), 531(i)
Conversion (Christian), 462, 578. *See also* Christianity
Conversos, 401–402
Conway, Anne, 528
Cook, James, 581
Copernican hypothesis, 522, 525, 529
Copernicus, Nicolaus, 522
Corn, 466, 467(i)
Coronation, of Napoleon, 645(i)
Corregidores, 461
Cortes (Spanish parliament), 400
Cortés, Hernando, 449, 457–459, 459(b), 459(i)
Cortés, Martín, 459
Cosmology, of Aristotle, 520
Cossacks (Russia), 498, 499, 545
Cottage industry, 560–563
  putting-out system in, 561
  urban artisans and, 567
  workers in, 561–562, 561(i)
Cotton industry. *See also* Textile industry
  slavery and, 540(i), 573
Coudray, Madame du, 611, 612–613(b)
"Council of Blood" (Netherlands), 435
Councils (Christian), 356
  of Constance, 357
  at Pisa, 356–357
  of Trent, 418(b), 430, 431
Counter-Reformation, 427
Coup d'état, by Napoleon I, 644

Court (households and palaces), in Italy, 376
Court (legal)
  in France, 533, 621
  Ottoman, 505
Court (royal), 490–491(b), 490(i), 491(i)
  of Louis XIV (France), 488–489
Courtier, The (Castiglione), 380–381
Courtiers. *See* Nobility
Court of Star Chamber (England), 400
Cowry shells, as currency, 581
Cradock, Fanny, 601
Craft guilds, 361
Cranach, Lucas
  the Elder, 411(i), 417(i), 418(b)
  the Younger, 418(i)
Cranmer, Thomas, 424
Crécy, battle at, 350
Credit, in Spain, 493
Creole, use of term, 576
Crime. *See also* Law(s)
  fur-collar, 366
  in Later Middle Ages, 341
  by nobles, 366
Crimean Tartars, in Russia, 545
Critical method, for government, 532–533
Cromwell, Oliver, 508, 509(i), 511
Cromwell, Thomas, 424
Crops. *See also* Agriculture; Farms and farming
  in Columbian Exchange, 466–467, 467(i)
  land-reviving, 556
  rotation of, 555, 556
  in 16th and 17th centuries, 554
Crossbow, 350
Cross-dressing, by women, 590–591
Cryptograms, Black Death and, 345
Cuba, 455, 457
Cults, of Supreme Being, 640, 640(i)
Cultural relativism, 473
Culture(s)
  Black Death and, 347–348
  in Enlightenment, 530–531, 535–537
  French, 489, 640–641
  overseas expansion and, 472–475
  worth of, 540
Curie, Marie, 528
Currency, cowry shells as, 581
Curriculum, in elementary schools, 595
Cuzco, 459, 460
Czech people, in Bohemia, 427
Czech Republic. *See also* Bohemia
  Hus and, 356, 357, 357(i)
  Wyclif in, 356

Da Gama, Vasco, 451, 452(m)
Daily life. *See* Lifestyle
D'Alembert, Jean le Rond, 534, 537
Dance of Death, 347–348, 349(i)
Danish phase, of Thirty Years' War, 483
Dante Alighieri, 367, 368
Danton, Georges Jacques, 635, 643
Dark Ages, use of term, 378
David (Michelangelo), 388(i)
David, Jacques-Louis, 645(i)
David d'Angers, Pierre, 626(i)
Death
  in late medieval literature, 347–348
  in Later Middle Ages, 338, 340(i), 349(i)
Death rate. *See* Mortality
"Debate about women," 396
Debt
  in France, 624
  in Renaissance, 375
  Spanish, 493
Debt peonage, 572–573

Decameron, The (Boccaccio), 347
Dechristianization, in France, 638
Declaration of Independence (U.S.), 623
Declaration of Pillnitz, 634–635
Declaration of the Rights of Man and of the Citizen (France), 629, 629(i)
"Declaration of the Rights of Woman" (de Gouges), 631
Deductive reasoning, 527
Defensor Pacis (Marsiglio of Padua), 356
Defoe, Daniel, 564
Dei, Benedetto, 375
Deism, 607
Demography. *See also* Population
  in 17th century, 558–559
Demons, witchcraft and, 435
Denmark. *See also* Scandinavia
  Protestant Reformation in, 422
  Russia and, 500
  sciences in, 529
Denmark-Norway, Protestantism in, 422
Deregulation, economic, 568
Desacralization, of French monarchy, 622
Descartes, René, 526–527
Descent from the Cross (Van der Weyden), 389
Dessalines, Jean Jacques, 647, 648(b)
Determinism, of Spinoza, 530
Dialogue on the Two Chief Systems of the World (Galileo), 525
Diaz, Bartholomew, 449, 452–453
Dictators and dictatorship, in Puritan England, 508–509
Dictionary (Bayle), 530
Diderot, Denis, 534, 540, 542–543(b)
Diet (food)
  bread in, 481
  in 18th century, 598–601
Diet (political)
  Imperial (1530), 422
  of Speyer (1529), 412
  of Worms (1521), 411
Dijon, revolt in, 486
Diplomacy. *See also* Balance of power
  in England, 400
  in Italy, 378
Directory (France), 644
Discovery. *See* Age of Discovery; Expansion; Voyages
Discrimination
  female workers and, 568
  Jews and, 549
Disease
  Black Death as, 341–348
  in Columbian Exchange, 464
  18th-century death rate and, 559
  in New World, 460, 461–462
  venereal, 591
Diversity, Ottoman, 503–504
Divine Comedy (Dante), 367, 368
Divine right of kings, 487. *See also* Absolute monarchy and absolutism
Divorce
  in France, 630
  Protestantism and, 417–419
Doctors. *See* Physicians
Domingo de Gúzman. *See* Dominic (Saint)
Dominic (Saint), 403(i)
Dominican Republic, Taino people in, 455
Donatello, 389
Drama, by Shakespeare, 474
Drogheda, rebellion at, 509
Dualism
  Cartesian, 527, 528
  legal, 366
Dublin, England and, 424

Dutch. *See also* Dutch Republic; Holland;
     Netherlands
  British Navigation Acts and, 569
  England and, 509
  farming and, 556–557, 557(i)
  government, 511–513
  independence and, 494(i)
  New World and, 460, 472
  Spain and, 494
  trade and, 471–472, 513
Dutch East India Company, 446(i), 471, 578
Dutch Republic. *See also* Dutch; Netherlands;
     United Provinces of the Netherlands
  in 17th century, 511–513
Dutch West India Company, 468, 472
Dynasties, in 17th century, 483

Earth. *See also* Astronomy; Universe
  circumnavigation of, 457
East Africa, 444(m)
East Anglia, social crises in, 341
East Asia, trade with, 445
Eastern Europe. *See also* Orthodox Christianity
  absolutism in, 494–495
  armies in, 486
  Black Death in, 343–344
  Jews and, 549
  Reformation in, 422, 427–428
  serfdom in, 482, 482(i), 555
Eastern Orthodoxy. *See* Orthodox Christianity
Eastern Roman Empire. *See also* Byzantine Empire
  plague in, 342
East India Company. *See* British East India
     Company; Dutch East India Company
Eck, Johann, 410–411
Eckhart (Meister), 359, 359(i)
Economic deregulation, 568
Economic liberalism, 568
Economics, Renaissance patronage and, 374
Economy. *See also* Trade
  Black Death and, 347
  global, 470–472, 569–581
  Hundred Years' War and, 354
  mercantilism and, 489
  peasants and, 480–481
  scientific revolution and, 528
Edict of Nantes, 434, 486, 488
Edict of Restitution, 483
Edict on Idle Institutions (Austria), 606
Edinburgh, Enlightenment in, 534–535
Education, 369. *See also* Literacy; Schools;
     Universities
  Black Death and, 348
  in Edinburgh, 534
  Erasmus on, 385
  humanist, 378, 380–381
  Locke on, 531
  Pietism and, 607
  in Prussia, 544
  Rousseau on, 594–595
  for women, 380, 533
Education of a Christian Prince, The (Erasmus), 385
Edward (Black Prince, England), 350
Edward I (England), 341
Edward II (England), 341
Edward III (England), 349, 350, 354, 368, 375
Edward IV (England), 400
Edward VI (England), 424
Egypt, Mamluks in, 445
Elba, Napoleon at, 651
Eleanor of Aquitaine, 349
Electors, of Brandenburg, 495
Elementary schools, 595
Eleonore of Portugal, 420

Elites. *See also* Aristocracy; Nobility
  agriculture and, 555
  colonial, 577, 578
  in France, 621
  Jansenism among, 608
  Renaissance culture and, 393
  in Russia, 503
  in Saint-Domingue, 647
Elizabeth (Bohemia), 528
Elizabeth I (England)
  on blacks in England, 394
  literature under, 473
  Mary, Queen of Scots, and, 425
  power of, 506
  religion and, 417, 423(i), 424–425
Elizabethan, use of term, 473
Emancipation, of Jews, 549
Embroidery, by women, 392
Emigration, from Black Death, 343
Emile or On Education (Rousseau), 594–595
Empires. *See also* Colonies and colonization;
     Imperialism; specific empires
  in Africa, 445
  in Asia, 578–581
  French, 489
  Mexica, 457
  Mongol, 497–498
  Ottoman, 503–505, 504(m)
  in Pacific region, 581
  Portuguese, 451–453
Empiricism, 526
Enclosure, 554(i), 556, 557
Encomienda system, 461, 462
Encyclopedia (Diderot and d'Alembert), 534, 540(i), 542
Encyclopedists, 534
England (Britain). *See also* British East India
     Company; London; Parliament (England)
  absolutism and, 506–511
  agriculture in, 556–558
  American Revolution and, 624–625
  Aquitaine and, 349
  Asia and, 578–579
  Black Death and, 342
  civil war in, 508
  colonies and, 463, 571, 572
  constitutional monarchy in, 510–511
  crises in 14th century, 341
  economy in, 569
  enclosure in, 554(i), 556, 557
  Enlightenment in, 534
  exploration by, 457
  exports from, 571–572, 571(f)
  food riot in, 480(i)
  foundlings in, 593
  France and, 399, 569
  French Revolution and, 633
  government of, 420, 510–511
  Hundred Years' War and, 348–352, 351(m), 354
  illegitimacy in, 588, 589–590
  India and, 578–581, 580(i)
  Industrial Revolution in, 572
  Ireland and, 366, 509
  Jews in, 549
  Napoleon and, 646, 650, 650(m)
  Navigation Acts in, 509, 569
  navy of, 486
  New Amsterdam and, 472
  New World settlement by, 460–461
  Peasants' Revolt in (1381), 339(i), 360–361
  popular revolts in, 486
  population in, 558(f)
  Protestantism in, 422–425, 607
  race and, 577–578

  Restoration in, 510
  rural manufacturing in, 561
  schools in, 369
  sciences in, 529
  Scotland and, 569
  slave trade and, 468, 575
  social crises in 14th century, 341
  Spanish-Netherlands war and, 435
  state and politics in (15th century), 399–400
  taxation in, 354, 361
English Channel, Spanish Armada in, 425, 425(m)
English East India Company, 578, 623
Enlightened absolutism, 541–549
Enlightenment, 518, 530–541
  children and, 531, 594–595
  coffeehouses and, 538–539(b)
  in France, 531–534, 632
  Jewish thought in, 530, 548(b)
  outside of France, 534–535
  philosophes in, 531–534
  popular literature and, 596–597
  in Prussia, 544
  in Russia, 544–546
  science in, 519(i)
  in Scotland, 534–535, 568
  women's rights and, 537
Entrepôt, 446(i)
Entrepreneurs, in 18th century, 600(b), 601
Epic literature. *See also* Philosophy
  Divine Comedy, 368
Epidemics. *See also* Disease
  Columbian exchange and, 464
  famine and, 340–341
  South American slaves and, 493
Epidemiology, plague and, 342
Equality. *See also* Rights
  in marriage, 416–417
  race and, 540–541
  Voltaire on, 534
Equiano, Olaudah, 578, 579(b), 579(i)
Erasmus, Desiderius, 385
Essay Concerning Human Understanding (Locke), 531
Essays (Montaigne), 473
Estate agriculture, 557
Estates (assemblies)
  in Bohemia, 495
  in Brandenburg and Prussia, 495, 496
  Dutch, 513
Estates (classes), in France, 620–621, 625
Estates General (France), 487, 625
Estates of Normandy, 481
Esther Before Ahasuerus (Gentileschi), 393(i)
Estonia, 482(i), 502
Ethiopia, trade and, 445
Ethnic groups. *See also* Diversity
  in Middle Ages, 366–367
Etiquette, in court of Louis XIV, 488–489
Eugene of Savoy, palace of, 491(b), 491(i)
Europe
  in 1715, 493(m)
  Afro-Eurasian trade before Columbus and, 444–448, 444(m)
  Enlightenment in, 531–535
  expansion of, 448–461, 552–581, 553(i), 569
  exploration and conquest by, 442, 443(i), 448–461, 452(m)
  inflation in, 468–470
  North American claims of (1755–1763), 572(m)
  Ottomans and, 504
  printing and, 385–387, 386(m)
  after Thirty Years' War, 484(m)
  witch-hunt in, 435–437
Evangelicalism, Methodist, 608
Évora, black people in, 394

Exchequer (England), 424
Excommunication, of Luther, 411
Expansion. *See also* Exploration; Imperialism
   European, 448–461, 552–581, 553(i)
   French, 646
   of Genoa, 447
   of Prussia, 543, 544
   of Russia, 545–546
Experimental method, 524, 526–527
Exploration,
   age of, 442, 448–461
   by China, 444(m), 445
   European, 448–461, 452(m)
   by France, 489–492
   Genoese, 447
   overseas, 448–461
   by Portugal, 448
   reasons for, 448, 452
   by Spain, 448, 453–456
   support for, 449–450
Exports. *See also* Trade
   English, 571–572, 571(f)
   French, 489
Extended families, 586

Fairs, urban, 597
Fairy tales, 596
Faith. *See also* Religion(s)
   reason and, 355
   salvation by, 409
Faith healing, 610
Fallow, elimination of, 555–556
Families. *See also* Marriage
   in 18th century, 586–591
   in handloom weaving, 562
   women and, 397
Famine
   in Later Middle Ages, 340, 340(i)
   peasant life and, 481
   in 16th and 17th centuries, 554
Farms and farming. *See also* Agriculture; Peasant(s)
   in agricultural revolution, 555–556
Farnese, Alexander (Cardinal). *See* Paul III (Pope)
Fascism. *See also* Italy
Fashion, in 18th century, 600(b), 601–602, 602(i)
Fate, Machiavelli on, 383–384
Faubourg Saint-Antoine (suburb), 567
Fedele, Cassandra, 382–383(b)
Feminism. *See also* Women
Ferdinand I (Holy Roman Empire), 422
Ferdinand II (Holy Roman Empire), 495
Ferdinand III (Holy Roman Empire), 495
Ferdinand and Isabella (Spain), 400
   Columbus and, 453
   Holy Roman Empire and, 420
   on Indians, 462–463
   Inquisition, Jews, and, 401–402
Ferrara, 377
Fertility, in 17th century, 558
Festivals, 597–598
   in French Revolution, 631(i)
Ficino, Marsilio, 379, 384
Finance, in France, 622, 624–625
First Coalition, 635, 638
First Continental Congress, 623
First estate (France), clergy as, 620, 625
First Step of Childhood, The, 594(i)
Fischer von Erlach, Joseph Bernhard, 491(b)
Fish and fishing industry, in Canada, 457
Flagellants, 347, 348(i)
Flanders. *See also* Holland; Low Countries
   France and, 492
   Hundred Years' War and, 350
   rural industry in, 561

schools in, 369
social crises in, 341
urban conflicts in, 361
Flemish language and people. *See* Flanders
Florence
   arts in, 376
   banks in, 374–375
   Black Death and, 342, 343, 347
   dominance by, 376–377
   economy in, 375
   Machiavelli in, 381
   republic in, 375
   same-sex relations in, 365
   wealth of, 378
Florida, 571
Fontenelle, Bernard de, 531(i)
Food. *See also* Agricultural revolution; Agriculture; Diet (food); Grain; Spice trade
   in Columbian Exchange, 463–464, 466–467(b), 466(i), 467(i)
   in 18th century, 598–601
   in England, 557
   population and, 558
Food riots, 480(i), 481, 486, 627
Forced labor. *See also* Slaves and slavery
   in American colonies, 461–462
Foreign policy, in Spain, 400
Foundlings, 592–594
"Four Horsemen of the Apocalypse," 338
France. *See also* French Revolution; Paris
   absolutism in, 434, 486–492
   American Revolution and, 623–624
   Aquitaine and, 349
   army in, 485
   Austria and, 420
   Black Death and, 342
   book trade in, 535(i)
   Catholic Church in, 606
   civil war in, 349
   classicism in, 489
   colonial empire of, 461, 571
   colonial trade and, 572
   constitutional monarchy in, 630–632
   crises in, 341, 621–622
   cultural revolution in, 640–641, 641(i)
   empire of, 489
   England and, 569
   Enlightenment in, 531–534
   estates in, 620–621
   expansion by, 646
   exploration by, 457, 489–492
   finances in, 624–625
   food shortage in, 481
   Fronde in, 487
   government of, 419, 631–632
   guilds in, 566–568
   Habsburg-Valois and, 422
   Hundred Years' War and, 348–354, 351(m)
   illegitimacy in, 588, 589
   India and, 580
   Italy invaded by, 378
   Jansenism in, 608
   Jews in, 549
   laws in, 349, 488, 629
   literacy in, 595, 596(m)
   mixed-race people and, 577
   Napoleon I and, 644–651
   nationalism in, 638–639
   New World settlement by, 460–461
   nobility in, 487, 488
   politics in, 397–399, 621–622
   popular revolts in, 486
   Protestant Reformation in, 422
   religion in, 407(i), 433–434, 486–487, 488

republic in, 635
revolts in, 486
separation of church and state in, 353
Seven Years' War and, 622
slavery and, 633, 642
and Spain, 492
state and politics in (15th century), 397–399
taxation in, 399, 492
Thirty Years' War and, 487
urban conflicts in, 361
wars under Louis XIV, 492, 622
wealth of, 569
wet-nursing in, 591–592, 592(i)
witchcraft and, 437, 609
women in, 646
Franche-Comté, 492
Franchise (vote). *See also* Voting and voting rights
   for free blacks in Saint-Domingue, 642
Francis I (France), 379(i), 399, 433
Francis II (Austria), 635, 646
Franklin, Benjamin, 624
Frederick I (Prussia), 496
Frederick II (Holy Roman Empire), 408
Frederick II the Great (Prussia)
   Enlightenment and, 534, 543–544
   Jews and, 549
   Russia and, 545, 546(m)
   Silesia and, 543
   War of the Austrian Succession and, 570–571
Frederick III ("the Ostentatious") (Elector of Brandenburg). *See* Frederick I (Prussia)
Frederick III (Holy Roman Empire), 420
Frederick William (Great Elector, Brandenburg), 495–496
Frederick William I (the "Soldiers' King") (Prussia), 496–497, 497(i), 543
Freedom(s)
   of religion, 422
   Rousseau and, 541
Freemasons, 537
Free people of color, 577, 578
   in Saint-Domingue, 633
Free trade, 569
Free will, Calvin and, 425
French and Indian War. *See* Seven Years' War
French language, 489
French phase, of Thirty Years' War, 483
French Revolution, 619(i). *See also* Guillotine (France)
   American Revolution and, 622–624
   background to, 620–625
   cultural revolution during, 640–641, 640(i), 641(i)
   dechristianization in, 638
   foreign reactions to, 633–634
   peasants and, 555
   politics and, 625–632
   second revolution in, 635–637
   total war in, 637–639
   women in, 643
Frescoes
   by Raphael, 390
   by women, 392
Friars, Luther as, 409
Frobisher, Martin, 457
Froissart, Jean, 350
Fronde (France), 487
Frontiers, ethnic tensions along, 366
Fur-collar crime, 366
Fur trade, 457

Gabelle (tax), 399
Galen (physician), 529
Galilei, Galileo, 524–525

Garden of Love (Rubens), 514(i)
Gattinara (chancellor), 420
Gays. *See* Homosexuality
Gender. *See also* Men; Sex and sexuality; Voting and voting rights; Women
   artistic genius and, 392–393
   clothing distinctions and, 601–602
   roles by, 396–397
   stereotypes of, 541
   witchcraft trials and, 435
General will, 541
Geneva, Calvin and, 425
Genevan Consistory, 426
Genius, in Renaissance, 391, 391(i), 392
Genoa
   Black Death from, 342
   Columbus and, 453
   republic in, 375
   slave trade and, 394, 448
   trade and, 447–448
Gentileschi, Artemesia, 393(i)
Gentry, beverages of, 601
Geoffrin, Marie-Thérèse, salon of, 536(i)
Geography (Ptolemy), 450–451, 450(i), 453
Geography, Kant on, 537
Geometry
   Descartes and, 527
   Kepler and, 524
George I (England), 511
George II (England), 511
George III (England), 623
German Confederation of the Rhine, 646, 646(m)
German language, in Prussia, 495
German Peasants' War (1525), 416
Germany. *See also* Holy Roman Empire
   Black Death and, 342
   cameralism principles in, 544
   clergy in, 346
   education in, 595
   Enlightenment in, 534
   guilds in, 567
   Habsburg-Valois and, 422
   mysticism in, 360, 360(i)
   Napoleon and, 646
   papacy and, 408
   religious war in, 421–422
   schools in, 369
   serfdom in, 482
   Thirty Years' War and, 485(i)
Germ theory of disease, 592
Gerritz, Decker Cornelis, 561(i)
Gesù, Church of, 430(i), 514
Ghana, 445
Ghettos, for Jews, 549
Ghiberti, Lorenzo, 387
Ghirlandio, Ridolpho, 455(i)
Gibbon, Edward, 593
Gibraltar, England and, 492
Gillray, James, 611(i)
Giotto, 389
Girls. *See also* Children; Women
   education for, 568
   work opportunities for, 587
Girondists, 635, 636
Glass-making, 601–602
Global economy, 470–472, 569–581
Glorious Revolution (England, 1688–1689), 510–511
Glückel of Hameln, 512–513(b), 512(i)
Goa, 453, 470
Gold
   in Africa, 445, 446, 452
   in Americas, 455, 468
Golden age, in Netherlands, 511

Goods and services. *See also* Consumer goods
   consumption of, 602–603
Gouges, Olympe de, 631, 638
Government. *See also* Law(s); specific laws
   absolutism in, 486–505
   central, 419–420, 485
   clergy and, 408
   constitutional, 506–511
   by English Puritans, 508–510
   enlightened absolutism and, 541–549
   of European colonies, 461
   exploration supported by, 449
   Montesquieu on, 532–533
   scientific research and, 528
   Voltaire on, 533–534
   women's roles in, 397
Goya, Francisco, 649(i)
Gozzoli, Bennozzo, 384(i)
Grain, 598–599
   fallow and, 556
   harvesting of, 555
   lack of, 341
   sales of surpluses, 482
Granada, 400
   Spanish conquest of, 448, 453
Grand Alliance, against Louis XIV, 492
Grand Empire (Napoleon), 649–651, 650(m)
Grasses, 556
Gravitation, 524, 526
Great Army (France), 650–651
Great Britain (England), 493(m), 569. *See also* England (Britain)
"Great chain of being," 521
Great Elector. *See* Frederick William (Great Elector, Brandenburg)
Great Famine, in northern Europe, 340
Great Fear (France), 629, 629(m)
Great Fire of London (1666), 574(b)
Great Northern War, 501
Great Powers
   Prussia as, 543
   Russia as, 502
Great Schism, in Catholic Church (1378–1417), 355, 355(m), 408
Greece, humanist studies of, 379
Greenland, 340
Gregory XI (Pope), 355
Grenadiers, in Prussia, 496, 497(i)
Grumbach, Argula von, 417
Guadeloupe, 460
Guanajuato, 468
Guanches people, as slaves, 448
Guilds
   craft, 361
   female, 568
   plague and, 347
   rural industry and, 566
   urban, 566–568
Guillotine (France), 635, 637(i)
Gunpowder, 451
Guns. *See* Weapons
Gustavus Adolphus (Sweden), 483, 485(i), 487
Gustavus Vasa (Sweden), 422
Gutenberg, Johann, 385, 386
Guzmán, Gaspar de. *See* Olivares, count-duke of (Gaspar de Guzmán)

Habsburg dynasty, 420, 493(m)
   in Austria, 420, 495, 546–549
   France and, 487
   in Hungary, 495
   popular education and, 595
   Spain and, 483, 494(i)
   in Thirty Years' War, 427

Habsburg-Valois wars, 378, 422, 433
Haiti. *See also* L'Ouverture, Toussaint; Saint-Domingue
   independence of, 642(m), 643, 646–647, 648(b)
   Taino people in, 455
Hall of Mirrors (Versailles), 490(b)
Hameln, 512–513(b)
Handloom weaving, 562
Harem, 505(i)
Harvests, in 14th century, 341
Harvey, William, 529
Haskalah (Jewish Enlightenment movement), 549, 549(m)
Health. *See* Disease; Medicine
Heathens, Christianity and, 472
Heaven, in Christianity, 409
Heine, Heinrich, 513(b)
Helgoland, 650(m)
Henry ("the Navigator") (Portugal), 449, 451–452
Henry II (England), 349
Henry II (France), 433
Henry III (England), 349
Henry III (France), 434
Henry IV (France), 399–400, 434, 486, 489
Henry V (England), 350–352
Henry VI (England), 400
Henry VII (England), 400
Henry VIII (England), 400, 422–424, 423(i)
Herder, Johann Gottfried von, 540
Heresy
   of Joan of Arc, 353
   witchcraft as, 435
Hevelius, Johannes, 523(i)
Hierarchy. *See also* Class
   of Christian church, 606
   gender, 396–397
   racial, 537–541
   in Renaissance society, 393–397
   of wealth, 395
Higher education. *See* Education; Schools; Universities
High Middle Ages, state (nation) in, 397
Hildebrandt, Johann Lukas von, 491(i)
Hispania. *See* Iberian peninsula
Hispaniola, 454(b), 455, 460
Historians. *See also* History
   on French Revolution, 621
Historical and Critical Dictionary (Bayle), 530
History, revisionism and, 620
Hogarth, William, 607(i)
Hohenzollern dynasty, 493(m)
Holbein, Ambrosius, 368(i)
Holbein, Hans, the Younger, 368(i)
Holland, 358. *See also* Netherlands
   agriculture in, 556
   France and, 646
Holy Office, Copernicus and, 429–430, 525
Holy Roman Empire, 397, 493(m). *See also* Germany; Habsburg dynasty
   Black Death in, 343
   under Charles V, 420, 421(m)
   government of, 420
   Napoleon and, 646
   Protestantism in, 413, 420, 422
   Switzerland in, 421
   Thirty Years' War and, 482–483
   witchcraft and, 437
Home life. *See* Households; Lifestyle
Homosexuality. *See also* Same-sex relationships
   in 18th century, 590–591
   in Middle Ages, 364–365
Honor, sumptuary laws for, 395
Horses, racing, 597
Horthemels, Magdelaine, 609(i)

Hosius, Stanislaus, 427
Hospitals
   in 18th century, 610–611
   foundling, 593
   for plague victims, 346(i)
Households, multi-generation, 586–587
House of Commons (England), 507
   cabinet government and, 510–511
House of Orange, 513
Hudson Bay region, 492, 570
Huguenots (France), 426, 433–434. *See also* Protestantism
   Edict of Nantes and, 434, 486, 488
Human body. *See also* Medicine
   scientific revolution and, 529
Humanism, 378–380
   Christian, 384–385
   education and, 380–381
   Protestantism and, 412
   in Renaissance, 378–380
   women and, 382(b)
Humans, origins of, 537
Hume, David, 511, 534, 535, 537, 540
Hundred Days, of Napoleon, 651
Hundred Years' War, 348–354, 351(m)
Hungary. *See also* Magyars
   in Austrian Empire, 495
   Black Death and, 343
   Ottomans and, 422
   Reformation in, 427
Hürrem (Ottomans), 505, 505(i)
Hus, Jan, 356, 357, 357(m), 427
Hussites, 356, 357(m)
Hypocrisy, of clergy, 356(i)

Iberian Peninsula. *See also* Portugal; Spain
   black people in, 394
   unification of, 402
Iconoclasm, in Netherlands, 434(i)
Identity, of racially and ethnically mixed people, 578
Illegitimacy, 586(i), 589–590
   foundlings and, 593
Imitation of Christ, The (Thomas à Kempis), 358
Immigrants and immigration. *See* Migration
Immorality, of clergy, 408
Imperial Diet (Augsburg, 1530), 422
Imperialism. *See also* Empires
   French, 649–650
   Portuguese, 453
   Russian, 499
Imports, British Navigation Acts and, 569
Inca Empire, 459–460, 464
Independence
   Dutch, 494(i)
   of Haiti, 642(m), 643, 646–647, 648(b)
   of Portugal, 494
   of United States, 624
Index of Prohibited Books, 430
India
   Anglo-French conflicts in, 571
   Britain and, 578–581, 580(i)
   in 1805, 581(i)
   Genoese expedition and, 447
   Portugal and, 470
   sea route to, 453
   sugar in, 465
   trade and, 444(m), 445, 453
Indian Ocean region, 445, 448, 453, 578
Indians. *See also* American Indians
   origin of term, 455
Indies, search for water route to, 455
Indonesia, 472
Inductive reasoning, 526

Indulgences, 409–410, 410(i)
Industrial Revolution, in England, 572
"Industrious revolution," 563(i), 566
Industry. *See also* Cottage industry
   in 18th century, 562(m)
   rural, 560–566
   in 17th century, 481
Inertia, law of, 524
Infanticide, in 18th century, 593
Infant mortality. *See also* Childbirth; Midwives
   in foundling homes, 593
   of indigenous American people, 461
   wet-nursing and, 591, 592(i)
Infantry. *See* Military
Inflation
   from Black Death, 347
   in Spain, 470–471
Influenza, 461
Inheritance, by women, 630–631
Inner light, 416
Inoculation, against smallpox, 559, 611–614
Inquiry into the Nature and Causes of the Wealth of Nations (Smith), 568
Inquisition
   Holy Office and, 429–430
   Netherlands and, 435
   Roman, 430
   Spain and, 401–402, 435, 606
Institutes of the Christian Religion, The (Calvin), 425
Instruction. *See* Teaching
Instrument of Government (England), 509
Integral calculus, 524
Intellectual thought. *See also* Art(s); Enlightenment; Literature; Philosophy; Religion(s); Renaissance
   in Enlightenment, 518, 530–541
   exploration and, 448
   humanism and, 378–380
   Jewish, 548(b)
   overseas expansion and, 472–475
   on race, 472–473
   scientific revolution and, 518, 519(i), 520–531
Intendants (royal officials), 461
Interesting Narrative . . . (Equiano), 579(b)
International trade. *See* Trade
Inuit people, in Greenland, 340
Inventions. *See also* Industrial Revolution
   in agricultural revolution, 557
Iran. *See* Persia
Ireland
   Catholicism in, 424, 509
   England and, 509
   legal pluralism in, 366
   linen industry in, 563(i)
   rebellion in (1641), 508
Isabella (Castile), 400. *See also* Ferdinand and Isabella (Spain)
Isabella (France), 349
Isabella of Este, 394
Islam. *See also* Arabs and Arab world; Muslims
   Black Death and, 343, 347
Istanbul. *See* Constantinople (Istanbul)
Italy. *See also* Roman Republic; Rome
   baroque style in, 514
   Black Death and, 342, 343
   city-states in, 376–378, 377(m), 513
   communes in, 375
   French invasion of, 378
   Habsburg-Valois wars in, 378, 422
   Inquisition in, 430
   popular revolts in, 486
   Renaissance in, 372, 374–384
   republics in, 375–376

   same-sex relations in, 365
   women in, 528
Ivan III the Great (Russia), 498
Ivan IV the Terrible (Russia), 498

Jacobean, use of term, 473
Jacobin club (France), 634, 635, 638
Jacquerie, 358–360
Jakarta, 578
James I (England), 473, 506, 507, 590
James II (England), 510
James V (Scotland), 427
Jamestown, 460
Janissary corps, Ottoman, 504
Jansen, Cornelius, 608
Jansenism, 608, 609(i)
Java, 446(i), 578
Jefferson, Thomas, 540, 647
Jena, battle at, 646
Jenner, Edward, 611(i), 614
Jesuit Priest Distributing Holy Pictures, 418–419(b), 419(i)
Jesuits, 431–433, 514, 606
Jewish Bride, The (Rembrandt), 512(i)
Jews and Judaism. *See also* Anti-Semitism
   in Austria, 606
   conversion in Spain, 401–402
   Dutch business and, 513
   in England, 509
   Enlightenment and, 530, 548(b), 549
   in France, 549, 632
   Glückel of Hameln on, 512–513(b)
   Mendelssohn family and, 548(b)
   in Middle Ages, 341
   in New World, 578
   in Ottoman Empire, 503–504
   plague and, 347
   racial ideas about, 472
   scientific thought and, 529
   as slaves, 448
   in Spain, 400–401, 401(m), 402
Joanna of Castile, Philip of Burgundy and, 402
Joan of Arc (France), 352–353, 354
John VI Kantakouzenos (Byzantine Empire), 343, 345, 347
John of Spoleto, 355
Joliet, Louis, 489–492
Jonson, Ben, on death of son, 593
Joseph II (Austria), 546, 547, 547(i)
   church and, 606
   Jews and, 549
   purification of religion in, 609
Josephine (France), 645(i)
Journal (Columbus), 448, 453
Journeymen's associations, 568
Journeymen's guilds, 361
Juan de Pareja (Velázquez), 469
Judaism. *See* Jews and Judaism
Judiciary and judicial system. *See also* Court (legal)
   in England, 400
   in France, 608, 622
Julius II (Pope), 387, 389–390
Junkers, 495, 497
Jupiter (planet), Galileo and, 525
Just price, 599

Kaffa, Black Death and, 342
Kant, Immanuel, 534, 537, 540, 541
Kepler, Johannes, 523–524, 525
Khan. *See* China; Mongols
Kingdom of Naples, 376, 377
Kings and kingdoms. *See also* Empires; Monarchy
   Catholic rulers in, 606
   in Spain, 400

Knights. *See also* Nobility
    armor of, 352*(i)*
    in English Commons, 354
Knox, John, 427

Labor. *See also* Forced labor; Gender; Serfs and serfdom; Slaves and slavery; Workers
    Black Death and, 347
    landless, 557–558
    peasants and, 358
    in putting-out system, 561
    in Spanish America, 461–463
    of women, 562–563, 564*(b)*
Lady with an Ermine (Leonardo da Vinci), 391*(i)*
Lafayette, marquis de, 624, 628
Lancaster, house of, 400
Land. *See also* Agriculture
    in France, 620
    in Ottoman Empire, 504
    ownership of, 555
    in Russia, 498
    in 16th and 17th centuries, 554
Landlords, in eastern Europe, 482
Language(s)
    Arawak, 455
    French, 489
    German, 495
Languedoc, houses of prostitution in, 363
La Plata, 461
La Rochelle, siege of, 487
La Salle, Jean-Baptiste de, 595
Las Casas, Bartolomé de, 462, 463
Last Judgment, The (Michelangelo), 388
Last Supper, The (Leonardo da Vinci), 391*(b)*
Lateen sail, 451
Later Middle Ages, 338, 339*(i)*
    Catholic Church in, 354–358
    famine in, 340, 340*(i)*
    social unrest in, 358–369
    society in, 358–369
    women in, 361–364
Latin language, humanist studies and, 378–379
Latitude, 451
Latvia, 502, 549
Laud, William, 507–508
Laura de Dianti (Titian), 394*(i)*
Lavater, Johann Kaspar, 548*(b)*, 548*(i)*
Law(s). *See also* Canon law; Law codes; specific laws
    ethnic tensions and, 366
Law (scientific)
    Boyle's law, 530
    of inertia, 524
    of planetary motion (Kepler), 523–524
    of universal gravitation, 526
Law codes, Napoleonic, 644–645
Laypeople, literacy of, 369, 387
Lay piety, 357–358
League of Armed Neutrality, 624
Legal pluralism, 366
Legal system. *See also* Law(s)
    peasants and, 482
    in Prussia, 544
Legislation. *See also* Law(s)
    in England, 354
Legislative Assembly (France), 634, 635
Leibniz, Gottfried von, 526
Leisure, in 18th century, 597–598
Leo X (Pope), 399
Leonardo da Vinci, 383, 390, 391*(b)*, 391*(i)*
Leopold I (Holy Roman Empire), 491*(b)*
Leopold II (Holy Roman Empire), 546
Leprosy, 341

Lerma, duke of, 494
Lesbians. *See also* Homosexuality
    subculture in 18th century, 591
Les Halles (Paris), 585*(i)*
Le Tellier, François. *See* Louvois, marquis de
Le Vau, Louis (architect), 490*(b)*
Lexington, American Revolution and, 623
Liberal arts, 378
Liberals and liberalism, economic, 568
Liberty(ies), Christian, 414–415*(b)*
Libraries, in Enlightenment, 537
Lifestyle. *See also* Children; Families; Marriage
    of common people, 552
    in 18th century, 584, 585*(i)*, 602–603, 603*(i)*
    in France, 619*(i)*, 638
    of Glückel of Hameln, 512–513*(b)*
    in Paris, 604–605*(b)*, 605*(i)*
    Protestant, 413*(i)*
    of sailors, 449
Lima, Spanish in, 461
Linen industry, in Ireland, 563*(i)*
Linné, Carl von, 537
Lisbon, 394, 453
Literacy, 597*(i)*
    in England, 595
    in Enlightenment, 537
    in France, 595, 596*(m)*
    of laypeople, 369
    popular culture and, 595–597
    printing and, 387
    religion and, 595
    vernacular literature and, 367–369
Literature
    death and, 347–348
    essays as, 473
    popular, 595–597
    of Shakespeare, 473–475
    vernacular, 367–369
    by women, 362–363*(b)*
Lithuania, 427, 549
"Little ice age," 340, 481
Liturgy, Protestantism and, 422
Llamas, 464
Lloyd, Edward, 539*(b)*
Lloyds of London, 539*(b)*
Locke, John, 510, 531, 534
Lollards, 356
London
    in 18th century, 571
    Great Fire of (1666) and, 574*(b)*, 574*(i)*
    same-sex subculture in, 590, 591
Longbow, 350, 353*(i)*
Longhi, Pietro, 586*(i)*
Long Parliament (England), 508
Lord protector (England), Cromwell as, 509
Lords. *See* Nobility
Lord's Supper, 412
Lorraine, 492
Lotto, Lorenzo, 373*(i)*
Louis II (Hungary), 427
Louis IX (France), 349
Louis XI "Spider King" (France), 399
Louis XII (France), 399
Louis XIII (France), 486, 487, 490*(b)*
Louis XIV (France), 488*(i)*, 530, 621
    absolutism of, 479*(i)*, 486, 487–492
    acquisitions of, 492, 492*(m)*
    Charles II (England) and, 510
    Versailles and, 488–489, 490*(b)*, 490*(i)*
    wars of, 485
Louis XV (France), 606, 621, 622
Louis XVI (France), 622
    arrest of, 634, 634*(i)*
    constitutional monarchy and, 630–632

    finances and, 624–625
    guillotining of, 635
Louis XVIII (France), 651
Louisiana, 460, 492, 571, 572
L'Ouverture, Toussaint, 642–643, 646–647, 648*(b)*, 648*(i)*
Louvois, marquis de (François le Tellier), 492
Low Countries. *See also* Belgium; Holland; Netherlands
    agriculture in, 556–557
    Hundred Years' War in, 350
    social crises in 14th century, 341
Lower Belvedere, 491*(b)*
Lower classes. *See* Class
Loyalists, 623
Loyola, Ignatius, 431–433
Lunéville, Treaty of, 646
Luther, Martin, 409–411. *See also* Lutheranism; Protestantism
    Bible translation by, 412
    On Christian Liberty, 412, 414–415*(b)*, 416*(i)*
    on Copernicus, 522
    German patriotism and, 421
    Holy Roman Empire and, 420
    marriage of, 416, 417*(i)*
    on religious radicals, 416
Lutheranism, 422
    Augsburg Confession and, 422
    in eastern Europe, 427
    Protestant revival and, 606–607
    Thirty Years' War and, 483
Luxembourg, 420
Luxury goods, 561
    spices as, 470*(i)*
    trade and, 447
Lyons, 486

Macao, 470
Machiavelli, Niccolò, 380, 381
Madeira Islands, 452, 468
Magellan, Ferdinand, 448, 452*(m)*, 456–457
Magistrates, in France, 621–622
Magnetic compass, 451
Magyars, 427. *See also* Hungary
Maine (French county), 399
Maintenon, Madame de, 489
Maize (corn), 466, 467*(i)*
Malacca, 445, 453, 470
Malay Archipelago, 444*(m)*, 456
Malay Peninsula, Portuguese and, 470
Maldive Islands, 581
Mali, trade and, 446
Mamluks (Egypt), 445, 447
Mandeville, John, 449*(i)*, 450
Manila, trade in, 470
Mannerism, as art style, 390
Mansa Musa. *See* Musa (Mansa)
Mantegna, Andrea, 389
Mantua, 377
Mantua, duchess of (Isabella of Este), 394
Manual on the Art of Childbirth (Coudray), 611, 612–613*(b)*
Manufacturing. *See also* Industry
    in 18th century, 560
    rural, 561
Maps
    cartography and, 450–451
    of English enclosures, 554*(i)*
    by Ribeiro, 456*(i)*
Maria Theresa (Austria), 546–549, 547*(i)*
    Catholic Church and, 606
    education and, 595
    Frederick the Great and, 543, 570–571
Maria-Theresa (France), 492

Marie Antoinette (France), 600(b), 634
Marie de' Medici, 487
Marina (Doña), 459(b), 459(i)
Maritime trade. See Seaborne trade
Market economy, in France, 620
Market gardening, 599
Marquette, Jacques, 489–492
Marriage
  age at, 361, 587
  changing patterns of, 588–589
  in 18th century, 586–587
  ethnic purity and, 366–367
  Luther on, 416
  in Ottoman royalty, 505
  Protestantism and, 413(i), 416–419
  women and, 361, 397, 416–417
Marseilles, 553(i)
  plague and, 342, 345, 559, 560(i)
  slave trade and, 394
Marsiglio of Padua, 355–356
Martial law, in England, 509
Martin V (Pope), 357
Martinique, 460
Martyrs (Christian), Joan of Arc as, 353
Mary I Tudor (England), 423, 423(i), 424
Mary II (England), 510, 513
Mary, Queen of Scots, 425, 427
Maryland, 460
Mary of Burgundy, 420
Masonic lodges, 537
Mass (Christian), 412
Massachusetts, 460
Masturbation, 592
Mathematical Principles of Natural Philosophy (Newton). See *Principia Mathematica* (Newton)
Mathematics
  Arabic learning and, 521
  Descartes and, 526–527
  exploration and, 451
  of Newton, 525–526
Maupeou, René de, 622
Maupeou parlements, 622
Maximilian I (Holy Roman Empire), 420
Mazarin, Jules, 487
Meat, in diet of common people, 599
Mechanistic universe, 527, 534
Medici family, 377
  Catherine de', 433
  Cosimo de', 377, 379
  Lorenzo de', 377, 387
  Marie de', 487
  Savonarola and, 378
Medicine
  in 18th century, 559, 609–610
  faith healing and, 610
  hospitals and, 610–611
  for plague, 344(b), 344(i), 345(i)
  scientific revolution and, 529, 529(i)
  surgery and, 610–611
Mediterranean region, Genoese trade and, 447–448
Memoirs (Catherine the Great), 544
Men. See also Families; Gender; Women
  clothing and masculinity of, 398(b), 398(i)
  gender roles and, 396–397
  marriage age of, 363
  same-sex relations among, 590
Mendelssohn family
  Dorothea, 548(b)
  Felix, 548(b)
  Moses, 548(b), 548(i), 549
Mercantilism, 489
  English, 571–572
  French, 489
  global economy and, 569

Merchant(s)
  in Afro-Eurasian trade, 445
  fashion and, 600(b)
  in Italy, 375
  oligarchies of, 375–376
  powers over poor, 563
Mercier, Louis-Sébastien, 604–605(b)
Merian, Maria Sibylla, 528(i)
Merici, Angela, 431
Merk, J. C., 497(i)
Merry Family, The (Steen), 511(i)
Messina, Black Death and, 342
Mestizos, in Latin America, 462(i), 463
Metals. See also Gold; Mines and mining; Silver
  Venetian trade in, 447
Methodists and Methodism, 593, 607–608, 607(i)
Métis, 463
Metric system, in France, 640
Metternich, Klemens von, Napoleon and, 651
Mexico, 457–459
  silver in, 461, 468
  Spanish conquest of, 449
Meytens, Martin, 547(i)
Michael Romanov, 498
Michelangelo, 372, 387, 388(i), 390
Middle Ages. See High Middle Ages; Later Middle Ages
Middle East. See also Arabs and Arab world
Midwives, 609, 611, 612–613(b)
Migration. See also Emigration
  of Africans, 573
  Black Death and, 343
  ethnic tensions and, 366
  patterns of marriage, illegitimacy, and, 588–589
  slave trade as, 579(b)
  of whites, 576
Milan, 376, 377, 378
Military. See also Armed forces; Soldiers
  in Prussia, 496–497, 497(i)
  Russian, 501–502
Millet system (nations), Ottoman, 505
Mind-body split, 527, 530
Mines and mining. See also Gold
  in Americas, 468, 471
  epidemics and, 493
  Spanish silver and, 572–573
Ming dynasty (China), 445, 453
Minorca, 492
Misogyny, in Renaissance, 396
Missions and missionaries. See also Monks and monasteries
  in New World, 578
Mississippi River, France and, 492
Mixed races, 462(i), 576–578, 577(i)
Mobilization, in French Revolution, 639
Modena, 377
Modernization, of Russia, 499–503
Modern world, Renaissance and, 372
Mogadishu, 445
Mohács, Battle of, 427, 428(i)
Mohammed II (Ottoman Empire), 446–447
Molière (Jean-Baptiste Poquelin), 489
Moluccas, 445, 456
Mombasa, 445
Mona Lisa (Leonardo da Vinci), 391(b)
Monarchy. See also Absolute monarchy and absolutism; Constitutional monarchies; Kings and kingdoms
  in England, 400
  female rulers and, 396–397
  in France, 397–399, 433
  in Prussia, 544
  women and, 349
Monasticism (Christian). See Monks and monasteries

Money. See Coins; Currency; Economy
Mongols
  Black Death and, 342
  Ming dynasty and, 453
  in Russia, 497–498, 545
  trade and, 445
Monks and monasteries. See also Friars; Missions and missionaries
  civic responsibilities and, 408
  English dissolution of, 424
Montagu, Mary Wortley, 611–614
Montaigne, Michel de, 473, 474, 593
Montcalm, marquis de (Louis-Joseph de), 571
Montesquieu, baron de (Charles-Louis de Secondat), 532–533, 534
Montezuma II (Mexica Empire), 457–458
Montpellier, 486
Montreal, 457, 460
Moon, Galileo on, 524(i)
Morality, in 18th century, 591
More, Thomas, 380, 384–385, 423
Moriscos (former Muslims), Spanish expulsion of, 493–494
Morocco, 452
Mortagne, Castle of, siege of, 353(i)
Mortality. See also Death; Infant mortality
  in 18th century, 559
  from plague, 343, 347
  in 17th century, 558
Moscow, 497–498
  Napoleon at, 651
Mothers. See also Childbirth; Children; Marriage; Wet-nursing; Women
  in 18th century, 593–594, 594(i)
Motion
  Aristotle and, 521
  Kepler's laws of, 523
Mountain, the, 635, 636
Movable type, 385, 387
Movement of peoples. See Migration
Mughals (India), 578, 580
Mulatto, 469(b), 577(i)
Mundus Novus, 456
Murillo, Bartolome Esteben, 466(i)
Musa (Mansa), 446
Music, baroque, 515
Musikiysky, Grigory, 503(i)
Muslims. See also Arabs and Arab world; Islam
  coffeehouses and, 538(b)
  navigation by, 451
  in Ottoman Empire, 503–504
  as slaves, 448, 465
  in Spain, 402
  trade by, 444(m)
Myconius, 368
Mysticism
  of Bridget of Sweden, 358
  in Germany, 360, 360(i)

Nagasaki, Portuguese trade with, 470
Nahuatl language, 459(b)
Nanjing, 445
Naples
  kingdom of, 376–377
  revolts in 17th century, 486
  wealth of, 378
Napoleon I (Napoleon Bonaparte), 644–651
  coronation of, 645(i)
  Europe in 1812 and, 650(m)
  at Waterloo, 651
Napoleon III (Louis Napoleon), Grand Empire of, 649–651, 650(m)
Napoleonic Code (France), 644–645, 646
Narva, battle at, 500–501

Naseby, battle at, 508
Nation. *See* State (nation)
National Assembly (France), 628(i), 634
    changes made by, 631–632
    formation of, 625–627
    as lawmaking body, 630–631
National Convention (France), 635–636, 638, 643
Nationalism
    in France, 638–639
    in Germany, 421
    in Hundred Years' War, 350
Nationality. *See* Ethnic groups
National state. *See* State (nation)
Native Americans. *See* American Indians
"Natural man," Diderot on, 542–543(b)
Natural philosophy, 520
Natural resources, in Siberia, 499
Natural rights, 623
Nature, classification of, 537
Navarre, 400
Navigation. *See also* Seaborne trade
    scientific instruments for, 521–522
    scientific revolution and, 528
    technology and, 450–451
Navigation Acts (England), 569, 571
    of 1651, 509, 569
    of 1660, 569
    of 1663, 569
Navy. *See also* Ships and shipping
    English, 486, 571
Nelson, Horatio, at Trafalgar, 646
Netherlands. *See also* Austrian Netherlands; Holland; Low Countries
    under Charles V, 434–435
    civil war in, 435
    Dutch Republic and, 511
    golden age in, 511
    Holy Roman Empire and, 420
    iconoclasm in, 434(i)
    rural industry in, 561
    sciences in, 529
    Spain and, 434, 435, 493(m)
    standard of living in, 513
    surplus grain sales to, 482
    uprisings in, 486
    wealth of, 569
New Amsterdam, 472, 569
New Astronomy, The (Kepler), 523
New Christians
    Jews as, 401–402
    Teresa of Ávila and, 432
New England, Cabot exploration of, 457
Newfoundland, 457, 492, 570
New France, 460, 571
New Granada, 461
New Haven, 460
New Model Army, 508
New Netherland, 472
New South Wales, 581
New Spain, 461, 578
New Testament
    Erasmus on, 385
    in German (Luther), 412
Newton, Isaac, 525–526, 525(i), 530
    Voltaire on, 533
New World. *See also* Americas
    diseases in, 461
    English settlement in, 460–461
    European "discovery" of, 455
    European impact in, 461–464
    French settlement in, 460–461
    mixed races in, 462(i), 576–578, 577(i)
    Spanish conquests in, 453–460
New York, 472, 569

Nice, 635
"Ninety-five Theses on the Power of Indulgences" (Luther), 410
Nobility. *See also* Aristocracy
    as bandits, 366
    clothing of, 601–602
    in France, 487, 488–489, 645
    as French estate, 620, 625
    in Hundred Years' War, 350
    Hungarian, 495
    in Italian Renaissance, 387–388
    peasant revolt (1525) and, 416
    in Prussia, 496, 497, 544
    in Renaissance, 395
    in Russia, 498, 544
    same-sex relations among, 590
Nogarola, Isotta, 382(b)
Nomads, Mongols as, 497–498
Normandy, in Hundred Years' War, 353
North Africa, Ottomans and, 504
North America. *See also* Americas; New World
    Anglo-French conflicts in, 571
    Dutch and, 472
    European claims in (1755–1763), 572(m)
    exports from England to, 571
    Franco-British competition over, 571
    Spain and, 421(m)
North Carolina, Roanoke colony in, 460
Northmen. *See* Vikings
Norway. *See also* Scandinavia
    Protestant Reformation in, 422
Nova Scotia, 492, 570
Novels. *See* Literature
Nuclear family, in 18th century, 586–587
Nuns (Christian), 408
    at convent of Port-Royal, 609(i)
    Ursuline order of, 431
Nursing. *See* Breast-feeding
Nutmeg, 471
Nutrition. *See* Diet (food); Food

Occam, William of, 355–356
Occult, astronomy and, 522
Occupations, in 18th century, 587
"Of Cannibals" (Montaigne), 473, 475
Of Natural Characters (Hume), 537
Ogé, Vincent, 633
Old Regime (France), 621
Olearius, Adam, 500–501(b)
Oligarchy
    Dutch, 513
    of merchants, 375–376
Olivares, count-duke of (Gaspar de Guzmán), 494
On Christian Liberty (Luther), 412, 414–415(b), 416(i)
"On My First Son" (Jonson), 593
On the Different Races of Man (Kant), 537
On the Dignity of Man (Pico della Mirandola), 379
"On the Immortality of the Soul" (Mendelssohn), 548(b)
On the Revolutions of the Heavenly Spheres (Copernicus), 522, 529
On the Structure of the Human Body (Vesalius), 529, 529(i)
Open-field system, 554–555, 556
Optics, Kepler and, 523–524
Orange, House of, 513
Orders. *See also* Clergy; Nobility; Peasant(s)
    social classes as, 395
Orléans
    duke of, 621, 622
    English siege of, 352
    Joan of Arc at, 352–353
Orlov, Gregory, 544

Ormuz, 453
Orphans, in 18th century, 592–593
Orthodox Christianity, in Russia, 498
Othello (Shakespeare), 474
Ottoman Empire, 446–447. *See also* Ottoman Turks
    absolutism in, 503–505
    in 1566, 504(m)
    Hungary and, 427–428
Ottoman Turks. *See also* Ottoman Empire
    Hungary, Vienna, and, 422
Overland trade. *See* Caravan trade; Trade
Overseas expansion. *See* Expansion; Exploration
Oxford, University of, 356

Pacific Ocean region
    Cook and, 581
    European empires in, 581
    Magellan in, 456–457
Pacifism, of religious radicals, 416
Pagans and paganism, denunciation of, 609
Paine, Thomas, 596–597
Painting
    baroque, 514(i), 515
    by women, 393
Palaces
    of absolute monarchs, 490–491(b), 490(i)
    Ottoman, 505
Pale (Dublin), 424
Pale of Settlement, 549, 549(m)
Palermo, 486
Palm Sunday, 608
Pamphlets, reading and, 596
Papacy. *See also* Catholic Church; Pope(s)
    in Austria, 546
    baroque arts and, 514
    in Catholic hierarchy, 606
    in Catholic Reformation, 428–431
    Charles V and, 422
    Luther and, 411
    taxation by, 408
    wealth of, 378
Papal curia, 408
Papal States, 376–377
Paper, printing and, 386
Paracelsus, 529
Pareja, Juan de, 469(b), 469(i)
Paris. *See also* France; Paris, Treaty of
    foundlings in, 593
    guilds in, 566–567
    lifestyle in, 604–605(b), 605(i)
    riots in (1792), 635
    salons in, 535–537
Paris, Treaty of
    of 1259, 348
    of 1763, 571
    of 1783, 624
Parish guilds, 357–358
Parlement of Paris, 487, 622
Parlements (France), 533, 621
Parliament (England), 354. *See also* House of Commons (England)
    Charles I and, 507, 508
    Charles II and, 510
    constitutional monarchy and, 510–511
    monarchy and, 400
    under Puritans, 508–510
Parma, republic in, 375
Partitions, of Poland, 545–546, 546(m)
Patriotism, in France, 645
Patronage, 374
    of Renaissance arts, 387–388
Paul III (Pope), 428–430
Peace of Augsburg, 422, 483
Peace of Utrecht, 492, 493(m), 570

Peace of Westphalia, 483
Peasant(s). *See also* Agriculture; Land; Peasant revolts; Serfs and serfdom
    in Austria, 547
    in France, 620, 635, 649
    literacy and, 596
    marginal religious beliefs of, 608–609
    marriage by, 587
    in Ottoman Empire, 504
    poverty of, 481
    proletarianization of, 558
    in Prussia, 497
    radical reformers and, 416
    rural industry and, 560–566
    in Russia, 498–499, 499(i), 502, 545
    in 17th-century economic crisis, 480–481
    social crises in 14th century and, 341
    Spanish, 494
    in Thirty Years' War, 483(i)
    weddings of, 589(i)
Peasant revolts, 358–361, 628–629
    in England (1381), 339(i), 360–361
Penn, William, 510
Pennsylvania, Quakers in, 460
People of color, free, 577, 578
Pepper, 447, 467
Persecution, religious, 433
Persia, Ottomans and, 504
Persian Empire, 446–447
Persian Letters, The (Montesquieu), 532
Peru, 459–460, 461, 467(i)
Peter III (Russia), 544
Peter the Great (Russia), 499–503, 503(i)
Petrarch, Francesco, 378
Petrograd (St. Petersburg). *See* St. Petersburg
Pharmacy. *See* Apothecaries
Philip II (Spain), 402, 457, 470(i)
    Armada and, 425
    empire of, 422, 434, 435, 468
    Mary Tudor and, 423(i), 424
Philip III (Spain), 494
Philip IV the Fair (France), 341, 349, 355
Philip IV (Spain), 486, 494
Philip V (Spain), 492
Philip VI (France), 349, 350
Philip of Burgundy, 402
Philippines, naming of, 457
Philosophes, 531–534
    salons and, 536
    on women's rights, 537, 541
Philosophy. *See also* Enlightenment; Intellectual thought; Science
    natural, 520
Phyllis Riding Aristotle, 396(i)
Physicians. *See also* Medicine
    childbirth and, 611
    in 18th century, 610
Physics
    Aristotle and, 521, 522
    Newtonian, 526
Pico della Mirandola, Giovanni, 379, 384
Piero della Francesca, 389
Pietism, 607
Pigafetta, Antonio, journal of, 448
Pilgrimage of Grace (England), 424
Pilgrims and pilgrimages, 408
Pisa
    Black Death and, 342
    council at, 356–357
Pitt, William, 571
Pius VII (Pope), 645, 645(i)
Pizarro, Francisco, 460
Plague. *See also* Black Death
    disappearance of, 559

in France (17th century), 481
hospitals for, 346(i)
in Marseilles, 342, 345, 559, 560(i)
medicine for, 344(b), 344(i), 345(i)
Planetary motion
    Aristotle and, 520
    Brahe, *Rudolfine Tables,* and, 523
    Kepler's laws of, 523–524
    Ptolemy on, 520–521
Plan of the English Commerce, A (Defoe), 564
Plantations
    agricultural slavery and, 395
    sugar, 452
    zones of (ca. 1700), 573(m)
Plants, in Columbian exchange, 463
Plato, 379, 381
Platonic ideas, 379
Plays. *See* Drama
Plessis, Armand Jean du. *See* Richelieu, Cardinal
Pluralism
    in church, 408
    laws applied to, 366
Plymouth colony, 460
Pneumonic transmission. *See also* Black Death
    of plague, 342
Poets and poetry. *See* Epic literature; Literature
Poitiers, battle at (1356), 350
Poland
    Black Death and, 342, 343
    Jews in, 549
    partitions of, 545–546, 546(m)
    Reformation and, 427
    Russia and, 500, 545–546
    serfdom and commercial agriculture in, 482
Poland-Lithuania, 427
Political prisoners, in France, 646
Political thought
    in Renaissance, 381–384
    Rousseau and, 541
Politics
    French Revolution and, 625–632
    popular action and, 486
    Protestantism and, 412
    revolution in (1775–1815), 618
    in 17th century, 486
    in western Europe (ca. 1450–1521), 397–402
Politiques (France), 434
Polo, Marco, 445, 454(b)
Poltava, battle at, 502
Pomerania, 483
Pompadour, Madame de, 622
Pondicherry, 580
Poor people. *See also* Peasant(s); Poverty
    diet of, 599
    in France, 621
    in French Revolution, 636
    Jansenism among, 608
    in rural areas, 560
Pope(s). *See also* Papacy; specific popes
    in Great Schism, 355
    from Medici family, 377
Popolo, in Italy, 375
Popular culture
    literature and, 595–597
    political action and, 486
Population
    Black Death and, 342, 343, 347
    decline in, 341
    in 18th century, 559, 559(f), 562(m)
    growth of, 448, 558–560
    of Prussia, 543
Poquelin, Jean-Baptiste. *See* Molière
Portrait of Baldassare Castiglione (Raphael), 381(i)

Portugal, 400
    and Brazil, 456
    colonies of, 461
    empire of, 451–453
    exploration by, 448, 449
    independence of, 494
    Indian Ocean trade and, 578
    Inquisition in, 436
    plantation slavery of, 573–574
    popular revolts in, 486
    slave trade and, 470
    Spain and, 402, 494
    trade by, 470
    Treaty of Tordesillas and, 456
    uprisings in, 486
    Venetian trade and, 447
    wealth of, 569
Potatoes, 466, 467, 599–601
    introduction into Europe, 560
Potosí, 468, 471
Poverty. *See also* Poor people
    in France, 627–628
    urban, 481
Power (authority). *See also* Absolute monarchy and absolutism; Constitutional monarchies
    expansion of rulers', 484–485
    of French monarchy, 488, 622
    religious, 412
    in Renaissance, 387, 388
Pragmatic Sanction (1713), 543
Praise of Folly, The (Erasmus), 385
Predestination, Calvin on, 426, 427
Pregnancy. *See also* Childbirth; Illegitimacy
    in 18th century, 588, 591
Premarital sex, 419, 588
Presbyterians
    charity schools and, 595
    in Scotland, 426, 508
Prester John, 446, 452
Price
    famine, epidemics, and, 340–341
    just, 599
    silver from Americas and, 468–470
Price revolution, 558
Priests and priestesses. *See also* Clergy
    Christian, 408
Primavera (Botticelli), 392(i)
Prime minister (England), 511
Prince, The (Machiavelli), 381–382, 383, 385
Principia Mathematica (Newton), 526, 530, 533(i)
Printing. *See also* Books
    in Enlightenment, 541
    growth in Europe, 386(m)
    of Ninety-five Theses (Luther), 410
    in Renaissance, 385–387
Printing press, 385(i), 396
Procession(s), Catholic, 608
Procession of the Magi (Gozzoli), 384(i)
Professionalization, of armies, 485, 485(i)
Profit, in Florentine banking, 374–375
Progress, Enlightenment concept of, 530
Proletarianization, 558
Property. *See also* Inheritance
    Locke on rights to, 510
Prosperity, in Italian Renaissance, 374–375
Prostitutes and prostitution
    in 18th century, 588, 590
    in Later Middle Ages, 363–364, 364(i)
    Protestants on, 419
Protectorate, in England, 508
Protest(s). *See* Revolts and rebellions
Protestantism. *See also* Christianity; Edict of Nantes; Huguenots; Lutheranism
    appeal of, 412–416

baroque art and, 515
Bohemia and, 356
Calvin and, 425–427
on Christian life, 413(i)
Copernican hypothesis and, 522
in England, 422–425
in English colonies, 460
in France, 433–434, 486–487
in Germany, 421–422
literacy and, 595
Lollards and, 356
Luther and, 409–411
marriage and sexuality in, 416–419
in Netherlands, 434–435
revival of, 606–608
scientific revolution and, 528–529
spread of, 422–428
Thirty Years' War and, 483
Zwingli and, 411–412
Protestant Reformation, 409–419
in Bohemia, 427
in eastern Europe, 427–428
in England, 422–424
German politics and, 419–422
Protestant Union, 483
Provence, France, 399
Providence, 460
Prussia, 493(m). *See also* Brandenburg-Prussia; Germany
absolutism in, 495–497
ethnic tensions in, 366
France and, 634, 635
under Frederick the Great, 543–544
military in, 496–497, 497(i)
Napoleon and, 646
peasants in, 482
Seven Years' War and, 543–544
universal education in, 595
Ptolemy, Claudius (scientist), 520–521
Geography by, 450–451, 450(i), 453
Public education. *See also* Education
in Enlightenment, 534
humanists and, 380
in Prussia, 595
Public health, mortality and, 559–560
Public sphere, 537
Pugachev, Emelian, 545
Purgatory, 409
Puritans, 426
Anglican Church and, 507–508, 510
charity schools and, 595
English rule by, 508–510
"Purity of blood" laws (Spain), 402
Putting-out system, 561
Pyrenees, Treaty of the, 494

Quakers, 416, 510
charity schools and, 595
in Pennsylvania, 460
Quebec, 460, 489, 571
Queens. *See also* Monarchy; specific rulers
Quilon, India, 445
Quirini, Lauro, 382(b)

Race and racism. *See also* Ethnic groups; Slaves and slavery
anti-Semitism and, 402
Enlightenment and, 537–541
European attitudes and, 472–473
ideas about, 472–473
mixed-race populations and, 576–577, 577(i)
in *Othello,* 474
in Saint-Domingue, 647

scientific justifications of, 473
in Spanish New World colonies, 462(i)
Racine, Jean, 489
Radical Reformation, 413–416
Radicals and radicalism, in French Revolution, 632, 635
Rákóczy, Francis, 495
Rape, 364
in 18th century, 589–590
Raphael (Raphael Sanzio), 390
Rationalism, 530, 534
Raw materials. *See* Natural resources
Razin, Stenka, 499, 545
Reading. *See also* Education; Literacy
in Enlightenment, 535, 537
revolution in, 535
Realism
in Renaissance art, 521
scientific observation and, 521
Reason. *See also* Enlightenment
Descartes and, 526–527
in Enlightenment, 530
faith and, 355
Rebellions. *See* Revolts and rebellions
Reconquista (Spain), 400
exploration and, 448
slavery and, 465, 469(b)
Recreation. *See also* Leisure
in 18th century, 597–598
Reflections on the Revolution in France (Burke), 633
Reform(s). *See also* Protestant Reformation; Reformation
in Austria, 546–547
of Christian Church, 355
ecclesiastical, 357
of education, 594–595
in Enlightenment, 533
in France, 649
plague and, 347
in Russia, 499–503, 545–546
Reformation, 406. *See also* Counter-Reformation; Protestant Reformation
art in, 418–419(b), 418(i), 419(i)
Catholic, 428–433
of Christian church, 408–419
in eastern Europe, 427–428
German politics and, 419–422
Protestant revival and, 606
Puritans and, 507
radical, 413–416
religious orders and, 409, 431–433
witchcraft trials and, 435–437
Reformed Church, 426
Refugees
to Geneva, 426
religious, in Holy Roman Empire, 422
Regents, Dutch, 513
Regulations
guilds and, 566
of women workers, 397
Reign of Terror, in French Revolution, 637–639, 643
Reinhart, Anna, 416
Relics, of saints, 608
Religion(s). *See also* Cults; specific groups
as artistic topics, 389
in Austria, 495, 546
education and, 595
in 18th century, 606–609
in England, 507–508, 509
Enlightenment and, 530
exploration and, 448, 452
in France, 407(i), 486–487, 488
French Revolution and, 632, 638

Hume on, 535
in Ireland, 508
of Kepler, 524
marginal beliefs and, 608–609
in Massachusetts, 460
in Ottoman Empire, 505
plague and, 347
Protestant revival and, 606–608
in Prussia, 544
recreation and, 597–598
in Russia, 498
science and, 525, 528–529
in 17th century, 483
in Switzerland, 421–422
violence over, 407(i), 433–437
Voltaire on, 534
Religious freedom, in England, 510
Religious orders. *See also* Monks and monasteries
in 18th century, 606
Reformation and, 409, 431–433
teaching orders and, 595
Religious toleration
Dutch, 513
for Jews, 549, 606
Religious wars
in Europe, 407(i)
in France, 433–434
in Germany, 421–422
in Switzerland, 421–422
Rembrandt von Rijn, 512(i)
Renaissance, 372, 373(i), 374, 395(i)
art and artists in, 376, 387–389, 390–393, 514
baroque art and, 515
economy in, 374–375
in Italy, 374–384
in North, 389
political thought in, 381–384
printing in, 385–387
scientific revolution and, 521
slavery in, 394–395, 394(i)
society in, 393–397
use of term, 378
wealth and nobility in, 395
Rent, for peasants, 555
Representation, American Revolution and, 622, 623
Representative assemblies, 354
in France, 625
Republic. *See also* Dutch Republic; England (Britain)
in France, 635
in Italy, 375–376
Republic (Plato), 381
Republicanism, 506
Dutch, 506
Research, scientific, 528
Resident ambassadors, 378
Resources. *See* Natural resources
Restoration, in England, 510
Revisionism, about French Revolution, 621
Revivals, Protestant, 606–608
Revolts and rebellions. *See also* Wars and warfare
in Ireland (1641), 508
against Napoleon, 649
by peasants, 339(i), 358–361, 416, 628–629
in Russia, 499, 545
by Saint-Domingue slaves, 632–633, 639–643, 639(i), 646–647, 648(b)
in 17th century, 486
in Spain, 494
Vendée Rebellion and, 635, 635(m)
Revolution(s). *See also* American Revolution; French Revolution; specific locations
agricultural, 554–558
in politics (1775–1815), 618

Revolution(s) (continued)
  in reading, 535
  scientific, 518, 519(i), 520–531
Revolutionary War in America. See American Revolution
Reymerswaele, Marinus van, 402
Rhineland, France and, 635, 637
Rhine River region, 495
  France and, 646
Rhode Island, 460
Ribeiro, Diogo, world map by, 456(i)
Rice and rice industry, 467
Richard II (England), Peasants' Revolt and, 361, 368
Richard III (England), 400
Richelieu, Cardinal (Armand Jean du Plessis), 483, 487, 488
Rigaud, André, 646–647, 648(b)
Rigaud, Hyacinthe, 488
Rights
  in France, 630–631
  natural, 623
  in Saint-Domingue, 633, 642–643
  for women, 537, 630–631, 634, 646
Riots. See also Food riots
  in 17th century, 486
Roanoke, English colony in, 460
Robe nobility (France), 487, 532, 621
Robert of Geneva. See Clement VII (Pope)
Robespierre, Maximilien, 633, 635, 636–637, 643, 643(i)
  dechristianization and, 638
  Reign of Terror and, 637, 643
Robin Hood, 366
Rococo style, 537
Rocroi, battle at, 494
Roman Catholic Church. See Catholic Church
Roman Inquisition, 430, 436
Romanov family (Russia), 499
  Anastasia (wife of Ivan IV), 498
  Catherine the Great and, 544–546
  Michael, 498
  Peter the Great, 499–503
Roman Republic. See also Rome
  Cicero and, 379
Romantic movement, 541
Rome. See also Roman Republic
  papacy in, 355
Root crops, 556
Rosaries, 431(i)
Rotation of crops. See Crops, rotation of
Rousseau, Jean-Jacques, 534, 541, 594–595, 594(i)
Royal African Company, 468
Royalists, in England, 509(i)
"Royall Oake of Brittayne, The," 509(i)
Royalty. See Kings and kingdoms; specific rulers
Rubens, Peter Paul, 506(i), 514(i), 515
Rudolfine Tables, 523
Rudolph II (Holy Roman Empire), 523
Rural areas. See also Agriculture; Farms and farming; Peasant(s); Serfs and serfdom
  industrial growth in, 560–566, 564–565(b)
  subsistence living in, 481
  wet-nursing in 18th century and, 591
Russia, 497–503. See also Razin, Stenka
  absolutism in, 497
  expansion to, 497–498, 498(m), 545–546
  German diplomat's account of, 500–501(b), 500(i)
  as Great Power, 502
  Napoleon and, 646–651, 650
  peasants in, 498–499, 499(i), 502, 503
  under Peter the Great, 499–503

Prussia and, 544
  society in, 498–499
Russian Empire, 493(m). See also Russia

Sacraments, marriage as, 416
Safavid Empire, trade and, 446–447
Sailors. See also Ships and shipping
  lifestyle of, 449
Sails. See also Ships and shipping
  lateen, 451
Saint(s). See also specific saints
  Joan of Arc as, 353
  relics of, 608
Saint Bartholomew's Day massacre, 434
Saint Basil's Cathedral (Moscow), 502(i)
St. Christophe, 460
Saint Diego of Alcala Feeding the Poor (Murillo), 466(i)
Saint-Domingue, 460, 577, 632(i)
  slave revolt in, 632–633, 639–643, 639(i)
St. Helena, Napoleon at, 651
St. Lawrence River region, 457, 571
Saint Peter's Basilica, 390
St. Petersburg, 502, 503(i)
Saint-Simon, Duc de, 489
Salic Law, 349
Salons, 535–537, 536(i)
Salvation
  Calvin and, 426
  in 18th-century religion, 606
  Luther on, 409
  Protestants on, 412
  Wesley on, 608
Same-sex relationships. See also Homosexuality
  in 18th century, 590–591
  in Middle Ages, 364–365, 365(i)
Sanchez, Juan, 432
Sanchez de Cepeda, Alzonzo, 432
Sanitation, childbirth and, 591
San Salvador (Bahamas), 453, 455
Sans-culottes (France), 636, 636(b), 636(i)
Santo Domingo, slave revolt in, 642–643
Savonarola, Girolamo, 378
Savoy, 635
Saxony
  education in, 595
  Protestantism and, 412–413
  radical Reformation and, 416
Scandinavia
  Black Death and, 342
  Protestant Reformation in, 422
Schism. See also Reformation
  in Catholic Church, 348, 355, 355(m)
Scholarship. See Intellectual thought
Schönbrunn palace, 491(b), 491(i), 495, 547(i)
Schools. See also Education; Universities
  elementary, 595
  humanist, 380
  Jesuit, 433
  literacy and, 369
Science. See also Mathematics; Scientific revolution
  in Enlightenment, 519(i)
  as natural philosophy, 520
  popularization of, 531(i)
  race defined by, 473
  society and, 527–529
  Spain and, 494
Scientific community, 527–528
Scientific method, 526–527
Scientific revolution, 518, 519(i), 520–531
  Enlightenment and, 530
  origins of, 521–522
Scotland
  agriculture in, 557
  Enlightenment in, 534–535, 568

France, England, and, 349
  imports from Europe into, 569
  literacy in, 595
  Presbyterian Church in, 426–427, 508
  social crises in 14th century, 341
  union with England, 569
Scots, as Presbyterians, 426, 508
Scriptures (Christian)
  education in, 595
  Luther on, 414–415(b)
Seaborne trade. See also Trade
  global economy and, 470
  Ottoman control of, 447
  Portuguese, 470
  routes to East and, 453–457
  Spanish, 470
  trading empires and, 465(m), 470–472
  wars over, 569
Second Coalition, 646
Second Continental Congress, 623
Second estate (France), nobility as, 620, 625
Second revolution, in French Revolution, 635–637
Second Treatise of Civil Government (Locke), 510
Segregation, of American natives from Europeans, 463
Self-government, in Ottoman Empire, 505
Senses
  Hume and, 535
  Locke and, 531
Separation of church and state, in France, 353
Separation of powers, 533
September Massacres (France), 635
Serfs and serfdom. See also Peasant(s)
  in Austria, 495, 547
  in eastern Europe, 482, 482(i), 555
  in England, 361
  in France, 649
  in Prussia, 544
  in Russia, 500–501(b), 500(i), 503, 545
Servants
  black, 394
  in 18th century, 586(i), 587
Servetus, Michael, 426
Service nobility, in Russia, 498, 503
Settlement(s), in Americas, 455, 461–470
Seven Years' War, 460
  European North American claims before and after, 572(m)
  France and, 622
  Prussia and, 543–544
Seville, 394
Sex and sexuality. See also Homosexuality; Prostitutes and prostitution
  in 18th century, 589–591
  master-slave relations and, 463
  premarital sex and, 588
  Protestantism and, 413(i), 419
  in urban areas, 361–365
Sextant, 523(i)
Sexual division of labor. See Gender
Sexual harassment, of women in service, 587–588
Seymour, Jane, 423
Sforza family, 377
  Ludovico, 391(b)
Shakespeare, William, 472, 473–475
Shi'ite (Shi'a) Muslims, 446
"Ship money," 508
Ships and shipping. See also Navy; Seaborne trade
  Black Death and, 341
  British Navigation Acts and, 569
  Portuguese, 450, 451(i)
  in slave trade, 574
  technological innovations and, 450
Shrines, 408

Siberia, 499
Sicily, riots in, 486
Siderus Nuncius (Galileo), 525
Siena, 375, 377
Sieyès, Emmanuel Joseph, 625, 626–627(b), 626(i), 644
Sigismund (Germany), 357
Sigismund I (Poland), 427
Signorelli, Luca, 398(i)
Signori (rulers), 376
Silesia, 483, 543, 570–571
Silk trade, 470
Silver
 from Americas, 461, 468–470, 471(i)
 China as buyer of, 470
 Spain and, 468–470, 572–573
Sin, Luther on, 409
Sistine Chapel, Michelangelo and, 387, 388(i), 390
Sixtus IV (Pope), 401–402
Skepticism, 530, 534, 607
Skin color
 categorizing people by, 394, 540
 inferiority of darkness and, 472–473
 in Saint-Domingue, 633, 642, 647
Slaves and slavery. *See also* Africans; Race and racism; Serfs and serfdom; Slave trade
 in Balkans, 448
 Christian conversions and, 578
 costs of colonial goods and, 601
 freedom and, 469(b)
 master-slave sexual relations and, 463
 in Ottoman Empire, 504
 Portugal and, 452, 465
 reconquista and, 469(b)
 in Renaissance, 394–395, 394(i)
 in Saint Domingue, 632–633, 632(i)
 sugar plantations and, 464–468, 464(i), 576(i)
 whites as slaves, 464–465
Slave trade, 394. *See also* Slaves and slavery
 in Africa, 446
 Atlantic, 448, 572, 573–575, 573(i)
 Dutch and, 468, 472
 England and, 468, 492, 570
 Latin America and, 463
 as migration, 579(b)
 number of slaves in, 468
 Portugal and, 394, 465, 470
 Spain and, 468
Slavs. *See also* Russia
 Mongols and, 497–498
Smallpox
 inoculation against, 559, 611–614
 in New World, 460, 461
Smith, Adam, 568–560
Smolensk, Napoleon in, 651
Snayers, Peeter, 494(i)
Social classes. *See* Class
Social contract, American Revolution and, 624
Social Contract, The (Rousseau), 541
Society. *See also* Families; Orders
 climate change, famine, and, 341
 science and, 527–529
Society of Friends. *See* Quakers
Society of Jesus. *See* Jesuits
Society of Revolutionary Republican Women, 638
Sodomy, as crime, 365, 590
Soho Square (London, 1731), 574, 575(i)
Soil, exhaustion of, 555
Solar system. *See also* Astronomy; Universe
 Brahe on, 523
 Copernicus on, 522
 Kepler on, 523–524
Soldiers. *See also* Armed forces; Military; specific wars
 in Thirty Years' War, 483(i)

Sorgh, Hendrick, 557(i)
South America
 Dutch and, 472
 Holy Roman Empire and, 421
 Magellan and, 456
 potato from, 560
 Spain and, 421(m)
South Asia, trade and, 445
South China Sea, 445
Southeast Asia, trade and, 445
Sovereignty
 of English Parliament, 510–511
 royal, 397
 in 17th century, 485
Spain. *See also* Exploration; Silver
 absolutism in, 492–494
 in Americas, 421(m)
 aristocracy in, 494
 Armada and, 425, 425(m)
 armed forces of, 494(i)
 asiento and, 570
 Atlantic exploration by, 448
 Black Death and, 342
 Catholic Church in, 400, 606
 colonies of, 461–464, 571
 Columbus and, 449, 450, 452(m), 453–456, 455(m)
 Creoles and, 576
 debt of, 493
 debt peonage and, 572–573
 Dutch and, 472
 economy in, 468–470, 493
 exploration by, 449, 450
 France and, 492, 569
 government in, 419
 Inquisition in, 436
 Jews in, 400–402
 mixed-race people and, 577
 Muslims in, 402
 Netherlands and, 425, 434, 435
 New Christians in, 401–402
 New World and, 457–460
 peasants in, 494
 politics in, 400–402
 popular revolts in, 486
 Santo Domingo and, 642
 silver in, 468–470
 slave trade and, 468
 state and politics in (15th century), 400–402
 Thirty Years' War and, 483, 494
 trading empire of, 470
 Treaty of Tordesillas and, 456
 unification and expulsion of Jews, 401(m)
 wealth of, 569
Spanish America, slaves in, 577–578, 577(i)
Spanish Armada, 425, 425(m)
Spanish Empire, trade and, 470
Spanish Inquisition, 401–402, 435, 606
Spanish Netherlands, 435, 492, 493(m)
Species, classification of, 540
Speculation, in England, 341
Speyer, Diet of (1529), 412
Spice Islands. *See* Moluccas
Spice trade, 447, 448, 453, 471–472, 471(i), 578
Spinning, families and, 562–563
Spinning wheel, 565(i)
Spinoza, Baruch, 530, 534
Spinster, origins of term, 563
Spirit of the Laws, The (Montesquieu), 532–533
Spirituality, purification of, 609
Sports, blood sports, 597
Sri Lanka. *See* Ceylon
Stadholder (Dutch), 513
Stålhammar, Ulrika Elenora, 591

Stamp Act, 624(i)
Standard of living. *See also* Lifestyle
 Black Death and, 347
 Dutch, 513
Starvation. *See* Famine
State (nation). *See also* Government
 absolutist, 484–485
 church relations with, 399
 in England, 399–400
 in France, 353, 397–399
 in Spain, 400–402
 in western Europe (ca. 1450–1521), 397–402
State-building
 in 17th century, 485–486
 in 18th century, 547–549
States General (Netherlands), 513
Status. *See* Class
Statute of Kilkenny (Ireland, 1366), 367
Statute of Laborers (England, 1351), 360
Steen, Jan, 511(i)
Stereotypes, of race and gender, 540–541
Sternpost rudder, 451
Strait of Gibraltar, 447–448
Straits of Magellan, 456
Strasbourg, 492
Stuart dynasty (England), 506
Subcultures
 homosexual, 590
 lesbian, 591
Succession. *See also* War of the Austrian Succession; War of the Spanish Succession
 in Spain, 492
Sudan, 445
Suffrage. *See* Voting and voting rights
Sugar and sugar industry, 452
 in Brazil, 464(i)
 consumption and, 601
 slavery and, 464–468, 464(i), 573, 576(i)
Suleiman I the Magnificent (Ottoman), 427, 428(i), 505(i)
Sultan, Ottoman, 504
Summer Palace (Vienna), 491(b), 491(i)
Sumptuary laws, 395
Sun-centered solar system, 523
Sunni Muslims, 446
"Supplement to Bougainville's Voyage" (Diderot), 542–543(b)
Supreme Sacred Congregation of the Roman and University Inquisition. *See* Holy Office
Surgeons and surgery. *See also* Medicine
 in 18th century, 609, 610–611
Swahili speakers, 445
Sweden. *See also* Scandinavia
 Napoleon and, 646
 Protestant Reformation in, 422
 Russia and, 500, 502
Swedish phase, of Thirty Years' War, 483
Swiss Confederation, 513
Switzerland
 Protestantism in, 411, 412
 religious war in, 421–422
 witchcraft and, 437
Sword nobility (France), 487, 621
System of Nature, The (Linné), 537

Tableau de Paris (Mercier), 604–605(b)
Tabula rasa (Locke), 531
Taille (tax), 399
Taino people, 455
Tariffs. *See also* Taxation
 in France, 489
Tartars. *See also* Mongols
 in Russia, 545

Taxation
  American Revolution and, 622, 623
  in Austria, 547
  in England, 354, 361, 508
  in France, 399, 492, 621, 624
  in Ottoman Empire, 504, 505
  papal, 408
  of peasants, 555
  in Renaissance, 402
  in Russia, 502
  in 17th century, 486
Tea, consumption of, 601
Teaching orders, 595
Technology. *See also* Industrial Revolution; Weapons
  exploration and, 450–451
  in Hundred Years' War, 354
  military, 353
Telescope, 524, 524(i)
Tempest, The (Shakespeare), 474–475
Ten Commandments, The (Cranach the Elder), 411(i), 418(b)
Tennis Court Oath, June 20, 1789, 628(i)
Tenochtitlán, 458, 458(i), 458(m), 459
Teresa of Ávila (Saint), 432(b), 432(i)
Territorial expansion. *See* Expansion
Terror, the, in French Revolution, 637–639
Test Act (England, 1673), 510
Tetzel, Johann, 410, 410(i)
Textile industry. *See also* Cotton industry; Woolen industry
  workers in, 561–563
Theater. *See* Drama
Theology
  of Calvin, 425–426
  of Henry VIII, 423–424
  of Luther, 409–411
  Voltaire and, 534
Thermidorian Reaction, 643–644
Third Coalition, 646
Third estate (France), 620, 626–627(b), 628(i)
  commoners as, 620, 625
  Estates General and, 625–627
Third of May, The (Goya), 649(i)
Third Rome, Moscow as, 498
Thirty Years' War, 482–484
  France and, 487
  Habsburgs and, 495
  phases of, 483
  religion and, 427, 483
  Spain and, 494
  United Provinces after, 511
Thomas à Kempis, 358
Thomas Aquinas, 520
Thought. *See* Intellectual thought
Three orders. *See* Orders
Tilsit, Treaty of, 646
"Time of Troubles" (Russia), 498
Titian, 390, 394(i), 399(i), 470(i)
Titus Andronicus (Shakespeare), 474(i)
Tlaxcala people, 458
Tobacco, 460, 601
Tofts, Mary, 607(i)
Toleration. *See* Religious toleration
Tomatoes, 466
Topkapi Palace, 505
Tordesillas, Treaty of, 456
Torture, in Inquisition, 436, 437
Total war, in French Revolution, 637–639
Tournai, 348(i)
Toussaint L'Ouverture. *See* L'Ouverture, Toussaint
Towns. *See* Cities and towns
Trade. *See also* Business; Seaborne trade; Slave trade
  Afro-Eurasian, 444–448, 444(m)
  in Asia and Pacific, 578–581

Black Death and, 341
colonial, 571–573
Columbus and, 453
Dutch, 513, 578
English, 571
French, 489–492
by Genoa, 447–448
in gold, 445, 446
with India, 453
medicine for, 344(b), 344(i), 345(i)
medieval, 341
in Renaissance, 374–375
in spices, 447, 448, 453, 471–472, 471(i), 578
by Venice, 447–448
worldwide, 569
Trade routes, in Age of Discovery, 445–446
Trading companies. *See* British East India Company; Company of the East Indies (France); Dutch East India Company; Dutch West India Company
Trading empires, seaborne, 465(m), 470–472
Trading states, in Africa, 445–446
Trafalgar, Battle of, 646
Training. *See* Education
Trans-Atlantic slave trade, 468
Transylvania, 427, 495
Travel. *See also* Expansion; Exploration
  literature on, 530–531
Travels (Marco Polo), 454(b)
Travels in Muscovy (Olearius), 500–501(b)
Travels of Sir John Mandeville, The, 449(i), 450
Treasure of the City of Ladies, The (Christina de Pizan), 362–363
Treaties. *See also* specific treaties
  in Swiss cantons, 422
Treatment, for plague, 344(b), 344(i), 345(i)
Trent, Council of, 418(b), 430, 431
Trials
  of Joan of Arc, 353
  for witchcraft, 435–437
Triennial Act (England, 1641), 508
True and False Churches, The (Cranach the Younger), 418(i)
Tsars (Russia), 498–499
Tudor dynasty (England), 400, 423(i)
Tuileries palace, 635
Tull, Jethro, 557
Turgot, Anne-Robert-Jacques, 567, 568, 622
Turks. *See also* Ottoman Empire
  Constantinople captured by, 447, 447(i), 498
  Hungary and, 427–428
Tuscany, 342
Tyler, Wat, 339(i)
Type, 385
Typhoid fever, 559
Typhus, 461, 559

Ukraine
  Jews in, 549
  Russia and, 499, 502
Unemployment, in Later Middle Ages, 341
Unification, of Spain, 401(m)
Union of Utrecht (1581), 435
United Provinces of the Netherlands, 435, 468, 511. *See also* Dutch Republic
United States, French Revolution and, 633
Universal education. *See also* Education
  in Prussia, 595
Universal gravitation, law of, 526
Universe
  Aristotle on, 520, 520(i)
  Copernicus on, 522
  Descartes on, 527
  Kepler on, 523–524

Newton on, 525–526
Voltaire on, 534
Universities
  Black Death and, 348
  of Oxford, 356
  scientific revolution and, 521
Upper Belvedere, 491(b), 491(i)
Upper classes. *See also* Aristocracy; Class; Nobility
  diet of, 599
Uprisings. *See* Revolts and rebellions; Riots
Urban VI (Pope), 355
Urban VIII (Pope), Galileo and, 525
Urban areas. *See also* Cities and towns
  Black Death in, 342, 347
  conflicts in, 361
  Enlightenment in, 535–537
  guilds in, 566–568
  in Middle Ages, 361
  popular literature in, 596
  religious violence in, 407(i)
  sex and sexuality in, 361–365
  women in, 361–364
Ursuline order, 431
Utopia (More), 380, 385, 423
Utrecht
  Peace of, 492, 493(m), 570
  Union of, 435

Vaccine
  for plague, 345
  for smallpox, 611–614
Vacuum
  Boyle on, 530
  Descartes on, 527
Valmy, Battle of, 635
Valois dynasty, 349
  Habsburg-Valois wars and, 422
Van der Weyden, Rogier, 389, 389(i)
Van Dyck, Anthony, 506(i)
Van Eyck, Jan, 389
Vasa family. *See* Gustavus Vasa (Sweden)
Vasari, Giorgio, 372, 378, 379–380, 391(b), 392, 420(i)
Vatican. *See also* Catholic Church; Papacy
  Sistine Chapel in, 387, 388(i), 390
Vegetable Market (Sorgh), 557(i)
Vegetables, in diet, 599
Velázquez, Diego, 469(b), 469(i)
Vendée Rebellion (France), 635, 635(m)
Venereal disease, in 18th century, 590
Venezuela, 456
Venice
  Black Death and, 342
  blacks in, 394
  dominance by, 376–377
  trade and, 447–448
  wealth of, 378
Vera Cruz, 457
Vergil, Polydore, 400
Vermuyden, Cornelius, 556
Vernacular languages, literature in, 367–369
Versailles palace, 490(b), 490(i). *See also* Hall of Mirrors (Versailles)
  court at, 488–489
  Estates General in, 625
Vesalius, Andreas, 529, 529(i)
Vespucci, Amerigo, 456, 457
Viceroyalties, in Spanish New World, 461
Vienna, 495
  coffeehouse in, 539(i)
  Ottomans and, 422
  palaces in, 491(b), 491(i)
Vikings, in Greenland, 340
Villa Capra, 390(i)

Villages. *See also* Cities and towns
  farming patterns and, 555
Ville-Marie. *See* Montreal
Vindication of the Rights of Man, A (Wollstonecraft), 634
Vindication of the Rights of Woman, A (Wollstonecraft), 634
Violence
  by popolo, 375
  religious, 407(i), 433–437
Virgil, 368
Virgin of Guadalupe, 578
Virtù, 379
Vocational training, for girls, 568
Voltaire, 532(i), 533–534, 536(i)
Voodoo, 642
Voting rights, for women, 510
Voyages
  of Columbus, 448, 453–456, 454–455(b), 455(m)
  European voyages of discovery, 448–461
  of Zheng He, 444(m), 445

Wages, for women, 563
Waksman, Selman, 345
Wallenstein. *See* Albert of Wallenstein
Walpole, Robert, 511
War of Independence. *See* American Revolution
War of the Austrian Succession, 543, 543(m), 546, 570–571, 580
War of the Spanish Succession, 492, 495, 569–570
Wars and warfare. *See also* Military; Navy; Weapons; specific battles and wars
  army size and, 485–486
  in France, 492, 622, 634–635, 638
  in Italian city-states, 378
  over maritime power, 569
  in 17th century, 486
Wars of the Roses (England), 400
Washington, George, 624
Water and water resources, improvements in, 559
Waterloo, battle at, 651
Wealth
  clerical, 346
  clothing and, 398(b), 398(i)
  from colonial trade, 572
  in European colonies, 576
  hierarchy of classes by, 395
  Hundred Years' War and, 350, 354
  in Italian Renaissance, 378
  mercantilism and, 489
  in Renaissance, 375, 395

  silver trade and, 468–470
  in third estate, 621
Wealth of Nations (Smith). *See Inquiry into the Nature and Causes of the Wealth of Nations* (Smith)
Weapons
  artillery as, 354
  in Hundred Years' War, 350, 353(i)
  technology and, 450
Weather. *See* Climate
Weaver's Repose, The (Gerritz), 561(i)
Weddings. *See also* Marriage
  peasant, 589(i)
Wesley, John, 593, 607–608
Wesley, Susannah, 593
West Africa
  slave trade and, 570
  trade and, 581
Western Europe
  Jewish emancipation in, 549
  peasants in, 480–481, 555
  politics in (ca. 1450–1521), 397–402
  state (nation) in (ca. 1450–1521), 397–402
Western Hemisphere. *See also* Americas; New World
  diseases in, 464
Westernization, of Russia, 502–503
West Indies, 460, 571
Wet-nursing, 591, 592(i)
What Is Enlightenment? (Kant), 541
What Is the Third Estate? (Sieyès), 625, 626–627(b)
Wheat, 467
White Mountain, Battle of the, 483
White people, as slaves, 464–465
William of Occam, 355–356
William of Orange (king of England), 510, 513, 590
Winter Palace (Vienna), 491(b)
Witches and witchcraft, European persecution of, 435–437, 436(i), 609
Wittenberg
  Luther at, 409, 410
  Ten Commandments painting in, 411(i)
Wollstonecraft, Mary, 633–634
Women. *See also* Gender; Marriage; Midwives; Nuns
  in arts, 392–393, 537
  childbirth and, 591
  as clergy, 417
  debate about, 396
  education for, 380, 533
  food riots and, 481
  as forced labor, 461
  in France, 349, 630–631, 630(i), 638, 643, 646
  gender roles and, 396–397
  in guilds, 568
  as humanists, 382(b)

  after Hundred Years' War, 354
  Lollards and, 356
  as medical practitioners, 609–610, 611
  Montesquieu on, 532
  in Ottoman Empire, 505, 505(i)
  Paris salons and, 535–537, 536(i)
  prostitution and, 363–364, 364(i)
  in Protestantism, 417
  Rousseau on, 541
  same-sex relations among, 590–591
  sans-culotte, 636(b), 636(i)
  in sciences, 528, 533, 533(i)
  as servants, 587–588
  in Spanish colonies, 463
  in urban areas, 361–364
  voting rights for, 510
  voyages of exploration and, 449
  witchcraft and, 435
  as workers, 361, 562–563, 564(b), 566
"Wonderful Effects of the New Inoculation, The" (Gillray), 611(i)
Woodblock printing, 385
Woolen industry. *See also* Textile industry
  decline in Later Middle Ages, 341
  female workers in, 563
  17th-century decline in, 481
Work. *See also* Labor; Peasant(s); Workers
  in Calvinism, 426
Workers. *See also* Labor; Peasant(s)
  in 18th century, 587–588
  indigenous, 572–573
  literacy and, 596
  rural, 480–481, 561–563
  Smith, Adam, on, 568–569
  women as, 397, 563, 566
Workforce. *See* Labor; Workers
Workplace, male, 361
Worldview, of Enlightenment, 518
Worms, Diet of (1521), 411
Wright, Joseph, 519(i)
Writing. *See* Literature
Württemberg, education in, 595
Wyclif, John, 356

Yiddish language, 548(b)
York, house of, 400
Young Woman Reading a Letter, 597(i)
Yucatec Mayan language, 459

Zacatecas, 468
Zapolya, Janos, 427
Zheng He, voyages of, 444(m), 445
Zurich, 412
Zwingli, Ulrich, 411–412, 416, 418(b), 421

Timeline | A History of Western Society: An Overview

	Government	**Society and Economy**
3000 B.C.E.	Emergence of first cities in Mesopotamia, ca. 3000 Unification of Egypt; Archaic Period, ca. 3100–2600 Old Kingdom of Egypt, ca. 2660–2180 Dominance of Akkadian empire in Mesopotamia, ca. 2331–2200 Middle Kingdom in Egypt, ca. 2080–1640	Neolithic peoples rely on settled agriculture, while others pursue nomadic life, ca. 7000–3000 Expansion of Mesopotamian trade and culture into the modern Middle East and Turkey, ca. 2600
2000 B.C.E.	Babylonian empire, ca. 2000–1595 Code of Hammurabi, ca. 1790 Hyksos invade Egypt, ca. 1640–1570 Hittite Empire, ca. 1600–1200 New Kingdom in Egypt, ca. 1570–1075	First wave of Indo-European migrants, by ca. 2000 Extended commerce in Egypt, by ca. 2000 Horses introduced into western Asia, by ca. 2000
1500 B.C.E.	Third Intermediate Period in Egypt, ca. 1100–653 Unified Hebrew kingdom under Saul, David, and Solomon, ca. 1025–925	Use of iron increases in western Asia, by ca. 1300–1100 Second wave of Indo-European migrants, by ca. 1200 "Dark Age" in Greece, ca. 1100–800
1000 B.C.E.	Hebrew kingdom divided into Israel and Judah, 925 Assyrian Empire, ca. 900–612 Phoenicians found Carthage, 813 Kingdom of Kush conquers and reunifies Egypt, ca. 800–700 Roman monarchy, ca. 753–509 Medes conquers Persia, 710 Babylon wins independence from Assyria, 626 Dracon issues law code at Athens, 621 Solon's reforms at Athens, ca. 594 Cyrus the Great conquers Medes, founds Persian Empire, 550 Persians complete conquest of ancient Near East, 521–464 Reforms of Cleisthenes in Athens, 508	Phoenician seafaring and trading in the Mediterranean, ca. 900–550 First Olympic games, 776 Concentration of landed wealth in Greece, ca. 750–600 Greek overseas expansion, ca. 750–550 Beginning of coinage in western Asia, ca. 640
500 B.C.E.	Persian wars, 499–479 Struggle of the Orders in Rome, ca. 494–287 Growth of the Athenian Empire, 478–431 Peloponnesian War, 431–404 Rome captures Veii, 396 Gauls sack Rome, 390 Roman expansion in Italy, 390–290 Phillip II of Macedonia conquers Greece, 338 Conquests of Alexander the Great, 334–323 Punic Wars, 264–133 Reforms of the Gracchi, 133–121	Growth of Hellenistic trade and cities, ca. 330–100 Beginning of Roman silver coinage, 269 Growth of slavery, decline of small farmers in Rome, ca. 250–100 Agrarian reforms of the Gracchi, 133–121

Religion and Philosophy	Science and Technology	Arts and Letters
Growth of anthropomorphic religion in Mesopotamia, ca. 3000–2000	Development of wheeled transport in Mesopotamia, by ca. 3000	Egyptian hieroglyphic writing, ca. 3100
Emergence of Egyptian polytheism and belief in personal immortality, ca. 2660	Use of widespread irrigation in Mesopotamia and Egypt, ca. 3000	Sumerian cuneiform writing, ca. 3000
Spread of Mesopotamian and Egyptian religious ideas as far north as modern Turkey and as far south as central Africa, ca. 2600	Construction of Stonehenge monument in England, ca. 3000–1600	
	Construction of first pyramid in Egypt, ca. 2600	
Emergence of Hebrew monotheism, ca. 1700	Construction of first ziggurats in Mesopotamia, ca. 2000	*Epic of Gilgamesh*, ca. 1900
Mixture of Hittite and Near Eastern religious beliefs, ca. 1595	Widespread use of bronze in ancient Near East, ca. 1900	
	Babylonian mathematical advances, ca. 1800	
Exodus of the Hebrews from Egypt into Palestine, ca. 1300–1200	Hittites introduce iron technology, ca. 1400	Phoenicians develop alphabet, ca. 1400
Akhenaten imposes monotheism in Egypt, 1367–1350		Naturalistic art in Egypt under Akhenaten, 1367–1350
		Egyptian *Book of the Dead*, ca. 1300
Era of the prophets in Israel, ca. 1100–500	Babylonian astronomical advances, ca. 750–400	Homer, traditional author of *Iliad* and *Odyssey*, ca. 800
Beginning of the Hebrew Bible, ca. 950–800	Construction of Parthenon in Athens begins, 447	Hesiod, author of *Theogony* and *Works and Days*, ca. 800
Intermixture of Etruscan and Roman religious cults, ca. 753–509		Aeschylus, first significant Athenian tragedian, ca. 525–456
Growing popularity of local Greek religious cults, ca. 700 B.C.E.–337 C.E.		
Introduction of Zoroastrianism, ca. 600		
Babylonian Captivity of the Hebrews, 587–538		
Pre-Socratic philosophers, ca. 500–400	Hippocrates, formal founder of medicine, ca. 430	Sophocles, tragedian whose plays explore moral and political problems, ca. 496–406
Socrates executed, 399	Building of the Via Appia begins, 312	Herodotus, "father of history," ca. 485–425
Plato, student of Socrates, 427–347	Aristarchos of Samos, advances in astronomy, ca. 310–230	Euripides, most personal of the Athenian tragedians, ca. 480–406
Diogenes, leading proponent of cynicism, ca. 412–323	Euclid codifies geometry, ca. 300	Thucydides, historian of Peloponnesian War, ca. 460–440
Aristotle, student of Plato, 384–322	Herophilus, discoveries in medicine, ca. 300–250	Aristophanes, greatest Athenian comic playwright, ca. 445–386
Epicurus, founder of Epicurean philosophy, 340–270	Archimedes, works on physics and hydrologics, ca. 287–212	
Zeno, founder of Stoic philosophy, 335–262		
Emergence of Mithraism, ca. 300		
Greek cults brought to Rome, ca. 200		
Spread of Hellenistic mystery religions, ca. 200–100		

	Government	**Society and Economy**
100 B.C.E.	Dictatorship of Sulla, 88–79 B.C.E. Civil war in Rome, 88–31 B.C.E. Dictatorship of Caesar, 45–44 B.C.E. Principate of Augustus, 31 B.C.E.–14 C.E. "Five Good Emperors" of Rome, 96–180 C.E. "Barracks Emperors'" civil war, 235–284 C.E.	Reform of the Roman calendar, 46 B.C.E. "Golden age" of Roman prosperity and vast increase in trade, 96–180 C.E. Growth of serfdom in Roman Empire, ca. 200–500 C.E. Economic contraction in Roman Empire, ca. 235–284 C.E.
300 C.E.	Constantine removes capital of Roman Empire to Constantinople, ca. 315 Visigoths defeat Roman army at Adrianople, 378 Bishop Ambrose asserts church's independence from the state, 380 Odoacer deposes last Roman emperor in the West, 476 Clovis issues Salic law of the Franks, ca. 490	Barbarian migrations throughout western and northern Europe, ca. 378–600
500	Law code of Justinian, 529 Spread of Islam across Arabia, the Mediterranean region, Spain, North Africa, and Asia as far as India, ca. 630–733	Gallo-Roman aristocracy intermarries with Germanic chieftains, ca. 500–700 Decline of towns and trade in the West; agrarian economy predominates, ca. 500–1800
700	Charles Martel defeats Muslims at Tours, 732 Pippin III anointed king of the Franks, 754 Charlemagne secures Frankish crown, r. 768–814	Height of Muslim commercial activity with western Europe, ca. 700–1300
800	Imperial coronation of Charlemagne, Christmas 800 Treaty of Verdun divides Carolingian kingdom, 843 Viking, Magyar, and Muslim invasions, ca. 850–1000 Establishment of Kievan Rus, ca. 900	Invasions and unstable conditions lead to increase of serfdom in western Europe, ca. 800–900 Height of Byzantine commerce and industry, ca. 800–1000
1000	Seljuk Turks conquer Muslim Baghdad, 1055 Norman conquest of England, 1066 Penance of Henry IV at Canossa, 1077	Decline of Byzantine free peasantry, ca. 1025–1100 Growth of towns and trade in the West, ca. 1050–1300 *Domesday Book* in England, 1086
1100	Henry I of England, r. 1100–1135 Louis VI of France, r. 1108–1137 Frederick I of Germany, r. 1152–1190 Henry II of England, r. 1154–1189	Henry I of England establishes the Exchequer, 1130 Beginnings of the Hanseatic League, 1159

Religion and Philosophy	Science and Technology	Arts and Letters
Mithraism spreads to Rome, 27 B.C.E.–270 C.E. Life of Jesus, ca. 3 B.C.E.–29 C.E.	Engineering advances in Rome, ca. 100 B.C.E.–180 C.E.	Flowering of Latin literature: Virgil, 70–19 B.C.E.; Livy, ca. 59 B.C.E.–17 C.E.; Ovid, 43 B.C.E.–17 C.E.
Constantine legalizes Christianity, 312 Theodosius declares Christianity the official state religion, 380 Donatist heretical movement at its height, ca. 400 St. Augustine, *Confessions*, ca. 390; *The City of God*, ca. 425 Clovis adopts Roman Christianity, 496	Construction of Arch of Constantine, ca. 315	St. Jerome publishes Latin *Vulgate*, late 4th c. Byzantines preserve Greco-Roman culture, ca. 400–1000
Rule of St. Benedict, 529 Life of the Prophet Muhammad, ca. 571–632 Pope Gregory the Great publishes *Dialogues, Pastoral Care, Moralia*, 590–604 Monasteries established in Anglo-Saxon England, ca. 600–700 Publication of the Qur'an, 651 Synod of Whitby, 664	Using watermills, Benedictine monks exploit energy of fast-flowing rivers and streams, by 600 Heavy plow and improved harness facilitate use of multiple-ox teams; harrow widely used in northern Europe, by 600 Byzantines successfully use "Greek fire" in naval combat against Arab fleets attacking Constantinople, 673, 717	Boethius, *The Consolation of Philosophy*, ca. 520 Justinian constructs church of Santa Sophia, 532–537
Bede, *Ecclesiastical History of the English Nation*, ca. 700 Missionary work of St. Boniface in Germany, ca. 710–750 Iconoclastic controversy in Byzantine Empire, 726–843 Pippin III donates Papal States to the papacy, 756		Lindisfarne Gospel Book, ca. 700 *Beowulf*, ca. 700 Carolingian Renaissance, ca. 780–850
Foundation of abbey of Cluny, 909 Byzantine conversion of Russia, late 10th c.	Stirrup and nailed horseshoes become widespread in combat, 900–1000 Paper (invented in China, ca. 150) enters Europe through Muslim Spain, ca. 900–1000	Byzantines develop Cyrillic script, late 10th c.
Schism between Roman and Greek Orthodox churches, 1054 Lateran Council restricts election of pope to College of Cardinals, 1059 Pope Gregory VII, 1073–1085 Theologian Peter Abelard, 1079–1142 First Crusade, 1095–1099 Founding of Cistercian order, 1098	Arab conquests bring new irrigation methods, cotton cultivation, and manufacture to Spain, Sicily, southern Italy, by 1000 Avicenna, Arab scientist, d. 1037	Muslim musicians introduce lute, rebec (stringed instruments, ancestors of violin), ca. 1000 Romanesque style in architecture and art, ca. 1000–1200 *Song of Roland*, ca. 1095
Universities begin, ca. 1100–1300 Concordat of Worms ends investiture controversy, 1122 Height of Cistercian monasticism, 1125–1175	Europeans, copying Muslim and Byzantine models, construct castles with rounded towers and crenellated walls, by 1100	Troubadour poetry, especially of Chrétien de Troyes, circulates widely, ca. 1100–1200 *Rubaiyat of Umar Khayyam*, ca. 1120 Dedication of abbey church of Saint-Denis launches Gothic style, 1144

	Government	Society and Economy
1100 (cont.)	Thomas Becket, archbishop of Canterbury, murdered 1170 Philip Augustus of France, r. 1180–1223	
1200	Spanish victory over Muslims at Las Navas de Tolosa, 1212 Frederick II of Germany and Sicily, r. 1212–1250 Magna Carta, charter of English political and civil liberties, 1215 Louis IX of France, r. 1226–1270 Mongols end Abbasid caliphate, 1258 Edward I of England, r. 1272–1307 Philip IV (the Fair) of France, r. 1285–1314	European revival, growth of towns; agricultural expansion leads to population growth, ca. 1200–1300 Crusaders capture Constantinople (Fourth Crusade) and spur Venetian economy, 1204
1300	Philip IV orders arrest of Pope Boniface at Anagni, 1303 Hundred Years' War between England and France, 1337–1453 Political disorder in Germany, ca. 1350–1450 Merchant oligarchies or despots rule Italian city-states, ca. 1350–1550	"Little ice age," European economic depression, ca. 1300–1450 Black Death appears ca. 1347; returns intermittently until ca. 1720 Height of the Hanseatic League, 1350–1450 Peasant and working-class revolts: Flanders, 1328; France, 1358; Florence, 1378; England, 1381
1400	Joan of Arc rallies French monarchy, 1429–1431 Medici domination of Florence begins, 1434 Princes in Germany consolidate power, ca. 1450–1500 Ottoman Turks under Mahomet II capture Constantinople, May 1453 War of the Roses in England, 1455–1471 Establishment of the Inquisition in Spain, 1478 Ferdinand and Isabella complete reconquista in Spain, 1492 French invasion of Italy, 1494	Population decline, peasants' revolts, high labor costs contribute to decline of serfdom in western Europe, ca. 1400–1650 Flow of Balkan slaves into eastern Mediterranean, of African slaves into Iberia and Italy, ca. 1400–1500 Christopher Columbus reaches the Americas, 1492 Portuguese gain control of East Indian spice trade, 1498–1511
1500	Charles V, Holy Roman emperor, 1519–1556 Habsburg-Valois Wars, 1521–1559 Philip II of Spain, r. 1556–1598 Revolt of the Netherlands, 1566–1598 St. Bartholomew's Day massacre in France, 1572 English defeat of the Spanish Armada, 1588 Henry IV of France issues Edict of Nantes, 1598	Consolidation of serfdom in eastern Europe, ca. 1500–1650 Balboa discovers the Pacific, 1513 Magellan's crew circumnavigates the earth, 1519–1522 Spain and Portugal gain control of regions of Central and South America, ca. 1520–1550 Peasants' Revolt in Germany, 1524–1525 "Time of Troubles" in Russia, 1598–1613

Religion and Philosophy	Science and Technology	Arts and Letters
Aristotle's works translated into Latin, ca. 1140–1260 Third Crusade, 1189–1192 Pope Innocent III, height of the medieval papacy, 1198–1216	Underground pipes with running water and indoor latrines installed in some monasteries, such as Clairvaux and Canterbury Cathedral Priory, by 1100; elsewhere rare until 1800 Windmill invented, ca. 1180	
Founding of the Franciscan order, 1210 Fourth Lateran Council accepts seven sacraments, 1215 Founding of Dominican order, 1216 Thomas Aquinas, height of scholasticism, 1225–1274	*Notebooks* of architect Villard de Honnecourt, a major source for Gothic engineering, ca. 1250 Development of double-entry bookkeeping in Florence and Genoa, ca. 1250–1340 Venetians purchase secrets of glass manufacture from Syria, 1277 Mechanical clock invented, ca. 1290	*Parzifal, Roman de la rose, King Arthur and the Round Table* celebrate virtues of knighthood and chivalry, ca. 1200–1300 Height of Gothic style, ca. 1225–1300
Pope Boniface VIII declares all Christians subject to the pope in *Unam Sanctam*, 1302 Babylonian Captivity of the papacy, 1309–1376 Theologian John Wyclif, ca. 1330–1384 Great Schism in the papacy, 1378–1417	Edward III of England uses cannon in siege of Calais, 1346 Clocks in general use throughout Europe, by 1400	Paintings of Giotto mark emergence of Renaissance movement in the arts, ca. 1305–1337 Dante, *Divine Comedy*, ca. 1310 Petrarch develops ideas of humanism, ca. 1350 Boccaccio, *The Decameron*, ca. 1350 Jan van Eyck, Flemish painter, 1366–1441 Brunelleschi, Florentine architect, 1377–1446 Chaucer, *Canterbury Tales*, ca. 1387–1400
Council of Constance ends the schism in the papacy, 1414–1418 Pragmatic Sanction of Bourges affirms special rights of French crown over French church, 1438 Expulsion of Jews from Spain, 1492	Water-powered blast furnaces operative in Sweden, Austria, the Rhine Valley, Liège, ca. 1400 Leonardo Fibonacci's *Liber Abaci* popularizes use of Hindu-Arabic numerals, important in rise of Western science, 1402 Paris and largest Italian cities pave streets, making street cleaning possible, ca. 1450 European printing and movable type, ca. 1450	Height of Renaissance movement: Masaccio, 1401–1428; Botticelli, 1444–1510; Leonardo da Vinci, 1452–1519; Albrecht Dürer, 1471–1528; Michelangelo, 1475–1564; Raphael, 1483–1520
Machiavelli, *The Prince*, 1513 More, *Utopia*, 1516 Luther, *Ninety-five Theses*, 1517 Henry VIII of England breaks with Rome, 1532–1534 Merici establishes Ursuline order for education of women, 1535 Loyola establishes Society of Jesus, 1540 Calvin establishes theocracy in Geneva, 1541 Council of Trent shapes essential character of Catholicism until the 1960s, 1545–1563 Peace of Augsburg, official recognition of Lutheranism, 1555	Scientific revolution in western Europe, ca. 1540–1690: Copernicus, *On the Revolutions of the Heavenly Bodies*, 1543; Galileo, 1564–1642; Kepler, 1571–1630; Harvey, 1578–1657	Erasmus, *The Praise of Folly*, 1509 Castiglione, *The Courtier*, 1528 Baroque movement in arts, ca. 1550–1725: Rubens, 1577–1640; Velasquez, 1599–1660 Shakespeare, West's most enduring and influential playwright, 1564–1616 Montaigne, *Essays*, 1598

	Government	**Society and Economy**
1600	Thirty Years' War begins, 1618 Richelieu dominates French government, 1624–1643 Frederick William, Elector of Brandenburg, r. 1640–1688 English Civil War, 1642–1649 Louis XIV, r. 1643–1715 Peace of Westphalia ends the Thirty Years' War, 1648 The Fronde in France, 1648–1660	Chartering of British East India Company, 1600 English Poor Law, 1601 Chartering of Dutch East India Company, 1602 Height of Dutch commercial activity, ca. 1630–1665
1650	Anglo-Dutch wars, 1652–1674 Protectorate in England, 1653–1658 Leopold I, Habsburg emperor, r. 1658–1705 English monarchy restored, 1660 Ottoman siege of Vienna, 1683 Glorious Revolution in England, 1688–1689 Peter the Great of Russia, r. 1689–1725	Height of mercantilism in Europe, ca. 1650–1750 Agricultural revolution in Europe, ca. 1650–1850 Principle of peasants' hereditary subjugation to their lords affirmed in Prussia, 1653 Colbert's economic reforms in France, ca. 1663–1683 Cossack revolt in Russia, 1670–1671
1700	War of the Spanish Succession, 1701–1713 Peace of Utrecht redraws political boundaries of Europe, 1713 Frederick William I of Prussia, r. 1713–1740 Louis XV of France, r. 1715–1774 Maria Theresa of Austria, r. 1740–1780 Frederick the Great of Prussia, r. 1740–1786	Foundation of St. Petersburg, 1701 Last appearance of bubonic plague in western Europe, ca. 1720 Growth of European population, ca. 1720–1789 Enclosure movement in England, ca. 1730–1830
1750	Seven Years' War, 1756–1763 Catherine the Great of Russia, r. 1762–1796 Partition of Poland, 1772–1795 Louis XVI of France, r. 1774–1792 American Revolution, 1775–1783 French Revolution, 1789–1799 Slave insurrection in Saint-Domingue, 1791	Growth of illegitimate births in Europe, ca. 1750–1850 Industrial Revolution in western Europe, ca. 1780–1850 Serfdom abolished in France, 1789
1800	Napoleonic era, 1799–1815 Haitian republic declares independence, 1804 Congress of Vienna re-establishes political power after defeat of Napoleon, 1814–1815 Greece wins independence from Ottoman Empire, 1830 French conquest of Algeria, 1830 Revolution in France, 1830 Great Britain: Reform Bill of 1832; Poor Law reform, 1834; Chartists, repeal of Corn Laws, 1838–1848 Revolutions in Europe, 1848	British takeover of India complete, 1805 British slave trade abolished, 1807 German Zollverein founded, 1834 European capitalists begin large-scale foreign investment, 1840s Great Famine in Ireland, 1845–1851 First public health law in Britain, 1848

Religion and Philosophy	Science and Technology	Arts and Letters
Huguenot revolt in France, 1625	Further development of scientific method: Bacon, *The Advancement of Learning*, 1605; Descartes, *Discourse on Method*, 1637	Cervantes, *Don Quixote*, 1605, 1615 Flourishing of French theater: Molière, 1622–1673; Racine, 1639–1699 Golden age of Dutch culture, ca. 1625–1675: Rembrandt van Rijn, 1606–1669; Vermeer, 1632–1675
Social contract theory: Hobbes, *Leviathan*, 1651; Locke, *Second Treatise on Civil Government*, 1690 Patriarch Nikon's reforms split Russian Orthodox Church, 1652 Test Act in England excludes Roman Catholics from public office, 1673 Revocation of Edict of Nantes, 1685 James II tries to restore Catholicism as state religion, 1685–1688	Tull (1674–1741) encourages innovation in English agriculture Newton, *Principia Mathematica*, 1687	Construction of baroque palaces and remodeling of capital cities, central and eastern Europe, ca. 1650–1725 Bach, great late baroque German composer, 1685–1750 Enlightenment begins, ca. 1690: Fontenelle, *Conversations on the Plurality of Worlds*, 1686; Voltaire, French philosopher and writer whose work epitomizes Enlightenment, 1694–1778 Pierre Bayle, *Historical and Critical Dictionary*, 1697
Wesley, founder of Methodism, 1703–1791 Montesquieu, *The Spirit of Laws*, 1748	Newcomen develops steam engine, 1705 Charles Townsend introduces four-year crop rotation, 1730	
Hume, *The Natural History of Religion*, 1755 Rousseau, *The Social Contract* and *Emile*, 1762 Fourier, French utopian socialist, 1772–1837 Papacy dissolves Jesuits, 1773 Smith, *The Wealth of Nations*, 1776 Church reforms of Joseph II in Austria, 1780s Kant, *What Is Enlightenment?*, 1784 Reorganization of church in France, 1790s Wollstonecraft, *A Vindication of the Rights of Women*, 1792 Malthus, *Essay on the Principle of Population*, 1798	Hargreaves's spinning jenny, ca. 1765 Arkwright's water frame, ca. 1765 Watt's steam engine promotes industrial breakthroughs, 1780s Jenner's smallpox vaccine, 1796	*Encyclopedia*, edited by Diderot and d'Alembert, published 1751–1765 Classical style in music, ca. 1770–1830: Mozart, 1756–1791; Beethoven, 1770–1827 Wordsworth, English romantic poet, 1770–1850 Romanticism in art and literature, ca. 1790–1850
Napoleon signs Concordat with Pope Pius VII regulating Catholic Church in France, 1801 Spencer, Social Darwinist, 1820–1903 Comte, *System of Positive Philosophy*, 1830–1842 Height of French utopian socialism, 1830s–1840s List, *National System of Political Economy*, 1841 Nietzsche, radical and highly influential German philosopher, 1844–1900 Marx, *Communist Manifesto*, 1848	First railroad, Great Britain, 1825 Faraday studies electromagnetism, 1830–1840s	Staël, *On Germany*, 1810 Balzac, *The Human Comedy*, 1829–1841 Delacroix, *Liberty Leading the People*, 1830 Hugo, *The Hunchback of Notre Dame*, 1831

	Government	**Society and Economy**
1850	Second Empire in France, 1852–1870 Crimean War, 1853–1856 Britain crushes Great Rebellion in India, 1857–1858 Unification of Italy, 1859–1870 U.S. Civil War, 1861–1865 Bismarck leads Germany, 1862–1890 Unification of Germany, 1864–1871 Britain's Second Reform Bill, 1867 Third Republic in France, 1870–1940	Crédit Mobilier founded in France, 1852 Japan opened to European influence, 1853 Russian serfs emancipated, 1861 First Socialist International, 1864–1871
1875	Congress of Berlin, 1878 European "scramble for Africa," 1880–1900 Britain's Third Reform Bill, 1884 Dreyfus affair in France, 1894–1899 Spanish-American War, 1898 South African War, 1899–1902	Full property rights for women in Great Britain, 1882 Second Industrial Revolution; birthrate steadily declines in Europe, ca. 1880–1913 Social welfare legislation, Germany, 1883–1889 Second Socialist International, 1889–1914 Witte directs modernization of Russian economy, 1892–1899
1900	Russo-Japanese War, 1904–1905 Revolution in Russia, 1905 Balkan wars, 1912–1913	Women's suffrage movement, England, ca. 1900–1914 Social welfare legislation, France, 1904, 1910; Great Britain, 1906–1914 Agrarian reforms in Russia, 1907–1912
1914	World War I, 1914–1918 Armenian genocide, 1915 Easter Rebellion, 1916 U.S. declares war on Germany, 1917 Bolshevik Revolution, 1917–1918 Treaty of Versailles, World War I peace settlement, 1919	Planned economics in Europe, 1914 Auxiliary Service Law in Germany, 1916 Bread riots in Russia, March 1917
1920	Mussolini seizes power in Italy, 1922 Stalin comes to power in U.S.S.R., 1927 Hitler gains power in Germany, 1933 Rome-Berlin Axis, 1936 Nazi-Soviet Non-Aggression Pact, 1939 World War II, 1939–1945	New Economic Policy in U.S.S.R., 1921 Dawes Plan for reparations and recovery, 1924 Great Depression, 1929–1939 Rapid industrialization in U.S.S.R., 1930s Start of Roosevelt's New Deal in U.S., 1933
1940	United Nations founded, 1945 Decolonization of Asia and Africa, 1945–1960s Cold War begins, 1947 Founding of Israel, 1948 Communist government in China, 1949 Korean War, 1950–1953 De-Stalinization of Soviet Union under Khrushchev, 1953–1964	Holocaust, 1941–1945 Marshall Plan enacted, 1947 European economic progress, ca. 1950–1970 European Coal and Steel Community founded, 1952 European Economic Community founded, 1957
1960	Building of Berlin Wall, 1961 U.S. involvement in Vietnam War, 1964–1973 Student rebellion in France, 1968	Civil rights movement in U.S., 1960s Stagflation, 1970s Feminist movement, 1970s

Religion and Philosophy	Science and Technology	Arts and Letters
Decline in church attendance among working classes, ca. 1850–1914 Mill, *On Liberty*, 1859 Pope Pius IX, *Syllabus of Errors*, denounces modern thoughts, 1864 Marx, *Das Capital*, 1867 Doctrine of papal infallibility, 1870	Modernization of Paris, ca. 1850–1870 Great Exhibition in London, 1851 Freud, founder of psychoanalysis, 1856–1939 Darwin, *On the Origin of Species*, 1859 Pasteur develops germ theory of disease, 1860s Suez Canal opened, 1869 Mendeleev develops periodic table, 1869	Realism in art and literature, ca. 1850–1870 Flaubert, *Madame Bovary*, 1857 Tolstoy, *War and Peace*, 1869 Impressionism in art, ca. 1870–1900 Eliot (Mary Ann Evans), *Middlemarch*, 1872
Growth of public education in France, ca. 1880–1900 Growth of mission schools in Africa, 1890–1914	Emergence of modern immunology, ca. 1875–1900 Electrical industry: lighting and streetcars, ca. 1880–1900 Trans-Siberian Railroad, 1890s Marie Curie, discovery of radium, 1898	Zola, *Germinal*, 1885 Kipling, "The White Man's Burden," 1899
Separation of church and state in France, 1901–1905 Hobson, *Imperialism*, 1902 Schweitzer, *Quest of the Historical Jesus*, 1906	Planck develops quantum theory, ca. 1900 First airplane flight, 1903 Einstein develops theory of special relativity, 1905–1910	Modernism in art and literature, ca. 1900–1929 Conrad, *Heart of Darkness*, 1902 Cubism in art, ca. 1905–1930 Proust, *Remembrance of Things Past*, 1913–1927
Keynes, *Economic Consequences of the Peace*, 1919	Submarine warfare introduced, 1915 Ernest Rutherford splits atom, 1919	Spengler, *The Decline of the West*, 1918
Emergence of modern existentialism, 1920s Revival of Christianity, 1920s–1930s Wittgenstein, *Essay on Logical Philosophy*, 1922 Heisenberg's principle of uncertainty, 1927	"Heroic age of physics," 1920s First major public radio broadcasts in Great Britain and U.S., 1920 First talking movies, 1930 Radar system in England, 1939	Gropius, Bauhaus, 1920s Dadaism and surrealism, 1920s Woolf, *Jacob's Room*, 1922 Joyce, *Ulysses*, 1922 Eliot, *The Waste Land*, 1922 Remarque, *All Quiet on the Western Front*, 1929 Picasso, *Guernica*, 1937
De Beauvoir, *The Second Sex*, 1949 Communists fail to break Catholic Church in Poland, 1950s	U.S. drops atomic bombs on Japan, 1945 Big Science in U.S., ca. 1945–1965 Watson and Crick discover structure of DNA molecule, 1953 Russian satellite in orbit, 1957	Cultural purge in Soviet Union, 1946–1952 Van der Rohe, Lake Shore Apartments, 1948–1951 Orwell, *1984*, 1949 Pasternak, *Doctor Zhivago*, 1956 "Beat" movement in U.S., late 1950s
Second Vatican Council announces sweeping Catholic reforms, 1962–1965 Pope John II, 1978–2005	European Council for Nuclear Research founded, 1960 Space race, 1960s	The Beatles, 1960s Solzhenitsyn, *One Day in the Life of Ivan Denisovich*, 1962

	Government	**Society and Economy**
1960 (cont.)	Soviet tanks end Prague Spring, 1968 Détente between U.S. and U.S.S.R., 1970s Soviet occupation of Afghanistan, 1979–1989	Collapse of postwar monetary system, 1971 OPEC oil price increases, 1973, 1979
1980	U.S. military buildup, 1980s Solidarity in Poland, 1980 Unification of Germany, 1989 Revolutions in eastern Germany, 1989–1990 Persian Gulf War, 1990–1991 Dissolution of Soviet Union, 1991 Civil war in Yugoslavia, 1991–2001 Separatist war breaks out in Chechnya, 1991	Growth of debt in the West, 1980s Economic crisis in Poland, 1988 Maastricht Treaty proposes monetary union, 1990 European Community becomes European Union, 1993 Migration to western Europe increases, 1990s
2000	Terrorist attacks on U.S., Sept. 11, 2001 War in Afghanistan begins, 2001 War in Iraq begins, 2003	Euro enters circulation, 2002 Voters reject new European Union constitution, 2005 Immigrant riots in France, 2005, 2009 Worldwide financial crisis begins, 2008

Religion and Philosophy	Science and Technology	Arts and Letters
	Russian cosmonaut first to orbit globe, 1961 American astronaut first person on moon, 1969	Carson, *Silent Spring*, 1962 Friedan, *The Feminine Mystique*, 1963 Servan-Schreiber, *The American Challenge*, 1967
Revival of religion in Soviet Union, 1985– Growth of Islam in Europe, 1990s Fukuyama proclaims "end of history," 1991	Reduced spending on Big Science, 1980s Computer revolution continues, 1980s–1990s U.S. Genome Project begins, 1990 First World Wide Web server and browser, 1991 Pentium processor invented, 1993 First genetically cloned sheep, 1996	Solzhenitsyn returns to Russia, 1994; dies 2008 Author Salman Rushdie exiled from Iran, 1989 Gehry, Guggenheim Museum, Bilbao, 1997
Ramadan, *Western Muslims and the Future of Islam*, 2004 Conservative elected as Pope Benedict XVI, 2005	Growing concern about global warming, 2000s First hybrid car, 2003 Copenhagen Summit on climate change, 2009	Movies and books exploring clash between immigrants and host cultures popular: *Bend It Like Beckham*, 2002; *The Namesake*, 2003; *White Teeth*, 2003; *The Class*, 2008

About the Authors

John P. McKay (Ph.D., University of California, Berkeley) is professor emeritus at the University of Illinois. He has written or edited numerous works, including the Herbert Baxter Adams Prize–winning book *Pioneers for Profit: Foreign Entrepreneurship and Russian Industrialization, 1885–1913* (1970) and *Tramways and Trolleys: The Rise of Urban Mass Transport in Europe* (1976). He most recently contributed to *Imagining the Twentieth Century* (1997).

Bennett D. Hill (Ph.D., Princeton University), late of the University of Illinois, was the history department chair from 1978 to 1981. He published *English Cistercian Monasteries and Their Patrons in the Twelfth Century* (1968), *Church and State in the Middle Ages* (1970), and numerous articles and reviews, and was one of the contributing editors to *The Encyclopedia of World History* (2001). A Benedictine monk of St. Anselm's Abbey in Washington, D.C., he was also a visiting professor at Georgetown University.

John Buckler (Ph.D., Harvard University) taught history at the University of Illinois. Published books include *Theban Hegemony, 371–362 B.C.* (1980), *Philip II and the Sacred War* (1989), and *Aegean Greece in the Fourth Century B.C.* (2003). With Hans Beck, he most recently published *Central Greece and the Politics of Power in the Fourth Century* (2007).

Clare Haru Crowston (Ph.D., Cornell University) teaches at the University of Illinois, where she is currently associate professor of history. She is the author of *Fabricating Women: The Seamstresses of Old Regime France, 1675–1791* (2001), which won the Berkshire and Hagley Prizes. She edited two special issues of the *Journal of Women's History* (vol. 18, nos. 3 and 4), has published numerous journal articles and reviews, and is a past president of the Society for French Historical Studies and a former chair of the Pinkney Prize Committee.

Merry E. Wiesner-Hanks (Ph.D., University of Wisconsin–Madison) taught first at Augustana College in Illinois, and since 1985 at the University of Wisconsin–Milwaukee, where she is currently UWM Distinguished Professor in the department of history. She is the coeditor of the *Sixteenth Century Journal* and the author or editor of more than twenty books, most recently *The Marvelous Hairy Girls: The Gonzales Sisters and Their Worlds* (2009) and *Gender in History* (2nd ed., 2010). She currently serves as the Chief Reader for Advanced Placement World History.

Joe Perry (Ph.D., University of Illinois at Urbana-Champaign) is associate professor of modern German and European history at Georgia State University. He has published numerous articles and is author of the recently published book *Christmas in Germany: A Cultural History* (2010). His current research interests include issues of consumption, gender, and television in East and West Germany after World War II.